MEN!

Critical acclaim for Isabel Losada's books

'Candid, thought-provoking, sassy and very, very funny.' *Daily Telegraph*

'Endearing.' *Independent*

'Very funny and never cynical.' *Ireland on Sunday*

'Great fun – yet always honest.' *The Bookseller*

'Swift, snappy and engaging.' *Sunday Tribune*

'Searching and honest.' *Independent on Sunday*

'Remarkably revealing.' *Mail on Sunday*

'Brazenly probing.' *Scotsman*

'Humorous and refreshing.' *Canberra Times*

'Isabel Losada has achieved the perfect combination of humour, poignancy and intellectual rigour.' *New Statesman*

'Compelling reading and the most uplifting experience.' *Western Daily Press*

'Full of a crazy joy . . . made me laugh out loud.' *Impact Cultural Magazine*

'Heart-warming and extraordinary . . . Losada writes perceptively and with humour.' *Wanderlust* magazine

'A truly inspiring read.' *Library Journal* (USA)

'The world must be changed . . . Isabel's story brings this truism to life in a vivid, funny, heart-warming, delightful way. It is a great read, a live teaching! I enjoyed it, laughed and learned a lot!' Professor Robert Thurman – Tibetologist and Buddhist Scholar, Columbia University, New York

'With large doses of humour delivered with a British accent and endearing humility, this book might just inspire you to change the world in your own way – whatever that may be.' *The Buddhist Review*

'With equal doses of whimsy and intellectual rigour, Isabel demonstrates how doing good can be a creative endeavour and one that doesn't have to be deadly serious to be sincere. Losada's inspiration is infectious . . . Hip and irreverent, *A Beginner's Guide to Changing the World* also pleases with its substance.' *Shambhala Sun* magazine

MEN!

Where the **** Are They?

Isabel Losada

First published in Great Britain in 2007 by
Virgin Books Ltd
Thames Wharf Studios
Rainville Road
London
W6 9HA

A catalogue record for this book is available from the
British Library.

ISBN 078-0-7535-1276-0

Text paper is from Sustainably Managed Forests and
Environmentally Friendly sourcing.

Registered in London No. 342489 Registered Office:
St Ives House, Lavington Street, London SE1 0NX.
To view our disclaimer, please follow this link:
http//www.clays.co.uk/disclaimer.htm

Typeset by TW Typesetting, Plymouth, Devon
Printed and bound in Great Britain by
Clays Ltd, St Ives PLC

All the people in my books are real.
In rare cases I change people's names to protect
their identity, but most appear as themselves, so
I would like to thank everyone who, in one
form or another, has played a part.

CONTENTS

THE PRE-AMBLE

WHAT WE ALREADY KNOW

This is not a book for women who think that finding a man is the solution to their problems. If indeed such women still exist. Personally, I'm not convinced that they do.

It is 35 years since Germaine Greer wrote *The Female Eunuch* and urged women to escape from their bondage as unpaid and miserable houseworkers, their brains stultifying through being alone with under-fives all day long, their bodies exhausted and their sexuality passive. Those days, for the majority of women, are long gone. We demand more, we are taking over the workplace, we expect equal pay and, where necessary, we have learned to behave as badly as men have always done.

The women that I know – and they do not represent all women, but I believe that they are the majority – are also thoughtful, empathetic and call themselves spiritual. This means, at the least, that they believe themselves to be responsible for their own state of mind; they have followed the developments of what was once called the New Age Movement; they have learned meditation; they have discovered the benefits of yoga; they eat well, taking care of their own health; they have forgiven their parents for the mistakes of their childhood; in short, they know who they are and they do not look to men to provide answers for them.

And yet – and yet ... of course ... we still want the companionship of men. We still want a good sex life, we still want the balance that naturally occurs when men and women work well together, we still want to care for men and – sometimes, to be cared for. Happy women know and accept all these aspects of ourselves. We want lovers, yes – but often more than this we want brothers, friends and playmates.

So I want to be very clear: this is not about looking for a man to 'make us happy' – I know that no such man exists. I know that happiness is inside me and that I'm the source of it. I even wrote a book on this: *The Battersea Park Road to Enlightenment* is about doing whatever we need to do to take full responsibility for our own happiness and enjoying the process. My next book, *A Beginner's Guide to Changing the World: For Tibet With Love*, was about looking outwards, engaging with the world and making a difference, with kindness and with time. And as I became more and more interested in happiness and contribution as subjects – I noticed a very strange phenomenon in London and everywhere I travelled; women alone – intelligent, happy, confident, dynamic, hard-working, radiant women. It may be partly that the men have abandoned them because the women no longer need looking after. But I don't believe that.

Personally, it's not that I know single and available men who are intimidated, but that I simply don't know any single men. Or not any that I or any of the single women I know would want to date. We are not including alcoholics, or men with other serious addictions or those that are forty and have never travelled or left home. We are talking about the men who can be the companions of the confident, joyful women whom I know. Whom we all know.

So this is the mystery. Where are they? And what are women to do about their absence?

THE QUEST

Well, someone had to do it, didn't they? Someone had to go out on behalf of all the single women and find some men for us.

There is an enigma – all women know this and one of us has to solve it. I've heard the question every day for years, 'Where are all the interesting men?' Are women who ask this question crazy, unreasonably fussy in their expectations or deluded? Or is the lack of interesting men a reality? And if so, what are we to do about it? I'm not talking about shagging. Most women can find a man that they could have sex with if they chose. That's not the problem. The problem is finding a man you'd like to have dinner with. This turns out to be a useful definition of 'interesting'. It can equally well apply to women. An 'interesting' member of the opposite sex, for the purposes of this project, is one who when you meet them you'd like to have dinner with them and, having had dinner with them you are glad that you had dinner with them and you'd like to see them again.

Oh, and there is a second criterion – they should be single. This word also needs to be defined. Single means not married, not 'separated' from a partner who is unaware that they are separated, and not living with anyone or in a relationship with any other person when that other person believes that they are in a long-term, committed and monogamous relationship. Tall order, huh?

I wish I had a clue how I'm going to do it. Which of course I don't. I'll start where everyone is always telling us to start – all those places that I recoil from in the assumption that a life spent with two of my friends who are contemplative nuns would surely be better than resorting to these options: online dating (cringe), singles' events (surely you have to be desperate?). I will go and visit the dating agencies; I'll interview the experts; I'll explore new territories. I want to go and spend time in all-male environments – with the builders, the bikers, the city financiers – anywhere that's ninety per cent men, to see if I can learn anything about these Martians.

I'm ambitious – I don't want to do this just for me. Of course it would be wonderful if, in the course of writing this book, I meet a man I would like to share a dinner with, my bed with and my life with . . . but I want to do more than that. I want to solve the problem for all of us. I want to be able to tell you, 'OK, so it's true that there are a lot of gay men in our cities (this is great if you are a gay man – but not so great if you are a heterosexual female). But it's no good moaning about it – I've found a place where there are straight men who appreciate women.'

A strange thing happened to me this week. I got on a bus, having made more than my usual effort to present myself, as I was on my way to a professional engagement, and a man smiled at me. Imagine that. I mean, I'm not 21 any more and I have no breast implants. I was confused for a moment, so confused that I forgot to smile back and just walked past in a kind of daze trying to make sense of this extraordinary event. At this moment he turned and said to the man sitting beside him, '*Oh, mais qu'elle est jolie!*' Then it made sense; of course – he was French. I couldn't remember ever hearing an Englishman turn and say to a friend, 'What an attractive woman.' It just doesn't happen.

You may hear a man yell, 'Whoa – nice tits!' but that's not quite the same, is it?

So I'm going out to explore. In a professional and determined way. It's a mission. I shall attempt to demonstrate courage and commitment. I shall be fair and compassionate. I am not anti-men – not at all – but I like them straight, intelligent and uninterested in spectator sports. Am I radical? I will attempt to demonstrate vulnerability and I will practise total honesty. I shall persevere in the challenge. I will not be downcast. I will keep going until I know where I can find great guys and I can ring up my 99 friends, report to my million readers, 'They do exist, girls! Here are the men.'

And – who knows? – I may even be able to pull off the happy ending . . .

Part I

THE USUAL ROUTES WITH SOME DIVERSIONS

1. YOUR PERFECT MAN IS WAITING TO HEAR FROM YOU

INTERNET DATING AND NOT MEETING GREG

After two days exploring internet dating, I'm ready to abandon the project and research a book on toads. It's absurd. Someone told me, 'Look at Match.com, it's the biggest and best internet dating site,' so I looked. Did I want to send an email to 'Shagamuffin', 'Trev69', 'Monkeyman', 'Bursting41', or 'Ohcrikey' (balding, remaining hair dyed bright orange)? I can tell you that the answer is no.

The whole thing invites judgements. If I feed in that I'd only like to meet people who have been university educated, have no body piercings or tattoos, don't smoke and live within ten miles of London, it informs me that there are no men matching my criteria.

And even then I'm in a bad mood with the whole concept. I don't think any of the men that I've been out with would have matched my criteria on paper. The last man I met that I became really fond of left school at fifteen and a previous boyfriend was bald. But I would never pick a bald man from a picture on the screen. I dated the man because of who he was – so the fact that he was bald didn't matter to me . . . but I don't want to choose a man with no hair.

Listen to me having a rant. These sites are too much. Yesterday – because I have been talking about this research on my website – someone emailed me some links:

www.love.org/christian_dating.htm
www.veggieromance.com
www.seniorfriendfinder.com
www.petpeoplefishing.com

I was not happy. I hold my Christian origins very dear to me, but I wouldn't recommend a Christian dating service unless the friend I was recommending it to was part of the Evangelical church, which I am not. The mere idea of it fills me with horror. I almost fell for a Tibetan Buddhist monk last year ... don't think I'd have met him on a Christian dating site, do you? And then look at this – Veggie romance? They have to be kidding. I am a almost a vegetarian, about 90 per cent, but I do occasionally have some fish or even, if I'm at a friend's house and they have cooked it, some chicken, but the mere idea of a dating site full of vegetarian men makes me want to rush out and buy something dead. I did look – ever ready to be proved wrong ... but 'Sensitiveman' and 'Naturalguy' were really not going to do it for me. Nor was I going to recommend them to anyone. Are you thinking terrible things about me?

As to SeniorFriendFinder – quite apart from the fact that I don't intend to consider myself 'senior' until I'm well past ninety – Why would I want to define myself that way? But I look and find that 'senior' here means 'over 25' and that the site seems to be mainly for people seeking 'couples or groups'. One day of this kind of research could be enough for me. Steering away from the groups option, I feed in 'male' between thirty and fifty. I am offered 'Bigman': 'Do you need a young man for no strings sexy fun?' or there is 'Hugs37': 'I'm called hugs because I like giving and receiving.' Both have provided photos and, for the first time ever, I can suddenly see a good reason for never having a hug again for the rest of my life.

What about www.petpeoplefishing.com? I love cats – I love dogs – but would I ever want to join 'PetPeople'? Would I ever want to go out with someone who defined themselves as a PetPerson? If someone asked me to define my personality, I believe I could come up with a long list of facts about myself as a product before I would list 'Cat lover'... OK, here goes:

Things I do
1. Mother
2. Author
3. Activist
4. Campaigner
5. Speaker
6. Actress
7. Broadcaster
8. Singer
9. Presenter
10. Journalist
11. Workshop facilitator
12. Researcher

Things I am
1. Stroppy (this is the first thing that comes to mind right now)
2. Intelligent (it's all relative)
3. Reasonably attractive (ditto)
4. Active (when not sitting at computer all day long)
5. Compassionate (unless on internet dating sites)
6. Affectionate (but not with 'Hugs37')
7. Kind (have discovered my limit today when looking at BaldKevin)
8. Not hugely overweight (for definition of 'hugely overweight' just look at some of the photos on these sites)
9. Spiritual (but don't want to put this word in any boxes)

10. Sexual (but don't want to do it 'Shagamuffin')
11. Independent (please, no men who advertise 'rescue me')
12. Arrogant (obviously, from the above)

Things I like
1. Silence and stillness
2. Intimacy
3. Sri Lankan food
4. Good-quality conversation
5. Books that make me laugh or think differently or both
6. The sea and swimming in it when it's rough and wavy
7. A piano, and a double bass or a guitar and live music without amplifiers
8. Laptop computers that work
9. Huge old trees
10. Stones
11. Mountains. Of all kinds
12. Dawn, dusk, sunshine in the daytime, stars in the night sky

People I like
1. People who love life and live life to the full. Risk takers
2. People who inspire me because they are funny or skilful or well informed or intelligent or musical – people who make me think 'I wish I could be like that'
3. People who are committed to making the world a better place
4. People who love their work, whatever it is
5. People who are good listeners as well as good communicators
6. People who are genuinely interested in other people
7. People who are curious about life and open to new ideas and new experiences

8. People who understand about personal responsibility and don't blame others for their problems
9. People who continue to be interested in learning, whatever their age
10. People who don't watch TV or hardly ever watch TV

Things I'm intolerant of
1. People who smoke – coz it hurts them – and it costs the NHS £982 million a year* to treat those with chronic obstuctive pulmonary disease (brought on by smoking)
2. People who are cruel and think that it's OK to behave like that
3. People who watch TV all the time (coz life is short and there is a lot that needs doing)
4. People who are racist, fascist, sexist, xenophobic, homophobic, ageist, or who in general think of 'us' and 'them' and who have never considered the inter-connected nature of existence
5. The world of advertising and its desire to convince us that our lives are not OK without 'things'
6. Waste
7. World government leaders not putting political support behind the Dalai Lama and the people of Tibet (well, OK I know the list is a bit random but I'm writing in the order that it comes to mind)
8. Football fanaticism. It's a game and an exciting one, but I think making it a religion is missing the point
9. Junk food, bad architecture, boring kids in school by not making education relevant to their lives, companies that pollute . . .

Gosh, the list could get long, couldn't it?
 Er – being too critical?
 Well, there we are – some lists that include my intolerances, but don't include the fact that I'm a cat lover.

---

* National Institute of Clinical Excellence, UK.

There are lots of sites that invite us to put ourselves in some kind of box:

How about – www.soulfishing.com for the black community? www.gefiltefishing.com for the Jewish community? www.picantefishing.com for the Latino community? Fetish? Chubby? Horny? www.GIfishing.com (love a uniform? they ask)? And then there are 'parents' . . . I am a parent – but don't define myself as such.

Why does the whole idea of all these labels make my hair stand on end in horror? I spend my life trying to avoid labels on myself and putting labels on other people. That awful question at parties, 'What do you do?' and the inevitable 'How old are you?' I mean – what does it matter? Some people of thirty or younger are past it. They have made up their minds about things; they have already entered the 'I know what I like – I like what I know' group. They have nothing else to learn and won't learn anything else. Then I have a friend in her eighties who plays the piano like a dream and travels and is full curiosity and has a genuine passion for life and an energy that positively bubbles out of her. She is learning new things every day.

Surely somewhere in the world there must be a good internet dating site, one that attempts to find out who you are rather than just nail you into a kind of label-coffin? I refuse to join any site that sorts me based on my feelings about body piercings, tattoos and star sign.

So, is there such at thing as a good internet dating site? I managed to do a search and the internet seems to think that the leading site in the world is – not surprisingly – one based in America called eHarmony. Harumph – I am still convinced that the words 'good' and 'internet dating site' shouldn't come into the same sentence. Undoubtedly the site reviewing the dating sites is also run by eHarmony. But I thought I'd give it a look. The site offers to find you someone with whom you match up on 29 different criteria and they start you off with a one-hour personality test. As if I can't think of things that I'd rather do with my evening.

But I did say that I wanted discernment – they were certainly offering it.

On every single personal characteristic I had to score myself from one to seven. How warm am I? (7?) How ambitious am I (6?) How modest (1?) How content, humorous, efficient, competitive, self-aware. Hundreds of these questions. What four qualities would friends pick to describe me? Well, if you asked my ex-husband . . .

Then I had the same again but asking about qualities I would like in a partner. Energy level 1–7, Intelligence 1–7, Sex appeal 1–7. Could I just answer 7 for all of them?

Then religion. Which of the world's great religions would I affiliate myself with? I tried to check all of them, but it wouldn't let me. I tried to check just Christianity, Buddhism and 'Spiritual', but it wouldn't let me. So I huffily ticked 'other'.

It was a gruelling session – true or false. 'I dislike some people' (well, doesn't everyone?) 'At times I have raised my voice in anger' – if you know anyone who has raised a teenager as a single parent and never raised their voice in anger please email me on my website. I'd like to meet them.

Interests A–Z. Oh, good grief . . . but does it mean that I won't have to meet people who enjoy 'collecting' and 'car maintenance'? I so hope so – as they would say in the US.

It was exhausting, this questionnaire, but at least it was intelligent. Were they really able to go through my answers and match me up with the perfect person for me, as the smiling pictures of happy couples of all shapes and sizes on the home page of their site showed?

I completed my personality profile, grumpily uploaded a photo, and went to bed. My perfect matches would start emailing me on the morrow.

I opened the email nervously. It didn't really feel like me as, although I had put up a genuine photograph, I had given my mother's name, Elizabeth. But there it was . . . they had found a match for me based on the hour-long personality profile. The email announced 'Elizabeth and George . . . there is someone we'd like you to meet'. So there I was – part of a couple. George and I had now only to make contact.

I opened George's details nervously. There he stood. My cyber prince charming. On his boat. Or on a boat of some kind. Another picture showed him in shades beside a large motorbike. Mmmm. Very curious. If the boat and the bike were his, I wondered, why would he advertise them? Was he advertising himself or what he owned? If they were not his, then advertising them was misleading. If they were his, then it was unwise. Had he not read that princes should disguise themselves as paupers and, only when they were sure that they were truly loved reveal that they owned a castle. Or a bike or whatever. Still, he lives in California. Things are different in the US. Somehow there it's considered OK – even commendable – to show off about how much money you have. So I'd cut him some slack on this point. Especially as he wasn't overweight or bald.

So now I was to send him some 'closed questions' from a long list they had provided for me. Closed questions are great because you don't have to think. I ask:

'What is your opinion of long-distance relationships?'

'What would you like a lot of: respect, money, fame or power?'

'How many books did you read last year?'

So far so good.

The following day his answers arrive:

'I would think if there is chemistry the two people would want to be together more often than not.'

'Money. But not in a filthy rich way, just enough to be able to travel without concern for having to work.' I smile . . . at least he is honest.

And books? He ticks 'More than 12'.

So far – so good. Then his questions.

'If you met the right person would you be prepared to relocate? Yes, I would.

'How trusting are you?'

These questions are easy when the answers are pre-provided. I choose 'I trust people and am able to forgive them when wronged'. But then he asks, 'How romantic are you?' and I have to leave the proscribed answers – all variations on 'very' or 'not at all' to say, 'To be honest I've always had trouble defining exactly what is meant by "romantic".' We are making progress.

The next stage is a list of 'must haves' and 'can't stands' in which you can list whatever you can't live without or with. George says that he must have someone who isn't afraid of risk and who lives life as an adventure; he says that he must have someone who is good at talking and listening. This is all good. But then I scan his interests and in amongst lots that is good and noble I spot 'bird hunting'. Horror. What is this? The search for women or the desire to kill innocent creatures? I skip the next stage and hit 'fast track'. This will get me through all the politeness, if he agrees, and get me straight to 'open communication'. The following day I see he has accepted. 'Good morning,' he greets me. 'This is a little scary. What about music? Let's say you could only choose three artists but you could take their whole body of work – which would you choose?'

'Hold on a minute,' I say. 'Before we move into art and music, I'd just like to ask . . . what exactly is "bird hunting"? I see you list it as one of your main interests. Please tell me that you don't mean killing creatures that sing?'

Another day comes and goes and he replies: 'I believe loyalists refer to it as "wing shooting". I believe that the Great Spirit designed us as hunters and we were not meant to graze in fields. We are meant to forage and hunt. It is our way. So to be on a spiritual path and also to connect with our animal nature is not such a bad thing, is it? Besides it's not always the bird who ends up disappointed. Trust me, plenty fly away to sing another day.'

I smile. Do I point out to him that there is a qualitative difference between disappointed and dead? Perhaps I shouldn't be too caustic.

'I'm afraid I think we have evolved slightly from the hunter state. We don't need to kill to eat and "The Great Spirit" in my understanding also believes that all life is sacred (or at least the little bit of the Great Spirit inside me does). How can I think of getting to know you when I know that creatures that sing on a day when you wake will not sing any more because you woke? And, as the Buddhists say "Once you have taken life from a living creature you can never give it back." You turn something that lives and breathes into a pile of blood and feathers?'

He replies with the same energy.

'To be clear – I don't enjoy the killing. I enjoy the traditions of it . . . the eighty-year-old shotgun, my English setter and coming as close to full-on communication as man and dog can. I enjoy the briars and thorns. I enjoy the field and the light on it and I enjoy cleaning the birds and eating them. I enjoy using the feathers to tie flies for fishing. I enjoy the adventure of travelling to a place to hunt. I am probably more of a conservationist than most people you know. I live in a wilderness area of incredible abundance and I despise people who hunt for any animals they cannot eat.'

OK, so he is a commendable huntsman. If there is such a thing. Another day goes by and I reply.

'I'm afraid we are never going to agree. In my mind conservation is not what you are doing. If you enjoy being in nature you can shoot things with a camera. I can think of many ways to spend a day . . . read a story to a child, take your dog for a swim, help to preserve the land that you love . . . or, if all else fails, better to stay in bed than to get up and go and destroy something. If I were there with you I'd want to come out with you and your dog and make noise to warn the birds of your approach and if you did kill one in spite of my efforts I would never want to make love to you again.'

I wanted to add a suggestion: 'Instead of the boat and the bike that I can see in your photos, why not post some snaps of you grinning and holding dead birds?' But I resisted. Instead I said, 'George, we are never going to agree on this. I never even kill ants. I'm afraid we will have to part. This is the end of my first ever cyber relationship. It's been quick, hasn't it?'

He wrote 'Good luck' and next time I signed on he had hit the close button. For the standard eHarmony reason he had chosen 'I feel our values are too different'. Too right they are. I opened my next match and there stood a man holding a large fish that he had evidently just caught as if to say, 'Look what a big one I've got.'

I know I'm being a hypocrite here because I have eaten fish and chicken in my life. On occasion I still do. I eat chicken very rarely and red meat never, but fish, well yes, I do sometimes eat some fish. I know that I could never pull one out of the water myself – I'd have to be starving before I could take something alive from its element and bang it on the head to eat it. But I still order fish sometimes if I'm in a restaurant. I can argue that George is a more honest man than I am. At least he is aware of the death of the creature and knows that its death is at his hands. Whereas I sit in my nice restaurant in my shiny city, totally apart from nature, with my holier-than-thou attitude . . . I know, I know, it makes no sense; either I should get off my high horse or I should stop eating fish and chicken totally. Very well . . . I shall have to give up chicken and fish totally. I've said that I'll try this before and failed, but if I'm going to be authentic at all, then the time, it seems, has come. If I want people to be consistent and have integrity then I'm going to have to demonstrate it one hundred per cent myself. I can cut everyone else some slack. But in this area it seems I can't cut myself any. And all this from my first two matches on eharmony.com.

I open up the new match from 'Russ' in Ohio with his very large dead fish trophy and hit 'I don't believe that our values are compatible'. I mean, it's rather sweet that he thinks he can impress a woman with the size of the fish he's caught. But hasn't he noticed that it's not in any list on the website of qualities that women look for? I go to the next match. Ah – here is a man photographed with a guitar. That's a bit more up the Battersea Park Road to Isabel's heart . . . but then I look at his requirements . . . 'Must want to start a family'. Ah, alas . . . been there, done that; it would take a lot to persuade me to consider having any more babies, much as I love them. And this man has it as a basic requirement. There are so many women out there looking for a man who wants to have children. One of them must have him . . . not me. Do I want to date an electronics salesman who lives in Ohio and doesn't supply a photograph? Nope. Do I want to date 'Randy' from Boise in Idaho who lists as his main interest 'recreational hockey'? No matter how fair I try to be, I just can't see it happening. I can't see me standing beside the hockey pitch shouting, 'Go Randy!'

And there it is again, the problem with all this choosing by label. Of course, if I were to love him first, I'd be very happy to go and stand by the pitch and support his desire to run around in circles, but I wouldn't choose this any more than I would choose a hunter or a 'real estate director'. So maybe we are narrowing it down. Maybe, in theory, I want a man who lives in a city and works in the arts. But that doesn't sound like what I want at all. And what do all the other women that live in cities want? We complain that we don't like city types, but do we really want men that live in the countryside? Can women who watch subtitled films date men who leave blank the question 'What was the last book you read?', presumably because they never read one? Could you live with a man who never reads books? It is all very confusing.

Then one day 'Greg' arrives in my in tray as a perfect match for me. His personality and mine have been put through the rigorous personality profile of eHarmony and they have decided that if Greg and I were to fall in love it would be 'for all the right reasons'. Greg lives in Los Angeles, California, is six feet tall and gives his profession as 'translator and filmmaker'. But – wait for it – Greg is good looking. I almost typed god looking. Yes – not too many marks to Freud here. Greg has two head shots . . . obviously proper, professional studio head shots. What is instantly noticeable is that he has hair. And he looks confident but slightly cheeky. He has a strong bone structure, perfect teeth (of course), smiling brown eyes and a general 'don't you want to spend the rest of your life with me?' look about him.

I scan down the personality review. One of the questions Greg has had to answer is what he is most passionate about. He says that he is passionate about movies, skiing, languages, travel, theatre, art, reading and eating out. The most important thing that he looks for in a person is 'intelligence'. Interests that their matching system has decided that we share are live music, friendship and conversation. The things that he can't live without include 'challenging projects that I feel passionate about', good friends and 'physical activity', ha ha. Suddenly I'm paying attention.

In fact, I'm in a panic. I look at the photo I've uploaded and quickly upload two more. I even upload a photo of myself shaking hands with the Dalai Lama. Well, I figure I'm allowed to be proud of it. I think – well, there can't be many photos with His Holiness (HH) in them. As I sit looking at his photo in stunned disbelief at how gorgeous he is and wondering what he's doing on this dating site, my friend Mark, who is staying, walks by. 'He's a good-looking bastard,' he says.

'Mmm, I'm looking forward to his first communication.'

'He won't email. He's clearly not real and let's face it . . . if he was, he wouldn't be interested in you.'

'What? He's real. He's a film director. eHarmony says we are a perfect match.'

'Then he'd be dating film stars ten years younger than him. You're too old. You're frumpy. You're not in Greg's league.'

'Too old????'

'If you go to the fruit stall in the market you aren't going to look at the back where all the wrinkly, mouldy ones are. Well, are you? You're going to pick the fresh, plump, juicy ones at the front.'

This was beyond the pale. I looked at his age. Four years younger than I am. (I refuse to tell you my age on grounds that I will incriminate myself.) But I have been honest on the site. Shit.

'He won't reply for the same reason that you don't want to date a man ten years older than you.'

'I wouldn't mind. And anyway, I'm only four years older than him. I'm looking for an interesting single man to have dinner with. I'm in New York in a few months. We could email and then meet for dinner, for goodness sake. I might make him laugh. Or something.'

'That's not the point. You won't hear from him.'

I ignored him and sent my closed questions. I decided I'd be a little bit girly and avoid the 'Do you prefer, respect, money, fame or power?' and asked some more demure questions. 'When in a relationship, how much personal space do you generally find you need?', 'How many books did you read last year?', 'What is your opinion of a committed long-distance relationship?' and 'What is your opinion of traditional gender roles?' The closed questions are a little bit naff, but I didn't want to look too keen and press 'fast track' right away, which would have led me straight to emailing. Besides which, I could have fun doing closed questions with Greg. Don't want to be hasty.

'Anyway, I don't believe he exists,' Mark taunted me. 'You don't have a cat in hell's chance of getting an email from him that says anything apart from "piss off, weirdo".'

So, a vote of confidence from my friend Mark, then. But I'm ever the optimist. I chose to believe that he did exist. Maybe he works as a translator in LA and is bored of drop-dead gorgeous women ten years younger than him. Maybe he was looking for something 'interesting'. Sigh.

So, I waited. Greg became a celebrity in the house. 'Has Greg emailed?' Mark said every time he called. I minded at first. After all, the other matches had all replied. I had 'requests for communication' from Tom in Charleston, Dan in Denver, Michael in Coppell, John in Delroy, Hubert in Mansfield, Norm in West Chester, Wayne in Honolulu, William in Tallahassee, Mehran in Vancouver and Randy in Lancaster. (No 'matches' at all from eHarmony from anyone this side of the pond.) But if all those men could reply, why not Greg? I would wake up in the morning and find myself checking to see whether Greg had emailed. No Greg. I'd go out for the day and come home in the evening, hope springing eternally. No Greg. He looked at me from the matches list – his gorgeous bone structure taunting me from among the very overweight characters with baseball caps and sunglasses carrying cats or cuddly toys. But no email from Greg.

I wanted to prove Mark's cynicism wrong and I felt that it was only fair that Greg help me with this by getting in touch. Perhaps if I pressed 'send/receive' one more time, an email would appear. But no email from Greg. I'd go away for the weekend and then come back. But no email from Greg. So there it was in my first two weeks – a microcosm of the entire dating world. An abundance of men that were fifteen years too old for me and listed 'my back yard' among their interests – literally I mean. A reasonable man that I could have considered but who I had 'irreconcilable differences with' and one who I'd really love to meet but who was evidently never going to reply. And, despite Mark's scathing comments, I moped – my photos really weren't *that* bad.

Then one day I signed on and found that Greg had communicated. He had 'closed' the matching process between us ... as I had done with so many of the others. There were standard boxes to tick and he had ticked two of them: 'I have too much going on in my life right now' and 'I am pursuing another match'. Mark laughed. 'You bet he is – one who is ten years younger than you are.'

And the strange thing is that I minded. I minded about a rejection from a man I'd never met on the other side of the Atlantic. I'd stuck up his photo on the pinboard and his name had become familiar in the house as an example of all that was most good and most bad about internet dating: I was supposed to be 'experimenting' with internet dating and 'doing research' but I still minded. I sat for a while and thought about all the women who had not had children and had never been married and who wanted to meet men more badly than I did.

This internet dating had a faceless cruelty about it that I didn't like. I didn't like being selected by age before any other criteria – or selecting men that way, either. I didn't like rejecting men who looked too old when maybe, if I met them, they'd be lovely. I didn't want to do this any more. I had two friends who had spent months trawling the UK sites, so I spent two weeks playing with those, too. But it's more of the same, isn't it? Absurdly time-consuming and rather grim. In this way it goes against my key philosophy that it's important to spend our time joyfully – internet dating sites just aren't fun. I wanted to find a different way to meet men . . . that would involve actually meeting men.

2. THE TOMS, THE DICKS AND HARRY

SOME THOUGHTS ON THE MARRIED MEN

Before we go any further with the narrative, I realise that, as a matter of urgency, I need to alert single female readers to a grave and possibly mortal danger and define some terms. I refer, of course, to the specific dangers posed by the married men. I know we have defined 'single' but we need to be aware that this definition is not shared by the married men out there. So let's be clear about this.

Once, when I was a married woman, I would have been startled by the mere idea of this chapter. My marriage vows meant everything to me; they were as precious as life itself. Bizarrely, I would have endured a lifetime of unhappiness, but I would never have broken them. This is an illogical position held by many. Better to be unhappy with me, your wife or your husband, or numb, than to be happy with someone else, no matter what the price. And I plead guilty to this. When my husband was with me, if he had said to me, 'I will never be really happy with you, but I've met someone with whom I believe I can be truly happy. Would you let me go?' I would have thought that he had gone crazy. It would have been his duty to stay with me. He had made a vow. He had promised. And that was it. The fact that he may have been far better suited to another woman and I, in my turn, may have been better off and happier without him, would never have crossed my mind.

Indeed, when it did happen that he had an affair with someone else, I was on moral high ground so elevated I should have known that one day I would be in the dirt looking up. I deserved it. I had been a very righteous wife. I had married in a church before God and any woman that got involved with 'my husband' . . . well, I would probably have spat on her if I'd seen her in the street. That was how I felt about her. There are countries where people like her were stoned to death and, metaphorically at least, I was ready to throw the first stone.

But those days are gone and now I know better. In my years as a single woman I have met so many married men that I see matters a little differently. A monk in the Taizé community in the South of France once told me that monogamy is as unnatural to the human condition as celibacy – 'Not many people know this,' he said. But I guess many single women do. Married men chase, wine, dine . . . married men lie and offer their services. One of my female friends tells me that 98 per cent of her married male friends have made passes at her. Some even offer their hearts. So I thought – just to provide a little clarity and so that you can avoid the mistakes that I have made – I would try to pass on to you the fruits of my experience.

For convenience I have divided the married category of male into the Toms, the Dicks and the Harrys. We will start by outlining the characteristics of the standard Tom, as they are the most numerous and easy to spot. They are clear and they are not liars – at any rate, not to the single women. A Tom speaks like this:

'You have to understand that I love my wife and couldn't possibly ever leave. She'd go to pieces without me.' (Note subtle feeling of compulsion: 'could not' rather than 'would not' and wife portrayed as helpless dependant.) Now, just when you think he is loyal as can be, he will add . . . 'But I could be free round about 2 p.m. Could I come over?'

Life is simple if you have a Tom in your life. They do not intend to leave their wives and they let you know, leaving you under no illusions. Everything is clear as can be. Good old Toms. There would be no danger of falling in love with one; they offer nothing anyway, except their bodies. I've correctly identified many Tom types and life with them around has always been simple. It's a straight choice . . . do you want to have an affair or don't you?

I remember the first Tom I ever met. I was a young actress and I'd just left drama school. I was nineteen. He was 28. We were working in repertory theatre in Worcester, I remember. He courted me like Cyrano de Bergerac. He wrote me love letters; he played emotional period scenes with me; he tapped on my window at late hours; he bought flowers, wine; he was the most romantic man I'd ever known. For me, there was just one stumbling block in the romance – as I kept reminding him, 'You're married!'

'So what? What my wife doesn't know won't hurt her, will it? And I'm not going to tell her. She's not here. But you are. I want you, you want me, so what's the problem?'

'You don't understand. You picked the wrong girl . . . I don't work like that. As far as I'm concerned, this woman is a kind of sister of mine even if I've not met her. I wouldn't like that done to me. How can you deceive her in this way?'

My denials seemed to further ignite his passions.

'You like me, don't you?'

'Yes . . . of course I like you.'

'And you fancy me, don't you?'

'That's not relevant. I told you quite clearly.' Amazement in my voice. 'How do you justify this in your mind?'

'I don't want to have regrets.'

'Don't you think you might regret being unfaithful?'

'Yes. But the way I see it is this. If I make love to you all night long I may regret it and if I don't make love to you all night long I may regret it, so I figure that I'd much rather make love to you and have regrets. Now you see that this faultless logic can apply to you too? It's the wanting you that is already an act of infidelity. As I'm here, we might as well be making love. What's the difference?'

'What?'

'If you say "no" you may regret it . . .'

'I'll risk it.'

'Can I just kiss you? We'll stop there. And whatever else happens is up to you. You are entirely in control here. I just want to let you know that you are the most beautiful and desirable woman in the whole universe . . .'

'Out! Get thee behind me, Satan.' I was a little more Biblical in those days. I have remembered his approach for many years. Like all the best temptations, it has a strong element of truth. It was easy then to say no to the Toms. I found them so shocking. So immoral. But things were so much more black and white then. I was nineteen.

I'm casting my mind back here quite a long way . . . have I ever had anything that I would call an affair with a Tom? No, I haven't. I've had the odd one-night stand, though. There was a Tom who lived outside London. He would book into a hotel and then ring me – usually telling me that he was on the Battersea Park Road and could he buy me dinner. I'd be at home working at my computer, not having spoken to a soul all day (authors who work and live alone must be a particularly easy source of potential companions for Toms), and I'd say, 'Oh OK . . . come in.' And I'd get bought dinner and flowers and wine. Now, don't misunderstand. I'm not pretending to be without blame. And I'm not proud of this behaviour. But I defy any woman reader who is clambering up onto her high horse, where I previously had gained such experience, to say no to dinner with a Tom.

A Tom is debonair; he dresses well, he speaks well, he understands women. My Tom was absurdly talented. He made me laugh, he cared about me. Oh, and did I mention . . . his wife didn't understand him? But I wasn't expected to believe it. That was just it. It was simple. He would come back after the meal and stay over . . . mostly we would just cuddle and once we did not. Just cuddle.

I remember when I had this first-ever one-night stand with a Tom I was racked with guilt for weeks. I wrote a long letter to his wife, which I knew I could never send, just to bring it home to myself what I had done. I changed the names and tried to get the letter published as a warning to married women. I had always practised 'do as you would be done by' and I felt I had betrayed this 'sister' of mine, some woman I had never met, who, no doubt, trusted him – and me, although she had never met me. I felt I had become some other kind of creature – a 'dangerous woman'.

I wouldn't hear from him for months at a time. But if I ever called (at work, of course) he would always ring me back. And he was genuinely fond of me, I know that . . . he still is. But I haven't spoken to him for years. I believe this Tom has a similar clear understanding with many of us single women. You are probably wondering if you know him.

You know the story about Moses going up the mountain to confer with God? They want to discuss the Commandments and Moses has gone to negotiate on behalf of the Israelites. Anyway, he ventures up and days later is seen returning, staggering down the mountain with the stones on which God has written the Commandments. 'It's good news . . .' he begins with a smile, 'I managed to get the Lord down to ten.' He proudly displays his ten Commandments. 'But there is also bad news.' A hush falls over the tribes of Israel. 'Adultery is still in.'

'Twas ever thus. I couldn't understand it before I was married. Coming from the theatre, where everyone slept with everyone and very little fuss was made, the fact that a quick bonk in the night was up there with murder and theft seemed a little . . . well, excessive. And then, when I was married my husband had an affair and left me with a little girl of two-and-a-half and with no family of my own to support me in any way, I began to understand why the Lord might have strong feelings about it. On the other hand, sex with other women while still married to one's wife can be harmless, even life enhancing – according to Toms. I know one Tom who has always slept with as many women as possible outside his marriage. Whether his wife knows anything about what he gets up to, I have no idea, for thirty years later he is with his wife still. They are happy together, for all I know. She knows he will never leave her and he never will. Pure Tom.

I have nothing to do with them any more. The occasional dinner with one and then I call him a taxi for his hotel. I know one 'lunch' Tom who works in the City and he and I are good friends. Again, he cares about me in his own funny way. He knows I sometimes feel lonely and isolated and he would 'comfort me' if I let him. But only in the afternoons. He'll invite me for lunch but never for dinner; he will never join me for any activity in the evenings or weekends. 'Those are family times,' he will explain, but if I'd like to see him on a weekday afternoon then he can always arrange to be away from work. I suppose I am interesting – sitting here at my computer in my own home. But I decline. 'It would be lovely to see you, Tom, under other circumstances . . . but I think not.'

One thing I can't complain about – there is never a lack of Toms in the world. I don't know if there are single women who lose their heart to Toms, but it would require a high level of foolishness. For they never deceive you. Or themselves. And, in their way of thinking, they never deceive their wives, either. They simply never mention anything. A life with clear compartments. And in the words of a true Tom, 'What the eye doesn't see, the heart doesn't grieve over.'

But then there are far more confusing men. The Dicks. A Dick is a man with dubious or ambiguous marital status. I became very confused by a Dick only a couple of years ago. A Dick, for example, may 'work away from home a lot'. He's married and he admits that, 'But we're separated. I see her of course, have to . . .'

'So are you planning on getting a divorce?'

'You don't have to any more. Once you are apart for two years, it's automatic. So, I'm separated. Is that all right then? Can I buy you dinner?'

Now here is an important point. Men dislike the lie direct. It still pricks at their conscience, so if they can avoid it, they will. Words become very important. One Dick once told me that, 'My wife never sleeps with me.' Now, careless me, I thought that meant that they didn't have sex any more. Be very careful and listen attentively. He didn't say that, did he? No, no. He said she doesn't sleep with him. Imagine my surprise when, at a later date, I find that he and his wife of fifteen years are still regular lovers. They just have two beds. Silly me.

Then there was a Dick who said that he and his wife had been separated for several years. I made a huge mistake. I imagined that he came into the category that I was looking for. Namely 'single'. But no. It was only after we had been dating for about six months that it transpired that his wife was totally unaware that they were separated. She had been living under the illusion that he was 'working abroad'. And of course he 'popped back regularly to see the children'. So, girls, if you ever meet a Dick and he tells you that he is separated, you need to ask, 'Oh yes . . . and does your wife know about this?' With this particular Dick, by the time I found out what exactly was going on I was practically living with him. 'Are you going to tell your wife?' Yes, of course he was, but not this week, as it was the anniversary of her mother's death. Or next month because she had some exams she was doing and he didn't want to upset those . . . or the next, because it was Christmas. And I would ponder to myself, 'Is it my business to tell him how to live his life or deal with his family? Could I insist that he told his wife?' I was very confused until I realised that his definition of 'separated' did not match mine and I ended it.

Beware of the Dicks, girls. 'Separated' can cover a wide range of states. Some men don't even mention that they have wives. They like to see how you will respond if you believe that they are single. One women I know confided to me, 'Oh yes, I was proposed to once by a Dick: he hadn't mentioned his wife.'

But with my Dick I was secure, as I never gave my heart to him. We had a load of fun and although it was a kind of emotional affair, it was a harmless one. He became a good friend who came into my life and then was thrown out of it. I think his wife, who lives abroad, thought that it was a particularly long stint in the London office. So, any man with a confused and confusing definition of his marital status – he's a Dick.

But then, just when you thought you knew how to keep your distance from all married men, there is a Harry. A Harry is very different from the Toms and Dicks in that he is not a womaniser. He may never have been unfaithful. He finds the lie direct impossible and the lie unstated almost as painful. He does not look at women outside his marriage – just as many women will not look at men inside marriages. But then one day all this goes horribly wrong – the carpet is gone from under your feet and you're on your knees. Any married man who is neither a Tom nor a Dick and who, for some reason (most likely to be lack of experience), defies the categories – by definition, he's a Harry.

And I have to pause in my writing. And breathe a little. For you see, I still love my Harry. Somehow, despite all my knowledge, wisdom and experience, a Harry fish got through my very carefully crafted 'no married men' net. It started innocently enough, as it would do . . . for unlike the Toms and the Dicks, a Harry never plans to be unfaithful. He sent an email. One of the advantages and disadvantages of having an author website is that I get lots of emails every day. And I try to reply to all of them. Very few of them get my particular attention, but Harry's did. It wasn't flirtatious, that first email, it was a purely professional enquiry. And I responded in a slightly less formal way, answering all the questions. There followed some well-written compliments about my books . . . I responded graciously. It didn't seem appropriate or necessary to me to quiz him on his personal details. We continued to email. Then one night I was caught unawares . . . I don't know if I was napping or what. But an email arrived that was so beautiful, it took my breath away. I was smitten. No matter what the consequences.

I wrote back. 'Harry, no one . . . no one writes to me like this.' Then I told him that if he was twenty stone, if he had bad breath and acne, or looked like Quasimodo, I didn't care. My heart was his. In my mind I was thinking, 'If he is paraplegic or deaf or has one leg? Will I mind?' And each time the answer was no. For some reason the obvious hadn't crossed my mind. He was none of these – but he was married. I was shocked and wary . . . but what was he to me? An amusing email correspondent I told myself, no more. And so the emails continued. They made me laugh in spite of myself. Perhaps I should have emailed, 'Stop making me laugh . . . you're married.' But I defy anyone who works from home to put a stop to emails filled with wit and joy. And what did he want, you may be asking? No more than I did, I think . . . emails to make him laugh on a daily basis. Entertainment and the pleasure of knowing that he was making me laugh.

Email is terrible. An obvious place for projection. Beware. I could see none of his faults and he could be what I wanted. He didn't correspond like a married man. Should I have said, 'I am experiencing an inappropriately high level of enjoyment from receiving your emails. Please try to be less witty'? Should he perhaps have said; 'I am enjoying our correspondence but, before I send you another line, may I remind you that I'm married?' Instead he just made me laugh and brought a wonderful joy to switching on my computer. He had won my mind somehow. He was so quick, so clever, so helpful on many matters. He'd sent me music he had written himself, photos he had taken. And this was all before we met.

The first meeting was an interesting one. He lived in Scotland so I didn't have to worry that he would be in London often. 'We have to meet . . . can I buy you dinner?' I was very, very wary. He wanted to meet me at the British Museum, 'to show you something amazing', at 2 p.m. I refused.

'What is this? No. I will not meet you at 2 p.m. anywhere half as interesting. You are a married man. I'll meet you at the time I meet everyone else that I am having dinner with. I'll meet you at 7 p.m., in a restaurant.' I should probably have refused to meet him. But by this time we had been emailing for about three months. He had become my chief source of laughter. Well, let's be honest here . . . some days, working from home, he was my only source of laughter. Would you have refused to meet him? Anyway, I figured the chances of us actually liking each other face to face were very small. Chemistry is a such a weird thing and just because he made me laugh in an artificial cyber world, I reasoned that this did not mean that I would ever want to see him again.

All that we needed was to not be attracted to each other and all would be well. He would be a good friend. We could keep up our emails and all perspective would be restored. It was worth meeting him to secure this hope alone. I was thinking, 'Dear God, let him be truly ugly.' I had slipped through his net too and I think he was hoping I would be very repulsive or deeply dull. Or was I deluding myself all along?

I have always been annoyed by the phrase 'soul mates'. Romantic tosh, I've always said. One girl who met and then married a man that I am very fond of announced, 'I have found my soul mate.' I thought, 'Well, I hope so – and I hope he has, too.' But what exactly is meant by this phrase? I have met several men in my lifetime with whom I've had a good connection. So what's a soul mate? Quasi-spiritual gobbledegook? An example of the early stages of projection when people do this infatuation stage of being in love – isn't that when people feel that they have met their soul mates? In actual fact no such thing exists and we may meet many kindred spirits in life. This is what I told myself. But then I met Harry.

I remember our first glance and the smile on both our faces. And then we started to chatter as if we had known each other for – not months, but many decades. That was how it felt. As if our friendship was as old as the hills. All those beliefs that maybe we have many lifetimes and we meet time and time again suddenly seemed to be the only logical explanation. A feeling of familiarity. Of content. That I would never need anyone or anything ever again as long as Harry would keep talking. Or listening. (How rare is a man who can do both?)

He was a couple of years older than I am, but evidently very fit. A man given to regular exercise and not overeating, someone who knows how to take care of himself. A man quick to smile and joke and slow to be serious. Who I reached out to touch as if I had known him for ever and he was mine to touch. That was how it felt. But you have remembered even as I was forgetting . . . he was married. The thing is, girls . . . and this is where you have to be so careful with a Harry – he didn't *seem* married. When you meet someone who is fully in the present moment, it is easy to be confused . . . for indeed in the time that they are with you they are not married. They are totally with you. He had that rare quality of being absolutely present; there was no mobile phone that rang, reminding us both that there were any other human beings on the planet beside us two.

We must have sat in the restaurant and talked and laughed for over four hours . . . we had covered a million shared interests. Primarily writing, which was our passion, travel – which countries we loved most and why, languages, music, politics, religion – contemplative Christianity, Buddhism, his work, my books, which he had loved, Eastern thought . . . but, now that I come to think of it, I don't remember discussing his family. Or my daughter. By midnight we were sitting in my lounge drinking coffee. We decided him going back to his hotel was stupid. We had known each other a thousand years. It doesn't happen often – you meet a soul that you really know that you know, does it?

Before you are too shocked, there was no sex. In theory, we were strangers still. And yet there is a deeper intimacy that can be experienced.

As I said, my Harry slipped through the net good and proper.

Over the next couple of months my life went crazy. For the first time in my life, or so it felt, I was truly in love with someone who was truly in love with me. It's not an experience that I would trade for any other living experience. (OK, daughter! Except childbirth, OK?) I would dream of him and he would dream of me. My heart would sing all day so loud that I had a smile fixed permanently on my face. I was living a new experience of heaven on earth. The paradise was an absurd foolish love song – a land of clichés, a planet in which I knew Harry and he loved me and I loved him and nothing else mattered.

Things were not so easy for Harry. The trouble with the Harrys is – and this is why you have to be so careful – they are the genuinely good men. They are not Toms or Dicks and never will be. They are not fools or experienced liars. They cannot deceive. Back in Scotland, Harry, like me, was in love and going crazy. He wanted to leave Scotland and come to England and be with me. He was miserable about the deceit and remember this is me, the hypocrite Christian Buddhist who doesn't believe in adultery. He couldn't bear it any longer . . . he went to his wife – and announced that he was in love and he was leaving. I was amazed, scared and utterly overjoyed.

I had adjusted, like a happy child, to the idea of a life with Harry . . . it was unexpected to find someone that I just wanted to be with, all the time, for ever. I had never felt so loved, so understood, so wanted. I had never brought anyone so much joy or received so much joy in the company of another person. I was ready to move to Scotland or Calcutta if he asked me to. If I had been offered the rest of my life as I knew it with all my friends and everything I have or the rest of my life on an island with Harry ... well, I would have called my daughter and said, 'You understand me making this choice, don't you, darling?' and she'd have said, 'I'm so happy for you ... go for it, Mother!' I'd have given up everything. This, I believe, is the foolish – some would say dysfunctional – state called 'being in love'. And I was in it, whatever 'it' is, up to the neck.

I could never have anticipated what would happen next. I had to go to Australia for a month on a book tour. Harry said, 'While you are away, things will calm down a bit here.' By the time I came back a month later (despite many phone calls and emails) he had changed his mind. 'I just can't do it,' he said, suddenly sounding like someone I didn't know, a Tom or a Dick. 'I have to stay ... I can't leave ... I have to be a good man .... I can't be that selfish ... I have to choose ... I have chosen. I'm staying. I'm sorry.'

And suddenly he wants to be my friend. Friend??? How am I to pretend to him, or worse still, to myself, that someone who I wanted to spend the rest of my life with is now, to me, as a 'friend' is? I feel as if I'm being asked to wander into a wood of self-delusion. How many of my friends do I want to share my bed with and know with an intense and joyful intimacy? Ann, the woman in the local laundrette for example, she comes to mind, she's my friend. Do they do brain surgery for this stuff?

And even if I could recast him in my life as 'friend', he was a friend that I wasn't ever to be able to see. It felt as though nothing else mattered. Everything I had learned in Christianity, Buddhism, meditation, a hundred excellent seminars, my own work – 'happiness regardless of external events', my beliefs about contribution, everything I stood for, it all meant nothing. I only wanted to see Harry.

I completely forgot about his wife and, yes, a son of thirteen. It was all about me. I turned my anger onto myself. What had I done? How had I 'created this'? Dreadful New Age-speak that holds us totally responsible for everything. Was I too strong? Too weak? Had I sent too many emails? Had I driven him away? I went over and over my personal responsibility, heaping condemnation on condemnation. I spoke to Harry and he just sounded guilty, wretched. I had somehow turned from someone he loved and wanted to be with to someone he felt guilty about. I had never asked Harry to leave his wife, I'd only asked him please not to lie to her. In the case of my Harry, the idea of leaving had been his choice, his decision, but now he didn't even respond to my emails.

I felt my belief in everything I had held to be good and true slip through my fingers. I didn't understand the universe any more. All his love – where was it? He didn't even ask what I was doing. 'If what we have isn't love,' I said, 'then I don't know what love is.' He just wanted to know whether I was over him so that he could stop feeling guilty. I had somehow become a mistake he had made. No explanations, no phone calls, nothing. I sobbed, my ego convinced that it was my failures, rather than any possible love for his family that had kept him away and denied us both the life that we could have had.

'What did I do?' I asked, like a dazed person, convinced that nothing short of ten years of therapy seven times a week in twelve-hour sessions could fix me.

One friend said, 'Actually it's not complicated at all . . . you don't have to analyse your subconscious or tear yourself apart.'

'I don't?'

'No. It's right there in your conscious mind how you set this one up.'

'It is?'

'Yes. You see, Isabel, if you meet someone and he has a French accent there is a reasonable chance that you will be aware.'

'That he's French. Yes. Oh. I see.'

'Yup. So there was a point, wasn't there, when you knew?'

'He was a Harry.'

'Yup. There was a simple fact about him you overlooked. He was married.'

And yes. There it was. I had known it and I had overlooked it. Somehow he slipped through my net and he was such a brightly coloured fish I didn't even care. I went on ignoring the fact and I allowed myself to love him. With a hundred per cent of my heart and soul.

So it goes like this, girls. 'May I buy you dinner/lunch/coffee or send you emails?'

'Well, this may seem a little odd, but may I ask ... are you married?'

And if the answer is no, just check ... 'Separated? Living with someone but temporarily going through a bad time? In any kind of relationship which the other person believes to be monogamous?' This may seem a little direct, but I'm sure they'll understand. If not you add, 'I'm single, you see, and I've been warned ...'

Now, I don't want you to misunderstand me here. I'm not saying that I'm the gullible innocent victim and that Toms, Dicks and Harrys are the bad boys. Not at all. But neither are the single women the evil seductresses that the wives would sometimes like to believe they are. Certainly I wanted to believe that when I was the wife. Many married women, mercifully, are less judgemental and righteous than I was. They are wiser. Human relationships, I now know, are very complex and I have now given up judging anyone. The 'rights' and 'wrongs' have to go out of the window and I think we all have to simply observe what is and to try to offer compassion and kindness whatever.

I hope this is all clear, we know our terms now, and I can save you some of the heartbreaking fuck-ups I've made.

So now we can proceed with the narrative.

3. A 'FRIGHTFULLY JOLLY' NIGHT OUT

SINGLES EVENTS AND MEETING MR DEADCAT

I raised the subject of internet dating on my website blog and emails started to pour in. Women who had hated it far outnumbered anyone who had had positive experiences; some people who just wanted 'a bit of a laugh' and were happy to spend a large amount of time in internet dating chat rooms seemed to find people to go out and meet; lots of horror stories of Toms and Dicks in disguise either looking for a way out or looking for women but with no intention of leaving; lots of men just wanting sex. For anyone who was looking for anything more serious it seemed to be more of a torment than a joy.

I know so many single women. I can think of a barrister, two single mums, three actresses, a couple of women in the publishing industry, a doctor, two nurses, two vicars, four students, three businesswomen, a grandmother, a teacher, an artist, a sculptor, a photographer, a doctor of science . . . well, I can think of a lot of women without even opening my address book. But if I held a party for these women I can't think of one available man that I'd like to introduce the women to. Of course I know a good range of Toms and

Dicks, gay men (give me ten minutes and I'll find you a hundred), asexual men who don't have relationships with either men or women for some non-specific reason ... an increasingly large number, men who lie a lot and sleep with lots of women (usually at least twenty years younger than them) never so much as contemplating monogamy – I know a couple of those. But, and here is the really strange fact; an available man who I want to have dinner with ... I don't know a single one.

It isn't a problem just in the UK, either. When I toured to promote my first book I spoke mainly to women journalists wherever I went. In Japan the women said to me, 'Japanese men no good. We like English men.' In Spain the women said, 'Spanish men are such pigs ... we don't like dating Spanish men.' In Italy the women said, 'We don't like Italian men ... where are the good men?' I stared at them hopelessly. 'Not in Spain, according to the women I met last week, or Japan, or Sweden, or Germany or ... I really don't know what to say to you.' And here I am, two books later, with this same problem.

I phone my friend Celia – a brilliant family barrister.

'Celia, do you know many single women?'

'I know five women barristers who are single. Very bright women, good careers, lovely homes – they have everything – except a man.'

'Do you know any interesting single male barristers?'

'I'd be dating him if I knew one. Why, what are you doing?'

'I don't know ... I'm thinking about it.'

'Well, when you have the solution, please let me know.'

So I go on thinking and talking to women and to men. I sit in coffee shops and watch people go by. I notice the huge difference in numbers between attractive women and attractive men. I know this is a superficial test – but try it some time. For 'attractive' I mean men or women who are not hugely overweight, who have thought for more than thirty seconds about the combination of clothes they have on, have washed their hair, have some kind of spring in their step or a smile on their face and look as if they may be an amusing dinner companion. It's a depressing task. Let's call it the PYLTHDW game, 'people you'd like to have dinner with', just by seeing them walk by. The game can be played by either sex and about either sex . . . just notice the difference between men who look interesting and women. Don't believe me – try it.

So I wonder what I would do about all this if it were a professional job. Mission impossible. I talked to girlfriends about it. 'Well, it's the Holy Grail isn't it? No one knows where they are.'

Then, while I went on pondering, I got invited to a singles event. In theory I could meet single men there, but the woman who has invited me says that the women there are usually wonderful but the men disappointing. She had never met any men there she was remotely interested in, but she kept going anyway in the hope that one month there would be a man there she liked the look of. This reminded me of my favourite definition of madness: 'Madness is doing the same thing and expecting a different result.'

Workshops I had taken (of the American 'get off your backside and sort your life out' type) were full of tips like these . . . another one of my favourites, which has to be recited in a schoolgirl singsong, is:

If you always do
What you've always done
Then you'll always get
What you've always got.
If you want something different
You've got to . . .

(take a deep breath and shout the last line to yourself really loud so that you will be sure to hear)

DO SOMETHING DIFFERENT!

This has to be shouted because we all seem to keep doing the same things and expecting something, one day, to change. Or I do. Was that Greg delivering my post this morning? Oh no . . . shit, it was the postman again.

Of course all I really want, still, is to be with Harry, but I also want to forget Harry and I've never been to a singles event before. So that's OK . . . I can justify it in my mind as not totally humiliating because it comes into the 'try anything once' box. So I look up the website of the company organising the event, www.thesinglesolution.co. uk. I've been warned about the age groups by a woman who'd been before.

'Everyone lies about their age, so in the thirties and forties group, the cut-off age is supposed to be forty-seven (by which time you are presumably beyond the pale). But you often see men who come to these evenings who are obviously in their fifties, or even sixties.'

Suddenly this question 'How old are you?' seemed to come up every day since I'd been exploring this issue. When I was trying to change the world no one asked me how old I was. I feel indignant on behalf of girlfriends who are fifty and look thirty-two on the one hand, and incensed at all the men want to date women twenty years (or more) younger than them.

'It's the same on the twenties to thirties nights,' my new friend continues, a flat resignation in her voice. 'The organisation let me go to one of those once when I complained that so many of the men in the thirties and forties group seemed to be sixty. I went to the twenties to thirties group and lots of the men were evidently in their forties wanting to date much younger women.'

All this conversation was ringing in my ears as I filled in the application form. I thanked God that I had not yet reached the end of my life. Age 47. The evening was in a wine bar in Moorgate, close to the City of London, presumably chosen so that people who worked in the City could go straight there and not go home first. They were charging £25 and the evening would include a brief bit of optional informal speed dating. 'A chance to meet eight men for three minutes each.' Drinks, of course, were extra, as was food, but the price seemed fair.

The evening comes. I find the pub, walk around the building and bump into a man who is evidently looking for the same place. Oh God, how embarrassing. A huge badge appears on my coat: 'I'm a sad loser who can't find a man – please feel sorry for me.' He sees the badge and is appropriately sweet and sympathetic. Evidently public school, he has that cut-glass accent that American women find so irresistible. But I do not find irresistible. He is (and I know I'm judging by appearances here – but everything about him makes me want to run away) gawky and buffoonish. He has a big smile and is obviously very keen to be considered charming.

I hold out my hand in a friendly way. I bear him no ill will as long as I don't have to date him. 'I'm Isabel,' I bark, in my usually doggy-tail-wagging kind of way.

'Oh – we don't give our real names at these events . . . we have sign-in names. Mine is Hampshire Jack.'

'Oh. I don't have a sign-in name, so mine is just Isabel. Which is my real name.'

'Honestly?'

'Yes. Honestly. Why pretend? This stigma about being single – well, someone has to come out, don't they? I mean, gay people walk down streets and celebrate, but single people hide. Don't you think that's strange?'

'It's just the way that they do it here.'

'Mmmm.'

We arrive at the venue. Upstairs is the bar for normal people, all sitting and drinking happily with their friends. But we have to pay £25 to go downstairs and join the social misfits. I sigh deeply and wonder about staying upstairs and drinking a bottle of vodka or gin in an evening. I can't face even talking to the smiling blonde wearing the T-shirt and taking money from people. I run off to the ladies', look in the mirror and wonder where the attractive woman I have occasionally seen there has gone. Instead there's some old witch character of about 97 vaguely hoping to be taken for 57. Mascara is running down my face from cycling earlier, making me look absurd. Lines and wrinkles have gathered together for a party on my face. 'Look how deep we can go' they wave at me from the edges of what were once my eyes.

I feel disinclined to wave back and just stand looking at them resentfully. Somewhere in my head I know that it's possible to improve the situation. Apply lipstick? No, don't want to look as if I'm making an effort. I apply a little lip balm and rub rather half-heartedly at the smudged mascara.

'None of us are twenty-five any more, are we?' says a woman staring at her reflection in the mirror next to me.

'What?' I look round, startled from my inner dialogue of complaints.

'We're not, are we? Twenty-five. Any more.'

'I'm not anyway. I believe some women are.'

'Oh yes. I suppose so.'

We approach the smiling singles-event organiser.

'Are you new?'

'Yes . . .'

'Well, if you could just put your name and your email address and your age here.'

I briefly contemplate screaming 'What is this obsession with age?' But instead I just fill in the form quietly and honestly and hand her my £25.

'As well as the speed dating option we have a flirt coach here tonight . . .' She looks at me with a sympathetic air. 'In case you need any tips.' I smile rather pathetically.

The crowded bar area would have looked perfectly normal if everyone wasn't wearing name labels that say (I kid you not) 'Essex Man', 'Mike69', 'Deadcat', 'Mr Nice Guy'. One of the organisers hands me a label.

'Can I use my real name?'

'Sure, some people do. Some people prefer to protect their real identities.'

'Why? To avoid the social stigma of being single?'

'I suppose.'

Someone has to fight back.

I write, 'Isabel Losada' on my label and flounce off to find a large glass of red wine and the woman who has invited me. I've never met her before, so I have no idea what she looks like. All I know is her name, which isn't on any of the labels. I already feel that I'm not doing this right, walking around looking at women's labels (most of which are pinned to their breasts).

I cast an eye around the room at the men – right next to me are two men who make me wish that I could draw cartoons. They're both thin, and almost bald and very smartly dressed in suits and ties; the suits are strangely similar and the ties, bizarrely, both red. The ties, I feel, are attempting to give them an air of confidence, but aren't quite up to the job. They both have thick spectacles and an earnest look about them. Maybe they're accountants, or bankers.

The numbers of men and women are about equal, the organisers had been careful to fix that. I glance round to see whether the assertion that the men are somehow not up to the standard of the women is true. And I can't say that it is. Not because the men there resemble a casting session for James Bond (now that's a good thought) but because a lot of the women look, I suppose, the same as I look, as if they wish they were somewhere else.

There are 'types' of men noticeable immediately. The public-school types like the 'chap' who had shown me in. The earnest types who count as 'gentlemen', like the two in the glasses with the red ties. The men who would always be described as 'lads', no matter what their age. There are a couple of those, who have a 'you fancy me, don't you?' look about them that it's hard to agree with. But the majority just look kinda 'normal' in a forgettable kind of way. Men that you would just walk past, which is what I suppose women had always done.

You are probably hating me describing these pour souls in this way, shouting 'who the hell does she think she is?' at the hapless book in your hands and contemplating hurling it across the room . . . but what would you have me do? I have to be honest with you. Maybe I am too choosy. Well, if so, I will have my punishment, which will be to share my bed with a ginger cat, a brown Labrador, a hot-water bottle dressed as a badger and a novel. So you can just watch it all unfurl.

I look around the room and notice that a flirting workshop's going on. I walk up to observe it in a superior manner. I certainly don't need to do this. A group of about ten women are sitting in a row opposite a group of men while a man, who appears to be gay, teaches the women how to make 'toffee eyes' at the men. He points out to the men that it's their job to notice and to do something about it. We have to be taught these things now?

I order some food and sit munching chips while carefully avoiding making eye contact with any of the men. A girl walks up. 'Ah, you're Isabel . . . I was wondering how I'd find you. My name is Christy. Well, it isn't really, but that's what I'm known as here. I've put your name down for the next session of the speed dating, is that OK?'

'Sure.'

'So what do you think?'

'I think the organisers have done a good job. I mean, it's crowded and I didn't expect it to be and the numbers are even, and there is a relaxed atmosphere and it's not too loud, which I like.'

'It's great as long as you don't talk to the men. One man over there just told me that this is his once-a-month night out. He literally stays in every other night and always looks forward to these events. I find that deeply depressing.'

'What does he do then?'

'I think he's an academic of some kind.'

They announce the start of the speed-dating event. The women are given a seat with a man sitting opposite them.

Once every three minutes the men have to move on. It's as easy as that. There are ten men and five minutes later I have forgotten at least seven of them. But I *love* speed dating. Many things appeal to me about it ... the girly part of me loves it that the women just sit like queens, while men have to keep getting up to move on. I like the fact that I can follow my daughter's directions for dealing politely with people who ramble. She gives the instruction to new lodgers for dealing with me, 'Nod and smile.' I could do this for the man who talked for three minutes about his IT business and the fact that he can take skiing holidays whenever he wants. Had I ever been skiing? I told him, quite honestly, that I had not. Then a man made him move to the next table. Another man told me that he much prefers this informal speed dating to the one where you have a card and have to put a tick in a box. 'This is much better, as you can go on talking with people afterwards at the bar if you've had an interesting conversation.' The third man talked about the false identity issue: 'you only give people your real name if you feel the chemistry is there. I think it's more than just the names. Everyone here has a false identity.'

'Why do you think that is?'

'You can be whoever you want here and protect who you really are.'

'Do you come here regularly, then?'

'Yes. I like being in a room where you know that all the women are single and available.'

I wince. But then he's moved on.

I can't remember a single word any of the other men said. They weren't unpleasant men. I didn't see any of them that looked like psychopaths and I'd have been happy to have been walked back to the station by any of them. But just as far as Moorgate station.

'So?' asks Christy.

'I love the system,' I say. 'And they seem harmless enough.'

'You'd be surprised.'

'What do you mean?'

'You know how I told you that the balance between men and women has become so bad that it's a real problem for some of the dating agencies? They just can't find men. Some of them are reducing the level of checking that they do and even offering free membership to men if they'll agree to take a certain number of women out. This is true, I promise you. There is one agency that I belong to, it's not cheap, and I was out with this man one night who told me that he had a free membership when I'd paid a fortune to join. And I wouldn't have minded, only that later on the subject of religion came up and he was a Satanist. He spoke about Beelzebub with what I felt was an inappropriate level of affection.'

I laugh, but I don't think I am supposed to.

'Did you tell the agency about this?'

'No. Do you think I should?'

'I can't believe that they are so desperate for men that they would be prepared to have Satanists on the books. I mean, equal opportunities is one thing, but introducing single women to men with a commitment to the study and application of evil is another, surely?'

'I suppose so.'

Then they announced the flirting workshop. By now I'm in a good mood and happy to try anything. I take my place on the end of the row and listen to the instructions with amusement and rapt attention.

'The good news, girls, is that it's all up to you. Men – they send the signals, you just have to notice and recognise that you are being signalled. Every woman has traffic lights on her head, guys, and she is at red, amber or green. So this is how you recognise a green signal . . . now, women, what you do is this. You are going to flirt with the man sitting directly opposite you.' I look up and see the IT salesmen from earlier. Mmm.

'What you do is,' he goes on with a smile and very high energy, 'you catch the man's eye and you signal this thought to him – you send him this silent message with your eyes: "You are really fit." Send it really clearly and then look away. It's very important that you look away after that length of contact or he'll feel threatened. Especially men in London, who are very shy.

'This is the signal, men. This means she likes you. The reason we call it toffee eyes is because if you notice any eyes sticking to you for longer than you would expect, that is a signal. The trouble is, as all girls know, men often miss these signals because the guys aren't looking at her eyes. Look at her eyes, gentlemen. Not anywhere else. This works all the way from one side of a crowded bar to another. So now let's do it.'

People shuffle uncomfortably.

'Women, look away, and when I say "toffee eyes", look up and send him the signal.'

This is quite something. I've never sent 'come and get me now' signals to a man who I'm totally uninterested in before. But I'm here to do the exercise and I guess the better I do it the more he'll learn. So I look up when I'm instructed and gaze at him as though he's George Clooney, Pierce Brosnan, Robert Redford, Mel Gibson, Robert DeNiro, Al Pacino and Harry all rolled into one. 'You are REALLY fit' I stare at him intensely, adding a coy smile for good measure. Then I look away and pay an inordinate amount of attention to the girl next to me. I look at the coach . . . anywhere, but don't want to glance back at him for as much as a second.

'How was that?' he asks the guys. The men complain that it's really quick. 'A woman would be unlikely to look at you for longer than that,' he says. 'She'd be afraid that you'd think she was a psychopath or desperate.'

I can sense the IT salesmen looking at me to see whether I'm going to glance at him outside the given moment of the exercise. I'm not. But if I'm going to play with the poor man I may as well do it well. This is an exercise, after all.

'Let's do it again,' says the coach. I keep my eyes firmly on the girl beside me. 'Toffee eyes.' I flash my eyelashes up across the room, 'You are REALLY sexy,' I signal for all I am worth. 'Sexy' is one syllable – one beat longer. Then I look away. I chat pointedly to the girl next to me. 'How's it going?'

'My man over there doesn't even know which woman he's supposed to be looking at.' Oh dear.

'Now, let's move on, guys, and you can see how different women do this differently.' The men get up and move on. The man who was supposed to have been looking at my neighbour has no clue where to look. I wave at him until he sees me, pointing at myself. At least he knows where to look.

'Now again, "toffee eyes".'

I glance up. 'YOU . . .' I signal for all I'm worth, 'are Johnny Depp.' I just have time to notice a perplexed look go across the face of the rather overweight and bald man on the other side of the room before I look away and speak again to the girl next to me.

'Don't look back at them after the allocated time,' I say to her, 'that will confuse them even more.'

I think some of the girls found it harder than I did. Ten years as a professional actress had to come in useful sometime. I remember as a young aspiring actress at drama school I had been cast once as Jane Eyre. Only my Rochester was a boy I abhorred with every ounce of me. The feeling was mutual. He played our love scenes with excessive amounts of unnecessary arm movement; he would bounce up and down on the stage, unable to put two feet firmly on the ground and wouldn't grace me with as much eye contact as I had just bestowed on the man across the room. I hated him. The man across the room was easier to send 'I adore you' signals to.

'Men, move around again,' says the coach. 'You see, men, how these signals feel different with different women – but it's all about the toffee eyes.'

I venture a question. 'I'm sure I heard somewhere that if you look at a man and hold eye contact he'll just walk straight up to you. Or maybe that was an instruction for a man? Some film somewhere?'

'Well, that may work in America or in Australia, but in London the men would run a mile if you did that to them. It's far too scary for them. I have my work cut out trying to get men to walk up to a woman after she has sent the normal signals, let alone a challenge like that.'

'But if a man is too scared to walk up to a woman who is flirting with him, then what's he going to be like to date?'

The women laugh. Then the men laugh.

'Fortunately that's not my problem ... this is a flirting workshop. OK. Let's do it a couple more times.'

So on we go. It's very interesting having all this information made specific. I did know this, but not as specifically as he has taught it.

'Now, girls, if you do this and he doesn't come up to you, you can repeat it a second time for the same duration. If he still doesn't get it, then you send a quicker "you're thick" glance. If he still doesn't come up to you then he's either painfully shy or dead and has been propped up.'

'Can you go up to him then? If he still hasn't come towards you?' one of the girls asks.

'You can.' Why would you want to?

'And if he doesn't speak to you?'

'Help him out by asking for some trivial piece of information.'

Mmm, like, 'Why does it say "Deadcat" on your name label?'

The session ends and I'm immediately approached by a man whose label says 'Tall, Dark and Handsome', which is interesting, because he isn't. Not any of the three. 'You were very good at that exercise,' he says and I notice that he has a problem with bad breath. Oh dear. I hope if I ever have bad breath someone will tell me right away. 'Thank you,' I reply, resisting the temptation to add, 'I'm an actress.' Instead I smile, 'It was interesting, wasn't it?' He buys me a glass of wine and I stay and make small talk with him and lots of the women and a few of the other men for the rest of the evening.

And that was my first experience of a singles event and some informal speed dating all rolled into one. I had a great evening out and I think I'd actually recommend it to men as a way of meeting women. Not all the women there were women I would have wanted to have met for dinner if I'd been a man, but I'd say that at least a third of the women looked fun and interesting. The venue had been smart, the organisation friendly, the activities very enjoyable. Unlike Christy, I wasn't disappointed with the evening at all.

But it felt horrible, artificial. It's that self-conscious feeling you get on stage if you know you are acting badly or if you have egg on your clothes and you think people are looking at it. The fact that the men knew that 'all the women are available' made it all feel vaguely humiliating and the fact that everyone assumed false names I found worrying. So I wouldn't recommend such evenings to any woman I know. And there had certainly not been any man there that I was going to stick toffee eyes onto in the hope of turfing out the dog, the cat, the book and the badger.

4. THE WRONG KIND OF MOAN

LIMITING BELIEFS, STATISTICS AND DATING AGENCIES

I'm not doing the singles weekends or the singles holidays. If the man that destiny intends me to spend the rest of my life with is on a singles weekend, then the stars will just have to run off course and I will have to die a lonely and sad old woman. Except I don't really think I will die a lonely and sad old woman because I have so many wonderful female friends in the same situation that at least, if we can never find a man we even want to have dinner with, we can all move into a big house together that would become a glorious celebration of being old batty females. We'd all have to wear purple. And have lots of cats. Growing cannabis in the garden would be an absolute must. Neighbours would say, 'What *do* they get up to in there?' And we could ensure that there were lots of rumours about us all. And we could run around the garden naked at night . . . and pretend to be witches and have big bonfires and make strange sounds to frighten the local schoolchildren. And we'd hold parties regularly, with champagne, to celebrate the fact that none of us were married to men who wore bedroom slippers, watched too much cricket and rarely spoke.

Now remind me – why did I want a man again? Ah yes, I remember – because, suffering from eternal optimism, I am still hoping to find one who doesn't watch cricket, which is why I will not be going to a singles weekend. No – the thought chills me and I know it's wrong to do condemnation before examination and I'm sure that there are some good singles weekends and singles holidays, but, just this once, will you let me off the hook? I'm missing them out, OK? I'd be afraid that the same man, whose only night out in the month is the singles night that I went to, has his only holiday every year with the singles holidays. Please address your letters of complaint about my stereotypical, outdated and inaccurate portrayal of singles holidays to the publisher, along with the stories of how you met your Mr Right ... your soul mate, on a singles weekend. It's inevitable now that I've decided not to go that that is where he is. But I'll risk it.

I want to do this and have fun. So I have to do something different. Which is turning out to be harder than I expected. The problem is that the voices of doom and gloom are everywhere. Every female I speak to between the ages of 21 and 81 wants to let me know that my mission is doomed to failure, that there are no single men out there who are worth dating, that the fact that I don't know any interesting single men is not unusual at all.

My friend Sally is convinced that my search for an interesting man is doomed. She says that he doesn't exist. More worryingly, she has proof ...

'Try this test, Isabel.'

'Mmm?'

'Ask anyone – *anyone*, this question: "Do you know one single man between the ages of twenty-five and say, fifty-five who, if you were single and female you'd want to date?" You'll find that they'll have trouble with the first bit, but if you throw in the second you'll have them. Mostly they'll say, "I know a single man," and then when you say, "Would you want to date him?" they'll hesitate and then add something like, "Well not really, he's a very sweet guy but he's forty-five and lives with his mother. Which wouldn't be bad, of course, if he'd moved back ... but in his case he never left in the first place." Something like that ... try it.'

So I sent the question out by email to a group of ten married female friends and ten married male friends.

'No.'

'No.'

'No.'

'None come to mind that I'd be interested in dating. I know one, maybe, but he's 57. But I know loads of interesting women.'

'No.'

'Isabel, the weird truth is that I don't know any attractive, eligible men (let alone in that age range) and in my experience nearly all single men are single for very good reasons . . .'

'I know one man. Personally he's not someone I would ever fancy in a million years, but he's sensitive and has a job and I'm sure he could make a good partner for someone. Does he count, even though I wouldn't be interested in him? Anyway, he's the one and only eligible man I know.'

'Dear Isabel – this is a question I can answer without pausing for breath. No.'

'I am now a single female again and I don't know any men that I would consider dating at all, let alone between the ages of 35 and 55, which would be my age range'

'No.' This from a married man. 'Most of the men I know are hopeless with women.'

Oh dear.

'I know one . . . but then I wouldn't want to date him myself. He is certainly not fit to date anyone of an even vaguely left-wing persuasion.'

Thought this was interesting.

'I did know one man who became available. Very good looking. Came out of a relationship – joined a dating agency and has now moved in with a much younger woman he met through the agency . . . in less than a month.'

Oh, good grief.

One male friend of 53 gave this answer: 'I don't know any. All the single men I know are not able to handle relationships. To have a good relationship needs experience, maturity and wisdom. Above all, they don't have a good sense of humour. Women like men who can make them laugh, but it's a more mature humour than men. Most of the men I know have a very immature, I'd go so far as to say stupid sense of humour, so if I was a woman I wouldn't want to date any of the men I know.'

This is may be a little harsh and this is, as you see, one of my male friends who prefers the company of women . . . but nevertheless, from a woman's point of view I thought it was an interesting answer. I was not feeling very encouraged, though.

Then there is this complication, 'It depends how you define single. I have a male friend who is 46 and left a marriage last year, but he's currently shagging a 24-year-old Russian ballet dancer. Well, to be more precise – two Russian ballet dancers. She asked him last week if he'd like to try a ménage-à-trois with a friend.'

I emailed back . . .

'So this guy is looking to give up these sexual frolics for a mature relationship with a woman near his own age? I don't think so.'

'No. I don't think so either. If I'm honest, lots of men I know have the same story. Sadly, it's very common and with the flood of passport-seekers this type of relationship will only rise. What I think you are observing is the decline in the importance of the family. Men don't want a loving, monogamous wife (it seems) when they can have a threesome with some young foxy chicks. Its consumerism superimposed onto relationships. Why work for anything of quality when the price of love is so cheap?'

I still think there are men of 46 out there who are at least open to dating women in their forties. I hear that Shere Hite – who is in her sixties – dates a man twenty years her junior, so maybe we'll have to start turning the tables? One woman said to me, 'Isabel, as it's known that men rarely get wiser with age, why not date them when they are younger?'

Curiouser and curiouser. And how's this?

'Isabel, this does not answer your question. My answer is ''no'' I'm afraid . . . I don't know any men I'd invite to my home for dinner who are single. But I thought you may like this. I want to tell you about my father, who is seventy. My mother died last year and she had been in a specialist hospital, so my father flew out when she died and they had the funeral at that time. When he returned a woman met him at the airport, who is also seventy. She brought her daughter along, I suppose not to seem too forward. She had been an old friend of my mother's. Anyway, they have been together ever since and married within three months. Once I'd got over the shock it rather made me laugh. She didn't hang about, did she?'

This was not the information I had been hoping for. Somewhere out there, someone must know a man whose wife need not necessarily have died in the last 24 hours.

Then finally a tiny sign of hope.

This reply came in from a male friend who is married himself. 'I know one. He's 43. Divorced. Wife kicked him out last year. Two kids, which the ex-wife has the care of.'

'Is he sleeping with any number of 24-year-olds?'

'Not as far as I know.'

Now you'll be very proud of me. I didn't ask, 'Why do you think the wife kicked him out?' I stuck to my question and asked, 'And you think he's OK . . . you'd consider going out with him if you were female?'

'I would, yes. He and I were at school together and he's godfather to my kids, so I think he's great.'

Brilliant. So in only twenty emails it can be done. I didn't ask his name . . . that wasn't the point of the random test. I just wanted to know that one exists.

He'd be amused no doubt, whoever he is, if he could read this. One was not a very good statistic, though. So I found a single female friend who owed me a favour and begged her to come to a library with me and look at some real statistics. Just how many available men are there in the UK?

Apart from the one divorced man above, I suppose you still don't believe that there are any, do you? I knew you wouldn't, so I have my evidence. Statistics don't prove much, but at least they can help us to deconstruct those beliefs a little. So here goes.

I drag my friend Jenny off to the library to consult the National Statistics and to sit at a computer looking at figures. The last year for which the figures are available informed us that in England and Wales alone there are over 12.5 million single men.

'Yes, Isabel, but half of those are under nineteen,' says Jenny, peering over my shoulder.

'Look, let's be positive,' I say. 'I'm trying to be encouraging.'

'OK, but get your facts right.'

We stare at the figures.

'Look at this . . . Divorce – divorced men remarrying in this year, 83,554 . . .'

I smiled.

'Jenny, do you think all these women dated the men when they were still married?'

'Who knows? Divorced women remarrying, 81,770.' So we're almost equal. Were these divorcees marrying each other, I wondered. What happened to the extra two thousand women? I scanned down the page . . .

'Decree absolutes granted to women, 114,665. And granted to men 51,691. Does that mean that over double the divorces are initiated by the woman?'

'It would seem so. Or that the men are lazier? Every year they've given since 1981 has twice as many divorces granted to women as to men. And look at this.' Jenny scanned through the figures . . . reasons for divorce . . . '68,859 "bad behaviour".'

'I love it. They just will not take the rubbish out, will they? Kick 'em out, sisters.'

'57,476 – separation for two years.'

'That means that they couldn't be bothered to argue about it.'

'286 – combination of more than one ground.'

'That means that they were determined to argue about it. The lawyers must love those.'

'654 – desertion.'

'That presumably means that they just walked out the door and never even gave a forwarding address.'

'16,831 – separation for five years.'

'They don't care whether they are married or not, evidently. Bunch of Dicks that lot.'

'What?'

'Oh, nothing.'

'And finally 32,084 – adultery.'

We don't seem to be very good at relationships, do we?

'But where are the figures for the single men?'

'OK. Men for this year – single, divorced and widowed: 4,899,000. Women: 3,893,000. So there you have it. A million more men. Roughly.'

'And that's in the right age group?'

'Twenty-five to fifty-five.'

'There are a million spare men?'

'No.'

Jenny sat at a computer and did clever things. '*The Times* on 4 February quotes figures that show 39,261 same-sex couples. This means 0.318 per cent of all couples are homosexual couples. But that's just the cohabiting gay couples.'

'Oh, hold on . . . I think I have the gay statistics sorted in my mind. The National Survey of Sexual Attitudes and Lifestyle still famously says that it's one in ten, roughly.'

'Oh yes? And how do they define "homosexual"?'

I'd checked this. 'They define homosexual in the survey as someone who has had homosexual relationships for three years or more. I've also asked gay men friends and the ones that I asked are happy with ten per cent as a general guide, although thinking it may be higher with more not wanting to own up.'*

'So we need to take another hundred thousand off the figure, then.'

Oh dear.

'And there are the men in prison . . . far more than women, surely?'

'The National Statistics say here that in this year there were 69,600 male prisoners and 4,400 female prisoners.'

Hey, prisons? Now there's a place. How about suggesting this as an advertising campaign at a singles agency? 'Do you have a forgiving nature? Don't mind if the man in your life has a dodgy background? Happy to put the past behind you? Agency seeks reliable women to take on thousands of single men. Look no further – become a prison visitor for the wrong reason.' Gives a whole new meaning to 'unavailable'. Maybe not, huh?

Back to statistics. 'So can you just tell me, Jenny – roughly? If we have a million single men and we take out

---

* Although *The Kinsey Report* stated rather famously in 1948 that between thirty and forty per cent of heterosexual men had had at least one sexual experience to orgasm with another man and the figure is hardly likely to have gone down since then.

the ten per cent homosexual and the male prison population, bearing in mind that this is not exact science as some
gay men are likely to be in prison, and then we take out
whatever you think the figure is for the cohabiting men,
How many are left?'

'We have roughly twenty-five per cent of 900,000 cohabiting. That's 225,000.'

Jenny does maths in her head.

'So????'

'Seventy thousandish in prison – leaves 605,000. This is
very approximate.'

'Sure. But it's still a figure I like – 605,000 is a figure that
I like very much.'

'It is? Why?'

'Because it is not zero.'

'That's true. Mathematically speaking it is much greater
than zero.'

Now, I know the research wasn't exactly of an academic
nature. Not exactly PhD-quality standard. But what else do
you need to know?

There are hundreds of thousands of spare single men out
there! Why on earth is it, if there are more men, that women
find it so hard to find them? I thought I'd go and ask a
professional, so I looked up Mary Balfour. Mary took over
the running of the leading London dating agency Drawing
Down the Moon in 1986 and since that time has seen
literally thousands of single women and considerably fewer
single men walk through her doors ... but she has still
managed to match up an impressive number of them. I
thought I'd go and have a chat with her and see if her years
of experience could throw any light on this, the greatest of
all modern mysteries.

Considerately, Transport for London has arranged for the
number 49 bus to run all the way from my door on the
Battersea Park Road to their door in trendy High Street
Kensington. The offices of Drawing Down the Moon are on

the top floor . . . thus ensuring that all wheezing smokers have given themselves away by the time they get to the door. I am not a smoker, but was still fairly refreshed by the eight flights of stairs. 'We can always tell the smokers before they get in the door.' She smiled.

Mary Balfour is red-headed, with a reassuringly soft and rounded face and a reassuringly soft and rounded body. She looks to me as if she is in her fifties and has a gentle, non-judgemental air about her. All her bits seemed to be her own and she didn't appear to have resorted to nips, tucks, Botox or any of the other widely available options for making women of 55 look 35. She seemed happy and is obviously running a business that she enjoys. She showed me into an attractively decorated room and had a companion arrive with coffee and biscuits. Then Mary asked me about myself and, I noticed, listened attentively. This quality of being able to listen well has become so rare that it stands out when I experience it. She was obviously giving me the professional once-over – body language, tone, timbre of voice, everything. Except I wasn't there to join her agency. I was after her knowledge and expertise.

'So, Mary . . . Where are all the men?'

Some rumours say that there is a crisis in the dating agencies where women are said to outnumber men by eight to two. But I had no means of checking this and I wasn't even going to ask Mary, because this was her profession and, even if the rumours are true, I could hardly expect her to admit them. But I could ask her about general trends.

'Why is it that there are *so* many women who can't find men?' I got out my pen and started to scribble furiously.

'The first factor is the ageism. Men want to date younger women and they fantasise about dating them younger still. A significant percentage are looking for women at least ten years younger. We have to train them out of that.'

I was thinking, 'Ten years?' Mmmm that's not what Christy at the singles night said, or my friend who has a mate shagging the two dancers. They seemed to think that twenty years was nearer the mark. Mary's just being nice.

'Secondly, men are just not as commitment-minded as women and not as likely to acknowledge their need for any kind of emotional dependency. They have it, of course, they just won't own up. Then there is the fact that men aren't in a hurry and women are. The number of women who come here and join up at thirty-nine and three-quarters is quite funny. The biological clock is screaming at them, which makes men nervous, understandably.'

'But don't men have a biological clock too?'

'Yes. But theirs doesn't start to ring until they are forty-seven. And then they'll look around for a woman of thirty-five who is good breeding stock. So it can be hard for us to persuade a man of forty-three to meet a woman of thirty-nine even if we think she'd be perfect for him. And they are scared . . . with good reason. Most of the men who come here have a friend who has been trapped. He's been told that she is on the Pill and so thought it safe to have unprotected sex with her and the next thing he knows she's pregnant and he has a relationship for the rest of his life with her whether he wants one or not. So men are very scared of that. Most men know someone who has had this done to them.'

'But I still don't understand how the age thing means there are no men out there.'

'It skews it all down the line. Women in their fifties who are often still in their prime and at the height of their careers are not interested in men in their late sixties unless they are rich, famous or charismatic.'

'Yes – it's interesting that charismatic is on the list, though. It's not just that they want them to be rich.'

'No. In fact, many of the women who come here have their own money. They don't need the men to be rich, they just want them to have money of their own so that if the woman wants to go on holiday, for example, she doesn't end up having to pay for him as well.'

They would have to be fairly well-heeled anyway to join the agency. The range of services offered by Drawing Down the Moon start at £950 a year and go up to £8,000 a year for the full-on personal matchmaker services. The prices offer everyone a kind of protection . . . someone would have to be financially self-reliant to be able to afford to join, so this protects the members from anyone being after anyone else for the money.

'Then of course homosexuality is a factor. No matter what people say, our personal experience is that there are more gay men than gay women. We once opened a gay section here and a year later we had two hundred and fifty gay men and eighteen gay women. I gave all the women their money back in the end because we just couldn't find enough women to find partners for them. Or maybe the women are just better at finding their own partners. I don't know.'

'So you get fewer straight men joining up than women?'

'Yes. We don't try to hide that. It's harder for us to find men than women. We now send out head-hunters, heart-hunters if you like. We have female staff and we'll send them out to social events, cultural and business events, exhibitions, singles events to look for men. We heart-hunt and we are happy to be open about this. We go out, find single men, talk to them and invite them to join us. We're always on the lookout. I was at a Prom last night and there was a man there alone with a book and I almost leaned over and used the book as an excuse to start a conversation with him. A man alone with a book is very likely to be single. I do it all the time. And I bring them in. My husband finds me very embarrassing.'

'But you wouldn't send your heart-hunters just to the local pub, then?'

'No. The women who come here are looking for intelligent, commitment-minded men. And there is a shortage of them. Interesting men. All women know this.' She smiled.

I suppose professional verification should be reassuring.

'I have a definition of an interesting man that I've come up with. I've even had it approved by males.' I offered it to her: 'An interesting man is a man who, when you meet him, you feel that you'd like to have dinner with him and, having done so, you're glad that you had dinner with him and you'd like to see him again. How's that?'

'It's fair, but you have to bear in mind that many men are lousy on a first date. They are nervous and so they talk and talk about themselves usually. Women have to share the responsibility for this, as we have been brought up to be good listeners, so we sit there and smile and give him all the signals to let him know how fascinating his prattle is when actually we may be thinking, "When is he going to stop?" We need to learn to interrupt and say, "So would you like to hear about me now?" or whatever.'

'But isn't that trying to change a man? From the first date? Not letting him be who he is? And taking responsibility for him? Doesn't sound like a good start.'

'No. It's just taking responsibility for your own experience and not allowing him to let himself down. The first time I went out with my husband he'd been going through a difficult time and he talked endlessly about his children. But if I'd judged him on that on our first date, I wouldn't be about to celebrate twenty-five happy years with him.'

I like that story. On the other hand, Harry prattled endlessly at our first (and last, as it happened) meal out together and it didn't stop me falling for him, because the content of his prattle was utterly engaging and so full of his passion for life and I could have delighted in listening to him all night long. Very different from the 'I'm going to tell you about my IT company' speech that I'd experienced at the singles evening.

'Aren't you just encouraging women to settle for something less than what they want?'

'No. We don't believe so. Women and men can both be as choosy as they want, but after the third or fourth date. Women are especially terrible at instantly dismissing men and the older they get the choosier they become. Psycho-therapists are the worst ... they arrive with a checklist. They know exactly what they want and there is no flexibility. Heaven help any man that they think is not in touch with his emotions. They go right to "Could I see this face on the pillow for the rest of my life?" before they've even been to dinner. Everybody jumps to conclusions too quickly.'

'But don't your clients see all the details and CV of people before they date them?'

'No. We don't let them do that or they'd just rule people out. We do a lot of the matchmaking ourselves and we encourage people to go on two or three dates. When someone calls us and says, "He's lovely ... I'd be really interested in having him as a friend ... he's just not the man for me," what this may mean is that he'd be perfect for her, but doesn't match up to her romantic ideal, so she's not prepared to give him a chance. If she gives him two or three dates, she may decide that she wants to go on seeing him.'

'What do you say to the accusation that interesting men don't join dating agencies?'

'They do. But we trawl the earth for them.'

It's still very confusing to me. You'd have thought the word would have got around male environments that there are many more women than men in these agencies and that men would be queuing up. Apparently not.

'So you still have more women wanting to join than men?'

'Yesterday I took phone calls from people who want to join. Seven women and one man. From speaking to them I was able to offer a place to the man and one of the women. We don't take everyone on who wants to join up. We can't take any women over the age of forty-five as we just can't help them. We can take men up to the age of fifty-two.'

I laughed. 'So a woman of forty-five is beyond the pale, then?'

'We are thinking of putting it up to forty-seven next year. Generally I encourage older women, in their fifties and sixties to try the internet. And we have another service called Only Lunch which is £1,350 a year and for that we find women a minimum of twelve interesting lunch or dinner dates. A man we'd be able to find many more.'

I love it. Do rich bachelors who live in say, Aberystwyth, know this? That all they'd have to do is sign up and a pick of London's specially selected women is here waiting to go to lunch?

'So are there any men you can't help?'

'Yes . . . smokers. We can't match smokers at all. Most women know that a man of sixty who smokes is likely to have problems getting an erection. Poor circulation, you see.'

I love it – male, sixty, yellow-stained teeth, smelly and can't get it up, seeks woman, twenty-five, for friendship and more. The truth behind the small ads.

I glanced at the clock. Mary was being generous with her time.

'So, just before I go then, Mary . . . what's your top tip for women all over the UK and all over the world? For meeting men? What to do?'

'Friendships.' She said. 'Pursue friendships. You may end up going out with someone who is a friend of someone else. It's a numbers game in the end. The more men you meet, the more men you meet, and if all else fails and you still don't meet a man that you want to commit to, at least you've got lots of new male friends.'

'Would you have a man for me if I joined up, Mary?'

She smiled and looked very professional. 'How old are you?'

I laughed. 'Aghhhh – is that a box I see appearing around me?'

'I can't match you if you don't tell me your age.'

As I left I noticed that the staff was exclusively female.

'How come no men work here?'

'Men don't want to work in dating agencies.'

'But why not? Surely what you do is psychology. Men become psychologists.'

'Yes, but not matchmakers, it seems. I always advertise to both men and women and some men come along at the interview stage, but it's usually only a handful and they are not as high quality as the women. So if you had the chance to employ a poor-rate candidate who was male or a first-rate candidate who was a woman, who would you give the job to?'

'Well, the woman, I guess.' I said. But at the same time I was thinking, I'd change the location of the ad. I'd change the wording. I'd word it in a way that would make the job more attractive to men and then maybe they could find a way to bring in more male clients. 'Fancy a woman who can stimulate your largest sex organ? (That's your brain, guys.) Want a good service? Text the experts.'

I'm not going to join her dating agency. I can't afford her prices and even if I could I'm not sure about the idea of going on dates with men that others have decided I'd like to meet. I'm not 39¾ and not very good breeding stock. I have friends who had joined and told me it was mainly very respectable City types. I couldn't think of a single guy I've ever dated who the agency would have taken on. All far too wild, or non-conformist.

But going to the environments where the men are; this sounded like much more fun. This has to be one part of the solution. I will start a collection of single men in my life to have as uncomplicated friends, as Mary suggests. I need to go where the men are to learn about the creatures. I shall go out into the field like a natural scientist and ethnographer and study them. I will spend time with them and take notes. And I will report loyally to you all my reports and observations. Maybe through this study of the gender I can understand them a little better and use this knowledge to help us track down the best of them.

Part II

EXAMINING THE GENDER IN ITS
OWN ENVIRONMENTS

1. 'CUPPA TEA, MATE?'

THE TRADES

One of the exclusively male worlds that I do find interesting is that of the trades: builders, plumbers, roofers, all that lot. Now, don't misunderstand me, I'm not saying that I find them sexually attractive – as a group there is nothing that makes me want to rip my clothes off for a group of men who, as generalisations go, are overweight, display large bum cracks and read the *Daily Sport*. I am attracted to them as males because they have skills and work hard.

This may seem weird to you. I can see that I'm going to have to face a dreaded word and a dreaded concept in this book – there is no avoiding it. The word, of course, is 'class'. It's funny, this is my fourth book: in an exploration of the world of twenty-first century nuns, the world of New Age spirituality and the question of what one person can do to make a difference, class wasn't relevant. Anyone can wake up one morning and decide to become a nun or a monk, get happy or explore how they can change the world. It makes no difference what your background is; they're just different starting points, each with its own specific challenge. There are many situations where, even in the UK, I'm happy to say, class makes not a tiny bit of difference.

In the world of male environments, however, the class issue can't be avoided. And those that work in the trades remain, by definition I suppose, working class. There are rare cases where 'middle-class' men sneak in to earn some of the takings, but they never seem to gain much admiration for it. But I have a different perspective on this. I come from a 'middle-class' (aren't these groups absurd?) background and have known many men in my lifetime who have been actors, writers, poets, fine artists, sculptors, even academics. The majority of the men I've dated have been in the arts; they have almost all been penniless.

The worst thing about being an actor, especially an out-of-work actor – and as an actor you are out of work most of the time – is that you have a skill that isn't worth anything to anyone. As the day ends you will have sent off a job application or two and made some phone calls in the hope of finding your next job. You have no result for your day's endeavour apart from the clarification of a worry about how you are going to pay the next food bill.

I have a good friend who was married to a man who was a musician. While they had three children young enough to need a mother at home, they lived in extreme poverty while my friend's husband sat and tinkled around on a keyboard, never bringing in a penny. This happens far less in working-class homes because, and OK, I know it's a generalisation, they are far less afraid of a hard day's work and don't mind getting their hands dirty. This man could have worked as a plumber for four days, kept his family off the poverty line, and still have written music on the other three days.

What is this middle-class nonsense that a hard day's labour is somehow 'beneath' us? And isn't it interesting that, while so many people complain about being unemployed or on low wages, the UK is short of 25,000 plumbers and a plumber can earn £40,000 a year and more than that in the South East. What are we to make of this?

Why are some categories of these men we are studying so unwilling to work up a sweat? Maybe some of us girls need to stop being so snobby and give some consideration to the guys who can do a little more than bang in a nail. So I thought I'd go and check them out for you. This would be my first attempt to find out what the real guys are doing with their weekends while we are all meditating.

Two minutes on the internet found me a weekend course, Introduction to Plumbing. I could bank on it not being exclusively female. I rang James at PPL Plumbing Training (www.ppltraining.co.uk) and he confirmed that yes, there would only be one other woman on the course.

'Where are you based, James?'

'York.'

'Oh. OK. Will I need anything? I've got overalls.'

'Just hard boots.'

'OK. I have those too. That's it?'

'Yup. We'll send you all the details. Be here at ten o'clock.'

The funny thing about turning up to a weekend course in plumbing is that you do not sit in a circle and go round and introduce yourselves and say what has brought you to the course at this point in your lives. No sign of a mat, a candle, or an opening prayer.

'Cuppa tea? Coffee?'

'Yeh. Thanks.'

The boss man, James, smiles amicably, but looks rather as if he wished he were somewhere else. There is a second man, Kevin, with a larger smile and eager to please.

'I'm a history teacher normally. I teach twentieth-century history, but I do a bit of plumbing too. Truth is that if I gave up the teaching I could cut the hours I work in half and double my salary at the same time. But I keep everything up.' Best ignore this comment at this stage in the day, I think.

Five rather grumpy looking guys arrive from GNER Electricians. Their bosses have decided that they need to do some plumbing this weekend. They don't look overjoyed about it. There's a young man from Zimbabwe whose father had been a farmer and was looking for a new job. Another punter called Rob who's doing up his property and wants to understand what the plumbers are up to. A young man called Happy and the other girl, who's also taking the course so she won't get ripped off by plumbers. But of course I only know this because I ask lots of questions. There were no introductions. There's also a third instructor, John, who's quiet and attentive. He's a property developer, but has made a point of knowing about property renovation and ended up teaching plumbing as a sideline. These guys are obviously onto something very lucrative.

James summons himself into action and they start on their intro. How to be a plumber. Now you can do this. Suck your teeth, shake your head, assume an air of overwhelmed despair and say: 'Going to be one hell of a tricky job, this. It'll take at least three days, I'm afraid. Don't know if I'll be able to get the parts. They'll be expensive. They're obsolete. This isn't going to be cheap, I'm afraid.'

Lots of teeth-sucking. Excellent.

We all tell our horror stories about being ripped off by plumbers and then we're down to the morning's 'lecture'. I have to use quotes as it wasn't exactly academic. At a speed obviously not designed for anyone to learn anything, he gave us an overview of the conventional ways into the industry and what the trade involves. There is, evidently, a little more to it than joining two pipes together; in theory a plumber should have a thorough knowledge of water regulations and drainage, an understanding and knowledge of all heating systems and the ability to be able to identify and rectify any problems with your plumbing. But here's the thing: unlike electricians, who are regulated and have to present you with a card from their professional body when they arrive, anyone can call themselves a plumber.

I could walk out of my two-day introductory course, place an add in the *Yellow Pages* and turn up at your house in overalls with my toolkit looking very professional and you'd be none the wiser.

The introduction is a mine of information that I feel sure would be of great interest to many seventeen-year-old males who are never told this. 'Any boy can leave school at sixteen and at seventeen he'll be earning £12,000 a year and by 21 he'll have "water regulations", be Corgi registered for central heating and be driving a BMW.'

What a weird world. Most middle-class kids at 21 have nothing but a huge student-loan debt and a degree in a subject that can't get them a job. They don't possess a single practical skill to earn a penny. So they end up taking jobs that they aren't interested in just to pay the rent and end up worse off than their working-class friends in the trades.

Here's a useful little quote for you in case you know anyone who wants to get rich. 'If you get into fitting solar heating panels, you are printing money.'

Or even, 'There is a huge demand for women plumbers because they are perceived as reliable and trustworthy.'

James moves on to practical matters and talks about joints. 'We don't cover soldering in any depth, but with all the new push-fits it's really not a problem. All new houses are plastic. In ten years you won't see copper or compressed fittings any more. The Yanks are all plastic.' Love it.

Then we're on our feet and into the workspace. I'm to put together some piping with two 15 mm 90° elbows, two equal Ts, a reducing coupler and a 22 mm stop end using olives and compression joints. Fun!

How to cut the copper without dropping the pipe cutter on my toe? How to hold the claw wrench firm with one hand so as to be able to turn the spanner with the other? How to make sure the pipes are fully home and the olives correctly compressed? This is boys' stuff. Strange really, an hour of concentration on a simple but fiddly task and I don't have to have a thought or an emotion at any time. Being a bloke has advantages – it was never like this in a goddess workshop. Then they put my construction under water pressure and, inevitably, water spurts out at entertaining angles and they all have a good laugh at me. I feel like their expectation of a female.

Lunch was a quick sandwich and then I'm shown my task for the afternoon: to plumb in a vanity basin. I stare at it in horror. A bare cubicle with a pipe at one end and a picture on the wall of what it needed to look like by the end of the afternoon. Connected. With copper piping with compressed joints. All going around corners and everything. And taps.

'You don't have to have the brains of an archbishop, but you do have to have the patience of a saint,' said Kevin cheerily as he watched me trying to get my tiny head around it.

'We chose that one especially for you,' says James. 'It's the fiddliest task.'

Oh, thanks James. The vanity unit is fixed to the wall and so it's inaccessible. You have to lie on the floor and work out how on earth you can get a spanner to the taps.

'How am I supposed to get this in here?'

'Ah, you need a crow's-foot spanner.'

Silly of me not to know that.

'Why won't these go on here?'

'To connect a tap, Isabel, you need something called a tap connector.'

'This is supposed to push into this, isn't it?'

'You need a bit of lubrication, love.' Ah well, there is one thing I could have worked out for myself.

I work for two hours. It's totally knackering. Now I know why the men who do this job are so keen on their tea breaks. After half an hour on this task I was ready for a twenty-minute break. Loath to let them see a pool of sweat breaking out on my face, I try to keep calm and do Zen plumbing. I look around and the GNER guys have all finished their tasks. While I've been struggling with my adjustable spanner, a toilet has been fitted, a sink's in place, a hand basin has water running from the taps, and the other girl had successfully plumbed in her bath ... only Happy and I are still struggling and swearing.

Then I remember something rather wonderful. On this job I get paid by the hour. So the longer I take, the more I get to charge. The fact that I'm working slower than anyone else makes me the highest paid. Most brilliant of jobs. Imagine that in anything else. Teaching? 'Sorry it took me all weekend just to mark the one essay, there was so much in it that I felt needed my attention.' Dentistry? 'To pull a tooth? Oh, about five hours I'd say, give or take.' Or even my job . . . 'No I'm sorry – can you tell my editor that it took me a week to write that page, so I'll be invoicing her for it separately.' I love it. But in plumbing this is how it is.

On the other hand, it's damned hard work, so the desire to finish the job, take the money and run is pretty huge. The testosterone seems to have become active in me. I don't just want to be a plumber . . . I want to be a good plumber and I don't want to finish last. Fortunately for me, Happy has run into some problem with his angles, so I'm not totally humiliated. Till they put the water on. Once again I've got five leaking joints and one that springs open like in a cartoon.

'OK, James . . . I guess I forgot to tighten that one.'

But I know what I've done wrong. I'm a new person for the weekend, one of the lads. I'm an amateur plumber.

It's all so very different in this man's world. There is something very clear about not caring. All these guys are here for the money and no one is pretending otherwise. No one stops at the end of the day and asks if we'd like to take tea together. They all bugger off and at 10 a.m. the following morning we're back. I manage to sneak a quick chat with the other girl, Alex.

'The thing is,' she says in a rather masculine kind of way, 'I'm having my house done up and I'm on my own with these blokes. It's not that I want to do it myself, but I don't want to get taken for a ride. Take yesterday . . . I plumbed in a bath yesterday afternoon and it took me two-and-a-half hours. So no plumber is going to be able to quote me three days for installing a bath is he? I'll say, "Look, I'm an amateur and I plumbed in a bath myself once in an afternoon." I'll pay for the course in one day's wages to the plumbers.'

There is a wonderful logic to this that I like. Don't you?

The second morning we're given lectures on water systems and how the water flows around your house. Direct and indirect supply. I have noted the only vital bit of information for you. Do you know why you should *never* drink out of your bathroom tap? I remember having a row with my first husband (we call him Slipperman) about this. I insisted that you shouldn't drink out of the bathroom taps because I had been brought up being told that it was 'different water'. But of course I didn't know why. My ex, on the other hand, informed me that I was off my head and it was all the same water.

Well now – twenty years later – I know why I was more right than he was. Do you? It is the same water, but the water in your kitchen tap comes straight in from the mains in the road. It is fresh(ish) and as clean as it will ever get. You can drink it if you are bold and given to taking risks. (Don't ask about how they 'purify' it!) But the water in the bathroom tap has been sitting for maybe three days in the tank in your loft. Most loft tanks do not have lids. Pay attention now. You need to check this when you've finished reading. In the bottom of the tank is, more likely than not, a dead pigeon, droppings from various creatures that may live in your loft or have lived there in the past . . . rats, bats, squirrels, birds of all kinds, flies – you name it. This has probably resulted in two inches of stuff at the bottom of the tank which we could politely call 'grime'. You brush your teeth in that water.

In short, the water that has been through this tank is not the same quality of water as that in your kitchen tap. So yah boo sucks to you, Slipperman! (Me? Not worked out my issues yet? What are you saying?) Anyway, go and have a look later. See if you can get some hunky plumber to get rid of your old tank and fit you a good clean new one that has a lid. You still shouldn't drink out of it, but at least you'll know what you are bathing in.

So there I am, sitting there waiting for my afternoon task – to fit an entire bathroom with copper compressed joints using flexi piping for the basin – when my phone rings. It's Harry.

Imagine the scene if you will. Losada in her overalls (large, baggy, navy blue and covered in paint) and large boots with steel toe-caps, a pipe-bending machine in one hand and a mobile phone in the other, rushing out to sit on the grass. An irrational pink haze appears around me, birds start to sing and, from nowhere quite discernible, music starts to play.

What did he say? You know, I've no idea. I can't remember. Something unremarkable like 'How are you?' I think. But I'm just so damned glad to hear his voice that I can't wipe a smile off my face that's bigger than the piece of pipe that I'd just bent. I just love his voice. Oh, listen to me. I'm glad that he can't see me, though. Not exactly the kind of outfit that would drive a man wild.

Then he rings off and says that he'll call straight back. What to do? I've a bathroom to fit. So – you'll be very proud of me I know – I put the mobile phone back in my bag and go to fit my bathroom. There's a lot of pipework to lie and joints to fit and I'm damned if any of them were going to leak today. I do not sit there pathetic and girly-like, waiting by the phone and get behind on my plumbing – no, no. I mean, a girl has to have some standards and for some reason I'm not going to let James, John, Kevin or any of my fellow plumbers have to finish the job for me. Instead I treat them to a spontaneous rendering of 'Singing in the Rain' while everyone else is just practising their expletives.

Why am I so entirely lacking in any kind of logic or common sense? Why should I be so pleased to hear from someone who I can never see and am never likely to be with? Surely my task is to forget this man, not be singing because he's phoned? Why should I like another human being so much that just hearing his voice talking about nothing in particular provides enough energy to plumb in a bath and a hand basin with every joint a model of perfection? Oh my goodness, I had just plumbed in a bathroom single handed.

'You've done a good job there, mate,' said Kevin appreciatively as he turns on the tap to test my system and remains surprisingly unrefreshed. 'Tape the compression joints?'

'Each and every one, boss.'

'Well, I'd give you a job. Do you do Yorkshires and end-feed?'

'Sure. What are they?'

'We're talking soldering.'

And the absurd man hands me a very large blowtorch. 'The next exercise with James is to make what you made yesterday morning but with soldered joints.'

These guys know nothing. I mean, putting large blowtorches in the hands of the guys from GNER may be one thing, but why on earth are they giving me one? No gloves, no mask, they haven't even told me to tie my long hair back. I realise how few women they have had on these courses.

Suddenly I'm soldering pieces of metal together and waving around a flame that isn't even visible. It wouldn't have been so bad if, every time I'd tried to turn the flame off, I'd known which way to turn the turny bit to get the flames to go down.

'The other way,' says one of the guys from GNER with a panic-stricken look on his face.

'You really need to keep an eye on me with this, James. I'm a liability to myself and others.' James ignores me and walks the other way. I keep going, now suffering only minor burns from the number of times I'd touched the metal.

'You can wear gloves to apply the lubricant if you like. It's not good for your hands that stuff, but we mostly don't bother.' Why is it still macho to put carcinogenic cream directly on your skin every day?

I vaguely wonder whether it would be worse for my hands if the flame touches them and I'm wearing the latex gloves. Will they melt and burn my hands all over and melt the latex into the burns? Or will it be worse to burn them without the gloves? I never had to consider these things in a tai chi class.

I watch the copper go all kinds of interesting colours and congratulate myself for concentrating on my soldering and not thinking about Harry's phone call. I move a cloth aside and don't set light to it. Maybe there is hope for me in a man's world? I'm making something useless. Then there it is. James runs water through it . . . and we're done. The punters disappear, leaving Alex and Happy and I looking at each other.

James presents us with certificates: 'PPL Plumbing Training Certificate of Achievement for Isabel Losada, who attended a two-day Intensive Introduction to Plumbing Course.' It should say 'and only wet everybody once or twice and did not set light to anything or anyone'.

'You going back to London now?' Happy pipes up.

'Want a lift to York Station, you two?' spurts Alex. See, this is the standard of jokes you get after I've been hanging around with the lads for two days.

I'm delighted to be travelling back with Happy. We sit on the floor in a corridor of a very overcrowded train back to London while he tells me his story. 'I was born and brought up in Nairobi and I've got an MA in business administration. I earn £25,000 a year now as an assistant manager of a large electronics store, but I'll double it as a plumber. I'm moving to Australia. I'm Sikh and there is a large Asian community in Perth.'

'I see. So you've got it all planned, then? When do you give up retail?'

'Immediately after the four-week course. My wages will double overnight and my wife will like that.'

'So you're married?' Even meeting single men to have as friends is hard.

'I've been married three years and I'm twenty-five. Before you ask, it wasn't an arranged marriage, it was a love marriage. This is best, as all women are alike anyway.'

'Are they?'

'I think so. If you can understand any woman, and what she wants, you're sorted.'

'What about men? Are they all alike?'

'No. Every man is different.'

'Do you understand women, then?'

'No.'

'What about your wife?'

'No.'

'OK. So since all women are alike and you don't understand them, let me ask you what you think she'll want to know when you get home.'

'She'll want to know what I did all weekend. All the details and she'll want to know if I met any women on the course.'

'What about if I was going back to a man? What would he want?'

'He wants to have his food, a beer and a shag and then go to sleep.'

'Is that so? Dinner and a quick shag? I thought you said all men are different?'

'Yes. For me it needn't be that quick. For example.'

I sat and listened most of the way home. It was really good hearing Happy's thoughts on men and women, having been brought up in Nairobi. He said that he thinks young men here are lazy, even his own community. 'None of the men want to work hard to make a living.' It's true. Certainly none of the second-generation Asian men that I knew in north London had become plumbers . . . but I knew a few with debts.

'So what are you going to do with your weekend's plumbing experience?' Happy asks as we pull in to Euston.

'Not sure. I'm thinking of exploring this whole area a little bit more. I used to know a guy called Steve who is a builder. He has a whole different perspective on life from mine and I learned a lot from him. I'm thinking of giving him a call.'

'On the building site?'

'Yes. I'm not totally unskilled. I've got a two-day training in plumbing.'

'I don't need plumbers at the moment. We're in the middle of a loft conversion. Can you fit Kingspan phenolic panels?'

'Absolutely.' Wot?

'OK. Right then. Totally unskilled manual labour with no experience and no muscle. That's £30 a day. Same as I give to my son and his friends when they help out. That suit you?'

'Perfectly, Steve.'

'And you'll have to sleep on site.'

'Er . . . with the other, er, men?'

'There's a caravan here. We'll put you in that. I'll speak to the clients.'

'OK.'

'And I wanted to chat with some of the guys. About women, and men, and stuff.'

'They all have plenty of opinions about everything. You may be shocked, though. Monday week?'

'OK.'

I donned my overalls and turned up for my briefing with Steve.

'So you're doing what?'

'Ethnography. Studying the species in their own environments.'

'I see.'

'What's my job?'

'Any good at mixing shit?'

'Mmm, sure, I'm good at that.'

'That is, you put four large shovels of building sand and one shovel of Portland cement into that mixer and do that

three times. This makes a mixture known as shit. This'll be
the only place you'll hear a man yell, "I need more shit."
Then you see them Thermalite blocks?' I thought I wouldn't
ask.

'Yes, Steve.'

'We need those fifty up in the loft. So when you've
finished mixing shit you could take them up them two
ladders.'

He walked me around the site. 'Watch your head at all
times. We don't wear hard hats here as it's only a small job,
but on a big site you have to and you'll see why if you don't
watch your head. That there is called a trap.' A trap on site
is not so much the problem of meeting Toms or Dicks as
stepping on a plank or in a hole that lowers you from the
first or second floor to the ground faster than you could ever
have anticipated. Then the lads started to arrive. Why are
men in trades so often called lads no matter what their age?

'This is Dave, who's a roofer, and his mate, Spud.'

'Mornin'. Nice overalls.' My overalls were paint stained
in a totally authentic splash-and-wipe fingers design.

'This is John, Jim, Bob. This is also Dave and this is also
Steve. I won't tell you what they all do coz it's not a lot
when I'm not looking, but you'd be surprised how many
roofers are called Dave.'

'So . . .' said one of the Daves, 'are you here to make the
tea, then?'

Ha! Reduced to my female role and it was not yet 8 a.m.
I grinned at them. 'I understand that making tea is the
client's job. I mean, that is the purpose of the client, isn't it?
To provide very large amounts of money and tea on the
hour? I'm stirring the shit.'

'Yeh, that's what we heard.'

They were friendly enough. But they had to be. I was a
friend of the man giving them the readies at the end of the
day. Nothing for it but to get my head down and work like
a Trojan for a couple of days until I had even some small
level of acceptance as one of the lads. None of them had

ever had a woman on site before, so I had to try not to be utterly pathetic.

Two days later the fifty Thermalite blocks were on the second floor, my arm muscles were developing nicely and I'd thought up some advertising campaigns:

- Insomnia? Forget drugs ... take Thermalite ... up two ladders.

- Weak, saggy arm muscles, girls? Bingo wings? Forget your local rip-everyone-off-a-lot gym. Just shovel cement.

- Bored of your desk job? Need to get out more? Travel to Wales on this unique earn-as-you-learn work-experience package. Must have endless repertoire of bad jokes.

'What do you call a man with no arms or legs who can play the piano?'

'I don't know, Dave.'

'A clever Dick. What do you call him if he goes for a swim?'

'I'm afraid I'm about to find out.'

'Bob.'

Sigh.

'What do you call a dog with no legs?'

'Is there something I should know about the chop saw?'

'Anything at all, coz he won't come,' shouts one of the Steves.

'No, Woodbine,' says one of the Daves.

'I'm sorry, you've lost me.' I was actually attempting to cut a 45 mm phenolic panel straight. This was going to be someone's home, after all.

'Coz you take him for a drag every morning.'

'What do call a Yugoslavian prostitute?'

Didn't think I'd go into the fact that there was no such place. 'I dread to think.'

'Slobber-on-my-knob-you-bitch.'

I think they were now at the level they'd be at without me on site. They could go on like this for hours. I swear they each had a five-hour repertoire of tasteless jokes.

Sometimes, when there was a quieter task, I'd manage to have a bit of real conversation. One guy, I'll call him Bob, although that's not his name, really shocked me and had views which, Steve told me later, were not unusual in the environments that he lives and works in.

'The nature of women is to try to control men. Whatever it is that you want to do, the woman tries to stop you doing it.'

'Such as?'

'Anything. Even going to the pub or going to the football. One way or another, my ex-wife tried to stop me playing football.'

'Why do you think that was?'

'Because she thought I had too much freedom. I was too happy.'

'Why wouldn't she want you to be happy?'

'I think all women want to stop men being happy. On a subconscious level. If a man is out training twice a week, he's having way too much fun. I'd be wary of a woman who is happy to let you go. It probably means that she's up to something. Most of my friends who are divorced, it's because the wife was having an affair.'

'Why do you think that is?'

'I think women get bored, whereas a man will settle down to domesticity.'

Or because more women are finally refusing the conventional role of mistress and housekeeper?

'Do you think most of your male friends would agree with your point of view?'

'Definitely. The current wife, she was nice before we got married, so I thought it would be different, but it's just the same.'

'And tell me, since you are the common factor in these two marriages, do you think there is anything you could do differently?'

'No. Women aren't going to change are they?'

Couldn't even begin to sort this one out. Anyway, he wasn't asking and I'm supposed to have learned not to give unsolicited advice. But such sad bitterness with no sense of personal responsibility was a weight heavier than ten of Steve's Thermalite blocks carried around every day.

'Well, for what my opinion is worth to you, I think it's possible to have happiness, equality and freedom in a relationship.'

'Oh yeh? On what planet?' Some place midway between Mars and Venus, I guess.

'Would you like some tea, mate?'

That night I sat in the pub with Steve. I was pondering human relations and trying to make sense of our inability to really love each other and seek genuinely for the happiness of those we love.

'You have to understand that ninety-nine per cent of working class men are doing a job they hate.'

As a working-class man himself, born and raised in an area of huge social deprivation, Steve had a right to his opinions.

'Men become cash machines.' He stared at his drink sadly. 'So the men become resentful of the women, who they blame for all this. And the man becomes valued based on the amount of money he brings in, which the woman then spends, running up endless debts on joint credit cards.'

'And that's it?'

'Try reading the *Daily Sport* every day for twenty years with no education.'

'Do working-class men – and OK I know we are speaking in huge generalisations, but in your experience – do they like women?'

'They serve a purpose . . . to raise the kids and shag on a Friday night. And the women don't like the men because they have no respect for them.'

'Why not?'

'Would you have for a man who hates his job, blames you, reads the *Daily Sport* and who only looks forward to going to the pub and getting pissed and when he comes home drunk and smelly complains because you don't want to be shagged by his fourteen stone for about one minute.'

'Then you can't sleep coz he snores so loud? You paint a lovely picture.'

'Let's just say that they don't expect much of each other. Or of themselves. There's not much thinking outside the box goes on.'

What I don't understand is why sheer boredom doesn't drive them to do something different, instead of just blaming their partners for what is wrong with life. But of course, that's not only a working-class tendency. One of the good things about not having a partner is the clarity. If my day isn't the way I'd like it to be I have no one to blame but myself. I have no option but to know that I'm one hundred per cent responsible for everything in my life.

The following day, while we were in a break from fitting tongue-and-groove moisture-resistant flooring panels, I found the obvious answer to all the stuckness, chatting to one of the other guys who was in a new and happier relationship. John had been in the trades from the age of seventeen: 'I do everything except the wires. I do a bit of plumbing. Worst thing that can happen is you get wet. Worst thing with the wires is you kill some poor bugger.'

'You work hard. I've been watching you.'

'Not really.'

'Aren't you exhausted at night?'

'Not really. I have a shower and sit on the couch for an hour watching the box.'

'Do you switch it off after the hour?'

'No. It's on all the time. I don't know anyone who doesn't have it on all the time.'

'Run that by me again. Everyone you know has the TV on all the time, every evening?'

'Yes, of course. And all day. Even if they're not watching it, it's on.'

'So is that what you do every night?'

'No. Some nights I'll take a pint of lager and sit in the garden. There's nothing much else to do, is there?'

So, how about we let him know? Address your letters:

'What Can John Do In The Evenings?'
John (Steve's friend)
Kabiray Builders Ltd
Somerset House,
Castle Street,
Alyn Crescent,
Caergwrle,
Wrexham LL12 9DR

Because unless he has a million answers he surely won't have enough.

'Do you enjoy your life, John?' He had been a pleasure to work with. Quiet and friendly, and stayed to help Steve clear up when all the others had buggered off.

'Sometimes it's a pain in the arse. Like when you work on your own and you don't get on with the people you work with.'

'That's funny, John.'

'You should try it.'

'I'm a writer, John. Writers have to get on with themselves. Everyone has to get on with themselves.'

Steve's face appeared.

'You two doing any work today? Can you show her how to use the laser saw without taking her fingers off, John? Those planks need cutting and we don't want blood on site. It would upset the client.'

So that was me sorted for the rest of the afternoon. Amazing, I was building three rooms in a roof. With a little help.

One night I got invited to the pub and some real stories

started to come out. I don't think this is bravado storytelling. I think this is true. About shagging the clients. I listened to numerous examples and laughed.

'Do you think most builders shag the clients then?'

'Yes. All those that get the chance, and most do get the chance.'

'I'll be working on a contract and I know if I make the right moves the opportunity is there. The husbands work in offices because they're the only ones that can afford us. They push computer keys all day and are pale, feeble and pathetic and usually can't put up a shelf.'

'Can't keep anything up at all.'

'And no idea how to grease a nipple.'

'Anyway, the builder turns up, tears the roof off her house and two weeks later she's got three new rooms in her house, her oestrogen levels have gone through the roof and she'll give the builder anything he wants.'

'This isn't true of all the women clients at home on their own all day, of course.'

'No. I see.'

'Just most of them.'

'So this is why you mostly don't wear tops in sunny weather then?'

'You get very hot working.'

'And the clients get hot watching.'

'So how many of you have had sex with your clients, then?'

'Couldn't say.'

'Obviously.'

'There are two blokes we know, work together, the older one goes for the mother, the younger one for the daughter.'

'Let's just say that they have a good success rate.'

Later I quizzed Steve again. 'But Steve, is all this true?'

'Yes.'

'And you? Do you sleep with your clients?'

'I don't. But I'm not saying that I haven't had the opportunity. Many times.'

I laughed. Steve was a good friend but I'd never considered him as a sex object. 'So how come you're not like the
others?'

'I like women too much. I've never wanted to take
advantage. These guys don't really like women somehow,
but they wouldn't admit that. You can't believe how
shallow men can be. Or how devious to get what they want.
It's true that men think with their dicks.'

'But that's only true sometimes, surely?'

'You don't understand how different men are to women.
You've done too many of them weird workshops. You just
see good in everyone, but some blokes are not nice at all.
On the big sites they'll get some new seventeen-year-old
boy on his first day, and stick a spanner up his backside or
paint his bollocks with whatever is nearby.'

'Such as?'

'Gloss paint would be most likely.'

'Some kind of bizarre initiation?'

'Yup. Very violent usually.'

'But isn't that called assault? Don't men go to prison for
attacking a seventeen-year-old?'

'He won't breathe a word, will he, or he'll never work
again. He has to come back the following day, hold his head
up and pretend it hasn't happened.'

'You're right. I think I understand men quite well because
I always look at the similarities between us; I mean, we all
want to love and be loved, don't we?'

'Love?' He laughed. 'Is that the same as sex? Love is the
woman's area. You are forgetting nature. Men have to
spread the seed as much as possible. Women have to try and
keep the man around to raise the kids. And men are often
brutes.'

'You're not.'

'I can be if necessary. When I was in the RAF a guy tried
to bully me. I knew I had a straight choice, get bullied by
him and then all the rest of them as well or earn respect by
beating the shit out of this bloke. So I nearly killed him. But

not quite.' He smiled. 'He didn't bother me again. Can't say I wanted to do it, but that's the way it is.'

Should I have been horrified to hear this or had renewed admiration? It's true, I don't think about these things. I've never considered the ability to cause grievous bodily harm an essential ingredient to being a man. But perhaps one of the things that women somehow know about men who are all feminine side is that they haven't learned to survive in the company of other men. Maybe these men know it themselves and so have no self-respect at some basic level. But I'm ashamed to still be discussing men in the context of violence. I didn't want to have to face this . . . but here it is. Is it natural that men are more aggressive or is it purely conditioning? I suspect it's ninety per cent conditioning but, at the moment, as Steve says, this is still the way things are. I suppose if you've grown up male you have to have some stance on competition and fighting, and the real killers, with no compassion, are not in the boxing ring but on the trading floors.

Interesting to me that two of my heroes, now that I think about it, are Gandhi and the Dalai Lama, both not only pacifist (although neither are known for a lack of courage) but also famous celibates. When Mohammed Ali was a pin-up was it men or women who had his picture on their walls?

'Tell you who knows a lot about women and a lot about fighting . . . you have a chat to Steve the Roofer tomorrow.'

After a couple of hours' work the following day I was allowed to steal away with Steve the Roofer, a good-looking guy of an indiscernible age, with a definite charm and plenty of confidence about him. He gave the impression that I didn't need to consider subtlety.

'So, Steve, Steve tells me you've been around a bit.' Well if I was writing fiction I wouldn't do a Gabriel García Márquez on you, and they'd all have different names, OK? I'd call Steve the Roofer Jack the Lad, but his name is also Steve and the story I tell you is true.

'I hear you know a bit about a subject I've been thinking about. Fighting.'

'Yeh, that's how I've earned my money.'

'What, boxing?'

'Kinda. But without the gloves. It's not legal.' He twinkled at me. 'But it's well paid and it's easy money. You don't know who you're going to fight – he could be fifteen stone, you see.'

'And you are?'

'Eleven. You've seen *Fight Club*, right?'

'Yes. But I thought it was a movie. I honestly didn't realise that this illegal fighting still went on other than with cocks.'

'No. Men too. Lots of it. All around the country.'

'So there's no attempt to match weight? Or experience?'

'No, you meet in a dungeon somewhere and you fight till one of you can't get up. If he's big he's going to get out of breath, so you just keep punching.'

'Do men die?'

'There are three points which, if you hit, you could kill him. The temple, the Adam's apple and the bridge of the nose. So you don't want to hit there. If you are fighting without gloves you just knock him about to wear him out and then one good swipe and he's gone. People bet all the time you are playing, they love it, the more blood the better. Especially the women, they crave for it, the more blood, the more they scream.'

'Don't the women cry sometimes?'

'No, they scream and get excited.'

'What about your wives?'

'They don't come. It's not the kind of thing you invite family and friends to. No one knows who you are. You come in and start fighting and people start betting. It's only people with money. We're talking thousands of pounds and the betting doesn't stop till the fight stops. If you put a thousand on me to win, for example, you may get three thousand back. But if I get knocked out, you lose. It's not a good way to live.'

'So, at the risk of asking a dumb question, why do you do it?'

'For the money. You've got debts so you just think about the money. That's the way out. You're scared, you're trembling, but then it just takes off. You don't think about anything when you're fighting. But the wives don't like it. That's why I've lost so many of them. They couldn't handle seeing my face half across somewhere else.'

'How many wives have you had, Steve?'

He threw me a huge, charming grin. 'Seven.'

'You've had seven wives?'

'Yeh, and some girlfriends too.'

If, as Samuel Johnson says, a second marriage is the triumph of hope over experience, does a man who has married seven times demonstrate the utter defeat of self-knowledge?

'Children?'

'Thirteen.'

'You're having me on.'

'No, really.'

'All by different women?'

'Two with the first wife . . . after that, all different women, yeh.'

In spite of myself I had to smile. The man is a charm-filled baby-making machine. Anyone want to have a good-looking baby but never see the father again? Address your letters to Steve the Roofer, Steve's friend . . .

'How old are they all?'

He launched off confidently, 'Twenty-four, twenty-two, twelve, six, eight . . . no, hold on.' He looked puzzled.

'God, can't think, some of them aren't wives, you see, they're girlfriends.'

This is why I don't write fiction. I mean, if I made this up my editor would say, 'Don't be absurd, Isabel. The writing has to have some credibility.'

I looked at him, trying to hide the exclamation marks coming out of my head, and wondering how all those children were doing with no father and what the reward might be from the Child Support Agency for an address for him.

'So, you were saying that the wives didn't like you fighting?'

'They'd say, "Don't do it," but when I walked in and put the cash on the table I'd see a big smile because there is spending money again. The money's there. You know this is probably the first time I've talked about all this. Anyway, I don't do the fighting any more.'

'I don't believe you. You're just saying that coz it's illegal. Why would you retire?'

'Coz there's blokes faster than me now. When I was doing it I had the speed and the knowledge. I'm past my fight-by date.'

'Oh, I see. Well, that reason I believe. How old are you, anyway?'

'I'm not telling you that. How old are you?'

'I'm not telling you that.' Strange, he was a charmer, but I still wondered how he had persuaded seven women to marry him and a further six to have more of his babies.

'So how do you feel about women now?'

'Love 'em. I've parted amicably from all my wives. I was never unfaithful to any one of them. I treated them all with respect.'

'So why did you leave them? All?'

'We fell out of love. If there is no love in the house it's not fair on the kids. If their parents aren't sharing the bedroom and that. The kids are the first ones to pick things up.'

'But don't you hurt them by leaving?'

'At first, yes, but better to hurt them a bit than to hurt them all the time if there is no love between the parents. Better to have friendship. Women are beautiful, they're not just put on the planet to cook and clean. They're not. Men used to be in control, now women are in control and it's about time.'

Now here was an unlikely advocate for women's rights. I wonder what the mothers of his children, all bringing them up without him, would have to say about his views and the consequences of them for his kids. But what do I know?

'So, Steve, you're single at the moment?'

'Yes.'

And here is the first single man that I've met in the project so far . . . any of you want to date him? But Steve wasn't going to need any help from me.

'I won't be single for long, I'm going to trap one.'

'Trap one? Have you got one in mind?'

'Oh yes. I've seen her down at the local pub.'

'How old is she?'

'Thirty-eight.'

'Does she know that you've had seven wives?'

'Oh yes. I never lie, no point, they find you out.'

So, as far as sowing his seed far and wide was concerned, in evolutionary terms this was the most successful man I'd ever met.

'So what's your advice for men then, Steve?'

'Women need to be charmed till you've trapped 'em and then treated with respect after.'

'And how do you trap them?'

'Just charm 'em. I've stood in a bar and a woman will walk straight up to me and say, "You've got lovely eyes," and that's it . . . she's trapped.'

'What's your advice for women on men?'

'Be careful. There's lots of idiots out there.'

All the week we'd been having a competition in creative uses of the staple gun. First tools had been stapled down, leading to loud expletives being bellowed across the site. Then it had progressed to lunch boxes, shoes, items of clothing; basically, anything that could be fixed down, if left for a second, was being fixed down. At one point, when one of the young lads, Jamie, was standing on a plank listening to his radio, one of the Daves had managed to reach over and fix his shoes to the plank while he was still standing in them.

The perplexed expression on his face when he realised that his feet weren't going anywhere was just too much and I laughed out loud. I should have known my moment was coming. No standing on ceremony for me. Jamie simply arranged for four of them to pick me up and staple-gun me to the wall by the overalls. I stood, wriggling and shouting all manner of abuse, on a chair, my arms and legs held out while two or three staples were placed through the cloth on each limb and on to a beam. Then they removed the chair and left me hanging, laughing but totally unable to free myself. Don't know what type of cotton they make the overalls from, but it wasn't ripping.

'That's it! No more tea for any of you! No more shit either! I shall take up cartooning and wreak my revenge.'

Boss man Steve, my mate, was grinning all over his face, knowing that my being stapled was a kind of approval.

'Nice work. Now I see I was wrong, lads, saying that you never do anything useful. I thought it was looking cluttered in here. It's a safety rule on site, Isabel, never leave things about. Have to keep the site tidy. Comfortable?'

'Absolutely.'

'OK. We'll go for lunch now then, shall we, lads?'

And off they all went, leaving me hanging about. It had been a good week. Now it was Friday I realised I rather regretted leaving behind me the simplicity of my life doing a loft conversion. Sure, it was hard work, but I felt fit and healthy and the transformation that we'd made to this property in a week was amazing. Well, I say 'we' as if my contribution had made a difference. But I promise you that in Gresford in Wales is a house where a large number of the insulation panels were cut and installed by me. Mmm, I wonder if they were going to come and get me down? I wriggled helplessly.

What was I learning about men through all this? So far, only the most obvious of lessons. I like them and they are very different from girls. Although maybe it's not so obvious, many of my friends complain that men don't communicate like women, instead of enjoying the differences. Hanging around up here was certainly better than looking at pictures of men on the internet or making small talk with City types in red ties. Even if I was going to miss lunch.

Then Steve the Roofer appeared through a hatch. 'Need a hand?' He produced a staple remover and gave me back the chair, easily removing the staples in about six seconds. 'Thanks.'

'Go back down that ladder. You haven't seen me.'

'Course not.'

I strolled out on to the grass. 'So who is making the tea round here, then?'

Out of all the men I chatted to about women and relationships all week, it was the conversation with Dennis the window fitter that I had on the last afternoon that stuck most in my mind.

'Steve tells me you're remarried, Dennis, and would be happy to brag about it.'

'Yeh, well I married my childhood sweetheart the first time, but it all went horribly wrong. So now I'm married again, I'm forty-three and my wife is thirty-five and pretty, too. That's the way things happen now, isn't it?'

'Is it?'

'Of course. If you sat ten people round a dinner table at least half or more than half would be divorced, wouldn't they?'

'I thought two out of three stayed together?'

'Yeh, but so many of those are unhappy and just bumbling along. People just bumble along until they're fifty but they're not happy, are they? I think once you've been divorced you learn a lesson.'

'So why don't more people move on then?'

'I think it's laziness. It's easier to go home and watch TV. People do whatever's easy – and then they die. Especially men. They're the worst.'

'Why are they any worse than women?'

'Because they're cowards. So even if a man is having an affair he'll deny it and make life miserable for his wife until eventually she is forced to make the decision for him.'

'Dennis, this is true. I've seen the national statistics and I can tell you that the vast majority of divorce proceedings are initiated by women.'

'It's obvious to me. As you get older you get married, don't you? And then you get divorced and then you get married again, don't you?'

'Really? I always advise keeping away from married men.'

'Why's that?'

'If a man or a woman are married and are still together then presumably it's because they want to be.'

'You're not accounting for the bumbling along factor.'

'If a couple aren't happy surely they should split up first and be living separately, not just splitting up when someone has an affair?'

'Oh yeh? And on what planet does this happen?'

This was the second time this week I'd heard that I need to be on some other planet. Some place between Mars and Venus where we all do our relationships differently.

'So you think I value marriage too highly? You're in favour of divorce.'

'Absolutely. There are far too many people bumbling along.'

What do you think? Have I been too careful in my warnings about the married men?

For a Tom, having affairs is simply one of the aspects of his bumbling along. He'll never change. But maybe the Dicks and the Harrys are at least attempting to stop bumbling. It could be argued that in order to avoid the 'watch TV and then die' life experience, that my warnings to single women about married men are wimpy and based only on my own experience. I'm told that in New York a first marriage is referred to as a 'starter marriage'. Maybe this is where we're all headed.

I think that, generally, Dennis is right and second marriages are happier than first marriages. I guess if all those second wives hadn't been prepared to take risks (moral, ethical, practical) then there would be thousands more bumbling along. As Jenny and I found, divorced men remarrying last year numbered 83,554 . . . and that's just the ones that got around to a formal second marriage. The statistics show that it's women who are the movers and shakers in all this. Men, according to Dennis, mostly only know how to sabotage marriages. They are not able to just sit down and say, in a calm and loving voice, 'I've met someone with whom I believe I could be happier, will you let me go?' And maybe that's because we women have yet to reach the point where we could reply, in a calm and loving voice, 'Of course. I'm sad that you've made this decision but glad to have shared ten years of my life with you. May you be happy, may you be well. My love goes with you.'

Some of us, maybe, could reach this unconditional, non-attached kind of love if a partner announces that he is leaving. I maybe know one or two women on the planet who love their husbands passionately, but would still be capable of responding like this.

And I know what you're thinking, you're thinking, 'Very convenient, Isabel, and if that happened, Harry could be with you.' But this isn't about Harry. It isn't about me. It's about the principle. Is Dennis right that far too many people are bumbling along on the way to death? And if so, is divorce no longer always a bad thing?

Should divorce now be celebrated?

It was Friday afternoon and Steve the boss was up to something. While they were all working on the downstairs extension, he was up in the loft. I looked in just in time to see him stapling the last of the week's wages, in cash, to the rafters with a staple gun. Each pile of money had a small piece of paper with a name attached.

'Quick,' he said as he removed every last ladder and staple remover, 'I've got to get out of here. Hide this, OK?' He passed me a staple remover.

'That's the week's wages? But how are they going to get the money out without tearing it if you take all the removers?'

'It'll be a bugger. Almost impossible, I'd say, especially as I'm taking the ladders too.'

We came down a ladder. Then he lowered it and put it in his van. 'Want a lift to the station? Here's your wages; I forgot to staple them up.'

He threw me a wage packet.

'Put your bag in here quick so they don't see. Don't hang about.'

'Bye, lads, have a good weekend. See you Monday,' he shouted cheerily.

'Hold on!' shouted one of the Daves. 'Where's the wages?'

'Don't worry, mate, it's all there, with the names and everything. I've left it in the loft.'

We drove off just in time to see a few faces notice that we were taking the ladders.

2. HARLEYS IN THE SUNSHINE

A BREAK WITH THE BIKERS

I wanted to find an all-male environment where all these silly 'class' groups mixed as equals ... something with lots of men but where class didn't make a jot of difference. And something that is not a spectator sport. More on how to avoid spectator sports later.

It happens that quite close to where I live there is a big and amazing shop that sells Harley-Davidson motorbikes. It's called Warrs and I have been known to go in there with friends just to gaze at the bikes. I can rarely get excited about a car ... far too much fuss is made about them, in my not so humble opinion, and they are destroying the world. I can't get too excited about a push-bike either, even though it is my main means of transport. A normal motorbike is a large and noisy push-bike without the advantage of free exercise. But there is something about a Harley.

It's not the hype – that's just silly. It's the bikes themselves. They are wonders of artistic and engineering genius. I mean, I'm a girl and even I can stand and say 'Wow!' when I see a Harley. Apparently there are groups of people that actually own these machines.

This seemed to me like a very explorable area. I'm determined to keep away from women for a while. Ballet school, theatre, independent TV companies, publishing houses, retreats, book clubs, writing workshops, tai chi workshops, tantric sex workshops, even the voluntary sector ... one hundred per cent of the things I've done in the last ten years have been oestrogen-fests. As Lorca shows in the amazing play *The House of Barnardo Alba*, women without men go mad, and my life is certainly a demonstration of that.

A day out with the guys was called for. I knew that, rather like the owners of Morris Minors, the Harley owners had a club. Well, actually, I can't think of any similarity between the owners of Morris Minors and Harleys except their willingness to join a club. A quick look at the website confirmed that all the local owners' clubs are thriving and that an eighty-mile bike ride was about to happen that very weekend.

I phoned someone calling himself 'Patch', which seemed an odd name for a biker, as I assumed he couldn't have the Long John version. Maybe a former hole in his leathers? I didn't like to ask. Stick to the script.

'Do you think there is someone who would like to take along a passenger?'

'I'll give big Dave a ring ... see what we can do.'

Big Dave called back only minutes later. 'Sure you can come ... you got a helmet?'

'No.'

'I see. I'll bring some stuff for you, then. We are leaving from Greenwich.'

'I'll be coming by public transport, so how do I ... ?'

'I'll meet you at Lewisham Station then. Sunday. Nine o'clock. Don't be late. We are never late.'

'OK, I'll be there.'

And that was it.

How can it be this easy to get to know a complete new swagger of men?

* * *

I set off at an unfashionably early hour on the Sunday morning to travel through parts of London I've never heard of. I mean, Mudchute, I swear to you, is on the Docklands Light Railway map. I sit on the deserted train and open one of the many books you'll find in the appendix. I am determined to become an expert and offer you the fruits of my months of study.

The page falls open where my bookmark was left, but my eye falls on an obvious question. 'Are you really ready to "open your heart" and meet your perfect mate?' I stare at it with resentment. While I can make jokes about the awful American New Age approach, I can also realise that there may be some value in the question.

The sodding book wants me to do a visualisation and 'open the door to my heart' (cringe). I sneak a quick glance at my door. There is a large sign on it: 'Private'. It startles me, as I am unaccustomed to such a sign. I'm used to seeing the door wide open and all sorts of strange people wandering in and out. Underneath, in smaller writing, is written 'Access Harry'. And there is large padlock, which I seem to have fitted to the door and given Harry the key. That blasted fish has swum off with it somewhere. I stare at the door petulantly and ask myself: 'Do I want the key back? Do I want to open the door?'

Nope. Absurdly, even the sight of Harry's name on the door fills me with joy. How ridiculous the human heart is. Will it not respond to any kind of logic? 'Harry is not available!' I remind the door. Ah, if only the lock would fall off or melt away at the sound of these words. But nothing moves. I stand by the door to see if I can budge it a little and I discover a strange thing. With the padlock still secure so that no one can get in, I can still release the door so that a little light and air can get in and out. Some progress perhaps. At least that should stop whatever is in there from going mouldy.

I emerged from the train to see three large machines. Next to them stood three large men.

'Hi, I'm Dave. This is also Dave and this is Pete.' (Honestly. No name changes.)

'Hello, I'm Isabel.'

Big Dave did not disappoint for a second. He was a big man in every sense of the word. He had the compulsory bald head, orange reflective Dirty Dog sunglasses so that I couldn't see his eyes, and lots of tattoos. I felt very happy and very safe. The other Dave was thinner and Pete was in the middle. They were all of an indiscernible age somewhere over forty and, as they were all wearing an impressive amount of black leather with various Harley motifs, there wasn't much to distinguish them one from another.

'Right, Isabel, here's your helmet and gloves. You been on one of these before?'

'A Harley? Never. I've been on other bikes but this isn't the same, is it?'

'Nope. I think you'll find this quite comfortable.'

The back of Dave's bike was a large, heavily padded chair with arms.

'Do I have to do anything? Lean the same way as you when you go around corners or anything?'

'Not on this, no . . . just enjoy the ride.'

Big Dave swung his leg over his bike and I clambered up, attempting to be ladylike. Then we were off to meet the ride.

We turned through the streets and up to Greenwich where about 28 other leather hunks stood by silver metal in the sunlight. Each black jacket had its own extraordinary decoration, the fronts of the jackets studded with metal and the backs ornamented with eagles and the names of the various clubs. I looked around for women. There were no women on their own bikes, and only three who were passengers and I didn't need to chat with them today. I had what I needed . . . a serious day of play with the guys and a wide, open road. Fantastic.

Once we were all met there was a dos and don'ts chat that lasted about four minutes. Big Dave and I were to take the back of the ride so I was announced 'End man' and given a fluorescent yellow jacket so that no one could miss me. It was great being on Big Dave's bike, as he was one of those in charge. Everyone knew him and he was obviously popular. The man who was going to take the front of the ride came and said hello and shook my hand. They asked what I was there for and I said I was 'exploring male environments'.

'Men and women sometimes have difficulty finding each other,' I explained, realising they would think me quite mad, 'so I'm trying to find out where all the men are.'

'Where are all the women then?' one guy asked.

'Doing yoga. Mostly,' I said. He grimaced. Obviously better to live and die a bachelor than explore yoga.

Everybody signed a document promising that they wouldn't sue the club in the event of an accident and that was the formalities over. Already I remembered why male company can be such a refreshing change. If this had been thirty women, five would have been late, nine would have had some concern about something on the bike that wasn't working properly, one would have asked if she could leave the ride early to go home and feed the dog, someone would have demanded to know the route we were taking and suggested an alternative route and why that would be better, two women would have asked what would happen if someone's bike broke down (even if this wasn't their responsibility) and, half an hour later we would all have had to know where we were going to be stopping for lunch and whether they sold alcohol-free drinks and vegan food. Here no one asked any questions – on with the ride.

Harley riders are self-confessed, unashamed show-offs. They like nothing better than to draw a crowd. And where you have a large collection of shiny Harleys you will also have a group of people admiring the machines, gasping, 'That's beautiful!' And when the bikes all start their engines we were giving them not only a sight to behold but also a pretty cool noise to enjoy. As we moved off it did make a din, but the bikes were so elegant and the riders so well dressed that nobody cared. As I was at the very back, I had the pleasure of watching the long stream of bikes sparkling ahead of us in the sunshine.

The watching public seemed a little confused. 'Bikers' are traditionally scary people ... but we were evidently not scary. When the woman on the bike at the very end waves, kids glance up at their parents, wondering whether it's OK to wave back. As I was on the last bike, friendly waving at the passers-by was an enjoyable public responsibility. I had just enough time to meet people's eye and wave. The young boys would be thrilled. The middle-aged couples would wave back with big grins and then, just occasionally, some elderly lady would look terrified. 'What me? Wave at you? You are in black leather; my dog and I are not even going to consider waving. You are a bad person.' So I'd smile even more broadly and wave some more.

It may seem a strange thing to say, but it was actually quite beautiful. When the bikes changed lanes they kept a strict formation and it was really impressive watching them weaving in and out. I loved not having a clue where we were going. The route, from a woman's perspective on these things (must re-do those blonde highlights), went something like: some roads, a long tunnel, a sign that said 'Welcome to Essex', lots and lots of beautiful countryside and then we were disturbing the peace in country villages that had names like Much Haddam and Baldock. I later saw the male version of the route. It read as follows: A102(M), A12, M11 to svs, A120, A10, A505. Are you any the wiser? I didn't care where we were going. I was very relaxed cruising off to someplace.

For anyone who is, yet again, thinking, 'Isabel is mad. I could never do this,' it wasn't in the least scary. The Harley owners were exemplary road users. They had a strict code of conduct, the speedometer didn't go over 60 mph at any point and any car drivers who cut up the formation were treated with the utmost civility. There was no overtaking any other bike at any point. The order we left in was the order that we arrived in.

I was sitting on a bike that had an 1,450 cc engine, whatever that means, and was called 'Ultraglide', and it certainly did. I had the curious sensation of being sat in a gliding armchair. I believe that twice in the seventy miles I recall a slight sensation that I could, if I exaggerated, call a bump. To add to the utter bliss of all this, Big Dave had a sound system on his bike. We were travelling along in a vehicle with no walls and no roof and yet I could hear every word of every song. I was happy to be in the present moment. Just to make sure I didn't miss it, Phil Collins sang to me, 'Oh, think twice, it's another day for you and me in paradise.' But he didn't need to remind me. I'd noticed already.

We arrived at our destination and took photos of the group. I had a huge smile. Three women and 28 men. I have never, in my entire life been in any group where the numbers were this way around. And I was thriving on the change . . . the men weren't good looking, they were mostly overweight and I'd decided the average age was probably over 49¾. But they were enjoying themselves in the most simple and uncomplicated way. Boys with toys.

Then we all strode off to a local pub for lunch. We took over an idyllic garden and I sat down to enjoy the ploughman's lunch and the bikers' banter.

'What brings you here?' They all looked at me.

'I'm going the places where the guys go to try and learn a bit,' I said. 'Do your wives ever come along?'

'My wife is just glad I've got a hobby,' said one. 'She is glad that I don't sit around all day watching TV and farting.'

'I see. So you come to get away from your wives?'

'I like the fact that I ride a bike and my wife doesn't.'

'I see.'

'I took my ex-wife out once,' another shiny black outfit says. 'I turned down the suspension almost completely and

went down a very long road with lots of potholes. That
made sure that she never wanted to ride with me again.'

'And that was the best sexual experience that she'd ever
had while she was married to him.'

'We like getting away from the women.'

'Yeh, like, "Why don't you paint a flower on your bike?" '
Raucous laughter. 'Or, "Try pink." '

'If I'd murdered my wife instead of married her I'd have
been free by now.'

'And you'd have had better sex in prison.'

'Whether you'd liked it or not.'

'That would make me not want to go to prison; I don't
want to be bummed.'

'That's what you say.'

I sat and listened in a mixture of amusement, horror and
confusion to what seemed to be a good natured mixture of
misogynist and homophobic banter. Can misogyny and
homophobia be good natured, you ask? I suppose not, not
any more than racism or any humour at the expense of
others can be . . . except that I had the feeling that they
didn't really mean any of it. I wasn't convinced that they
genuinely disliked gay men and more than they disliked
women. Unless, as Germaine Greer was saying in *The
Female Eunuch*, which I was also rereading for your reading
list in the appendix, at some level men hate women. It was
certainly confusing.

'I pulled up at the lights the other day and a bloke pulled
up beside me and said, "Oh, you've got a Harley. Would
you like to go for a drink?" '

They all roared with laughter. It was hard to not laugh
too and I wasn't trying too hard. It was strange. Not
aggressive homophobia. More like playful showing off.

'So did you go?' I asked. 'What happened?'

'He woke up in an alley with a sock in his mouth and a
condom up his arse.'

I don't share their opinion that that is funny. I got more
confused. I wondered if maybe the anti-gay jokes were

supposed to demonstrate to me that they were not gay. Why not address the matter directly?

'Gentlemen . . .' I smiled politely. 'Would it be fair to assume that you are mostly heterosexual here?'

'Yes. But we do all wear leather and do a lot of polishing and cleaning.'

More laughter and one put his arm around the other to demonstrate how not gay he was.

I couldn't help but notice that the two telling the most anti-gay jokes were the two with the most gay mannerisms.

'Shall we tell her about the Cillit Bang?'

'No!' said someone else.

Big Dave had said nothing. He was sitting there with his head buried in his hands with a look of quiet despair on his face.

'Have you heard about anal bleaching?' (Best not to work out who was saying what at this point.)

'No. I'm still using hamsters.'

'Felching is the term.'

I thought maybe I'd broach the subject of women.

'I know a hundred single women,' I said. I notice men sit up when I say this.

'Some of them may like to come along for a trip on the bikes one week. If I let them know . . . would any of you like to bring a passenger?'

'No fat ones.' More raucous laughter.

'Excuse me? I don't see any gentlemen here that are short of a pound or two.'

'No, we like wealthy women.'

That flip would have been good if it had been deliberate but no, he'd misunderstood.

'She means weight.'

'We don't like fat women. The bikes can't cope,' said a fat man.

'And I don't want to give a ride to any women that shaves more than I do.'

They all laughed at this, too. It was a bit much. I have a woman friend who has had a hormone imbalance for many years and resorted to shaving at one point. It was an agonising condition for her ... but I gritted my teeth and went on smiling.

'I want to meet a woman who likes rugby.'

More laughter. 'Some chance.'

I grinned obligingly. 'Actually, one of the single women I know likes rugby very much and she says that men are intimidated when she often knows more about rugby than they do. How do you think you'd handle that?'

He sloped off.

'What's wrong with that question?' I asked.

'He wants a man, obviously.' More laughter. Back to gay stuff so quickly?

A more moderate voice joined in.

'Hey ... J.K. Rowling ... what're you writing about?'

'A lot of women moan that they find it hard to meet men.'

'You mean a lot of women moan a lot,' said one of the women-haters.

Funniest joke of the day.

Now, I don't want you to despair of these guys. Dave hadn't said a word. And there were a couple of others: the quiet and gentle Andrew, who was listening and observing ... ready to step in, I think, if anything got out of hand.

And others on other tables who wanted no part of this rather obvious, er, 'humour'.

'Hey, write this joke down. It's a good one.'

'OK.'

'What do the donkeys at Blackpool have for lunch?'

'I don't know ...' I played along. 'What do the donkeys at Blackpool have for lunch?'

'An hour off.'

They all laughed. I looked at Andrew, who smiled at me sympathetically but wisely said nothing. The banter went on.

'Does that include the ones on the beach?'

'So ...' I smiled, ignoring them. 'Would you like me to invite a friend along occasionally?'

'Lots of the wives don't know that the bikes have passenger seats. They can be hidden in the tour packs on the back.'

'My wife wouldn't let me come if she knew I'd given some girl a ride for the day.'

What does he mean, 'My wife wouldn't let me come'? Do women really tell men what they can and can't do? Do men really allow women to stop them having fun just like they said on the building site? Are relationships really this bad?

'Oh come on,' said one, 'it would be good to have some women along. It keeps the flies off the sandwiches.'

'He doesn't mean it,' said someone quietly in my ear.

'It's OK. I understand.' But I didn't really.

'Look. All I'm suggesting is that if there are any guys who have bikes that can take two who would like to take a passenger along, I think I know some girls who would enjoy a day out, that's all.'

'We can find out if it would be OK to put it on the website,' said Dave. 'We'd have to check the insurance situation and everything.'

'OK.'

'So where do you think women should go, guys? To meet more men.'

'Lap dancing?'

'It's easy for women to meet men.'

'Is it?'

'Yeh. They just need to smarten themselves up a bit and make their skirts a bit shorter.'

I'll mention that later to my feminist academic friend who's just finished her PhD, then.

It was very curious. All the jokey homophobia and misogyny, and yet they were obviously enjoying having me around, even if I was just a good reason to show off to their mates. They didn't offend me with their absurd humour. But could any women I know date any of these men? The ones who were the wisest and the most thoughtful had said nothing. The quiet Andrew and the wonderful Big Dave who was looking after me for the day were both married, of course. Big Dave, I discovered, had five children. Some of the others, who were single, I wouldn't want to put in the same room as a woman. They gave the impression that they hadn't had this experience so far in life and, despite claiming to be straight, they seemed to prefer male company anyway. They had chosen a hobby that would leave them almost exclusively with men.

'So what was it that Richard Gere is supposed to have done with hamsters?' asked one.

Dave cracked.

'Well, I hate to break up the party.' Eighteen stone of him rose to its feet. 'But I'd like to be going now, Isabel.'

'Yes, Dave.'

I love it when someone else is in charge of me and I don't have to make decisions.

We were not going back as a group. Everyone would make their own way. So no cosy 60 mph on the way back. Dave found the M11 and the speedometer was soon dipping over 80 mph. It was the weirdest feeling, not unlike a mild vertigo at times. I was sitting in a chair with the ground beside me going by at 80 mph. The weird thing was being able to see the ground so clearly. I realised that it had the potential to make me dizzy if I thought about it.

When you travel in a car, you have the illusion that you are safe inside this little box. If the car crashes into something, there is, at least, the little box itself that may give you some protection. But you don't feel as if you are really in the world. You are in the box of your car. On a bike there is no such illusion. I knew for sure that I would only have to lean over sharply and suddenly and death and I would meet in a rather abrupt manner. Such were the thoughts that whistled through my head on the return journey. I stopped looking at the road and looked at the countryside instead, Dave's music completing the sensation of being in some altered state. I sat totally still, as in meditation, and remembered to breathe. And for once it looked as if time was passing at the speed the years go by.

Dave brought me to my front door. Neighbours looked out of the corner of their eyes as this huge bald mass of black leather steered his £35,000 bike into the drive. 'Cup of tea, Dave?'

'I don't like to impose.'

'Don't be daft.'

We sat in the garden with mugs of tea.

'So what should I make of all that, then?'

'You need to understand that underneath all that men are intimidated by women. You have to be so careful what you say and do. So many things can be misconstrued. You know, my daughter was competing in a gym competition and I wasn't allowed to go and photograph her?'

'Yes . . . I can see. But surely that's kids. It's not the same with women, is it?'

'It is the same. If you so much as make polite conversation it can be misconstrued. Men get reprimanded, cautioned, taken to court, taken to the cleaners.'

'So that's why men in England never smile at me?'

'Yup. You'll be more likely to be given a blank stare, straight ahead, without acknowledging your presence. A lot of guys don't understand women and don't know how to talk to them.'

'Yes. I think a lot of women are quite bad at understanding men, too. As has been said before, it's a miracle the race survives.'

'And there are very few happy marriages. After the woman is pregnant it often seems that the man has fulfilled any useful function he may have. It's amazing how headaches only come on after the woman is pregnant.'

'Oh dear. Are we that bad?'

'If you talk to a woman in the workplace anything you say can be turned against you. A woman can accuse you of putting a hand up her skirt and whatever the outcome, the man is in big trouble. People will always say there is no smoke without fire.'

'So you guys are scared of us?'

'Did you ever try offering a woman a seat on public transport?'

'If a man offers me a seat I say, "Thank you".'

'This is one response, but not the most likely one. Women are hard work. The guys enjoy themselves because they are in their own company and they don't have to be worried. You're all right, but there are so few places now that men can go that women haven't taken over. This is one of them.'

'I see.'

'But there is a pub evening once a month of the Harley Owners' Group. It wasn't a typical day today and some of the guys who were talking I've never seen before. It's a totally different group that go to the pub. Why don't you come along and meet them?'

They are a weird and wonderful bunch these bikers, to be sure. The night I went to the pub, Big Dave or Very Big Dave, as I had started to call him, brought his steed around to collect me so that I could arrive in the necessary amount of style. He had also decided that I needed to be lent some 'colours' (a jacket with all the appropriate patches) so that I could blend in.

Some of the men are almost comically elderly. I never imagined this. I began to wish that I was a photographer, as it was a mass of long, grey hair. One man I chatted to, who was 35, said that he must have brought the average age down by half when he joined. It is funny, though. If you have a mother who is widowed and interested in meeting a man in his late sixties or seventies, you may not have thought of suggesting that she take up riding a Harley. One couple who came in were a genuine delight to behold. Assuming they were married.

'Oh yes . . . we've been together forty-one years. We met in 1960.'

'He had a bike and I thought, "I fancy a ride on that."'

'It was a 1,200 Harley, built in 1951. Anyway, we started to ride together a lot in Canada where I lived and one day she said, "I'm going home now, are you coming?" She meant England, but I said, "OK," and I've been here and with her ever since. But I wish I had that bike now . . . it would be worth a fortune.'

Groups of men stood around the wonderful machines outside speaking some language that was obviously going to require study. I really think that only the male of our species is able to utter phrases like,

'I've got Vance and Hines ovals; they have the Screamin' Eagles on.' or 'Ah, but what about the slash-cuts?'

And I wonder how many females on the planet could answer this question, 'Just exactly what is the main benefit of extending the rake on the forks?'

I staggered into the pub in search of red wine and some conversation that I could comprehend. Big Dave introduced me to Paul, the chief of this particular chapter, and we sat down to discuss the wonders of the Harley. I explained the nature of my project and the fact that I was 'exploring male environments'. Paul nodded approval. Obviously this was the best of them, in his estimation.

'Riding a Harley is one of the most acceptable activities that a man in his thirties, forties or fifties can go off and do with other men that is fun and isn't frowned on by anyone because it's so aspirational. It's a strange thing. Almost everyone would love to own a Harley. With other bikes there is a sense of anonymity, but with a Harley there is a relation between the bike and the fact that the rider is a free spirit. Freedom and fun are two of the things that Harleys stand for, everyone knows it. In France even the grannies will stop and admire them. I like being acknowledged for being a free spirit.'

'That's it.' I nodded enthusiastically. 'Yes. Exactly, that's what I love about them too, about being here, about the whole Harley ethos. I just love it; I love the fact that it's completely cross-class, I love the fun and freedom thing. It's *so* different from the female environments that I've mixed in where, obviously, we do nothing except sit around and talk about our feelings.'

What's happening to me? Am I cracking anti-women jokes too now?

'Have you thought of riding a bike yourself?'

I felt my skin go a lighter shade of pale.

'Wot? Me?'

He laughed. 'Why not?'

'I'm not big and butch enough. I'm quite happy wearing a pink cashmere cardigan, sitting on the back, being looked after by Very Big Dave.'

'Yes, but there is nothing quite like riding one yourself. Shame that you'll never get to experience that.' What? Harumph. Says who?

'Isn't it scary and expensive and difficult?'

'You can do the Harley practical test at a place called Rider's Edge in six days. Then you could always hire a bike when you wanted to and ride it yourself.'

'But I've never even taken a theory test. When I passed my car licence they had only just invented road signs.'

'Oh, the theory test is easy. Go on . . . it would be good to have a woman in the chapter.'

'Mmmm. I'll think about it.'

So much for a harmless evening at the pub.

There is something about the phrase, 'Shame you'll never get to experience that.' It certainly makes one sit up, doesn't it? The fact is that, in this lifetime, we have a limited number of heartbeats left.

If we are lucky there will come a time when we are ninety and living in an old people's home. If cancer doesn't bump us off sooner, we will then have ample leisure to sit and reflect upon our lives and the things that we never got to experience. The aged tell me that the worst thing is the regrets . . . the things that they wish they had done. 'I wish I'd moved to the seaside,' 'I wish I'd spent more time with my children,' 'I wish I'd learned to paint,' 'I wish I'd travelled . . . but now I can't. My legs won't let me.'

But here I am in the present, still living the life that one day, if I'm lucky, I'll be looking back on . . . and it seems to me that the selection of things that I may regret break down into two neat groups. In the first group are those things outside my control: not having had brothers and sisters, not having had a son to keep my lovely daughter company or even not having had the chance to spend today with Harry. This last example springs to mind. For some reason. Not that he's on my mind at all.

The second group of potential regrets is all those things that we can do something about but, unless we take action, are also likely to end up being things that we wish we had experienced. I would love to be able to play a Bach prelude, but I can only play half of one. I can sit down at any piano anywhere and play half a prelude . . . isn't that absurd? I've known this half a bit of Bach for years, but I've never taken the time to sit down and memorise the other half. I can imagine that in my old people's home (and I can't write this sentence without stopping each time to add 'Insh'Allah', 'God willing') there will be a piano, I can be sure, and if I'm not careful, I'll be sitting at it playing half a prelude. I'll have lost the music by then, and the ability to commit new passages to memory and the other old dears will be driven battier by me never being able to play to the resolution.

OK, so I'm getting carried away with this example. But there are all the other things that I know I could have and do if I am just disciplined and put my mind to it. I can learn Arabic, I can learn how to make chapattis well, and I can do everything in my power to travel and live the fullest life I know how. These just require me to make a choice and take action.

Now, one of the great mysteries of life, as we all know, is into which group the vexed question of 'men' should be put. For all of you that are 39¾, it may well feel that meeting a man that you want to have babies with comes into the category of things outside your control. As indeed, ultimately, it does. However, and here's the fun part . . . if you don't want to be very cross with yourself when you are ninety, at least you want to know that you did everything that you humanly could do to find someone that you wanted to live your life with. And you had a damn good time doing it.

The belief that meeting someone is totally outside our control and in the realm of the mystical is still around. We are advised to 'just go on living your life' in a non-specific kind of way and 'when the time is right' (?!) 'he'll turn up'. It's a kind of quasi-spirituality, a requirement to trust in 'fate' or 'the universe'. In Christian or conventional religious groups from any faith, 'God will bring along the right person at the right time'. Both these views mean that we are cast back into a fairytale and can stand around singing 'Some Day My Prince Will Come' and sweeping up the cinders.

As you see, I don't subscribe to this view. I'm all for trusting the spiritual world under whatever terms you prefer, but, based on statistics alone, unless you move to China, the chances are no man is going to miraculously turn up and find you. We have to be joyfully pro-active, positive and yet not attached to results. On the lookout and yet learning and growing anyway and having a damned good life. I'm not saying that chance doesn't play a part ... but you have to be in the right place to give chance a chance, don't you? Look at my absurd life, for example. I spend most of my days sitting at my computer and sending emails to a bunch of people across the world that I'm never likely to meet. The only man I see daily is the man in the post office. I am very fond of him, but he's Muslim and happily married with two children, and his wife and her mother also work in the post office. So my chances there would seem to me to be limited, even from the most optimistic perspective. Especially as all we ever discuss is stamps.

The man in the local supermarket doesn't really do it for me and the owner of the laundrette is female. So if someone tells me that 'the perfect man will turn up when the moment is right', I ask them where exactly I am to expect him? Somewhere between my house and the post office? I mean, I haven't studied maths, but the statistical chances of me meeting someone that I want to share my bed and the rest of my life with on the corner of Battersea Park Road seem to me to be fairly low.

So I don't listen to all those who tell me that meeting someone should be left to 'fate', 'God', 'destiny', 'the universe' etc., and instead I will move this challenge to the second group of potential regrets: 'Things that we can do something about by making choices and taking actions'. If I take action but never meet anyone, at least I won't either be able to be angry with myself or angry at destiny. Nor will destiny be mad at me, as I gave it a chance and had a damn good time, too.

The advantages of this approach as opposed to the wait-around approach, I contend, are fourfold:

1. We'll be amazing people out there doing amazing things, grabbing life by the er . . . horns, and we'll be truly attractive for that reason.
2. We'll be living lives that we love and inspire others.
3. There will always be lots of friends around in the meantime, coz positive energy is attractive to all.
4. We'll have such a good life that it will matter far less whether we meet someone or not or, when we look back, whether we met someone or not.

And just think – if we were all approaching a group hundredth birthday party tomorrow and some bright spark like Losada had come up with the idea of writing a list of things that we wish that we had done . . . well, I'll admit that I may end up with 'Spent ten years with Harry' on my list. But, dammit – I will not have 'Ridden a Harley-Davidson'. Why would I want that there? Why would you want that there? Why would anyone blessed with two arms and two legs not want to go and ride the open road?

So the only thing is to listen to Paul and put aside my stereotypical views about it not being very 'feminine'. I don't care if my inner girly isn't happy about it and wants the prince to be driving the charger . . . I'll ignore her and learn to ride myself. And when a young nurse pushes me, in my dotage, in a direction that I don't want to go . . . I'll be able to wag a bony finger and say, 'That way, young woman! I used to ride a Harley-Davidson, you know!'

And she'll be so impressed that she will then respectfully push me where I want to go.

Besides, Paul is right and if I'm on this mission to study the male species, then I have to study them on their own territory as one of them, don't I? A Venusian sometimes has to adopt strange behaviours in her attempt to learn to understand the creatures from Mars.

The official Driving Standards Agency textbook for the motorcyclists' theory test is 319 pages long, so I hope you're impressed by my hard work and dedication. What I want to know is, am I not the only person in the country that now knows the difference between a toucan crossing and a pelican crossing? What about this question 'At a puffin crossing (I jest not), which colour follows the green signal?'

And your next question in the short taster of the theory exam: Which three emergency services have blue flashing beacons? a) Coastguard, b) Bomb disposal, c) Gritting lorries, d) Animal ambulance, e) Mountain rescue, f) Doctors' cars?

We are all supposed to know these things, cyclists and pedestrians too.

Now here are the answers and if you didn't know them, please pick up a copy of the Highway Code next time you're in a bookshop or buy one from www.dft.gov.uk. It's only £1.99 and you can put it on the loo. Never let it be said that the books of Losada don't make a positive difference in you life.

1. At a puffin crossing (which is a crossing with an infra-red sensor to detect pedestrians crossing), steady amber follows green.

2. The emergency services that have a blue flashing light are a) Coastguard b) Bomb disposal and e) Mountain rescue. Powered vehicles used by disabled people have amber flashing lights, as has any slow-moving vehicle. A green flashing light is a doctor on call.

So, by filling my head with facts like these I managed to get through the theory exam. I sent a text to Paul at the local chapter group: 'I'm through!'

Within a minute a message came back. 'Congratulations. When are you going up to Rider's Edge for the practical?'

The Harley Training Centre Rider's Edge is truly a male environment. There is only one specialist training centre outside America. It happens to be in Wales. Most people who learn to ride a bike just take something called a Compulsory Basic Training test, but with one of these licences you can only ride a lightweight bike. The Rider's Edge course offers a whole lot more than this. The training is run by specially licensed former police riders at an amazing centre at the Royal Welsh Showgrounds with six miles of private roads. This course is the business. If I am ever to ride a Harley, this is the course that I have to take . . . and pass.

I arrived in at the centre, called a local cab service and said to the driver, 'Do you know any local landladies that run a B&B but that like to have guests?'

'There's Mrs Davis, but she's seven miles from where you are.'

'Tell me about Mrs Davis.'

'She's elderly, about seventy, and she lost her husband two months ago.'

'So, she'd be glad of a bit of company, then?'

'Yes, but she's had a fall and broken her wrist, so she may have trouble making up the beds and all.'

'Please tell her that if she'll have me I'd love to come and I'll give her a hand with the beds and fix my own breakfast.'

It would give me great joy to sit and listen to Mrs Davis talking about her late husband for several hours if she wanted to and I wouldn't have to say anything at all. He rang and Mrs Davis said that I'd be the first guest since her husband's death, but that she'd be delighted to welcome me.

I walked into the training centre, suitcase in hand, heart in mouth, secretly looking forward muchly to tea with my new seventy-year-old landlady with the broken wrist.

I really enjoy being surrounded by men. Perhaps I'm still getting over all those years at ballet school and in the theatre. I loved all the instructors at once, as they all had wonderful Welsh accents; those lovely, soft, lilty, accents that sound like the voice-over for Ivor the Engine. They were ex-police drivers: funny, disciplined, careful and conscientious. They never teach with more than two learners to each instructor. There were four guys and me. I was the odd one out and so had an instructor all to myself. I liked my instructor immediately: he was old enough to be my father, with a lifetime of experience with bikes and he also took the intermediate and advanced courses. I was *so* happy and so excited. Pictures of smiling punters holding certificates were pinned to the walls along with thank-you letters about the numerous successes. They checked our eyesight and our qualifications before sitting down for an hour or two more theory until finally they said, 'OK. Shall we go and get on a bike, then?'

Oh, joy of joys – we were going to be allowed to sit on a motorbike! We climbed into lots of protective clothing, walked around to the bike sheds and stood in admiration; the shed was full of everything from little 125s to the largest and most expensive Harleys. One of the instructors was talking, 'This is the throttle, this is the back brake on the right pedal, this is the clutch.' I loved it. A course where I could learn a new skill instead of examining my over-observed navel.

'This is the front brake, but you'll learn the correct way

to use this. You have to be gentle with it, as you'll see. The most important control is the clutch . . .'

The guys were nodding as if all this was obvious. I just felt excited. The first exercise was to push the bike around and get the feel of it. 'You always stand on the left of the bike.' My bike was shiny and red. We pushed them outside and were eventually allowed to sit on them. 'Now paddle the bikes forward with your feet.' Then we were introduced to the joy of the ignition key and allowed to start the bike and go forward a couple of feet. Oh boy, this was fun. Who'd be a girl?

We drove our bikes up and down. I amazed my instructor by doing a perfect U-turn on my first drive down the driveway. We were on private roads, so it was all wonderfully safe. Then we all split up and I was left with my instructor.

'You're doing very well on that,' he said. 'Now, throttle off, clutch in, left foot down. Yes. Perfect stop.' I was enjoying myself, hadn't quite got the hang of the clutch, but I had no fear of the machine and it seemed to show. 'OK. We're going to go down to the training area now. So just follow me, nice and slow and you can see how the bike feels in second and third gear. Just nice and gently.' I was fitted with headphones so that he could talk to me as I was driving along. With the Welsh accent, and the mountains around us it was all just perfect. I couldn't think of anything I'd rather be learning.

'Now just move gently up into second. Yes, that's right, and slowly release the clutch. Good. A little wide on that turn. We'll go straight up here. Good. A little more throttle. Good. Now on this stretch you can see how much smoother the bike is in third. Left foot under the gear level ready . . . good . . . and clutch out. Good. Excellent, Isabel. You're a natural. Excellent tight turn there. Make sure you come down properly through the sequential gears. Good. And down to one. And if you come to a stop beside me here. Good. Excellent stop. Perfect. You can't imagine how hard it is to teach some people to do that.'

'What? Put their left foot on the ground?'

'Some people find it hard, but you're taking to this easily. Do you ride a pedal bike?'

'Every day.'

'That will help. How does it feel to you?'

'A bit bumpy, I don't seem to be able to control the gears and the clutch at the lower speeds.'

'I might try you on a Buell after lunch. They are larger, but smoother and easier to control. Would you like to try that?'

'I would, yes.'

We drove up and down and round and round. I was still struggling with the clutch control when we went back for lunch. I compared notes with the others. The boys were doing fine. One of them had already fallen off twice: 'I haven't hurt myself, but it's made me more nervous than I was.'

'It's quite normal to come off a couple of times,' said a Welsh whisper. 'All part of the learning curve.'

'How are you doing, Isabel?'

'I'm struggling with the gears a bit but I'm enjoying myself.'

We set off for the afternoon session, which was to be slow riding. Around cones in figures of eight, etc. I was given my slightly larger Buell bike. An American bike, descended from a Harley, but lighter. I drove off happily with my Welshman talking in my ear. 'Now we're going to turn right here. Steady. Now move up into second. Excellent. I see you are even indicating. Very good, now we are going to turn left at the bottom.'

I brought the bike to the turn, but I was in third gear and I couldn't seem to move down the gears fast enough to make the left turn. I steered to the left and instinctively pulled the right brake with my hand as I do every day of the week. The bike came off the road and on to the grass – oh shit, I'm out of control. Time is all over the place. What's happened to the tense? Is this slow motion? How to think?

Grass? Big machine? I pull the throttle in some misguided attempt to get the bike to stand upright. The bike is not a horse, doesn't understand me and goes faster. I'm skidding and I seem to be leaning over to the left. What now? I'm sure I should have let go. Why haven't I let go? Why does any part of my subconscious feel that I need to protect a bike from grass? Why is the sky there? Did something stupid just happen? Ah, I'm on the ground with a bike on top of me.

'Are you OK, Isabel?,' a wonderful Welsh voice was saying in my headphones. I nodded and shouted, 'I'm fine,' as he rode up. 'But I think I've twisted my wrist in some way.' I held in the air something rather odd looking that had previously been a wrist. Only my hand didn't seem to belong to me any more. 'Oh dear,' I said, 'It doesn't hurt.' My hand was sticking out at a weird angle as if it had taken to doing a bird imitation in a game of shadows.

'No, it won't hurt now . . . but give it five minutes. I'm afraid that's a fracture. It looks like a double fracture. No more riding for you for a while.'

He looked at me. I think he was as perplexed as I was.

'What did I do?'

'You used the front brake and then I think you pulled the throttle.'

'Why did I do that?'

'I've no idea, I'm afraid.'

'I'm so sorry.'

'No, I'm sorry.'

'No really, it's not your fault, I should have told you how dim I am.'

'It's not your fault, either; everyone makes mistakes. I've called an ambulance.'

'How many people have done this course this year?' My wrist started to scream at me.

'Hundreds.'

'And how many broken limbs have you had?'

'You really want to know? Only the one. You're the first.'

* * *

I suppose that, as the idea was to seek out new experiences in male environments, being put on a stretcher and carried into an ambulance by three burly Welsh ambulance drivers must be a kind of success. Especially as one of them was then called upon to speak to me in a soft, intimate and reassuring voice for the hour-long bumpy journey to Hereford Hospital. Or this is what I told myself – it wasn't quite what I'd had in mind.

I had this long journey to amuse the ambulance driver, between gulps of the gas Entonox, and I told him that I remembered my teacher saying quite clearly in the morning not to touch the front brake and to control the speed with the clutch. And I told him that if he could write down what I was saying then I'd later have a record of the effect of the gas on my remaining brain cells for a book I was writing. And he smiled at me, in a patronising kind of way, as I was evidently deluded, and continued to speak to me in a professionally reassuring voice, and wouldn't write anything down. And the Entonox made it feel as though the pain was still there but I was somewhere else, curiously observing all this; like a writer writing about it but not being in the scene, or an actor saying the lines of the character and at the same time finding that they are not the character, but have wandered off to consider what's for dinner after the show.

Then everything got hazy. It wasn't ambulance men but doctors peering down at me. Extracts of conversation that I'd rather not have overheard in my life would have to include, 'Can I have some help? We've got a Colles fracture to pull out here.' Are you feeling sick yet? They filled my arm full of something and told me to look the other way and think of Harry. Or I think that's what they said, but I'd breathed a lot of gas by this time. A yanking went on while various doctors seemed to fight over who owned my arm, they wrapped something around it and before I knew where I was, I was being dispatched with a large plaster cast and a bag full of painkillers.

'We'll be forwarding the bill for those.'

'Oh really? Yes, doctor. Thank you, doctor.' He wasn't good looking.

In the waiting room John from Rider's Edge had driven all the way to pick me up, rescue me, and take me back to my new home at the B&B.

Mrs Davis opened the door with a huge smile. 'It's lovely to have you. I'm a bit handicapped at the moment, you see – I've broken my left wrist.'

From under my jacket I produced my broken left wrist.

'Well, I never. I wouldn't have believed it.'

That evening, I sat with the cat and listened, with the greatest of joy, to stories about Mrs Davis's late husband; she had to put her fork in my cheese on toast to hold it still so that I could cut it, and later, although she is seventy and I am not yet seventy, with her one good hand, she helped me undress so that I could go to bed.

'Go straight to your local hospital when you get back to London,' they'd said to me. 'They'll want to x-ray it to check that it's setting straight.' So I went along and an elderly and evidently experienced male scowled at the x-ray.

'We can do better than that. Be here tomorrow morning at 7.30 a.m.'

Now something has gone wrong and it's not the fracture. Just when I was in an all-male environment and making some progress, and you thought the narrative was zipping along nicely, we are trapped in a time warp. It's 7.30 on a Tuesday morning and here we are. I'm supposed to be on this research project for you and for me, and instead, we're in a waiting room. I suppose if you set out to look for the Holy Grail this is to be expected. I have time to reflect on life, men and the present moment.

This waiting room is painted pastel blue which, I suppose, is meant to be calming. There are twelve rather uncomfortable plastic chairs and one small table. On the table are eight one thousand-piece jigsaws. Do you suppose there is something about the length of this wait that I don't know?

It's curious, this pain thing. I can now confirm that our attitude to it is one of the differences between us, the creatures from Venus and those strange beings from Mars. Consider the men on the building sites – every week there is an accident of some kind. And what about racing cars for a living, fighting professionally like Steve the Roofer or going off to war? Am I am now experiencing, quite accidentally, one of the differences between us? Gary, my stuntman friend, is totally unfazed by broken bones. I remember him telling me that he's been in hospital twenty times and sometimes with five or six bones broken at a time. 'One of the hazards of the job,' he'd say. But I really don't like this. I'm really not happy at all. And I wonder if women have some gene in them that naturally makes them want to take care of the men and the children and themselves? It's not that long, in evolutionary terms, since men had to go out and put their lives in danger every day just to bring back the food. So it seems that, just as they have some inner drive to court physical danger, we have some instinct to avoid it.

Do the women adventurers that climb mountains, sail round the world, or throw themselves out of planes for a living simply ride over that delicate little voice that says, 'Fuck! Get me out of here . . . this is a *bad* idea?' whereas men either don't have this voice at all or, if they do have it, they don't hear it or don't choose to listen?

You may smile, but we modern spiritual women often speak of 'listening to ourselves' or 'honouring the inner voice'. It would all be different if men listened when an inner voice said, 'Listen Jim, this going off to make war with the Klingons thing, it's really not a good idea. You might get hurt.'

Eight o'clock. I'm looking forward to the general anaesthetic. If astral travel is available on the NHS, my astral body will be out of here before they can say, 'Colles fracture.' I'll be off to see Harry. Pop up to Scotland the cheap way and see what he's up to. How his clothes are looking on him.

Had a sweet call from a Dick this morning. Said he'd have the operation for me if he could. Funny old world.

It's airless, timeless in this pastel-blue ward with the plastic chairs and the jigsaws. I look at them – country cottages mostly, with roses growing up by the door and, in a frenetic, livid sprawl someone has written, 'This jigsaw has 23 pieces missing.' Ha ha. Think I could learn the lesson from that jigsaw without taking the time to put the pieces together. If you imagine that you can put together the perfect picture of living in a cottage with roses and some Martian, you need to be warned in advance that the picture may have 23 pieces missing.

Speaking of imperfect pictures, did I tell you I'm going to see Harry this Sunday? Ah – I didn't mention it? Please don't be cross with me. I know, I know, I'm supposed to be setting an example and demonstrating an enlightened version of the letting-go process to you and instead I'm utterly hopeless. He's just too gorgeous.

He phoned you see. (After I'd emailed to let him know about my success on the first day of the bike course, and mentioned my fracture.) He asked if I'd like to have lunch with him on Sunday. He has to come down from Scotland on business.

'I'll understand if you want to say no.'

What was that voice in my head yelling, 'Yes!!!!!' a deranged voice yelling at me like a maniac in case I have the stupidity to say no.

'What was that?' I questioned the inner voice, which I had thought was supposed to be one of wisdom.

'Yes! Say yes!!'

'Harry – er, I think it's a yes, actually.'

'Really? In spite of everything?'

'Yes. In spite of everything.'

And I know it's stupid. And I know how it looks. I'm having lunch with a married man who has let me know that he's not leaving. May as well hand out free packets of ammunition to the critics and the book reviewers. Just cut and paste the following sentence: 'What woman in her right mind would have lunch with a married man who has decided to stay with his wife?'

And even leaving the critics aside, what girlfriend would advise, 'Oh this is a good idea, Isabel. Rush off and renew all your feelings for him? As if having your arm broken twice isn't bad enough, you want to get you heart re-manipulated too?'

I have no defence. Neither to critic nor friend. My only plea is for mercy and to let you know that no one disapproves of this more strongly than I do. Except possibly Harry. One of my current flatmates is very blasé, 'I don't know why you are so worried. Lots of my friends see married men.'

'But I don't. And Harry's never done this either. We're both very unhappy with deceit of any kind.'

But my desire to see his smile has overruled all my objections – practical, logical and ethical. Please remember me in your prayers.

Ho hum. 9 a.m. Wonder whether I've caught MRSA yet.

My mobile rings. It's a Tom. He makes me laugh, and I remind him that he's married.

Leaving me here is evidently a form of torture. 'Put the fracture patients in a room for a couple of hours with no painkillers and no breakfast. If they haven't gone home by the time we get there, Nurse Jones, then we know that they really must want to have the operation.'

9.14. Doctor comes in and tells me that they'll only operate today if a bed becomes available. I explain that I have to give a talk to 400 women in just over 36 hours.

'It's a charity event ... the Ladies' Lunch in Aberdeen. They've paid £40 each.'

'If a bed becomes available, we'll operate today. If not, I'm sorry.'

Then he makes me sign a form saying that I realise that the operation can result in nerve damage and the metal pins

that will hold the bones together may cause infection. He
has a yellow silk tie. I decide I don't like it much. Which
year of medical training is it that they do the empathy
removal?

He pottered off. Why are male doctors only good looking
on TV?

9.30. Two hours. The jigsaws *are* intended for use. Still,
at least I'm not thinking about Harry.

If only life were more like the movies or I was making this
up.

> *A man with a broken right wrist wandered into the
> waiting room, 'Hello.' He smiled. 'My name's Mat-
> thew.' He held out his left hand to shake my right hand
> ... 'Does your wrist hurt?' he asked. 'It does rather.' I
> blushed because he was so attractive.*
>
> *'Yours?'*
> *'Mine does too, yes.'*

And there it is. The first start of the potential happy ending.
But no. Reality is that it's 10 a.m. and it's just me and the
jigsaws. I pull two plastic chairs together, put my feet up
and ponder on reality a little.

Let's review the 'Where are the interesting single men?'
research so far. I have managed to establish some things.
The internet is only really likely to work for you if you are
under thirty, just want to have fun and have a lot of spare
time to while away in the evenings. A lot of what goes on
there is just for sex and not with any thought to a long-term
relationship. The UK sites are also full of Toms and Dicks,
according to the stories that were sent in to my website. It's
also likely to bring a lot of upset, frustration, projection
and, if you're lucky, rejection too. If you persevere with a
hundred per cent determination (and, to be fair, everyone
knows someone who met a partner on the internet), you
may eventually locate an enjoyable dinner companion. You
will have to be diligent and determined, though. I have one

friend who had two friends working on finding someone for her and they were online all day, every day for two weeks. She met someone, but she's 23, blonde, skinny and lives in New York. I also have a female American friend who is 45 and met her husband through the internet. She'd been internet dating for two years. I wish I'd made that up.

The worst thing about the internet is that it's no fun. It's hugely time consuming, you don't necessarily actually get to meet any men, and they can't find a label for the mystery of human chemistry. Which is why I'm just not prepared to give any more time to it.

But one of the advantages of the internet is that you don't actually have to meet any men that you don't want to meet. This, in turn, is the disadvantage of singles events. If you feel inclined to turn up at one of these, you are put instantly into the desperate category. The other problem with singles events is, as my friend Sam so succinctly puts it, 'If you want a Gucci handbag, you don't go to Marks & Spencer to check remaindered leftovers.'

The same is true of the many and various dating agencies. Instead of examining men like products on your computer, you can end up paying large sums of money to have someone else make your choices for you and feel disappointed with you if you don't want to go on a second date with Mr Sweet-but-very-dull-who-talks-about-cricket-a-lot. If you are a man looking for a woman, then I would recommend the dating agencies.

So far I've decided that if you are going to move on from all that and get yourself where the guys are, then you'll at least get to learn about them by direct experience and enjoy male company which, I find, is so different from female company. This may have different disadvantages, such as the sometimes (how shall we put it?) less-than-sophisticated behaviour that men can demonstrate when in groups. The element that I most enjoy about being in groups of guys is the often uncomplicated fun. On the other hand, which is not a phrase that I'll be able to use for at least six weeks, I am beginning to see why there aren't many women in these places. We have a different type of conversation and we don't want to get our hands burnt. Literally.

Now, if I were to apply a little feminine thought and analysis to all this, as part of my research into men as a group, I might ask why male environments seem to be so two-dimensional and superficial. What do I make of all that 'We're so straight and love to keep away from women' behaviour of some of the guys on the first Harley day? What does being masculine mean to men now? Is the kind of aggression that Steve was forced to demonstrate in the RAF really biological? Is it still about not showing or communicating your feelings? Do men still have to separate themselves from emotions that would be considered weak – fear, sadness, dependency, vulnerability – in order to be considered appropriately masculine?

To a woman all this is now a cliché. But it seems that many men haven't worked anything out at all and are just hopelessly confused. So many are still making decisions based on defining themselves by external success rather than inner reflection and the quality of their relationships. Along with ignoring negative emotions, the good and healthy use of emotions gets lost, too.

The men of whom all these generalisations are most true would logically feel safest in all-male environments where it's understood that some subjects are out of bounds and there aren't any annoying women about to challenge them. 'No dear – you don't have to feel embarrassed about crying – we're at a funeral – it's called emotion.'

But women can be unbearable – go on and on about these subjects and are guilty of not letting men be however they want to be. As Big Dave says, women are hard work. However, of one thing I'm certain, men are better off with women around and vice versa. And what we all want is kindness and understanding, surely?

11.30. A nurse comes and gives me a wrist tag with my name and date of birth. Well, if it's my destiny not to come around from the general and to become an unfortunate statistic, there will at least be no danger of anyone left wondering how old I was.

I'm asked if I'd like any pre-medication in case the operation happens today. 'I thought I was having a general anaesthetic?'

'Yes, but some people are in such a state of nerves that we have to give them something to calm them down before they have the general.'

I smile sweetly and say, 'No, I'm sure a general will do the trick nicely.'

11.31. Where were we? On a more pragmatic level, apart from the fact that I'm in hospital, the experiment with the Harley community is interesting. I do have, as Mary Balfour has suggested, a new range of male acquaintances in my address book. The fact that I can't go riding with them is certainly a problem and the fact that, yet again, all the sane ones are married is another. It seems extraordinary that I've been on this project for two months and I don't yet have one new male friend in my address book who is single and who I'd like to have dinner with.

12.00 noon. Oh goodness me, someone's coming. Nurse Nwamaka wants to know whether I'd have any objection to going on a men's ward. Another movie opportunity, dammit.

They wheeled me into the men's ward. 'Well, hello. I wasn't expecting to meet you here,' said a Mr Clooney, his leg strapped in the air in a most ungainly manner. I smiled at him – thank God I didn't look that stupid. 'My name's Isabel.' I shook his hand and wondered how he managed to be quite so attractive with his leg wired up.

Alas, the difference between movies and life.

The man in the bed opposite is called Faisal, he's 22 and has had his jaw broken in a street fight. Apparently the occurrence of young men admitted because of street fights is common on the ward.

'Nurse, does a bed mean that I'll be operated on today?'

'Only if no emergencies come in.'

Faisal sees me writing and asks, perhaps lacking the wit and style that Mr Clooney could have entertained me with, 'Are you a writer?' I contemplate the existential nature of this question and decide the answer has to be 'No.' I'm not even my thoughts, my body or my feelings, according to Buddhism, let alone being a writer. But I nod.

'You'll be in a lot of pain when you come back.'

I smile at him.

'You'll have long nails in and everything and the bruising will be terrible – all up your arm. You'll be black and blue.'

'Thanks, Faisal.'

So I start to feel nervous. More than that, I start to feel sad and sorry for myself.

I can't even find a solution to the men situation for myself, let alone for us all. I have no solutions for all the women who have written to me. Maybe I can just settle down in my comfort zone with my girlfriends and give up even trying to understand the male species, let alone find out where the interesting and available ones hide themselves. On Faisal's TV masses of them are cheering like lunatics in Trafalgar Square. What has happened? Has peace broken out? Is the Dalai Lama back in Tibet? Has someone found a cure for cancer? No. A cricket match has been won.

'Not won, actually. Just tied,' says Faisal. Why am I interested in the creatures? Why are any of us interested?

Of course I know Toms and Dicks who aren't interested in cricket. And Harry isn't interested in cricket. I give in and think about Harry and feel more sorry for myself.

Can I get out of this plot line please? Can I have a holiday? Can I stop being the heroine? Can I be the wimpy stay-at-home friend of the heroine who always gets the guy? Can't I live with Harry in a country cottage with 23 pieces missing? I mean, I can play that role.

So I go to sleep. And at 4.30 Nurse Nwamaka wakes me up to let me know they'll be sending me to sleep to operate. And I've never felt so happy and grateful in all my life.

So I get bits of metal put in me and then speak, with my arm in plaster, rather unconvincingly perhaps, about the joys of risk-taking to wiser and more sensible women in Aberdeen. On the way back, Paul from the local Harley group rings.

'About the ride around Brittany. I'd like to confirm your ticket? It'll be about fifty of us. You're qualified to ride yourself now, right?'

'Not exactly.' I relayed my tale of left bends, throttles and front brakes.

'On the first day?'

'Yup.'

'Oh, bad luck.'

'No, I don't think it was bad luck. I think it was stupidity. No fun riding through France with fifty men on bikes for me.'

But of course, biking aside, I'm expecting to be swept off my feet all over again. With my arm in plaster, and my heart held together with sticky tape, before I can even think about the next fun male environments I can explore in my handicapped state . . . before I can do anything sensible or intelligent or logical . . . this Sunday, is another kind of make or break. I'm seeing Harry.

3. A JOLLY GOOD FAMILY AND A GOOD JOB, TOO

THE UPPER CLASSES

OK, head down, more generalisations coming ... but we'll discuss the error of generalisations in the next chapter. For now I'm just going to go on making them and hoping that the fact that I know I'm generalising, and the fact that I'm drawing your attention to it makes it slightly less reprehensible.

In spite of the wonderfully rich cultural diversity in Britain there is still a strange group of people in London that will not be ignored. It's ridiculous to have to call them this, but they make up the category called the upper class. Their parents (they always have parents) either have money inherited through land ownership or they have worked hard, made a fortune and joined this, the posey set, because they can afford to do so. The impostors used be referred to in derogatory terms as 'the noveau riche'. They had the money but not the 'class' of the those who had always been rich. Now there are so many that have made their own money it's all got confused. But a classless society? We don't have one.

Anyway, whether the money is new or old, all parents know what they want to do with it. They want to give their children the best possible education and, traditionally, this has always been considered to be public schools. So generations of little boys (and girls too, but we're studying the boys) were sent off to be turned into little men. Taken from their parents too young and forced to learn that if they showed any feelings they would be bullied. Among the English upper classes this has been considered to be the best start in life.

In some senses it is a good start if you have a very narrow definition of education. But if it's a preparation for life, then some radicals would argue that knowing how to relate to women might be useful. Why would you put your son in an institution that only has boys? They will grow up – they do grow up – into hard-working, well-connected, successful individuals. They are blessed or cursed with a sure sense of their own superiority and no clue how to relate to a woman. London is full of them.

I have a theory that these men are another group that don't really like women because, even if they are heterosexual, they are just not at ease with them. They want to marry one, they want a wife and family but, given the choice between a night out in the company of their wife or with the 'chaps', they will always choose male company because that's what they've grown up with and that's what they know. Your average Frenchman, who has grown up in a mixed school, would always choose the company of women because he loves women and is endlessly fascinated by them. Your average English public schoolboy is not.

I have a single female friend who has moved here from the US and thinks this type of Englishman is gorgeous. She thinks they are all Hugh Grant. Once she asked if she could use my garden to make lunch for her latest crush. 'You must meet him,' she said. She arrived early and prepared the most wonderful lunch, laying it all out in the garden with a touching attention to detail. She had invited me to join them so that I could give her my impressions.

He arrived late after a five-mile run because he was training for something. We sat down to eat lunch and he talked a lot. Explaining that he was meeting some rowing companions later so couldn't stay for coffee, he left early. My friend asked me my honest impression. 'You just don't see it, do you?' I said. 'He isn't interested. It's not personal. It's not that he doesn't like you. He doesn't like women.'

'Isabel, he's totally straight, I assure you.'

'I didn't say he wasn't. I just can't help noticing that he doesn't really seem to enjoy women. He wasn't listening to you. He wasn't asking questions. He was having lunch with two intelligent and articulate women, neither of us that ugly, and he barely made eye contact. He didn't ask you any questions about what you are doing. Or me. He's happier with his male friends and he's rushed off to them. Don't you see?'

His behaviour had been what would have been called rude if he had been aware of what he was doing. But he wasn't. He didn't intend to be rude; to not notice the trouble that she had gone to, to not care. And it wasn't that he wasn't interested in her sexually. He was. But it was obvious to me that he was one of those that didn't want to give his time or attention to women.

In spite of me writing like this, I don't like stereotypes. I fight against them. I look for exceptions. And of course there are many. I even know two men with 4 × 4s and double-barrelled names who read the *Guardian*. But, apart from those two, it has to be said that this strange sub-group of men does exist.

'They're not really a sub-group,' said Jenny when I mentioned this one day.

'Yes, they are. Surely they only exist in south-west London?'

'And on their country estates, in business and in the City.'

'But nationally they are still a sub-group and they certainly need a little study. They are so . . . er, odd.'

One night some local acquaintances were going out for drinks in London's super-trendy Fulham. This isn't usually an area I would go to. But in the course of my research I was interested to go and listen. Fulham is a known haunt of the latest generation of public-school boys with their very particular views on life. Also, to make the evening more fun, one of my favourite neighbours was going along. Daisy is a 12-plus model and one of the most beautiful women in London, so it's always entertaining spending the evening with her and watching the men fall over their feet as she walks by. There is a bar/restaurant in Fulham called Brinkley's (www. brinkleys.com) where a lot of this 'set' hang out. One of them had heard that I knew lots of single female women and said that he would bring along a male for every single female I could bring. He rang and questioned me on the phone, 'What sort of girls will you be bringing? And how many?'

'What do you mean "what sort"? Rupert, you mean what age.'

'Yes, and jobs, you know, that sort of thing.'

'You want them all to be blonde, rich, twenty-five, and to want to have sex like a rabbit?'

'Yes. No, seriously, colour of hair doesn't matter.'

If only it was wit and not the truth he was speaking.

'What sort of men will you be providing, then?'

'Men with a jolly good family and a good job, too.'

I ask you, 'a jolly good family' – what are these words 'jolly good'? I have to get out of south-west London. Please remind me.

'How are we going to talk, Rupert, if it's a noisy bar? Are we going to book tables so that we can actually speak to each other?'

'Don't worry. It'll be fine.'

Meanwhile I rang some friends. Jenny and Daisy would come, and I rang some younger female friends just to be obliging.

The noisy bar environment is designed to favour superficial assessments of people. Daisy, as I said, is one of the most beautiful girls in London. Jenny is one of the most brilliant and I can be interesting to speak to on a number of topics, but to discover this about Jenny or myself, you'd have to actually talk with us. And this also applied to some other girlfriends I'd invited ... all pretty, but not professional models. We had not walked in the door before a pack of men circled Daisy, giving cursory politeness to all the rest of us. It was a formal mating game and I looked round to see if I could spot David Attenborough.

'And here we see the males on heat, who pick out the youngest female likely to produce the best offspring and begin their mating dance around her. The young female watches their displays with a total lack of interest while the older females look on in thinly disguised disgust at the obvious nature of the male's performance.'

Did you ever see the card with a male peacock spreading out his tale very proudly while two female peacocks watch. One of the females is saying to him, 'Just cut the crap and show us your willy.'

Obviously none of these men had read the book which was number one that week on the Amazon bestseller list, *The Game* by Neil Strauss, about how to pick up women. I am going to be recommending this to you in the appendix because, the amazing thing is, if you look at what he's advising men to do, you can see why it would work every time. A quite horrifying world in which men introduce themselves to each other along with a number indicating how many women they've slept with. 'I'm Tom ... 998.' But it's essential reading, nevertheless.

I'm not familiar with these mating environments, as I've never really enjoyed noisy bars for exactly the reason that you can't listen to people or have anything but the most obvious conversation. These guys wanted sex or wives, but presumably the wives are picked on looks and sexual performance alone. My definition of 'interesting' wasn't being shared by any of the crowd tonight. A few female friends of Rupert's were there. They looked infinitely mateable material. They all had blonde hair and were very attractive, with expensive, beautifully cut clothes and short skirts. I didn't get a chance to actually speak with any of them, as they were a whole table away and the music was too loud.

I looked around for the most interesting-looking of Rupert's single friends. There was one who didn't look like the rest and looked a little older and wiser. With the instant decisions that we make in these places, I could tell he wasn't my type, but I was curious to see what he would have to say about the difficulty of meeting single available men in London. I introduced myself and asked my standard questions.

'My name's Thomas.' He shook my hand formally, which seemed rather strange. 'Surely it works both ways? Men have trouble meeting women, too.'

'Do they?'

'I can only speak for myself, but hanging around with Rupert, he spends a lot of time in bars in London and all you meet is women who are incredibly shallow.'

'Shallow? In what sense? Are you sure it's not the environment that's shallow?'

'No. They are more interested in the size of your wallet.'

'Than the size of your penis?'

'Yes. They care more about the wallet. They all want to be wined and dined and they'll take you for a ride. If I want to see Rupert and his friends make fools of themselves with lots of raucous women, I know where to go. But I'm in the Army. We think about things. I can't bear the superficial nonsense.'

'You're in the Army? And you're public school?'

'Yes. The officers have a different set of values. My soldiers have fathered children by women, none of whom they are married to, and don't see anything wrong with that, whereas the officers have a greater sense of responsibility. Talking personally, I wouldn't marry until I felt it was absolutely right. The whole ethos of the family is paramount. Not everyone has this sense of responsibility.' He looked around him.

I had stumbled, not so much on a fish out of water as an officer out of barracks. It's not every day, I suspect, that you can meet someone like this in Brinkley's. Around me men shouted raucously and women laughed rather too loud. Jenny had cupped her hand over her ear and was attempting to hear what a man was saying to her. Daisy had wedged herself in a corner with her friend to protect herself from the increasingly more obvious courtship display.

'How long have you been in the Army, Thomas?'

'Sixteen years.'

'All your adult life, then?'

'Yes.' And public school before that. Heaven help him.

'So how come you're here tonight?'

'I've been placed in London.'

'Do you find it hard to meet women, then?'

'I've been in Sweden. I don't speak Swedish and I'm not particularly attracted to Swedish women. The women I've met in London don't want to be with someone who has no control over their own destiny. They prefer a man who works in the City, has at least a million a year and is probably a coke-head.'

Bitterness, however, draws nobody to us.

'Go on . . .' I said. 'Do you mind if I write your words down? It's just that I don't often meet men like you. I don't think my friends do, either.'

'No, that's fine. Someone needs to say these things. I challenge you to find someone in the City who is not dysfunctional. They do what they like. They have no personal responsibility. And they hit women, too . . . I could tell you stories of domestic violence in the City. But I won't.'

'So you feel that in the Army you have a higher sense of personal responsibility? Would you live with someone outside marriage?'

'Yes, but only if it was part of a path towards a possible marriage. In the City the core values are money and power. Ours are service to others. Women aren't interested in that.'

'Hold on . . . I'm listening to you. You see being in the Army that your core value is service?'

'Yes. Selflessness is a quality that is scorned or at least it's certainly not given the weight that it should be given. What do women care about professional men who put their lives on the line for others?'

'Thomas, many of the women I know aren't interested particularly in money as a key value. But they don't look upon a life in the Army as a life of sacrifice in which men are prepared to sacrifice themselves for others . . .' – there is no way to sugar the pill here. Give it to him straight – '. . . they look upon it as a life of obligatory and sometimes blind obedience to a questionable authority in which men are prepared to kill others, thus perpetuating violence and war in the world.'

I could hardly expect that to go down well.

'That's just ignorance. They don't know any better.'

I had offended him so much that he left. Should I have said, on your behalf, that we are grateful?

I turned to Rupert. 'I'm afraid I've upset your friend. He left.'

'Oh, don't worry about him. He's moody.'

'He probably has a right to be. We haven't seen what he's seen.'

I rang Rupert days later to try and get Thomas's number to call and apologise if I'd been insensitive, but Thomas wouldn't give out his number, which is a shame, as I think it's good for people with totally opposing views to listen to each other sometimes. Thomas evidently didn't think so.

'Anyway,' said Rupert, unconcerned about his friend's departure, 'what are you asking him? Ask me . . . have I ever done it up the arse? Yes.'

'Was that with a man or a woman, Rupert?'

'What?'

'I was reading recently that a high percentage of men have been brought to orgasm by another man at some stage in their lives.'

'I have never been brought to orgasm by another man. No – I've only done it up the arse of women.'

Romantic, isn't he?

'What's your next question? Do I like going down on a woman? The answer is yes. As long as she shaves, I love it.'

Now, if you are over 35 this may come as a surprise to you. My friends in their twenties and early thirties have informed me that they are expected shave off *all* their pubic hair now ... or just to leave one thin line known as a 'Brazilian'. Apparently it's inconsiderate to have hair between our legs, as a man may have to get one in his mouth. I consider this rather outrageous, especially considering what we put in our mouths and the places it's been. I have a male friend whom I share my bed with sometimes but don't have a sexual relationship with. He's a cuddle buddy. Anyway – seeing me getting out of the shower one day he proclaimed, 'Well, I'm never going to go down on you unless you shave more than that off.' This may be too much information for you, but I want you to know this, as I think it's quite shocking. My pubic hair is not in the least excessive and has always grown in a small, neat triangle which I've always kept trimmed and have rather enjoyed. He wanted me to shave it all off?

'Er – may I point out that I have never invited you, anyway?'

So he and I agree to differ. But I include this as I thought women were supposed to be more sexually liberated. I can see my daughter's friends will feel obliged to do yet more hair removal. As if underarms, legs and bikini lines weren't bad enough. But if you are female and over 35 you need to know that it's now considered obligatory 'all over the world' (apparently) and if you are going to have younger male lovers you'll need to know this. But back to the bar.

'Isabel, this Rupert is a pain in the neck,' said Daisy. 'He keeps trying to grope me and put his hand up my skirt under the table.'

'Now we see the male attempting to mount the female at a hugely inappropriate point in the mating ritual. He has repulsed the female, she's disgusted and is leaving. He's going to have to think of a better approach than that to interest the most beautiful female in the group.'

Surely gorillas would understand a mating ritual better than this? As well as being beautiful, Daisy is also very bright, has an excellent degree and speaks three languages. He had obviously not considered this.

Daisy stared at her phone, looked at me and said, 'I've just had a call from someone, so my friend and I are leaving, OK?'

'Of course.'

I turned to Dr Jenny.

'Have you had enough?'

'Yes.'

The conversation had turned to the shoot that was happening the following weekend. Why being a member of the 'upper classes' seems to be inextricably linked with killing, I've never been able to understand. Foxes, deer – there was no way I was even going to visit these environments. Maybe I could learn more about the male species in them ... but the closest I wanted to get was plates. I could consider shooting plates.

But I know what you are thinking ... you want to know what happened at the meeting with Harry, don't you? You're even annoyed with me that I kept you waiting an entire section to tell you.

Here I am trying to do a serious piece of pragmatic research and find some explanations and solutions for us all, and all you want is to know what happened with Harry.

What is this? The amazing pull of the romantic narrative . . .
I could be unfolding the secrets of nuclear science here and
you'd still want to know about Harry. Do you know, just
in case you read my last book . . . there I was dealing with
support for the Dalai Lama in what I seriously believe to be
the most important point in international politics today, and
I'd get to the end of a lecture or a talk, and a woman in the
front row would invariably put her hand up and say, 'What
happened with the monk?' Forget the solution to the war on
terrorism, forget essential differences between men and
women – just get on with the romance.

We'll have to jump back in time a little. When I was on
my way to meet Harry I took some notes.

Every cell in my body is singing. There is a joy swimming
through my veins that seems to intensify the quality of the
universe. Everything is more real, more vibrant, more . . .
Oh my goodness, I'm looking forward so much just to
seeing his face that I almost don't care what words do or
don't come out of his mouth. Just listen to me. Bewitched,
bothered and bewildered, right?

I wonder if he has any speeches prepared: 'Isabel, I'm
sorry about what happened, but I've realised now that all
contact between us has to stop. You are a drug that I have
to break free from.' If he begins such a speech I'm going to
have to get up from my seat and leave. I mean, what reply
is there? 'Yes, and I'd like to live with you for the rest of
my life, too, and I've never changed my mind for a second?'
I'm so looking forward just to seeing his smile. How absurd
the human heart is. My editor should throw this section out.
'Isabel, you can't include this, it's ridiculous.' Maybe I'll
even get to touch his hand. How old am I? I must try not
to have any expectations of the meeting, neither hopes nor
fears. Not that I can even imagine what form a hope would
take. He's made it quite clear that I'm supposed to have
given up on hope. It's not as if he's flying down from
Scotland in order to see me. He has a business meeting here

and is fitting me in. Maybe I've been reframed as an unfortunate error in his life that he wants to put properly behind him in order to avoid any amusing emails in the future. Damn it. I still don't understand what the universe has against me. What did I do wrong?

It's not as if men don't ever decide that being married for thirty years with one set of problems is enough and they're ready for a new set of alternative problems. That they are ready and able to move on ... so why the hell do I have to find one that decides it's impossible and the only way forward is for everything to stay the same? Damn. Damn. You know I'm looking forward to seeing him whatever he says? To seeing his face and remembering more precisely the shape of his head. Maybe he'll start his speech, 'We must never meet again.' And I'll be smiling and he'll think I'm acknowledging what he's saying and actually I'll be smiling just because I'm so enjoying the sound of his voice. I know I sound absurd. As if I've put him up on some huge pedestal. But it's honestly not like that. I could write you a long list of his faults, but a man can have many faults and weaknesses, they can even watch rugby or football, and women still can love the creatures. How talented we are.

Harry, like the rest of them, was born and lives on Mars and many of the things that I'm learning about men in this project are as true of him as of any of them. I may smell blossom, but I don't believe I'm wearing rose-tinted spectacles. I'm sure he'd drive me crazy in many ways and I him ... but I'd still like to be with him. He once asked if I liked him more because he wasn't available and I said, 'No, I don't. That's the one thing about you that I really can't stand.' Why do women like unavailable men? I mean what's the point of a relationship if you can't play, travel, work, sleep, cook – what's the point of a relationship where you can't even phone? No, unavailable men are boring playmates. God, I'm looking forward to seeing his face, his smile, his hands. Did I say that?

Maybe I can get myself to some higher spiritual perspective on all this. Maybe things do happen for a reason and, whatever the outcome today, things happen as they should. A broken wrist, a broken heart ... what's a break or two in terms of a lifetime?

The bus is edging along in the traffic as I sit here writing on the top deck. And there he is at the bus stop by the restaurant. A casual red shirt. Blue jeans. He's early. I can actually watch him looking around as the bus edges forward. Is there a way I can bottle tenderness? I have far, far more than is appropriate.

And now, we're back to today and me sitting here with the neighbour's brown Lab that I'm dog-sitting, my cat and me attempting to think intelligent thoughts. I didn't take notes during my lunch with Harry, you see. I didn't even rush home and pick up my notebook.

It doesn't surprise me now that I remember so little of our conversation. Harry wanted me to do the talking so that he didn't have to, and I didn't want to push him to talk. At one point he said, 'That's one of the things I love about being with you. It's so easy. And I don't need to explain things.'

I had no desire to spoil the simple pleasure of his presence by asking any questions about anything. The closest I got was, 'You don't have any speeches prepared, then?'

'No. No speeches.'

The waiter was French. I speak French and Harry doesn't, so I had the simple pleasure of impressing him by jabbering a paragraph or two. Harry told me about a trip he'd been on, and I told him about the Harley guys. We chatted about everything and nothing. Aren't men weird? Women would never do this. They'd say, 'So?' 'How are you?' 'Where are we now?' Lesbian relationships must be so exhausting. Imagine two people who want to talk about everything and bring feelings into every conversation. But Harry was very clear – he wanted to see me and know my news, but he didn't want to talk about anything that mattered and if he loved me for anything it was for not saying, 'So? How're things?'

And I was as happy as a little child, just being with him. When the meal was over I saw him to his train. Suddenly it was like a scene from a modern film version of *Brief Encounter*. We got to the station and his train was right there. So he said, 'It's better like this. No goodbyes.' He ran onto the platform but, before he was able to get on the train, the doors closed and locked. I was the happiest girl in London. I have to say 'girl', as that's how I felt. We had another hour before the next train where we could sit and drink coffee and talk about nothing.

But the thing about this film scene is that once I'd got over the fun of being in the same frames as Harry, I sat down later to watch. There were lots of things that I simply hadn't noticed at the time. If I'd been directing, when the doors closed in front of Harry's face, he would have stood still and a gentle smile would have broken across his face. He'd have walked back and said, 'You see? No matter how hard I try and escape, the universe is with you. Maybe it's a sign?' That's not what I saw.

The doors closed in front of his face and he looked from left to right up and down the platform to see whether they were going to open again. At the time I'd been so busy laughing I hadn't seen it. He walked up to me and said, 'Another hour till the next one.' And I made a joke and said, 'Yeh, how gutted am I?' But he didn't look happy. How could I not have noticed that he'd wanted the doors to open? Now I keep pressing rewind I think he looked tortured. He was standing next to a woman he loved but just feeling guilty; taking responsibility for everyone's happiness except his own. I could shake him – re-direct the scene, say, 'No . . . you don't have to play it like this. We can have a different ending.' But without him, my playback machine offers no such facility.

All the love I have for this man, all the tenderness, has now become useless. He says that he has made his choice. This is

147

a hard one for me because, even though I think it's the wrong one, if I really love him I must want for him what he wants, or says he wants when he wants it. Mustn't I? If I'm really to love him in a totally unconditional and non-attached way, then I seem to be called to walk the other way.

If a man says to a woman, or a woman to a man, 'I've met someone with whom I believe I can be happier,' then, as I said earlier, true love must let that person go. I can see that. Is this the same? Here is a man making a choice that he believes to be the right one and, whether I agree or not, even if I can see another way, I have to respect his decision. I suppose.

So here is a new challenge. To somehow take all that tenderness I feel for Harry and use it to take the dog for a walk. Or something. And then what? How does this work? Do I just hope that somehow this abundant fountain of tenderness will dry up? I have no experience of trying to learn how not to love. I tell myself that loving someone is wanting the best for them and honouring their choices. It's not as if Harry has asked me, 'What do you think, Isabel?' No. He hasn't asked me. I've made it clear what I'd like and the universe isn't doing what I want. One girlfriend said to me, 'Isabel, you must trust the universe.'

'Jane, you don't understand. I'm not even on speaking terms with the universe.'

The funny thing is that if I write, 'So that's it, then,' I know that even you are left hoping he'll come back into the story later. But that may be next year or in five years, ten years or never. Shit, isn't it?

It is worth getting up at six in the morning on a Saturday to get out of the city. It doesn't matter which city you are escaping from and it probably doesn't matter where you are going to. It's the escaping that counts.

It was 7.30 a.m. on a frosty November morning and a train was speeding through a fairytale white landscape. Not snow, but frost. Peeping through from under the white there was a palette of greens, yellows and browns from leaves not yet fallen. They were too cold that morning. They weren't going anywhere. I was though, sitting cosily on the train on my way to Hungerford to follow up a most surprising lead.

I had an email on my website from a woman who says that she lives her life surrounded almost exclusively by men. This is unique. If I had a pound for every email I've had asking me where the men are I'd be in first class. She got my attention.

'I live with men and my social activities revolve around men. The only other female I see apart from one female co-worker is my mother.'

'What do you do?'

'I run an outdoor activities centre. You know the sort of thing – we organise off-road 4×4 driving challenges, archery, quad biking, and clay-pigeon shooting.'

'And socially? Your social life is also all men? What do you do?'

'I work at the local rugby club. Would you like to come down?'

Another all-male environment – another trip to Mars. Had to go there.

I arrived at Hungerford Station and, like a true city girl, looked around for a cab rank. There was nothing. No bus stop, no mini-cabs, just one solitary couple getting into their car. 'Er, can you tell me where I can find a taxi or a bus or any other Homo Sapiens?'

'You're not from round here, then? Hop in and we'll run you into Hungerford.'

It's another world outside our cities. People are friendly. They talk to each other. They offer lifts to total strangers. The couple dropped me near other forms of life and I then ordered a cab to drive me through the stunningly beautiful white countryside to get to Moordown Farm. The sky was a clear blue, the air crisp and an autumn sun was just taking the chill factor from the air. Or at least I think it was air.

It was certainly something unrecognisable from the miasma outside my window in Battersea.

We drove up to be greeted by two waggy-tailed dogs and Vicky.

She walked forward and held out her hand. 'Hello, we've had a cancellation of one of the stag parties, I'm afraid – so instead of thirty-three men and me, today it's only fifteen. And all the instructors.'

She showed me into a pre-fabricated hut.

'So what do you do exactly, Vicky?'

'I organise the business and I instruct all the men.'

Steve, one of the workers, walked into the room. 'We are building a Land Rover with a front on both ends.'

'Why?' I had to ask.

'It's a team-building exercise. It's drivable and steerable in both directions, but neither end has all the driver needs. So instead of thinking as an individual, you have to co-ordinate the different driving tasks. One person has the throttle and another has the clutch. And so on.'

'Unless you co-operate with other people you can't go anywhere,' said Vicky.

'A bit like life really, then?'

'Exactly.'

Then fifteen men arrived back covered in mud from various outdoor pursuits. They were a young stag party of various aspiring Rupert types from London, in good spirits and happy to let me gatecrash. It was rather fun, as I've never been to a stag party before and I liked them because they weren't going to kill anything. Vicky had asked them if I could join in the 4 × 4 driving and the clay-pigeon shooting, so four of us set off with an instructor, to take a truck over some rather extraordinary terrain that had been specially created to enable you to kill yourself and four others fairly easily.

Exploring male environments is dangerous, but it is fascinating watching how groups of men relate to each other. It really is totally unlike groups of women.

The instructor explained to the first man, James, why he needed to keep the gears in first at all times and not rev the engine to go up hills.

We set off. It was marginally more terrifying than a fairground ride. At least in a fairground you know that the track is fixed in some way. We juddered along. James was keen not to lose face, while his male friends in the back taunted him in that way blokes do when they are got together.

'Left hand down, old chap. No, *left* hand *down*. Yes, that's the right left. Jolly good.'

These 4 × 4s can climb up hills so steep that when you are climbing them all you can see is the sky. Then you reach the top and suddenly all you can see is the ground as you go down the other side. Just as I was wondering how it was possible for a two-and-a-half-ton vehicle to drop vertically without killing us, the truck magically righted itself and the instructor was saying, 'Now, James, take a left up that bank. Keep well away from that ditch there, easy over the brake.'

'That's the ditch on the other right there,' taunted the guys in the back so that James had to keep driving and smile. He looked gripped by panic. If the truck had had women in there is a fair chance that they would either have been screaming or they would just get out.

I'm sure if I did this sort of stuff for Channel 4 I'd be a millionaire by now.

At one point we were left waiting for the other truck to catch us. The stag told us the difficult time he'd had finding his future wife: 'It wasn't so much a question of me picking her up. She picked me up.'

'Tell us.'

'It was a work party and as it ended we were all organising the taxis to go home and she said, "We don't need a taxi for Charlie because he's coming home with me."'

I love it. I wonder if this girl went to public school? That's the way to do it, girls. Just pick one you like the look of and then call a cab. It's hard not to be won over by such joyful assumption-making. Just as Harry knew, I think, that I'd fall in love with him. Damn. I mentioned Harry again.

'That was seven years ago. I've been seeing her ever since. I've never done any of the dating stuff. Speed dating and all that palaver. I think that's for people who can't get a partner any other way.'

I loved it. This from a man that didn't even take the risk of ordering the cab. Amazing what some people know with no experience, isn't it?

'I'm not sure that's always so now,' said one of his friends. 'I went on a speed-dating night once to try it out – lots of the guys are really hopeless, so if you go along as a bloke and you are half-decent, you get the pick of the women.'

I suppose it's encouraging that opinions differed on this. 'What about you?' I asked the third man present.

'I wouldn't go to those events. I just wouldn't feel comfortable,' he said.

So ... one out of three from the micro-sample in the truck would try something new. It's a start, I suppose. Then we were off to the clay-pigeon shooting. This is what groups of men do with their weekends. Weird, huh?

We arrived in a field with four 'cages' for shooting from. At the other end of the field were the machines that fired the clay plates, which sailed up into the air over the cages in perfect arcs.

The instructor handed out guns and told us how to hold them. My new habit of not being able to pursue any activity beyond day one was obviously setting in.

'I'm sorry,' I said to the instructor, 'my newly healed wrist is too weak. I can't even lift this gun, let alone fire it.'

'Women just don't have the muscle,' one of the guys said. The chaps stepped forward for their lessons.

It was fascinating to watch and study the men trying to hit the target. Because the target is moving, you have to keep the gun moving, past the target and then fire when you can't see anything, which is counterintuitive. The guys wanted to see the clay before they shot at it. So those that were able to relax and do what he said hit the clays. Those who tried to control themselves, the gun and the instructor missed every time.

And the competitive, testosterone-driven face-saving was primal. As if they were fighting for pecking order – and this was just a stag party . . .

The instructor could stand next to the man with the gun and push it up to follow the flight path of the clay and say 'now' and if they relaxed and pulled when he said, they'd hit it. But for one of the men this loss of status was just too much. He had missed the playfulness of the rather wonderful instructor and had a sense-of-humour failure, which of course made his shooting worse. Such fun watching a bunch of male egos together.

'Do you find it different teaching women?' I asked one of the instructors. 'Or are we pretty much the same?'

'No. Women are much better. They listen. They don't assume that they know better than the instructor before they start.'

Now he said this, OK? It's very politically incorrect to say that men and women are different. Feminists have spent years proving that we are the same. Well, now we have established that we are equal in terms of brainpower and girls are leading boys in school in most subjects most of the time . . . maybe now we're there we need to look at this again.

Why, for example, rugby? I'm not even going to discuss football at this point . . . That afternoon Vicky was to take me to my first ever rugby match. Newbury was playing Nottingham at home. That is, Newbury was at home. Do I have that the right way around? You can see how much I know. I say 'my first rugby match', but it was just the second half, which didn't seem to matter much, as I believe that what I saw in the second half very much resembled what happened in the first.

Now I know I'm laying myself open to be shattered like a clay plate, but I just don't understand. I think I'm missing the necessary part of my brain. We walked in and it was very pretty. A floodlit pitch at an early dusk. Trees in the background. And lots of people with scarves and hats shouting a lot. Vicky went off to find some hot drinks. I tried to understand why anyone would want to come here regularly. I was suddenly a creature from Venus very lost on Mars again.

It's true that there were a lot of very large men running around. Most of them seemed to be twice the width of any man I know. Legs like tree trunks. One girl told me that she went there just to watch the thighs and it's true that they were certainly something to be admired. Watching the Olympian beings was made particularly amusing because the day was so cold; now that the sun was going down they were actually steaming. They ran up and down and threw themselves on top of each other. Then, when there was a heap, all the rest seemed to want to throw themselves on too.

I've just started reading the next book for the appendix by Professor Simon Baron-Cohen called *The Essential Difference* (there are no limits to my dedication to our subject), about the difference between men and women. He points out that from a very early age, pre-school, boys are rougher in their play and more likely to get involved in horseplay with other boys. I looked at them now, and yes, his comments did make sense. And I know that some women play rugby and football, and I know some men do yoga, but that doesn't demonstrate anything, because there are always exceptions. The fact is that the vast majority don't. The vast majority of women really wouldn't want to spend their afternoons running round a field in a competitive sport, throwing themselves in heaps and hurting themselves and others.

I've probably got you hopping mad now. But you have to understand that, at this point in this epic tome, your narrator is in the middle of a discussion on my website about how we as individuals can contribute to saving the rainforest. This interests me . . . participation interests me. Playing sport I can understand. But grown men standing around watching while other men have fun? It's lost on me.

I turn to the man next to me. 'Who's winning?'

'Nottingham. That's the scoreboard up there. Oh, go on. Go *on*. Ooooooohhhhhhh!' He was jumping up and down with frustration.

'Which colours are Nottingham, then?'

'Yes, yes, go on, our man . . . no, no. What is he doing? In the stripes is Nottingham. No! No!'

I stood totally calm and detached from the proceedings.

'Isn't it a lovely evening?'

'What? Oh yes. Come on, COME ON! Ooooouph!'

'So who are you supporting, then?'

'Yes, yes, yes . . . no, over there. Me? Oh no! Newbury.'

'The home team?'

'Yes. In the blue,' he added.

'Oh! Yes!' He jumped up and down with excitement as a ball was put over a white paint line. Accidentally forgetting himself, he grabbed onto me in his excitement. I grinned rather sheepishly and he let go.

'Do you come here often?' I smiled. 'I mean, most weekends?'

'I'm the president of the Newbury team. Have been for ten years. So, yes. Ohhhh.'

He kept his eye, heart and soul glued to the action.

'Are these guys professional, then?'

Vicky arrived with a cup of coffee. 'COME ON, NEW-BURY!' she bellowed with the rest of them. I wondered whether she realised that she'd been in these male environments so long that she seemed to be trying to outdo them.

I stood between Vicky and the president watching the field as the tree trunks ran up and down.

'Ooooh, *go onnnnn!*' yelled the president.

'Oooh, yes!' or 'Oooh, nooo!' yelled Vicky. And I could see, in theory, why they were excited. The teams were very equally matched and each time one scored it meant that team would win unless the other scored again and the time was running out. The president patiently explained to me about tries and conversions. And I was happy to be there. It was fun. As much fun as you can have, I guess, watching events over which you can have no influence other than to look on. Vicarious excitement, vicarious success, vicarious failure – vicarious risk-taking. 'We won!' or 'We lost!' That good feeling of being part of a group, but all you do is shout.

Now, I know I'm thinking too much here. But spectator sports ... I just don't get them at all. I'd rather paint a pensioner's garden fence. The only reason I would go would be to support one of the players if one was a husband, son or close friend. But even then I imagine they'd say, 'Go and do something useful with your afternoon. You really don't have to come and stand in the cold and watch what I'm doing.'

I'm not getting this, am I?

Thank God I did once know a Harry who said, 'I have absolutely no interest in rugby, football or spectator sports of any kind.' This is deeply reassuring because I do sometimes need to be reminded that there are men out there who aren't interested in this and who, like me, totally miss the point.

We wandered into the club house after the game. Oh, did I mention that the home team won? It was an exciting finish, but of course I end up feeling sorry for the team who lost. All that huffing and panting and then no climax. In the club house I had the familiar feeling of being in the wrong place that I used to experience in the days when my ex-husband played cricket and I used to stand around with the other cricket wives trying so hard to be interested in cricket.

From my perspective these club houses are just like pubs. Places where people talk but no one ever really says anything. A kind of companionship but without anyone really saying what mattered or how they really were. A place where it's OK to answer 'How're U?' with 'Fine, and urself?' How do I explain to myself the fact that I felt more at home in the middle of Tibet sitting with nomads whose language and culture I knew nothing of than in a very friendly club house with a group of elated English people in the country in which I've spent most of my life?

We had drinks and everyone said nothing lots of times to everyone else before we drove back to the farm to pick up some bits. A large group of genuine Ruperts were there, young men in identical flat green caps gaffawing loudly, and on a cart were sixteen dead pheasants, one dead rabbit, one dead pigeon and one dead rook. I stood and stared at them. The beauty of the plumage gone. Strings around their necks, eyes bulging.

I was speechless for a couple of minutes as I just stood looking at the men and the dead birds. Vicky walked up. I asked her, 'Why did they shoot the rook? They can't eat him, surely?'

'Rooks count as vermin.'

How I hate that phrase. My neighbours say it about the slugs, the pigeons and the squirrels.

Then a gaggle of young women came out and joined the men in the flat caps.

'The women weren't shooting, surely?'

'No. They are just along to beat and for the men to show off to. They're young, that lot. They are all public school and in their first year at university – no shortage of money. They like their shooting. Are you ready to go the station?'

'Yes please, Vicky.'

We drove through the countryside. Vicky talked without stopping about all the men in her life. I half listened. She told me that she never has a female lodger, only men.

'Even my dog is male,' she said. 'I wanted a male dog.'

It was reassuring at least to know that I wasn't the only person who had gone a little mad. Women without men may go crazy, but I think women need women for balance too. Or I

certainly need both in my life. I wished Vicky goodbye. I
would like to go back and take some friends to play. I would
bring, ideally, a mixed group of friends, to shoot bits of clay
and ride buggies and 4 × 4s at silly angles. But the cart full of
dead birds left me still confused about the men with their guns.

The more I went into all-male environments, the more I
really saw how different we are. When I got home I sent an
email to Professor Simon Baron-Cohen, the man who had
spent twenty years studying the difference between men's
brains and women's brains. I certainly had some questions
I wanted to ask him.

But before that (as they say on TV) – the City. I had an
invitation to go and experience for myself this very special
male environment, which I had long heard described to me
as the ultimate in testosterone locations. And the heart of
the City? The trading floors themselves. Many people point
out that it is big business now that runs the world, 'The
politicians are just puppets . . .' apparently.

I have a vast and extensive knowledge of how trading
works. Here is my detailed analysis. Are you concentrating?
Prices of things go up and down and the idea is to buy them
when they are low and sell them when they are high. If you
sell at the right time, you get very rich. If you mess up, you
can lose impressively large amounts of money. That's the
gist of it.

I'm going to omit the names from this section in order to
protect the not so innocent. The bank I was visiting has a
very large building in the centre of the City. It has about
four trading floors with between 1,000 and 1,500 people on
each floor; about ten per cent of the traders are women.

Of course, I'd been expecting men waving their arms
about and lots of shouting. That's all gone. Now it's just a
huge room with rows and rows of computers. On either side
of each computer are further screens with charts of numbers, graphs and lines going up and down. In front of each
computer sits a very sallow-faced man.

'I leave home before six, and I'm usually sat here by 6.45 a.m. We work twelve-hour days and we don't leave the workstation for breakfast or lunch. You sit down here in the morning and you don't leave till seven in the evening.'

One of the white faces had been allowed to turn away from the screen to talk with me.

'So you have to give your life away?'

'Yes. We are very well paid, but we sell our souls.'

'We're monkeys,' said the next very pale face.

'What do you earn?' I asked rather directly. 'I don't mean personally, of course . . . I mean on average . . .'

'There's a basic salary, between £80,000 and £100,000 per year – that's standard. But then you also get an annual bonus and that can be anything from about £250,000 and in some cases is up to £15 million.'

'Per year?'

'Yes.'

'It's good money,' said one.

'Shame about the soul.' I smiled. Strange, surreal world. Men who want for nothing, but are in prison.

'I have a friend who is an accountant and he works the same hours I work for £65,000 a year,' said one. Curious, isn't it? They tell themselves that everyone has lives like this really, with twelve-hour days, which isn't true. The accountant can go home early if his son's in the school play.

'My girlfriend is a doctor,' said another. 'She works longer hours than I do, including weekends often, and she makes £40,000.'

But can you really compare being a doctor with a job in which the only reward is money?

'Why not work here for a couple of years and then get out?' I asked. 'Wouldn't that be perfect? Make a couple of million and then run before you get to forty?'

'You wouldn't want to be a trader beyond the age of forty. We all talk about leaving, but we're dependent on the money.'

'So when do you hope to escape?' I asked one who looked a bit older.

'Two years. We always say another two years. It's a rolling two-year horizon. Because of the money, you see. Excuse me a minute.'

He spoke through a hands-free phone attached to his head and adjusted some numbers on the computer.

'How much higher will he go, do you think? Ask him if he'll go to 3.7 but don't scare him off.'

He clicked around some more.

'I'm so sorry.' He turned back to me politely. 'We've just done another £300 million there.'

'Good grief,' I said. 'These are some pretty large sums of money you're dealing with here on behalf of this bank, then?'

'Let's look at this morning,' he said. '£25 million, £200 million, £1 billion, £500 million, £50 million, £50 million.'

'What happens if you make a mistake?'

'If you lose half a million it will be overlooked. If you lose a million that's not good. I made a mistake last week. Got a figure wrong. But I called the guy back and he didn't hold me to it. Most people are decent. You come up against some bastards, but they aren't the majority.'

I love it. Things that it's OK to say to say your boss here . . . Ooops, sorry, I lost half a million this morning.

That's OK. Think nothing of it, but don't do it again, OK?

On the other side of me another sallow face was saying, 'I'd want £44 million on the Delta.'

'The problem we have is,' said the first face, 'we'd like to leave, but we don't know what else to do. You look at the salary you'd be earning and you think, "If I just stay here another year I could earn in one year what I'd earn in ten years doing that." So you end up staying. Men who do leave go and buy a helicopter, fly around for a year, get bored with not working and not knowing what to do and come back.'

'Another two years?' I asked.

'Exactly. You've got it.'

'The thing is, you see.' I smiled. 'There are other values to a job apart from the money. There are other reasons to work.'

They looked at me rather blankly.

'Yes, I suppose. If you could find something that you really loved, but we've been here since university. We have no other life experience, no transferable skills.'

'We have absolutely zero transferable skills,' the man next to him agreed. 'We know nothing about anything else.'

So this is what they call a 'limiting belief'. They even have them here. This one is obviously put about on the trading floors to keep men at their stations.

'What else could we do? Any salary you look at is laughable compared to what we earn here.'

Er, they could work out how to get His Holiness the Dalai Lama back into Tibet and make a contribution to world peace. They could create a plan to save the rainforest. They could work with drug-addicted teenagers in inner cities. They could teach. They could volunteer. They could work out how to give something back.

I didn't say any of this. I just listened to them.

One had some photos of the most beautiful house I think I've ever seen. On the beach, of course.

'What's this amazing building?' I asked.

'It's a holiday home. I'm just buying it today. The price is there . . .' It was $1,850,000.

'You only have the one holiday home, then?' I enquired.

'So far.'

'Ask him what car he drives,' said one of his friends.

'What car do you drive?'

'It's the new two-seater Daimler.'

'Cost him something over £80,000,' said his friend.

How bizarre this all was. I could bring about a stressful ten minutes for myself if I checked my bank balance and realised that, at best, there will be no holidays for my daughter and me this year or next. On the other hand, I can walk out into the sunshine in ten minutes, and sleep until seven tomorrow morning. I thought about these men at home with their wives. In the hard times it must be very difficult not to end up resenting the partners who are out there living lives and spending the money.

'Well, at least you don't have rows about money at home, then?'

They laughed rather too loudly.

'There are a lot of predatory females out there who want men that work in the City just for the money.'

Just as Thomas, the Army officer I'd met in Fulham, said, then. But there is a certain justice to the way it works. Men who pursue money are themselves pursued by girls pursuing money. Instant karma.

He went on, 'The best marriages are with women who are in the same business, because they understand. Women throw themselves at us. We get treated like footballers.'

Listen to that for the ultimate way to treat a man – 'like a footballer'.

'When you go out to the nightclubs, the women stand around in the VIP lounges and you hear the most terrible stories. Guys who've gone back with a girl, the first night and she's pregnant and she wants a million or a wedding ring.'

'Hold on, do you know anyone personally that this has happened to? I mean, they're not just stories.'

'I do.'

'So do I,' said his friend.

How well these guys must know each other. Or not, I suppose. They work twelve-hour days side by side for ten years or twenty.

'And another thing is that a lot of the women are basically high-class prostitutes. Only they don't look like prostitutes. You meet a woman in a nightclub and she seems really lovely and you start a conversation with her and suddenly she's discussing the price.'

'That happens a lot, too.'

'You're serious? Where are these places?'

'Oh, all the best clubs ... China White's, Pangaea, Mo*vida ... in the VIP lounges. Many of the women in these places ... you just can't tell any more.'

Look at this, girls. We're 'predatory'.

'So the women go out hoping to meet guys from the City?'

'Or any men who have money.'

That's what I've been doing wrong, then. I've been considering personality. I knew I must have missed something obvious. Not.

'You'll have to excuse me – something's come up here.' He suddenly looked very stressed. I clocked the look on his face and made a hasty retreat.

'Thank you for chatting with me.'

He waved while not taking his eyes from the screen. I hope he hadn't just lost the bank a billion.

I walked across the trading floor and looked at all the faces. As I'd been told: almost exclusively white, male and most were in the 'first half of life', aged between 21 and 41. How strange to feel sorry for millionaires. The main thing I noticed was how bad the air conditioning seemed to be. The air was as stale as an overheated department store. Some say this alone will kill them prematurely.

And why do they end up sitting there for all the best years of their lives? Is it, as Jenny said to me one day, 'All about ego. The one that makes the most money wins. They use money to gauge success because it's so measurable.' Perhaps. But I would also take a different view. They are there, I think, because they believe that to have money will make them happier, and will make the women in their lives happier. They are there because they love their wives and their families and are, in some sense, sacrificing these years so that they can be providers *par excellence*. So, ironically, they are willing to become what they called 'monkeys' for the love of women and children.

Sadly, I think it's another example of men and women misunderstanding each other. Sure, women want money – but only until they realise that it can't buy them anything worth having. Thomas had told me, from personal knowledge of people he knows, that domestic violence is a huge problem in the City. The men think they want money until they realise that it won't make their wives love them any more. Someone needs to go there and tell them they are singing the wrong song. It's not 'Money Makes the World Go Around' but 'All You Need is Love' that has the truer refrain.

Why are men and women so consistently failing to understand one another? I was looking forward to my trip to see the professor.

I arrived in Cambridge in an optimistic frame of mind, little realising that this time I was going to get what I was seeking. Part of the answer.

The taxi drove into Trinity College. Here was the very courtyard that Eric Liddell and Harold Abrahams had raced in and were later immortalised in *Chariots of Fire* when Ian Charleson and Ben Cross did the same. Who won that race? You know, I can't remember. I remember John Gielgud as the dean, peering down superciliously, a wonderful portrayal of the arrogant paternalistic superiority of academia at its worst.

Professor Simon Baron-Cohen isn't a bit like that. Simon's large and impressive office looks out on the famous quadrangle and, as well as the compulsory thousand books, has an armchair and a large and comfy sofa. I knew what he looked like, as I'd Googled him before my arrival. How's this for a new line in illustrated books? You can have a look at him yourself if you like . . . www.autismresearchcentre. com (autism is his speciality) and look under staff and there is his face. He's young for a professor, or looks it. About forty? I didn't like to ask. A kind and open face easily given to smiling, with the compulsory receding hairline and spectacles. Healthy, energised, not stuffy or dull at all. Photos of three gorgeous children displayed proudly in frames for all to see.

Our email correspondence before my arrival had been very jovial. I'd read his book on the difference between men and women. But I don't want to misrepresent him. So I thought I'd give you the terrible truth from his mouth and not mine. He made me tea and I thought I'd go straight to the point . . .

'So, Simon, apart from the bits . . . what is the difference between men and women? I've been looking at men in their own environments – in the wild, if you like. I like them a lot, but I find I'm having some trouble understanding the creatures. And I know a lot of women who feel the same.'

'There are differences between male and female brain anatomy that are as definite as the fact that women can have children and men can't.'

'Mmm?'

'One difference is that females have a stronger drive to empathise and males have a stronger drive to systemise.'

'And what does that mean exactly?'

'Empathy is defined as the drive to identify somebody else's thoughts and feelings and to respond with an appropriate emotion.'

'And systemising?'

'Is the drive to analyse or construct a system.'

'What's a system?'

'Anything that is governed by rules that takes input and produces output. The drive is to analyse the rules that relate input to output.'

'So women like to understand people and men like to understand things?'

He winced. 'Well, that's a simplification of it, yes.'

'You mean that we are different biologically? Our brains are differently wired?'

'Yes. There is a lot of evidence now for this. Studies come

out every month showing the differences between the sexes in brain structure and brain function.'

'Hold on a minute. Doesn't this put the feminist movement back fifty years?'

'Well, I was worried about that and I waited five years before publishing my book because I was afraid that it would be dismissed as politically incorrect. But today feminists don't deny that there are biological differences. No one suggests one sex is better than the other. We are just different. I mean, we know that we are different hormonally and genetically. Now we are beginning to understand the psychological differences.'

'So – to take the first thing that comes to mind: why are so many men interested in spectator sports? I can understand why men want to play, because it's fun. But to watch others play?'

'This is an interesting example because it's universal. Men all over the world, and a small percentage of women, like to watch sport. Sport has at least three systems in it.'

'It does?'

'Take football. There is the league table as one system. "Our team is fourth and if we get one more point we may go up one position in the table. Or if this other team play badly they may get relegated to the lower division."'

'Yes . . .'

'Then "technique" is another system. Physics, the motor aspects, what happens if you top-slice the ball. And the team itself, which is a bit like a machine . . . a system. Each player is like a cog and can affect the overall efficiency of the system. Spectators, who are mostly men, will stand on the sidelines endlessly discussing which player should be in or out to get the best result.'

I began to want to take a nap.

'Why does it matter? Why do they care whether the team goes up or down?'

'That's a social hierarchy. Primates consider social hierarchies important. It changes your life.'

I look blank.

'You don't believe me? There is lots of evidence that the lives of non-human primates are radically affected by their position in the hierarchy. The top male will have first access to food and mates.'

'But aren't we supposed to have evolved?'

'Position in a social hierarchy is a life-and-death struggle of universal importance for males. Part of the claim of evolutionary psychology is that we haven't evolved to a point where these things no longer matter . . .'

Oh, good grief.

'. . . on the contrary, there may be circuits in our brains that we share with our primate relatives that go back millions of years and still affect our behaviour as humans today. Evolution has shaped men's and women's brains differently. There are exceptions, of course. A small percentage of women are interested in league tables and you are talking to a man who has no interest in football.'

'Pleased to meet you, Simon.'

'We have devised a questionnaire – it measures your empathy quotient, or EQ, out of eighty and your systemising quotient, SQ, out of eighty. Would you like to find out where you lie on the scale?'

'Sure.' I sat and patiently filled in all his questions and worked out my scores.

'My total score for systemising is one. My score for empathy is seventy.'

He smiled.

'Well, you're exceptionally low on the systemising score . . . hold on . . . I have the figures here . . . Yes, you're in the lowest one per cent for systemising and in the highest one per cent for empathy. No wonder you start to fall asleep when I talk about league tables. Someone with the opposite profile would fall asleep if you started to talk about the quality of relationships and human interactions.'

'Mmm. Yes, I think I was married to a man with that kind of profile for seven years.'

'Men with a higher drive to systemise are the majority.'

'So this means that most men are likely to have less empathy than most women?'

He opened his wallet and produced a simplified little chart. 'I carry this around because I can't always remember the exact percentages.'

	Extreme of type E	Type E	Type B	Type S	Extreme of Type S
Women	6	44	36	14	0
Men	0	17	33	44	6

With my minimal drive to systemise, I looked at his little chart carefully.

'How many people have you tested?'

'Throughout the research? Thousands.' He pointed to the box in the top left-hand corner. 'You're in that group – an extreme empathiser.'

'Where are you?'

'I haven't taken the tests because I'm too close to them, but I suspect I'm in the B group,' he said rather carefully.

'So this is why women get so frustrated with men?'

'Yes and vice versa. A male systemiser is anxious because there is a big game on and he doesn't want to miss a single minute of it and it's due to start in 3.5 minutes. And a female empathiser is anxious because she wants to talk . . .'

I remember this . . .

'About why he hasn't spoken for the last three days.'

'If they both stopped to notice that the other person thinks differently from them it might lead to a better relationship.'

'Ah,' I said. 'There are probably a million rows going on even as we speak.'

'Yes, "It makes me so angry that you're always pottering off to your shed to fiddle with your tools" . . . she could realise that the tools are systems and it's important to him that they be organised and looked after.'

'So it's not his fault that he's anal?' I teased him.

'Ah, well, that's your choice of word . . . I wouldn't say that. I'd say "preoccupied".'

I laughed. We do have to be careful, don't we?

'OK, Simon. "Preoccupied".'

'She is preoccupied, too, but with a different topic. Relationships and the quality of them. Intimacy.'

'So it's not the fault of women when men don't communicate their feelings, then? I've heard this for years, "We bring them up." '

'No. Obviously nurture is important, but so is biology.'

'I remember I bought my daughter a Meccano set. I remember I really tried hard to encourage her to play with it, but she just wasn't interested. She preferred painting pictures.'

'Many parents say this. They try to avoid gender-specific toys, but it doesn't work. And this is pre-school and even in families without televisions.'

Suddenly lights started to go on in parts of my brain. I had flashbacks over the last week. The image of the sixteen pheasants hanging by their necks suddenly flashed into my mind. 'So men shoot birds because they lack empathy?'

'Those men or women who shoot birds do that because they have reduced empathy. It's not that they lack it completely, but to kill an animal you need lower levels of empathy. As a strong empathiser you'd find it very hard to kill any animal or bird.'

'I go to great lengths to avoid killing an insect. I can kill mosquitoes, but even then I hate to do it.'

And, dammit, I was thinking of Harry again. Of how he hates it when they cut down trees. Of how he understood when he phoned one day and I was upset because the neighbours were cutting down a healthy tree in the communal garden and I'd been outvoted in my attempt to save it. Of a conversation we once had about gardens and letting plants and animals be – cut back less, let grow more.

I dragged my brain and soul back to Cambridge and looked at Simon's chart.

'So can the situation be improved? Is empathy an inborn drive? Are most men who have less of this eternally hopeless, or can they learn?'

'Empathy is not one hundred per cent biological. There's plenty of scope for learning, experience and training changing your empathy levels. Only of course many men wouldn't be interested in learning to be more empathetic. It's the biological component . . . that's the controversial bit.'

'A lack of drive in this area? So that's why, when I was once persuaded to attend a past-life seminar, there were so few men exploring this area? They're just not interested coz it can't be proved, just as I have such a lack of drive to understand the inner workings of my computer. All I want is for it to work. I don't care how it works.'

'That's it.'

'So when a feminist writes a book like *Men: The Darker Continent* and lays the problems of the world at men's feet . . . she's right?'

'Well, let's not get things out of proportion . . .'

No, professor.

'. . . systemising has led to many wonderful achievements, like modern technology.'

Yes, professor.

'But yes, I'm sure that many of the world's problems are the result of doing things based on systemising rather than empathy.'

My brain was starting to buzz.

'So, Simon, to succeed on the trading floors it would be useful to have a high drive to systemise and a low drive to empathise because then you won't care too much about the consequences of your actions on other people?'

'Yes. And in war you might think, "We'll have to bomb a hundred thousand people but we'll win," so lower empathy helps. For someone like you, even one death would be too many, but Blair made a decision to bomb Iraq, where there would be a hundred thousand deaths. That has to be a systemising decision ... We take this action ... but it removes Saddam. And we can think of plenty of other examples of problems in our society that result from lack of empathy.'

'Domestic violence.'

'Rape.'

'Bullying.'

'These are the extreme cases, but even the way our society "drops" old people who are no longer useful to us as workers is an example of a systemising approach to the workplace. It's certainly not based on empathy or compassion.'

Oh my goodness, how interesting. And this is why – in Tibet, teaching compassion and empathy is the most essential part of the Tibetan Buddhist education system. I thought of individuals. My last male lodger, an expert systemiser, spent hours and days playing with his computer, yet he had to be taught how to speak to a woman. I'd say to him when he complained that he couldn't handle parties, ' "To get over your shyness all you have to do is think about the person you are meeting and not about yourself. Try being genuinely interested in other people!" '

And even then with male friends like him . . . . men don't necessarily have genuine interest in the woman, they just work out what you have to say and do to get the result you want. The most extreme example of this is what Neil Strauss wrote about in *The Game* – the men that have worked out a system for getting women into bed. But aside from just pulling a woman for a shag, a relationship is a lot more complicated, as a woman is a very unpredictable system.

'Why do so many men talk so much about themselves on a date? If they are good systemisers, they should surely have worked out that they need to listen a bit too?'

'Talking too much is a sure sign of reduced empathy. Good empathisers are good listeners. That doesn't mean that all you do is listen, since that wouldn't be a dialogue, but knowing how much to listen and how much to talk, and how to respond in a sensitive way requires empathy. If you really care about another person's thoughts and feelings, you can't just listen to the sound of your own voice. That's not a dialogue, that's a monologue.'

'I've been looking at men in all-male environments.'

He smiled. 'That's a good place to see how shocking the extremes can be. I was out with my son walking in the New Forest last week and we came across a model-boat club. Even I was shocked after twenty years of research. Grown men park their cars by a lake. They open the hatchback and have ten different types of model boat in the back and all the tools for the petrol-driven engine. They tinker with one of the engines for hours and then wade out in those green rubber waders that go up to the top of their thighs, stand in the water for fifteen minutes and zoom the boat around the lake. Playing with 1. The speed, 2. The figure-of-eight path, 3. The waves. They like to see how they can make it spin and turn or race. Then they put it back in the car, spend hours cleaning it, checking all the parts, cleaning each component, organising the tools and then they repeat it all with the next boat. There is very little dialogue between members of the club. And that's a Sunday. My little boy loved it, but he's ten. These are grown men.'

'Mmm. I'd be willing to wager that some of them are single and belong to internet dating agencies.'

'What my son and I saw was probably just the tip of the iceberg. If you followed them home, you'd find a whole workshop that supports their hobby.' He hesitated for a second. 'I assume,' he said, remembering himself. 'And of course some women may be members.'

'Of course. Best not to generalise about model-boat club members.' I laughed. 'But you didn't happen to see any women members?'

'No.'

I remembered all the Harley guys standing around comparing exhaust-pipe sizes. Saying things like, 'Just exactly what is the main benefit of extending the rake on the forks?'

It all made sense now: systems, hierarchy, no obligation to empathise with anyone – perfect.

'It was the same at the shooting club. The difference between one trigger mechanism and another ... all I was thinking was, "You could kill something with that."'

'Look at the chart. Of every ten men three are Type B (balanced), two are type E, so their empathy is stronger than their systemising. Four are Type S (they have lower empathy than systemising skills) and one will be an extreme systemiser.'

He didn't like to say 'with very poor or practically no empathising skills'.

He went on, 'You have a related issue. According to your scores, you are in the six per cent of women who are extreme E.'

'So what are my chances of finding men with my level of empathy?'

'There are no men like you.'

I laughed.

'Thanks for that, Simon.'

He looked rather taken aback for a moment as he realised what he'd said.

'But when I say "zero" I mean less than one per cent,' he added kindly, 'who are an extreme of Type E.'

'It's not that I mind dating computer experts, it's just that the conversation is so limited to systems and themselves. The definition of an interesting man that I had was "a man who when you meet him you know that you'd like to have dinner with him and, having had dinner with him, you know that you'd like to see him again". This seems to be a hard test, as so many men just talk about systems or themselves. I met a man last week in a group and he was talking and talking and a woman was trying to speak and he just wouldn't let her. He went right on talking. I finally looked at him and said, "Will you let the woman speak?!" Later she said to me, "That's my husband."'

'Men with a drive to construct and analyse systems is the largest group – forty-four per cent. Seventeen per cent are Type E, with a stronger drive to empathise. Thirty-three per cent are Type B and their empathy is as good as their systemising ... but it is rare to find men with a score of seventy. And of course men with a high empathy score are more likely to already be in relationships.'

'So should I just give up?'

'You need to look for these men in the right places. Certainly not in all-male environments.'

'So what are the right places?'

'Psychotherapists?' Now he was smiling at me. Oh, good grief.

'Did you hear about the two psychotherapists who meet on their way into work? One says "Good morning." And the other wonders, what was meant by that?

'That's why I've enjoyed men who are not like that intense. I like systemising men. I don't even mind if they don't want to talk about emotions.

'I just want a level of empathy that means they want to talk and listen, they enjoy intimacy and they don't want to kill things or play with engines or computers all day. For me to be interested in a man, he has to care about people, I suppose. So you're right. And I'm sure most of the women I know would like a man who cares about people too.'

'You sound as though you would prefer a man who is people-centred. The areas where people take an interest in other human beings and in communication. Writers who care, journalists, teachers ...'

'Teachers?'

'Of course, a maths teacher may just like maths. He may not care about the students. But on the whole people who have chosen to work with other people care about them.'

A gentleman of a lower social status knocked and came into the room. I know he was of lower social status because he was wearing a bowler hat and had come to collect Professor Simon Baron-Cohen's post. I had to smile.

'Did you say that we had evolved beyond hierarchies?'

'I wish.'

Simon had to rush off. He had agreed to go and hear one of his students give a presentation and was keen to support him. I, with my high empathy, understood and he, knowing my scores, knew that I'd understand.

'It would be useful if it was possible to take one of your charts on a date and say – please could you fill this out.'

'It would take some of the romance out of it though, wouldn't it?'

Simon dropped me at Cambridge station and I sat on the train attempting to think through the consequences of this extraordinary meeting. It was nothing too major. It just felt as though I had been almost completely wrong about everyone, had failed to notice and understand the most key difference between the sexes. And had been looking for interesting men for us in all the wrong places.

I was a little bit stunned by all the new connections in my brain after my meeting with Simon. So much of what had bewildered me about much male behaviour now seemed to make sense. I wrote in an email to Simon a few days later:

'I've always believed that ''people do the best that they can with the knowledge, understanding and awareness that they have at the time''. And I still believe that – so there is no point ever in being angry with anyone or with ourselves because, as they say in some circles, ''if we knew better we'd do better'. What you have provided is an explanation as to why the awareness of men is often so different in quality and in priority from us lot in the other sex.'

Simon's work explains why the men on the building site felt that women just wanted to stop them having fun. It explained the shooting, the ruthlessness of *The Game*, of why Rupert didn't see that putting his hand up Daisy's skirt wouldn't do it for him, it explained behaviour that sometimes seems to women nothing less than inexplicable stupidity. It even explained the war. I understood now why there were fewer men in publishing and why so many of the male writers I met at book festivals were gay. I understood why I want to fall asleep and feel frustrated and sad if I'm out to lunch with male friends and they talk about boats or cars without listening to each other. I realise that when I'd written about the rugby match 'I just don't get it . . . I seem to be missing the necessary part of my brain', I was closer to the truth than I realised. And most especially, Simon had explained a lot about the public-school-educated men in the City and in that bizarre social enclave known as south-west London.

In a sense I felt relieved by all this. I felt I genuinely understood them better. But in a sense I felt sad. I don't like statistics. If I'd looked at the odds against me I'd never have got my first book published. And I don't like stereotypes. I'm not racist or ageist or any of those. But if I wasn't careful this could become, in my thinking, a new kind of sexism and, in the case of the 'upper classes', definitely classist.

I now had an academic explanation of how all these men who have been to public school have had the empathy trained out of them and why they try so carefully to conserve their identity within a social elite. Hierarchies . . . systems. I'd had this way of seeing the world and the differences between the sexes explained and it may have validity, but it's a way of understanding the status quo that I don't welcome. It's a systemising approach to human beings rather than an empathetic one.

I want to share this phone conversation with you. It's with a male who is as upper class as you can become without reaching royalty. He is public-school educated and, in theory, should be an example of the stereotype, but of course he is nothing like it. He should be everything that I don't like. He even shoots. Except I love him very much. I won't give you his real name – it wouldn't be fair. But you can listen in on a conversation. Just when I'm in this position of trying to figure all men out and especially the upper classes, he and his wife invited your narrator to dinner at his magnificent house in . . . well, let's call it Diddington-Under-Bogbury. You know that estate, right? So that bit I made up – but the rest is word for word . . .

'I'd love to come . . . and er, while you're on the phone . . . do you mind if I ask you some rather strange questions? I've been meeting lots of men recently who are in the, er, well the . . . upper classes. I don't understand them.'

'That makes two of us,' he replied with his delightfully upper-class accent. 'There are a good many things I don't understand. Those chaps who work in the City – get up at six and don't get home till after dark. They never see their children and have two weeks of life a year. When will men realise that time is more important than money?'

'I don't know. And a lot of public school guys with double-barrelled surnames . . . I don't understand the way they are with women.'

'They only want to marry their own caste. It's almost like Crufts. Women have to be the right pedigree. Rather limits the options. I was lucky to find my wife.'

So Simon is right about social hierarchies and the importance of maintaining your position. That's what Rupert had really meant by 'what type of women are you bringing along?' He meant what pedigree as well as 'do they bang like rabbits?'

'From the outside, looking up, as it were, I have to say that all the men seem so . . . well, lost. Is there a crisis of male identity in the upper classes or something?'

'Oh yes, absolutely. There's no money any more, you see. Even until five years ago you could make a lot of money running, say, a thousand-acre estate, which is not a massive holding, but does very nicely. That would have produced £100,000 a year, but now that won't keep the roof on the house or even heat the hall. So now there is an increasing temptation to marry out.'

'But I don't understand. Surely if you're at the top you can only go down?'

'There is more money down. There is no money in land any more. The girls never had any money in the old families, anyway. My sisters had nothing. I inherited all the land. In my day the girls weren't even educated.'

'What do you mean, "in my day"? How old are you?'

'I'm forty-five.

'In my year at Eton at least forty came on to Oxford. But now you can't get into Eton or Oxford because it's so terribly tough.'

'What? You mean you have to be bright?'

'Yes. So what's the point of being upper class any more: you can't automatically go to Eton, you can't get into Oxford without having to sit exams like everyone else, the merchant banks don't exist any more, fox-hunting has been banned, agricultural incomes have collapsed and the House of Lords has pretty well been abolished. There are no benefits left.'

I chuckled. 'You're very funny.'

'And the odds are that you'll attract some gold-digging girl. My wife loved me in spite of my money.'

That line was pure Oscar Wilde, but he actually said it.

'It's all a mystery to me. You're so kind and lovely and I know you do so much for a million charities . . . but then you hunt and shoot.'

'We've always been on the land. It's part of the life. That reminds me, would you prefer partridge or pheasant for dinner?'

'You're pulling my leg?'

'No really. We have some partridge from a shoot last weekend.'

I hesitated, not wanting to admit that I'm vegetarian. It seemed so predictable of me. I'm a stereotype arty author, I suppose. Maybe I should ask for lentils.

'Oh . . . you're vegetarian?'

'Afraid so. Sorry.'

'That's absolutely fine. Don't worry for a second.'

'I wouldn't have believed I could like someone quite as much as I like you and your wife, even though you shoot. In some ways you are the stereotype, in so many other ways you defy it. That's the thing about stereotypes, they don't exist. There are always so many exceptions.'

'Delighted to be of assistance to you.'

'Thank you for your time.'

'Anything else, my dear?'

Yes. The future.

'Well, there was one more thing . . . I was just wondering, your little son – will you send him to Eton?'

'After five generations there? If he can get in. Of course.'

Part III

PLACES TO GO, PEOPLE TO MEET

1. THE GAME OF TEN PLACES: SOME RESEARCH FOR US ALL

So Simon says, 'Do something different,' And we must evidently do what Simon says. My idea of going into male environments has been valuable in terms of ethnographic observation and understanding, but not in the least useful in terms of finding a range of dateable specimens. It seems to follow a staggeringly basic logic, now that I come to think of it, that the all male environments are full of men who either don't like women, don't understand them, or at least are more at ease with other men.

So what are the environments where men and women mix and where there may also be the possibility of an interesting conversation? Where are the intelligent communicators, the men I'd love to meet and you'd love to meet because we wouldn't be bored for a second?

I propose a game that we can all play. I'm calling it the game of ten places. Ten places where we can all meet intelligent men. We want to know where intelligent people go in the evenings, the ones who don't watch TV.

'Ah . . . you're after the intelligentsia now then?' said Jenny.
'What exactly is the intelligentsia, doctor?'

'Go look it up in a dictionary.'

It's not a word you hear much nowadays, is it? But intelligentsia has a definition outside and beyond the Russian history books.

The dictionary informs me that the people in this group are 'the intellectuals, referring to professionals such as lawyers, doctors, engineers, professors, scientists' and er, writers.

Ah yes, the intelligentsia, including some, but not all, writers.

Every major town and city has some groups like this. I always get the impression that there are private members' clubs where they hang out. One has to be invited to join by other members. I say 'one', as I think one does say one, doesn't one? And, furthermore, the membership of these elegant and elite groups is, of necessity, absurdly expensive – to keep out the wrong kind of writers, for example.

So let's concentrate on finding places we can all go to: without huge expense, where we at least stand a reasonable chance of having an intelligent conversation. My attempt at logic goes like this ... if there are more than one or two interesting single men in our cities, what are they going to be doing with their evenings? Going to singles' events? I think not. Standing in loud and smoky pubs where they put hopeful hands up skirts and conversation is reduced to monosyllables because no one can hear anything anyway? No. Pubs are rarely the places where the intelligentsia are to be found. They are too intelligent. Ditto nightclubs.

So this is the experiment. Using London as my test city, I want to find ten locations where regular events (lectures, debates, discussions) are open to the public. Please repeat this experiment in your own city. Find all the most intelligent spots and if you are successful email me c/o the website, www.isabellosada.com, and together we can produce some lists for all of our use. I'll use London as a testing ground, but the experiment can be repeated by you in your own town and I'll put the answers together on my website. So this list of ten places will be changed and updated on the site – as will the one in whatever town you live in. Depending on how many of you want to play . . .

Here are some of the criteria you may like to consider:

1. Don't go to anything that you don't have a genuine interest in. We are not going out to look for guys, but we are going out 'doing something different' in interesting places where we may also stand a good chance of at least having an interesting conversation.
2. When choosing an event location to visit, information about the make-up of the crowd can usually be obtained if you are friendly when you book. 'Can I ask how many people you are expecting? Are your visitors mainly in their twenties, thirties, forties, fifties, sixties? Is it mainly women or men?'
3. You need to be interested in the subject being discussed, but don't feel that you need to be well informed. No one knows about everything and you may be inspired to learn more by attending a talk and hearing an erudite speaker. Personally, I know practically nothing about practically everything, so I consider all subject areas open to me.
4. If you have a friend to take along it's easier, but you are then likely to talk to your friend. I recommend pushing your comfort zone by going alone and talking to strangers. After all, it's not hard to smile and say, 'Interesting wasn't it?' (Neil Strauss says that you shouldn't go alone, as you look as though you have no friends . . . but he also says any friend you go out with should be less attractive than you are, so you may not want to play 'The Game' by his rules.)
5. If the talks are free, so much the better. But don't shy away from £7 entry. We pay that at the cinema and did we ever meet anyone new sitting in the dark?

So . . . those are my thoughts so far. Let's see how it works out in the real world.

PROSPECT

There is a magazine called *Prospect* that does an excellent (but by no means inclusive) list of many of the most intelligent events in London – and some around the UK, too. You can find it online at www.prospect-magazine.co.uk. As I said, I'm not going to do anything that I don't have a genuine interest in, but, at the same time, the purpose of the exercise is to spot where some men are. I'll keep an eye on the crowd and report back to you.

I looked at the *Prospect* list and came up with a list of talks and discussions that interested me. The first one that I spotted was a talk at the British Library, www.bl.co.uk. It has a theatre that seats 250 and plenty of room to mingle afterwards. There was a lecture that caught my eye, an evening on the work of T.S. Eliot, whose plays I've always adored and most of whose poetry has left me feeling ignorant and confused. I rang and asked the woman in the booking office lots of questions.

'And, finally, can I ask about what sort of punters you'd expect at an event like this?'

'They will be almost completely women, white, middle class and over the age of fifty.'

Good grief. I felt my interest in T.S. Eliot drain away with surprising speed. How about 'The Science of Love' at the Institute for Cultural Research, www.i-c-r.org.uk, with Dr Glenn Wilson? He was going to discuss 'The principles of sexual attraction and arousal and investigate the conditions that promote the experience of romantic love and the brain areas and neurochemistry involved'. You mean he could explain to me why I still care about Harry? I phoned them immediately ... 'That was last week.' So I'm never to understand it.

OK, so how about the Royal Society for the Encouragement of Arts, Manufacturers and Commerce, www.rsa.org.uk?

'The RSA runs a programme of projects and lectures based around five challenges:

- encouraging enterprise
- moving towards a zero-waste society
- fostering resilient communities
- developing a capable population
- advancing global citizenship.'

All sounds very impressive. It has an evening about a charter on creativity, innovation and intellectual property rights with two hundred people attending. And it's FREE. So we'll start here.

THE RSA

My arrival at the RSA happens to coincide with my reading of another of the books I'll be recommending to you, *Men in Love: Men's Sexual Fantasies – The Triumph of Love Over Rage*. It is the most explicitly sexual of the books so far. The author, Nancy Friday, collected two thousand letters in which men wrote graphically and explicitly on the details of their sexual fantasies. She chose two hundred for discussion in the book. It is definitely a book you need to read, or at any rate, it was a book that I needed to read. It has given me cause to put my sexuality under examination and I've come to realise just how incredibly dull I've been. Sex with total strangers I've picked up in a bar that night? With my relations? Foursomes? Animals? With other women? With a man but with me wearing a strap-on willy? Well, call me unimaginative ... I've done none of these things.

I have never deliberately flashed my naked crotch (American spelling, I believe) at a man as a means of picking him up. This I was reading about only last night. I haven't even been tied to the wall by a man who has all the appropriate paraphernalia especially fitted in his home. I have never assisted a man with a desire to wear nappies and wet himself. (You don't want to know how common this is.) Then there is what they call 'water sports'. Why would a man be sexually aroused by having women urinate on him? This isn't rare either. But I'm left at a loss to understand it.

I did dress up in my school uniform and role play occasionally for my ex-husband who, having been a secondary teacher, was given to all the usual fantasies.

'Oh, sir! You'd like me to sit on your knee while you mark my essay? Oh, sir!'

Reading *Men in Love*, I've come to the conclusion that my sex life has been very tame and is making me look at men from a whole new perspective. Has that man ever done it with a cow? Does he long for group sex with men and does he tell his wife? Does he get more turned on by high-heeled shoes than by vaginas? These are some of the very inappropriate thoughts passing through my mind as I sit innocently in the coffee bar at the RSA eating cake.

Fancy me having enjoyed sex as an expression of love and intimacy! How girly can you get? I looked around, wondering whether I could see any men who, even in theory, I would like to broaden my sexual experience with. In the corner sat two vicars in full black gear with dog collars. I promise, I'm not making any of this up. Two men in their sixties sat in another corner deep in debate. Three well-dressed women chatted and drank wine. On the table next to me two men read newspapers. They seemed to be waiting for a casting for Humpty Dumpty. I couldn't see any other reason for wearing those clothes and letting your girth reach such an astoundingly comical size.

Then a friend of mine walked in. I'd decided to go alone to force myself to talk to strangers, but as I couldn't see any I wanted to talk to, I was glad to see her. My friend, female, whose name I can't give you as you'll see, sat down and I amused her by telling her of the double purpose for my visit.

'How do I describe you?'

'I once described myself as "a lively pensioner" in a personals ad. It was a mistake. Be sure to tell your readers that if they ever write a personals ad they should never include the word "lively". And another time I wrote "sensitive" – best to avoid that word too.' I laughed. My friend is both lively and sensitive, but maybe I have a different definition, despite Nancy Friday's influence. 'I've been coming to the RSA for years and I can tell you that the gentlemen that come here come in pairs. They are not all business colleagues.'

'Oh please! I can't believe I'm hearing this.'

'I've decided I much prefer talking with the gay ones, anyway. They are so much more humorous. What's the alternative?' She threw a glance at the Humpty lookalikes on the next table. I sighed as we made our way up to a packed auditorium.

On the stage sat three extremely prestigious men. John Howkins, the project director of the Adelphi Charter (and lots more qualifications), James Boyle, William Neal Reynolds professor of law (and lots more qualifications) and Sir John Sulston, Nobel laureate, amongst other things. I sat back to be entertained and educated.

The charter being discused was to protect our right to the free access of information. Did you know that nearly a fifth of all human genes have now been patented? I have to use this phrase again. I am not making this up. Talk about systemising of ideas . . . One company, Incyte Pharmaceuticals/Incyte Genomics has the intellectual property rights for two thousand human genes. What this means is that if you are doing research on breast cancer, for example, a situation may arise whereby you will not be able to afford access to the information you need.

So I was listening. As well as looking at the audience. I'd say the crowd was about fifty-fifty men and women . . . so better than a T.S. Eliot night, then. But my gaydar was very confused. In case you don't live in a major city and haven't heard this before, your 'gaydar' is your inner device, more or less accurate depending on your model, which tells you whether a man or woman is straight, gay or flexible.

After ten years working in the theatre I used to trust my gaydar totally. But now something was very wrong – I was having trouble spotting men who looked straight. A guy holding hands with a man who looks very like him is a bit of a giveaway ... but guys on their own, reasonably well dressed with hair, who smile back when you smile at them? It was all very confusing.

'Surely they can't all be gay?' I whispered to my friend.

'I've really no idea any more.'

Meanwhile, the men on the stage all looked straight to me. Is that libellous, do you think? I mean, could a gay man sue you for saying that you thought he looked straight? The first speaker, John Howkins, was what you may think of as a typically charming British gentleman. A bit feminine for my taste, gentle and probably went to public school. I couldn't equate him in my mind, for one second, with ever having had a single one of the thoughts detailed so graphically in *Men in Love*. The second speaker I found terrifying. He was funny, he was arguing for freedom of information and I agreed with everything he said, but not with the way he said it. He was so 'right' despite his left-wing views and he reminded me of the men in another of the books in the appendix, *Men: The Darker Continent*, in which Heather Formaini rather convincingly blames men for all the problems of the universe. And if you'd offered me a million pounds to guess whether he was gay or straight, I would have had to flip a coin.

Now, I want you to know that I don't normally sit in lectures thinking about the sexuality of the speakers – I normally listen to the lecture, but if you read a three-hundred-page book on male sexuality, you may find that it rather influences the way that you see human relations for a while.

The third speaker was wonderful. If he'd been born with a 'drive to understand systems' he'd made good use of it. Sir John Sulston is the man who got up one morning and mapped the human genome. That is, on Monday he identified all the approximately twenty to twenty-five thousand genes in human DNA. On Tuesday he determined the sequences of the three billion chemical base pairs. On Wednesday he mapped this information into databases. On Thursday he found a way to improve the tools for data analysis. On Friday he considered the question of the transfer of all related technologies to the private sector, and got a headache while considering the ethical, legal and social issues that arise as a result of all this. On Saturday he won a legal case to keep all this information in the public domain. And on Sunday they gave him a Nobel Prize. I may have this a bit wrong. It may have taken more than a week, but that's about the gist of it.

But as well as all this, there was something lovely about him. He was unassuming and softly spoken certainly, modest . . . well if you've done that lot, I guess you can be. But he also reminded me of my uncle, or how my uncle looked when I was a child. Reading Nancy Friday is worrying because she's a Freudian analyst. Freud puts your entire sexual history down to your formative experiences as an infant. If you go along with Freud, the unconscious rules us still. This is especially worrying in my case, as my sexual development is supposed to be heavily dependent on my relationship with my father. And I didn't have a father. I did have an emotionally and physically absent uncle whom I saw about once a year. I have never given Freud much credit, but now I looked at John Sulston and wondered. Like my uncle, he was heavily bearded. Unlike many women I've always rather liked beards, even white ones. Might this be because as a very young child I enjoyed the very rare visits from my uncle? Can our formative experiences really influence our whole lives and does the fact that I grew up in an all-women household (I was brought up with no brothers or sisters by my late mother and late grandmother) with cats account for the fact that I'm currently living in an all-women household with cats? God, I hope not. Next time I'm looking for a lodger, I'm now determined that I'll give the room to a man. 'Male? Know how to wash up? The room's yours.'

I've never particularly gone for older men and, looking at John Sulston, I questioned myself. How old a man would I be prepared to date and why? Or why not? If I met a man like this one speaking, who had a well-balanced masculine and feminine side, who was confident yet unassuming, a man I could genuinely admire and yet who was softly spoken, would I rule him out if he was more than ten years older than I am? Or more than ten years younger? What about you? What's your limit either way? Or if you have a partner and he/she left, what would your age limit be for dating members of the opposite sex, both older than you and younger? Or can't we say any more? Shere Hite is sixty and has a lover more than twenty years younger than she is.

Sir John Sulston was saying that ethics must not become subservient to economics. And I was thinking what a privilege it was to be in the same room as such a man. How I wished him well in all that he did and how little of our communication is with words. A timbre of voice, a way of standing, a gentleness in the eyes. What is that famous statistic? Eighty per cent of communication is non-verbal?

The talk ended and half the audience, including my friend, left immediately. I wandered down with the other half to mingle a bit. In the queue for the wine I was approached by a rather overweight man, straight evidently, in networking mode. He quizzed me on who I was, what I did and more or less what I could do for him. I humoured him for a while and then escaped. The room was mainly men, but they did seem very intent on talking to other men. I wondered whether I had aged more and faster than I knew or whether I looked particularly unattractive tonight. Whatever the reason, evidently no one else was going to approach me. So I walked up to the next man that smiled at me and chatted to him for the rest of the evening. He was elderly and, I wasn't surprised to find, American. One of the directors of the Wellcome Trust, who told me what it had cost to help John Sulston win the case to keep the map of the human genome in the public domain. I laughed at the figure, which had plenty of zeros.

'Ah, it wasn't the ethics that won the case then?'

'Maybe they played a role.'

After we'd been chatting for about ten minutes, a man walked up and glowered at me, letting me know in no uncertain terms, that I'd been talking to this important man for far too long. I was required to say goodnight.

'Well, lovely to have met you, then.'

'You're not coming to the dinner?'

'No. I'm not on the guest list.' Nor wanted on it by some, it seemed.

I picked up a leaflet of future free lectures and escaped out into the warm night air. And that was the end of my first evening at the RSA. I'll give them seven out of ten for lecture value and four out of ten for the possibility of meeting interesting men. I've been back for two more RSA talks, which have managed to be intellectual without being interesting, and the crowd somehow lacks energy. We can do better.

THE TATES

The second event I went to was at Tate Modern – www.tate.org.uk. Tate Britain, Tate Modern, Tate Liverpool and Tate St Ives all give a good selection of lectures, debates and discussions. Some of them are wonderfully silly . . . video installation, for example, has never really been my thing. Listen to this: there was a talk scheduled by Pipilotti Rist about her work. To be fair, I may have loved it, but I wasn't to get beyond the blurb.

'Her digital utopias captivate, float and shimmer with saturated colour and animated camerawork, just as they reveal the darker dimension of their own desires and aspirations. Rist remixes our cultural assumptions about feminism, the body, fantasy and reality, and the very technology that creates her work.'

Those are all themes that interest me. I went to a lecture on architecture instead.

I arrived early enough to notice that the crowd was, this time, ninety per cent students. Not what we are looking for, is it? I mean, it's hard for students not to meet other students. If you are under 21 and not meeting interesting guys, unless you are studying nursing or hairdressing, then you can't be trying. I know women complain that men under thirty are absurdly immature and not fit for dating . . . but they are easier to locate at least, right?

I spotted an interesting-looking man from right across the room. 'Wow, great energy!' I thought to myself, which is weird, as I couldn't see him very well, but I could somehow sense his energy. How do we do that? Answers on a postcard, please.

I watched him. He was wearing a dark suit, quite plain and casual/smart with a red silk scarf. He looked good because he looked relaxed and comfortable. He walked through the crowd and down to the stage. I had, inevitably, picked out the main speaker. In fact, I had picked out one of the leading architects in the world.

Bernard Tschumi, French, is currently designing the Museum for African Art, New York, The Museum of Contemporary Art, São Paolo, and the New Acropolis Museum, Athens.

The last one is an amazing project: a museum under the Acropolis to house the Greek treasures that we know as the Elgin Marbles, and which the British Museum currently has no plans to return.

I sat in the lecture hall and enjoyed looking at his weird buildings and envied him his amazing three-dimensional creations that people can walk around in. Such complex and wonderful architecture; the meeting of aesthetics with engineering and, in a wonderful and imaginative building, with the senses. I suppose it does require a meeting of systemising skills with empathy and imagination. A man like this is easy to admire. And I thought about walking up to him after the talk and saying, 'Are you having dinner now? Can I come along?' I am capable of doing such things, and I've made some of my most interesting friends through being outrageous, but for some reason, that night, I didn't quite dare.

I know! If I'm only going to pick out the Nobel laureates and world-leading architects I'm (a) limiting my options slightly and (b) not really representing your interests. There were a lot of students at Tate Modern . . . but to be honest, I don't think I did the Tate justice. The opportunities for strolling around galleries on a weekend and looking at the visitors as well as the art are well known. You can do this as a game. Almost like one of those 'What the bleep do we know?' exercises from the Californians who believe that we create our own reality. Literally.

So it works like this. You go out and instead of thinking, 'I wonder if I'm going to meet anyone interesting today?' you 'bleep' it. You programme your own day – now I know this sounds crazy, but there really are lots of people who believe this. You decide 'today I'm going to meet someone interesting' – they call it an 'essential contact' – at the gallery. So when you go out you are not looking at the art and wondering whether you'll meet someone, you are wondering *which* person is your essential contact. Then you spot him, the person who you'd like it to be, and so you make it happen because you know it will.

I've never really been sure about all this stuff, it seems a bit 'self'-centred to me, to say the least. But then I'm caught because, a bit like prayer, it is most effective for the one who really believes. There is the mystery. How powerful are our beliefs to shift our experiences? What do we make of the teaching of Jesus Christ when he said that if you have faith the size of a grain of mustard seed and you say to a mountain, 'Move!' it will move? What do you think?

I'm saying this because I once did a form of this exercise on an advanced seminar with Insight Seminars. The exercise was simply to go out of the door, make an essential contact and be back by 5 p.m. So I went to Battersea, as I was about to move here, and chatted to people and met a man who helped me plumb in my washing machine when I moved, which was pretty essential at the time . . . but not quite what I had in mind. So I guess I don't get too many marks for this exercise. But there was a woman on the course (if I remember correctly her name was Tina) who decided that she was going to meet her future husband. She went and sat in a park (I am not making this up) and a man walked up to her and started to chat. They are now married and have two children. So there may be a mystery here somewhere. I'm not saying that these people are right, but certainly, to an extent we do create our own reality with our expectations, far more than we could ever imagine.

But can I create an audience of attractive and available men at a talk at the British Library on the works of T.S. Eliot? I don't think so. If you go to the galleries, do take a friend and be sure to enjoy the art. Any interesting meetings have to be a game and a bonus.

THE FRONTLINE CLUB

So, where next? I thought maybe an interesting kind of journalism. World affairs. There is a place in London called the Frontline Club, www.thefrontlineclub.com, which is a club for frontline journalists who risk their lives to do their jobs. The membership is (can you believe this in London?) sixty per cent male. 'Yes, but, Isabel, I'm not a frontline journalist.' Ah, but you don't have to be. I rang them up and all you need is an interest in current affairs. And to be proposed and seconded by members of the club. How would you do this here or at any club where you didn't know anyone? Well, you'd have to go to some events, meet some people and ask. Life is for the adventurous risk-takers and you'd need to be one of those to hang out with these guys anyway.

But for the purpose of looking at these ten locations, I don't want to join, I just want to go to an event. This club has events every week which are open not only to members but also to the public. How's this for a pretty good example?

'Tragedy and Betrayal in the Middle East: how to escape history in Iraq with Robert Fisk. Fisk will detail how a more in-depth view of events yields a quite different interpretation of present events as reported in the mainstream press.'

Fisk will be the only person I've ever heard speak who has interviewed Osama Bin Laden three times and even photographed him smiling benignly at the camera. (The photo appears in his book.) I hadn't followed his column in the *Independent* but I do have a genuine interest in gaining a better understanding of Middle Eastern affairs. So, the possibility of meeting new men and an interesting evening – this fulfils my criteria.

This was undoubtedly the most educated and literate bunch of people I had ever sat in a room with. There was a feeling as we all piled in that we could have started the revolution. International journalists, leading Arab speakers, people who looked convincingly as if they knew what was going on in the world. What an amazing crowd. They all looked engaged with the world around them, and more than just knowing about it, they looked as if they cared. It was a relief to me just to be in a room with such people. I stood and enjoyed looking at them.

I complimented one woman on an elegant jacket she was wearing. Instead of saying, 'Oh? Thank you,' and addressing me rather coolly as people sometimes can, she held out her hand immediately and said, 'Hello. Very pleased to meet you. My name's Poppy. I work with the ISM'

I couldn't pretend that I understood her.

'Er?'

'The International Solidarity Movement. Have you ever been to Palestine?'

'No.'

'If you ever want to go, get in touch with us.'

'What do you do exactly?'

'Volunteering. In Palestine. We're a Palestinian-led international non-violent peace movement. We resist the occupation of the West Bank using only non-violent direct action.'

'Ah yes, I'm familiar with the principles of non-violent action.'

'Look us up sometime: www.ism-london.org.uk.'

'I may well do that. And I'll tell some of my, er, friends about you in case any of them are looking to do something a little different.'

'Bye, then. My seat's at the front.'

Robert Fisk was inspirational. He began: 'Our job as journalists is to tell the truth. To challenge the centres of power when they lie. This was the great failure of journalists after September eleventh. If there is any crime the first question a policeman asks is, "What was the motive?" but no one asked this question. We were allowed to ask, "Who did it?" "How?" "Where were our attackers from?" but to ask "Why?" was to be anti-American, unpatriotic.'

I never remembered reading anything that really explained the motive beyond, 'Because they hate America.'

'When I interviewed Bin Laden in his camp, built by the CIA [this was pre-September 11th, of course] he told me that his plan was to reduce the USA to a shadow of itself.'

The CIA built Bin Laden's camp? This was evidently news to no one in the room apart from me.

I ventured a stupid question. 'How come we don't know more about the other side's point of view even if we don't agree with it?'

'The last taboo subject is America's relationship with the Middle East.'

'And with Israel,' some man in the audience added.

'It isn't just about American patriotism, either. When I asked, in London, "Why did they blow up the twin towers?" I was accused of being undiplomatic.'

Fisk's talk encompassed the grand sweep of world history and the relevance of major events to current affairs. As he started to draw to a close we learned that he is not optimistic about US and UK withdrawal. 'Iraq is now more dangerous and more chaotic than it has ever been.' He should know, he has lived there all his adult life. 'The idea that we are moving forward to democracy and freedom is a lie.'

'But the Iraqi people want freedom?' asked a woman in the back row.

'Yes, of course they want democracy and human rights, but they also want freedom from us.'

'People don't care about Arab Muslims,' interjected an American man who introduced himself as a journalist.

Fisk agreed. 'Whatever people think about oil, they are certainly not thinking about the Iraqis.'

He ended his talk by saying that he had never been as pessimistic about the Middle East as he is now and added that he is against all violence, by everyone, ever, under any circumstances.

So good to hear those words. We gave him a standing ovation. People then stood up and ordered wine and we could actually talk to each other. Why don't cinemas do this?

I stood in the queue waiting to congratulate him. Two guys behind me were chatting. One said to the other, 'I'm going to Soho now to have a bite to eat and then meet some friends, would you like to come?'

I swung round with a smile. 'Why, thank you. I'd love to.'

The Arab friend of the speaker smiled at me. I laughed, 'Oh, you weren't talking to me?'

'We'd be very happy if you'd like to join us. This is Paul from the BBC World Service. I'm Ahmed.'

'Thank you, I'd love to. I'd love to hear what you both thought of tonight's talk. This is a subject about which I know and understand so little.'

We reached the front of the queue. And I shook Robert Fisk's hand warmly. I thought about the degrees of separation we have from each other. In shaking the hand of the Dalai Lama I had been one handshake from Mao, whom His Holiness had met as a young man. In shaking the hand of Robert Fisk I was one handshake from Bin Laden. The world is small.

'I was encouraged,' I said, 'to hear that you don't agree with violence under any circumstances. Tell me, do you think that putting pressure on our government to encourage China to put real political commitment behind Beijing's talks with the Tibetan Government in Exile would be the most logical way forward in the war on terrorism?'

He looked in despair at world events. 'I don't know anything about Tibet. It's not my area.'

'No. I see that. But the Dalai Lama, you see, has stuck to the non-violent path and . . .'

I saw his eyes glaze over. I was another person with my own favourite cause wanting to tell him about something about which he felt he could do nothing. He saw no connection between Tibet and the Middle East, nor between the Dalai Lama's teachings on hope and his personal despair. Never mind.

'Wonderful talk.' I smiled at him. This is what he wanted. He was too exhausted for anything else. 'Congratulations.'

'Thank you.'

The guys behind me shook his hand and then said, 'Shall we go then?' I cast an eye round the room and it was so full of interesting-looking people I was loath to leave, but they wanted to go, so I had dinner with Paul and Ahmed. And we discussed world events. Or they did and I listened and asked stupid questions. I tried to impress Ahmed with the fact that I've had four lessons of Arabic and could write the word 'Salaam' like this سلام on a napkin. After the evening we'd just been to, the fact that one author in London could write the word for peace in Arabic seemed like some tiny symbolic gesture in the face of the accusation of total indifference that had been so successfully made earlier in the evening.

'Why are you learning Arabic?'

I loved his assumption. 'Hold on, I didn't say I was learning Arabic, I said that I was trying to learn Arabic. I'm not sure that's the same thing. But I'm learning because it's a beautiful language. I'd say that's the main reason.'

'There are many beautiful languages.'

I wasn't going to get away that easily.

'And the script is beautiful too.'

'So is Chinese.'

No escape.

'OK, well, and it's because I love the passion of the Arab peoples. I've always experienced such warmth and whole-hearted generosity and welcome from any Arabs I know and I hate the fact that now, in a game of word association, the word that would come to most people's minds after "Arab" is "Terrorist" or "Extremist" or something derogatory. OK?'

He gave me a gentle smile.

The men I was having dinner with both spoke four languages. So I soon turned the conversation back to listening to them. With some horror I paid special attention when the talk turned to men, women and relationships.

'The West is a polygamous society in denial,' said my acquaintance from Egypt. 'The majority of the men I know in the UK who have power and money have both wives and families and several mistresses. Women are only interested in powerful men.'

'Henry Kissinger said that power is the greatest aphrodisiac,' Paul interjected.

And somehow Harry appeared at the table. 'What do you think, Isabel? Do I drive you wild because I'm powerful?'

I sat there smiling at someone who wasn't there. His power over me was based entirely on his smile. On his energy. He had no power, no position. I would have taken him in with nothing but his coat. Then I noticed a silence. I think someone who was physically at the table may have asked me a question. I had no idea what it was, so I asked one of my own.

'Don't you think that women want interesting men who are available?'

'For "interesting" read "owner of a company",' said Ahmed. 'Here women don't seem to care as long as he's powerful. They just want to shag the boss. The men don't care either. Men don't realise that their actions leave a trail. It's like a man taking a piss against a wall and he thinks because he's facing the wall that people don't see the consequences.'

'That's what you think of men in the West?'

'Yes.' He had been drawing a picture on the paper table mat while we ate. 'Look, don't you think this image of a man pissing against the wall is a good image of men in the Western world?'

It was hard to gauge which was greater, his anger or his bitterness. Neither quality made him attractive. I could see why the women wouldn't be queuing up and the reason was not his lack of power or money. I tried to lighten things a little.

'So, your advice to single women in London would be to go to Egypt?'

'Oh, yes. But surely you must know that both women and gay men have been going to Egypt for the men for years?'

'Well, no. This is certainly not an angle that I had considered. Aren't there problems with cross-cultural marriages when the custody battles over children cover different languages and different cultures?'

'Those are the ones that you read about in the papers,' Paul spoke up. 'You don't read about the happy ones. Several of my friends live in Damascus with their husbands or wives from Europe and there are no problems.'

'Really?'

'No more than in any other marriage. And I think sometimes they are better marriages because they know they have to work to make it successful.'

So there is one unexpected alternative solution from an evening at the Frontline Club in London. Have we really given any serious consideration to different cultures? Maybe it will come to that. I would be willing to bet that any women of thirty who moved to Damascus and enrolled in a university to study would not have to wait until she was 39¾ until she met a man she wanted to have dinner with.

Onwards and upwards.

CAFÉ DIPLO

In South Kensington is the French Institute. It shows French films and, every other Saturday morning, hosts a morning lecture with coffee and croissants. The talks, Café Diplo – www.monde-diplo-friends.org.uk, are almost always in English and there is every opportunity to mingle afterwards and even to stay for lunch and chat to the speaker or anyone else who seems interesting.

Now may I take the liberty of reminding you of the first principle of the game of ten places? 'Don't go to anything that you don't have a genuine interest in.'

Following a great evening at the Frontline Club, I'd had this talk with the Arab lecturer Sami Ramadani recommended to me. He is an exile from Saddam Hussein's regime who campaigned for democracy in Iraq but strongly opposed the US-led occupation.

I sat that morning and listened to the best explanation of the US and British presence in Iraq I had ever heard, followed by an explanation of why there could be no disengagement, only 'digging in' and the inevitability of Iraq turning into another Vietnam. He spoke with a well-informed grace, without bitterness but with a sadness that left us all close to tears. I was amazed and delighted to have heard such a speaker. Incidentally, as I know you like solutions, you may like to know what Professor Ramadani sees as the only solution to the occupation: 'for the people to turn against their governments as they did with Vietnam'. (He had earlier put a very convincing case of how, in order for Western governments to control, we have to 'divide and rule' by turning the various factions against each other.) So the inevitable point I'm leading to is that, once again, it's up to us, the people, to bring about change.

Did you know that the whole spectacle of the bringing down of the statue was stage-managed? I saw the pictures in the newspapers and watched it on TV and I believed it was a local Iraqi crowd. But here is what happened. The streets around the statue were sealed off and a group of exclusively young males were brought in and paid to pull down the statue and cheer. Now do you believe me? How do I know this, you ask? Not from Professor Ramadani, but from a film made by a group of pro-American Arabs who were working at the time for Al Jazeera TV and made a film called *The Control Room* about the events of the invasion and the occupation. Can you believe that we could be fooled with something as simple as bringing down a statue and then pretending it was local Iraqis . . . do they think we are fools? Well, I am. I believed it.

It was a memorable morning and we all got to stay to lunch. But here's another sad bit of the story and I'm really foxed as to why this should have been the case. From the point of view of our research, I'm somewhat confused in having to report to you that the audience was eighty per cent white, middle class, over fifty and female. There were some men present, but most of those were over sixty. I would have thought that in a political subject area intelligent males would be keen to hear an alternative point of view from the opinions in most of the mainstream media. But apparently not.

As Sami Ramadani left I gave him a little card. On one side I wrote *The Control Room* made at Al Jazeera TV. See if you can find this film'. On the other, for the second time that week, I wrote 'Salaam' in my best Arabic calligraphy. He glanced at it and smiled. I told him about the film and then asked a question that I don't believe he was expecting: 'On a different subject, may I ask you, why do you think it was mainly women here today?'

'I think women care more about the suffering of the Iraqi people. The men don't care, do they? Why would they care that our children are dying because the drinking water is polluted by sewage and our hospitals are bombed? They are all engaged in some form of sport on Saturdays, aren't they?'

I winced. I suddenly wanted to defend them ... maybe they worked harder all week and at the weekend wanted to see their children? That's the compassionate answer, or maybe they don't like being passive and sitting listening? Or maybe they're at the supermarket. It's true that most of the women there had been older, so maybe they had more energy to go and listen to a speaker on a Saturday?

So that's why I said be sure to be interested in the topic, because wherever the interesting single men of 25 to 55 who live in South Kensington are on a Saturday morning, it isn't considering world events at the French Institute.

THE INSTITUTE OF CONTEMPORARY ARTS

Went to the Institute of Contemporary Arts in the Mall three times. Maybe I was unlucky or is it just me? They are strangely pretentious (and that isn't a word I use very often). They consider the work and the talks there 'radical' but for some reason, although I can do weird and surreal, I can even handle obscure, here I don't see radical, I just see wanky. I've been similarly unenthralled by the talks I've been to and there is no opportunity to discuss them afterwards with other punters as, when you come out of the talk, everyone leaves straight away. There is only a very noisy bar area where it would be impossible to have anything but one of those smile-nod-and-shout-a-bit conversations.

Thinking that maybe I was being unfair to the ICA, I rang them up and, to my surprise, they agreed with me. 'No, this isn't a place to meet people. It's true that most people leave straight after the talks. The only way you could meet people here would be to bring a large group of friends and arrange to meet someone else who brought a large group of friends. This is a great place to come with people you already know, see a good film and then the bar's open until one in the morning. But I agree with you, it's not a good place to meet anyone new. It's difficult to meet new people in bars and clubs.'

So there you have it. But they do have the most wonderful selection of amazing films. And maybe the current programme of talks will have something radical and juicy . . . and maybe after they read this they'll find a way for people who come to talks to meet each other afterwards. They are at www.ica.org.uk.

THE ROYAL INSTITUTION OF GREAT BRITAIN

I love the Royal Institution of Great Britain. If you are reading this in the US, or anywhere outside London, here it is . . . www.rigb.org. This place is very impressive. But I certainly didn't think so at first. A friend had recommended the ultimate 'systemising' evening – 'Codes and Code Breaking' with Dr Simon Singh.

I arrived at the RI early for dinner before the lecture and was shown into a library full of men in dinner jackets. Now you may think that congratulations are in order. Isabel has finally located for you a room full of well-dressed and intelligent men. Except that the average age of the men must have been 97. They had evidently had fun casting the scene for the film I had just walked into, *Isabel's Latest Disaster*.

The men were sitting hunched in their dinner jackets, peering over their spectacles. There isn't a single man in the room who is not wearing spectacles.

'What an elegant sling,' said one who, for the number of his wrinkles, had obviously been given a speaking role. I had tied a scarf around my Tubigripped arm and was attempting to wear the offending item like an accessory.

'Thank you. It's the latest fashion, you know.'

He looked at me rather quizzically, not really understanding my attempt at humour. I escaped to the ladies', where I met a woman who complimented me on my coat.

'Thank you. Do you mind my asking, do you have any particular interest in code-breaking?'

'No, but my husband is an old fart and loves dressing up in a dinner jacket and standing around looking important. I should have left him years ago when I discovered his preference for shagging hounds, but I never got around to it and now look at the mess I'm in ... I'm 80 and actually married to one of those characters in the library.'

She didn't really say that, she just looked as though she wanted to. We went into dinner. Seats had been allocated and I sat next to a professor someone, a chemist who had made his money through an artificial flavour enhancer that is injected into meat. Long live vegetarians.

On the other side was a younger man and his wife. He asked me, quite from nowhere, what I thought about Fermat.

'Fermat?'

'A mathematician, round about 1500–1600 – you know, surely? As in Fermat's Theorem.' Ah – a systemiser speaks to an empathiser.

'What's a theorem?'

'It's a mathematical proof. He found one but then wrote in his book, "I have discovered this fantastic proof but there isn't room in the margin to write it down."'

'Wasn't it a wind-up?'

'It took three hundred years to be sure it wasn't a wind-up and some chap at Cambridge two years to prove there was a proof.'

'What was he trying to prove? In words that I may understand.'

'Well, you know $X^2 + Y^2 = Z^2$?'

'Absolutely.' Not. Looks like a description of a system to me.

'That's Pythagoras. And what Fermat said was that it's not true for any value other than two.'

'Why would this guy at Cambridge want to spend two years trying to solve this? How will this help mankind?'

'Not a clue. It was a problem that had to be solved.'

'For its own sake? In a wanky academic kind of way?'

'Absolutely.'

'This is all very male stuff isn't it? A love of systems?'

'Yes. It's also a proof of how completely dull men are.'

I was quite shocked to hear him say this, out of the blue, when I thought I was learning about theorems.

'You think men are dull?'

'Of course. This can't be news to you.'

'I quite like them.'

'Well, it's a question of taste, I suppose,' he said, 'but I certainly wouldn't marry one or entertain any kind of relationship with one.'

'Why not?'

'What's to like? There is not one attractive quality about us.'

I smiled.

'No really, this is a serious point. Men are self-centred and narrow minded. What do they talk about? Beer, football, computers, cars ... Would you find any of these subjects interesting?'

I laughed. 'But you are talking to me about mathematics. So you're not all like that. But tell me please, if you weren't here with your wife and father-in-law [the chemist] but were single, where would you be?'

'Mmm. I'd be down the pub being bored to death by a group of men talking about beer, football, computers and cars.'

'But why? Why wouldn't you be doing something more interesting?'

'Laziness and comfort.'

What do we do with them?

'Well, laziness I can understand, but I'm not sure what you mean by comfort.'

'Blokes together in a non-stressful environment.' Ah – just as Big Dave had told me, then.

'So you'd rather be bored than stressed?'

'On a Friday night? Yes. It's easier to be part of a crowd than to bother to be an individual. I'd like to think that I'd go to art galleries and intelligent talks like this one, but the truth is that I'd be too tempted to stay home. Would any bloke go to a gallery on his own?'

'Why not?' I said in some exasperation. 'Is a man so pathetic he can't look at art alone?'

'Yes. That's what I'm saying – blokes are.'

'Oh nonsense,' I replied. Just wish I had more evidence to back up my optimism.

A bell rang in the main auditorium; it was a full house and three-quarters male. Here the men were all ages, so obviously only the library is for the dinosaurs. Out walked Simon Singh, master systemiser, onto a stage where, in 1832, Michael Faraday explained the use of the electromagnetic induction system to another crowded full house. The atmosphere was expectant, excited and slightly geeky.

Singh began his lecture about Enigma and told us how codes and how code-breaking won us the war. Strange to think that if it wasn't for a little group of men with an obsessive interest in figures, numbers and patterns, we'd all be speaking German.

Some of his talk was so complex it left me feeling as though I was in infant-school maths. And sometimes he had easy ways to demonstrate mathematical thought.

'An astronomer, a physicist and a mathematician were holidaying in Scotland. Glancing from a train window, they observed a black sheep in the middle of a field. "How interesting," observed the astronomer, "all Scottish sheep are black." The physicist responded, "No, no – some Scottish sheep are black." The mathematician gazed heavenward in supplication, and then intoned, "In Scotland there exists at least one field, containing at least one sheep, at least one side of which is black."'

After all the generalisations that have flown around in this book I am delighted to bring you this story about a sheep and to conclude from this mathematical example that the only thing I can accurately demonstrate from my conversation at dinner is that there exists in the world one man who sometimes talks about beer, football, computers and cars. And even he admits it's boring and he's only there because he's lazy. I think this is very important to remember next time you see a pub full of men; you're only looking at one side of them.

I was not sure that my mind was fully on the lecture. Singh demonstrated a code and talked about data-encryption standards and the man next to me inadvertently grunted out loud with satisfaction. He was in his early thirties. An extreme systemiser, perhaps? I wonder if I could go out with anyone who is so excited by key distribution?

Singh was saying, 'And this was the greatest break-through in cryptology in two thousand years.' But I lost track of his talk and don't know what was. When I was at drama school they told us that a good actor has always to please three different people in the audience:

One that can hear but can't see.
One that can see but can't hear.
One that can both see and hear but doesn't speak the language.

As a speaker Mr Singh had a fourth possibility to contend with – one who can see, hear and speak the language, but doesn't understand the subject. So to manage to send me away smiling despite the fact that most of his talk meant nothing to me was quite an achievement.

I was waiting to see whether there would be enough mingling later for me to be able to recommend this fine and historic institution to you as a place where, after the talk, you can go and have an intelligent conversation. And I can. We trundled down the stairs where everyone consumed sand-wiches and wine for the rest of the evening. It is exactly as you would imagine. A time machine. They don't appear to have altered anything since 1799 when it opened. Your American friends would love it here. The Great Britain that they have seen in the movies – here it is. The chandeliers, the huge oil paintings, olde books on endless shelves and everyone seems to know everything about everything. One can almost imagine that Britain still has an Empire. Of course, it doesn't feel like the real world, and I wouldn't want it to be, but it was fun for an evening. I chatted to a man called Giles. He asked, 'Are you going to come to my ball?'

I smiled. I don't remember anyone ever using this phrase to me in my life before tonight. 'Tell me about your ball, Giles.'

'It's a charity ball at the Natural History Museum, next year. I run a charity for research into liver and pancreatic cancer. There will be five hundred people.'

'The Natural History Museum? That's quite a venue. What will they charge you?'

'£30,000. Our costs are £120,000, but that will be covered by sponsors, so all the money from the tickets goes to the charity.'

'How much will you charge per ticket?'

'£150.'

'I see. Wow. So what will people get for their donation?'

'An eight-piece live band, a three-course meal, celebrity appearances and, of course, a champagne reception with canapés.'

'And is this an annual event?'

'Absolutely.'

When people called 'Giles' do fundraising, they don't mess about.

'So?'

'I'll mention it, Giles. I may have some friends around the UK who may like to do something different and make a charity donation so that they can come to London and come to your ball. Do you have a website?'

'Yes, it's www.blucharity.org.'

So what do we think? Not a cheap way to meet new people, but certainly sounds like a fabulously grand evening out. You may consider yourself invited, with or without a prince. Didn't think I'd stop to question him on whether he insists on equal numbers of men and women ... it's a charity, after all. He was looking at me with confusion. I guess he could tell that I didn't quite fit in among the oil paintings. 'So what brings you to the RI?'

'I'm visiting different places in London where you can meet interesting people. Specifically, interesting men.'

'How are you defining interesting?'

I reeled off my well-practised definition, 'For the purposes of this project, an interesting man is one who, when you meet him you think that you'd like to have dinner with him and later you are glad that you had dinner with him and would like to see him again.'

'That's good. It's a good litmus test, dinner, you have to have real conversation.'

'Exactly.'

'Better than meeting someone in a club.' I'm so glad that he said that.

'So you like the definition, then?'

'I do. Have you been to the Royal College of Surgeons?'

'No. What's the crowd there like?'

'A varied bunch of pseudo-intellectuals who are actually just a bunch of nice guys.'

'Is it mainly men, then?'

'No, I'm using the term generically.'

'Oh, so women are included in "nice guys"? Generically?'

'Yes.'

Let this one pass, shall we?

'What kind of evening would you recommend?'

'You're not a doctor?'

'No. But I'm interested in health, obviously.'

He went on, 'They did an evening this month on breast cancer awareness, but I don't think that would be much good for meeting men. I'd come to something macho. Open-heart surgery, brain surgery, trauma, something like that. Don't come to gynaecology or dermatology; don't come to anything that has an "ology" in. In medicine they are less interesting by far. But I would say this, I'm a surgeon.'

Oh dear. Hold on. All we know is that somewhere in London is one surgeon, one evening, who held these views.

'I'll look them up. And I'll consider your ball, Giles. I may even tell some friends about it.'

'Thank you. Jolly nice to have met you.'

It's that word 'jolly' again . . . that the Ruperts use.

As he left, an older man walked up and said hello. I smiled.

'Your bow tie, sir, is very splendid.'

'So, madam, is your bottom.'

He made me laugh. I'd been bending over to write down the details of Giles's charity. I was a little shocked. I always expect my elders and betters to behave well.

'Can I ask how old you are, sir?'

'I'm sure you can.'

'I mean, may I ask how old you are?'

'You may.'

'How old are you, sir?'

He smiled politely. 'Would you like some more wine?'

'Yes, please.'

There were some extraordinarily odd-looking men in the room. I thought a little gentle observation would amuse my new companion. 'That gentleman in the blue waistband is rather unfortunate in his appearance, isn't he?'

He glanced around and chortled jovially at the unfortunate, and at me. 'It's called a cummerbund.'

'What? A nose that shape? Mine's called retroussé.'

'No, the "waistband".'

'He'd be the perfect casting for Tweedledum or Tweedledee.'

I don't normally make fun of people; it must have been the three glasses of red wine.

'Or both. Spielberg would cast him as both. Using fancy camera work.'

'And two different-coloured cummerbunds.'

I was beginning to dislike myself. Just in time, the man's wife appeared and glanced at his smile disapprovingly. Maybe what Bob on the building site said is true and wives really don't like their husbands to have too much fun.

'We need to be leaving now, George.'

'Yes, dear.'

He looked at me like a sentenced man whose time was up. Ah, the joys of marriage. I can't believe, if I were ever married to Harry, that when he was well past 65, I would pull him away from a laughing conversation with a younger woman.

Oh, for heaven's sake – look what I just did. I can't even get through a section about the Royal Institution without mentioning Harry.

THE ROYAL COLLEGE OF SURGEONS

I looked up the Royal College of Surgeons, but at the time of writing this there was nothing going that interested me or that I didn't have to be a surgeon to attend. Dedicated to the quest I am, but I draw the line at an endoscopic anatomy workshop or a lecture on open surgery of the shoulder. But if you are a doctor or have an interest in medicine, this has to be a great place to check out.

GRESHAM COLLEGE

You have to look hard to find likely places. How are you doing in your town? There is a little jewel in London called Gresham College (www.gresham.ac.uk) in Holborn, in the City. They have been giving FREE public lectures there for over 400 years. It's not always an excellent mingling opportunity, in that most of the time people just go to the lectures and leave, but sometimes they give away drinks, too. They're not allowed to charge for anything because Sir Thomas Gresham said so. The fact that he died in 1579 makes no difference. So, free lectures for us all. Good old

Sir Thomas. I put myself on their email list and couldn't resist going to hear what Professor Raj Persaud had to say about the 'Psychology of Attractiveness'. What attracts us to members of the opposite sex?

Well, girls, here is something that will not amaze you . . . apparently women rate 'intelligence' as one of the key factors. Women and men were both asked how important intelligence was for them as a factor in these types of relationship: 1. a one-night stand, 2. a short-term relationship and 3. marriage. Women said that intelligence was the major determining factor in all three situations. Men said that intelligence was important for marriage, less so in a short-term relationship and it seems that for a one-night stand any carbon-based life form will do.

I'm not surprising you here, am I? Prof. Raj went on to say that women use humour as a judge of intelligence. A good sense of humour is indicative of an intelligent man. Maybe this was news to some of the men in the audience. He wouldn't have got away with these revelations in a small group of women at dinner. They'd have said, 'Yes, Prof. Now tell us something that we don't know.'

He told us how not to seduce George Clooney. If you ever bump into George between your home and the supermarket don't say, 'I really loved you in *ER*.' Why not? Well, again, isn't this stuff obvious to women? Isn't it men that are really bad at so called 'pick-up lines'? You don't say that because that's what 99 per cent of the women who meet him for the first time are going to say. You need to be a little more clever, to demonstrate some kind of genuine interest, make an observation on some obscure film that he was in early in his career that he thinks everyone has forgotten about. So there you have it. Of course, this tip also works for anyone who is used to being flattered.

Dr Raj pointed out that if you go on lots of dates and they don't work out, you may like to look at what you are doing. But he doesn't understand. He's male and happily married. What he doesn't know is that the problem for women is finding a man who we'd like to date in the first place. Most women know what to do with them when we've found one. He played us the seduction scene from the film *Groundhog Day* and showed how Bill Murray could mess up a seduction scene even when he had numerous chances to live the same evening over and over again. The point he was making was that we need to look at what we are doing and try to learn from our mistakes. In other words, 'If you always do . . .' (Repeat mantra and don't forget to shout the last line.)

There were a few more bizarre little pieces of information that may come in useful sometime, so I'll pass them on. I know I'm digressing again, but who knows when you may need to know these things? Why do we women wear eye make-up? Well, to make our eyes look bigger. We know that. But why do we want our eyes to look bigger? Apparently because, again on a subconscious level, we are all programmed to want to take care of babies and babies, of course, have larger eyes relative to head size. So we are innocently speaking directly to the man's subconscious and saying, 'Take me home and take care of me.' Ha ha, I hope I have some feminist readers hopping with rage.

Blusher. Ever since ancient Egypt women have been making their cheeks red. I thought it was something to do with arousal, but it's an even more basic subconscious message than that. Apparently women's skin is redder when they ovulate. So by making our cheeks redder we are signalling, 'Breeding material . . . pick me.' We can think of this next time we apply blusher.

A man is more likely to be attracted to you or you to him if you share facial characteristics. If you take a photo of someone and, with a bit of clever morphing, give the photo characteristics of the opposite sex, apparently we'll all say, 'I like that person.' So it seems that we are looking for ourselves. A worrying thought. We feel most attracted to those faces that look most like our own, or so research shows. Although while he was saying this, a man with a very unfortunate face and very, very thick spectacles was mumbling, 'No, no,' under his breath. Obviously for him the prospect of meeting a woman who looked like him filled him with horror.

I sat there thinking of the words of a friend who met Harry who said, 'You are a female version of him. You two have the same energy, the same personality, the same love of humanity ... you even look alike.' I noticed that my mind had wandered off to Scotland, chastised it and demanded that it return to the lecture.

Our tendency to like things that are like us extends to the absurd, it seems. People are told about the 'mad' Russian monk Rasputin and asked how they feel about him. Then they are told that he shares a birthday with the person being questioned. Apparently if we think he has the same birthday as us, we change our opinion of him for the better, the reason being that we decide that anyone born on that day can't be all bad. What simple creatures we are. And it gets more absurd still. We are more likely to want to date someone if they share the same first letter of our second name. So I am more likely to want to date 'Paul Lifeless' than 'Paul Mysterious'. How crazy are we?

But then Professor Raj started to be really interesting. He says that we place too much importance on attractiveness and not enough on compatibility. It works like this: people come to him who have met someone they are attracted to and they ask, 'How do I know whether he is my Mr Right?'

He says that it is very likely that he is Mr Wrong. And here is a way to check. You can work out what the top ten things are that you absolutely couldn't live with. So even if you met a George Clooney who was a millionaire, you still couldn't live with him if he did the things on your list. So – let me see, cruelty to animals is the first that comes to mind for me.

1. Cruelty to animals or children (or anyone).
2. Someone who isn't kind, all the time, to everyone.

3. Someone who has no interest in other people, other cultures or travel.
4. Someone who doesn't wash. (OK. I'm writing in the order I think of them.)
5. Someone who expects me to do one hundred per cent of the cooking. *'Sorry, George – you're not willing to do half? There's the door.' 'Oh, Isabel, can we just eat out every night? I have so much money and what are we going to spend it on?' 'Oh, OK then.'* But in real life I'd like to share the cooking.

That would be my top five. So the idea is that, no matter how attracted you are to someone, if the things on the list clash, eventually they will drive you apart. So compatibility is ultimately more important than mutual attraction.

'It's not in the easy times,' Prof. Raj told us as he ended his evening, 'that you'll know whether a relationship will make it . . . it's how you'll deal with a crisis.'

'But we haven't had a crisis,' a woman in the audience shouted out.

Prof. Raj smiled at her. 'Then generate one.'

But his last piece of advice I wholeheartedly agree with. I may even have said something similar myself. What is the best way to be in order to seduce people? In order to have people fall over themselves to be with you? Have fun. Enjoy life. Because if you do that, people will always want to be with you and be a part of that. So, he says that the best pick-up line ever is, 'Are you having fun?' because whatever the answer is, you have just associated yourself with the magic commodity. Fun.

THE ROYAL GEOGRAPHICAL SOCIETY

I like evenings where someone is doing something positive and I found an amazing talk that was happening at the Royal Geographical Society – www.rgs.org. This is yet another place in London where talks happen and you can mingle in the bar before and after the talk and meet people. The RGS tells me that the crowd here can be divided into two groups: the armchair travellers – people with an interest in geography, travel and exploring remote places on the planet, and the people who actually go.

'Holiday this year, dear?'

'Yes, dear, how about the South Pole this year?'

I found a talk about the rainforest. A man called Hylton Murray-Philipson doing what he can to save it. I got in touch with him and, bizarrely, he had heard of my efforts to save Tibet from my last book. There should be some kind of club for individuals who attempt to change the world, only of course the speaker at that night's event was considerably more successful in making a difference than I was. He had just raised half a million for Rainforest Concern, (www.rainforestconcern.org), a small charity working with indigenous people who live in the Brazilian rainforest. Now he was speaking to six hundred people about the protection of this outstandingly important natural environment. So not all men with two second names like to shoot things and play rugby.

I dressed up and bought a ticket. The audience was obviously made up of very powerful and influential sorts. The men were all wearing suits and seemed to be there with their elegant wives. I took along my beautiful neighbour, Daisy, the model not keen on Ruperts, and two friends of mine who are Druids and believe in the protection of the forest as a matter of spiritual importance as well as ecological necessity. The four of us didn't really fit in, but nobody seemed to mind.

Call me naïve. Do you know, I actually thought the rainforest was protected? I thought that they had brought in laws to stop the destruction and illegal logging. So I sat, with a curious feeling of déjà vu, to hear that the main culprits of the destruction are the Chinese, who are building roads all through the forests. They showed us a map of Brazil and, instead of what I'd thought was there, and what you see on an atlas, which is a continent of green, what is actually there is an elaborate network of roads with trees in between. And it's still being destroyed at a rate of nine football pitches a minute. Hylton began his talk.

'The roads marked in red are still mud roads, but all those marked in yellow have been tarmacked over so that trucks can roll up and down and take what they want. Of course, most of the logging is illegal, but when there isn't a policeman for the nearest five hundred miles, it's impossible to enforce.'

He showed us pictures of the untouched forest, the richest biodiversity on earth ... then pictures of what happens when it is cut down to raise beef or grow soy beans.

And as I sat there listening to the passion of this quiet and gentle man who had lived with indigenous people and come back determined to make a difference, I felt some great joy restoring me. Here was a man who was demonstrating everything that is good about being human. In male form, too. It was like sitting listening to a mathematical proof. He wasn't giving a presentation on cars, computers or cricket. He wasn't guilty of any of the crimes that I was hearing men accuse other men of every day. Or we hear politicians accused of. He wasn't cynical or angry or aggressive. I rather wished that I was the astrologer in Simon Singh's story and then I could have concluded that all men are gentle, care about the world and are doing all that they can to make it a better place.

When he finished I turned to Daisy. 'So what do you think of this place? I mean, would you consider coming here again?'

'I think it's a great place.'

'You don't think – for someone in your twenties – that it's a bit stuffy and dull?'

'No, I don't. His talk was brilliant, I'm really interested and I'm sick to death of the London nightclubs full of coke-heads. Everyone I know does drugs all the time, so it's really difficult to have a good conversation.'

I'd heard this before from friends in their twenties. They prefer parties in Paris, where there is far less drug-taking and more dancing. My cuddle buddy Mark says that when he goes out clubbing all night long he doesn't take anything and is the only one who dances all night on a natural high; the crowd he goes out with thinks he's weird. But I still have trouble believing it's quite as universal as they all tell me it is.

'Come on, Daisy, you're exaggerating . . . they can't all do drugs every time they go out.'

'No. OK. Ninety per cent of the clubs, then, ninety per cent of the time. I'm sick of it. I've had a much more interesting evening here.'

Goodness – approval for my quest for intelligence from the stunning 24-year-old.

After the lecture Hylton invited us to join fifty of them who were going for dinner. He introduced his wife, Noo, and the elder of his two sons and they were all so lovely I forgot the other reason I was there. We sat, the Druids, Daisy and I at a table with a group of women from Brazil and we discussed how we (you and I), as individuals, can contribute to saving the rainforest. We put together a list of ten ways and I was totally absorbed, as I love to explore ways that, as individuals, our actions can bring about change. By the end of the dinner we had this list:

Ten Things You Can Do to Save the Rainforest

1. Get healthy. Don't eat beef, because the rainforest is cut down to raise cattle. If you must buy beefburgers, check they don't come from South or Central America and at least insist that the poor cows were British. (Or locally produced, wherever you are.)
2. If you must buy a car, buy a Smart car; voted most environmentally friendly car by *Ethical Consumer Magazine*, huge fun and easy to park, too. A friend of mine has a yellow one . . . www.smart.com or better still, carpool, www.car-pool.co.uk.

3. Be noble. If you are going to buy furniture, buy second hand, recycled furniture or bespoke furniture from a local supplier using reclaimed or FSC (Forest Stewardship Council)-labelled (sustainable) items. See www.fsc-uk.info.

4. Make enemies. At work, insist on recycling of course, but you can also find out whether your organisation is using paper from a sustainable source. If it isn't, ask them to, then give them a month to swap and if they don't, organise a friendly office petition. Don't be critical, but do be gently persistent. These guys are good . . . www.greenstat.co.uk.

5. Go on holiday. A range of amazing ethical holidays in Brazil can be found at www.sustainabletourism brazil.org.

6. Leave work all together. Have a grown up gap year and volunteer to save the rainforest. Here are two organisations you can call and ask about volunteering – www.btcv.org.uk, or www.questoverseas.com. Both offer short- or long-term adventures.

7. Blow your nose with care. The Greenpeace site www.saveordelete.com is encouraging a total boycott of Kleenex, which uses virgin paper from ancient forests to make tissues!

8. Buy real food. The advantages of buying locally farmed organic food are manifold. It isn't wrapped, you know where it's come from and it tastes better. This company will deliver to your door, and they'll send ethical tissues and organic milk in real glass bottles that you return to them: www.farmaround.co.uk.

9. Save our soy beans . . . much of the Brazilian rainforest is cut down to grow soya (international production is 110 million tons annually). If you buy soy products, check where they come from and always buy organic soy, as non organic soy is produced in Brazil. Also then, wherever it comes from, you are not encouraging the use of pesticides.

10. Put your feet up. And read a magazine. If you buy one year's worth of the *Ethical Consumer Magazine*, www.ethicalconsumer.org (£30, and you get online access to www.ethiscore.org and all the back issues, too), you can check up on everything before you buy it and become truly knowledgeable.

I sat in the taxi on the way home thinking of all the things I could do with this list. I could put it on my website and give it to friends to put on their websites. I could give it to Greenpeace, Rainforest Concern and Friends of the Earth for them to play with and adapt. I could work out changes that I could make in my life personally in response to Hylton's inspiring talk. It had been a truly wonderful evening.

And it was only then that I remembered ... I was supposed to have been going out to see if there were any interesting available men there. I had got so carried away with the joy and passion of the evening and chatting to the women at the table, I had completely forgotten why I was there. The moral of this story? Well, the simple truth is that no matter what they tell you in the songs, the movies, in literature and the arts – there are some things more important than meeting the opposite sex. Hoorah.

OK. Back on the job. I was still worried that the places I've been exploring in the hope of arriving at 'intelligent' locations have become stuffy and full of suits, so I phoned Daisy to ask her if I should, after all, be going to nightclubs.

'Absolutely not. They're great for dancing, but certainly not for meeting intelligent or interesting men. And even if they were intelligent, you wouldn't know, because they'll be on something and when people are on coke they all behave like coke-heads. I never expect to meet anyone that I'd want to date in a club.'

'But, well, apart from the Royal Geographical Society, the places that I've been going ... the brainy places, you wouldn't be interested in going to any of those, would you?'

'Who says?'
What? The Royal Institution for example?'
'Sure I would.'
So in a little additional venue-checking, I decided to take Daisy to the Royal Institution. A night was coming up on 'Mind Magic'. I certainly needed a little magic at this stage.

THE ROYAL INSTITUTION

Dr Richard Wiseman couldn't fail to be a good speaker. He had started life as a magician (systems) and then become a psychologist (empathy) – as good a training for a high-quality speaking event as you could wish for. He cajoled us with magic and then mystified us with the psychology of how and why it worked without giving away any of the secrets of the Magic Circle, of which he is a member. He included stunning optical illusions, including one in which he shows a video clip – he focuses your attention on counting basketball passes and you fail to notice a man in a gorilla costume walk through the clip, pound his chest and walk off again.

'This does, of course, have some relevance to scientific and medical research . . . if we are so focused on looking for one thing that we fail to notice a gorilla, who knows what we may be failing to notice while we are looking for something else?'

Don't like to imagine the relevance this may have to this project. Have I failed to notice some really wonderful potential gorillas? Probably. Dr Wiseman has written a book on luck, so at the question-and-answer section at the end I decided I'd ask him about the relevance of this to our search.

'I'm writing a book about how interesting members of opposite sexes can best meet each other . . .'

'Well, hello!' he said in a sexy voice and made the audience laugh.

'I wonder if you can comment on what role luck may have to play in this process?'

The audience laughed again. I went on, 'Or any other comments you may like to make?'

'Ah, yes – well, let me tell you a story. We were doing some research for the book. We interviewed two groups of people – one group who consider themselves to be very lucky and one very unlucky. It was interesting because in the unlucky group we had a man who had won four million pounds on the lottery.'

The audience evidently envied the man his misfortune.

'When I interviewed him I said, "Excuse me asking, but we don't have many four-million-pound lottery winners in this group – could you tell me how that is an example of you being unlucky?"

'"But I was unlucky!" he complained. "It was a typical example of my bad luck. I chose all the right numbers but some other bastard chose them, too. If he hadn't done, then the prize wouldn't have been split and I'd have won eight million."'

And while you are smiling – how and when do we all do this? What he basically seemed to be saying is what I've always believed – that we create our own luck by what we do with circumstances. This much we know. But sometimes all the optimism in the world couldn't seem to create opportunities. I leaned over and said to Daisy, 'How many attractive men can you see in the audience?'

'None.'

'Oh come on . . . what about him?'

'He looks like a psychopath.'

'He does not!' I looked again. 'Well, maybe a little bit like a psychopath . . . What about him, then?'

'No, he's too nerdy.'

'Or him?'

'He looks like a scientist.'

'He probably is a scientist.'

'Isabel, you're asking the wrong girl. I like my men Latino – there are none of that sort here.'

So it seemed that, yet again, I was having a good evening in the wrong place.

Then the talk ended and Giles came up and said hello, he of the charity ball whom I'd met at my last evening here. 'Hello, this is Katie, my partner and this is my father.'

'Hello. This is Daisy.'

Goodness, it seems I know people who go to the Royal Institution. We chatted for a while and, as there were no drinks after the lecture that night (which is very annoying – if you go, you need to check this), they invited us to join them for dinner and walked us around the corner to a casino that had a restaurant attached. I noticed large numbers of men sitting around tables. I wondered whether any of them had really come out hoping to meet interesting women, but were gambling their money away instead.

We sat down for a meal. While Daisy, Katie and Giles discussed surgery, I talked with Giles's father, a distinguished gentleman of nearly sixty. Inevitably he asked about my project and I told him that men and women often seemed to have difficulty meeting each other and forming good relationships.

'That's because men are liars,' he began. Isn't it interesting how many men think so badly of other men?

'What do you mean?'

'I mean they con women into believing things that they don't really mean or don't really think.'

'You think men do this?' I stayed neutral and just asked questions.

'I think all people do it, but men use it as a way of getting women into bed and women fall for it all the time.'

'What kind of lies do you think men tell women, in your experience?'

'What women want to hear.'

'Like what?'

'Ninety-nine per cent of men, for example, aren't interested in star signs, but if a woman says during a dinner, "I'm a Leo, what are you?" he will feign an inordinate interest in star signs or whatever the girl says on any subject. He will pretend to be interested even if he hates the subject.' Ha ha – has he been reading *The Game*?

'So you see that as lying?'

'Yes. I don't think women do this. Have you ever pretended to be interested in football?'

'No.'

'But men will deceive because they have an ulterior motive.'

'What about a straight lie?' What I call a 'lie direct' when speaking of Toms and Dicks. 'Such as "I have a boat" when they don't have one.'

'Most men won't do that. They'll protect themselves psychologically, so they'll say that they haven't lied about something because she didn't ask the right question.'

'Such as "Do you have a wife?" for example?'

'Exactly. And they lie to their wives all the time. I know married men who sleep with a lot of single women regularly with no intention of leaving their wives and the single women seem to let them. For some reason.'

Ah – he was going to tell Tom stories.

'I have a friend who has told his wife that he likes to play golf on a Saturday afternoon. But Saturday is actually his shagging day. This is true. Every Saturday he shags a different woman. He went to the trouble of going out and buying a set of golf clubs and he muddies them up on the way back from his shags and then cleans them every week, when he gets home, in front of his wife.'

You've got to laugh haven't you? 'One week his wife said, "You must be getting very good at golf," and of course he'd never played a day in his life, but he went out and got himself some golfing trophies and had them engraved with his own name on.'

'Honestly?'

'Honestly. That's what they do.'

'You don't see this as unusual behaviour, then?'

'No, I could tell you a million stories like this. This man has a friend who liked the golfing model, but didn't want to fork out on a set of golf clubs, so he decided he'd say that he wanted to take up cricket. All he had to buy was cricket whites. But it went wrong. His wife said one week that she'd like to come and watch him and he couldn't think of an excuse quick enough. So he took her to where a local cricket club were playing and he stood all afternoon, just outside the boundary, pretending to be an extra fielder, when he didn't even know the cricket team.'

'And he got away with this?'

'He got away with it until tea time, when it would have become obvious that they didn't know him, so he managed to convince her that they didn't need him any more and they could go home and of course she didn't know anything about cricket, and she believed him.'

Oh dear. How much we love our men and will believe in them.

'She never found out?'

'No, it worked really well for him. She'd been so bored that she never asked to go again. But you've got to be lucky, I suppose, to pull that off.'

'Or just have a woman who believes in her husband.'

'I know men that make up complete false identities to pull off one-night stands. But I'm not telling you anything you don't know already, surely?'

'I've met lots of men who tell the truth.'

He turned to Daisy. 'Surely you know men who make things up to get women into bed?'

'Of course, I've met footballers, millionaires, Concorde pilots.'

I turned to Katie. 'This is too general, surely? Katie, do you think men lie more than women?'

'Yes, it's too general.'

Giles added, 'We'd have to consider a large variety of people in a large variety of situations.' Thank goodness they had been at Simon Singh's talk on mathematics.

Katie said, 'And even then you wouldn't know if the sample was typical and you couldn't prove they were lying or not when they said that they were.'

But Giles's father was insistent. 'Yes, but it's common knowledge that men are liars.' In the same way that some people know that all Scottish sheep are black?

As Daisy and I chatted about these stories on the way home, I realised just how complex those situations are, which I had listened to laughing, and how difficult it is to draw any conclusions from them at all. One of the things we could notice is the lengths the men in the stories were prepared to go to in order to have sex but avoid upsetting their wives. And what about the levels of self-deception involved in both cases? Could the women really notice nothing week after week? Could the men really justify the deceit to themselves?

Personally, I don't believe that men are any better or any worse than women. Through my work in a million seminars I know that once you strip away all the masks and 'behaviours', you find that everyone just wants to love and be loved. We all want to be accepted for who we are. So I'm not making any judgements. But I am trying to take a look at the differences. Lying is based on what? On fear.

Once, when my daughter was younger, I discovered that she had lied to me. I phoned a wise old friend to ask her advice. She said, 'What you have to consider, Isabel, is why she has lied to you. What is she afraid of? Of your reaction if she tells you the truth?'

If a man lies in an attempt to seduce a woman, it is because he believes he will not be accepted for who he really is or that he doesn't live up to some image of what he thinks a woman wants? Alas for human relationships. The men in these stories that have no interest in golf or cricket have weaved complex webs for, no doubt, complex reasons. Do they care deeply for the wives who, for yet more complex reasons, aren't interested in sex any more? Are the men afraid of being thrown out and of being alone? Are they simply afraid of losing their housekeepers? Or are they maintaining, at all costs and with very little credibility, their image of themselves as 'good' men?

I think women can lie just as well as men can. We just lie in less obvious ways. Men and women are both masters of self-deceit. So I don't think we can be angry or upset with anyone if we stop to look, with a genuine attempt to understand, at what is going on. We have to start with total honesty with ourselves followed by courage to communicate openly with each other. If we hold back from this because we have judged ourselves as bad people or because we are afraid that the other person will judge us in this way, then we are putting our desire to live up to an image (a false one, of course) before the truth of our own hearts. In this way we are all lost and no relationships can be real.

Our relationship with ourselves is the starting point, and to consider whether we want intimate relationships with others where we can't be honest. As Gandhi said, we can 'be the change that you want to see in the world'. So all we can do is be honest and kind to ourselves and honest and kind to others. Whether we are male or female – that's the power we have.

So I think the game of ten places has to be an ongoing project and a way of opening up the whole discussion of how people meet each other. As a reader of *Men!* you are now a part of this. Do we really want to go on meeting people in pubs and clubs where appearance is the only thing that matters and even if, like Daisy, looks are on your side and you are 24 and so beautiful and curvaceous in all the right ways that you can make a living from your looks – even then meeting people in this way doesn't serve us. Is it any wonder that so many relationships and marriages are unhappy if this is the way we meet each other and an entire generation now also has to be drugged before they can pluck up the courage to speak to each other?

In the locations that we are looking for, conversation is necessary, it is required and enjoyed. People are likely to be sober (although there will probably be a glass of wine or two about – but not to excess). The ten places will not be mainly women or exclusively men, although a mixture, like the Frontline Club, that is more men than women is preferable.

I'm aware that this idea could take a year if I went on visiting ten venues in London to find the best ten and even then the ones at the start would probably have changed or closed by the end of the year. The only way to keep this current is through my website. And we need to keep it current for your city, too.

The game of ten places is an ongoing game. I guess we all need to start playing it. A bit like *Desert Island Discs* . . . women up and down the country need to meet up in pubs and home-groups and, instead of complaining that it's impossible, discuss the game of ten places.

'And which are your ten places for Edinburgh?'

'Oh, Henderson's vegetarian restaurant is at my number one . . .'

'No – I love it there, but for meeting men the Filmhouse in Lothian Road has to have it and Fiona has Word Power bookshop at number one. They have events there and everything.'

Women have to stop discussing the problem and start combining forces to discuss the solutions. But meanwhile, as we all start to play this game, I feel one more radical solution is called for. I have a solution to the problem of spectator sports, an environment that is mainly but not exclusively male, an idea to get us away from the Toms, Dicks, Harrys and Ruperts . . . a way for us to get away from grey cities . . . that may just take us to a different world. And one that has men in, too. Take a deep breath.

Part IV

DIVING IS THE NEW FOOTBALL –
GOING DOWN

1. DEEP BLUE IN BIRMINGHAM

I'm going to make a very risky statement. Stick my head up above the crowd, notice that the wind is blowing the other way, the tide is against me and every single other cliché that says basically, don't say this – but I'm going to anyway . . . you may shoot me down: 'Spectator sport is boring.' I know there are women who have discovered that being part of a huge crowd at a football match has a thrill to it – yeh, yeh, blah, blah, yada, yada . . . and does sitting watching TV have a thrill to it as well?

Let's imagine that you are in the position that I was in when I was married. As a young actress I worked six days a week in repertory theatre and only saw my husband one day a week, just as anyone who works hard and whose partner works hard is only really likely to see them at the weekends. Do we really want to share our weekends with men who spend them sat in front of a television watching football, cricket, rugby, horse racing, car racing, or even people racing?

I've a sneaky feeling that I represent the vast majority of women who actually find spectator sports of all kinds dull. But no one dare admit it any more. It's become so universal that we feel obliged to accept it. Just as women are the ones who get pregnant, men are the ones who watch sport on TV. As if it was genetic. As if an obsessive interest in the rise and fall in the league tables of a group of men they are never likely to meet was normal behaviour. When did this microchip get added to the male brain? In Shakespeare's day, from the plays that I've read at least, men seemed to be more interested in the art of seduction.

We have a Larson mug in this flat that shows a family sitting on a sofa, father, two kids and the dog, all staring at the wall. Underneath is written 'In the days before television'. Whatever happened to family days out? Whatever happened to husbands and wives studying something together? Massage? Photography? Cooking? Wine tasting? Art? Languages? Music? (Making it, that is.) Sex?! (Having it, that is.) Whatever happened to voluntary work – to going out with the British Trust for Conservation Volunteers (www.btcv.org) and saving a river or a forest? What happened to our communities? To the concept of contribution (www.do-it.org.uk)? Does it all boil down to the response of Professor Sami Ramadani, giving his fascinating and moving lecture about Iraq to an audience of mostly women: 'Men are involved in some kind of sport at the weekend, aren't they?' TV and sport? Is that all there is, dammit?

But don't misunderstand me . . . I'm not anti-sport. Sport is life-enhancing. What I'm against is spectator sport. There is an additional consideration of this problem. We can't change men. Or anyone. Our job is to love people as they are. Obviously it is not appropriate to go out with a man who loves watching the football at the weekends and then try and persuade him to do something different. No, no, none of that. Then we start to behave like the wife of Bob on the building site who says that women just want to stop men having fun. Never try and prevent a man doing what he loves. If you do that then he should leave you and find a woman who will love him for who he is.

But this means that we have to be very careful where we meet them in the first place.

If you want to have an enjoyable and active relationship with the man you love you may like to consider that sports break down into two groups: those that you can play too and those you can't. Football obviously is the worst example of the second group. But then there is the first group, the activity sports, which may or may not be competitive. In the competitive group there is always tennis, badminton, squash – but often because strength is a factor, few women can compete equally with men in these sports. But then there is another group that is a whole lot more fun: paragliding, climbing (this is fantastic – I've done a little, it's not competitive, although it can be and it involves going to amazing places and trusting other people with your life), or even parachuting (you have to try this as, if you have a man who has never done it before, he'll be just as scared as you are). But if all these things leave you a little breathless and terrified and you are still looking for a man who enjoys a wonderful, non-competitive sport that you could enjoy together on equal terms, then I have the solution for you. Scuba diving. We are going to make a special study of this. We shall make diving the new football for those who want to have good relationships. For couples that want to learn a skill together, explore a new element together, experience wonder together, and maybe, if you save up, see the world together.

Dr Jenny, my lodger, a woman of many mysteries who has been doing her best to keep out of this story, suddenly spoke one day – out of the blue, so to speak, 'You should look at diving. That is definitely an alternative male environment that women can enjoy. I've been thinking about it. There is this big diving show that comes up twice a year. There's one this weekend. You should go.'

Lost in contemplation of my persistently non-rotating wrist, I looked up at her in amazement.

'All you have to do is get on a train and go to Birmingham.'

The National Exhibition Centre has to be the most massive building I've ever been in. The Dive Show, with only 16,000 punters expected, is a small event for them.

I walked in and sat down to manwatch and then had to buy coffee, as I was convinced that I must, finally, have gone mad. Am I so blinded by love for Harry that my vision of other men is being distorted? I don't mean metaphorically. I don't mean 'how' I'm seeing them – I mean what I'm seeing. This isn't what I meant by a solution at all.

It was, indeed, about ninety per cent men but, for a start all the men had either no hair, bizarrely short hair or shaven heads. Can it be so long since I've seen thousands of men in one place that I don't know what they look like any more? Shouldn't there be more variety? Don't some men still have longish hair? And another thing. They were all overweight. This was not me deducing wrongly from one overweight man at this exhibition centre that they were all round ... this was far more alarming. This was me sitting, clinging to my sanity by a thread looking around thinking, 'No, surely, this can't be true, there must be fit, healthy men with hair? Shouldn't at least one of them be good looking? Or one side of one of them?' I dug some music out of my bag and decided to disappear into a world full with the absurdity of Frank Sinatra. So, with Old, Blue Eyes singing to me, not without a certain irony I thought, his *Songs for Swingin' Lovers*, I went for a wander.

The exhibition hall was made up with innumerable stalls: they were selling wetsuits, drysuits, snorkels, everything you could ever need for a life sub-aqua. There was a dazzling display of ads letting you know that if you book your next diving holiday with this company, in that country, your reward will be to see more fish.

Location shots of the Bahamas, Tenerife, the Philippines, Honduras, the Red Sea flooded my eyes as Frank caressed my eardrums. Wonderful underwater photos were every-where, and video screens showing films of goggled faces (different from Googled) weaving in and out of the seaweed. The various diving schools in the UK were there, as were an impressive number of conservation organisations (check out www.sharktrust.org). Then there were the toys – underwater scooters! A little machine that you hold on to and it whizzes you along.

'Oh, cool!' I said to the man selling these. 'Isn't this very ecologically unsound?'

'No, totally environmentally friendly.'

'What happens if you let go? Does it just go whizzing along for ever?'

'No, if you let go it stops, see?'

He obviously thought he had a sale. 'Can I interest you in one?'

'I'd love one. But I've never been underwater in my life.'

'Then what? . . .'

'I'm just admiring all your toys.'

Underwater cameras. Underwater video. What have I been doing all my life?

This looked like the best hobby in the world. There was just one problem . . . the men. I spotted a girl in a wheelchair on one of the stands. As I looked at her she smiled up at me.

'Is that a diving accident?' she asked, looking at my Tubigripped wrist.

I turned Sinatra off and sat down to chat with her. 'No, I came off a motorbike. Don't ask. Was yours a diving accident?'

'I was going diving, but I fell over in the car park.' A kindred spirit obviously. She was very approachable.

'May I ask you some questions?'

'Sure. I'm a diving instructor, so I should be able to help you.'

'Well, actually it's not the diving. I think I'm going mad.'

'I'm definitely the right person then.'

'The men here. Am I hallucinating or are they all hairless?'

She laughed. 'No, you're not mad. They cut it all off because they're divers, it's a pain in the water. Your hair would drive you mad. I can guess you're not a diver, as you'd have cut it all off.'

'Oh. Well, thank God, I really thought I was making it up. And aren't they all overweight too? Am I imagining things?'

'It's a very rufty-tufty sport/hobby, whatever. Not a lot of women want to do it. You can't be concerned about hair or make-up. You'll always look a frigging mess and if you wear a drysuit you'll smell. And as for the men in diving, well . . .'

Oh dear. Am I really hearing this again?

'. . . they're not your tall, dark and handsome types. More a breed unto themselves. Or breeds unto themselves.' We glance up. 'There are different groups, different pedigrees.'

Only a couple of weeks ago I was hearing that the upper classes divide us into pedigrees and here she was, not in the least upper class, doing it with divers.

'The tekkies, that's your worker dog, a sort of Springer spaniel or even a Doberman. They have no fear and they're quite scary and very focused. They like deep, dark water. Then there's the recreational UK divers. Labradors, all of them. Absurdly loyal and you'd trust your life with them. They're your friends.' She hesitated again and whispered, 'But you wouldn't want to go out with them.' As she spoke she pointed out men around us. 'Then there is the poodle family. Your gadget men. They have every toy going and usually more than one just in case. Always dive with a poodle, because if you've forgotten something, he's bound to have a spare. I went diving with a poodle in Cornwall and he brought his daughter's drysuit – which none of us could possibly have fitted into in a million years – but he brought it just in case. That's your gadget poodle man all over.'

Oh goodness, it's Simon Baron-Cohen's systemisers in their diving manifestation – the model-boat men with their tools all over again. The stall beside where we were sitting had gadgets, so she pointed out some of her favourite poodles. Is it sexist to talk like this? Or diverist? I don't know any more.

'They're not very lean and lithe, are they? Not very fishlike.'

'No. Stout with a big belly. The "nine months pregnant" look.'

'Why's that? Surely they get exercise diving?'

'A little, but they are big beer drinkers and they like their bacon sandwiches. It's a lower middle- and working-class sport. I've never seen an upper-class man in diving.'

Now even hobbies can be sorted by class?

'But, I don't understand, all those expensive holidays?'

'Oh no. That's warm-water diving you are thinking of. All the men you can see here are UK divers. Cold-water divers. You're looking for warm-water divers. You're in the wrong place. This lot are quite different. Warm-water divers are OK. For this lot it's an obsession. They dive all through the year.' So it looks as though I'm here to learn about strange male behaviour again.

'So these men all dive in the UK? On the coast?'

'Not necessarily. There is a place called Stoney Cove in Leicestershire, the mecca of UK inshore diving. If you go to this lake on a Sunday you can watch the water level rise as three thousand people, ninety per cent overweight men, disappear into the water. It's basically a big muddy pond.' Model boats without the wellies.

'But if you have a genuine interest in cold-water diving at least it must be a good place to meet men?' I struggled to be positive on our behalf.

'Not really. They wouldn't notice a woman unless she looked like a Page Three model and wore a short skirt. The women there have no make-up and are talking about peeing in wetsuits.'

'Warms you up, presumably?'

'Yes. It's frowned on, but it fills your day and I enjoyed it on a freezing March dive. But look – no sane woman would want to go out with a UK diver. They dive every weekend.'

'All through the winter?' Good grief. What's this, low systemising and low empathy too?

'Yes. The divorce rate in the UK diving community is very high. Apart from the fact that some of the male instructors are notorious womanisers who use their position to be more attractive to new open-water students, even if they don't do that, the wives get fed up with it. What women wants to spend her weekends in a muddy pond?'

'Do you dive in it?'

'Yes. But I'm an instructor. I get paid to dive in it.'

'Can you see anything?'

'Not by the time three thousand people have kicked up the silt. But warm-water diving is different. The Red Sea is a totally different environment.'

'So is that one a good one to meet men in?'

'Definitely. And a better breed of male, firmer bodies and all bronzed. Except they all live on the other side of the country.'

'You mean the south of England?'

'I'm afraid it's an example of the north–south divide. Southerners, warm-water divers mostly, are less hardcore – some would say wussy, of course.'

'So can you tell the difference between the UK and the holiday divers as they go by?'

'See those T-shirts?'

One said 'Fuck Nemo, Find Me'. And the other 'Dive naked, things look bigger underwater'.

'Yes, I see them.'

'Terrible T-shirts, shaven head, overweight, big boots and buying gadgets. Classic UK diver.'

Oh dear. So we are avoiding this area of the sport, then. I really would like to have been bringing you some good news about one sort of Englishman at this point in the narrative. But there's more.

2. THE SUBLIME TO THE RIDICULOUS

PATRICK MUSIMU AND NO TEXT

There were a number of talks and seminars going on at the Dive Show, so I thought maybe I should visit some. The main one was a lecture by Nigel Marven, who has fronted several TV shows about diving, none of which I'd seen. He told us that he only got the job in the first place because he was working as a researcher on a David Attenborough series and just happened to be in the right place at the right time. One day someone said to him, 'You're quite funny and go close to animals, why don't you present a series for us?'

He was witness to the fact that sometimes you can be very lucky. In my humble opinion, he certainly wasn't auditioned based on his speaking skills. How can you present a lecture on a monotone with no punctuation? 'And here I am meeting Gerald Durrell it really was a fabulous time and may I have the next slide please and I had to bring the owls and this is where I learned to dive and may I have the next slide please . . .'

I was so bored I actually had to get up and sneak out of the back. I snuck off to see if I could find the organiser's office to ask a little about the warm-water-diving world. I walked in and introduced myself to a wonderful smiley lady called Liz. I told her about my T-shirt filled morning.

'Ah yes, well, the warm-water-diving scene is different. As it happens I have a very large number of women friends who have met husbands and lovers on diving courses and I think there are good reasons for that. I met this man at my diving college who was doing the course at the same time, we kept in touch after the course and we're married now.'

'You're a good ad for warm-water diving, then. You went out on your own, did you?'

'Yes. I wasn't single actually, I was living with someone, just kinda bored. We'd been together seven years and I'd only ever been on holiday with him. It was my first trip abroad on my own. I guess it was the classic seven-year syndrome.'

'So you were still with the first one and you lined up the second before you left the first?'

''Fraid so. I didn't plan it like that. I just went diving. Funnily enough, you see it quite a lot in diving both ways around. It often happens when one person in a relationship is far more adventurous than the other. That's why I think it's common in diving for good reasons. The adventurous one decides to go off and do something new and exciting. When they go diving they meet other people who are prepared to go off and do adventurous things.'

'Lots of people who are "doing something different"?' Hoorah.

'It's easy to make friends because there are about eight people on a course and you are sharing the experience of learning. I went on my own and he was on his own. Diving is a good sport for equality because it's not to do with strength, so men aren't necessarily better at it than women are.'

'I wouldn't be able to kill myself on the first day then, or break my arm?'

'The whole training is about safety.'

'Are you on commission?'

'Who for? There are hundreds of different schools and hundreds of different places to dive. I'm not being paid to say this. I just think it's a great sport.'

Hooray. So maybe this could work for us . . . but be sure it's warm-water diving.

Meanwhile, back in the exhibition centre, there seemed to be something two dimensional, rather, kind of, well, systemising about it all. Admittedly a weekend about diving into another element, which lacked the said element, was going to be a rather limited experience. But it wasn't just that we weren't diving – there seemed to be a purely pragmatic approach to life all around me. After so much spiritual work over the years, or even after a bog-standard 'Mind, Body, Spirit' exhibition, it felt as if everything had moved from three dimensions to two. With no sea, it seemed to lack any connection to any kind of spirituality in any form. I felt as though a whole part of me was not required to be present. Maybe it was my 'drive to identify somebody else's thoughts and feelings and to respond with an appropriate emotion', as Professor Simon would say. There was nothing here to really engage me . . . except gadgets. I could see why there were so few women here.

But then I walked into a talk by Patrick Musimu, sat down to listen, and began to smile. Here was the right talk in the wrong place.

Patrick Musimu is, in one sense, interested in systems. But when one of those is your own body, it all becomes a lot more interesting. He is the world-record holder, four times over, of the sport known as freediving. In this sport you breathe in and go down under the water with no breathing apparatus and win based on how deep you go. It's not just a question of how long you can hold your breath (seven minutes, twenty-one seconds in Patrick's case), but the effect of the water pressure on your body, which increases with depth. If you get it wrong you come up dead. Patrick held the world record, which was 117 metres, but then realised that he was not competing to win. He was exploring his own metal and physical boundaries which were imposed only by his own belief system and by what others tried to tell him that the limits of the human body are. Now, our belief systems and how they limit us or serve us is a fascinating area. Anyway, he grew tired of all the paraphernalia of international competition.

'Federations are one of the systems that chain us and limit us. They guide our thoughts like the news fills us with propaganda and we end up believing it. They impose limits on our thinking. I wanted to show that we can live outside the systems. That we have choice.'

So Patrick announced that he would dive to a depth of two hundred metres . . . but he would do it his way. The diving world laughed, they knew that what he had announced was impossible. But Patrick was on a different level. He was reprogramming his brain.

'The concept of breathing as a means to exist is now foreign to me,' he announced to a room full of sportsmen who were listening for diving tips.

'I'm overwhelmed with joy when I realise I'm alone,' he said and divers looked at each other, wondering what he was talking about and what relevance this had to freediving. Then he showed us an independent video of the dive he'd made where he'd proved that we define our own limits. At the start of the video he walked out to the boat with his wife, their small baby, a couple of technical people to help with the dive and an underwater cameraman who was kitted up with tanks. No tanks for Patrick.

We saw him lower himself into the water and the audience fell silent as the soundtrack to the dive started. It was a sung prayer that began, 'My sins are like mountains and my good deeds are few,' and he kept on going down and down, 'I turn to you with my heart full of shame,' and we watched as he went down, 'My heart is full of tears.' It made me want to pray myself, even though I could see that he had come up alive. 'Bestow your goodness and mercy upon me . . .' The music went on, the singing went on and still he was going down. In the film during the descent, he tapped his fingers against a kind of metal line, apparently to let himself know that he was still conscious. 'Send your mercy and blessings on the prophet and upon those who follow him.' And still he went down. Eventually he made a movement to indicate that he was ready to go up. When he reached the surface the equipment showed that he had dived down to 209.6 metres. Patrick comes from Zaire and, six years before, had never been in the sea nor known that it tasted salty.

He took questions from the audience of sportsmen.

'But didn't it frustrate you that your depth wasn't recognised by the International Diving Federation?'

'Everyone knows that I did it,' he stated simply, 'what difference does it make whether it's official or not? Training for this I've discovered and entered a new dimension. I'm not interested in competition – it has no personal value. I am competing with myself.'

'Is it true that you put water in your lungs when you dive?'

'No, I store it in my sinus and middle ears.'

'How is this possible?'

'You spend nine months in the womb in water. You have to teach your body that you don't need air.'

'When you are down there, don't you want to take a breath?'

'No.'

'Doesn't it bother you that there was so little international coverage because the dive wasn't official?'

'When you touch heaven, you don't really want to have to give a soundbite.'

It was so funny. He wanted to discuss spiritual things and they were all asking about competitive success.

I knew nothing about diving, but I was interested in what he had learned. I asked my question, 'So, do you leave your body when you are down there? Is it true, in your experience that, as the monks teach, the mind and the body can separate?'

The audience looked round. I morphed into a loopy New Age lunatic with long skirts and sandals. Patrick just answered my question.

'Yes. Other people, the monks, reach these levels of understanding with nothing. I need the water to help me.'

Then he went back to answering technical questions about the dive. I smiled and wondered why he was there. Someone asked about his training. Many people had come to him and asked for help, but when they found that he wanted to train them without going near water they lost interest.

'What are your plans for the future?'

'I plan to start breathing.'

I once met a man who had meditated every day for an hour for twenty years. Attempting to seize the opportunity for some instant enlightenment I asked him, 'What have you learned?' He smiled at me and said, 'Use a cushion.'

I'm not saying that I'm the only one who could understand Patrick ... but he looked and sounded as though he should have been at a talk with Anthony Robbins or Deepak Chopra and I'm more used to those ways of thinking, even if I have no knowledge of his sport. One young male diver in a bright orange and green T-shirt asked,

'How do you train to hold your breath for seven minutes and twenty-one seconds?'

Patrick replied, 'How do you get yourself in the right state of mind to live the best that you possibly can for the majority of the time?'

Fantastic answer. Very Californian. Only, as it turned out, Patrick had never heard of any of these teachings; he had learned them himself through his own experience and passion for life and the human body. I acquired a press pass so that I could sneak into the organiser's lounge. I was very interested in meeting this extraordinary example of the male species.

I found Patrick sitting in a corner, looking, once again, as if he was in the wrong place. I sat down next to him.

'Do you have the feeling, Mr Musimu, that you are giving the right talk to the wrong audience?'

He looked at my eyes carefully. 'You are the person who asked about the separation of mind and body?'

'Guilty.'

'Yes. There is always a larger group that only want to know the technique and a smaller group that understand some of the things that I'm trying to say.'

'You are giving a human-potential talk. Anthony Robbins and Deepak Chopra would like to meet you.'

'Who are these people?'

There are so many different worlds on our planet.

'They are two of the best-known teachers of human potential in the world. They teach what you teach. Only they teach it as a concept. You practise it. They say "limits are only in our mind" – you demonstrate it. What are you speaking here for?'

'What do you think?'

'I've really no idea.'

'Money. I can't afford to accept speaking engagements free of charge unless it's for humanitarian or scientific reasons.'

I laughed. 'You're not serious. You have done what was believed to be impossible, defied human and medical beliefs, and you are here because you need the money?'

'Ask me what I'm doing tomorrow.'

'What are you doing tomorrow?'

'Sitting at a desk.'

'You are writing about all this? That's fantastic.'

'No – I'm doing telesales.'

I laughed.

'I'm writing, too, but I don't know how to go about being published.'

'I'm a writer, Patrick.'

So we sat there while he talked to me about the human body and how you have to get the permission of your body if you want to push it to extremes and you have to know and understand how it works. Thinking I could do a favour for his wife, I casually suggested that he may like to extend his understanding of the human body in the direction of tantric sexuality.

'Did you know that it's supposed to be possible to learn to make the orgasm implosive instead of explosive so that you can surf it like a wave and maintain it for as long as you choose? This would seem like a good area that you and your wife may enjoy exploring together.' I've never had the chance to explore this myself. Oh Harry!

A faraway look came over Patrick too. Followed by a grin. I hope I planted a seed there. Then he quizzed me about writing and I explained my understanding of the writing process and the world of international publishing and I was so proud and so happy that I possibly knew something that could in some way be of assistance to this extra ordinary man. And that was a deliberate gap between extra and ordinary. For once it is even possible to say unique without exaggeration.

I was on the biggest high just from meeting him. Why couldn't I have met a thousand men like this – or a million? One for every woman who wanted one. But sometimes it's good to know that one man this inspiring and interesting lives and walks on the planet. He's what most people would call crazy, of course . . . but I can relate to that.

I was hovering around about a foot off the ground with joy . . . I lost my head. And did something stupid that I hadn't done for months. Without thinking I took one of the crazy risks I take sometimes, just hoping he'd understand. I sent a text to Harry. I'd been turned into a little kid, all excited and wanting to tell my best friend about meeting Patrick. But then nothing happened and my mood went plummeting down like a replay of the film I'd just seen. Except when I got to the bottom, instead of swimming blithely back to the surface I sat on the rocks and made up stories about why he wasn't replying. Do men do this too, or is it only women that are this absurd?

The process of making up stories is an interesting one and, in theory, I'm 'trained' not to do it. What happens is that a real event occurs, and instead of just sticking with the known event, i.e., no reply . . . the mind makes up ridiculous stories, fretting all the while. 'Harry hasn't replied . . . that's it. He never wants to hear from me again or speak with me again.' Or, 'Harry hasn't replied, he must be angry with me.' Please note that it is not necessary to have any reason or logical basis for a supposition of anger at this point in the story-making. 'Harry hasn't replied . . . he must have barred calls from my number.' 'Harry hasn't replied, he must be preparing a text that says "please don't text me any more" and can't think of what words to use.' Then gradually, the longer I looked, pathetic and crestfallen, at my phone (there was a time when the replies were instant) the more elaborate the stories became. 'Harry has lent his mobile to his wife and she has picked up the text. I have met Patrick and then used the experience to make another woman unhappy. She is probably crying and shouting at him even as I sit here.' My head sank lower and lower in shame. I'd just wanted to hear his voice, to hear his laugh – what kind of a fool am I?

I sat and looked at my phone and drank tea. One of the organisers came up to me, all excited, 'I can't believe that you got to talk to Patrick for all that time. Isn't he the most fit man in the world?'

'What?'

'He's a sex god. That muscle tone . . . didn't you notice how wonderful his body is?'

'No. I wasn't thinking of him like that. He's married. I don't look at married men like . . .' Sigh. Oh dear. Should I say – most of the time I don't notice married men? Apart from when I did? 'What I mean is, I wasn't thinking of him in a romantic sense at all. He's married and I was just enjoying talking to him as one person to another. He's good looking I suppose, yes.' In a non-Harry kind of way.

' "Good looking I suppose!" Isabel, you have just been sitting for about an hour with the most desirable pick-up in the diving world and you are telling me that you didn't notice him? That's like saying that you didn't notice that George Clooney was good looking. Or Brad Pitt. Only, in the diving world, Patrick is a lot more exciting than either of those. What did you talk about?'

'Spiritual things, mainly. And I suppose I did mention tantric sex . . . but I was thinking of his wife. I was enjoying the possibility of passing on an idea about some physical research that they could do together.'

'You are either a saint or a madwoman,' she said and flounced off, exasperated with rage and envy. I wrote her words down.

We know the answer to her though, don't we? I skipped saint and have put a lot of time into exploration of 'madwoman'. I take risks for love. I watched her go, looked down at the photo I'd been given of Patrick and me and then looked at my phone. No text from Harry.

That night there was an exhibitors' party that the friendly Liz had invited me to. I could just about lever my eyes from my phone for long enough to look up and see smiling faces and decide that maybe it was a good idea. 'We'll probably be the only women there,' she said. This was true, but the room was full, literally I fear, with about five hundred overweight men in T-shirts. Liz took one look and left. I decided I'd stay for a drink. There were three men in suits who looked out of place, so I sat down with them. They were from Holland, talking to each other in Dutch; they seemed pleasant enough and they were bi-lingual, as all educated Dutch are. I chatted with one of them, the subject inevitably turning to the men that we were both looking at.

'Something happens to men in the diving world before, in the middle of, or after a divorce. As their lives start to fall apart they decide to become diving instructors.' He looked at them rather disdainfully. 'It's a way for them of feeling free. So they quit their desk jobs and go full time. I'd be willing to bet that most of the men in this room are in the middle of a divorce. It's the same all over the world.'

'At least they are living life.' I remembered the thoughts of my philosophising builder friend again. 'At least they aren't bumbling along in dead marriages and watching TV.'

'Ah. So that's why my marriage is healthy – because we don't watch TV?'

'Yes. I'd say so. If you're not watching TV you must be doing something more interesting. Do you have children?'

'I have one of four and coming in March, another son.'

'You see? That's because you weren't watching TV.'

'That man – he is just after a divorce.'

'What's wrong with divorce anyway?'

'People don't fight for their marriages any more.'

'Oh, I think they do.' I have friends that work really hard at their marriages. 'No one wants a marriage to end in divorce. I think it's just that people don't know how to be happy and they think it's because of who they are married to.'

We sat looking at the room full of shaven men drinking massive amounts of beer and becoming more like each other. I asked him, 'So you wouldn't recommend men in the diving world, then?'

'Diving is good if you meet the other people on the diving courses, but you must never date the instructors.'

'Why's that?'

'Each course lasts between four and six weeks and then it's a new group of students so you know, in advance, how long the relationship will last.'

I laughed.

'But it's true,' he said vehemently. 'In our schools . . .' (I didn't like to enquire too closely what organisation he was with) 'to be accepted as a course director we have a number of requirements.'

'Yes?'

'One: you need to be divorced. Or at least in the middle of a divorce, but we prefer the divorce to be complete. Two:

we require the applicant to have a minimum of four children by at least two wives.'

'Or girlfriends?'

'No, no, wives. Three: he should have absolutely no money. We only accept bouncing credit cards.'

'Four,' the suit next to him interjected, 'the brains must be at least one metre below the chin.' I looked blank for a second. 'Oh, I see, a metre.'

'About three feet. He has to be very active in that area.'

'And,' said the second, 'as a daily discipline we require him to stand in front of the mirror every day jerking himself off.'

God – what is this? A kind of man-hatred again?

'I'm sorry,' I said. I'd stopped smiling. I didn't understand his aggression. These men in T-shirts looked harmless enough to me. He misunderstood me and explained.

'They don't see, "I'm overweight and I have no thoughts and no interests" – they see "Look, I'm good – it's still working." You know the old joke. For a little sausage you have to buy the entire pig.'

Isn't it odd how men speak about other men? I tried to lighten the atmosphere a little. 'So, gentlemen, you don't respect the men that work in this industry much, then?'

'It's our choice to have them as customers.'

'But hold on a minute . . .' Now I'm defending divers from men in their own industry?

I tried to be a little balanced. 'Let's say there is a man whose wife dies of breast cancer'' (this will be many of us girls, after all) 'and the man has given up his desk job because he has realised, through his loss, the futility of a life making money. He has become an instructor because he loves diving all over the world and maybe he even has a commitment to marine conservation, and he wants to share his passion with others. He doesn't shag all the female students because he has a sense of responsibility and also he wants a serious long-term relationship, not just a casual shag. He's ready for that and he respects and likes women. He's even able to love them. Now where is he?'

They looked at each other.

'He's not here.'

An elderly gentleman walked over. 'This is my father,' said one of the Dutchmen. 'We are going for dinner now. Would you like to join us?' I glanced at my phone. Nothing. 'Sure, why not?' Maybe I could find out why they hate men so much.

We drove to a restaurant and I include this bit in the story just so you know how completely stupid I can be. The old man was funny and very charming. We ordered dinner and started to chat. Quite soon it transpired that we didn't agree on anything at all. Not only did they not like divers or men in general, but they didn't seem to like anyone much. They kept a home with large walls and dogs trained to kill anyone that came over the wall.

I was horrified and tried to tell them why. 'If I lived in your town and I had a son who had developed an addiction to heroin and, in his desperation, he was trying to steal your video recorder, you'd have him killed, would you?'

'Of course – if he comes on to my land.'

'You agree with capital punishment, then?'

'Yes. Certainly.'

Now here is an interesting situation. Three men are buying you dinner. All seem relatively civilised and they're being pleasant. But gradually, as the evening wears on, you realise that you are sitting at dinner with three raving fascists.

'If they are going to keep letting these coloured people into Europe, what can we do?'

'I'm sorry?'

It was only then that I realised something odd about the diving world. It had no black or Asian people at all. Now I'm not meaning for a moment that there are more than three racists in the whole diving world. I suspect that the reason that there are zero black and Asian men along is that they can all think of better things to do with their weekends than diving into muddy ponds. But the result of this is that the three 'gentlemen' that I was sitting at dinner with didn't have to encounter anyone who might shift them from their bigoted views.

'It's the same all over Europe. It's all these immigrants. That's why we train our dogs to kill.'

So at what point do you get up from the table? Was I to go on sitting there nodding and smiling?

'Gentlemen, I do not believe that the colour of someone's skin makes them any more or less likely to steal your possessions. And I don't believe that there is any situation in which a man deserves to die because he is misguided enough to want to commit theft. Are there not a million examples of young men who have got into trouble and then later gone on to benefit their fellow human beings despite having come from troubled childhoods?'

'What would you do if they broke into your home?'

'I would hope that any drugs that they may have taken did not so separate them from their own humanity that they would hurt me. But as to my possessions? What are objects? Let them take them. I wouldn't want them killed.'

'I would be delighted if the dogs killed a man who had entered my land. If he comes over my wall, I kill him.'

'What about compassion?'

'You give these people what they deserve. They shouldn't be in our country anyway. They are not like us.'

They were talking at me, not to me. 'There is evil in the world. People are evil.'

Would you have left by now? Or would you still have been sitting there with society's requirement to be polite still dictating your actions? I lived with a man once and I always felt that if someone had said, during a dinner, 'I think this or that group of people should all be shot,' he would have said, 'Could you pass the salt?' I started to debate inside my head. Isabel, do not sit at table with these people, even if they are buying your dinner. Sometimes you have to make a stand. Literally. I got up out of my seat.

'I'm sorry, gentlemen. You have been most kind to me personally, but I can not sit at table with you. I disagree with you profoundly, I find your lack of humanity distressing and your views abhorrent.'

I put a £20 note on the table and walked away. Then I felt guilty and turned back. I felt for a moment that I'd been very rude. As bad as they were. Surely I should be civil? So I shook their hands.

'Thank you. For bringing me here and for your kindness to me. I hope the conference goes well for you.' I shook the hand of the old man I'd previously considered charming. I felt sure he would be the worst of them.

The restaurant called a taxi and as I waited I examined my actions. Then I wondered why I had shaken their hands. I find I'm sitting at table with racist fascists and I still shake their hands? 'Well thank you, Herr Hitler, it's been a lovely dinner.' What was I thinking of? Then I thought some more. They had been so vindictively unpleasant about the divers earlier and I'd got into a car with three of them. They could have driven me anywhere. Done anything with me that they wanted. And there were three of them and one of me. Why am I so trusting of the universe? I mean, I usually reap what I sow and my trust is usually honoured, but I'd only have to be this stupid once. I thought I could judge character, but I'd been very wrong about these three men. I'd been very stupid. I was vulnerable and anything at all could have happened to me.

I stepped outside, away from their gaze. There were some young men hanging around outside. I smiled at them. They were so young. On the lookout for girls. One was staring at me as if he wanted to say something but didn't know what to say. Spotty, self-conscious, at least he stopped me thinking about what could have happened to me earlier. I smiled at him. 'Are Brummies friendly?' I asked. 'I'm from London, you see.'

'Yeh,' he said. 'With the ladies.'

'What do you mean?

'It's the blokes. That's where all the violence comes from.'

'Why are they violent?'

'They are jealous of each other.'

'What are they jealous of?'

'Money, drugs, girls, cars, valuables, anything. If they are jealous they take things.'

'With violence?'

'Violence or being a Judas.'

'What's that?'

'Pretending to be someone's friend and then stabbing them in the back when you need them most. There's lots of immigrants round here see. Foreigners. We can't get college or jobs or nothing coz of them.'

'How old are you?'

'Seventeen.'

'Can I ask you a weird question?'

'Go on, then.'

'What do you think being a man is?'

There was a long pause while he thought about it. Then he said, 'Dunno, really. Not having to depend on anyone else.'

'What do you think being human is?'

'That's just what we are, innit?'

'Yes. You and me. And the immigrants. And the foreigners. We're all just human.'

The taxi arrived. A kind and gentle Asian cabbie with a strong Brummie accent. I tell him about my evening. About the men who hate anyone not white, about the boys who say the same. 'There's a lot of that round there. That was a bad area you were in. Lots of drugs. There are better areas.'

We got to the hotel I'd booked into for a night. I paid him and then handed him an extra £5 tip. I just wanted to be nice to someone. To let the world know that kindness was still about.

'Buy yourself a drink,' I said.

'I can't. I'm fasting.'

'You're fasting?'

'It's Ramadan.'

'Of course it is. Allah be praised.' Thank God, so to speak, for Allah.

I checked into my hotel room. Took out my phone. Sat on my bed and cried. All I really wanted was a text from Harry.

3. MEETING ANGELS

THE SCUBA TRUST KICKS ASS

The following morning I went to Patrick's talk all over again. At this point in the project it was good just to be in the presence of a man who inspired me. I heard him say his great sentence again: 'How do you get yourself in the right state of mind to live the best that you possibly can for the majority of the time?' and I felt better just listening to him.

I came out and went in search of coffee, knowing rationally of course that this is a substance that can help me live the best I possibly can, and then something happened to me that happens very rarely and, outside London, has never happened before. A woman approached me, smiling. She was probably in her early thirties, ginger hair, a round face and a big smile. She blushed and said, 'Excuse me for speaking to you and I'm probably about to make a fool of myself but er, are you Isabel Losada?'

The fact that I had been given a press badge that said 'Isabel Losada' had probably been a bit of a giveaway.

'Sort of,' I said. 'Some version of her anyway.'

'Oh, I love your books. I didn't know you were into diving.' She sat down with her drink.

'I'm not.'

'But you're working here?'

'In a sense, yes.'

'So are you going to go diving?'

Somehow I'd managed to avoid thinking about this. 'I, er, I don't know. I'm a bit afraid of things at the moment, I just broke my wrist you see and I, er.'

She laughed. 'Hold on a minute – I've read your books and I learned about going outside the comfort zone from you. I practise it all the time. You've helped me do things I never would have done. Really. I mean, you talk about it all the time in your books.'

'Er, thank you. Er, yes I know I do. I, er, it's just that, I, er.' I could hardly say, I haven't had a text from Harry.

'Are you afraid to go diving?'

'Right now . . . I'm sorry, I'm really pleased to meet you and I'm really glad that you've enjoyed my books. What's your name?'

'Sarah.'

'The truth is, Sarah, that I've had a weird year and I'm finding that I'm scared of things for the first time in my life. I'm feeling a pull towards embroidery, sewing, things that involve minimum physical danger. Things where no parts of me, internally or externally, can get broken.'

'Diving's not that dangerous. I mean, it can be, but mainly at advanced levels. You should try it, really.'

I knew what was wrong with me really. Irrationally I wanted to go diving with Harry. Who probably wouldn't want to go anyway. Even if he answered my texts. Time I pulled myself together. Did what Patrick said in his talk. Remembered who I'm supposed to be. Practised what I preach. All that. I ordered another coffee.

'Diving isn't dangerous then, Sarah?'

'I remember I once heard that it is as dangerous as ten-pin bowling.'

'Are there many fatalities in bowling?'

'I think it's statistically more dangerous to stay at home.'

261

'OK, Sarah. You're right, of course. And I do have another subject that I'm exploring alongside the diving. So if I trained and did some warm-water diving, what would I need to do?'

'Go and see them at the British Sub-Aqua Club. They'll sort you out. Gosh, I'm so glad I met you. I'll tell my friend who bought me your book.'

I smiled gratefully. 'Thank you. I'm glad I met you, too. Cod moves in mysterious ways.'

'What?'

'I think I needed a push, that's all.'

How weird. I looked round, but she was gone. Maybe sometimes angels really do appear to move us along in the right direction. It seemed more plausible than me meeting a reader of my books at a diving exhibition in Birmingham.

The fact is that there was/is a part of me that doesn't want to go diving. It's an irrational fear rather like the fear that I had before I jumped out of an aeroplane. A fear based on an imaginary experience that turned out to be nothing like the actual experience of skydiving. And the irony is that when I went to learn to ride a Harley I wasn't scared at all, when perhaps a little more fear would have served me.

I passed a lady in a wheelchair who'd been sitting in the same place all day collecting for some charity. I doubled back and put some money in her tin.

'What are you collecting for?'

'The Scuba Trust. It teaches people like me with disabilities to dive.'

'Really? May I ask what your disability is?'

'To learn to dive my main disability was that I was petrified of water. But apart from that I have severe rheumatoid arthritis and I also suffer from cellutius. On land my feet swell up, as you see.'

She showed me her horribly swollen feet, all red and sore.

'I can't walk on land. But in the water I can wriggle my ankles. So with fins I can move quite well.'

'Goodness. Well, that's inspiring. Rather takes away any excuses I may have thought I had about learning. Or anyone else that I might know. Thank God I don't have a fear of water . . . how did you get over that?'

'Very slowly. But the worst problem was finding a doctor to give me medical permission to dive. You have to have medical certification so they can teach you and the first doctor I went to – he took one look at me and said, "Oh no, you're far too disabled." So I thought about it and just decided to go to some different doctors. The third one said yes. The Scuba Trust is very good. I have two helpers when I'm training and an instructor. I'm training for my IAHD certificate, that's the International Association of Handicapped Divers.'

'You are seriously inspiring. So what other disabilities do your fellow students have?'

'There is a sixteen-year-old diabetic and the oldest must be sixty. That's Alan. He's wheelchair bound. He has the shakes and his speech is slurred. It should be a sad story, he was a builder and he fell off a roof, but he's determined to get the qualification. And one girl was in a car accident and has had half her brain taken away . . .'

There we could all be. 'Half her brain and she's still alive?'

'Half her body doesn't work very well. But she's still very much alive and she'll get her certificate.'

'I keep meeting angels here today.'

She held out her hand. 'My name's Doreen, what's yours?'

'Isabel.'

'Pleased to meet you, Isabel. So, are you a diver?'

'Not yet, Doreen, but I think I'm going to have to be now that I've met you. I mean, I don't have an excuse, do I? No one does.'

'I learn once a month in a pool in Dorking and then my husband and I have just been out to the Dahab in the Red Sea. I've only been diving a year, but it was amazing for me the first time they took me in the water.'

'How did they do that if you can't walk?'

'They wheeled me into the sea in my wheelchair and kitted me up in the water. It was really wonderful. We went out to the Dahab. I've been out twice now with my husband. I was the first handicapped diver the instructor had taken out and he was so pleased with himself. When I first got in the water my head was jigging around so much he pulled me out again, he thought there was something wrong with me, but I was just so excited looking at everything I wanted to turn my head in every direction at once. I even saw a scorpionfish. You have to try it.'

'Thank you, Doreen.'

Two steps on from her was the stall of the British Sub-Aqua Club. I walked up and found a smiling female face. It was Mary Tetley, the operations manager.

'Hello. Can I help you?'

'Yes. I wonder if you can tell me a little about the world of warm-water diving?'

4. HOW TO ALIENATE YOUR READER

WRITING BY THE RED SEA

And that is how, for once, today, I am sitting by a pool, looking out over the Red Sea and writing to you. As author experiences go, I can recommend it. Why it has taken me about five years to work out that I don't have to spend January in rainy, freezing Battersea, I don't know. Under the circumstances, I think it's very generous of you to still be reading. This is about different ways to meet men and it sure beats the internet. Please try not to hate me, because I'm going to share all the secrets.

It's absurdly cheap to get here (flight £80 in January) and I'm being looked after by a little company called Longwood Holidays (www.longwoodholidays.co.uk) and yes, that was a deliberate plug because they've been lovely and the local rep who works for them has even bothered to learn Arabic, so she has my admiration. In high season it may not be quite this relaxed: the weather is perfect but not too hot and somehow they have just the right number of guests at the hotel . . . which is hardly any.

You need to know all this because I'm about to recommend this trip to you, not for the Hotel Intercontinental, nor for the town – if you want to see Egypt then I wouldn't recommend Hurghada, which has been created for the tourist industry rather than for the locals – but because this is the best and safest place in the world to come and learn to dive. When I walked up to Mary Tetley at the British Sub-Aqua Club and told her about my adventure with Harley-Davidsons, I asked her if she could send me to a really safe school. She chose the Divers' Lodge (online at www.divers-lodge.com) – I got in touch with them and here I am, sitting by a pool. It's an odd time to be writing to you, for I'm neither at the beginning of the story nor at the end. I'm in the middle of my week, the middle of my course, and you are a great reassurance to me as – the miracle of time being what it is – I can be sure that as you are reading this, I have finished my course, so to speak, and as no one would be likely to publish posthumously, it seems likely that I've survived. Furthermore, I have good news to send into the very same future. To come here and not meet any men would be impossible.

The only woman I've seen all week is Jane, the amazingly lovely girl who works at Divers' Lodge. When I asked Jane if there was anything that I could bring her from London, she asked for a packet of PG Tips and a copy of *Hello* magazine. She has an office surrounded by the Red Sea. Literally. Their little building is on the end of a pier. They have one classroom, three tiny offices and a store for wetsuits. They also have a wicker hut in which the wetsuits are hung up to dry. (As it happens, this doesn't turn them into drysuits – only into dry wetsuits.)

Goodness, the sun has moved and is now shining on me. In order to continue writing I'm going to have to move one foot to the next chair. Have to order coffee to assist me. OK.

The little straw hut is far too small and doesn't have nearly enough space to hang all the soggy suits, even in January. The little centre has no toilets and it could all do with a coat of paint ... it doesn't look too promising. It's one of the oldest and best diving schools in the whole of the Red Sea.

When you go into town, ignore the tourist shops. Why anyone would want to bring home a miniature pyramid or a plate with a picture of Cleopatra on is a mystery to me. Aren't our homes cluttered enough? But what Hurghada does have is no less than three recompression chambers. In the unlikely event of there being any kind of diving accident the emergency services would get you into a chamber faster than you could say 'nitrogen bubble'. This is another reason this is the place to come.

But then you have to meet Wessam. Even if I never go into the sea again, it would have been worth coming out here for the experience of meeting this wonderful, warm, funny and overweight Egyptian man. Just imagine any carpet seller in the world and you've got him. This centre teaches the highly respected technical diving courses that have raised levels of awareness about the number of international fatalities in this more extreme form of diving. It's all happening from this modest little pier. It even turns out that divers from this centre were the safety team when Patrick Musimu made his extraordinary freedive.

So I feel in very safe hands when I turn up for my first day, all of which was to be spent in the classroom. Of course my group isn't typical. When smiley Lizzie from the exhibition centre had taken her course it was with twelve English male holidaymakers in peak season. I can report that my group is also all male, except they are all locals. Of the six men, three are called Mohammed, and they are all impressive, as the course is in English. If I pass the course I can dive anywhere in the world.

The day is full of wondrous surprises – the 'oxygen' tanks don't contain oxygen. Apparently if you went down with a tank of pure oxygen it would poison you.

'Does anyone know what's in the tanks?' asks Wessam.

Your narrator, ever seeking to demonstrate her brilliance in a room full of men, raises her hand.

'Air?' Aren't you glad you bought this book now? Aren't you just impressed with the knowledge and brilliance of your narrator?

I think Wessam was hoping for a more technical answer but he smiles obligingly and says, 'Yes, that's right and what is the air made up with?'

Apparently what we breathe is 21 per cent oxygen and 79 per cent nitrogen with other odds and ends drifting in and out in trace amounts. Or in the case of carbon monoxide in our cities, not-so-trace amounts.

And here is another fact. I have to tell you this because it's just so wonderful. Did you know that, because the water reflects the light, if you dive down below five metres you don't see any more red, below ten metres and you can't see orange, fifteen and you can't see yellow, below twenty metres green disappears, then at twenty-five blue goes, until eventually below thirty metres everything is grey. Unless you take a lamp and then all the colours appear again because they were there all along – you just couldn't see them. So the red fish was still red ... he just looked grey. How weird is that? So if no one takes a light down, is he still a red fish?

It's a bit like the joke that a bitter male told me. If a man stands in the middle of a forest and makes a statement, and there is no woman anywhere within earshot, is he still wrong?

My notes from my first-day theory of diving are all about how much air you have to have to dive at certain depths, but as a newly qualified diver you're not going to dive below twenty metres anyway, you'll always have the required fifty 'bar' of air left and you always dive with a partner or 'buddy'. Here is a sentence of wisdom from Wessam that I rather liked, 'You can't dive together alone.'

By the end of the day I understand most of what I need to know and am looking forward to putting on the silly wetsuits and sitting on the bottom of the hotel pool. That night one of the Mohammeds tells me how I can take the local bus into town and escape from the tourists to chat to you.

Weird new world . . . somehow seem to now be in a place that only has men in it. In the middle of Allah knows where, with just enough information to stand a reasonable chance of seeing my hotel again, but I feel a million times safer and happier than I did in Birmingham.

It's not worth describing the view to you . . . from where I'm sitting looking out it's a wide road with tourist shops. That's it. This town, created for tourists, was once a small, idyllic fishing village, but the original homes have been knocked down to be replaced by a McDonald's, a KFC and the usual collection of quick pizza cafés. Except there are also real cafés like the one I'm sitting in. We are 98 per cent men and they are almost all smoking their hookahs (or 'hubble-bubbles' as they are sometimes wonderfully called). It's not hashish, just flavoured tobacco, so when the smoke wafts towards me it smells of cherries or apples. I'm high, certainly, but it's being 'somewhere else' that does it for me, not the passive smoking of shisha. Wish I'd made more progress with my Arabic . . . the few sentences that I do know: 'peace be with you', 'God willing', 'please', 'thank you' and a few more serve me well. It's more than most of the tourists, I guess. I can even say, 'Thank you, my love,' but I think better of it.

Why am I so happy here, sitting watching people in a place where I don't speak the language? I love it that the men greet each other with warm handshakes and kisses. I love it that all the prissy and self-conscious physical inhibition between men doesn't exist here. I love it that they are engaged in twos or threes or groups in what is evidently genuine conversation. I watch the two men in front of me with an inappropriate level of fascination. They are talking as loving brothers might talk . . . but they are evidently not brothers. What shocks me so much is that this should surprise me. Why is the art and enjoyment of conversation among men so diminished in our culture that it has become a clichéd joke among women?

Even our pubs now almost all have TV sets in ... so instead of sitting on a couch at home and watching sport they go out with other men and watch sport. Or else they often engage in a form of conversation based on meaningless argument – a kind of intellectual tit for tat. Shakespeare had a great phrase that he used to describe bad acting, 'sound and fury, signifying nothing'. More talk than listening – airing of one's own opinions as if they were not already aware of them. Or some just engage in what we could call 'banter', like the endless joke-telling of the guys on the building sites or the strutting one-upmanship that you sometimes find in the upper classes.

But this? Men sitting together all evening, not a TV in sight, enjoying each other's company, looking at times thoughtful, at times sad, at times focused, as their conversation flows quite naturally from business to family to the concerns and developments in each of their lives. Why have I never seen men in England talking like this? Or is it not just England? Is it Britain? Or Europe? Or the West?

The waiters come by and stare at my writing with admiration, just as I would admire their beautiful Egyptian characters. The waiter speaks to me. 'Where are you from?' The same question the world over ... the monks asked me this in Tibet.

'From London.'

'Oh, London? Nice!' and he takes mint tea and shisha to the next table. Another five men arrive, the older men wearing Arab clothes, so elegant, so much more dignified than the ubiquitous Western suits.

Of course I do realise that there is another side to all this male camaraderie. Where are the women? At home cooking, cleaning and looking after the children, I fear. It would be lovely to imagine that they are also involved in passionate conversation and I hope they are ... I fear the truth is probably more mundane. Many of them will be watching TV.

Besides me there is only one other Western women in the café. She is blonde, well dressed in a rather ostentatious way and obviously 'with' one of the local guys. He looks fairly pleased with himself. I guess they'd all like one like her.

We are all watching the dumpy, overweight tourists waddle by. They are shopping ... buying faux Egyptian objects that they couldn't possibly need and most of which are probably made in China.

What happened to me? Why am I so comfortable as a misfit? I guess I've never liked conformity or being some-where that I'm expected to be a certain way. That's one of the joys of being a foreigner somewhere else. You are outside the box. In this café they don't know what to make of me and I like that. Perhaps they imagine that I don't know that this isn't the sort of place that women come to alone. Perhaps they imagine that I'm looking for a man. Ha ha.

'My name's Said,' says the waiter as he wanders by. He looks at me as if he hopes that I'll say, 'You want sex, Said? Or wife? Good English wife?' But I just smile at him and keep scribbling black ink onto white paper. They take turns to stop and gaze at me – wondering if I'm writing about them. I am, of course.

'What do you do?' Then I remember some of my Arabic; I know how to say 'I'm a writer' and the word for book – *khitab* – and feel very pleased with myself. A well-dressed Arab comes up and speaks to me in his perfect English, 'Good evening, you are writing?'

'Yes.'

'Do you live here?'

'No, I just arrived here.'

'Welcome to Egypt. I hope you enjoy your visit.'

'Thank you. Tell me, this substance that everyone is smoking ... is it legal?'

He laughs. Absolutely. It's just tobacco. Mine is apple flavoured. Would you like to try some?'

Why not? 'Yes, I suppose I would.'

He calls the waiter to bring me a new mouthpiece, which is hygienically wrapped. He takes it out of its bag, fits it on the end of the tube and hands me his hubble-bubble. For the first time in the evening I feel like a tourist. Smiling, they watch me. I inhale and listen to the bubbles – so much more fun, no groovy sound effect with cigarettes. Nothing much happens to me. I don't pass out or anything – I just feel as if someone has filled my lungs with apples and nicotine instead of oxygen and nitrogen. I'm not a smoker. Inevitably I lose any cool and cough a lot.

'It's an acquired taste,' he says politely.

'Is it worth acquiring?'

'Definitely not.'

'I'll leave it to you, then. Goodnight. Is there any advice I need for the local bus?'

'Yes. Don't let them charge you more than one Egyptian pound.'

That was the second day – two days ago now – from where, you may recall, I am still sitting writing to you by a pool with another cup of coffee finished and the sun beginning its own descent towards the sea. That morning we put on dry wetsuits and jumped into the pool here. It's a weird feeling sitting on the bottom of the pool, all kitted out with air tanks, watching the bums of stately German ladies in their pool workout, joggling about to Elvis Presley singing 'Hound Dog'.

The trick to this part of the course is simply to remember that you have to breathe through your mouth. It seems that some people have difficulty remembering this. As one of the exercises is to take off your mask and put it on again, it's an insuperable barrier for a small percentage.

But I managed it and I hadn't found a way to break any limbs in the pool, either. We bobbed around, the Moham-meds and I, practising taking the breathing apparatus out of our mouths and putting it in again, all safety exercises to increase confidence should anything at all go wrong underwater. So far so good – we learned hand signals; the thumbs-up sign for OK doesn't mean OK, it means 'I want to go up'. And the above-water sign for 'not OK' means 'going down?' The dancers' 'give them the old razzle dazzle' routine here doesn't mean 'look how talented I am coz I tap dance', it means 'I have a problem'. And the 'om' sign with first finger to thumb, which I'd previously been taught as a hand position for meditation the other way up, here means 'OK'.

So it was lunchtime on day two and I had no broken limbs, there wasn't a woman in sight and I was learning a new skill and getting a suntan. This diving is a good idea.

In the afternoon was our first dive in the ocean. But not an ocean dive – just a dive off the end of the pier to practise all the skills again. I did them all right first time. This is looking promising. If I can do them, you can too. That's for sure.

At the end of the day, when the Mohammeds had dispersed to their various wives, I said to Jane, 'You can't abandon me to eat in the hotel with the elderly German tourists. I mean, I like Germans, but this lot are all very bored. I keep wanting to mention the war and sing numbers from *The Producers* just to liven things up.'

'When I told the team that you were an author, one of our technical divers said that he'd like to meet you. Would you mind having dinner alone with a stranger?'

Mmmm. A couple of questions spring to mind.

'Well, Jane – this may seem like an odd question . . . but is he married?'

'No.'

Still checking.

'In the middle of a divorce or a separation of unclear definition?'

'He's never been married.'

'Is he living with someone who is going to be upset if she hears that we've had dinner?'

'No. He's not even going out with anyone.'

This is a good start. What comes after – once bitten, twice shy?

'And he's interesting?'

'That's him over there with the goatee.'

I looked around and saw a man with the body of a Greek god pulling off a drysuit. He looked as though he could enjoy a different woman's sexual appetite every week for 52 weeks of the year.

'He's a bit of a Don Juan, isn't he?'

'Hisham? No. Not at all. He was in his last relationship for three years and since it ended he hasn't dated.'

'You amaze me.'

Then he walked up and held out his hand.

'Hello.'

'I need help in getting away from the hotel tonight and I hear that you've volunteered for "looking after the guest" service – or maybe Jane volunteered you?'

'Not at all. I heard that you write books and I enjoy reading them . . .'

Was this a set-up? 'Did Jane tell you to say that?'

He looked confused. 'If you'd rather not, I'll understand. Perhaps you'd prefer to eat with Jane?'

I have grown too cynical.

'No, really, I'd be delighted. Thank you.'

And at this point I'm going to go in from the pool and write you the rest of this bit of the story later.

5. AN INTERESTING DINNER DATE

APRICOTS TOMORROW

Good grief. Dinner tonight with a man who looks interesting and who isn't married or living with someone or dating someone who thinks they are in a long-term monogamous relationship and who isn't having sex every week with two 24-year-olds despite the fact that he evidently has the opportunity to.

If, having had dinner with him, he is interesting, and I'm glad I had dinner with him and I want to have a second dinner with him, I will have achieved one of the goals I set myself. I'll have proved to myself and to you that it's possible.

Hisham is a kind of living proof of the theory of reincarnation. He is evidently both a Russian – an intensely bright and earnest young man sat in a library for hours every day with Karl Marx working out how to bring about the revolution, and a Parisian – sitting with Jean-Paul Sartre, creating ontological tomes. He was/is deeply existential. 'Life is absurd,' he would say regularly in the conversation and I kept wanting to giggle. Instead I just said, 'Is it?' and smiled warmly. Maybe it is if you are working as a technical diving instructor and just don't fit the world. The conversation turned to my book and I told him that I was recommending the sport of diving to women.

'I notice that it's mainly men that dive.'

'There are two kinds of women who come here – some come to find men, which they do through diving, and others come for the diving and still find men. We have a guarantee – if you don't find a man, you can have your money back.'

Ah ... but maybe he's referring to a quick shag, and that's not what we're after, is it? We can find that from any pub or club in any town in the UK. Remember we've been especially warned about the instructors. Jane had been painting Hisham a little whiter than my cynical London cuddle buddy would ever believe.

'So how are they – your five-day relationships?'

'I have none.'

'Why not?'

'I have to know a woman. I'm not interested in five days.'

'But you're male. I heard at a lecture in London that for many men a "carbon-based life form" will do for sex. Isn't knowing the woman optional?'

'Not for me.'

'So – you're telling me that you've worked here as an instructor for six years and you haven't slept with a single woman from any of your courses.'

'That's correct. But I was in a relationship and I've not been out of it for so long and I'm possibly the only instructor in the whole of the Red Sea of whom this is true.'

'That's a relief. I was about to have to alter everything I thought I'd learned.'

'A good diving instructor will spot all the potential relationships in a mixed group on day one, put everyone into the appropriate buddy pairs and keep the best-looking female student for himself.'

'This has to be the best profession in the world for men, then?'

'Yes. Except I became too well qualified. I mainly teach instructor level and technical diving.'

I laughed. 'So – all men, then?'

'Exactly. And some of the European women who come here . . . I am surprised that the instructors can remember their names, because after fifty-two weeks they all look the same, whereas the local girls aren't allowed to have any sex until they are married. So many marry very young.'

'And that's kept to? I mean, none of the teenagers have sex?'

'It's kept to. Apart from the very rich families, where they all do what they want.'

'So you are in the wrong place for your personality.'

'Yes. I should have lived in the eighteenth century.'

'I was thinking earlier that you probably did. You should go to Paris. Or Russia.'

'I could do. I have friends I've taught to dive who are in the Russian mafia. They are always inviting me to fly there.'

'Why don't you go?'

'You know, Russian men are worse than the Arabs in the way that they think about women.'

'How so?'

'Let me put it this way . . .' He acquired a heavy Russian accent. 'Women are there to be fucked.'

I laughed. 'You must excuse me speaking to an Arab in positive ways about his own – but I heard that Arab men treat their wives with great respect?'

'Oh yes. They call it a sacred relationship. They marry them at twenty, start to have children at twenty-one and by the time she's thirty she's overweight, bored and stays at home all the time. Then he starts to have affairs with other women. All this is normal if it is him – but if she is unfaithful the sky falls down around her. I am very sarcastic about Arab society. I have little respect for the status quo, because it doesn't work.'

'Neither does ours in Europe.'

'How can you have a healthy relationship if you only see

your prospective partner in the company of your parents and you can't sleep with them beforehand?'

'But, Hisham, often even if it's a love marriage it doesn't work.'

'Love is overrated.'

'You're very funny.'

'I'm quoting Al Pacino.'

'If you hadn't owned up, I wouldn't have known it wasn't your own perspective.'

'It is. I think being in love is just like the feeling you get when you eat large quantities of chocolate. I love chocolate and when I eat it I notice that it's exactly the same feeling.'

'Have you ever been in the state that is called being "in love"?'

'Yes, just the once. It was like Swiss chocolate.'

'What were the symptoms of being in love?'

'I can't say.'

'I can.'

'You have been in love, then? What was it like?'

[Enter violins – crescendo builds, the entire string section of the orchestra plays ascending fifths.] I waved off the background music. I paused. I smiled. 'It made the world the way it could be. You know that lovely saying "may you live every day of your life"? It was like that. It made every day real, vivid, magnified – every second. Just knowing him. And every second I spent with him I cherished. I still cherish them. You see, if I just start to think of him . . . watch the size of the smile appear on my face? See it?'

'Yes I do.'

'That's his. That's what happens when I think about him.'

'And to me when I think about good chocolate.'

'If you offered me a week in Egypt learning to dive or a week in a dark basement with rats and Harry – I'd take the basement. So would the rats.'

'Obviously you are still in love with him.'

Oh God. What did he just say? I struggled to defend myself. 'Hold on. I wasn't talking about him. Was I? It's just that you asked me about falling in love.' After all my efforts to forget him – it's that obvious, even to a stranger. There was a long pause while I tried to persuade the smile to leave my face. I even enjoyed talking about him. I looked up at Hisham. 'It really was better than chocolate.' I thought this was a winning comment.

'Are you sure?' he said. 'Have you tasted the right kind of chocolate?' He's good, this guy. Then he looked pensive for a moment. 'I think the problem that I have is that I compare all the women I meet to Sarah, who I was in love with.'

'I know. They don't match up, do they?'

That's the irony of this whole quest for me. It's about men and how you and I can meet them but, for my part, I don't really want to meet men. Not with all my heart and soul. Somewhere, in another dimension, is a door. I've forced the door open, broken the chain and taken down the notice that said 'Access only Harry' and, just as I did all that, I swing around and find a new notice has appeared hung on the door that I've so carefully wedged open: 'Harry preferred'. In spite of everything I just want to be with Harry. To be diving with Harry. To be in this café with Harry.

But Hisham was very cute. He looked up at me. 'Two weeks ago I had an email from Sarah saying that she's met someone else.'

Ouch.

'Bitch. How dare she?' I smiled sympathetically.

The tender pain of the fragile human heart.

'I replied and I said "I'm happy for you" and I meant it, but . . .' His voice trailed off.

'Yes. Harry said that he'd be happy for me if I met someone else. I'd have hit him, but we were at different ends of the country at the time on the phone . . . so I think I just said "mmmm" or something. What did you want to say to her?'

'I didn't know. I didn't tell her what I was feeling because I didn't know.'

I knew. I know every nuance of what I feel.

'Was I supposed to be angry or sad?' He didn't understand – he was asking me – yet not really asking. I listened. 'I remember it felt like hovering in the water. In the middle of deep, dark water. I put Chopin on.'

There was a pause while we looked at each other. The two rejected ones.

'But had you already ended it?'

'Not really. Not formally.'

I didn't like to ask any more questions.

There was a long pause while we just sat, and then he said, 'I can't believe you've been listening to me talking for two hours. You're a stranger and I know I'm not drunk. You should be a private investigator. You'd just smile at a man and give him a couple of beers and he'd tell you everything.'

We sat on the local bus and he took me back to the hotel and dropped me off. I was still wondering if we'd been set up. Had Wessam and Jane decided to take care of me a little better than their job description required?

Whatever the circumstances, I had finally achieved one of my goals. Met a man who fitted the description: 'A genuinely single man who, when you meet him you think that you'd like to have dinner with him and, having had dinner with him, you're glad that you had dinner with him and you'd like to see him again.'

It had taken nine months and I'd had to change continents. But I'd achieved it.

6. UNWISE LIES TO EQUALISE

It's not just me, is it? When you are one woman in a group of men you have to try especially hard not to let the side down, particularly in an Arab country, where the wives normally have to stay at home. I had to be on top form today. Having had years in various forms of self-awareness seminars that teach, in one way or another, that the mind is in charge, I've always tried to have a positive attitude to boats.

'Now, Isabel,' I say to myself in a determinedly cheerful voice, 'just because you've had problems with seasickness in the past doesn't mean that you can't get into this little boat and have a great morning.' I have discovered either that positive focus has a measurable limit to its efficacy or that I'm a bad subject. A small boat, a rough sea and I have never managed to co-operate.

So this morning Wessam is smiling at me. The sky is a clear blue, the sea looks as it may have done the day after Moses had put it back together, there wasn't a wisp of a breeze and I was asking for seasickness tablets.

'You cannot be sick today. There is no wind.'

'Oh but I can. I have the most incredible talent. You've no idea. Everyone has some kind of talent. Being sick on boats is mine.'

I pulled out sea wristbands from my bag, swallowed two tablets and recited the top tips: 'Keep looking at the horizon. Stay warm. Drink water. Don't go down below if you can avoid it.'

We were going out to sea and I was as excited as a kid. This could be my first ever day on a small boat when I wasn't going to turn green and long for solid places. All my diving equipment was my responsibility but, even after two easy days, I knew what I needed and how to make all the necessary safety checks on my own and my buddy's equipment. And I was the only woman on the boat that day. I'm still not quite sure why this pleases me so much . . . only that I really am doing all this, and it really is in an enjoyable male environment.

Hisham was on another boat that day teaching technical diving in French, but I had my adored carpet seller Wessam as my buddy to take care of me. We set off across a clear blue Red Sea and something amazing happened. I felt fine. I was having another unique experience. I was at sea in a tiny boat and I was smiling. 'Well, Isabel, you never cease to amaze me. Maybe there is hope for you yet,' said some part of me to another part.

'Look, there's the reef,' said one of the Mohammeds, pointing to a dark-green patch in the water. I realised that I had no idea what a reef was. I'd thought that they were all over the bottom of the sea, places like this . . . but no, this reef is like a little island surrounded by just a sandy bottom . . . just like an oasis in the desert. In these oases the coral grows and all sorts of sea plants for the fish to feed on. It's a bit like swimming down into a life-sized tropical fish tank.

By the time you've got all the gear on, which included in my case 14 lbs of weights to help you go down and a jacket that fills with air to help you come up and an air tank and various tubes and fins (what we call flippers and they insist that you call fins), walking isn't the easiest thing. It's all rather clumsy, until you step into the water and then all the weight disappears. Going down isn't hard as a beginner because there is a mooring rope and you use that to guide your descent.

There is only one possible problem that can occur. I'd found it. If you have a cold your ears can't sort out the pressure. On a good day it's simple, as all the men were demonstrating, you simply pinch your nose and blow very gently and your ears will sort it out on their own. It takes a second.

This process, known as equalising, makes a dive completely comfortable. As long as you can do it. We went down the rope – Wessam was making the 'OK?' signal and I was thinking, 'Are my ears supposed to feel this cross?' I had no clue, so I went on going down. My ears felt odd, but I decided to ignore them. All around me fishes were getting on with their day jobs.

There has to be a God and He/She has to have a great sense of humour. I mean, the design of some of these creatures is just so wonderfully silly. Little minimalist pieces of life with black and white stripes are one thing, but a parrotfish? If you imagine Barbara Cartland as a fish, you have it. Too much colour, all pinks and clashing purples . . . a badly dressed fish. But somehow, under-the-water fashion has a certain gay, carefree quality. Everyone wears colour, has a silly face, a ridiculous headdress or rather overstated floaty bits and doesn't care.

What has happened in our cities that we all wear black and dress alike? We want to hide our true colours? Our brilliance? We want not to be noticed? I tell you, we could learn a thing or two from the fishes: a little dot in peacock blue, a wispy thing in a deep mauve, they don't hesitate to enjoy orange, they flaunt yellow and are happy to contrast one green with another. They party with diversity. They swim by, saying, 'And look at me!' 'And look at me!'

We sit on the bus, men and women in cities, saying, 'Don't notice me, don't speak to me.' And we contrast black with black. What has happened to us?

Wessam is a joy to me down here. Above the water he's a clown, always playing the fool, teasing and open to being teased. Below the water he's a different person. Utterly focused and professional. I love the fact that above the water I make fun of his disappearing waistline. He's just got married and in only six months is already following the Arab tradition of becoming a roly-poly smoker. The overeating begins immediately the wedding ends.

'My wife cook very good,' he complains.

'You eat very good,' I laugh at him.

But below the water he's in his element and I'm his pupil. He watches my every move in the water in case I do something stupid. Even at this shallow depth, my life is in his hands. If I did something stupid, like press the button that inflates my jacket for too long, I could go shooting up to the surface and injure myself. So he keeps an eye on this foreign woman – so noisy above the water and so blissfully silent here.

He links my arm and makes a sign to look, pointing down. There in the sand is a spotted stingray, beautiful, round and flat. A kind of tastefully decorated inverted plate with a tail. I've only seen them in pictures before, or in aquariums . . . what a simple joy this is. I wave at it with my fingers. It ignores me and gets on with whatever it's doing. Eating the nutrients it finds in the sand, I believe, makes up the day's employment.

Then a huge bunch of transparent straws swim by, then a collection of little bits of mirror and then some pulsing bits of purple. I'm so busy looking at them all I've quite forgotten I'm underwater and breathing.

Eventually Wessam makes the thumbs-up sign which means, as you'll remember (no extra charge for the diving lesson in this book – it's all included in the retail price), that it's time to go back to the surface. We reach the rope and make what's called a 'controlled ascent', going slowly, giving ears, lungs and nitrogen in the blood time to adjust. Five metres from the surface we rest for a 'safety stop', three minutes of waiting to listen to my ears popping and complaining. Then we're up.

Gosh. I've just made my first ocean dive.

Now wouldn't you rather be doing this with a man that you love than watching him watching other men playing football? And wouldn't you rather meet your next suntanned lover here?

The second dive of the day didn't go so well. I guess I was overambitious, but a war broke out between me and my ears. While the Mohammeds disappeared below me, I was struggling with the simple process of equalising. I was trying to pretend that I didn't have a cold. Just as I'd tried in the past to pretend that I didn't really get sick in boats. But Ms Can-do-anything-I-really-put-my-mind-to was in trouble again.

Going down is supposed to be easy. It is in some circumstances, right? In diving you go down a little, equalise and then go down some more. If you can't equalise your ears, you go up until your ears are happy and then try again. But they just wouldn't play. I think, on reflection, that my left ear tube was completely blocked with cold. I didn't want to give up though. So I spent ten minutes going up and down while rowing with my ears.

'Oh, just pop, will you?'

'Ow!'

'Well, just equalise and then it won't hurt at all. It's easy.'

'Ow. Go up!'

'No – we're going down. This is diving. That's down.'

'Ow. Go up!'

'Oh, for goodness sake. OK. I'll go up a tiny bit – there is that better?'

'Don't know.'

'Are you popping?'

'No.'

And all the while Wessam is making the 'OK?' sign and waiting for me to respond 'OK'. They don't have a sign for

'I'm great but my ears aren't following my instructions'. There is only a sign for 'I have a problem' (the razzle-dazzle dance routine hands). But if I do that, he'll go up. So I just shrug my shoulders. This is not in the book of underwater signs.

Question marks are swimming around his head. I decide to try another method of equalising not in the textbook. I remove the breathing apparatus from my mouth, pinch my nose and swallow. This seems to work, but Wessam is making very clear 'don't do that' signs. 'Do not remove the regulator' – he wags a finger at me as to a dim child and points at the breathing apparatus in my mouth. I'm not supposed to do this as it then involves holding my breath and the golden rule of diving is that you don't hold your breath underwater.

Now I do want to emphasise that this is a *very* simple process. This is not what will happen to you. The guideline is clear. If you have a cold, don't go diving, because it makes clearing your ears hard. So you simply don't dive until the cold is gone. Unless you are stupid. Then you try and dive anyway.

I'm trying anything I can think of to get my ears to co-operate. I've done loads of holding my breath trying to equalise for the best part of eleven minutes. But finally I've made it and we're sitting on the bottom on the sand with flecks of colour winking at us.

Then he takes my hand to go off on the dive. We are supposed to swim right around the reef. The only trouble is that, after a virtual eleven minutes doing it all wrong because of my cold, I'm in no fit state to enjoy the dive. Having not been breathing naturally for all that time, I now just feel strange and light headed. I'm not sure whether I have too much oxygen in my blood by this time or too little, but I know I don't feel completely relaxed, as I should do.

'Just breathe slowly and normally for a bit and you'll be fine,' I advised myself. 'No – it's no good. Your ears still aren't happy and you've thrown out all your air balance, you silly fish,' I said to myself. 'You're supposed to feel totally comfortable and relaxed. You're not comfortable. Go up. You have an enjoyable dive or no dive.'

I looked at Wessam and very bravely admitted defeat. I put one arm across the other in the sign that means 'end the dive'. He looked utterly perplexed, but copied my sign to confirm and I nodded. He took me up.

When we got to the top he said, 'What happened? We were at the bottom.'

'I know, but I just wasn't comfortable.'

'You must not take out the regulator. Why did you do that?'

'I know. But I couldn't equalise.'

'Why not?'

'I don't know.' I did know, but I didn't want to own up. 'I just wasn't relaxed and comfortable.'

'Then you did good to end the dive. Don't worry. We go again tomorrow.'

So I won back a few Brownie points for being a sensible female. But I was in a very bad mood with my ears.

That night was my second dinner with Hisham. Imagine, a single man that I want to have dinner with more than once, and I'm not writing fiction. I listened to him talking about his life, his childhood in war-torn Beirut and the frustrations of his present life in Hurghada.

'I don't go out in the evenings because I know there's no point. I'm not going to meet anyone I want to talk with in Hurghada.' (Sound familiar?)

'So what do you do in the evenings?'

'I listen to Chopin. I come home very tired and fed up from listening to banal human-being conversation. I put Chopin on.'

'How? How do you listen to Chopin? Teach me how.'

'First you have to find a working cigarette lighter, which is hard for me because I don't smoke.'

He's funny, isn't he?

'Then you turn off all the lights and try and remember where you left the candles. Hold up the lighter high so you can find the candles and then light them. Turn on the Chopin.'

'Do you sit down or lie down to listen?'

'It should be midway between the two.'

'Ah. A semi-recumbent position?'

'What's that?'

'Midway between the two. Now, what are your favourite pieces of Chopin?'

'The "Polonaise". Then the "Funeral March".'

'After a bad day?'

'No. Many people find it sad, but for me it's full of joy. Then there's the 'Barcarolle" and Mozart and Vivaldi. My two favourite pieces of Mozart have very similar themes and the numbers of the pieces of work are similar too, I can never remember which is which.'

He looked at me, confused once again that he was talking so much. 'At one point you have to let me shut up talking so that I can listen to you. How do you make me talk like this? That's what I'd like to know.'

'I'm interested. I have a genuine interest in people.'

'That's rare.'

'So I'm told. I have another question.'

'OK.'

'What's an interesting single man like you doing in a town like this?'

'Can I pass on this one?'

'Yes. But why do you want to pass?'

'Because I've been asking myself this question every day for the last year and a half and I don't find the answer yet.'

'So I'll show you a trick. I know that you don't know the answer. But if you did know the answer, what would it be?'

He smiled.

'For the diving. I'm here for the diving. The beauty of the diving overcomes everything. You are learning about entering a silent world. Sometimes when you breathe quietly you can hear the parrotfish nibbling on the coral.'

'Why are they nibbling the coral? Do they eat it?'

'Some of the corals, yes. And the turtles break the coral with their beaks.'

'Don't turtles have teeth?'

'I don't think so. The turtles are vegetarian, like you. They only have beaks. Not like you. They eat turtle grass.'

I sat and listened to this young man from Lebanon talk about the wonders of the sea and I felt so well and happy that he wasn't interested in football, computers, making money or killing innocent creatures.

'So you enjoy teaching?'

'Yes. I love to show people a world they didn't know. Today I was teaching the Frenchman and we just sat on the bottom and watched a whole wall of glassfish swim by. I could see that he had to remind himself not to smile too widely or the water would get in his mask. My friends who work in cities and make a lot of money don't have what I have. I have no money at all and they have everything – but I have the sea every day and they don't.'

'Do you have any plans for the future?'

'I would like to open my own diving school in Marsa Alam. But it isn't going to be easy. I have a potential partner, he'll put in the financial side and I'll give all the diving skills.'

'I love it. So while he's working in a city preparing his half, you've been diving to prepare yours?'

'Exactly.'

We were sitting in a little local family-run restaurant. As we finished our food they brought apple shisha for him and mint tea for me. I sat and just looked at him. I couldn't understand why a piece of highly intelligent tri-lingual eye candy like this would be interested in a woman who was . . . well, let's just say that he's thirty; I am . . . a bit older than that. He didn't even want my passport as he had, rather sensibly, no desire to live in Europe.

Then again, I couldn't understand why a piece of intelligent not tri-lingual eye candy like me would be interested in him for anything more than entertaining conversation and laughter. So we took the bus back to the hotel and I thanked him for my second enjoyable dinner.

I closed my eyes that night and saw rising bubbles, black-suited figures and fish. I was happy, but my ears weren't. I would have gone on ignoring them but now I could actually hear them complaining. My left ear was now letting me know that I'm alive by amplifying every heartbeat. 'Pum-pum, pum-pum.' And my right ear itched. I had to own up.

'Wessam ... ears not happy,' I said at 8 a.m. the following morning as the Mohammeds prepared for their second day on the boat. I was seething with jealousy. I knew what he would say.

'OK. You go to doctor. When you are better we do next dive, OK?'

Damn. Blast. Fuck. Shit. Trotsky. Big smile ...

'Of course, Wessam. That's fine.' (Pum-pum, pum-pum.)

'We will take you to the doctor.'

'Thank you, that's very kind.' (Pum-pum, pum-pum.)

'Doctor will do this.' Wessam looked in my ear, peered at my face and then said, 'Don't dive.' He complained, 'They say this to me and I say, "You crazy man. I am diving instructor, how can you say 'don't dive'?" Then the doctor look in my ear again and say, "OK. Don't dive – one year." '

So when the doctor looked in my ear and said, 'You have inflamed middle ear – don't dive – three days,' I was pleasantly surprised.

When I told Wessam he said, 'How did this happen? Why you have inflamed middle ear?'

'Well,' I admitted petulantly, 'I had a bit of a cold, you see, and I didn't like to mention it because I knew that you'd say, "Don't dive." '

'So now you have three days on land. Call me Sunday.'

Oh dear, three days by the pool, resting. Now you are thinking that you want to be a writer, huh?

* * *

Two days later I had a third dinner with Hisham. He seemed to have had a hard time with some of the women he'd known. Just as, you and God know this, I've had a hard time with some of/most of the men. So I invented a game. As we walked back from dinner I suggested that we play, completing the sentence, 'One of the things I don't like about women/men is . . .' It kept us talking for about two hours.

Hisham: 'One of the things that I don't like about women is the way that so many of them scream when they see each other again after a separation of about two days. It's so false.'

Isabel: 'One of the things I don't like about men is the fact that so many of them seem to have lost any pleasure in genuine conversation.'

Hisham: 'One of the things that I don't like about women is the way that they have made shopping into sport.'

Isabel: 'One of the things I hate about men is the way that they've made sport into religion.'

Hisham: 'One of the things I hate about women is that they fake orgasms and imagine that this is helpful to men.'

I laughed. I told him the famous statistic that ninety per cent of men say that a woman has never faked an orgasm with them coz they can tell the difference, but eighty per cent of women say they have faked orgasms. Go figure.

Isabel: 'One of the things I hate about men is that they so often have ego and performance linked to making love so strongly that women end up faking orgasms just to keep the men happy. Or they are honest and risk leaving the man thinking that either he has failed or there is something wrong with her.'

As a species we don't seem to have learned much about sex for all our liberation, do we?

Hisham: 'One of the things I hate about women is that they are interested in gold, diamonds and money.'

Isabel: 'One of the things I don't like about men is that they so often seem to behave as if money were the best measure of success as a human being.'

You'll find that you can play this game for hours.

Hisham: 'One of the things I hate about women is that they all play games. They are never direct. Never honest.'

'Except when they are.'

'What?'

'Except when they are. I never play games. I'm completely honest. It has always got me nowhere and, only recently, lost me a man I loved. But I'm always honest. Completely, stupidly honest.'

'I see.'

Isabel: 'One of the things I don't like about men is the way that they all seem to belong to someone else.'

'But not this evening.'

'No. Not this evening.'

And we walked all the way back to the hotel, linking arms and chatting like teenagers and we smuggled him up to my room (this isn't allowed under Egyptian law) and we drank coffee. And that's all we did. We sat on my balcony, looked at the sea and drank coffee. Hisham said, 'They won't believe it at the diving centre that we just talked. If I tell them, I can be sure that they won't believe me.'

'Why not?'

'If any man managed to get into a woman's room it would be to have sex with her. And even if he didn't have sex, he would pretend that he did.'

'So the truth is unbelievable?'

'Exactly.'

'Isn't it odd that this is what is normal now? We've only just met and yet we're supposed to be shagging like rabbits.'

'Everyone expects this. That's why the hotel rules say that I shouldn't be in your room.'

'So the hotel expects it, too?'

'All over Egypt it's the law. We're not allowed to be in here together unless we are married.'

No wonder Arabs have a reputation for being obsessed with sex. Of course, if it's forbidden it becomes more dangerous and therefore more exciting.

'If we were in Amsterdam no one cares what you do, so they all smoke strange substances and pass out instead and in London at many of the clubs people take coke which, male friends inform me, often prevents you from being able to get an erection.'

'Here, sex is the required behaviour.'

We looked at each other. And at the bed. I did fancy him like crazy and he didn't seem uninterested in me. But dammit, neither of us was ready for that much intimacy. I smiled at him and said, 'I'm really enjoying knowing you, Hisham. And drinking coffee.'

'Me too.'

And then we did the one thing that we knew no one would believe and maybe even you won't believe. We pecked each other on the lips like parrotfish. He went home – and I went to sleep.

7. PRESSURE TO BE NEUTRALLY BUOYANT

Today I saw a lionfish! This is everything I promised you. Beats the hell out of watching sport, there are men here *and* I saw a lionfish today!

So, after two days enforced sunbathing, sitting by the pool and swallowing anti-cold products with anti-inflammatories while writing to you, I was allowed back in the water today. I don't mind admitting I was very nervous this morning. In the last two days I've read all the theory. This is a bit like reading all the things that could go wrong with an aeroplane before sitting on one.

Did you know – Losada meanders off on one of her famous digressions – all that stuff they show you on a plane about inflating your lifejacket and blowing the whistle is all just show? The number of times an aeroplane has landed safely on water? (Think about it.) In the entire history of aviation the answer is nil. It's not possible. But they go through all that performance every day all over the world just to make us feel better and think, 'OK, well, if I've got a whistle on my lifejacket then I'll be OK.'

The training manual I've been reading offers no such empty promises. In one attempt to cheer the reader up from all the gory details of what can go wrong it says,

'Fatalities from decompression illness are rare in recreational diving.'

Oh? Rare are they? That's all right, then. It lets me know that if I hold my breath I could explode my lungs. If I equalise while going up I could burst my eardrums. If anything went seriously wrong and nitrogen turned into bubbles in my blood I could get paralysed. They're not sparing on the details. I guess other sports don't have a training manual that says, 'If you fall off the mountain/cliff/ nasty high place you could die,' or 'You're going to buy a CAR??? Are you mad? Do you know how many people are killed on the roads every year?'

But when you learn to dive they make sure that you know it all. To say that they are 'very safety conscious' is an understatement. All this meant that I had my heart as well as my breathing apparatus in my mouth when I took my 'giant stride' off the boat into the water this morning.

As it happened, I had a different instructor. Wessam, my cuddly carpet seller, was off to Cairo on business and I had been allocated to learn with Hisham. Another huge problem . . . like the sunbathing, really. On the other hand, I was now doing exactly what I'd been told not to do at the Dive Show in London. I was going out with my instructor, somehow, despite my determination to stick to the advice I'd been given. (Well, after two dinner dates it kinda counts as dating even if we're just talking, doesn't it?) But we'd had the dinners first and then he'd become my instructor. Does that count?

And then I got to see Hisham in the water. I guess for anyone who dives regularly watching someone's first dives, as he was watching mine, must have told him a lot about me. Just as we learn from watching a man dance, or cook or drive a car in a city. I'd laughed at him because the sun was shining and he was putting on a drysuit. There is something very sweet about a man tucking in a sweatshirt and putting on socks to go diving. I almost wondered whether he was still wearing his pyjamas under his tracksuit and, as his day went by, he simply added more layers or removed them again. The drysuit amazed me, no loss of dignity for him while I pottered around the boat in my bikini wishing some parts of me were flatter and some parts were less flat.

'Let's go diving,' he said, calm as a millpond, while I wondered why it was quite so hard to get my fins on. And then, 'Hold your right hand over your mask and breathing regulator and your left hand over your weight belt and take one giant stride forward.' Splash, splash and we were in the water. No problem with the ears this time – I just swallowed and they popped happily and I practised my 'om OK' sign all the way down to the sand.

There were exercises that I had to complete for my qualification: taking the mask off, following an underwater compass, removing my breathing apparatus while remembering to breathe out . . . all fairly straightforward. And then we were off to explore. I can't remember the names of all the fishes. It was suddenly like Bruce Forsyth's *Generation Game* – they all swam past me in and out of the million coloured corals and before I had time to remember that this one was fat and blue with black spots and this one was little and green with yellow stripes, I'd seen another dozen little beings swim by.

I had to learn what's called 'neutral buoyancy' – that is, being in the water and going neither down, which could damage the corals, nor up. So while I struggled, adding a little air to my jacket to get me to go up a little or releasing a little to get me to go down, I watched Hisham who hung in mid-water suspended by some invisible means, like the fish.

I would suddenly find myself dropping down close to some amazing anemone and would have to kick to avoid it. He barely moved in the water. Or he'd let me lead. Once or twice I'd be so engrossed in examining a giant clam that when I looked up he wasn't there. I'd look right and left and see no black figure, only fish. I thought, 'Ah, this must be part of my test. I know what to do. The theory book said that I search for one minute and then if I don't find him I make a controlled ascent and then search at the surface.' Then I looked and there he was – right behind me pointing out a timid little face hiding under a rock.

You see, I don't want to describe all these fishes to you. I really want you take a man you love and go and see for yourself. Or, failing that, a girlfriend whose company you enjoy. Or, failing that, go alone. I'll put the details on my website for you. After all, Doreen went, and she can't walk.

I saw table coral and wonderfully weird Sinularia, I delighted at my first ever encounter with Goniopora and stopped in amazement to examine Sessile Xenia. Of course, I'm playing now. I know that you haven't a clue what any of these mean. But then, just as I was looking at these, along came a napoleonfish. Just type napoleonfish into Google Images and have a look at the extraordinary creature. And yet it's not just seeing the creatures – not like birdwatching, when you are on the ground looking through your binoculars saying, 'Wow – isn't she beautiful.' With diving you are in their world. By the simple act of learning to breathe down there you have become a fish. So they swim up and look at you and then swim away, just as they do with other fish.

Hisham and I had four dives like this in two days, each lasting about thirty minutes. The weather was wonderful, I was eating lunch on the boat, getting a suntan and passing more tests each day. I had to show I could inflate my jacket in the water, take it on and off while bobbing around at the surface, and take off the 14-lb weightbelt at the surface, with the waves doing a merry dance, without dropping it. I nearly humiliated myself and dropped it – which would have meant that Hisham would have had to go down to retrieve it – but one of the Mohammeds took it, so I managed to save face. It was all going a little bit too well. It was beginning to feel like fiction.

Last night I had dinner with Hisham again. I couldn't decide whether to tell you this part or not. It would have been so easy to have left this out, but I want to be honest with you and this is all part of the story – life is complex when people make it so. We were still only talking and sitting at dinner. I was going on listening and still, with his permission, writing down some of the things he said. We had moved on from 'love is overrated' but now it was like swimming down to a place where no light reached and everything went from grey to black darkness. Now I was diving with him into his nihilistic philosophy.

'Life is absurd', 'life is pointless', 'nothing has any meaning' – a blind person passed and Hisham said, 'Why doesn't someone who is blind just kill themselves? If I was blind I'd kill myself.'

'Oh really? So because someone is blind they have no reason to live? What about deaf people? Should they all kill themselves too?' I tried not to be angry at this absurdity.

A little girl ran by all full of life and energy and he said, 'I never want to have children. If I had a little girl like that she'd probably get raped and abused and then be totally fucked up all her life.' What had he seen in his life – what does growing up in a war zone do to a mind that it chooses to follow this path?

I replied, 'Or – if you had a child she might not get abused, but grow up full of laughter. Or even if she was abused, she might get over it and become a doctor and successfully treat thousands of people in her lifetime. Or just make one person laugh one day.'

'I never want children in case they suffer. Why would you want to bring anyone into this world? Why would you want to live in this?'

'For the pleasure of life itself?'

'Life is overrated.'

I smiled. But he was deadly serious. Deadly. Or serious and deadly. Or maybe just dead. I couldn't work it out at first.

He said, 'I can't leave here.'

'Yes you can. I thought you said that you had friends in the Russian mafia who would send you a ticket to get out.'

'I can't accept help from strangers. I won't ask for anything. That's charity.'

'No it's not, if it gives people pleasure to make you a gift.'

'That's the way you see things. I won't accept anything from anyone.'

'That's just pride. Get over yourself.'

'You can't understand me.'

'Why do you assume that?'

'No one can.'

'That's only your belief.'

'I don't have beliefs. I don't believe in anything.'

'That's a belief, too. That you can't leave Hurghada, that's also a belief.'

'No. It's a reality.'

'If we leave this restaurant and keep walking, by morning we won't be in Hurghada any more. Forgive my stupid example, but I'm just trying to demonstrate that a negative belief is still only a belief. Life is full of miracles. Of possibilities ... but I think we have to create them. I ...' My voice trailed off. I was starting to sound like Pollyanna talking to JeanPaul Sartre.

'What do you think life is for?' he asked with a tone of voice that let me know that whatever I thought was misguided.

'Well, I ...' I hesitated. 'I believe it may be so that we can learn unconditional love.'

'That's absurd. To put the words unconditional and love together. It doesn't exist. All love is conditional.'

I started to sound like a tape recorder.

'Again, that's your belief. Not mine. I didn't say it was easy. If we give food to a beggar that is not an action done with any hope of return. There are no conditions – it's just a loving action.'

'That's not love. That's pity.'

'They say that pity is akin to love. It's a kind of love.'

'I don't see the point.'

'Of love?'

'Like I said, it's just a chemical reaction, like eating chocolate.'

This was becoming absurd. I turned to swim sideways across the current, just like it said to do in the theory book if the current got too strong.

'Hold on. The fact that eating chocolate may produce a chemical change in the body that feels like love doesn't disprove love itself. That's not logical.'

What is this? I have to argue for the existence of love?

'Don't you phone your mother because you love her?'

'No, I call her because she changed my nappies and I feel obliged.'

'And you're prepared to go on record saying that? I can write that down?'

'Absolutely.'

'Doesn't it give you pleasure to hear her voice and make her happy?'

'Pleasure is overrated. Don't you agree?'

'No. I don't agree that pleasure is overrated or that love is just chemicals or that people are absurd or that life is overrated. I think it's underrated. I think we underrate people and we underrate everything. You told me earlier that people underrate the porter in your block and speak down to him just because of his job. Well, I think we underrate all people. The guys on the boat who are not instructors but 'just' crew. The chefs, the cleaners, all the people who nobody rates. Even those stray dogs over there – they have a huge potential to love and enrich the lives of human beings, but they are just left in the road. People and animals and birds and fish and plants and corals and the passing of time ... it's all underrated. People are not cherished, we don't appreciate others as we could or love others as we could. "Love one another." According to Jesus, that's what we're here for.'

'I don't believe in Jesus.'

'I see. Nor his teachings, I suppose. Well, who do you believe in?'

'No one.'

'Whose teachings do you believe in then?'

'No one ... Jesus, Buddha, Mohammed, they all just made things more complicated.'

'OK then, let's take a more recent example – Gandhi?'

'He didn't do any good at all.'

Oh, please. Suddenly it felt like a scene from *Life of Brian*, 'What have the Romans ever done for us?'

'Hisham ... surely these people tried to teach us about love, just as you teach about diving.'

'These people knew nothing about love.'

'You think not? Well, I can't speak for Mohammed, I don't know his teachings well enough, but I think when Jesus said, "Pray for your enemies," that's an example of unconditional love. When you're being nailed on a cross and still not condemning your persecutors ... well, that seems like a pretty good demonstration of unconditional love to me.'

'That's just a story. There's no such thing. It's absurd to put those words together. It's better to be alone with Chopin.'

So what do you think? Is this man better to be left alone with Chopin?

8. FINNING, WINNING AND BEING WON

I hadn't gone home cross. Just sad. Sad that someone who had so much going for them was determined to be so black. No matter what he's seen. I tell a story in *A Beginner's Guide to Changing the World* about a monk who leaves Tibet after many years of having been tortured in Chinese prisons. He is given an audience with the Dalai Lama and, during the meeting, he tells His Holiness that in all his years in captivity (about 25 of them) he saw only one danger. The Dalai Lama asks what that was and he replies, in accordance with Buddhist teachings, 'The danger of losing my compassion for my torturers.' There are so many examples of people who have endured the most horrendous suffering and seen great human cruelty, and yet still believe in human goodness. The Arabs have a saying, 'If you can't be a lighthouse, at least be a candle.' And it makes me feel sad when people waste their energy cursing the darkness.

But the following morning – no matter how black Hisham was about humanity – it was sunny and warm, and he had a theory exam to set me. The Mohammeds had all long gone while I was sitting by the pool, and now I was in the classroom on my own with my test paper. My practical ocean water dives were all done. Now all I had to do was get through this exam. I wasn't happy. There were maths questions . . .

'What is the minimum surface interval required between a dive to 20 metres for 29 minutes followed by a dive to 14 metres for 39 minutes?'

And even though it was multiple choice and I had a chart to work this out, I was straining my brain like the innumerate stage-school child I am. I had to pass the exam . . . by this time I almost felt that I was representing all the forces of human good in the world. Only Hisham was hovering around wanting me to pass, too. 'Just ask me if you don't understand any of the questions.'

I sat and concentrated, forty questions. I had no idea what the pass mark was, but I could only do my best. I handed in the paper and went to sit on the boat, drink coffee and chat with Jane.

'So you're all done, then?'

'Yup. Back to Battersea the day after tomorrow.'

'Has diving won you?'

'Yes. It's definitely the way to go for individuals who want to do something different and have magical adventures and for couples who want to spend time together and share their passions. It's not that expensive as a holiday and it's definitely worth saving up for.'

'Has Hisham won you?'

'What?'

'I just wondered. He seems interested and usually he isn't.'

We sat on the sunny deck of the little boat looking out over the sea. 'I never do this,' she said, 'take a coffee break, sit in the sun.'

'If I lived here, Jane, I'd definitely date Hisham for a while, because he's wonderful, but he's also very black in his thinking sometimes and I'm not sure that I really want . . .'

What do I not want? To have to argue for the existence of unconditional love?

'Anyway,' I went on, 'I don't live here. I'm not planning on moving to Egypt and Hisham doesn't want to live in Europe . . . but, Jane, I've really enjoyed getting to know Hisham. He's a very good man, a very precious one. It's a shame that he doesn't believe in people, or human goodness, or love.'

'What does he believe in, then?'

'Only fish.'

I suppose he must have guessed we would be talking about him. He strolled over in cream-coloured trousers and a loose green jacket, his curly hair shining in the sunshine. In London they'd pay him to walk down a catwalk looking as he did. He smiled – in spite of his non-belief system, he believed in me.

'Congratulations. You've passed.'

'I have? You mean I didn't mess up?'

'Well, you didn't get one hundred per cent – some of the maths questions at the end we'll have to go over with the diving charts and the tables – but you got eighty per cent and that's a pass mark.'

'Fantastic . . . well done you.' Jane was proud of me. How lovely. Then Wessam waddled up, all smiles. 'Well – due to my good lessons I hear you passed.'

'Of course. I had two amazing instructors. I wouldn't have dared to fail.' (Pressure or what?)

'I like happy endings,' said Jane. 'Oh well, I guess I'd better get back to work now, then.' She and Wessam walked back into the office, leaving Hisham and I sitting looking at each other.

'I'm sorry about last night. I spoiled your evening. I have the day off tomorrow.'

'That's good. I'd love to see you.'

So yes. OK. I'll own up. We spent the day doing what boys and girls who are attracted to each other do best. I made him smile. A lot. He made me smile, too. I have one more person in the world that I'll try to love unconditionally . . . whether he believes that it's possible or not.

And now I'm back in Battersea. It's sunny here today and I've just realised what I did wrong in all this going down. I messed up on one of our definitions didn't I? I thought I'd been so clear, but somewhere in the story I muddled up the words 'single' and 'available' didn't I? I forgot I was looking for an *available* man. With all the married men around, I started to think that all I was looking for was a single one ... but I wanted an available one. Available has to mean geographically available (in the same continent preferably) and emotionally available (wouldn't prefer to be alone with Chopin).

I know another man apart from Hisham who isn't married any more and knows that I love him to pieces ... heaven knows, I've been telling him for about twenty years. But he never does anything about it. That one would rather be alone with his dog. I know a third who says he loves me but would rather be alone with the trees. These are the emotionally unavailable men. A geographically unavailable man is one thing – but do you cross the world for an emotionally unavailable one?

I know what you are thinking, because I've had letters before. You are split now into two camps: those of you that are thinking, 'Yes, Isabel – go! Sell everything ... he just needs to be loved a bit,' and those of you that are thinking, 'No rescuing anyone, Isabel ... if he wants to be with Chopin, leave him with Chopin and if he wants to be with you, then he'll make it happen.'

You are both right. Only he won't make it happen, because he believes that it's not possible and, in this way, we create our own reality. I believe anything is possible unless he believes it isn't. That happiness is possible ... unless he believes it isn't. And I could be happy even with someone that doesn't believe in happiness ... because I do believe in it. But would I choose that? I think not, don't you?

So where does all this leave me? Where does it leave us? It is possible to meet a man that you want to have dinner with more than once. And I have found for us a world where, all over the world, the people who love adventure are meeting together on boats and going diving. It's a male environment and a magical one ... but if you decide to explore it, go in peak season. Don't date the instructor. And if you go and find Hisham – give him a kiss from me.

Part V

A PONTIFICATION – SPIRITUAL FEMINISM

1. THE SOLUTION: TANGO WITH THE STATUS QUO

So. I've done a lot of thinking about this men situation over the last nine months. I've been out and looked, haven't I? I'm sure the critics will accuse me of all kinds of things, but they can't accuse me of not having looked (apart from in the nightclubs – but, well, thanks to Neil Strauss and *The Game* I really felt I didn't have to).

I have good news and bad news. When I started I thought that the fact that women complain all the time that there are no interesting and available men was a group limiting belief. It isn't . . . there really aren't many. This is good news, because I hope I've proved that you're not mad. If you are a single woman and you're having trouble meeting interesting and available men – don't be surprised. If you know women who are wonderful and they think they are single because there's something wrong with them – please buy them this book so that they really know it's not just them. They don't need seminars or therapy – really. But this leaves single women with a very important question. If we *really* want to find one (39¾) what we are prepared to do differently?

My daughter turns out to have one of the best and most logical solutions. Leave the country. There is a huge marketing opportunity available for anyone who wants to start an international dating agency for women. Men can find Thai wives or Russian wives any day that they want them . . . but where are the agencies for women? Someone could have a lot of fun setting one up and deciding what the criteria would be – after all, it wouldn't be just looks. Er . . . would it? I'm not doing it, but surely someone will – remember, you heard it here first. China?

The British dating agencies are going to have to do something different . . . they just don't have enough men. And, did you know, when people do meet through dating agencies, they'll still never own up. Isn't that absurd? Mary Balfour at Drawing Down the Moon hasn't had a single couple she can use for her own publicity because the men are never prepared to go public. 'Sometimes the women will,' she says ruefully, 'but the men won't.' Gay people walk through the streets with banners but single people still won't come out?

The situation gets worse in our cities and interesting women over 45/40/39¾/35/30 continue to have careers and interesting, fulfilled lives without men in them. Last night I was out to dinner with friends. We were five single women and one couple. Yesterday in the papers were stories of women in New York having eggs frozen. They are reported to believe in their early thirties that it's highly likely they will never meet a man that they'll want as a father to their children. And I've heard the same in London.

Doing radical and exciting things with our lives is one solution. They have to be fun and joyful – like diving was. I had the following email on my website yesterday on the ongoing subject of where the men are:

'I spent two months at Everest base camp and went climbing in the Himalayas. There were ten women there and about 250 men. One day I noticed that one of the men had long eyelashes and now he's the father of my child.'

That's what I mean by radical solutions. By living for two months with 250 men she certainly increased her odds, didn't she? And, if you do decide to go travel, I'm told, by a Polish man, that in Poland the men are wonderful and in Croatia I noticed that the men don't look bored, as they do in the UK. This may seem crazy, but the situation here, as we all know, isn't changing. Unless we change it. And how could we do that? There is one thing that we all need to do. I do have one solution.

After months of thinking about this I am going to adopt a change of tone here and sound a little serious. You'll forgive me I hope, but I think it's called for. I speak to myself as much as to everyone. OK. Take a deep breath – are you sitting comfortably? Fasten your seatbelt. Any solution to all this mess is going to have to be radical. Ready?

HONESTY?

In 1970 feminists like Germaine Greer were calling on women to stand on their own feet and not be dependent on men financially or emotionally. We have made progress financially. As an author I'm often invited to all-female reading groups where I hear that a majority of the women are the leading financial earners in the house. This is not unusual. But have women achieved any level of emotional independence? Are we less needy? Or, to quote a frequent male complaint, less whiny?

During the same historical period in which laws have been passed in our land to make discrimination in the workplace an offence, another change has taken place. The word 'religion' has become a bad word and the word 'spiritual' has become an overused one. The vast majority of women aged ten to seventy probably consider themselves spiritual, with their own personal definition of the word (above seventy women may be happy to be called 'religious').

So are women really more 'spiritual' now? Where has all this spirituality got us? What does it mean? Has it taught us to be better people? Has it helped us to love one another better? Perhaps in some ways it has. But here is where I think the talk needs to meet the walk. I'd like to call for some radical integrity and consider the impact that it would have on us and on the men around us.

I said at the end of the story with the golfing and cricketing husbands that the only power we have is to follow Gandhi in his famous teaching, 'Be the change that you want to see in the world.' That is the point at which spirituality, relationships and human happiness touch. We have to be honest ourselves. Not easy. I have lied. I have colluded with men who have been unfaithful to their wives. And who has benefited? Not me, not the wives and, in spiritual terms, certainly not the husbands. The men may benefit in the short term, but by sneaking a quick shag and then going home to brush up their consciences and their golf clubs they aren't exactly discovering quality or depth in relationships, are they? Ahmed says that this is a polygamous society in denial. From what I have observed, that doesn't seem to be making us happier.

Let's imagine a different way forward. Imagine if, slowly but surely, just as we have found our feet financially and carved out our rightful position in the workplace, women decided that they didn't want to be lied to, or lie to other women any more. Is our new 'spirituality' just a belief system about feeling good ourselves, or can it impact on the levels of human happiness around us? For example, if all the women who are having affairs with married men (and, sadly, the number is huge, believe me) said, 'Not if you are going to lie to your wife.' What would happen then? If more of us offered and asked for radical honesty there would be a lot more divorce. Many fewer unhappy, long, lingering, 'blundering along' marriages, and, ultimately perhaps, a lot more happy ones.

The extraordinary Neil Strauss, the author of *The Game*, achieved something quite remarkable in his book. He had so many women that he created a genuine harem. He dated eight women, and his sexual activities often included threesomes, but (and here is another conclusion that I didn't expect to reach in reading a book about a pick-up artist) bizarrely, he earned my admiration because he didn't lie to any of them; they all knew about each other. None of them could be upset, as he never cheated. He explained the set-up and they had a simple choice – they could join in or not. No one was ever deceived. Ultimately, he met a woman he wanted to date uniquely and phoned the other eight and told them that it was over. Again, he never lied to them. Now, if a man can be that clear with eight women, it seems to show that telling the truth is not an impossible goal in human relationships.

It's a terrible realisation to have come to, but the most significant reason that there are almost no available men is because so many women are prepared to accept deceit and have affairs. My sisters – we (the mistresses and the wives) are enabling these male cake-eating habits. And it is my contention that nobody benefits. I hope I can show that, as Tolstoy said, 'The one thing necessary in life, as in art, is to tell the truth.'

First of all, why are women so often lied to? If your husband or boyfriend lies to you, why is this? Is it because he's afraid you'd throw him out, jettisoning various of his possessions in a rapid trajectory through sundry windows, with elegant expletives offered to fuel the neighbours' gossip for years to come? Because he's afraid that you'll drag him through the courts, that he'll end up living in a hole in the ground and be allowed to see the children once a month, if you feel magnanimous? Just that you'll leave him? Or is there another whole layer beneath this one?

Margaret Mead writes in her book *Male and Female* that if we observe our closest animal relatives, the primates, we could notice that the male does not feed the female. Even when she is heavily pregnant and can hardly walk, she still fends for herself. He'll fight for the right to take her sexually and to protect her, but he will not nurture her. I'm not convinced that women ever really understood that.

Again, speaking to the women here – despite our belief in our own equality, when it comes to keeping a man, sometimes women will do almost anything and put up with almost anything to prevent him leaving. I know three men who stay with their wives because the wives are so hopelessly dependent (can't drive, for example, or use a computer, are alcoholic, or suffer from a million and one emotional problems) that the men don't know how to leave. They have affairs with more independent women, tell them about how unhappy they are with the women at home, and the single women sympathise and open their legs. We're not really so spiritual, are we?

Buddhism, for example, teaches us to look to ourselves for maturity, to not 'need' others in any negative sense. How do we achieve spiritual and emotional maturity? I believe that it's about acknowledging our freedom, our choices and our personal responsibility. Following a spiritual path is about working out how to live a joy-filled life, to serve others, not to be dependent. And, as the men would say – stop whining, pleading, nagging, bitching, bribing, humiliating, manipulating and emasculating men.

I'm sorry if that sounds harsh. But I've spent so much time with men in the last year, and there is so much pain that we exacerbate with our expectation that they should play a part in our wholeness. They will not. They cannot. They don't know how and it's not their job. Their job is to love us because they choose to, because we are whole and magnificent women – and that's up to us.

I'm not blaming women for the fact that so many men lie to us (as you'll see later, when I talk to the men directly) but I am looking squarely at the role we play and our responsibility.

Kahlil Gibran compares a healthy relationship to two trees growing side by side – not leaning on each other, and simultaneously strangling and being strangled. If you are together through necessity rather than choice, you have both grown lazy. He has taken you for granted and you have taken him for granted. If he's shagging a younger woman while 'respecting' you and you're turning a blind eye for any number of reasons, well, it may be domestic convenience but it isn't happiness, is it?

I suggest that our new spirituality is deeply flawed. When we begin to achieve emotional independence we will be the kind of women that men won't have to lie to. This will mean that men will love us without feeling trapped or suffocated. Emotional independence would also enable us to love men freely and, if necessary and that is what they really want, to help them to be free.

So, let's look at honesty as a product of spirituality and personal responsibility and where it would lead us in human relationships.

The Office of National Statistics shows that women are already the chief initiators of divorce. Rather than finding this depressing, I am amazed to be concluding that, in order to increase the sum total of human happiness and for everyone's benefit (especially the children's), I think we need more divorce. But a totally new kind of divorce; one without acrimony, pain or lies. To achieve this we will need to be braver, wiser, warmer people.

I know that many couples give up too easily, but I'm not talking about celebrity marriages arranged as a publicity stunt, or thoughtless marriages that last a year. I'm assuming that most people who get married and make a vow promising that they will only be with that one person from now till death makes that vow because they want it to be so.

If we believe that the majority of people want their marriages to work, let's look at what happens when they go wrong and a couple cease to be good for each other. They don't even delight in each other's presence. Sadly, it takes most of us about 0.1 seconds to think of unhappy marriages.

Is it possible for a woman to let a man go and send her love with him? I'm not saying it's easy. It's not easy living alone. But neither is it easy to live with a man who has ceased to communicate or who wishes that he was somewhere else. We need to divorce with compassion and – yes, I believe that I can demonstrate that it's possible – with love. Any true definition of spirituality has to be about the practice of unattached and unconditional love.

NO FIG LEAVES

If we want to have quality relationships then they have to be based on honesty with ourselves and with others. I remember hearing a talk once about the true meaning of Adam and Eve being naked. It isn't about the absence of fig leaves. It's about having the courage to show who we really are. Of being, as it says in the scriptures, 'naked and not ashamed'. Being real. Isn't that scary? And sexy? And beautiful?

So, about telling the truth – men, and women too – if you don't want to be with someone any more . . . you simply tell them. It's that hard and that easy. But you don't have to attack them. Part lovingly, gratefully, with thanks, with compassion. It's really not impossible.

I'm aware that I'm in danger of you thinking that I don't understand or that what I'm saying doesn't apply to your situation. That I'm talking bollocks and that I have no experience. So here are two stories – my own and one other.

My divorce wasn't easy. I had no family and a small daughter of two and a half. When my husband and the father of my child left, I felt as if I'd been ripped in two. But he didn't destroy my trust. We were unusual. The most important thing I'd offered alongside my marriage vows, and asked for from him, was total disclosure. And he honoured that.

Seven years into the marriage he said, 'I've met another woman. I need to go away and spend time with her to try and find out what course of action I'm going to take.' If we hadn't had this agreement to be honest or he'd had less respect for me or less integrity himself, he'd probably have done what most men do, taken the easy option and just lied. He'd have gone on seeing her ... I'd have been more and more unhappy, his mistress would have been more and more unhappy and our daughter would have spent her most formative years surrounded by adults who would rather have been somewhere else.

In our case what happened was a lot more unusual. I said, 'Where will you go?'

They were going to stay in the empty house of a mutual friend. For two weeks. Every night I knew where he was. I sat remembering our wedding; we had stood in a church and he had told the angels and archangels and all the company of Heaven that he would stay with me. I thought he would come back to me in tears of remorse.

He did shed a few tears when he came back – but I think he was also trying to hide the spring in his step.

'How was it?' I asked.

'It was extraordinary.'

I didn't ask for details. But I was still glad that he wasn't lying to me.

There was a long, difficult period that followed where I observed his struggle with compassion. He still loved me in some ways and he certainly loved his daughter. He was torn in two. I watched him and thought, 'I'm glad I'm not in his position.' My role was easy, all I had to do was suffer, but he felt responsible for four people's lives. I didn't beg or plead. He spoke to her and listened to her sobbing on the telephone. Sometimes he was sobbing, sometimes I was. Our daughter can hardly not have sensed some of this.

Something had to shift, so he moved out to stay with a friend of his and said he wouldn't see either of us for at least three months. I was convinced that he would come back. But he never came back. Eighteen years later he is still with her and not a single day passes now when I don't have words with those angels and archangels and thank them for his choice. It was a courageous one; he followed his heart and he deserved the happiness he found. I would have gone slowly mad living with him, but I didn't know this at the time. He has everything in common with her and nothing in common with me. He likes to stay at home and watch TV a lot and so does she. I like to go out and have adventures.

But the reason I'm telling you more personal information than you need is just to point out one thing. He never lied to me. It's possible.

How many times have we listened to men and women, always in great distress, say, 'I don't even mind that he/she had an affair [sob] so much [sob]. It's the lies! [wail] I feel so stupid, so humiliated, everyone knew except me [crumple into convulsed heap of misery].'

Often, being lied to hurts more than the infidelity. And then, so often couples throw coals onto burning fires. They make the agony worse. They throw around blame and recriminations, the one who is being left (still more often the women) will cry 'But don't you love me any more?' and the man, in his anger, pain and guilt will shout 'No! I don't love you any more!' Of course it's not true. Not by any definition of love worth having. What does it mean 'to love'? Many books exist on that subject, but at the very least, love in a long-term relationship means to care about someone. Can we really live with someone for ten, twenty, thirty years and cease to care about them? Only if we are forced to harden our hearts to justify our actions.

The one being left often creates this. They drive the 'guilty party' away by going crazy, being hysterical, throwing every stone that has been stored up for years, 'Now I remember that time when you smiled at that girl on the 27 bus – you were probably shagging her too, you bastard. You've never loved me, you bastard . . .' etc. In my old street I used to hear these rows through the wall.

Can we learn to go on loving someone and still leave them? Can we learn to go on loving someone and let them go? Or, as in my case, with Harry, let them stay? Can we even begin to discover what is meant by unconditional love?

I know of a couple in Bath – and this is a true story – where a woman was living with her husband and two children. She was very surprised to find that she had fallen in love with another woman and they began a sexual relationship, which she couldn't bring herself to tell her husband about. It was made worse for her by the fact that her husband and new 'friend' got on very well. However, at the same time she could hardly bear to confess to her new lesbian lover that she was still sleeping with her husband. Again – something had to change. She had to tell the truth.

Eventually she told them both. And – listen to this as an example of male maturity – the husband, although shocked, was most concerned for the consequences on the children. So they worked out a way that everyone could be happy and benefit. The husband bought the house next door and moved into that. The woman stayed in the marital home and the lesbian lover moved in, contributing all her finances to make the new house purchase possible. Meanwhile (and I love this detail), they knocked an inner door between the two houses so that the kids could go from house to house without getting wet. They knocked down the garden fence to make one larger garden. They all remain one extended family. With this attitude from the husband, I was not surprised to learn that the husband soon met another woman who moved into the second house with him. At the time of going to publication everyone is genuinely happy with this arrangement and is grateful for everyone else. The children have four parents who all like each other. Can you imagine? What made this true-life story possible? The courage to be honest from the wife and the courage to have compassion and understanding from the husband. No jealousy, clinging or possessiveness anywhere in the story. Hooray.

THE ETERNAL TRIANGLE – THREE SOLUTIONS

Now you may be laughing at this idea of honesty. But, actually, as I said, women are already taking steps in this direction. Asking for honesty, offering it, sometimes demanding it. I think women need to be still more mature and change the way we set men free . . . we'll all be better off.

'But this still means that bastard husband of mine gets to shag his new Sheila, twenty years younger, and I'm left at home with that cat?' I can see my older female readers ready to murder me. OK – so let me reply to you directly first.

THE WOMAN LEFT BEHIND

Let's look at it a little closer. Firstly, unless you throw him out, right now, he has everything. You know his favourite food and how he likes his eggs cooked, you know the date of his mother's birthday and you allow him his little peccadilloes. Is it really serving him as a human being to be serving him his eggs sunny side up? Years ago, in his classic bestseller, *The Road Less Travelled*, Scott Peck attempted to define love as wanting to see the growth of the other person. In this context we mean the emotional growth, the psychological growth, growth in ability to empathise, to appreciate others, to be vulnerable and real, to have compassion, spiritual growth – or, if you don't believe in all that, simply to be a better human being and to be able to love better.

The truth is that your husband is stagnating in the protected greenhouse environment you have created. He needs to go out to face a storm or two. He will learn more as a human being and appreciate more without you. Women complain that men don't get wiser as they get older – we play a part in perpetuating that. Look at what happens to him if we throw him out to live with his mistress.

Let's assume for a moment that Sheila is 25 and he is, well, a fair bit older than that. This is fairly typical. Well, she may want sex every night and every morning too, which will make him very happy – but let's also give her the benefit of the doubt. She's no fool and she's picked a man you picked yourself once, so give her some credit. She isn't going to iron his shirts; she'll tell him he can do them himself or pay to have someone else do them. She may cook him a meal as a party piece just to show that she can and then she'll say, 'Now your turn . . . what are you going to cook me?' She will refuse to mother him: 'Your turn to clean the flat.' She will be full of demands and expectations – he will become her project. I've actually heard women say, 'He needs a makeover.' She'll want to change his clothes, his eating habits, his hobbies . . . all those things that you have long ago learned to accept, she'll kick up a fuss about. 'You mean you don't floss??? Eweeeewww, how gross!' If he comments that he used to enjoy Morecambe and Wise, she'll say 'Who?' She also hasn't heard of *The Goon Show*, thinks *Dad's Army* is stupid and doesn't know that Bill and Ben are flowerpot men. In short – he pays a price for all that sex.

He'll humour her and find it charming at first, this interest in what shirt he wears . . . he'll lap up the attention, the fact that she hangs on his every word and thinks that he's so clever. But he's having to grow up. He'll start to realise that he's traded what was once an equal partner for someone who feels more like a daughter. It's not so easy. And there is another factor. If he's unfaithful, she is far more likely to walk or show him the door. All the other Sheilas in his life have had to go. Most of his friends have to become her friends. His old married friends are angry with him. Both the men and the women resent the fact that he left. They claim sympathy for the one left behind (often increasing the feeling of victimhood). Unless his old friends are very enlightened, none of them will have thrown a divorce party for him and the ex-wife. The truth is that they are jealous – but they won't admit it. Possibly not even to themselves.

Meanwhile, Sheila has scratched the car, run out of money and wants him to come to yoga with her. He'd never have been seen dead in a yoga class before, but now he's there, prancing around saying to himself, 'This isn't too bad, actually,' and wondering whether he can have a beer after a yoga class or whether that will be frowned on. 'Now you are putting toxins into your body, sweetie – just after you've done it so much good.' Ha ha.

You get the picture? He has a lot of learning to do. He's having to open his mind to new ideas and take them seriously. He has to listen to her in a way that he has never listened to you. He can't get away with anything. In short, he's having to grow up and work out how he can negotiate and make this new version into a younger, sexier version of you. He's genuinely happy – and you may still like to remember him in your prayers!

OK, so – the 'woman left behind'. Options for the bright woman of fifty (or over thirty-five in some cases)? You know the expression that you hear a lot in this case? It's 'trying to make the best of things'. Yeuk. Don't you feel depressed reading that? It's what T.S. Eliot calls 'living and partly living'. Not this route – I don't recommend this. There is a line in scripture about being hot or cold but never lukewarm – 'because you are lukewarm, I spit you out'. It's living death. Don't do that.

Then there is the despair option. Watch TV, start drinking, don't bother to give up smoking, don't have the smear test, eat too much, don't bother to exercise. Despair doesn't have to be drastic ... it doesn't have to involve jumping out of a fourth floor window as an attractive woman of 52 did in central London last week. No, it can be far more subtle than that: 'Why bother to exercise?' 'I enjoy smoking' (some women will actually add 'it's all I've got'). Make an effort to see friends – but a half-hearted effort. Remain bitter so that he has to feel guilty for ever. Punish him with your own ill health and despair – punish everyone. I don't recommend this option either.

Then there is the option that I recommend, option three, and I'm talking now to any woman of any age who has been left. You have just received your freedom. Get down on your knees and give thanks to all those angels and arch-angels and any other gods or spiritual beings that you happen to think may exist. Then you may enjoy taking an inventory of everything that was wrong with the life you had with him – this may be thirty years? Every compromise that you made to please him. Every pleasure you gave up. What about the fact that you used to enjoy painting or poetry until he made some derogatory comment one day? You can wear what you like, see who you like, eat what you like. You can design the next fifty years of your life – creating means to have everything that you could never have before so that any change from what's on your plan can only be better. And make damn sure every non-fucking day is an adventure. With this attitude it is very unlikely that many fucking opportunities will be missed. The world is yours, sweetheart! He ain't ever going to say 'no' again and if you meet new men you'll have different rules and they'll all be your rules.

For some women this will not be easy. The comfort zone has become very small. Bad habits of not taking risks have crept in. Fear is dominant. Well, my sisters – the only fourth option is to stay at home and transform. The woman who can do this, make no changes in her life, not be bitter alone and be truly happy is a rare creature indeed. Sooner or later we will all be eighty and have to do our inner work as our legs won't carry us out of the door. If you are able to transform who you are unaided, then I salute you. Except you wouldn't be holding this book in your hands. You'd be reading the Upanishads, the annotated Torah or St Julian of Norwich. Losada wouldn't get a look in. Of course, I recommend taking our spirituality seriously before we reach eighty, but for those of us who are still less than this age I recommend a different course of action. Personal transformation through meditation plus blasting the comfort zone.

So, where was I? Ah yes, option three – a life of adventure, discovery and celebration. If you want to fuel your tank with a wonderful expression from the man with the ridiculous name, Chuck Spezzano – 'Happiness is the best revenge' – that's permitted. (Not encouraged – I'd rather do the right thing for the right reason. But certainly permitted.)

OK. So how do you do this if you are afraid to go out of the door? The answer is very simple. You take small steps. Every day you stretch yourself a little. If you are afraid to drive a car because your husband did the driving for ten years. Take a driving lesson. You need to know that fear and excitement are very similar emotions. The day that you are afraid, you are not bored. You are alive. Every time anyone invites you to do something and you feel fear – do it. If no one invites you, create your own adventures and invite people to join you. If my elderly uncle, with a pacemaker inside him, can do a parachute dive on his 75th birthday, what's your excuse for not trying new things? If you watch too much TV, I would recommend going cold turkey. Put the TV in a cupboard high up and put a cold, dead turkey where your TV was. This will remind you that this is how you'll look soon. Between now and then, do you just want to watch TV? I don't think so. You need a new bunch of friends (they'll probably be younger than you, coz many of your married friends have probably become a little set in their ways and – now that you come to think of it – a little dull. Oh God, were you like that?? Yes! You were – but those days are gone). They are bored and stuck, you see. You are not bored or stuck. You've been set free. Your ex didn't approve of you doing WHAT? Well, start there, then!

And you would probably never have . . . insert your own list of dreams and number them one to a hundred. And please don't complain that you don't have enough money. One day we'll all have as little as the cold, dead turkey, so there is no better time to learn about the uselessness of possessions than now. Learning to live dreams without money certainly makes it more of a challenge. But better be happy living in an old houseboat than be miserable in a luxury apartment. You don't need me to list dreams for you. Do you want to travel and not pay a fortune? How about teaching English for a while in a school for orphaned girls in Tibet? If you'd like to do this, email my website as I know an organisation that can arrange this.

Want to enter a different world? Do something you never dreamed of? How about scuba diving? 'I'm too old' – not according to Doreen. Too unfit – not according to Doreen. Afraid of water – well, so was Doreen. There are no excuses. I think the Scuba Trust trains people with worse disabilities than you have. Nothing is standing between you and the world (any more) except your own mind. And you can reprogramme your own mind. Really you can. Create wonderful adventures, take small steps and then congratulate yourself all the way. All the way around the world. Don't think of reasons why things aren't possible. Consider new ways in which they can be possible (www.vso.org.uk) and, if you have children, make sure you hear them say, 'I can't believe what she is doing now.' Be outrageous. Start your life.

THE OTHER WOMAN

So now I'd like to speak with the women who are sleeping with the married men. I know what he says to you about how helpless his wife is, I've heard every line of it. But that 'wife who doesn't understand me' that he tells you about? That's the same woman I was just talking to. As long as everyone believes she's helpless and he goes on telling her lies, she's never going to start living her life over, is she? And it's you (and me, as I've played your part) denying her that opportunity.

Neil Strauss wrote to me in an email: On fidelity: the best wisdom I learned from a pick-up artist is that three things necessary in any relationship are – 'honesty, trust, and respect'. You can't have love or a healthy relationship without these things. And the destructive power of cheating is not the act itself, but the way it sabotages the honesty and trust in the relationship.

It's not getting anyone the quality of relationships that we could have. Do you imagine that he's not lying to you, too? And you know what you can do differently? You can leave him and not collude any more. I can write this directly to many women I know in this postion.

You don't really want it like this, do you? He doesn't cherish you. What you really want, what every women wants and deserves, is a quality relationship. No matter how good the sex is, does it really make up for the fact that he leaves you and goes home to his wife? (I'm not writing this for the group of women who actually like this arrangement – that's another whole bowl of chicks.) It's interesting that Harry once asked me if I liked him more because he's not available. Why would I want a man who feels like a soul mate who I can't go diving with? Does he think I'm crazy? Life is too bloody short.

Why do you want a man that you can't wake up and find there in the middle of the night? Who you can't watch sleeping? Why are you choosing a situation where you can't plan a holiday? You can't phone him when you want to? Why are you choosing to be with someone when you can't meet his friends? You can't see him on his birthday? You can't introduce him to your granny (unless you lie to your granny too).

Now the objection here is a little different. I can hear many women saying, 'But you don't understand. I love him.' Yes – well, here is the Losada test for this one. Please, just as an exercise for me, be a little more clear with yourself, will you? Take away the word love for a second, as we none of us use it too precisely, and put in another word. You certainly don't mean that you want his spiritual growth. So what do you really mean? You care for him? You adore him? You need him? You 'can't live without him'?

OK – let's look at these in reverse order! You can't live without him. You respond every time you hear that song, 'I can't liiive . . . if living is without you oo ooo, I can't giiive . . . I can't give any moore.'

Yes, you can. You can live without him. You can't live without air or food. Let's get real here. You may *feel* as if you can't live without him. Or don't want to. I've been here, too. I don't want to live without Harry. But to say that I can't? That's not true, is it? I don't mean to be unsympathetic – I don't know the story, but the image of the woman killing herself that was on the front of the papers recently is clear in my mind. There would have been a love story there somewhere. Very few intelligent women kill themselves over money. I'd be willing to bet that she just felt that she couldn't live without him, whoever he was.

But look at what she could have done. She could have gone to Tibet and taught in that school I was just telling you about. If she had a terminal illness she could have worked in a hospice. We can live without these men, sisters!

Did all those feminists of the last generation die just so that we could have the vote and then sit around with beliefs like 'I can't live without him'? Find yourself sitting feeling miserable because the married man hasn't called? Well, who has the power here? YOU DO, sister! You say to him, 'Enough already. No more lies. Either you tell your wife what's happening and grant her a divorce, or you don't see me any more. I look forward to seeing a photocopy of the decree nisi. I love you and I'd just like you to tell her the truth for all of our sakes. No one is happy.'

He'll say, 'Have you gone mad? I'm happy. You're happy. She's happy. Why do you want to destroy everything we have?' He'll accuse you of being selfish. Or, if he's lucky, he'll have big guns . . . he'll be able to say, 'I couldn't do this to the children.' You'll be accused of putting your own selfishness before the lives of the children. One Tom even said to a woman I know, 'Isn't the little happiness that we share enough for you?'

Bear with me, men – I'm not against you – I love you and I'll get to you later, and I'll get around to talking about the children.

Now I'm talking to the 'other woman'. I was just saying what he'll accuse you of if you ask to see a decree nisi –

certainly of that most inadmissible of crimes, being 'unreason-
able'. If he loves you (or the quality of the sex you provide)
then he'll accuse you of practically anything he can. You'll
find that he knows all your weak spots. He'll make you feel
guilty, or try to dissuade you with humour. Or, worse still,
he'll sulk and say, 'OK – you're obviously not interested in me
any more. I won't call again.' Nothing is worse than feeling
misunderstood, so if you're not careful you'll be hooked back
in. But you hold your ground – you want to see the decree so
the deceit will end. If she phones you and says, 'I really don't
mind you having sex with my husband,' well, that's another
story. Better email me and we'll discuss that – I can't go into
all the possible scenarios here and that doesn't happen often.

It's a risk, of course. If it's the sex he wants and not you,
he will easily find a less 'demanding' woman who will
provide. You will have learned the truth about him. You'll
learn whether he's a Tom, a Dick or a Harry. Whichever,
you were allowing him to eat the cake and have it, weren't
you? The problem is how you live your life without him.
Well, that's the same couple of paragraphs as for the wife,
the woman left behind. If you're lucky, you're a little
younger than she is. One of my friends has a mother who is
finally kicking her husband out. He's been having an affair
with his secretary for twenty years. She's sixty – it will be
harder for her than for you.

He told you he'd leave his wife? Well, you'll see now,
won't you? Meanwhile, welcome aboard. You are no longer
part of the problem – you are part of the solution. Let's call
you a spiritual feminist, shall we? Let's make this a new
possibility. A spiritual form of feminism in which women
are honest because they have learned enough about spirituality, meditation and personal responsibility to be able to
stand on their own two feet or sit on their own meditation
cushion . . . without collusion in other women being lied to.
And because they love men more than this.

I can actually hear you screaming, 'But what about the
children?!!'

BUT WHAT ABOUT THE CHILDREN?

Right – the children. So children need stability, a 'stable home' and to know that their parents love them. Some psychologists would say that it's more important for them to see that their parents love each other. But – leaving that aside – they need to know that they are loved. The word 'divorce' tragically spells the beginning of the end of some children's lives. This is all parents' greatest fear. They love their 'kids' (in this situation they always seem to be called 'kids' whether they are three or seventeen), possibly had divorced parents themselves, and will go to any lengths to avoid inflicting this suffering. Or so they tell themselves. I know several men who, realising that their marriages were over when the children were two, decided that they had to 'stick it out' until the kids were eighteen. You hear of women who say, 'I don't care what you do but I don't want to hear about it.' And they stay together 'for the sake of the children'. They play charades. For ten years or more, or less. And this game of happy families is played 'for the sake of the children'. Really? It's an overused cliché, so I'm overusing it.

A short digression. When my daughter was younger I had a friend who was a single father and bringing up three young children on his own while I was on my own with my daughter. Sadly, we were not in love, but we were the best of friends and we'd often take the four children out to play. We had no money but we'd do picnics and take bus rides. We even created a very good descant recorder group with him and myself, my daughter and the two eldest of his children. We'd play in the park and buy ice cream, and every time we went out, people would come up and say how happy we all looked. 'It's so lovely to see a happy family,' they'd say. They could see that we weren't pretending anything. We never had the heart to tell them the truth. We wanted them to believe it. Isn't that wonderful and sad all at the same time?

Now I know it's not always easy raising a family, and couples can't be expected to be happy all the time like we were. But children aren't stupid. Do you think a child of three or even younger can't sense whether the atmosphere they are in is a genuinely happy one or not? They may not have words for it, but they know. Do you think they can't sense bitterness? Do you think they don't know that something may be wrong with sarcasm? Do we really imagine that a child can't sense energy just as well as an adult can? Only it's worse because they don't understand. They study their parents' faces, every vowel intonation they absorb like a sponge, every nuance of mood and furrowed brow they see. And the children are unhappy, but they don't know why. As they get older they become more confused because many charade-playing parents tell their children that they are happy; the children assume that their environment is normal, so something must be wrong with them.

If Slipperman had stayed, I would never have said to my daughter, 'I hate your father.' Of course not. But neither would I ever have learned how to pull my socks up, take full personal responsibility and determinedly turn myself into the person who she now describes as her favourite inspiration.

How can children grow up happily when the adults around them don't cherish each other? How can they grow up happily and with good role models for positive relationships of their own if their own father needs to lie to their mother (or vice versa) and she knows but doesn't like to think about it? While they both justify this slow suicide for their children's sakes? Don't you begin to feel you can't breathe just reading this?

Did any adolescent *ever* say to a parent, 'Mum and Dad, I realise that you haven't loved each other since I was a toddler and I realise that you sacrificed the best years of your life and suffered for years for my sake and I'd like to thank you'? To identify with the adolescent for a phrase – bollocks did they.

Ask any child who is old enough to understand what they want for their parents and they just want them to be happy. Really happy. Not pretending. Imagine that atmosphere. A house with real joy. Real appreciation, with every moment treasured, every breath, every second valued – because we have so few heartbeats left. Which house would you want your children to grow up in?

'We hide it well,' says a voice of one woman I know. You insult your children's intelligence. It feels good to write this, as it's hard to be this brutal to any one specific person. Everyone is doing what they think is best under the circumstances. But I don't believe lying and 'putting on a brave face' is good for the children. Which model of 'normal' relationships would you want your child to learn, consciously and unconsciously?

OK, so you'll allow me that a child growing up in the oppressive atmosphere of an unhappy marriage may not be a good idea, but you do all right. Surely that is better than 'ripping a child's life apart' with the big D-word? One man told me that he'd read in a study that children do better in marriages that stay together where the adults row than in divorced families. How pessimistic is that?

We are recreating divorce, remember? We are being responsible grown-ups, continuing to care for each other and to treat each other with love and respect. Why are children so upset by divorce? Only because the parents are devastated by it, because they say terrible things about the other one, fight over the children or make the children choose.

Only last week a man called me who was in the middle of a divorce court and said, 'I'm just fighting my ex-wife.' He didn't say 'negotiating with'. I'm afraid the adults have a lot of work to do. But let's imagine a situation where the adults are behaving like adults and allowing the children to be children. What is actually happening? One parent is moving out of the family home and getting another home. Or they may be selling the family home and buying two very small flats. Or they maybe selling the very small flat and one of the parents may be renting a room.

If no one is having hysterics about this and Mummy is saying, 'Daddy is going to have a dog at his house and we are going to have a budgie in ours,' where is the attention of the children going? 'What kind of dog?' I'm not saying that the children wouldn't rather have both the parents downstairs on the sofa smooching . . . but if that isn't going to happen, then at least let them experience two happy homes. It is the job of both the adults individually to ensure their own happiness by whatever means they need to. They have no one to blame any more. What kind of teachers are we for our children if resigned misery is what they have to look forward to?

It may be strange, but I actually believe that this could benefit the children, or the child. It's a bizarrely common fact that fathers who move out often spend more time with their child or children than they did before the split, or vice versa if the child lives with the father. They all learn about emotions and are forced to express them and talk about them in a way in which 'charading' families will not. Our friend Professor Simon Baron-Cohen has come up with a list of 412 different emotions. Many parents don't know how to discuss emotion with their children and often fathers still don't know how to have emotionally literate conversations. But there is nothing wrong with being sad or afraid, as long as it is expressed. The irony is that after living in a family playing charades, a child can even feel relief that someone is admitting that they feel sad.

Bad times wake kids up to good times; sadness teaches us when we are really happy; fear teaches us the meaning of courage; anger teaches us about vulnerability; suffering teaches us gentleness and compassion. There is nothing wrong with these experiences . . . they are part of what children need to learn about in life. They are as valuable as education – as long as the adults around them know how to handle them. It's not knowing about fear or sadness that stultifies people's development.

It's simple stuff – name the emotion that you or the child is feeling, talk about how it feels a bit, then listen. This 'reflective listening' (as it is called) creates emotional maturity, EQ, and children who are not afraid of their own thoughts and feelings. But to give your child/children these benefits, you have to avoid hurling vindictive or negative angry bitterness around. Anger can be OK, but you can't pronounce, 'Your father is leaving us!' and burst into tears, letting children know that their world is at an end. Parents have to sit down together without acrimony and explain that one parent is moving out, but won't be far away. (Through the wall, in the case of the family in Bath that I was telling you about earlier.)

And of course there are other benefits. The two homes will now take on different house rules so the children will have to learn new flexibility. In this home they watch TV – in this one they don't. In this one they are allowed to stay up later, but have to eat weird food. In this one you can put your feet on the furniture, but you have to tidy up more often. In this home there are always lots of adult visitors who expect them to sit at table and have conversations, but in this house you can do painting any time you want.

They have two educations and if everyone is friendly, or as friendly as possible to everyone else, the children are closer to what they really need – a community. Different points of view are enriching. And if they see their parents happy and they have a dog in one house and a kitten in another, then how are their lives destroyed? They are not. And would they prefer that their parents had not split up? Probably. And would they be better off playing charades, as they were while the parents demonstrated how to hide emotions and not express what they were really feeling? I don't think so.

A WORD FOR THE MEN

And finally, a word for the men. I bet you think that I think you are the baddies. The problem, the creators of all this mess. The liars, the cheats, the villains. No – I don't think that. As you know – and I hope I've made it clear in this book – I like men and, bizarrely perhaps, I feel I understand them. I don't know, perhaps I was a man in a recent former lifetime or perhaps it's because I've been both mother and father to my own daughter. Perhaps it's because I've spent so much time with men on this project or because I'm heterosexual? Whatever the reason, I'm not angry with the men at all.

Despite the title of this book and the scarcity of interesting, single, available men, ultimately I don't see that much of a difference between us both. Our bodies are different and, according to Simon and all the most recent research, our brains are different. Your ability to put different parts of your lives in different compartments may be different and maybe you don't listen as well and can read maps better like the books say. But I think our hearts are pretty much the same. Fear is the same for men and women; pain, sadness, joy – these are all the same. Even if the sex is different, men still want to love and be loved, you still want to feel appreciated. I think men are doing the best they know how, just as women are. But the fact that I'm not mad at them doesn't mean that I don't have some things to say.

So this is for any man who has a wife and a mistress or two or three – the Toms, the Dicks, the Harrys – and for any man that is in a marriage or a relationship that he doesn't want to be in. And my message is simple. Life is short. Get real. Leave.

It should be clear to you if you've read what is above that your wife is not the helpless dependant that you've made her out to be. And if she is, you're not helping her get over that. I even know one man, in Ireland, whose wife has been an alcoholic for ten years. He has a son, so to buffer the son from the problem, he has never left. He knows he can't rescue her or change her behaviour – but instead of finding a genuine solution he has simply ignored it and slept with other women. The more hopeless she becomes, the more trapped he feels. It would have been easier for this woman if he had left ten years ago.

I know another very unhappy man whose wife is over sixty. They've been unhappy for at least ten years . . . if he'd left when she was fifty it would have been a million times easier for her. I know a third man who is still young but who has decided to stay in his dead marriage for 'about another ten years – for the sake of the children'. Oh, please!

What is it with you guys? Is it fear? Is it complacency? Is it laziness? Is it a lack of guts? Or are you afraid to feel guilty? Is it the money? Or as Prof Simon suggests, the loss of social status? You know what I think – no matter how much you insist that it's the love of the children or the fact that you 'really care for your wife', I think it's your image of yourself that you don't want to change.

I'm not saying that any man in this situation is a 'bad' man, any more than any woman. But I do think that there is a level of self-deception that is quite staggering. You can bet that the man I wrote about earlier in the book, the one with all the golfing trophies, likes to think of himself as a 'good husband'. One male friend has a wonderful phrase he's invented – it's one on from 'white lies' – it's 'compassionate lying', lying to protect the other person. What a load of poor self-deception is that? This man is a 'good husband' and a 'good father'? And the other one who has decided to stay ten years 'for the sake of his two kids'. Guys! Who do you think you are fooling?

What has happened to you? Don't you know the difference any more between genuine happiness and a life of self-deception? Please don't make women into children . . . and that is what you are doing. The more you take responsibility for the women, the weaker and more helplessly dependent they become. Do you seriously think that your wives are going to go crazy if you leave? (Sure, they might – for six weeks.) Why do the statistics show that you'd rather be caught out playing away than sit down and say, 'I've met someone and I want to leave. I'm sorry.' Why is it so hard?

One of my male friends said, 'If he's got a wife who cooks for him and a twenty-three-year-old Bolivian girlfriend who can suck a golfball through a hosepipe, why would he want to change anything?' As we've seen in the book, many men don't rate other men very highly, while often making exceptions of themselves.

But, call me old fashioned . . . I still think that if you have the chance of a harem of nineteen-year-olds or a challenging and fun relationship with a woman of the same age as you are (shock, horror!), most of you will, ultimately, want a partner. Are all men who say that sex with love is more interesting than sex with strangers lying? I don't think so. More novel with strangers? Yes. More exciting? Perhaps. Better? No.

One of the reasons that there are so few interesting and available men is because none of you have the guts to leave. You wait until a younger woman comes along and is prepared to have sex with you while you are still married. And even then you do nothing – because you don't want the responsibility for the divorce? How pathetic is that?

And then you lie to cover your tracks . . . really, guys, you can do better than this. Currently no one I know can think of a single man who has left a marriage when there hasn't been a third party involved. What about this expression, 'Women leave a marriage for themselves, men leave for another woman.' It's not good, is it?

How can I defend you, my brothers? You can do better – just as the wives can and the other women can. You can learn to love your wife and leave her. You can stop lying to her and you can stop lying to your mistress, too. If you are going to pass all the emotional responsibility to women like this and force a situation where they have to make all the difficult decisions, then you may as well have stayed at home with your mothers.

Buy the song – 'Make a new plan Stan, Slip out the back Jack, Don't need to be coy Roy' – just be kind, and leave with love and compassion. If she screams at you and calls you a bastard, don't be surprised, but don't yell back. Just say, 'Yes, I've lied. But I'm not lying any more.'

Don't fight her in the courts. If you can't agree the finances, then get some good mediation. Put the kids first. Be generous. This is the same girl you courted not so long ago. Treat her the way you treated her then and she may surprise you. I'm not recommending this so that you can go from one bed to the next. Find a place for yourself, somehow . . . get yourself free.

So that's it. That's all sides of the triangle. If we want this all to change, each person involved in any of these situations (or knows someone who is and can pass this on to them) has the power to make a difference. Each person who decides that they choose to be real, to be true to themselves and unconditionally loving with others, is part of a shift. No one would be deceived or lied to, we could genuinely support each other, be open with our children and we'd all 'be the change that we wish to see in the world'. Does it sound as though I'm painting a utopian ideal? Nope – this is simple. I'm just asking for more honesty.

And when we can make the changes that I speak of: when a mistress asks for the truth or leaves, and when a wife stands up, stops being dependent and helps the unhappy man go, and when a man who is in a dead relationship tells the truth, leaves and learns to live alone . . . then there will be fewer unhappy, bumbling-along marriages with 'every day a little death' (Sondheim). If, one person at a time, we can 'be the change we'd like to see', then the sight of a joyful happy family will no longer be something to comment on and there will be some interesting and available men out there, for me, for the hundred single women I know in London, for the million female readers of this book and for every intelligent single woman over 35 anywhere in Western society.

THE EPILOGUE

So what became of Hisham and Harry? They are both different kinds of life lessons and evidently I'm a slow learner.

When I got back from Egypt I thought a lot about Hisham – his love of the sea and music and his antipathy towards the human race. I found I wanted to send him some music. So I looked carefully and chose a beautiful double CD of Yo-Yo Ma playing the Bach cello concertos. It is solo cello; deep, dark and brooding, moody yet serene. I knew that Hisham would love it. I wrapped it in purple tissue paper and gold ribbon and sent it, with a letter, off to Egypt. I know that it arrived safely at his local post office, because they let Jane know, at Divers' Lodge, that a parcel arrived that Hisham needed to sign for. But here is what happens if you try to love someone who doesn't want loving. He never collected the parcel. He told Jane that he couldn't be bothered. Jane emailed me to ask if she could have the CDs and I said she could, but they wouldn't let her take them and she couldn't persuade Hisham to make the short journey to find them. For all I know, they are there still, in their tissue and ribbon. So that is Hisham. Being unavailable to receive a gift is a high level of unavailable.

And Harry?

Well, I spoke to Harry a month or so ago about this book and he asked if I was dating someone new. He doesn't want to be in touch with me any more or for me to love him any more. He said, 'You're spoiling the memory.' He wants me in his past. Ouch.

I said, 'But, Harry, I've finished the book and, when I see the sky, I still think of you.' He said, 'But I don't want the story to end like that, with you still thinking about me and me here and you there . . . that's not how it should end.'

Too right it isn't. But Harry doesn't understand. I don't write fiction . . . apart from when I do.

[Insert background music: symphonic, lilting strings] Roll – fiction . . .

So I made him angry for a while, because I couldn't forget him. But his problem was that, in spite of feeling angry, he couldn't forget me either. One day I heard a tap on my window . . . I looked up and there he stood. My Harry, with a smile on his face the size of a Cheshire Cat's.

I opened the door. 'Hello. Tea? Coffee? Are you staying? Or just visiting?'

'Er, staying, I think. Is that OK?'

'Sure.'

'Wife and son aren't too happy about this, but they'll get over it. Son wants to know if he can come and stay with us next weekend in London. He may be visiting a lot. He'll be half living here. Is that OK?'

'Of course.'

[Pause]

We looked at each other. I was smiling with tears pouring down my face. It was like a fairytale.

'Is this my happy ending then, Harry?'

'Yes, I think it is.'

    'How did you make it happen? How did I make it happen?'

    'I just told the truth. To everyone. And my wife is brilliant . . . she wants me to be happy. I always said I wanted to change my whole life. She knew. And you? You were just so honest, so real – so non-fiction.'

    'Thank you. So what was it, then? Tea or coffee? Chocolate biscuit?'

And the non-fiction ending? Well, the thing I love about real life is that we never know, do we? Word's got around about my determination to date men who aren't married, so they seem to show up occasionally now. I have a date next week with an unmarried man. I may want to just have dinner with him once or, if he doesn't mention spectator sport, I may want to see him twice. My daughter is living at home for a while and we have a new lodger, an Italian male who washes up, pays the rent and is wonderfully uncomplicated.

I am fantastically free, and working on this project has certainly helped me to appreciate that. The joy of being single is that we could meet someone extraordinary any day of the week. I could take off or be whisked off tomorrow for an adventure anywhere in the world.

Rachel Billington, the author, said on my radio this morning that the phrase she hates most is 'you must move on' – 'Where,' she asked, 'are we to move on to?' I laughed. I'm with her on that. Harry may be cross with me for still loving him. But I'm not cross with myself. Maybe my dinner companion next week will make me laugh and be available and I'll soon wonder what I saw in Harry. Or maybe not. But my secret of happiness has always been to celebrate everything – the pain, the loss, the heartbreak, the failures and the successes – and to just go on loving anyway.

My agent just emailed and said that she had dinner with two interesting available men last night. I've replied with my details and those of my most fun single female friend. Who knows? Let's see if the men have the courage to respond. Interesting and available men are hard to find, it's true, but reliable builders are out there and teenagers who love to get up early. Everything is possible. So be honest, be happy, sit squarely on your meditation cushion, and keep looking. The world is ours.

APPENDIX ONE: THE ON-GOING STORY . . .

So this is where you get active.

THE GAME OF TEN PLACES

I would like to make some lists of the best ten places to meet interesting men in the town or city where you live and create a reference for women in your town. Where would an interesting and available man in your town be?

If you and a girlfriend (or even you alone) would like to go out and visit ten different locations in your town (not including pubs and clubs) then please send your 'Ten Places' list to: tenplaces@isabellosada.com

We hope to have all the lists available online for everyone to compare notes!

MEN! AND HONESTY . . .

If you have any other comments on this book or ideas on where or how you think that interesting and available men can be found – please send them to men!@isabellosada.com

Please don't write and say 'They are everywhere, just walk outside.' I know . . .

If you have thoughts on a new kind of divorce or

comments about the concept of feminist spirituality please email me on women@isabellosada.com

If you would like to get in touch with me personally I do attempt to answer all my emails. It's another form of madness. You can reach me care of the 'Contact' page of www.isabellosada.com.

If you email and I don't reply please either forgive me or try again.

Very best wishes,
Isabel Losada, London, 2007

APPENDIX TWO: THE READING LIST

Here are some of the books that I've been reading while I've been working on this project. It isn't an extensive or academic reading list (many academics cheat and just list all the books on the subject, most of which they haven't read).

I've actually read all these, so, in the order in which they come to mind, here is some further reading on our subject, should you choose to consider this mystery further.

Men: the Darker Continent, by Heather Formaini. First published in 1990, this is about as bad as it gets in terms of the bad news. If you are in any doubt that men are responsible for all the problems in the world, Heather Formaini will remove your last shred of doubt. Depressed me for a week ... I still love men, but she is horribly convincing.

The Game: Undercover in the Secret Society of Pick-up Artists, by Neil Strauss. I was so horrified by this concept when I read a review, I made a point of ordering it from the library in order not to give Neil one more sale. And the book is shocking – but it's also funny, fascinating psychology, very well written, and explains why I didn't include bars and nightclubs. He's a very good writer and deserves all the success that the book has had. Essential reading for women, I'd say.

Men are From Mars, Women are From Venus, by John Gray. Overwritten and dated – explains things with numerous obvious examples as all American psychology books do, and at times infuriating. However, read it with a pinch of salt and your sense of humour and it does still have some genuine insights.

Simply Irresistible: The Psychology of Seduction – How to Catch and Keep your Perfect Partner, by Professor Raj Persaud. This is the book about which Dr Raj gave his entertaining evening when I was playing the game of ten places. If you'd like to read more about any of the points he mentioned that night, then here are his writings on attraction in full.

The Essential Difference, by Simon Baron-Cohen. This really will help you understand men better and also has all the charts in the back so you can find out for yourself just how much empathetic ability and systemising ability you have.

Men in Love: Men's Sexual Fantasies – the Triumph of Love Over Rage, by Nancy Friday. Don't say I didn't warn you . . . I only made it to page 316, but I still think it's essential reading in the quest for us to understand each other better. And it will make you think about sex for weeks!

Y: The Descent of Men, by Steve Jones. Mainly about genetics and chromosomes. Interesting stuff if you are of a scientific frame of mind. And he tells us that in China there are eighty million men under thirty with no hope of marriage. (So if you haven't chosen your university degree yet, take Chinese and start packing – then set up a dating agency and you'll be a millionaire soon.)

The Female Eunuch, by Germaine Greer. The classic, first published in 1970. Never having read this, I considered it essential background reading for this project but, much to my surprise, she wasn't so much anti-men as anti the entire status quo and I loved her book for that. Also, it's brilliantly argued and alarming to see that some of the things she'd worked out then we still haven't sorted out today.

The Future of Men, by Marian Salzman, Ira Matathia and Ann O'Reilly. Published in 2005, this book studies men from the point of view of how to market to them and sell to them. If you have any kind of business that sells to men, then I'd recommend it.

Why Men Don't Listen and Women Can't Read Maps: How We're Different and What to do About it, by Allan and Barbara Pease. A light and easy read. Will mean that you'll have an excuse not to read maps in the car any more . . . just hand the map to him and ask instructions from the next passer-by. Prof Simon's book says the same things, but explains it all greater detail.

Men: The Truth, by Steven Appleby (cartoonist). And if you only buy one of these books then this would have to be the one.

APPENDIX THREE: EMAIL FROM THE BLUE

-----Original Message-----
From: Hisham
Sent: 13:47
To: Isabel Losada
Subject: Bach

Dear Isabel,

Months later and you write and ask why i never picked up the music. OK. Please take the time to read my explanation, and i hope you will understand it. This will be a very long e mail, by my standards at least . . . :-)

The reason why i didn't pick up your present for me, was not, of course, that i didn't want to wait in a queue. For Bach, i'd wait for a very long time. i just didn't want to have any emotional involvement with you. So at that time i felt that this would be the best way to make this point very clear. i know that you got the point that i wanted to make but since i lost what would have been a wonderful friend.

As for the dark side of my character, well, what can i say? It is surprisingly lifting. The last 6 months I've spent working all the time at sea, I have changed a lot. But it all started before that. It started when I have met this crazy woman who believed that she could change the world . . .

Well, this is very difficult for me, saying that i am sorry, sorry for not picking up your present for me, for not answering your e mails and messages, for not giving you a decent explanation for my actions, and every other thing that I have done towards you.

I wish you all the best, and i do sincerely hope to see you again some time just to say sorry in person.

I know that this is very surprising, even I am surprised at my self . . .

May the sun always stay shining in your face, and the wind keep blowing behind your back . . . I am not sure if i have quoted this properly . . .

a very big hug
hisham

p.s. mind you i still believe that love is over rated and biochemically it is the same feeling as eating large quantities of chocolate . . . :-)

PS even before you ask – i don't mind you using this for your book if you want to . . .

ACKNOWLEDGEMENTS

All the people in my books are real. In rare cases I change people's names to protect their identity, but most appear as themselves, so I would like to thank everyone who, in one form or another, has played a part.

Special thanks are due to Steve Hands and all at Kabiray Builders, Mary Balfour at Drawing Down the Moon, PPL Plumbing Training, Warrs, Harley-Davidson UK, Anthony Simpson, Professor Simon Baron-Cohen, Professor Raj Persaud, the British Sub-Aqua Club, Divers' Lodge – Hurghada, and John Lenkiewicz of the Institute of Sexuality and Human Relations for his endorsement of the emotional legitimacy of my conclusions.

I would like to thank Mark Farley of Waterstone's, Julian Rafot at the Pan Bookshop and Matthew Perren in Edinburgh for wise advice whenever I need it; Daisy, Peggy and Albert for listening, Jenny for tolerance and good advice, and John and Christy for their remarkable support.

I am indebted to Rosemary Davidson, Jenny Parrott, Alice Lutyens, Camilla Goslett and Jonathan Lloyd and, further along the road, to Rowan Lawton and Caroline Michel. Also a thank you to Lesley O'Mara for her faith in my work. Finally I would like to thank Ed Faulkner, Kate

Quarry and all the energetic and imaginative staff at Virgin Books.

My daughter Emily Lucienne is a constant source of enthusiasm, encouragement and love. Thanks to Hisham for allowing me to quote him unedited – such openness is rare. Most especially I would like to thank the man who is not called Harry. Ani Ahpbec Jden. Shuf fakterni habibi.

Emma gazed at him.

"You said you can rec̶̶̶̶̶ ̶̶̶̶ ̶̶̶̶̶ ̶̶̶̶̶̶"

Ridge nodded. He suspected that if anybody could teach him to read, it would be Emma. She was determined and intelligent, and too pretty for his peace of mind. Being stranded in the small cabin with her was sweet torture. He hoped her lessons would steer his thoughts in other directions.

Ridge clasped her hand, tugging her to her feet. He miscalculated his strength and she flew upward, into his arms. She pressed against his chest and his body reacted with all the subtlety of a tomcat in the springtime.

Startled, Ridge looked down into Emma's uptilted face expecting to find disapproval. Instead, he saw the reflection of his own desire and he instinctively drew her flush against him. Emma was so close he could smell the first tendrils of her passion. Pleasure swirled through his brain, obliterating everything but his need.

"I want you, Emma," Ridge whispered.

Emma's legs wobbled but his corded arms kept her upright. She knew intimately what he wanted, as her own body begged for the same. But once they gave in to lust, it would be impossible to undo . . .

A ... ON FOR LEARNING

To Find You Again

Maureen McKade

BERKLEY SENSATION, NEW YORK

This is a work of fiction. Names, characters, places, and incidents either
are the product of the author's imagination or are used fictitiously, and
any resemblance to actual persons, living or dead, business
establishments, events, or locales is entirely coincidental.

TO FIND YOU AGAIN

A Berkley Sensation Book / published by arrangement with
the author

PRINTING HISTORY
Berkley Sensation edition / July 2004

Copyright © 2004 by Maureen Webster.
Cover art by Judy York.
Cover hand-lettering by Ron Zinn.
Cover design by George Long.
Interior text design by Kristin del Rosario.

For information address: The Berkley Publishing Group,
a division of Penguin Group (USA) Inc.,
375 Hudson Street, New York, New York 10014.

ISBN: 0-425-19709-3

BERKLEY SENSATION™
Berkley Sensation Books are published by The Berkley Publishing
Group, a division of Penguin Group (USA) Inc.,
375 Hudson Street, New York, New York 10014.
BERKLEY SENSATION and the "B" design
are trademarks belonging to Penguin Group (USA) Inc.

PRINTED IN THE UNITED STATES OF AMERICA

10 9 8 7 6 5 4 3 2 1

Alan, for your faith and love.

Natasha, for your support and confidence.

And much thanks to Deb Stover, Kathleen Crow, Von Jocks, and Susan Wickberg for your suggestions, critiques, and margaritas.

ONE

"*AMAZING grace! How sweet the sound . . .*"

The voices of the Sunset Methodist Church members blended with wheezy organ notes to circle Emma Louise Hartwell with its rhythm. Emma's lips moved with the remembered words, but no sound came forth. Although she held her head high, and, aimed at the front of the church, her gaze followed dust motes, which drifted aimlessly through sunlight slanting in between boards covering one of the windows. Next week the shutters would be removed, heralding the church's official recognition of spring.

Emma shuddered as the four walls closed in on her, and her heart pounded like a war drum. She should've waited until next Sunday to make her first public appearance. At least, then, she would have the illusion of freedom as she looked through the glass panes. Now there was only warped wood and shadowed corners, so unlike . . .

No! She didn't dare think about that, not while surrounded by those who had judged and sentenced her even though they didn't know the truth. Of course, if they knew everything, her total condemnation would be assured.

Her attention wandered across the congregation, and

she recognized many people from her childhood. Biddie Little, the organist, who still hit the wrong key at the most inopportune time. Thomas Lyndon, the owner of the Sunset Bank and Trust, who had his nose so high in the air that Emma wondered how he could walk without tripping. Sally Warner, a childhood friend, who was now married to George Orton, another of Emma's classmates, and already with two children—another reminder of the time she'd lost.

A hushed scuffle between the Morrison children caught Emma's attention. The boy and girl were tugging and punching at one another as their parents ignored them.

A Lakota child would never be so disobedient during a religious ceremony. They were taught from infancy to remain quiet and to honor their elders, as well as to revere their traditions and rituals. But then, the Lakota children wouldn't have had to sit on hard benches surrounded by four walls for two hours either. Emma, who'd grown up attending Sunday service, found herself anxious to escape the confinement. However, the intervening years had taught her to remain still and silent, like a mouse when a hawk passed overhead.

The final hymn ended with a concluding groan of the organ, and Emma herself nearly groaned in relief. She wished she could forego decorum and run outside like the children, but this was the first time she'd attended service with her family since her return five months ago. Her mother said they had wanted to spare her the pitying looks. Emma believed her parents wanted to spare *themselves* the town's censure. However, enough time had passed that they hoped for a parcel of acceptance.

Familiar townsfolk greeted John and Martha Hartwell, as well as their fair-haired daughter Sarah, but only a few acknowledged Emma's presence. Even Sally and George, whom she'd known for years, didn't stop to visit with her, but only sent her guarded nods, as if she had a catching disease. Still, Emma could understand their wariness. They had all grown up with the same stories she had heard about the "red devils."

But they hadn't lived in a Lakota village for almost seven years.

Emma followed her family to the doorway where the minister stood, shaking hands with the members of his flock.

"Fine job, Reverend," Emma's father said. He'd spoken those same words to the minister every Sunday that Emma could remember. It was another one of those oddly disconcerting reminders that some things hadn't changed.

"How is Emma doing?" the reverend asked.

Emma bristled inwardly, but kept her outward expression composed and her eyes downcast. They talked about her as if she wasn't standing right beside them. She hated that, but had promised her parents to remain as inconspicuous as possible.

"She's fine, Reverend," Martha Hartwell replied.

Emma risked sneaking a look at her mother and recognized the strain in her forced smile.

"We're thinking of sending her to visit her aunt back in St. Paul," her father interjected.

Emma gasped and opened her mouth to protest, but his warning look silenced her. Her cheeks burned with humiliation and anger. Her parents were going to rid themselves of their embarrassment one way or another. And they hadn't even deemed her important enough to discuss their plans for *her* future. Bitterness filled her and the air suddenly seemed too heavy.

"Excuse me," Emma whispered and stumbled past her sister, her parents, and the minister.

Her face burned from all the looks—pitying, accusing, and morbidly curious—directed toward her, as if she were a wolf caught in barbed wire. Her eyes stung, but she lifted her head high and held the tears at bay with the same stubbornness that didn't let her despair overcome her. She had lived a life that few white women could even imagine. Nobody had a right to judge her.

Nobody.

Although her long skirt and petticoats encumbered her

movements, Emma continued marching down the road, away from the church and the townspeople who now seemed like strangers. She knew her father would be angry and her mother disappointed in her behavior, but they had no right to treat her like a simpleton. She was twenty-two years old and perfectly capable of taking care of herself. Her parents, however, didn't see it that way. They saw a daughter who'd become a blemish on the oh-so-respectable Hartwell name, and it was their responsibility to remove the rot.

The sun's rays were warm, but the breeze chilly as it struck Emma's face and cut through her long cape like it wasn't even there. Her hair, done up in a proper bun beneath her bonnet, escaped its confines and tendrils whipped about her cheeks.

She rounded a bend and her gaze blurred as the tears finally defeated her control. Now that she was out of sight, she surrendered to the anguish twisting in her belly, making her gasp for air. But she didn't slow her pace. She prayed to God and Wakan Tanka, the Great Mystery, to escape the suffocating life that was now hers.

Nobody knew what she had left behind when she was returned—not even her family.

Pain arrowed through her breast and Emma stumbled. A firm hand caught her arm, steadying and shocking her.

"Easy, ma'am."

She whirled around and the stranger released her. The man hastily removed his hat and fidgeted with the brim. He wore brown trousers with a tan buckskin jacket and a red scarf around his neck. Thick, wavy brown hair hung to his shoulders and his dark blue eyes were steady, but guarded. The man's black-and-white pony stood patiently on the road, its reins hanging to the ground.

"I'm sorry if I startled you, ma'am. It's just that I saw you stumbling-like and thought you might be sick."

The man's voice was quiet and husky, as if he didn't use it very often.

Emma's cheeks warmed and she dashed a hand across

them to erase the telltale tear tracks. "No, that's all right. I didn't hear you."

A cool spring breeze soughed through the tree's bare branches and Emma shuddered from the chill beneath the too-light cape.

The man removed his jacket, revealing tan suspenders over a deep blue shirt, and awkwardly placed it over her shoulders. "You shouldn't be out here, ma'am. You'll catch your death dressed like that."

Emma's fingers curled into the soft material and the scent of cured deerhide tickled her nose with memories of another life. She caught herself and tried to hand the jacket back to him. "No. I can't—"

"I'm fine. You're the one who's shivering like a plucked sage hen."

She almost missed his shy, hesitant smile.

Trembling from the cold and from her thoughts, Emma snuggled back into the coat, grateful for the warmth. "Thank you," she said softly. Besides the leather, she could smell woodsmoke, horses, and the faint scent of male sweat in the well-worn jacket. "You're right. It was stupid of me to run off like that."

The man dipped his head in acknowledgment, and his long hair brushed across his shoulders. His gaze dropped to the hat he turned around and around between work-roughened hands. His reticence was oddly comforting.

"Are you from around here?" Emma asked.

"Yes'm. About four miles northwest."

That would make him a neighbor.

The steady clop-clop of hooves directed Emma's gaze to the road. A man dressed in a cavalry hat and pants and a sheepskin coat rode into view. He drew his black horse to a halt.

"I was wondering what happened to you, Ridge," the man said, eyeing Emma like she was a piece of prime rib.

She shivered anew, but this time it wasn't from the cool wind.

"Ease off, Colt," the man called Ridge said without force. "The lady needed some help is all."

"She all right?" the man asked.

"The lady is fine," Emma replied curtly. She'd had enough of people talking about her like she was invisible to last a lifetime.

The clatter of an approaching buckboard put an end to their stilted conversation and Emma's heart plummeted into her stomach when she spotted her father's stormy expression.

The soldier backed his horse off the road as the wagon slowed to a stop beside them.

"Get in, Emma," her father ordered in a steely voice.

Words of refusal climbed up her throat and she swallowed them back. She wouldn't humiliate herself or her family in front of two strangers. With tense muscles, she returned her Good Samaritan's jacket. "Thank you."

She kept her chin raised and her backbone straight as she climbed into the wagon's backseat, which was covered by a thick blanket. Ridge's hand on her arm aided and steadied her until she sat beside her sister.

"Stay the hell away from my daughter, Madoc. She doesn't need the likes of you," her father ordered.

Shocked, Emma only had a moment to give Ridge a nod of thanks before her father whipped the team of horses into motion.

She knew she was in big trouble by the fearful looks her sister kept casting her. Her mother, too, was pale. There would be little mercy from her father for embarrassing the family with her abrupt departure from church, and for her improper actions with the man called Madoc.

A man her father thought wasn't good enough even for her.

RIDGE Madoc kept his anger blunted as he placed his hat on his head and shrugged into his jacket. He caught the lingering scent of the woman's flowery perfume, and his belly coiled with heat. Frowning at his body's instinctive, but unwelcome reaction, Ridge accepted his horse's reins from his friend.

"Did you recognize her?" Colt asked as Ridge vaulted into the saddle without the use of his stirrups.

"Not 'til Hartwell showed up." Ridge shifted, the leather creaking beneath him. "She was the one rescued from the Lakota a few months ago."

"The one everyone's calling a squaw woman," Colt said as they rode toward Ridge's place.

Ridge glanced sharply at his friend, seeing beyond the coolness to the anguish below. Colt's wife had been killed by a band of renegades in Texas four years ago when they'd been stationed down there.

"Might've been better off if she was killed or never rescued at all," Colt added quietly.

Ridge mulled over his friend's words, seeing some truth in them. Miss Hartwell was carrying more than her share of shadowed ghosts. He'd seen them in her pretty brown eyes. But he'd also seen strength and determination in her pint-sized body. Miss Hartwell was a fighter. "Don't you think that's her decision?"

"Would you want her back if she'd been your wife?"

Uncharacteristic impatience made Ridge snap back, "If she was, I'd just be happy she was alive."

"Even if other men'd had her?" Colt's voice was soft, almost gentle.

Ridge ground his teeth together at the thought of Miss Hartwell being forced to submit to such indignity. "It wasn't her fault."

"There's a lot of folks who figure a white woman should kill herself before letting an Indian touch her."

"And there's a lot of Indians who think the same about the *wasicu*."

Colt only grunted a response.

Ridge took a deep breath then let it out slowly, calming

his mind and body the way he'd learned from the People when he was a young man, before he met Colt in the War. Although the two men had been to hell and back together, they disagreed on the Indians' place on the ever-decreasing wilderness. Both had their reasons.

Ridge had spent time with various tribes. He'd even fancied himself in love with a Sioux maiden one time, but he had no horses to gift her parents. In the long run, it had been for the best. Ridge respected most of the Indians he'd encountered, but his path didn't lie with them.

Ridge and Colt rode in silence, which grew more comfortable as they neared Ridge's place. Coming around a rocky bend, Ridge beheld his one-room cabin, which looked small and insignificant in the shadows of the Bighorn Mountains. He'd grown up here, although the run-down building he'd lived in had been burned to the ground by his own hand when he'd returned. Too many memories had been locked in that shack, and most all of them were bad.

"Looks good, Ridge. You must've been working some on it since I been here last," Colt commented, breaking the late morning's hush.

"Added the lean-to at the end for wood and fixed up the barn some so Paint had a dry place out of the weather." Ridge angled a look at his friend. "It's been what, two months?"

Colt shrugged. "I reckon. Army keeps me pretty busy with the growing Indian troubles."

Ridge understood too well. That was one of the reasons he'd quit his job as a scout. The other was this place—it was his now, free and clear. His stepfather had finally died a little over a year ago—Ridge figured meanness had kept him alive when he should've been dead and buried a long time ago. Ridge had only been six years old when his ma married Harry Piner, and twelve when she'd died. Three years later, Ridge'd had enough of his stepfather's violent temper. He had run away and never looked back. Until now.

"So, you gonna put me to work before you feed me?" Colt asked.

"Damned right. You gotta earn your grub," Ridge shot back with an easy grin.

"Tell me why I came here to work on my only day off in three weeks."

"Because I make the best venison stew this side of the mountains."

Colt chuckled and slapped Ridge's back in easy camaraderie. Then the two men took care of their horses before starting to repair the sagging corral fence.

EMMA endured the awful silence all the way home by thinking about the man who'd been so kind to her. Madoc. The name sounded vaguely familiar, but she couldn't place it. The other man, his friend, was in the cavalry. She'd seen enough of those uniforms that early morning when her peaceful existence had been shattered. She shut down the nightmarish memories before they carried her back into oblivion, where she'd lived for so long after she'd been returned seriously injured to her family's ranch.

The wagon rattled into the yard and her father halted the horses in front of the house. He hopped down and helped Emma's mother, then her sister. Emma didn't wait, but clambered down herself, earning a disapproving scowl from him.

"Wait in the study, Emma," he ordered. Then he exchanged a brusque look with her mother.

Gritting her teeth, Emma nodded curtly and followed her sister up the steps to the wide veranda. Sarah opened the arched door and they entered the spacious house. As Emma started upstairs to her room, her younger sister grabbed her arm.

"You're supposed to wait for Father in the study," Sarah said.

"I'm going to change out of my church clothes first."

Sighing, Sarah trailed after her, right into Emma's bedroom, and perched on a dainty spindle-footed chair.

"Father's not at all happy with you, Emma. Running away was bad enough, but talking with Ridge Madoc . . ." Sarah shivered. "Father says his mother was a tramp, and the apple doesn't fall far from the tree."

"Father says a lot of things." Emma reached up to undo the tiny pearl buttons at the back of her dress. "Who's his mother?"

Sarah shrugged. "All I know is she was married to Harry Piner."

Emma struggled to place the name. "The mean old man who lives in that shack just north of town?"

"Yes, but he died last summer. Then, right before you came home, Mr. Madoc claimed the place. Father was angry because he wanted the rest of the land, but since the rightful heir showed up, he couldn't get it."

Emma paused to look at her sister. "What do you mean, 'the rest of the land'?"

"Father's been buying pieces of Mr. Piner's land over the past few years. Whenever the old man needed money for whiskey, he'd come to Father and sell some more."

"But Mr. Madoc won't sell what's left?"

Sarah shook her head. "He plans on settling there."

No wonder her father didn't want Madoc anywhere near her. Besides having bad blood, he had also thwarted her father's plans for the land. Still, Mr. Madoc had been kind to her, and Emma had found little kindness since she'd returned.

She moved to stand in front of her sister, her back toward the younger woman. After a moment, she felt Sarah's fingers undoing the remaining buttons.

"Thanks." Emma couldn't get the confining dress off fast enough. She hung it in her armoire, and removed two of her four petticoats, placing those in the closet, too. She rummaged past the dresses the seamstress in town had made for her over the last few months, and picked out one of her past favorites, a somewhat faded green-and-blue paisley smock.

"You're going to wear that?" Sarah asked, staring at the old dress like it was a dead snake.

"I like it."

"Father hates it."

"He doesn't have to wear it." With the buttons up the front, Emma didn't need Sarah's help. The fabric stretched taut, threatening to undo the button between her breasts. The first time she'd worn the old dress upon her return, she noticed she'd gained an inch or two in her bosom, although the rest of the dress was loose.

"So why does this Ridge Madoc have a different last name?" she asked, oddly curious about him.

"I heard Father and Mother talking about him one time. I guess his mother was married to Mr. Madoc's real father who owned the place first, but that was before we moved here," Sarah replied.

"Emma Louise! Get down here!" Her father's bellow thundered from the foot of the stairs.

Sarah's eyes widened. "Now he's even angrier with you."

Emma shrugged, almost surprised by her unconcern. "What can he do to me that hasn't already been done?"

Her sister gasped.

Emma strolled out of her room and down the stairs where her red-faced father stood. Martha Hartwell stood a few feet behind her husband, her lips set in a grim line.

"I thought I told you to throw out that rag," he said, motioning to her dress with a slicing motion.

Emma began to cross her arms, felt the fabric tug across her chest, and instead, clasped her hands in front of her. "It's *my* dress. I can do with it what I please."

Her father's eyes sparked with anger, and a muscle clenched in his jaw. "The study."

Still wrapped in indifference, Emma walked into the dark paneled room with heavy, navy-blue velvet curtains on the two large windows behind his desk. She glanced longingly at the overflowing bookshelves. Without the books, she wouldn't have survived her confinement over the past several months.

Emma settled into a wingback chair in front of the desk, sitting with her feet flat on the floor and her hands resting in her lap like a proper young lady. She would've preferred to sit with her legs folded beneath her, but she figured she'd provoked her father enough for one day.

Her mother perched on the twin of Emma's chair, her face pinched with worry. Her father, however, didn't appear the least bit anxious. No, he was spitting mad.

"What do you have to say for yourself, young lady?" he demanded.

She met his glowering eyes without flinching. "You and Mother have no right making decisions which affect my life without talking to me first."

Her father blinked, apparently startled by her forthrightness. "You're our daughter and you live under our roof. That gives us the right."

"Would you ship Sarah off without talking to her about it?"

"Sarah is not you."

Boiling anger and hurt engulfed Emma as she gripped the armrests. "What you mean is that Sarah is still clean and pure, but poor Emma is used and soiled." Her nostrils flared and her fingernails dug into the armrests. Long-held silence exploded in defiance. "I am not a *thing* you can cast aside and forget about. I have a life. I have hopes and dreams."

"Which will never be realized around here," Emma's mother interjected almost gently. "No respectable man will have you."

Emma's stomach caved and she stared down at her fisted hands, which had somehow ended up in her lap again. She absorbed the pain of her mother's words, praying her expression didn't reveal her anguish. Once upon a time when she was a young girl, Emma had dreamed of meeting a handsome, dashing young man and living happily ever after. A part of her still yearned for that happy ending, but fate had stolen that wish, leaving no hope of ever realizing it. She raised her head and turned to the older version of herself. "Thank you for sharing that with me, Mother."

Her mother flinched, and even Emma was shocked by the depth of her own bitterness.

"That's enough, Emma Louise," her father ordered. He stood and paced behind the desk, his body silhouetted against the windows. He'd taken the time to remove his jacket, but still wore one of his white church shirts with a string tie and vest.

The regulator clock ticked loudly in the muffled silence. Emma concentrated on its steady rhythm—tick-tock, tick-tock—to block out the other sounds swirling through her head, but the memories were too powerful to be denied any longer.

Pounding hooves.
Gunshots.
Screams.
Blood.

Her heart hammering, Emma stared at her hands, almost surprised to find they weren't scarlet stained. Instead, she noticed how they'd finally lost their dried parchment texture, but weren't nearly as smooth as they'd been seven years ago.

Her father stopped pacing, but remained standing behind his desk. The silence was so intense that when he rubbed his jaw, Emma heard the rasp of his short whisker stubble against his hand. "Maybe it was wrong of your mother and I to make plans behind your back, but we were only thinking of your best interests."

Emma bit her tongue.

"As you know, your aunt Alice is a widow with no children. Your uncle left her very comfortable financially, and we doubt she'll ever marry again. She's willing to let you move in with her and begin a new life."

It wasn't that Emma didn't like Aunt Alice. She did. She

admired her aunt's independence and used to enjoy watching her put her brother—Emma's father—in his place. There were few people who could tangle horns with John Hartwell and come out unscathed and victorious. His older sister was one of them.

Emma took a deep, steadying breath. "I'm fond of Aunt Alice, but I want to stay here. This is my home, where I was raised. I don't want to leave."

Her father's stern expression faltered and Emma caught his helpless look directed toward her mother. Emma had no doubt he loved her—still loved her after everything that had happened, but didn't know how to show it. The only time she'd seen him truly emotional was when he'd come to the infirmary at the fort after the cavalry had brought her in, wounded and weak from blood loss and shock. For the first time in her life, Emma had seen tears in his eyes. Since then, though, he'd gone back to his characteristic detachment.

Her mother leaned forward to lay a hand on Emma's. "Believe it or not, we don't want you to leave either. Your father and I discussed this for weeks before we contacted Alice. But surely you must see it's for the best. In St. Paul, no one knows of your time with the . . . Indians." Martha Hartwell's voice quavered. "Although you won't talk about what happened while you were with them, we can imagine how you must've suffered."

"I was treated well." That was true. Emma hadn't told them much about her years with the Lakota tribe. At first, it had been because she hovered on death's door for a week after coming home. In the days that followed, her body healed but her mind had shut down after the horrific visions and sounds she'd experienced the morning the soldiers attacked the village. And now it was too late to tell them. Everyone seemed to think they already knew, and anything Emma said would invariably be seen as the ravings of a madwoman.

"They're a lot like us," she finally said. "The children play, the women cook and clean, and the men hunt and protect the women and children. Parents love their children and want them to grow up to be good and responsible adults, too."

"They're heathens," her father said curtly. "They murder women and children."

Emma smiled, but there was no warmth behind it. "Then I guess the whites and Indians have more in common than most folks think, don't they?"

Her mother gasped. "You sound like you're defending them."

"They stole you away from us, away from your home," her father added, his husky voice revealing both anger and distress.

"They saved my life," Emma corrected.

"And God knows what they made you do while you were with them," he continued as if she hadn't even spoken.

"They didn't make me to do anything I didn't want to."

Her mother squeezed her hands. "Thank God. We prayed that you wouldn't be forced to—" She broke off.

But Emma knew exactly what she meant. She had lived with that fear for weeks after she was carried into their camp, not realizing she wasn't a captive. She was treated decently and her adoptive parents had cared for her and protected her. And when the time came, Emma hadn't been scared. Nervous, yes, but not frightened.

Not of Enapay.

She'd chosen to hide that fact from her parents and Sarah. They wouldn't understand. Nobody would understand unless they had walked her path.

"We're relieved," her father broke the stillness. "That way, when you do find a man to marry, he won't know."

"Know what?" Emma asked.

"Of your circumstances."

Dare she tell them? Did it matter?

"Please let me stay," Emma pleaded, ready to put an end to the conversation.

Again, the mute exchange between her mother and father. Emma was beginning to hate those secret looks.

"In two weeks you will go on an extended visit to your aunt's," her father proclaimed. "That'll give you some time to prepare."

Emma wanted to kick and scream, to throw a tantrum unpleasant enough that her parents would change their minds. But she wasn't five years old, and John and Martha Hartwell truly believed they were doing the right thing for their eldest daughter.

There would be no changing their minds about this.

Emma nodded even as every muscle in her body rebelled against the simple motion. "Two weeks."

"Two weeks," her father repeated.

"It's for the best," her mother reiterated, as if trying to convince herself.

Emma stood and walked out of the room. Her legs moved as if someone other than herself was controlling them. Keeping her mind and expression blank, she climbed the stairs and entered her room, locking the door behind her. Once there, she opened a dresser drawer and dug beneath her underclothing to find what she sought. Her fingers recognized the soft leather and they closed around a small moccasin.

Slowly she brought it out and hugged it to her chest.

Two

DUSK was falling as Ridge and Colt sat in companionable silence in the cabin. They had turned two chairs toward the stove and were drinking coffee after finishing the pot of venison stew Ridge had made.

"How're Pres and Sarge doing?" Ridge asked.

Colt stretched out his long legs and crossed his ankles. "They're getting tired. They would've come with me, but the colonel's got them going out again, looking for those Indians that hightailed it off the reservation."

Ridge scowled. "From what I heard, most of 'em were women and kids. They ain't going to hurt anyone."

"Maybe, maybe not. But I guess there were a few young bucks with them—the kind that got something to prove."

Ridge stood, plucked a rag from a nail on the wall, and used it to pick up the hot coffeepot on the stove. He raised the pot to Colt, who nodded and held out his cup. Ridge topped it off, then refilled his own. After returning it to the stove, he sat down and tipped his chair back so that the two front legs were off the floor.

This was Ridge's favorite time, when he could sit back and enjoy some peace and quiet after a day's work. When he'd been with Colt and the others in the army, evenings were spent in easy camaraderie, usually playing poker for matchsticks and drinking coffee.

Ridge had left those days behind. His last order had been to find an Arapaho village. After he found it, the peaceful camp had been destroyed by soldiers drunk on glory and vengeance. It wasn't a battle as much as it had been a massacre. Even now, Ridge could see and hear the carnage. It made him sick to remember.

"You should've stayed on," Colt said in a low voice.

A cold fist wrapped around Ridge's spine. "No. I couldn't."

"Maybe if you had, they wouldn't a done the same thing to that Lakota village."

"They didn't listen to me before." Ridge sipped his coffee, his stomach churning with guilt and bitterness. "Why would the next time be any different?"

Colt continued as if his friend hadn't spoken. "The Hartwell woman almost got herself killed." His lips turned downward in disgust. "She was dressed just like one of them, acted just like 'em, too, from what I heard."

Reining in his anger at Colt's disapproval, Ridge pictured the woman with the fawn-colored eyes as she thanked him for his coat. It was a damned shame her life was ruined. No white man wanted a "squaw woman."

He became aware of Colt's scrutiny.

"You ain't thinking of ignoring Hartwell's warning, are you?" Colt asked.

Ridge shook his head. "Nope. Miz Hartwell's got enough problems."

"Damned shame she's ruined," Colt said, unknowingly echoing Ridge's thoughts. "She's a pretty filly, but no man in his right mind's going to want to get hitched to her."

Ridge's hand tightened around his cup. He recognized the truth in his friend's words, but that didn't mean he had to like it.

Colt finished his coffee and glanced out into the disappearing daylight. "I'd better get back to the fort. Colonel

Nyes wants us to check on those folks settling along the river tomorrow so we'll have to leave early. Wants to make sure they haven't had any Indian troubles."

"My guess is they haven't. Too far west."

Colt nodded. "Yep, that's what I figure, but what the old man says goes."

"Nyes must be running out of Indians to kill if he's looking for more." Sarcasm sharpened Ridge's words.

"I don't like the colonel, but I can understand his position. The man has his orders, just like the rest of us," Colt said with a hint of defensiveness.

"A man like him can hide a whole lot of hate behind orders."

Colt's jaw muscle clenched. "Maybe it is a good thing you quit."

The two men parried sharp looks until Colt turned away to retrieve his hat and jacket. Ridge sighed and donned his, also. They'd been friends too long to let a difference of opinion get between them.

"I reckon it was," Ridge said quietly.

Colt dipped his head in acknowledgment. They walked out to the stable where Colt's horse was penned next to Paint. While the cavalry captain saddled his gelding, Ridge leaned a shoulder against a post.

"I appreciate you coming out to help me, Colt," Ridge said.

Colt paused long enough to give him a crooked grin. "You'd do the same for me."

Ridge smiled. "I reckon, even though your venison stew tastes like chewed-up leather."

"And how the hell do you know what chewed-up leather tastes like?"

"I've eaten your stew."

The two men chuckled as Colt led his horse outside. Ridge extended his hand, and Colt clasped his forearm as Ridge did the same.

"You take care, soldier," Ridge drawled.

"You, too, pard."

Colt mounted in one fluid motion, lifted a hand in farewell, and urged his horse into a trot.

Ridge folded his arms on the top corral pole and watched his friend swallowed up by the dusky shadows. He took a deep breath and let his gaze wander across his land.

His land. That sounded good, even if instead of five hundred acres, only one hundred remained. Damn Harry Piner for selling off what was rightfully his.

Ridge didn't remember much about his real pa, but what he could recollect filled him with both warmth and soul-deep loneliness. He recalled his pa lifting him onto the saddle in front of him and the two of them riding around the yard as his ma had watched with a gentle smile; helping clean the tack and the smell of oil and leather and his pa's wool shirt; carrying in two pieces of wood because he was too small to handle anymore and his pa's big hand patting his shoulder to thank him for helping fill the woodbox.

Then his pa had died and his ma married Piner. It hadn't been bad the first year. Harry had seemed like he cared for them, and had tried to make the ranch profitable. However, the harsh winter and falling market prices had seemed to conspire against him. He started drinking, and his temper grew shorter, especially with his stepson and later with Ridge's ma. His violent outbursts often left both mother and son with painful bruises.

In the end, Ridge's ma gave up, and twelve-year-old Ridge was left with his stepfather's mean temper and painful lessons learned with a leather belt or a fist. When Ridge turned fifteen, he ran away and never looked back.

Until now.

His father's ranch was almost lost by Harry Piner. It was up to Ridge to make things right. He planned on rebuilding, which meant finding a way to buy back the land Piner had sold to Hartwell for a pittance. Then Ridge would find a respectable woman to marry and raise more Madocs who'd make his ma and pa proud.

The major obstacle in getting started was money. He needed more than he had to buy the blooded bull he had his eye on down in Cheyenne. The rancher who owned the bull said he'd give Ridge until June to come up with the cash. After that time, he'd put it up at auction.

He knew Colonel Nyes would hire him back in a heartbeat—experienced scouts were hard to come by. But Ridge didn't want anything to do with the army and Nyes's solution to the "Indian problem." With spring coming, the big ranches were going to need more help. He'd find a job at one of those and save his money.

The wife and children would have to wait.

EMMA dropped her needlework to her lap, pressed her head back against the settee, and closed her eyes. She'd slept little the previous night after a vivid dream about wolves and mountain lions, and through it all, the sound of a crying wolf cub. The nightmare had left her shaken and anxious, and Emma had learned not to ignore such omens. Although she wasn't certain what the vision meant, she knew she couldn't go to St. Paul. Her journey lay in a different direction, one she had ignored for too long—at first by blaming the winter, then by trying to forget. But not a day passed that she didn't draw out the child's moccasin and imagine how much he'd grown.

Although that path held numerous perils, she had no choice. The plan to leave was dangerous to contemplate, even alone in the front room when her mother and sister were in town shopping, and her father in his study with the door closed.

A tap-tap on the front door startled her and she waited a moment, expecting her father to answer it. When he didn't come out of his office, she realized he probably hadn't heard the quiet knock. She debated whether to get the door herself or to inform her father of the visitor.

A month ago, there wouldn't have been any hesitation—she would've disappeared into her room while her father saw to their caller. But Emma'd had enough of cowering in corners. All it had gained her was a one-way trip to her aunt's. It was time she started making her own decisions and facing her fears. No longer would she shame her husband's memory, or hide from her son's fate.

She laid her needlework aside and went to the front door. Taking a deep breath, she swung it open and her eyes widened at the sight of the man on the porch.

"Mr. Madoc," Emma greeted, trying to hide her startled pleasure at seeing him again.

Ridge Madoc appeared equally surprised and he quickly removed his wide-brimmed hat. Obviously, he hadn't expected her to answer the door. "Ma'am. I, uh, came to see Mr. Hartwell about a job." He shifted his weight from one moccasined foot to the other, like a schoolboy called up in front of the class.

Emma caught her frown before it could form. "Did he ask you here?"

Ridge shook his head, then brushed his longish brown hair back from his brow. "No, ma'am. I wanted to see if he was doing any hiring."

Emma glanced over her shoulder, grateful to see that the study door remained closed. "He doesn't handle the hiring. Our foreman, Bob Tucker, does that."

"Do you know where I might find him?"

"He told my father he'd be staying around the yard this morning, keeping an eye on the mares that are due to foal." Emma looked past Madoc, shading her eyes against the bright sun. She couldn't spot the foreman, but had an idea he'd be in the far barn. Emma made a quick decision. "I'll take you to him."

"You don't have to."

She smiled at his flustered expression. "It's all right. I need to get out of the house before I go crazy anyway. Just give me a minute to get my coat."

Giving him a nod of apology, she closed the door. Although she'd lived outside the strictures of civilization for years, Emma didn't dare invite him into the house without a chaperone nearby. Of course, she could've gotten her father, but he would have a fit if he knew Madoc was here.

The only chance Ridge had of getting a job was to talk to Mr. Tucker directly.

She donned her coat, remembering to wind a wool muffler around her head and neck. After finding her gloves, she tugged them on and slipped outside, bumping into Madoc's solid body.

He caught her shoulders and steadied her.

A shiver passed through her at his strong, yet gentle grip. "You catching me is becoming a habit," she said, keeping her voice light.

He released her and stepped back, his expression anxious. "Sorry, ma'am. I didn't mean any disrespect."

Emma risked placing a gloved hand on his sleeve. "That wasn't what I meant. I'm grateful for your assistance." She smiled behind her scarf, and hoped he could see the sincerity in her eyes.

Ridge studied her a moment, then a slow smile stole across his lips. "My pleasure, ma'am."

Although Emma knew he was only being polite, she liked his diffident smile and the sound of his husky voice. She started down the porch steps and heard Ridge follow. As they walked across the yard, he kept half a step behind her, which made conversing difficult. She slowed her pace so he could catch up, but he slowed accordingly and continued following her.

At least he didn't mind being seen with her. Most respectable people did.

"Were you in the army, too?" she asked, turning her head to glance back at him.

"Yes, ma'am."

"When did you get out?"

"Last year."

She'd slowed even more while they'd talked, and Ridge finally ended up walking beside her.

"Why did you get out?" she asked.

"You sure ask a lot questions, ma'am."

Chagrined, Emma risked a glance at him and instead of irritation or anger, she spotted a twinkle of amusement in his eyes. It made her feel only marginally less guilty about asking such personal questions. "I'm sorry. It's really none of my business."

His humor disappeared. "It's all right, ma'am. I'm just not used to talking about myself."

"I can understand that." Emma had found the less said about her life with the People, the better.

She increased her pace, but Ridge remained beside her instead of fading back again.

"I fought in the War Between the States," he finally said in his husky timbre. "After my enlistment was up, I signed back on as an army scout and stuck with that until—" He angled a look at the blue-capped sky, then settled on the buttes in the distance. "Until it didn't seem right anymore."

Emma's stomach knotted. "Were you the one who led them—" The knot moved up and threatened to strangle her.

"No." His answer was immediate, telling Emma he knew what she was trying to ask. "I quit last fall."

Relief flowed through Emma like a swift-running river. It was important to her, knowing he hadn't been involved in the butchery; her instincts weren't wrong about the soft-spoken man. They arrived at the barn and Emma said, "Mr. Tucker's probably in here."

"Thank you, ma'am." Without another word, Ridge slipped inside the building.

Emma was tempted to follow, but her upbringing stopped her. Proper young ladies did not get involved in men's discussions. She laughed without humor. Nobody saw her as proper any longer, although her father insisted on continuing the charade for appearance's sake.

She trudged back to the house, hoping her father hadn't noticed her absence, but if he had, did it matter? Passing by Ridge's horse tied to the hitching post in front of the house, Emma paused to pat the horse's neck. She slipped off a glove and ran her palm over his velvety nose.

She tipped back her head to gaze at the blueness unbroken by clouds, and to breathe in the fresh scent of the awakening earth. It was the Moon of the Greening Grass and soon the countryside would be filled with infant wild-flowers and leafing trees.

And what of her son? Was Chayton playing with the rest of the children? Was he scampering after butterflies among the blooming flowers and laughing in delight?

Or had Chayton been struck down like so many others the night the soldiers had come to the village? The pain struck her then, like a knife twisting in her belly and she breathed in short pants to stem the tears.

She had refused to think about the possibility of her son's death, unwilling to open her heart to the overwhelming grief. But now, she could no longer bury the soul-deep anguish. Her arms ached to hold her son and her ears kept searching for the sound of his voice. He'd been such a happy child, eager to explore, his pudgy legs propelling him from one adventure to another.

Burning tears stung her eyes and she swiped her arm across her face. Crying wouldn't help her—she'd done enough of it the past five months and it had achieved nothing but a one-way trip away from everything she held dear, especially Chayton. Her baby . . .

Emma sensed someone approaching and glanced back to see Ridge Madoc returning. The stiff set of his shoulders and the tight lines in his face told her the outcome of his talk with the foreman hadn't been favorable.

She stepped away from his horse, pulled her glove back on, and waited until he drew even with her. "He didn't hire you," she stated.

"That's right." The clipped words were a sharp contrast to his usual drawl.

He jumped onto his horse's back and fitted his toes into the stirrups.

Emma grabbed the reins before he could escape and placed a hand against the horse's neck as she gazed up at Ridge. "I'm sorry."

He stared down at her and his eyes softened beneath his hat brim. "I'll find a job."

"Couldn't you go back to scouting for the army?"

His mouth twisted up again. "No, ma'am. I've had a bellyful of killing."

Emma released his horse's bridle and crossed her arms, hoping to hide her sudden trembling. "I'm glad," she said softly. "Goodbye, Mr. Madoc."

Ridge touched the brim of his hat with two fingers and nodded. "Ma'am."

Emma watched the former scout ride away. *He* would know how to find the remnants of her tribe, but convincing him to help her would be difficult. It would entail her having to tell him about her son and late husband, and she wasn't strong enough for that.

Although the sun was warm, the ever-present wind was cutting and she reluctantly returned to the house. To her stupid needlework and her useless existence.

EMMA stood in a shadowed corner of the town hall, trying to remain inconspicuous. She had fought a long battle with her parents to allow her to attend this dance, and won only because they believed she'd be leaving for St. Paul in a few days. If they suspected she only wanted an opportunity to speak to Ridge Madoc, their permission would've never been granted.

She closed her eyes to block out the expected, but still hurtful, snubs and listened to the music, which was overlaid by children's laughter and the buzz of conversation. The sounds carried her back, to before her life with the People. She used to love attending socials, pretending she was the belle of the ball. She'd slip outside and, in the shadows, dance with an imaginary beau. In her pretend world, she'd been graceful and coquettish, knowing the right words and expressions to charm a man.

No matter how hard she tried, Emma couldn't return to her make-believe world. It, like so many other things, had been lost to her.

At least her sister Sarah still had her dreams and the possibility of them coming true. She'd danced twice with

William Lyndon, the banker's son; Sarah had confessed her pining for him to Emma.

"Marybeth told me he was an army scout."

Startled, Emma's eyes flew open. Two women stood about six feet away, their heads close together as they conversed behind their palms.

"His name is Pony Cullen," the other woman said to her companion, as if imparting a deep dark secret. "Colonel Nyes says he's his finest scout."

Emma followed their gazes to a tall, rail-thin man wearing a well-worn pair of uniform trousers and a brown shirt. When he turned to refill his cup from the men's punch bowl, she saw his face was pockmarked and sharply angled.

Suddenly, he lifted his head and stared straight at her, as if he knew she was studying him. Emma should've dropped her gaze, but his caught her, held her, like a cat toying with a baby bird.

Out of the corner of her eye, she saw the two gossiping women now had their sights on her. Idly, she wondered what the scandalmongers could come up with which hadn't already been whispered behind her back.

Cullen finally turned away, freeing Emma. She searched the room, hoping Mr. Madoc had shown up, but she couldn't spot him. The women had said Pony Cullen was a scout—would he work for her? Or should she stick to her original plan of asking Ridge Madoc?

Before she could decide, Cullen ambled out the back door. Emma figured he had to answer the call of nature after drinking so much "punch." Now would be an ideal chance to talk to him in private.

Ignoring the two gossiping women, Emma followed after the scout. The evening air nipped at her cheeks and she shivered from both the chill and nervousness.

After waiting a few minutes in the cool darkness, she spotted Cullen returning from behind the building. Before her courage escaped her, Emma strode purposefully toward him, hoping to intersect his path in the relative privacy beside an ancient oak tree.

"Mr. Cullen," she called.

He stopped and raised his head. From her distance, Emma couldn't read his expression. As she neared him, a knot began to form in her belly. "My name's Emma Hart—"

"I know who you are," Cullen interrupted.

Emma's cheeks burned. Of course, everyone knew her. "I heard you were a scout."

She was close enough to see Cullen's gaze rake over her, and the knot expanded.

"You heard right," he said.

"I'd like to hire your services," Emma stated, imitating her father's no-nonsense business voice.

"What kind of services ya lookin' for?" He licked his thin, dry lips.

Emma's fingernails bit into her palms. "I'd like to hire you to find some Indians."

Startled surprise was followed closely by cruel chuckles. "Got so you liked them bucks, huh?"

"What?"

Cullen stepped closer, leaving less than a foot between their bodies. "You don't need to go lookin' for one of them. I can give you what you need right here."

Emma recoiled, bile rising in her throat as his meaning became clear. "That's not why—"

Cullen grabbed her wrist and yanked her against his chest. The stink of tobacco and sweat made Emma's stomach roll. "You're no better'n a whore now, Miz Hartwell." He deliberately slurred her name.

Emma struggled to escape his grip. "Let me go!"

"Go ahead and yell. Ain't nobody gonna help a squaw woman." He tangled his fingers in the hair bun at the nape of her neck and jerked downward, forcing her head back.

Emma opened her mouth to scream but Cullen's lips smashed down upon hers. Her cry died in her throat as terror and disgust gave her added strength. She shoved at him, but he only tightened his hold on her hair. Her scalp burned and tears of pain trickled down her cheeks.

She hadn't survived a near drowning and seven years with the People only to be beaten, or worse, in the town she grew up in—a place she should've been safe. Anger replaced her fear and she stomped down on his foot with her heel. He muttered an oath and his grip loosened. She pulled away, only to have her arm grabbed. His fingers dug into the tender flesh and Emma had no doubt there'd be bruises.

"So, you like it rough?" Cullen grinned down at her, exposing yellowish-brown stained teeth. "I do, too."

Tendrils of panic snaked around Emma's chest as she struggled to escape. Although the two busybodies had seen her leave, Emma doubted they'd say anything if she didn't return. And even if they did, who would lift a hand to help her?

Emma Hartwell had committed an unforgivable sin seven years ago—she'd chosen to live.

$\mathcal{T}$HREE

ORIGINALLY, Ridge'd had no intention of attending the dance in town that Saturday night. What little he knew of dancing was associated with Indian ceremonies and he didn't figure that type of dance would be looked upon too kindly.

But although he hated politics, he knew how it worked. If he was to become a respectable member of the community which had shunned him as a child, he had to rub elbows with the local folks, even those he didn't like.

He rode down Sunset's main street as his gaze wandered across the numerous buggies, wagons, and saddle horses lined up and down the road. It looked like everyone from a twenty-mile radius had come in for the dance.

A block from the meeting hall, he dismounted and tossed the reins loosely around a post. Even this far from the dance, he could hear voices and the occasional rise of fiddles above the hum of conversation. The sound reminded Ridge of a disturbed beehive.

He tried to swallow, grimaced, and stuck a finger between the paper collar and his neck, and tugged. If the dance didn't kill him, the shirt damned sure would.

Ridge adjusted his hat and trudged across the street like he was headed to a ladies' tea party. Against his better judgment, he sidled into the crowded hall. Removing his hat, he ran a hand over his head, ensuring the leather tie still held his long hair back. He searched the many faces and nodded to those who met his gaze. Many of them returned his nod of greeting.

Howard Freeman, owner of the hardware store, crossed through the mess of people to greet him. Freeman grinned broadly and extended his hand. "Must be some special occasion to get you into town."

Ridge shook his hand and smiled with genuine warmth. "Seeing you dressed up like a Thanksgiving turkey is more than reason enough."

Freeman chuckled, his fleshy chins resembling a turkey's wattle. "Look at you! I almost didn't recognize you wearin' a store-bought suit."

Ridge smoothed a hand over his vest self-consciously and resisted the urge to tug at his collar again. "I reckon you won't see me wearing it very often. Damn thing's gonna choke me."

Freeman laid a fatherly hand on Ridge's shoulder. "I always said it ain't the clothes, but the man wearin' them that counts."

Ridge noticed Hartwell and his wife chatting with Thomas Lyndon, the mayor as well as the bank president. Hartwell caught his eye, scowled, and turned away. Ridge frowned—the two men were probably scheming to force some small farmer into selling out to the mighty rancher.

"Maybe not, but men like Lyndon and Hartwell don't see it that way," Ridge said, his lips curled in distaste.

"They ain't bad men, Ridge, just used to things bein' a certain way." Freeman clapped him on the back. "You shouldn't be standin' around jawin' with me. In fact, I think Grace is just waitin' for some fella with two left feet to ask her to dance."

Ridge followed Freeman's pointing finger to the man's daughter, a red-haired gal with freckles dusting her nose and cheeks. She was standing by the refreshment table, watching the dancers as she swayed to the music. "I don't know anyone with two left feet, but I reckon I could handle her."

"Just don't be handlin' too much. Even though you're a friend, you're still a man and she's my daughter," Freeman warned, his eyes narrowed.

Ridge held up his hands, palms out. "I'll behave."

"See that you do." Freeman winked and moved away to greet someone else.

As Ridge wandered through the crowd, he spotted Hartwell's youngest daughter dancing with a boy he recognized as the banker's son. At least they'd be able to marry off one daughter well.

He swept his narrowed gaze across the room, looking for the elder Hartwell girl. Not that he expected to find her—the merciful thing would be to leave her at home, safe from the narrow-minded folks. But Miss Hartwell didn't strike him as one to back down. He admired her for that.

Strangely disappointed when he didn't see her, he continued to ease his way through the crowd, bumping and jostling and mumbling apologies as he made his way toward Grace Freeman.

Suddenly his path was blocked by a man wearing a dark blue double-breasted coat with the insignia of a cavalry officer. Silver eagles with spread wings decorated his shoulders.

"How've you been, Madoc?" Colonel Nyes asked, his voice politician-smooth.

"Busy." The word came out tersely.

"I heard you were working for the Circle C, getting a hired hand's wages." Nyes took a sip from his punch glass, which had more than punch in it by the smell of the officer's whiskey-scented breath.

"You heard right."

"I thought you'd be working on your own place." The colonel smoothed his pale blond mustache with his thumb and forefinger over and over, a smug habit Ridge hated.

"I'm doing both."

"We both know you could be earning twice as much working for me."

Ridge laughed without a trace of humor. "Blood money. No thanks, Colonel."

Anger glittered in Nyes's narrowed eyes. "Since when do you care about that? I've heard rumors about what you did before you joined the army. This isn't much different."

Ridge stiffened. "Anybody ever teach you not to listen to rumors?"

"Rumors are often reliable fonts of knowledge. Surely you should know that, Madoc." Nyes eyed him closely. "I can use someone with your talents. We've got murdering redskins on the loose and you can help us find them."

"So we can be the murderers instead?"

Nyes stared at him with something akin to disgust. "I never figured you'd go soft, seeing as how you never had any trouble killing undesirables before."

Ridge fought the urge to smash his fist into the colonel's aristocratic nose. "Go to hell, Nyes."

The pompous bastard smiled. "That's your destination, Madoc."

Ridge spun away before his tenuous control broke, and nearly plowed down a couple dancing at the fringe of the swirling bodies. The room was suddenly too damned hot and he fought his way to the nearest door, forgetting about Grace Freeman and everything else in his need to escape. Stumbling into the cool night air, he breathed deeply to exorcise the sleeping demons Nyes had stirred.

Raised voices caught his attention and he searched the shadows for the source. A man and a woman stood close to one another about thirty feet away, beneath the outspread limbs of an oak tree, telling Ridge he was an uninvited witness to a lover's spat. He clapped his hat back on his head, intent on going home where he heard only the wind and the coyotes.

"Let me go," the woman cried out.

Ridge recognized the voice and the desperation in the

tone. Even before he made a conscious decision, he was striding toward Miss Hartwell. The man was gripping her arms and had pinned her against the tree as he nuzzled her neck. She was struggling to escape.

Ridge grabbed the taller man and jerked him away from her. The man flexed his hands at his sides as he stared down at him. Ridge balanced on the balls of his feet and his hands closed into fists. "Come on, Cullen. Or is it only ladies you can beat up?"

"She ain't no lady, Madoc." The scout Nyes had hired to replace Ridge motioned toward Miss Hartwell. "She spread her legs for them; I figger she'd spread 'em for anybody."

Rage poured through Ridge's veins and he swung, catching Cullen on the jaw and spinning him around. With a roar, Cullen charged and Ridge tried to sidestep him, but the man managed to knock him off-balance. Cullen followed with a blow that snapped Ridge's head back. Although Cullen was rail thin, he had deceptive strength. Ridge staggered and ducked, barely escaping a second fist aimed at his face. He kicked Cullen in the groin and the scout dropped to the ground, clutching his privates.

Ridge leaned over the fallen man. "Keep your filthy mouth shut and your goddamned hands off Miss Hartwell." Ridge grabbed a handful of Cullen's greasy hair and jerked his head back so they were eye-to-eye. "You understand?"

Cullen stared at Ridge, his narrow-set eyes flat and filled with pain and hatred.

Ridge tightened his hold and felt a measure of satisfaction when Cullen grunted. "I said, you understand?"

"I understand," Cullen said through clenched teeth.

"Good. 'Cause if I hear about you bothering her again, I won't be so forgiving."

Ridge released him and backed away. He watched while the sorry son of a bitch pushed himself to his feet and stumbled away. Only after Cullen was gone did Ridge give his attention to Miss Hartwell. Her face was silvery-white in the moonlight and one sleeve had been tugged down, leaving a pale shoulder bared. Ridge had to restrain himself from going after Cullen. "Are you all right, Miss Hartwell?"

Wrapping her arms around herself, she managed a small nod, but her voice was surprisingly steady. "Yes, thank you, Mr. Madoc."

The woman had grit, but she was shy of brains coming out here with Cullen.

"You should get back inside."

She glanced in the direction Cullen had gone, then looked back at Ridge. "It's not what you're thinking."

"You don't know what I'm thinking, ma'am."

Her lips thinned. "I didn't lure him out here and I didn't invite his attentions."

Ridge, starting to feel the ache from the scuffle, shifted restlessly. "Then what were you doing?" The question came out more accusing than he'd intended.

The woman straightened her backbone and raised her chin. "I offered him a job. I want him to track down the Indians I used to live with."

Ridge cussed inwardly and reined in his temper. "I'd sooner trust a rattlesnake than Cullen."

"I realize that now. I made a mistake."

"Why do you want to find them?"

She glanced away and her spine stiffened even further. "That's none of your concern."

"Fine. I suggest you get back inside now." Ridge leaned over to pick up his hat and slapped it against his thigh before settling it on his head. "Evening, ma'am."

He turned to leave but she caught his coat sleeve.

"I *have* to find them," she said with quiet intensity.

He met her scrutiny with his own and read the sincerity and desperation in her eyes. His gaze flickered across her shoulder and he spotted bruising on her milky white skin. Rage burned through him anew at the evidence of Cullen's violence. Gently, he reached out and pulled the dress back into place, hiding the signs of Cullen's attack.

Miss Hartwell's eyes widened, and he heard her soft inhalation of surprise and saw the delicate flare of her nostrils. Ridge forced himself to release the cloth and stepped back.

"The best thing you can do is forget about 'em and move on with your life, ma'am," he said quietly. He touched the brim of his hat and strode away.

All the way across the street he could feel Emma Hartwell's sharp gaze drilling into his back. She was a fool to want to go back to the Lakota. There'd be some hot-headed braves who'd blame her for what had happened to them and vengeance wouldn't be pretty or swift. Although her life wasn't the best here, at least she was alive and safe.

He tightened his saddle cinch and mounted up, but before riding out, he took one last look. Miss Hartwell was walking back into the hall, her proud carriage bowed. He shrugged aside the whisper of guilt and deliberately turned away.

A full moon lit the night and a breeze stirred the leafless branches to create fluid shadows on the forest floor. A baby animal yipped, cracking the brittle silence, and an owl's hoot immediately followed. Moments later a wolf pup emerged from the scanty brush. He raised his head and let loose a pitiful howl that wavered and waned in the silvery darkness.

A mountain lion's roar answered the forlorn call and the young wolf whimpered. The pup rose but immediately collapsed onto the dead leaves blanketing the earth. He whined, calling for his mother but only the owl, perched on an overhanging branch, heard the cry.

The owl tipped its head, and its bright, round eyes focused on the weak animal. "The fearsome beast comes, little one," the owl spoke to the pup.

The small wolf shuddered with both fear and exhaustion.

The mountain lion stalked into the clearing, his eyes glittering in the moonlight. His nostrils flared and he swung his head unerringly toward his prey.

The pup laid there silently, as if knowing there was no

hope. *The lion padded over and batted his shoulder with his massive paw. The wolf pup whimpered as he rolled over and over to finally rest on his side. The mountain lion bared his teeth as if smiling, and picked up the pup by his scruff and tossed the young animal into the air.*

The pup dropped to the ground and yowled in pain. The cat stalked back and continued its cruel game with his helpless prey.

A full-grown wolf jumped into the clearing, startling the mountain lion away from his toy. The wolf laid back her ears and growled at the larger animal. The mountain lion snapped at the wolf, angered by the interruption, but the interloper refused to desert the pup.

The cat roared and leaped toward the wolf, who jumped at the same moment. The two animals met in a clash of sharp teeth and razor-like claws. The wolf drew first blood and the shrill screams of the mountain lion filled the forest. The cat sprang at the wolf and buried his teeth in the side of her neck. The night echoed with the cries of a battle that would be fought to the death.

And the pup lay unmoving on the cold, barren ground. . . .

"No!" Emma screamed, her eyes flashing open as she jerked up in bed. The dream held her in its talons for a brief moment longer before releasing her and fading away, leaving an aching emptiness in its wake.

Sweat covered her brow and rolled down the scar between her breasts. Her hands shook as she drew them across her face.

The bedroom door flew open and her sister ran into the room, her robe flapping behind her. "Emma, are you all right?"

Emma nodded and clasped her sister's hand, pulling her down to perch on the bed beside her. "I-I had a dream."

"More like a nightmare," Sarah guessed.

"No. A vision. I saw—" Emma closed her eyes, knowing to continue would only make her sister think she was crazy. She met Sarah's puzzled gaze. "You're right. It was only a nightmare." She gave her younger sister's hand a final squeeze and released it. "I'm all right. You can go back to bed."

"Would you like to talk about it? I know I always feel better after I talk to someone." Sarah brushed a strand of hair back from Emma's damp forehead and kept stroking her brow gently, like their mother used to do when they were children. "I had nightmares for weeks after you disappeared. I kept hearing you cry for help, but I could never find you." A tear slid down her wan cheek.

Emma's own eyes filled with moisture and she wrapped her arms around her little sister. Sarah's shoulders shook as she cried soundlessly against Emma's neck. Emma hadn't even considered how her absence might affect her sister, who'd just turned thirteen when she'd disappeared. Her memories of Sarah were those of a brat, throwing a tantrum when she didn't get her way. Their father had spoiled her, giving her gewgaws and making allowances for her, something he'd never done for his eldest daughter.

Emma remembered her resentment at the unfairness, and the deep-seated bitterness flared briefly. But the past was gone; in fact, it seemed a lifetime ago. There was no doubt her sister had been changed, too, by Emma's disappearance.

"At first I was scared," Emma said softly as she continued to rock the younger woman. "After I was brought to the village, I was taken care of and adopted by Talutah and her husband Fast Elk, the brave who found me. They'd had a daughter who would've been my age but had died only a month earlier." Emma easily remembered the fondness and patience her adopted parents had shown her as they taught her their language and customs. "They live in a harsher world, which is why their ways seem so barbaric to us. But deep down, they're a lot like us."

Startled, Sarah drew back to look at Emma. "You can say that after what they did to you?"

Emma cupped her sister's tear-dampened face and peered into her eyes. "They saved my life, Sarah. I know people around here say I was their captive, but I was free to leave if I'd wanted to. But where would I have gone? I was miles from any town. I lived with them and didn't allow my fear to turn into hatred, and I became friends with them. After a while, I learned to enjoy my new life."

She wished she could confess everything—her marriage, her child, how she came to love her adoptive parents—but fear kept her from doing so. Sarah might understand or she might not. Emma couldn't take that chance, especially now that she knew what must be done.

Sarah clasped her hands. "I'm glad, Emma. I'm glad they saved your life and I'm glad you're home."

Emma's throat tightened and she hugged her sister one last time. "Thank you for coming to check on me."

Sarah rose and smiled tremulously. "You used to do it for me when we were little. Goodnight, Emma."

"Goodnight."

After Emma heard her sister's bed frame creak in the room next to hers, she threw back her covers and rose to sit in the window seat. Pushing aside the curtain, she gazed into the darkness, lit only by a slivered moon. In two weeks the moon would be full, just as in her vision.

And Emma was certain it was a vision, sent to her by Owl, the messenger. For the past week, he'd been trying to tell her something. Now she understood. She had to find Chayton, the wolf pup in her vision, before he was killed by the lion.

Who was the mountain lion? Or had the large cat only been the symbol of approaching death? The unease she'd been experiencing throughout the past days bloomed to full-grown dread.

She'd been preparing to escape before she was forced to travel to St. Paul, but she'd wanted to find a guide. Her aborted attempt to hire Cullen had been a desperate measure.

Even now, in the security of her own room, Cullen's dirty words retained their power to humiliate her. Emma drew up her knees, laid a burning cheek on their coolness, and wrapped her arms around her legs.

She closed her eyes, remembering how grateful she'd been when Ridge Madoc had come to her assistance. But then she'd seen the look in his eyes. He thought little better of her for being alone with a man in the darkness. Maybe he figured she deserved what Cullen had done. But, no, if he thought that, he wouldn't have interfered. He'd heard her cry out and had acted like a gentleman to help her. But as much as she wanted to make Ridge the hero, he, too, couldn't look past her being a "squaw woman."

However, for a moment, when he'd so carefully fixed her dress over her shoulder, Emma couldn't deny the empty yearning in her chest. After Enapay had died, she'd buried her needs and found solace in caring for her child. But sometimes, in the middle of the night, she remembered how her husband had touched her and made her body writhe until he filled her and quenched the fire in her belly. When those memories became too powerful, Emma would touch herself under the curtain of darkness and find the release her body so desperately craved. But it was never enough. Ridge's touch reminded her of dark nights and shared pleasures.

A breeze jangled the shutters and Emma ached with fear for her son. How could she have left him behind? It didn't matter that a soldier's saber had wounded her or that terrible screams and horrific sights had paralyzed her. She should have searched until she found Chayton or died trying. But that choice had been taken from her when a soldier had recognized her white features and whisked her away from the decimated village.

Emma tried to quash the torment rising in her breast, but a tiny sob broke free. She had a choice now, and she chose to search for her son. Dear God, she prayed he was still alive.

She would leave tonight under the cover of darkness. There was no time left to secure a guide, but at least she knew where to begin her journey.

* * *

DAWN colored the sky coral, pink, and orange as Emma rode into the main encampment on the reservation. Exhausted, she kept her horse to a plodding walk as it wove in and out of the haphazard tipis. A skinny yellow dog yipped once, then slunk away. Emma's nose wrinkled under the barrage of rank sweat and both human and animal excrement. The smell was nothing like the village where she'd lived—the people there had kept themselves and their camp tidy and clean.

She recognized hopelessness as the culprit here, where the Indians had given up and surrendered in exchange for handouts from their captors. Some of the Lakota on the reservation no longer even tried to retain and practice the old ways, which were frowned upon by the Bureau of Indian Affairs agents.

Moisture filled Emma's eyes, and she blinked back the tears. She couldn't help them and to feel pity would only insult the proud people. Women and men wrapped in blankets crept out of their lodges and stared at her. Emma searched the impassive bronze faces, hoping to find someone she recognized, but nobody looked familiar.

By the time Emma reached the end of the village, she was trembling so much she could hardly draw her horse to a stop. She slid off her mount and her legs wobbled. Her feet were numb in the snug riding boots, which she hadn't worn since she was fifteen, and her thighs beneath the split riding skirt were irritated and chafed. She would've gladly exchanged her civilized garb for moccasins, a deerskin dress, and leggings.

An elderly Indian stepped forward, his shoulders hunched, but his eyes keen.

She faced the old man and bowed her head. *"Tunkasila."*

Although she couldn't see him, she could feel his surprise at her use of the Sioux word for grandfather.

"Táku eniciyapi hwo?" he asked.

"I am called Winona by the Lakota," she replied, continuing to speak in the language she'd learned. She risked lifting her head and when the old Indian didn't give her a disapproving look, she grew bolder. "I seek my son. Five moons ago my village was attacked by horse soldiers." Emma couldn't control the shudder of horror at the memory of that night.

The elderly man studied her for a long moment, then turned and motioned for her to follow. A young boy materialized beside her and took her horse's reins. Emma gave him a brief smile and allowed the boy to lead the animal away.

Keeping her gaze aimed downward, she followed the old man to his tipi.

"*Timá hiyúwo,*" he said and disappeared inside.

Emma loosened her chinstrap and allowed her hat to slide down her back, to rest between her shoulder blades. Taking a deep breath, she accepted his invitation to enter and ducked under the deerskin flap, praying he could give her the information she sought.

$\mathcal{F}$OUR

RIDGE herded nine cattle into the canyon to join the other fourteen head he'd found that morning. He halted his horse under the miserly shade of a scrub oak growing next to a small stream. He dismounted and allowed Paint to drink.

Although it was early April, the midday sun was comfortably warm on his head and shoulders. Most of the snow had melted, but a few pockets remained, hidden in enclaves steeped in cool shadows.

He hunkered down beside a riffling brook and cupped his hands to drink the icy cold water. After wiping his mouth with his sleeve, he rose. His stomach growled, reminding him he hadn't eaten since dawn. As he unwrapped some dried venison from the cloth in his saddlebag, he caught a plume of dust to the east. As he chewed the jerky, he squinted at the dust cloud and the horse creating it. The rider rode unerringly toward him and Ridge tensed.

He narrowed his eyes until he could make out the nearing figure. John Hartwell. What the hell was he doing here?

Ridge kept his arms hanging loosely at his sides, but his muscles coiled. Did Emma tell her father about the fight between him and Cullen the night before last? And, if so, was Hartwell planning to thank him or shoot him?

Hartwell halted his horse on the other side of the four-foot wide stream. He didn't wear his usual suit, but typical range gear, although his wool trousers and waistcoat were newer and of better quality than a hired hand's. Hartwell's cheeks were flushed, and sweat mixed with dust streaked his face. He remained in the saddle. Ridge figured the man enjoyed looking down on folks.

Ridge nodded a mute greeting.

"Madoc." There was more hospitality in a rattlesnake's reception. "I've got a job for you."

Anger came directly on the heels of surprise, and Ridge laughed, a cold, harsh sound. "I wasn't good enough to work on your ranch, so what makes me good enough for this job?"

"You were a scout," Hartwell said tersely. "I need you to find my daughter. Emma ran away Saturday night."

The night Ridge had found her alone with Cullen. He ground his teeth and felt the tug of his jaw muscle. "Maybe she ran off with some fella."

Hartwell shook his head impatiently. "My other daughter said she had a nightmare. It upset her but she wouldn't tell Sarah about it." He looked away, embarrassment and a hint of humiliation in his expression. "Sarah thinks she went back to the savages that kidnapped her."

After Emma's confession about trying to hire Cullen to find her adopted tribe, Ridge wasn't surprised. But he wasn't about to confess that to Hartwell. He shrugged. "They're probably scattered seven ways to Sunday."

"I'll give you a hundred dollars to find her and bring her back home," Hartwell offered.

A hundred dollars. That was more than he would make in three months working as a ranch hand, and the balance he needed to purchase the bull. But what about his land—the land Hartwell had practically stolen from Harry Piner.

"On one condition," Ridge said flatly. "You sell me my land back at the same price you paid for it—fifty cents an acre."

Hartwell's mouth gaped and his face reddened, but this time it was with antagonism instead of embarrassment. "That's extortion."

"That's business," Ridge shot back. He lowered his voice and smiled without an ounce of warmth. "You know all about business."

Hartwell's knuckles were white as he gripped his saddle horn and a vein in his forehead pulsed angrily as he glared at Ridge.

"Your daughter for my land. Your choice, Hartwell." An eagle's cry sliced through the tension and Ridge glanced up to spot the mighty bird soaring high above them—a favorable sign.

He looked back at Hartwell to find the man still mulling over his offer. Ridge's lips curled in disdain. A man who had to consider a choice between his daughter and some land was a miserable excuse for a human being.

The rancher's eyes blazed. "All right."

"I want it in writing." Men like Hartwell respected words on paper.

"Damn you, Madoc. My word's good."

Ridge merely stared at him.

Hartwell capitulated with a snarl. "Come to the house and I'll have a contract ready to sign."

Ridge relaxed. "Why didn't you get me yesterday? She's got a day and a half lead now."

Hartwell glanced away and rubbed at a patch of dust on his cheek. "I tried to find her myself, then I went to Colonel Nyes. The son of a bitch said they'd keep an eye out for her during their patrols, but didn't want to expend the manpower to find a—" He clamped his mouth shut, but Ridge knew what he was going to say.

It looked like he and Hartwell had something in common after all: a mutual dislike for Nyes.

"She's not in her right mind, Madoc," Hartwell confessed in a low voice. "But she's still my daughter."

In the few instances Ridge had talked to Emma Hartwell, she hadn't seemed crazy. He also had a feeling the woman had reasons no one but herself knew for wanting to find those she'd lived with. But a hundred dollars and the chance to recover his land at a dirt cheap price was more than reason enough to take the job. Bringing Emma Hartwell back to her own folks was the right thing to do, too, even if Ridge didn't care much for her father.

Ridge mounted his horse. "I have to tell the foreman I'm leaving; then I'll meet you at your house in an hour."

Hartwell nodded, relief in his haggard expression.

EMMA patted her mare's neck soothingly as she tracked the progress of a black bear and her cub a hundred yards away. Although she knew a sow with her young could be dangerous, Emma also knew that as long as she didn't make any threatening moves or try to get close to them, the bear would ignore her.

The sow stopped and lifted her nose to scent the air. Fortunately, Emma was downwind. She watched the cub rollick in the clearing, oblivious to the dangers surrounding it. He had his mother—she would take care of him.

Unlike Chayton, whose mother had abandoned him.

No! She hadn't. Not voluntarily. When she'd finally recovered physically, her mind had remained sick from the horrible memories of that night. And even if she'd had the strength to look for Chayton, the winter weather would've denied her the opportunity.

But now, with the arrival of spring and the information she'd gained at the reservation, Emma knew the general location of her people. Or at least those who weren't killed the night of the attack, she thought with a bitter tang.

She'd asked about her son, but the old man hadn't known anything about him. If Chayton were still alive, he'd be with the group which was now headed northeast.

Sunlight sprinkled through the trees, dappling the meadow. A droplet on a spider's web captured the sun and wove it into a tiny colorful rainbow. A gift for those who truly saw. The tribe's shaman had taught her that, and Emma had listened.

As she stared at the water drop, the colors swirled, then coalesced into the image of a brown eagle riding the wind high in the sky. The eagle soared closer and closer until Emma found its keen eyes staring directly into hers.

She gasped and blinked. The image disappeared and only the droplet remained. Someone was searching for her. It shouldn't have surprised her.

Five days had passed since she'd left the reservation. She knew her father would send somebody to find her and bring her back. Shivering despite the warm air, Emma hoped she wasn't leading the army straight to the reservation runaways, only to have the soldiers finish what they started.

The bear and its cub disappeared into the brush, and Emma urged Clementine, her horse, through the meadow. The mare danced nervously, tossing her head at the fresh bear scent, but Emma handled her with a firm hand.

Emma trusted the intuition she'd gained while living with the People. The shaman had said she possessed a second sight, a rarity among the *wasicu* who did not understand. But Emma embraced her fledgling gift. Now she prayed it would lead her safely to her son.

RIDGE knew he was close. After four days of trailing the surprisingly trail-savvy woman, he had come to admire and respect her skills. Few white men, let alone a woman, could travel such distance in such a short amount of time and manage to cover their tracks so well. There'd been times when he'd followed a blind trail, only to have to backtrack and find the real one.

The sun had set two hours ago, but Ridge knew he was near his quarry and had chosen to continue on, hoping to find her that night. He was rewarded for his persistence when he smelled faint woodsmoke on the breeze. Following it led him directly to her.

Ridge surveyed the small camp and spotted her bedroll a few feet from the glowing embers. Her horse was fifteen feet away, hobbled and grazing contentedly. Ridge dismounted and ground-tied Paint. Moving on soundless moccasins, he entered her camp. Her horse raised its head and snorted, but was too accustomed to being around people to raise an alarm.

Miss Hartwell slept on her side, facing the fire's remains, and her blanket was tugged up to her chin. The orange glow of the embers reflected reddish-gold strands in her honey-brown hair and illuminated her winged brows and slightly upturned nose. Her lips were pressed together, with the lower one slightly fuller than the upper, giving the impression she was pouting.

Suddenly, Ridge wanted to discover if her lips were as soft and sweet-tasting as they appeared. Before his mind could offer an argument, he was drawing nearer to her.

The woman threw off her blanket and charged upward. Orange glinted off silver metal and Ridge felt a blow, followed by a sharp burn across his forearm. He reacted without thought, grabbing the wrist of the hand that held the knife and wrapping his other arm around her waist. He squeezed her wrist until the knife thudded dully on the ground.

She fought in his arms, flailing arms and legs, and they rolled across the dirt, ending up with Ridge straddling Emma's waist. He locked his ankles down on her lower legs and imprisoned her hands on the ground above her head. Lying atop her, Ridge could feel her breasts rising and falling against his chest and his body reacted instinctively to her feminine curves.

Ridge gnashed his teeth and willed his blood to cool. "Settle down, Miss Hartwell. It's Ridge Madoc."

The moment he said his name, she ceased struggling.

"Mr. Madoc?" she asked.

"Yeah," he answered curtly, sitting up so she wouldn't feel him so intimately against her belly. "You gonna behave?"

Her stiff muscles relaxed beneath him. "Yes."

Releasing her hands, he shifted off her, kneeling to her side. With the fight drained from both of them, Ridge could now feel the blood soaking his sleeve and dripping onto the ground. The throbbing in the gash told him it wasn't a mere flesh wound.

Damn.

"I'm surprised it was you," she said quietly as she sat up.

"What?"

"I knew my father would send someone. I didn't think it would be you."

Ridge shrugged, then hissed when the movement sent an arrow of pain through his wounded arm.

Miss Hartwell scrambled to her knees and gazed down at his injury. "Your arm. How bad is it?"

"Could be better."

Her annoyance disappeared, replaced by concern. "I'll build up the fire so I can take care of it."

Ridge didn't argue, knowing it needed to be cleaned and maybe sewn, too. She completed her tasks quickly without speaking. Although Ridge wasn't accustomed to being around a woman, he felt little awkwardness with Miss Hartwell. She didn't prattle on and on about this and that, but worked efficiently with a minimum of commotion.

"Move closer to the fire, Mr. Madoc," she ordered.

Ridge did so and worked to remove his jacket and shirt so she wouldn't have to cut the sleeves off. The woman assisted him, easing the two pieces of clothing off the wounded arm.

Without any sign of embarrassment, she ripped a camisole dug out of her saddlebag into three pieces. Upending her canteen, she wet one and began to clean away the blood around the wound.

Although Ridge usually preferred silence, he found he wanted to hear Miss Hartwell's voice. "Where'd you learn to use a knife?" he asked.

"Fast Elk, the husband of Talutah. I lived with them." Her brow furrowed, but she didn't look up. "There were a

handful of young Indian men who felt the same way as
Cullen, only it was because I had white skin."

Ridge wasn't shocked by her matter-of-fact statement.
It didn't matter what color a man was, there were always
some who enjoyed hurting folks. "You must've been a
good student."

She glanced up. "Fear is a good motivator." She returned her attention to the wound.

The night's silence surrounded them with only the fire's
crackling and the occasional coyote's yipping disturbing
the serenity. Ridge kept his gaze on Miss Hartwell's bowed
head as she cared for the injury with surprising expertise.
He had an idea this was another thing she'd learned when
she was with the People.

"I'm going to have to stitch it," she announced.

"Figured."

"It's going to hurt."

"I've been cut before," Ridge said. "I've got a bottle of
whiskey in my saddlebags. You can use that to soak the
needle and thread in."

She nodded and rose gracefully to disappear into the
darkness. It wasn't long before she reappeared leading
Paint. After tying his reins to a low-slung branch, she retrieved the bottle.

Kneeling by the fire, Miss Hartwell dribbled some of
the liquor across the needle and thread. She recapped the
bottle and was about to set it to the side.

Ridge reached for it with his good hand. "I could use
some before you start."

She eyed him mutely as he took three long swallows and
shut his eyes to enjoy the burn and growing numbness that
followed. A small hand took the bottle from him and set it
aside.

"Do you often drink whiskey?" she asked.

Ridge opened his eyes to find the lips he'd been admiring earlier thinned with irritation. "Only when a crazy
woman attacks me with a knife."

She bent over his arm and pushed the needle through a

flap of skin on one side of the gash and tugged the thread through the bead of blood welling from the tiny hole. Ridge averted his gaze and ground his teeth.

"I'm sorry," she finally said when she was half done. "I didn't know it was you."

"Who'd you think it was?"

"I didn't think. I only reacted."

"That'll get you killed," Ridge said, studying the fiery hues of red and gold in her hair as she stitched the wound.

"Or the person who's foolish enough to try sneaking up on me when I'm sleeping."

In spite of the situation, Ridge grinned. "Yes, ma'am. That, too."

He felt rather than saw her reluctant smile.

Long, graceful fingers moved the needle cleanly through skin. There was no hesitation in her movements, only a steady economy of motion. He wondered if she'd been so calm and quiet before she'd been taken, or if she'd learned patience with the Lakota, just as he had.

She finished and tied off the thread. As she reached for a piece of the torn-up camisole, he looked down at the neat black stitches that held the cut together.

"You do good work, ma'am," he said.

"The wound or the stitching?"

He spotted a hint of amusement in her eyes. "Both."

She wrapped the cloth around his arm, smoothing the material with an experienced hand. It'd been a long time since Ridge had been near enough to a woman to smell her and he savored Miss Hartwell's musky feminine scent, overlaid by trail dust and sweat.

"I'm going to make some tea that will help with the pain," she announced as she tied off the makeshift bandage.

"You don't have to—"

"I know, but I feel bad enough that I was the one who injured you."

While she poured water into a battered pan, Ridge stood to care for Paint.

Miss Hartwell rose and halted him with a touch on his wrist. "What're you doing?"

"Gotta unsaddle my horse."

"I can do it."

"No, ma'am. A man takes care of his own horse unless he's dead or dying."

She glared at him. "Fine. But don't be surprised when your wound starts bleeding again."

"I'll be careful," Ridge groused.

Miss Hartwell didn't say anything more but settled down to ready the tea leaves to steep once the water was hot. Using his uninjured left hand, Ridge took three times as long to unsaddle and rub down Paint. By the time he finished, he was exhausted and the tea was ready.

Miss Hartwell handed him a steaming cup as he lowered himself to his saddle, which lay on the ground by the fire. "Thank you, ma'am." Although he wasn't a tea drinker, he took a sip and swallowed, enjoying the warmth and slight bitterness as it flowed down his throat.

"I'm not going back, Mr. Madoc," she said quietly, but with an edge of steel.

"Your family wants you home."

Anguish flashed in her eyes. "I miss them, but I can't go back. Not yet."

"Why?" Ridge finished his tea.

She stared into the flames. "I have something I have to do first."

"What's so important that you'd abandon your own family?"

She laughed, but it was a raw, hurtful sound. "Abandoning family. That's what this is all about, Mr. Madoc."

"I don't understand, Miss Hartwell." Ridge peered at the woman and her figure blurred. He squinted and managed to clear up the picture for only a second. His eyelids flickered downward and he fought to keep them open.

"You should get some rest, Mr. Madoc. You lost a lot of blood."

"Home. In the morning," Ridge slurred.

"Yes, Mr. Madoc. In the morning you can go home."

He felt a gentle pressure on his arm, guiding him to lie down. A blanket settled over him, and small, competent hands tucked the material around him. "Thank you, ma'am," he murmured.

His last memory before dropping off was that of a woman's tender touch feathering across his brow.

When Ridge awakened the next morning, groggy and confused, the sun was high above the horizon. And Emma Hartwell was gone.

$\mathscr{F}$IVE

ADJUSTING the canteen and bedroll straps crisscrossing his chest, Ridge followed the suspiciously distinct trail Emma had left behind. He knew her skill at hiding her tracks firsthand, yet she wasn't making any effort to hide the two sets of hoofprints now. Why?

He should've been more wary of her willingness to help after she'd knifed him, but he hadn't expected someone like Miss Hartwell to be so treacherous. The woman he'd found stumbling near town nearly two weeks ago wouldn't have attacked him. Nor would she have drugged his tea.

Even as young as he'd been, he remembered his pa's strict lesson on treating women with respect and courtesy. He'd always said it didn't matter if the woman was a lady or a whore, Ridge always tipped his hat and opened doors for her. Emma Hartwell was no whore, despite what many of the townsfolk thought. Yet she hadn't acted like a lady either.

So how should he treat her?

Like a bounty.

Ridge cringed inwardly. She wasn't anything like those men he'd hunted for the price on their heads. Most of them had been more like animals, and when he'd defended himself, it was more like putting down a rabid creature than shooting a man.

After he joined the army, he swore he'd never return to bounty hunting, although he'd been tempted over the last month. The money was a whole lot better than chasing cattle around all day, but tracking down murderers and thieves was a dangerous job. Too dangerous for someone who had a reason to live.

Ridge stumbled over an exposed tree root, jarred his injured arm, and bit back a curse at his uncharacteristic clumsiness. He'd been walking steadily for over three hours, feeding off anger and humiliation. However, his emotions were starting to drain and he couldn't ignore his arm's throbbing or the stinging blisters on his feet.

The ground was littered with boulders jutting out of the earth and Ridge lowered himself to one with a groan. His feet nearly groaned in relief.

He was getting soft. A year ago a little cut wouldn't have taken so much out of him. A year ago he wouldn't have been wounded and left afoot by a gal, either. At least she'd left his saddlebags, canteen, and rifle so he wouldn't starve or be helpless against a wild animal.

He tucked the canteen between his injured arm and his side, then used his other hand to remove the stopper. Raising the canteen to his lips, he took a few sips of the cool liquid. The water helped clear his foggy head, but he didn't dare drink too much. He wasn't certain how far he'd have to walk, but he *would* find Miss Hartwell, even if he had to track the woman halfway to hell. Then he'd haul her crafty little backside back to her daddy's ranch—tied belly down across her horse's saddle, if he had to—and collect the one hundred dollars.

A wolf's bay sounded from nearby and Ridge jerked his head up, searching for the wild animal. The sun slid behind a gunmetal gray cloud and another howl ripped through the stillness. A shiver skidded down Ridge's spine as he rose. It was uncommon for a wolf to howl during the day. He turned slowly, making a full circle, as he sniffed the air and squinted to see around the surrounding rocks and trees.

Nothing.

Clutching the rifle more tightly in his good hand, Ridge slung his canteen and saddlebag over a shoulder. Puzzling over the wolf, he continued following the trail, which had grown fainter across the rocky ground.

The horses' tracks became clearer as reddish soil replaced the rough land. Ridge increased his stride. Clouds continued to blot out the blue skies, urging him faster. If it rained, he'd lose the tracks completely, as well as his chance to find Miss Hartwell.

Half an hour later, Ridge rounded a corner and nearly stumbled into Paint. The horse, his reins wrapped loosely around a bush, raised his head as he munched a mouthful of grass.

Ridge grinned and laid a gloved hand on Paint's neck. "You're a sight for sorry eyes, fella."

Paint snorted and tossed his head, then lowered his muzzle to tear up some tender spears of grass. As the animal ate contentedly, Ridge examined him, sliding a hand along his flanks and down his legs, but didn't find anything amiss. It appeared the woman wasn't completely heartless. She probably only wanted to slow Ridge down to make good her escape.

He spotted a piece of paper caught between his saddle and the blanket, and tugged it out. He recognized his name written on the folded sheet, opened the paper, and stared at the letters for a long moment. Swallowing hard, he crumpled the note and tossed it away.

After tightening Paint's cinch and ensuring the bridle was fitted correctly, he shoved his toe into the stirrup and hauled himself up carefully. The stitches in his arm pulled and he clenched his jaw. It was merely another reminder of why he wouldn't return without Emma Hartwell.

The woman owed him.

* * *

THE Lakota elder had told Emma to ride north and east if she wished to find her adopted people. Although they'd had only a six-day head start and most of the survivors were women and children on foot, Emma wasn't surprised she'd been unable to catch up to them.

Generations of nomadic living had given the Lakota the skills and tools to disassemble their homes and be ready to journey in less than an hour. The first time Emma had witnessed the entire village preparing to abandon a site, she'd been terrified that the Indians would kill her and leave her body behind. After being reassured she wouldn't be harmed nor abandoned, Emma had resolved to do her share rather than to be a hindrance. It had been the beginning of her acceptance, and she had grown to have an abiding respect for their ways.

Emma halted her horse with a slight draw on the reins and gazed out across the vast expanse of land. North and east covered a wide swath of territory. Would she ever find them in the sprawling wilderness?

If only she'd been able to convince Ridge Madoc to help her. However, that option was lost to her, especially after what she'd done to him. Wounding him with her knife and then putting sleeping herbs in his tea hadn't been enough. She'd also taken his horse. He wouldn't be happy, but she hoped her note convinced him she wasn't going back until she attained her goal.

A chill slipped inside her jacket and goose bumps danced across her arms. She glanced up at the clouds, dark and swollen with rain, and worry sent another shiver through her. What if Ridge didn't find shelter? He was already injured. What if the wound became infected? She had cleaned it well, but infection was common even with minor cuts.

She turned in the saddle, resting one hand on her horse's rump as she studied her back trail in the fading light, and was pleased to see no evidence of her passage. She'd left a trail a child could follow when she'd taken his horse because of her guilt-stricken conscience. Surely he had found the animal by now, read her note, and headed home.

After she left his horse, she'd circled around and resorted to covering her tracks once more in case he was pigheaded enough to follow her. She suspected he wasn't a man to give up easily, which would've been an admirable quality under different circumstances.

Clementine snorted and stamped her front hooves. It was time to quit woolgathering and continue her search. She urged her mare northeast and prayed she was moving closer to her son.

A cold drizzle started at dusk, forcing Ridge to push Paint harder. Rain would wash away the faint signs of Emma's trail. She'd returned to covering her tracks, which told him she meant for him to find Paint. He didn't know whether to be grateful for her thoughtfulness, or annoyed for giving him cause to feel guilty for taking her back home.

After hours of following the almost-nonexistent trail, he caught sight of a small flickering fire. He was too far away to tell if the body moving around it was Emma's, but he suspected it was.

He dismounted and tied Paint in some sparse shelter. Stepping carefully onto the wet ground, he drew closer to the flames until he recognized the figure. He'd found his prey. Again.

His attention on Emma, he accidentally kicked a stone and it skittered across the hard ground. As quiet as the sound was, the woman must've heard it. She froze and lifted her head to peer into the darkness.

His heart pounding, Ridge remained still, ignoring the light rain that continued to fall. Her wary gaze skipped across him and she finally gave her attention back to whatever she was preparing over the tiny fire. He'd do well to remember her keen senses in the future, as well as her uncanny vigilance.

Letting out his pent-up breath, he sidled closer until he stood only ten feet away, hidden by a tree trunk. With no intention of taking a chance this time, he withdrew his revolver, but didn't cock it. As furious as he was, he recoiled at the thought of even shooting a warning shot if she tried to escape. He only hoped she didn't know that.

He stepped into the slight clearing.

Emma froze.

"Miss Hartwell," Ridge said, his voice a cool parody of politeness.

Emma stared at him, her expression revealing nothing. Then she leaned over and deliberately stirred the contents of a small kettle hanging over the fire. "Mr. Madoc. Would you like some stew?"

Ridge caught his smile before it could grow. The woman definitely had spunk. "What'd you put in it?"

She glanced up at him and her eyes held the hint of a twinkle. "I didn't know I'd be having company."

"Then I reckon you'd best step away from the food until I'm done eating." He motioned with the barrel of his gun. "Move back."

"What're you going to do?"

"Something I should've done last night. It would've saved me a mess of trouble." He motioned with his chin. "Back."

Her eyes flickered to his revolver. "Are you going to shoot me if I don't?"

This time he did smile, but it was without warmth or amusement. "Don't worry. I'd just graze you, ma'am."

Her lips thinned, her humor fleeing. "I doubt my father would appreciate you bringing me back with a bullet wound."

Ridge snorted. "Your father could barely choose between his precious land and you."

Emma flinched and her gaze fell, but not before Ridge spotted her humiliation at the plainspoken truth. It was as if she'd suspected all along, and his words confirmed her father's opinion of her. Suddenly he felt like the lowest vermin for hurting her with his rash words.

"Step back, ma'am," he said, gentling his voice slightly.

She left her improvised spoon, a stripped twig as thick as her thumb, in the kettle and did as he ordered.

"That's good enough," Ridge said when she was some feet from the fire. "Now put your hands on your head and leave 'em there."

She glared at him, her eyes sparking with fury and helplessness, and Ridge was relieved to see the bleak anguish had vanished. He could handle an angry woman, but a teary-eyed one scared the hell out of him.

With her damp hair straggling in clumps about her face and her clothes limp from moisture, Emma should've looked like a drowned rat. However, the rain made her long skirt cling to the curve of her legs, and her jacket hugged the fullness of her breasts. Her wrath only made her more breathtaking.

Clearing his throat and mind, Ridge concentrated on the task at hand. He retrieved the pieces of rope he'd brought with him and approached her warily. Her narrowed gaze followed him and he was reminded of a trapped animal.

"Sit down, but keep your hands on your head," he ordered.

Emma remained mute as she lowered herself to the ground. Without the use of her hands, she plopped clumsily onto the wet, unforgiving ground.

"Now roll over onto your belly and put your hands behind you," he said.

Her mouth fell open with indignation.

"Just do it, ma'am," Ridge said before she could speak. After his lousy day, he wasn't up to any verbal sparring.

Pressing her lips together, Emma laid flat on the ground. After a moment's hesitation, she placed her hands at the small of her back.

Ridge closed in behind her and squatted down. "Easy, ma'am. I'm not going to hurt you unless you force me to."

She lifted her head and glared at him over her shoulder. "But only a flesh wound."

Ridge smiled, knowing full well she could see him. "That's right, ma'am."

Despite his injured arm, he made quick work of tying

her wrists. He could feel the tension in her shoulders and arms, and wished he didn't have to resort to old bounty-hunting methods. But she'd already proven herself untrust-worthy, and he couldn't chance losing her again. Her return meant a prized bull and the beginning of a cattle herd.

He shifted around to straddle her hips and grasped her ankles, pulling them upward like he was tying a calf. She twisted like an eel, trying to dislodge him or make him lose his grip on her.

"Damn it, woman, stop fighting or I'm gonna hurt you," he warned.

Emma struggled even more.

Ridge leaned back, placing more of his weight on her hips, and wrapped his good arm around her calves. Her dress draped down to reveal heavy stockings with black lace-up boots beneath the single petticoat. The boots weren't made for hard riding, and the kid leather was al-most worn through where the stirrups had rubbed. He sus-pected she had her share of blisters, too, but also figured she'd chew glass before admitting it.

Because of his injured arm and her resistance, it took longer to truss her. Once done, he released her legs and pushed himself upright, barely containing a groan. "I'm going to get my horse and bring him on into the camp."

"You can't leave me like this." Emma rolled onto her side to stare up at him accusingly.

"Yes, ma'am, I can. I'm tired, sore, and hungry, and I don't want to have to be watching out for your tricks."

"Fine." Her tone said just the opposite.

Ridge adjusted his hat. Every fiber in his body rebelled against leaving a woman tied up and on the wet ground, but she'd brought the situation on herself. If she'd agreed to go back with him without any fuss, they could be sharing a meal instead of acting like two cats fighting over the same piece of dirt.

He spun around and strode off to retrieve Paint. Return-ing five minutes later, he noticed the woman had managed to wriggle over to a tree and sat crookedly against the bole. Her clothes were smudged with dirt and mud, as was her face.

"That doesn't look too comfortable," he commented, working the saddle's girth loose.

"It's better than lying facedown in the mud," she retorted, her grimy chin out-thrust.

Ridge laid the saddle on a rock. "You do look a mite dirty there, ma'am."

If her eyes could shoot bullets, he'd be six feet under. He turned his attention to removing Paint's bridle. "What's so dang important about finding them?"

Emma remained mute. Ridge figured he'd have an easier time coaxing a rattler off a warm rock than getting Emma to talk. Not that it mattered to him why she wanted to go gallivanting around the country looking for people who didn't want to be found.

Ridge hobbled Paint and then concentrated on rubbing down the horse with the saddle blanket. Once that chore was done, he stepped over to the small fire and added branches from the pile Emma had gathered to feed the hungry flames. He leaned over to sniff the kettle's contents, and everything blurred. Dizziness swirled through him and he nearly pitched forward into the fire. Bracing his legs, he waited for the light-headedness to disappear. His wound's blood loss and his long trek were catching up to him.

"Are you all right?" Emma asked.

"Yeah," Ridge lied. He wasn't about to admit to Miss Hartwell any weakness. "What's in the kettle?"

"Rattlesnake."

"Kin of yours?"

An unladylike snort met his ears. Miss Hartwell had more than her share of starch in her ladylike backbone. "More likely yours."

"At least you haven't lost your sense of humor," Ridge said dryly. "I'm going to have some stew, then I'll feed you."

"I can feed myself if you untie me."

"That's not going to happen, ma'am. I don't take kindly to folks who knife me, then drug me." He dug out a tin plate and spoon from his saddlebag. "Makes me mad and when I get mad I get stubborn."

"Ornery," Emma corrected.

Ridge shrugged. "I reckon that, too, but you gave me reason enough." He returned to the cookfire and spooned some stew onto his plate, always keeping one eye on the woman. He sat on the ground as he shoveled a bite of food into his mouth. It was better than anything he could've thrown together. "It's good, ma'am."

"I'm glad you find it to your liking." Emma's voice could've frozen water. "I hope you're going to leave some for me, or is that part of your plan—starve me so I'm too weak to cause any trouble."

Ridge pretended to consider her suggestion while inwardly amused at her tart words. "That ain't a bad idea."

"My father would probably appreciate it."

Ridge glanced sharply at the woman and found her lips curled into a cynical scowl. "I told you I'd feed you."

"And I'm supposed to take your word for that?"

"My word's good."

He glared at her when she looked like she was going to continue arguing, and she lapsed into silence.

Ridge finished eating though he hardly tasted it. How had he ever thought Emma demure and retiring? She had the uncanny ability to both fluster and anger him in the same breath. It was at least a four-day ride back to Hartwell's ranch. If he had to, he'd gag her for the entire trip.

He straightened to refill the plate for Emma, and barely stifled a groan. Between the knife wound and his achy muscles, he wanted nothing more than to lie down and sleep.

After carrying the food to Emma, he sat cross-legged beside her. "Hungry?"

"No."

"Eat anyhow. I don't want you swooning."

"I've never swooned in my life."

Ridge rested his hands on his knees and held the plate between them. "Not even when the Indians got you?"

"Not even then," she replied quietly.

"Most women would've."

"So I've heard." She paused. "I also heard most women would've killed themselves rather than stay with them."

Ridge met Emma's amber eyes. "I never could understand that. I figure living is the important thing."

"Then you're not like most white people."

He shifted uncomfortably. "Better eat afore it gets cold." He raised a spoonful of stew.

Emma, her gaze never wavering from Ridge, opened her mouth and he stuck the spoon inside. He watched as her lips closed around it, and he drew the spoon out. The full lips remained together and she chewed almost daintily.

Suddenly realizing he was staring, he looked back at the plate as he refilled the spoon. He kept a tight rein on his thoughts, concentrating on his injured arm's ache instead of Emma's tantalizing lips. He lifted his gaze to her eyes once, only to find her cheeks flushed beneath the grime, and he glanced downward again.

Some minutes later he scraped the plate clean. "More?"

She shook her head. "But I would appreciate some water."

Nodding, he found her canteen and held it up so she could drink. When she was done, he placed it back on her saddle, which rested on the ground not far from the fire, along with her bedroll.

Night cloaked them in darkness except for the glow of the fire. All Ridge wanted to do was curl up and go to sleep, but he had to clean up the camp, change the dressing on his arm, and decide what to do with Emma.

"If you let me loose, I'll wash the dishes," Emma volunteered, and added with an accusatory tone, "Besides, I'd like to clean up and change my clothes."

"A little dirt never killed anyone."

"I give you my word I won't try anything."

"Why should I believe you?"

"Because my word's good," she threw his earlier declaration back at him.

"I got no reason to trust you, ma'am."

"I never gave you my word last night." Then she added quietly, "If I had, I wouldn't have run out on you."

Despite his previous objections, he considered her request. He didn't like the idea of her sleeping in damp, muddy clothes. She could catch a cough or worse. He'd seen it happen too often.

As if reading his mind, Emma sneezed once, then a second time.

He knelt behind her. "Don't give me any grief, Emma. I'm not in the mood," he said, leaning close to her ear.

"I won't," she replied, her voice husky.

He untied her wrists, but had her release her own ankles. Standing, he leaned a shoulder against the tree she'd been sitting against. "No dallying."

Emma nodded, but didn't meet his gaze.

She cleaned the kettle, plate, and spoon with practiced ease, and Ridge knew she hadn't learned that living in Hartwell's fancy house either. Once the kettle was spotless, she refilled it with water to heat over the fire.

"I'm going to change my clothes," she said.

Ridge's first impulse was to turn around and give her privacy. But he suspected if he did that, he wouldn't see her again. He kept his stance relaxed, but his breath came in shorter bursts as he resisted the images that invaded his thoughts. "Go ahead."

"That's hardly proper, Mr. Madoc."

Ridge barked a sharp laugh. "If you haven't noticed, ma'am, nothing about this is proper."

"You can't expect me to undress in front of you."

"That's exactly what I expect." He could see evidence of Emma's inner battle in her frown and wrinkled brow. "We don't have all night."

Although her actions were of surrender, her clenched teeth and blazing eyes told Ridge another story.

Keeping his face blank, he watched her remove her jacket. Her fingers shook as she unbuttoned her blouse and slipped the soiled shirt from her smooth shoulders. The firelight cast flickering shadows across her slender neck and the slope of her breasts, disappearing beneath her white camisole. When her hands went to her skirt, Ridge's heart stepped up its pace even more. Once she'd undone the hooks, she skimmed the skirt down her slender hips and legs. She gracefully lifted one dainty foot, then the other as she stepped out of the pool of cloth.

His breathing grew rougher. It'd been a long time since he'd been with a woman and his body wasn't shy about reminding him.

Emma glanced up and her gaze ensnared his. The black circles in her eyes nearly covered all of the light brown, inviting him to dive into their depths and never come out. Her lips parted as if she too were having a hard time finding air.

Ridge's blood pounded sluggishly in his ears, drowning out everything else. The night faded until only Emma remained. Emma, lit by firelight and resembling a beautiful wild creature with her full lips parted and her breasts straining against the thin-clothed camisole.

A soft whimper escaped her, startling Ridge back to cold reality. He dropped his gaze and tried to ignore the throbbing in his groin, which far surpassed the discomfort of his arm.

He listened to Emma as she donned clean, dry clothes and when he thought she was done, he finally raised his head. Emma was kneeling by the fire, her back to him. She dunked a cloth into the warm water, wrung it out, and wiped her face.

Ridge joined her and removed his jacket.

Emma's eyes widened and although she tried to hide her fear, he found it in her white-knuckled grip of the damp rag.

"I'm only going to change the dressing on my arm," Ridge reassured her, annoyed that she thought so little of him.

Her fingers eased their pressure on the wet rag. "I'll do it."

He tilted his head in question.

"I won't try anything." For the first time since he'd caught her, her smile was genuine. "I promise."

Ridge unbuttoned his shirt and slipped the injured limb from his sleeve. He extended his arm to her.

Emma unwound the dressing, which had dried blood on the inner layers. "You broke open the wound," she scolded.

"It happened while I was walking."

Emma darted a glance at him as her cheeks reddened, but she didn't apologize. They both knew she wouldn't have meant it.

"Some of the skin around it feels hot," Emma said. "It doesn't look like it's infected, but I'd like to put something on it that'll draw out the bad blood."

"It won't knock me out?" he asked warily.

"No."

He nodded. "Go ahead."

Emma retrieved a buckskin bag from her saddlebags and opened it to dig out some dried plants. Cupping the herbs in one hand, she dribbled some water over them with the other. Once the mixture held together, she daubed it on the stitched gash.

Ridge sucked in his breath at the stinging sensation.

"It only hurts for a minute or so, then it'll start to tingle," Emma explained.

By the time Emma finished rebandaging his forearm, even the tingle was nearly gone.

"I could make you some tea for the fever."

"No tea."

"Suit yourself."

Ridge redonned his shirt and jacket. The camp was in order and Emma was dressed in dry clothes. He moved Emma's bedroll and saddle to the other side of the fire, then picked up the two lengths of rope he'd used to bind her. "Come here," he ordered Emma.

"What?"

"You heard me."

She didn't move. "What if I promise not to try to escape overnight?"

Ridge smiled. "My faith only goes so far, ma'am."

She continued to stare at him. "So does mine. How do I know you're not planning to—to use me?"

Ridge scowled. He didn't like her thinking he was the same as Cullen. "Because if I planned on using you, I would've done it by now."

She crossed her arms. "But maybe you've thought about it."

"Don't be calling the kettle black, Emma," Ridge said, his patience fast disappearing. "I wasn't the only one thinking."

Emma attempted to hold his stare, but surrendered with a barely discernible murmur. She walked over to her bedroll and lowered herself like a lady sitting down to afternoon tea. Her spine ramrod straight, she placed her hands at the base of her spine.

"In front," Ridge corrected. "Or you'll never get any sleep."

Puzzled, she held out her hands. Ridge forced himself to tie her wrists, tight enough that she couldn't wriggle free, but loose enough that they wouldn't cut into her tender skin.

"Take off your boots," Ridge said.

Using her tied hands, she removed her boots awkwardly. He set them beside his bedroll.

He plucked his lariat from his saddle and wove one end around the rope binding her wrists. Stringing out the rope, he tied it to the tree Emma had been sitting against.

"What're you doing?" Emma demanded.

"Making sure you don't go anywhere."

Once he had her secured, Ridge returned to his own blanket and saddle on the far side of the fire. "This way you can't reach me or any of the supplies. You can't even get close enough to the fire to burn the rope off." He laid down on his side, facing Emma. "Go to sleep."

She remained sitting up, her shoulders stiff.

Ridge closed his eyes, but kept his hearing focused on

Emma. It was a long time before she finally settled into her bedroll amidst some muttered Lakota curses.

Only when he heard her breathing even out did he allow himself to find sleep.

$\mathcal{S}$IX

CORAL and red filaments twined through the eastern sky, announcing the sun's return. Winona allowed herself a few moments to enjoy the gentle flow of life beginning to circulate around her. An owl hooted quietly, as if recognizing the reverence of a new day, and wings rustled as the creature left its perch.

A child whimpered and Winona cocked her head toward her own shelter, but a mother's hush came from a tipi twenty feet away. It wasn't Winona's son; he remained sleeping soundly.

She picked up a basket from beside her tipi and walked the path leading to the river. Her toes struck a soft object and she bent down to pick up a small moccasin. Smiling, Winona realized it was the one her son had been missing last night. Chayton hated to have his feet covered, and always tugged his moccasins off and left them on the ground. She tucked the tiny leather shoe into the belt where she carried her healing herbs.

Following the narrow game trail to the river, Winona enjoyed the freedom of this life. She still remembered her old home and the girl she'd been, but it was like someone else's *past, no longer hers. Her clearest memories were those of her husband and the child they'd created. Winona's footsteps faltered. She missed Enapay and had mourned her husband's death nearly two years past, but she had Chayton to care for and love. Although she'd received marriage offers after she became a widow, she'd declined them. Perhaps later, but for now she lived for her son and the joy he brought her.*

The vibration of the earth startled Winona and she froze. The tremors grew more distinct until they became thunder—the thunder of horses' hooves. Gunshots rang out in quick succession, followed by horrific cries and screams of terror. The colorful woven basket slipped from Winona's fingers and bounced lightly on the ground, forgotten.

"Chayton!" Winona raced toward the village, oblivious to the thorns that scratched her arms and legs, leaving tiny blood trails in their wake. Breaking through the brush, she barely noticed the horse soldiers with their guns and sharp sabers. Pushing through panicked people and horses, Winona didn't see the blade arc toward her. Nor did she feel the blow or the blood that immediately welled from the wound between her breasts.

She had to find Chayton!

Struggling to her feet, Winona couldn't figure out why her legs wouldn't obey her or why her eyes became blurry. A horse's foreleg struck her shoulder and she lifted her head to gaze into a white man's shocked face.

He leaned down, grasped her wrist, and dragged her up onto the saddle in front of him. She cried out, struck at him with her fists but the iron band wrapped around her waist didn't loosen. Her chest burned and it hurt to breathe. Her limbs grew heavy.

No! She had to stay awake. Had to find Chayton.

As consciousness receded, a mountain lion's scream rent the air. . . .

Emma jerked upright, but something tugged at her wrists, sending her back to the ground. Did her captor tie her onto his horse? No, she wasn't riding. She lay panting, struggling to separate dream from reality. Opening her eyes, she focused on the dim form of a sleeping man on the other side of orange embers.

Ridge Madoc.

Emma bit her lip to keep from crying out her despair. Despite the night's coolness, perspiration rolled down her neck, adding more moisture to her sweat-drenched collar. Her heart beat so hard she thought it might jump out of her chest.

The dream-memories faded, but the terror lingered. Her stomach cramped with remembered helplessness. She didn't know if Chayton was alive or dead, and the not knowing tore a hole in her heart.

A tear escaped and slid across her temple and into her hair. When Chayton was learning how to walk, she'd forced herself not to hover like an overprotective mother. Children had to learn from their mistakes or they would never gain wisdom. Harsh lessons, perhaps, but Emma respected the Lakota way and tried not to dishonor her husband's memory. But every bruise Chayton had gained, Emma felt tenfold.

What if Chayton no longer walked on this earth? What if he had been murdered by the soldiers?

Emma's throat thickened and she fought to breathe without weeping. She had survived because she hadn't given in to useless tears. But no matter how hard she fought to hold back the agonized grief, she lost the battle.

Tears flowed and her shoulders shook with long-hidden sorrow. She cried for the fifteen-year-old who had her girlhood stolen. She cried for the young woman who struggled to be accepted and loved in an alien culture. She cried for the wife who lost her husband, and the mother who lost her son.

"Emma?"

Ridge's tentative voice startled her. She'd forgotten she wasn't alone in the night's darkness. She could barely make out his prone figure on the other side of the fire's remains. He was partially upright with his elbows braced on the ground, his head turned toward her.

"Is everything all right, ma'am?" he asked.

She bent over to wipe her tear-streaked face on the coarse blanket, then cleared her throat. "Yes."

Emma held her breath, hoping he would lie back down and leave her alone to grieve. She felt his searching gaze on her and remained still.

"Might help to talk about it," he finally said.

"There's nothing to talk about."

Ridge sat up and crossed his legs beneath him. "My ma always said, 'Ridge, there isn't any shame in having nightmares. It's only your heart telling you to share your problems.' "

Emma tried desperately to keep her emotions bottled inside, but Ridge's compassionate words defeated her. Her breathing hitched, sounding like a strangled sob, but she would allow no more tears.

She heard a faint "damn" from Ridge and then her hands were enfolded. The rope was unwound from her wrists and callused fingers rubbed them. "It's okay, Emma. Everything's gonna be all right."

Nothing would be all right until she learned of Chayton's fate.

She struggled to escape when Ridge awkwardly patted her back. "Leave me alone." Much to her shame, her voice was as weak as her resolve.

He didn't speak but firm hands settled her against his chest, his legs outstretched with her cradled between them. He wrapped one strong arm around her shoulders and the other around her waist as he held her close. Resting his chin on her crown, he rocked her gently. He crooned words in a language Emma didn't recognize, but the tone was soothing and comforting. She borrowed his strength as she rebuilt the shattered wall around her memories.

For five months she'd kept her secrets, harboring them within her heart. Not even her family—*especially* not her family—would understand how she could've loved an Indian. A white woman wasn't supposed to submit to heathens, but Emma hadn't submitted—she'd embraced the

Lakota way, which was even a greater sin in most people's eyes.

She wouldn't—couldn't—tell Ridge. He might be more open-minded than most folks, but to see pity in his face would be just as humiliating as seeing disgust. However, she was more determined than ever to find those she'd lived with for over six years.

Giving in to temptation, Emma remained in Ridge's capable arms a few moments longer. She relished his warmth and security after months of feeling isolated, despite living with her parents and sister. The steady rhythm of his heart beneath her ear helped her relax muscles she hadn't realized were tight with tension. It would be so easy to fall asleep in his arms.

Emma forcibly roused herself and sat up. Ridge immediately released her, but not before she heard his sharp intake of breath. His wound. She'd forgotten about it while she'd wallowed in self-pity.

"Did I hurt you?" she asked, her breath misting in the cold air.

"It's nothing, ma'am."

Although Emma couldn't make out his expression, she sensed the ache was more than "nothing."

"Let me make sure it didn't start bleeding again," she said.

He shook his head, tucking his injured arm close to his side. "It didn't."

Emma knelt in front of him, her backside resting on her heels. She tugged her jacket tighter around her and crossed her arms, placing her hands in her armpits. "Thank you."

Ridge glanced away, as if embarrassed. "Wasn't nothing, ma'am."

Emma smiled. "Maybe not to you." Her smile disappeared. "I have to find them, Ridge." It seemed ridiculous to call him Mr. Madoc after she'd spent the last ten minutes within his capable arms.

"You don't know where they are," he stated.

"I know the general direction. With your tracking skills, you might be able to find them."

Ridge allowed a tight grin. "Seems to me you have more than enough savvy to find them yourself, with you knowing how to hide your tracks and all, ma'am."

"Hiding a trail and following a trail aren't the same. You see things I don't." *And I see things* you *don't,* she thought, remembering her visions of the wolf, the lion, the eagle, and the owl.

"Your father hired me to bring you home."

"He didn't give you a time limit."

"Don't go playing with words, Emma. We both know what he meant."

"It means you'll get paid whether you bring me back before or after I find them," she insisted.

"I don't have time to be running around the country after you," he argued. "I got work to do back at my place."

"How much is he paying you?"

"One hundred dollars," Ridge replied after a moment's hesitation.

"How would you like to double that?"

He narrowed his eyes. "How?"

"You find my—" She broke off, shocked she'd almost given away her secret. "My people and I'll pay you another hundred dollars."

"And where're you gonna get a hundred dollars?"

"Do you think I'm lying?"

"Ma'am, I think you'd say or do damn near anything to get what you want."

His words cut deep, especially knowing he was right. "Maybe. But you will get the extra money. I swear it."

He didn't refuse her outright, which gave Emma hope. She pressed her advantage. "Think of how much more two hundred dollars will help you and your ranch than one hundred."

He scowled, but didn't reject her offer. Emma remained silent, intuitively knowing she'd pushed him as far as he would go.

"How long do you plan on visiting with the People once you find 'em?" Ridge asked.

Emma squelched a smile of victory and considered his question. "Long enough to make sure they're all right and to say my goodbyes."

"A day? Two days? Five?"

Irritation quashed her growing sense of relief. "Five, maybe more."

"How much more?"

"I don't know."

"One week, Emma."

She opened her mouth to argue, but clamped it shut. Ridge had a stubborn set to his grizzled jaw. "One week," she repeated, but didn't promise.

"Then we go back to your ranch, and you and your pa'll pay me."

"That's right." Emma's own jaw ached with tension. Her plans were dependent upon whether or not she found Chayton. If he wasn't with the first group they stumbled across, she planned on continuing her search. And if he was there, she wasn't certain whether she'd stay at the village or bring Chayton to the ranch.

Ridge stood, his movements more graceful than Emma would've expected for an injured man. "You'd best get back to sleep. We'll have a long day tomorrow, ma'am."

"Do you have any idea where they might be?"

"Maybe."

"Where?" Emma demanded, coming up on her knees.

Ridge squatted beside the coals and coaxed them back to life with some small twigs. Then he added a handful of larger pieces until the fire illuminated his face, which possessed a calmness Emma didn't share.

"Where?" she repeated with more impatience.

"Places I remember from when I lived with them."

Emma's mouth gaped. "You lived with the Lakota?"

"Long time ago. Things were different then."

"Were you a captive?"

"No."

"Then—"

Ridge held up his hand. "Go to sleep, Emma."

She studied his expression, which gave away nothing. "That's why you were such a good scout." She didn't intend for it to come out accusingly.

He merely stared at her, until she looked away. She smoothed her bedroll, anxious to have something to do.

"Are you going to tie me up again?" she asked quietly.

"Do I need to?"

"No."

Ridge tilted his head, but didn't speak.

Self-conscious, Emma settled in her makeshift bed and pulled the blanket up to her chin. Her cheeks felt stiff from dried tears, and her body ached, but it was a good ache, like she'd spent the day scraping buffalo hides with the other women after a successful hunt.

"Goodnight, ma'am," came Ridge's soft drawl.

After a moment, she whispered back, "Goodnight."

ACCUSTOMED to waking at dawn, Ridge opened his eyes to find the first streaks of light appearing in the dark blue sky. He turned his head and spotted Emma's head peeking out of her bedroll. He hadn't expected her to run off again, but she had a habit of doing things he didn't expect.

The fire had died down, but embers remained because of the late night addition of wood. He stifled a sigh and rose to answer nature's call. When he returned to the camp, he recoiled the rope which he'd used to tie Emma to the tree, and set it beside his saddle.

Fifteen minutes later, he leaned over, intending to awaken Emma by touching her shoulder. His bandaged arm reminded him that wasn't a good idea and he drew back. "Wake up, Emma," he said in a low, firm voice.

She immediately stirred and lowered the blanket from her face, revealing eyes more alert than Ridge expected. Glancing up at the lightening sky, she levered herself to a sitting position. "You shouldn't have let me sleep so late."

Ridge allowed a slight smile. "Sun's just coming up. Most folks would call this early."

Emma wrapped her arms around her drawn-up knees, keeping the blanket over her lower body. Her lips tilted upward. "True. Mother and Sarah think dawn is the middle of the night."

"What about your father?"

Emma's smile disappeared and she pulled her knees closer to her chest, as if protecting what lay within it. "He'd be eating breakfast now."

Ridge cursed himself for bringing John Hartwell's specter between them. "Coffee?"

"When I get back," Emma said, throwing her blankets off.

"Where're you going?"

Emma stood and gazed down at him, amusement in her twitching lips. "Where did *you* go when you first woke up?"

Ridge's face heated and she laughed lightly.

"You heard me?" Ridge asked.

Emma shrugged. "I'm a light sleeper, remember?" She leaned down and patted his shoulder. "Don't worry. I didn't peek."

Ridge kept his attention on the tin cup he clutched in his hands as she walked into the brush. He wasn't used to women teasing him about such personal matters. Hell, he wasn't used to being around a woman, teasing or not. It was going to take some getting used to.

A few minutes later Emma returned and Ridge handed her a steaming cup of coffee.

"Thank you." She eased down on the ground and sipped the hot bitter liquid.

Ridge expected her to talk, to ask him about the time he'd lived with the Lakota, but she remained silent. He had his own questions for her, but it didn't seem right badgering her when she seemed content to let him keep his secrets.

It wasn't until they'd saddled their horses that Emma spoke.

"I know this wasn't what you signed on for when you agreed to find me, but I'm grateful for your help," Emma said, meeting his gaze squarely.

Ridge shifted under her direct look, feeling exposed and vulnerable. He adjusted the brim of his hat and eyed the fat fluffy clouds. "Like you said, ma'am, two hundred dollars'll do more than a hundred."

Her eyes flickered downward, to where the reins were threaded through her gloved hands. When she looked up again, her expression was neutral. "They're headed northeast."

Ridge nodded. "Figured so by the direction you'd been riding."

"Do you think we'll find them in the next day or two?"

"Maybe, but might be closer to two or three." He felt a twinge of irrational annoyance. "I promised you we wouldn't go back until we found them, and I aim to keep that promise."

"I trust you."

Although Ridge's chest tightened with her soft declaration, he couldn't fully believe her. As sure as he knew the mountains wouldn't fall down overnight, he knew Emma Hartwell was hiding something.

He only hoped her secret wouldn't get them both killed.

THE spring day warmed as the sun rose higher in the endless blue sky. Emma opened her jacket and loosened the wool scarf from her head so that it draped around her neck. Before they'd hit the trail that morning, she'd pinned her hair into a bun at her nape to keep the strands out of her face.

Content to bask in the uncommonly warm rays, she didn't attempt to speak with her former captor. She also suspected Ridge was a man who didn't tolerate empty conversation, which suited her fine. However, her gaze often strayed to his easy rocking motion, which belied the thin slash of his lips and clenched jaw. She wondered if his memories of this area were pleasant or something he preferred to forget. She opened her mouth to ask, but abruptly chose silence. It would be discourteous—in both white and Indian societies—to ask such a personal question.

"They aren't there," Ridge announced in the late morning.

Startled by his voice's intrusion after hours of silence, Emma glanced at him. "What?"

A minute shift of the reins and Ridge halted his pinto pony. Emma drew up beside him, their stirrups brushing.

"One of the places I thought they might be holed up." He pointed to a line of trees a mile or two away. "If they were there, I'd've seen some sign by now."

Disappointment weighed heavily on Emma as she slumped. She knew it was unrealistic to think finding them would be so simple after just a week of searching, but she'd hoped that with Ridge's knowledge it would be easier. However, the people she'd lived with were desperate and wouldn't settle for a traditional camp location. Food wouldn't even be their major consideration—concealment and security would be until they found a larger group to join.

Ridge's gloved hand settled on hers as it rested on the pommel.

"We'll find them, Emma," he assured.

The weight of his hand was comforting and something else—something that dipped into her belly and lay there warm and tingly. She lifted her gaze to meet sincere midnight blue eyes and managed a smile. "I know you'll do your best."

Ridge searched her face and Emma's cheeks heated. He abruptly removed his hand and his attention drifted forward again. Emma's mare followed without urging.

While she'd lived with the People, they'd ranged for miles in the wilderness, following the food supply. She kept hoping to spy something that looked familiar. Instead, her attention kept wandering to Ridge and the way he set the saddle and the keen eyes that saw so much more than even her own. It was obvious he was comfortable in the untamed land. Perhaps even more so than so-called civilized towns. He was a man she could admire and respect, but it saddened her to think his thoughts weren't nearly as charitable of her.

Emma took a deep breath and let it out slowly, then inhaled again, filling her lungs with fresh air. Clearing her thoughts like the shaman had taught her, she pictured the bright, pure air swirling through her body, illuminating the dark, stale places. She imagined the life pulsing around her, from the most insignificant ant to the greatest buffalo. All were connected as one through Mother Earth, each an integral part of the cycle of life and death; of rebirth and transformation.

An increasingly familiar scent intruded—Ridge's unique blend of deerhide, woodsmoke, and honest labor. His masculine essence triggered a new awareness to her body that she tacitly ignored.

Emma placed her unwelcome attraction to Ridge into the far recesses of her thoughts. She couldn't afford to be sidetracked from her mission by long-denied needs, especially with a decent man like Ridge Madoc. But then, it was his very decency that attracted her even more powerfully than his muscular body, smooth-shaven features, and clean scent.

Ridge slowed and Emma's horse came abreast so they rode side-by-side.

"I've missed this," Emma said quietly. At Ridge's questioning glance, she waved her hand outward. "This. The land. Quiet. Peace." A magpie flew past and the sunlight turned drab feathers to shiny blue. "Freedom."

Ridge remained mute, but Emma knew he'd heard her.

"Do you miss it?" she asked curiously.

"Sleeping on the ground, eating cold biscuits and tough jerky, not being able to take a long, hot bath?" He flashed her a wry smile. "Yeah, sometimes I miss it."

Emma laughed softly. "Yes, bathing in a mountain-fed stream isn't one of my favorite things either." She sobered and her gaze wandered across the wilderness. "But it wasn't a bad life. The People, they care for one another, watch out for each other's children." Her breath hitched in her throat. "They share their bounty with the rest of the tribe. When one suffers, everyone does. Not exactly how the whites see things, is it?"

"Two different kinds of people, Emma," Ridge began. "For one, the world is there for the taking and folks want the biggest piece they can get their hands on. It's like a grown-up marbles game—whoever has the most wins. For the People, they look at things different. Respect for the land and honor of one another and those who came before them are their beliefs. Without them, they don't have anything."

Although surprised by his relatively long speech, she nodded, her gaze turning inward, to the reservation camp she'd visited before starting her search. "But that's changing."

"It's the way of life, Emma. Things're always going to change."

"But that doesn't make it right."

"I never said it did," he said patiently. "But you and me can't stop it, so it doesn't do any good to get all riled up about it."

Emma's thoughts turned to her son, a child of both worlds, but embraced by the Lakota. If she took him back to her parents' home, what kind of life would he have? But if she and Chayton stayed with the Indians, how much longer would her adopted people remain free? And she didn't want to raise her child on a reservation, unable to walk freely on the same plains as his father's ancestors.

"Maybe if enough people got riled up about it, we *could* change things," Emma said.

"Maybe." Ridge didn't sound hopeful.

Emma leveled her gaze at him. "Would you?"

Ridge rubbed a wind-weathered cheek with a gloved hand. "I'm a simple man, Emma. All I want is a piece of land I can call my own, some cattle to run on it, and a good woman to share my life and raise my children."

"What if someone stole your land, scattered your cattle, and hurt or killed your wife and children?"

He met her gaze. "Your pa already stole my land."

Emma flinched. From what she'd heard, her father hadn't exactly stolen the land, but what he paid for it was equivalent to cheap beads and cheaper blankets. She didn't know how to respond to Ridge's bitter statement so she chose silence.

Her thoughts returned to the People and where they might be headed. She knew there were a number of Sioux further southeast, in the Black Hills of the Dakota Territory. However, many of the Tetons preferred the Powder River basin. Was that where her adopted people were going? Or was it Canada where the U.S. government couldn't touch them?

"What about Canada?" she asked.

"I already thought of that, but figured they'd more'n likely stay on land they know. The next camp I'm checking is about fifteen miles from here," he said, keeping his gaze aimed forward. "I should know if they're there once we get within a few miles of it."

It would be a long fifteen miles.

$\mathcal{S}$EVEN ·

BY nightfall, Ridge was certain the Indians were nowhere near the second possible camp. His next guess was some fifty miles away and it would take the better part of a day to get there, provided the weather cooperated. As he unsaddled his horse, Ridge raised his head and sniffed the cool air. There was a change coming. He suspected winter was going to make another appearance.

He and Emma prepared their camp, moving around one another in companionable silence. Emma volunteered to make their supper, which consisted of rabbit, biscuits, and gravy. A jackrabbit had jumped out of a patch of brush in front of them that afternoon, and Ridge's shot had been true.

By the time the meal was ready, Ridge's stomach was grumbling. He accepted a tin plate with three biscuits slathered with gravy and a large portion of the roasted rabbit. Emma had used some of her dried plants to spice up the meat, giving it a rich flavor.

"That was real good, ma'am," Ridge commented after he mopped off his plate with the last biscuit.

He volunteered to clean their plates; Emma didn't argue. When he returned from the stream, she was sitting near the fire, her legs to one side and a blanket wrapped around her shoulders. If not for her light skin and honey-brown hair, Ridge would've thought she was an Indian.

As he approached her, he noticed an open book held in her hands.

"Thank you," Emma said quietly as she looked up. The fire's glow glossed her face with warm tints. "I hope you don't mind if I read for a little while."

Ridge shook his head. "You don't need my approval, ma'am."

She tucked a finger in the book to hold her place and closed it, then rested her chin on her fist to simply look at him. Ridge tried to ignore her steady gaze, but his body felt it all the way down to his marrow. He lowered himself to a nearby log and opened his saddlebags to slide the clean plates and forks back into them.

"I know I don't need it," she said. "But it would be rude of me to ignore you all evening."

Ridge barked a short laugh. "We aren't at some ice-cream social, Emma, so there's no need for you to be so polite-like." He finished fastening the saddlebags' straps. "You don't owe me anything but one hundred dollars once I get you home."

Her mouth pursed, like she just bit into a rotten apple. "You'll get your money."

"I know."

The fire crackled between them, occasionally snapping and shooting sparks into the air.

"Would you like me to read aloud?" Emma asked quietly.

He kept his gaze aimed downward, afraid she'd see how much her simple offer touched him. He cleared his throat. "If you'd like. It won't bother me."

"I hope you like humorous stories." She smiled and mischief glittered in her eyes, along with the firelight. She dipped her head and began. "*The Celebrated Jumping Frog of Calaveras County* by Mark Twain."

Ridge watched the movement of her bow-shaped lips as

she formed the words effortlessly. The sight mesmerized him, and tempted him to run a gentle finger along the full lower lip. He could imagine the softness, like a wild rose petal.

He closed his eyes, afraid temptation would overwhelm his common sense, and merely listened. He liked Emma's mellow voice as it rose and fell in a pleasant cadence. The only other woman who'd read to him had been his mother, and her voice hadn't been as easy on the ears. Emma had a way of making the story sound like something special and magical.

The story was about some gambler who trained a frog named Daniel Webster to jump. To Ridge, training a frog to jump seemed a useless thing to do, but the Twain fella had written it in such a way that it made Ridge chuckle and shake his head.

Of course, Ridge wasn't certain it was the story or Emma's way of reading it that made it so amusing.

Some minutes later Emma stopped and rubbed her eyes. "I thought I could finish it this evening, but I'm afraid it'll have to wait for another time."

Although disappointed, Ridge shrugged.

A breeze kicked up, stirring the fire and sending sparks swirling upward. Emma shivered and closed the book. "Winter's reminding us it's still here."

"Feels like it," Ridge murmured.

"Did my reading aloud bother you?"

He jerked his head up. "No. You've got a pretty voice." He suddenly realized what he'd said and snapped his mouth shut.

Emma smiled and laid her hand on his coat sleeve. Despite the clothing between them, Ridge fancied he could feel the warmth of her delicate fingers. "Thank you. I've always enjoyed reading. It's one of the things I missed most when I was with the People." Her eyes focused inward. "Sometimes when Enapay returned from a raid, he would bring me back a book."

"Enapay?"

Emma's eyes widened and he heard a catch in her breath. "He was a friend."

Suspicion followed closely on the heels of unexpected jealousy. "Sounds like more'n a friend."

"If he was, that's my business," Emma said without meeting his gaze.

Ridge eyed her warily. Was Enapay the reason Emma needed to find the tribe she'd lived with? And if he was, was it any of Ridge's concern?

"We'd best turn in," Ridge said.

Emma placed her book in her saddlebags as if it were gold bullion. But, then, maybe books were Emma Hartwell's treasure.

Without exchanging another word, Ridge and Emma slid into their respective bedrolls.

Ridge pondered Emma's slip and his own reaction to it. It was only natural for a man to want to protect a woman, even when the woman didn't want protecting. A lot of folks already suspected Emma had been sullied by the Indians, but if she'd chosen an Indian lover, her life would be made more hellish by neighbors and so-called friends.

What if she *was* trying to return to an Indian lover?

Unsettled, he turned on his side so his back was to the woman.

THE temperature fell rapidly overnight, and the following morning Emma and Ridge moved through their morning tasks quickly, eating jerky and leftover biscuits, and drinking icy water for breakfast. They readied their horses to head out just after sunrise.

Few words were exchanged between Emma and Ridge, and unwieldy silence hung between them. The horses tugged at their bits and danced nervously at skittering leaves as if sensing the tension. Emma kept a snug hold on the reins and tried not to think about the previous night's blunder. She'd been so careful for months. Why had she slipped up last night?

Because Ridge Madoc makes me feel too comfortable.

He could've continued questioning her about Enapay, but he hadn't. He also hadn't looked at her any differently this morning, although she had expected him to renege on their deal. However, he'd surprised her again. Any other man wouldn't have been so tolerant. Especially her own father.

The day remained cool as Emma and Ridge traveled through terrain which became more barren with every mile. The mountains were over their left shoulder, and the winds that swirled down from the snow-capped peaks battered at Emma, despite her warm coat, muffler, and scarf. During a short rest in the late morning, Emma added a blanket to her shoulders. Ridge cocked an eyebrow at her, but nodded when an especially vicious wind swept through, the bitter cold cutting to the bone.

Midafternoon brought an unholy scream that made the hair stand up on Emma's arms. The blood drained from her face as she cast about fearfully for the source of the inhuman sound. Or was this a vision reminding her of the danger ahead?

"Mountain lion," Ridge said, his breath misting through the scarf covering the lower half of his face.

Relief flowed through Emma. Ridge had heard it, too, which meant it wasn't part of her dreams. However, it still unnerved her.

"It's all right, Emma," he added. "It's half, maybe three-quarters of a mile away."

He obviously thought she was frightened of the animal, and Emma wasn't about to disabuse him of that notion. How could she explain her dreams without making him think she was crazy?

"Springtime. He's probably looking for companionship." Emma forced lightness into her tone.

"Not likely. They would've mated by now and the female would be carrying the young."

"Don't they mate for life, like wolves?" she asked, intrigued despite herself.

Ridge shook his head and his eyes twinkled above his wind-ruddy cheeks. "They're just like alley cats."

Emma recalled the hideous howls in the early spring from the feral cats, and her cheeks heated beneath her wool muffler. "Oh."

Ridge chuffed a quiet laugh.

Emma couldn't help but smile and her tension eased.

Half an hour later, they arrived at a river swollen with spring melt from the mountains. Chunks of ice streamed by occasionally, carried down from higher elevations.

"We'll have to find a better place to cross," Ridge said.

Emma's heart thumped loudly, and she fought the panic rising in her breast. "Good idea. This doesn't look safe," she agreed, raising her voice to be heard above the river's raging current.

Ridge turned his horse downstream and Emma followed, hunching her shoulders. They rode for nearly a mile before the river widened and the current slowed.

"How deep is it?" Emma tried to keep her gaze averted, but her attention kept returning to the streaming torrent.

A crease formed between Ridge's eyebrows. "If I remember right, not more'n two or three feet. The horses shouldn't even have to swim."

Emma studied the meandering expanse. Although it wasn't nearly as fast-flowing as upriver, fear clawed at her throat. Ever since she'd nearly drowned that fateful day seven years ago, she'd had an irrational fear of water. She hated crossing anything larger than a stream, but living with the Lakota, she'd been forced to do so or be left behind in the wilderness.

"Are you all right, Emma?" Ridge's concerned voice broke through her heart-pounding fear.

"Fine," she answered too quickly.

"If you're scared, we might be able to find a better place farther downstream or—" He paused deliberately. "We can go back."

"I'm not scared," she snapped.

Ridge scrutinized her and Emma held his gaze, unwilling to let him use her fear as an excuse to abandon her quest.

"All right," he said grudgingly. "Take off your boots and stockings, and carry them around your neck so they don't get wet."

Emma didn't want to expose her feet to the cold air and colder water, but recognized the wisdom in Ridge's suggestion. She dismounted and removed her boots. She glanced at Ridge to find his back to her and she quickly rolled down her heavy black stockings. Bunching the stockings, she placed them in her shoes. She tied the laces together and placed them behind her neck.

Before she could return to the saddle, Ridge joined her and cupped his hands. After a moment's surprise, Emma smiled gratefully and placed her bare foot in his warm palms. He raised her up and she gracefully swung her right leg over the saddle. As she fitted her right foot in the stirrup, Ridge gently guided her left foot into the other one, but didn't immediately release her.

Emma gazed down at him, but could only see the top of his hat and his wide, competent hands covering her bare foot. His thumb brushed across the sensitive instep and her toes curled as pleasure raced through her veins.

Ridge abruptly released her and mounted his horse. He, too, had tied his moccasins together and draped them over his neck. After one quick look at Emma, Ridge kneed his horse down the sloped bank and toward the water. The animal balked and Ridge kicked the gelding's flanks. With a snort and toss of his head, Paint entered the cold mountain water.

Emma's hands trembled and her body tensed tighter than a bowstring. If she wanted to discover her son's fate, she had no choice but to follow. Emma used the end of her leather reins to lightly slap Clementine's rump and the mare leapt forward, only to stop sharply at the edge of the river.

Emma sailed over the mare's neck to splash into the river. The icy cold water shocked the air from her lungs, and she frantically scrambled to her hands and knees in the shallows. She gulped in air as her body trembled.

"Emma, you all right?"

She blinked the droplets from her eyelashes and focused on Ridge, who'd ridden back across the river. Her heart racing and her lungs screaming, she could only nod.

He dismounted, getting his own feet wet in the shallow water. "What happened?"

"Uh, Clementine balked. Stupid of me. Flew over her head," Emma managed to gasp out.

Ridge frowned as if he didn't believe her, but only held out his hand. She accepted it gratefully and he tugged her to her feet.

"Your shoes are gone," Ridge said.

Emma's hand went to her neck but there was nothing there. They were the only shoes she had. "They can't be far." She frantically searched for the boots, but couldn't spot them.

Ridge scowled. "The current must've caught them. C'mon." He helped her up the steep bank, to where Clementine stood calmly, as if she'd done nothing wrong.

The cold breeze struck Emma, ripping away more heat from her chilled body. She wrapped her arms around herself and shivered.

Ridge released her and retrieved the blanket from her saddle. He wrapped it around her shoulders and picked her up.

"What're you doing?" Emma asked, struggling weakly to escape his arms.

"You might cut open your foot." Ridge carried her to a large rock where he eased her down. "I'll be right back."

When he rejoined her, he carried a second pair of moccasins. He knelt down and, with an economy of emotion, tugged the first deerskin boot, then the second, on her nearly numb feet.

"Thank you," she murmured.

"They're a mite big on you, but better than nothing. And since the river's not any deeper'n a couple feet, you won't get them wet."

"Are you sure?"

Ridge nodded. "I was all the way across when I looked back and seen you in the water."

"Sorry," she mumbled.

"It's all right," he said gently.

Emma's nerves jangled, but the terror she'd felt only minutes earlier loosened its stranglehold with Ridge's soft-spoken words. She leaned forward and rested her forehead against his chest. "I-I thought I was g-going to drown," she stammered.

"The water wasn't deep enough to drown in, but you did get soaked." He rubbed her back. "There's a shack only a mile or two from here where we can spend the night."

Emma nodded as she felt the first snowflake land on her cheek.

"Can you ride?" he asked.

"Yes."

Ridge helped her to her horse, then gave her a boost into the saddle. She settled uncomfortably on the cold seat, her wet clothes bunching around her legs and thighs.

"Here." Ridge held the reins up to her.

She accepted them and watched Ridge mount his black and white horse. He nudged the animal closer to her.

"Stay right behind me, Emma," Ridge said. "We'll cross slow and easy-like."

She closed her eyes momentarily against the renewed fear, but nodded gamely.

"Remember what I said. Stay close," he repeated.

Keeping her gaze on Ridge's back instead of the churning water, Emma followed him. Her heart sounded louder than the rushing water as she clung to the saddle-horn, her knuckles white. Her mare moved farther into the river. Goose bumps covered her skin and her teeth chattered, although Emma wasn't certain if it was from dread or the cold.

Ridge's horse scrambled up the opposite bank and out of the river. Clementine followed without prodding and Emma was once again on solid ground.

"Are you doing all right?" Ridge asked, his brow furrowed in concern.

She nodded, lightheaded with relief to have the crossing behind them. "Just c-cold."

"We'll be at the shack in five or ten minutes."

"Thank heavens," she murmured.

By the time they arrived at the small cabin, Emma's teeth were chattering uncontrollably and she had little feeling in her fingers and toes. Although her mind was sluggish, she knew she had to get out of the wet clothes and into something dry.

She started to dismount, then felt herself lifted from her horse. Blissful warmth radiated from Ridge and she snuggled against his chest. Closing her eyes, Emma imagined she was back in her tipi wrapped in heavy buffalo robes.

Ridge lifted the latch and the door swung open, the force of the wind causing it to crash against the wall.

He carried Emma inside, and the near silence was eerie after the dull roar of the blizzard. As his eyes adjusted to the darkness, he spotted a rough frame bed. Although it was bare and narrow, it was better than the dirt floor. He checked for mouse nests, found none, and lowered Emma to the thin mattress.

"Stay here. I'm going to get a fire going," he said to her.

She rolled onto her side and pulled her knees up to her chest. "So cold."

"I know. Just give me a few minutes and I'll have the place warmed up."

He went outside and moved the horses around to the lee side of the building, where he found a stack of firewood. He quickly hobbled the horses and loosened their girths. Promising to return to remove the tack, Ridge tossed Emma's saddlebags over his shoulder, then loaded his arms with wood and carried it into the cabin. He glanced at Emma who was still lying curled up on the bed—she appeared to have fallen asleep. He knelt beside the iron stove in the center of the single room. Five minutes later a fire blazed in the stove's belly.

Certain the fire had caught, he closed the stove door and rocked himself to his feet. Finding a lantern with some kerosene left in it, he lit the wick and pale yellow light filled the small cabin.

Now that he could see the room, he searched Emma's saddlebags for dry clothing. He found a skirt and blouse, but no undergarments. After a quick search of the cabin, he unearthed two old woolen blankets in a crate and laid them on the end of the bed, along with her clothing.

He debated whether to touch Emma while she was asleep, but decided it would be safe since he'd seen her knife in a saddlebag. Besides, she needed to change into dry clothing.

He shook her shoulder and she blinked blearily at him.

"You have to take off your wet clothes, Emma."

She nodded and her hands went to the buttons on her coat, but she only fumbled with them, as if she couldn't get her fingers to do what she wanted.

"Let me, Emma."

After a moment, she nodded in surrender and remained pliant as he removed her jacket, then the soaked blouse beneath it. Her damp camisole lay against her skin, so translucent Ridge could see the tan circling her peaked nipples through the cloth. He swallowed hard and ignored the undeniable charge of lust through his veins. Keeping his gaze averted, he skimmed the undergarment off and tossed it aside. He covered her naked breasts, glancing at them only once as he buttoned her blouse. Steeling his reaction to her feminine body, he removed her skirt and petticoat with the same impersonal motions and slipped on the dry skirt.

His gaze traveled to her face where he met half-lidded eyes. "Thank you," she whispered, her expression as trusting as a child's.

"You're welcome," he said, an odd lump in his throat.

He eased her back down on the bed, her eyes already closing, and covered her with the dry blankets. Fighting the urge to kiss her brow, Ridge dragged a shaking hand across his forehead. Although he was tired, he was glad he still had the horses to take care of. He needed the distance from Emma to cool his hot blood.

Half an hour later, Ridge finished laying out Emma's wet clothing around the tiny cabin. He'd changed out of his damp buckskins into some men's clothes he'd found in the same box as the blankets. Although the pants were a little snug and the shirt hugged his chest, he was glad for the dry clothing.

Ridge added more wood to the fire and stretched, popping his spine in two places. Outside, the light gave way to darkness. The wind continued to blast, and the cabin creaked from the assault. Spring blizzards weren't uncommon but this one had caught him unprepared. They wouldn't be continuing their journey for a day or two, maybe longer.

Ridge considered making something to eat, but exhaustion won out. The bed looked inviting, even without Emma in it. But she was there and it wasn't proper to be lying beside a woman who wasn't your wife or a whore, even if he had seen her in her full glory.

Sighing, he laid down on the floor close to the stove and crossed his arms over his chest. He'd slept in a lot worse conditions.

BEING on his own since the age of fifteen, Ridge was a light sleeper. Even the absence of sound often awakened him because of its peculiarity. This time, however, it was Emma's restlessness that woke him.

Ridge rolled to his knees beside the bed. Emma's face was damp and he rested his palm lightly on her brow. She had a slight fever.

He massaged her blanket-covered arm. "Easy, Emma."

She turned toward him, but her eyes remained closed.

Her agitation eased and Ridge breathed a sigh of relief. He rose and added more wood to the fire, then laid back down on the floor.

Emma grew restive again, and Ridge debated for only a few seconds before climbing onto the narrow bed beside her. Leaving the blankets between their bodies, he lay on his back, his side touching hers.

She snuffled and rolled halfway on top of him, hiding her face in the crook of his shoulder. It was sweet torture to hold her softness and feel her breasts against his chest. He was sorely tempted to skim his hands below her blouse and cup them in his palms. The cold had pebbled her nipples earlier. Would his touch do the same?

Ridge's eyes shot open. This was Emma Hartwell, a woman who trusted him with both her life and her virtue.

But what if there was no virtue to protect?

Ridge shoved his doubts aside. It didn't make any difference. He wouldn't take advantage of a good woman who'd already had a world of hurt in her life. He rested his chin on Emma's crown and focused on the blowing wind.

Within moments, he was asleep.

*E*IGHT

EMMA shifted in the warm cocoon as she was lured toward waking. She ignored the pull and snuggled deeper into the arms that embraced her. In fact, there was an entire wall of solid heat behind her. She smiled to herself.

An erection lay nestled against her buttocks and, caught between wakefulness and slumber, Emma pressed against familiar hardness. Desire meandered through her veins and settled in her belly. She knew it had been a long time since she'd lain with her husband. He must have been riding with a raiding party and returned last night while she'd been asleep. Unlike many warriors who were gone for days, her husband didn't awaken her to spill his seed in his wife immediately after his return. He was a considerate lover, concerned with her pleasure, too.

Through the lazy haze of passion, Emma felt the thrill of hands stroking her bare stomach and moving higher to her breasts. She tingled with need, knowing the pleasure that awaited her by joining with her husband. Rolling onto her back, Emma reached for the hem of her deerskin dress . . . only to encounter cotton.

Bewildered, she opened her eyes to see not Enapay, but

a stranger looking down at her. She rolled away and was caught by a strong arm.

"Easy, Emma. You'll fall off the bed," the man said in a husky voice.

Memories returned. *Ridge Madoc. Traveling. The river. Icy water.*

She searched the dim room, not recognizing anything, except the man lying in bed with her. "Wha—how'd we get here?"

He leaned back, placing more space between their bodies. "We rode here, remember?"

She had to think a moment. "My horse threw me into the river. You came back and then you led the way across." She shifted so she wasn't in danger of falling off the bed. "You said you knew where there was a cabin."

Ridge smiled, his teeth uncommonly white against his dark growth of whiskers. "This is it. It ain't much, but it's out of the weather."

"I'm just glad it's warm. Thank you." She glanced down, noticing her blouse was mis-buttoned and it was different than the one she'd been wearing. So was the skirt, and she wasn't wearing any undergarments. She pressed her thighs together. "Did you—?" She motioned to her clothing.

He glanced down and murmured, "You were asleep, so I dressed you in dry clothes."

Ridge levered himself off the crowded bed and Emma couldn't help but notice how snug his clothing was, especially the trousers. The material outlined his hard length. Her cheeks warm, she raised her gaze. "It seems I owe you another thank you."

Ridge knelt in front of the stove, his back to her, and opened the stove door. The fabric of his shirt threatened to split across his shoulders and hugged his firm torso down to where it was tucked into his trousers. Her body pulsed with unfulfilled passion and she wished she were brave enough to kneel behind him and wrap her arms around his lean body.

"You don't owe me anything, ma'am. It's part of the job." He added the last piece of wood.

Although his words were true, they hurt, and erased her desire completely. "I'm still indebted to you," she said lamely.

He turned to look at her over his shoulder. His gaze was steady with no sign of the hunger she'd glimpsed moments earlier. "One hundred dollars worth."

Humiliation made her cheeks burn, and she silently scolded herself. Lying so close in the narrow bed had made Ridge's maleness react as nature intended. Any other woman would have produced the same response. Ridge had made no secret of the fact that he was leading her to the Indians only for the money. So why did his businesslike manner disturb her?

"Are you hungry?" he asked.

"Yes," she simply replied.

"There's some cans on a shelf. We can open one of those."

Emma watched as he looked at each can, then set one filled with tomatoes on a tiny rickety table. "Tomatoes for breakfast?" she asked, frowning at his choice.

Ridge shrugged. "Why don't you pick what you'd like while I check the horses?"

Emma stood and had to wait a moment for a wave of dizziness to pass. She was aware of Ridge's scrutiny and waved a hand at him. "I'm fine."

He didn't say anything, but donned his moccasins and coat. He paused by the door. "There's an empty can under the bed you can use while I'm gone." He left the cabin and cold wind shimmied across the floor.

Emma quickly found the can and did her business, then placed it outside the door. Before checking out the tin goods, she found her only remaining pair of black stockings in her saddlebag. Flushing slightly, she drew them on, along with the now-dry undergarments Ridge had removed and hung up to dry. She also tugged on Ridge's oversize moccasins to keep her feet warm.

Emma brushed her hair and tied it in a ponytail that fell halfway down her back. Now that she was dressed decently, she padded to the corner of the cabin. She picked up the cans and read each label, then picked out two—peaches and hominy—and placed the tomatoes back on the wall shelf. Although she liked tomatoes, she couldn't fathom eating them in the morning.

By the time Ridge returned bearing an armload of wood, Emma had opened the tin cans and had the hominy heating on the stove. She also used water from the canteens to make a pot of coffee.

"Smells good," Ridge commented. "I seen a kettle that I'll use to bring some snow in."

"Does it look like the storm will be ending soon?" Emma asked.

He shook his head, his expression grim. "Not likely, ma'am. Maybe tomorrow."

Emma turned back to the stove so he wouldn't see her disappointment, and began to mash the hominy.

"They won't be able to travel, either," Ridge said, guessing her thoughts.

"I know, but I've been looking for so long."

"Everything will work out the way it's supposed to, Emma."

She knew Ridge couldn't offer her any more reassurances, and was glad he didn't insult her by trying. She wouldn't despair, not after coming all this way.

After Ridge brought in a snow-filled kettle and put it on the stove, they ate the simple meal at the small table. Emma had the only chair, and Ridge sat on an empty cracker keg that had been beside the bed.

As the blizzard continued unabated through the long morning, Emma busied herself by exploring the shack. But there was little to find except for two pairs of wool socks. She donned a pair over her stockings, which made the moccasins fit a tiny bit better.

Ridge finally changed into his own clothes, which relieved Emma. She had found herself eyeing him far too often in the too-small shirt and trousers.

Ridge kept the potbelly stove full of wood. The heat kept the cabin comfortable, but the fierce winds drove through the cracks in the walls. He plugged some of the worst ones with mud he made from melted snow and dirt from the floor, but the room remained drafty.

Near noon, Ridge opened the door to bring in more wood, and a four-foot snowdrift greeted him. They were lucky it didn't cover the door. He hauled in five armloads of wood and Emma carried them from the door to the stove, where she made a neat pile. It gave her something to do, as well as assuaged some of her guilt for being so useless yesterday.

With the last armload, Ridge stomped the snow off his boots and removed them by the door. Emma handed him the other pair of wool socks she'd discovered.

"Thanks," he murmured.

"You're welcome." She crossed to the stove and stirred the contents of a small kettle. "I made some lunch, if you're hungry."

Ridge's stomach growled, eliciting a wry smile from him. "Guess I am, ma'am."

Emma had combined some of her seasonings with the tomatoes to make a decent soup, and had mixed up sourdough biscuits to go with it. It wasn't a feast, but it filled them.

After their lunch, Ridge brought out a folded map and opened it on the table. Emma joined him, leaning close to see the squiggles and lines.

"Where are we?" she asked, pointing at the map.

Ridge stabbed a point. "Here. About fifty miles southwest of the Yellowstone River."

"So that crooked line is the Yellowstone River?"

He nodded. "And this one here is the Tongue and this one the Powder." He dragged his finger upward. "I'm thinking the Lakota group went this way."

Emma nodded, hoping he was right. She leaned closer. "Where's the fort?"

"Fort Fetterman, where we came from, is back here." He pointed to a square south of their location, and then motioned to another square almost due west. "That's Fort Logan."

She straightened. "Why don't you write the names on the map? It'd be easier to follow."

Ridge refolded the map. "I know where everything is."

"But—"

"It's my map, Emma, and I like it the way it is," he said curtly.

He collected his revolver and rifle, along with his cleaning supplies and brought them to the table.

Sighing, Emma went in search of something to do and retrieved her book. She sat at the table across from Ridge.

"You can read out loud, if you'd like," he offered.

"It won't bother you?"

He shook his head. "It's better than listening to the wind howling." He grinned boyishly. "Besides, I want to find out what happened to Daniel Webster."

She smiled, inordinately pleased. "So you *were* listening."

His eyes twinkled. "I told you I was. Go on."

Amused by his eagerness, she began to read. As she did, the blizzard disappeared from her thoughts and only Ridge's occasional snort of laughter drew her out of the imaginary world of Jim Smiley, Daniel Webster, and Simon Wheeler. Half an hour later, she closed the book.

"That Twain fella sure knows how to spin a yarn," Ridge remarked. He'd finished cleaning his weapons while she read, and had leaned back in his chair for the remainder of the tale.

Emma gazed into his twinkling eyes and nodded. "Last month I read his first book that related his journey to Nevada to look for gold. I enjoy his humorous slant on his fellow human beings."

Ridge eyed her with something akin to awe. "You sound like you've read a lot of books."

She shrugged, embarrassed. "I suppose I have. Before I lived with the Indians, I used to read all the time." She gazed unseeingly at the stove, her mind going back to the day her life was irrevocably changed.

"Why'd you fall off your horse, Emma?" Ridge asked curiously.

She blinked at the unexpected question. "She stopped fast and I went over her head."

Ridge's eyes were somber. "You're a good rider. What's the real reason?"

Emma stared down at her book, debating whether to tell him or not. She took a deep breath and raised her head. "I'm terrified of crossing rivers."

"Why?"

"I was fifteen years old. I'd ridden to my secret place so I could read without Mother or Sarah bothering me. There was this huge oak tree beside a river. We'd gotten a lot of rain and the water was higher than usual and it was moving fast, just like the river we crossed yesterday. I was walking along the bank when the ground gave way under my feet. I fell in."

She shuddered, remembering too well how the fast-flowing water bore her downstream, and how exhausted she became trying to break away and swim to shore.

"My dress was so heavy, it kept dragging me down. It took everything I had to keep my head above the water. I don't know how far the current carried me until it began to slow and I managed to crawl out. The next thing I remember is waking up to find an Indian standing over me." In her mind's eye, she pictured the savage warrior who became her adopted father.

"I'm sorry." Ridge laid his hand on hers.

She gazed down at the veins that textured the back of his hand and the long slender fingers more fitting of an artist than an army scout. "Don't be," she said softly. "He and his wife treated me like their own child." She traced one of the narrow white scars that crisscrossed his knuckles. "How'd you get these?" she asked.

He shrugged. "Got them when I was a kid."

Her fingers found another scar on his palm. "How about this one?"

A corner of his lips quirked upward. "Made the mistake of sticking my nose in where it didn't belong. The man who did it ended up teaching a stupid boy how to survive in the wilderness. Tracking, hunting, trapping, and anything else involved in staying alive."

"How old were you?"

"Fifteen." He drew his hand out from between hers. "Are you going to read some more?"

"I need to give my voice a rest." Grinning, she pushed the book toward him. "But I wouldn't mind listening to your voice."

Ridge shook his head and rose so abruptly his chair almost tipped over. "No, ma'am. You don't want to listen to this croaky voice."

Emma rested her cheek on her propped up hand. "You have a beautiful voice, Ridge."

His face reddened. "A man's voice can't be beautiful, Emma."

"Yours is," she insisted. "Read the next story. Please?"

He turned away, shaking his head. "I've got to check the fire."

Emma frowned, not understanding his reticence. He obviously enjoyed stories, yet he didn't want to read. Her gaze caught the canned goods on the shelf and recalled how Ridge had chosen tomatoes for breakfast. She thought of his map and how well it was marked, yet no names were written on it.

"Do you know how to read, Ridge?" she asked softly.

Ridge remained squatting in front of the stove, his back to Emma. The silence stretched out until he answered in a voice so soft Emma had to strain to hear him.

"No."

Ridge stared into the stove, at the reddish-orange embers that writhed like a nest of disturbed snakes. His face burned, but the fire wasn't the reason. Memories. All bad. Words he'd buried. Anger he'd swallowed. Pain he'd hidden.

A hand on his shoulder startled him and he barely restrained the instinct to jerk away. Her fingertips made small indents in his skin, each one a gentle brand.

"There's no need to be ashamed," Emma said quietly.

Her words reminded him why she stood so close and why he couldn't stay. He straightened and gazed down at the woman's upturned face. Her eyes were wide, filled with sympathy, and he wished he hadn't looked at her.

"I'm not," he lied.

Emma folded her arms across her waist, her stubbornness revealing itself in her bold stance. "Many men and women are illiterate."

Even though Ridge didn't know how to read, he did understand words and illiterate was one he hated. Ignorant was another. However, they weren't as bad as "simpleton" or "idiot" or "half-wit." He'd heard them all, mostly from his stepfather, but also from his classmates and the teacher who hadn't believed him. It was only his mother who had believed him.

He stalked over to his saddlebags, needing something to occupy his hands and thoughts, but found himself idly playing with a strap as he struggled to escape the memories' harsh blows. He heard Emma come up behind him but didn't turn around.

"Schools were scarce in the Territory," she said.

Ridge kept his neck bowed as his fingers stilled their restless motions. "I grew up in Sunset, same as you."

A frown tugged at her pretty lips and questions flashed in her eyes, but she only asked, "Your parents didn't let you attend?"

He bit the inside of his cheek and tasted blood. "Let it be, Emma."

"I only want to help."

It tore at his gut to hear her wounded tone. But all these

years he'd hidden his failing from everyone but Colt
Rivers, who'd helped him hide his condition from the
army. "There's nothing you can do," he said, less gruff now.

"I could teach you letters and how to read," she offered,
then smiled. "I used to dream about being a teacher before—" Her smile faltered.

Ridge gripped his saddlebags to keep from hugging this
tenderhearted woman whose cheeks pinkened with uncharacteristic shyness. He could see her as a child, pretending to be at the front of a classroom and calling up
imaginary students to read or answer a question.

If only it were as simple as she believed.

He closed his eyes, wondering if he had the strength to
confess. He owed it to Emma to try. He guided her to the
table and held the chair for her. Although her expression
was puzzled, she sat with her hands knotted in her lap and
remained silent. That was one of the things Ridge liked
about her—she didn't badger him with a passel of questions, but let him speak in his own time.

He perched on the barrel, his hands on his knees. "It
wasn't that I didn't go to school," he began. "For three
years I did. I learned my letters and numbers. It's just that
when they were all together, they didn't make any sense."

A furrow appeared between her eyebrows. "What do
you mean?"

Frustrated, Ridge dug his fists into his thighs. "Book
pages looked like a jumble of letters. I tried sounding the
words out like the teacher said, but I never could get them
right. And when I tried writing them, I got the letters all
mixed up." He shook his head. "The teacher figured I was
either lazy or stupid."

"You aren't either," Emma argued, her eyes blazing
with indignation. "From what I've seen you aren't afraid to
work and you're one of the smartest men I've met."

Although he was warmed by her belief in him, it was
misplaced. His mouth was bone-dry and he tried to work
up some moisture. "At first the teacher said I was doing
them wrong to be contrary." He ran a trembling hand

through his long hair and smiled, although amusement was far from his thoughts. "He broke a lot of rulers on me."

Emma's gaze darted to his fists, and Ridge stilled the impulse to tuck his hands behind his back.

"The scars on your knuckles." Her face paled. "I'm sorry, Ridge."

"It wasn't you who did the deed."

She laid a soft hand on his knee. "I'm sorry you were punished for something that wasn't your fault."

Ridge shrugged aside her concern. "The teacher tried. He'd make me write letters over and over until my hand hurt so bad, I couldn't write anymore, but I still couldn't get it right."

"What about your mother and father?"

"Ma used to read to me and I'd try to follow along. And my stepfather—" He peered out the window beside the bed. Snowflakes dashed by, chasing one another as they raced to the earth. "He thought I was lazy and stupid."

And beat the hell out of me with his leather belt.

"Will you let me try?" she asked softly. "I promise we'll stop whenever you want."

No, Ridge didn't want her witnessing his humiliation. Besides, she'd just think he wasn't trying, just like everybody else.

He stalked to the door and shrugged into his sheepskin coat. "I'm going out to check on the horses and bring in more wood."

He plunged outside before Emma could speak. The wind stole his breath, and he turned his back to it, struggling to breathe against the assault of frigid air. He punched his hands into his pockets and lowered his head against the brittle sheet. He trudged through the drifts, most of which were higher than his knees.

In his haste to escape Emma and the memories she evoked, he'd forgotten his gloves and a scarf to wrap around his face. He wouldn't be able to stay outside long without risking frostbite. He checked the horses and found them huddled together, their backsides to the wind that tore around the corner of the cabin. There was little snow buildup on the lee side so the animals could forage. The horses had drunk the melted snow Ridge had brought earlier, and he picked up the battered tin pan to refill. The metal was so cold it seemed to burn Ridge's fingers and he dropped it, cussing. The horses skittered away.

"Easy," Ridge soothed, running a hand along Paint's neck, then along Clementine's withers. Once the animals were resettled, he tugged his jacket cuff over his hand and picked up the pan, silently cursing his idiocy in leaving his gloves in the cabin.

Idiot.

That was one of those words that had sent him out here like a dog with its tail tucked between its hind legs. Even now, almost twenty-five years later, the remembered jeers made his gut tighten with bottled-up anger and hopelessness. He knew Emma would never taunt him, but if he accepted her offer to try to teach him, she would soon realize the truth.

He was stupid.

$\mathscr{N}$INE

HIS ears began to grow numb and Ridge tramped back to the cabin, pausing by the door to fill the pan with clean snow. With a ball of dread in his belly Ridge entered the cabin, and warmth and peacefulness surrounded him.

Emma was standing by the stove and turned to face him as he set the metal pan on the floor beside the door. He removed his coat, prolonging the moment before he would say no to her generous, but misguided, offer.

"More water for the horses?" she asked, her chin motioning to the pan.

Ridge nodded.

She crossed the floor to pick it up and set it on the stovetop. The snow on the bottom of the pan sizzled and crackled on the hot surface, unusually loud in the cabin's silence.

"I could've done that," Ridge said, unaccountably irritated.

"I know."

She remained by the stove and stared into the pan. Ridge couldn't read her expression, except that she seemed thoughtful. He joined her, standing on the opposite side, and held his chilled hands over the rising heat.

"When I lived with the Indians, my adopted father brought back a horse from a raid," Emma began conversationally.

Ridge lifted his head, but found her gaze aimed at the melting snow.

"The horse tried to bite anyone who came near it. It also had these horrible scars on its back and withers." Emma hugged herself. "Fast Elk said it had been beaten for so long, it had forgotten how to trust. So when anyone came near the poor animal, it expected pain. Fast Elk worked with that horse every day for weeks to get it to trust him."

She paused and worried her lower lip between her teeth.

Ridge knew where she was headed with her story and sighed impatiently. "So your adopted father finally got the horse to trust him and the animal became his favorite pony."

Emma lifted her head and her eyes revealed sadness. "No. The horse never learned to trust and we used him for meat that winter."

Ridge drew back, startled by her blunt words. "So what's your point, Emma?"

She met his gaze unflinchingly. "The point is that the horse refused to trust anyone, and it died because of its stubbornness."

"You can't expect an animal to understand, Emma," Ridge said, not bothering to hide his annoyance. "If it only knows pain from people, it has no reason to let anyone get close."

"That's right. But we're people, not horses."

Ridge saw only sincerity and compassion in her expression. He knew she wanted to help him, but she didn't know that in doing so, she'd only be hurting him.

"Please let me try to teach you," Emma implored.

"You don't know what you're asking, ma'am."

She stepped around the stove and clasped his hands. There was unexpected strength in her grip. "I'm asking you to trust me, Ridge."

He had no defense against her softly spoken words. Although he suspected she was hiding secrets—secrets involving the very Indians they searched for—he trusted her with his. He ignored the tightening in his chest and nodded slowly. "I'm not holding you to any promises," he assured her. "A lot of folks have tried, including my own ma."

"Then I'll be in good company, won't I?"

Her smile thwarted any other arguments he had, and he wished he had the right to take her in his arms and kiss her. "Yes, ma'am."

Emma rubbed her palms together. "First thing is to find something to write on."

"You want to start now?"

Challenging eyes met his. "Do you have something better to do?"

He fumbled around for an excuse to stall his lessons. "I should take the melted snow out to the horses and bring in more wood."

He expected Emma to argue, but she only said, "We'll start whenever you're ready."

"After I do the chores," Ridge felt obligated to add.

This time Ridge took the time to bundle up warmly and, despite himself, found he was growing excited about Emma's offer. What if she could accomplish what no one else had? What if he could actually learn to read and write?

No! He wouldn't let himself hope, only to have that hope crushed yet again. So many times he'd thought he could learn. He'd even come to recognize a few words, like his name and some smaller words. But picking up a book and reading it like Emma did was something beyond his abilities.

Half an hour later, he finished the chores and returned to the cabin with the last armload of wood. Emma sat by the table, biting her lower lip between her teeth as she studied the open book before her. Her braid tumbled over her shoulder and draped her left breast. One of the blankets hung like a sack on her, and his too-large moccasins stuck out from beneath her skirt. But her spine was straight and her slender neck curved enticingly, inviting him to kiss the pale skin. She was a fetching woman, her natural beauty made more evident by her lack of a fancy dress and slippers.

Ridge took a steadying breath and joined her.

"What're you doing?" he asked.

She glanced up, startled. "Trying to figure out how to begin. It's been a few years since I attended school and I don't want to do this wrong."

"It's not like anyone else has done it right," Ridge said with an unexpected swell of bitterness.

"Then we'll both figure out the right way."

His reservations returned twofold, and he knew he should back out now while he still could, but hated to be the one to dim the bright enthusiasm in her eyes. It was a sight better than the unhappiness he'd glimpsed in their depths too many times in the past few days.

He lowered himself onto the barrel.

"Can you read or write at all?" Emma asked.

Her question was cautious, like she was tiptoeing around a family of skunks.

"My name and some words. Not much," he admitted.

She turned the open book so it lay in front of him. "I'd like you to see if you can read the title of this story."

Ridge's heart clamored into his throat, just like when Mr. Porter instructed him to read in front of the class. He cursed himself for being so skittish. He wasn't seven years old anymore and Emma wasn't going to rap his knuckles with a ruler when he got it wrong.

He licked his lips and leaned over the page, which was filled with a terrifying mishmash of letters. Focusing on the largest letters on the page, he began. "The s-stier fo the dab—"

He shoved the book across the table in frustration and Emma caught it before it fell off the edge. He should've known it would be like this—feeling like he was that dumb kid again and standing at the front of the class as the other children laughed at him.

A trickle of sweat rolled down between his shoulder

blades. He squeezed his fists so tightly they began to cramp. "I'm stupid. I told you," he said hoarsely.

She clasped a clenched hand. "It's all right, Ridge." She scooted her chair nearer to the barrel, so her shoulder touched his arm, and dragged the book back into place. She pointed to the first word he'd stumbled over. "Can you read the letters of the word?"

He fought the urge to shove both the book and himself away from the table. For Emma, he'd try. He concentrated on the book and not on Emma's clean scent or her soft hair, which was almost close enough to tickle his nose. "S-T-Y-O-R."

Her brows folded downward. "That's S-T-O-R-Y. Story."

"No, it's not." ·

Her frown grew, and Ridge recognized that look. It was the same one everyone else had right before they told him to stop making things up. But instead, Emma asked, "What about numbers?"

"What?"

"Can you read numbers?"

He shifted uncomfortably. "I know numbers but it's the same as the words."

"What do you mean?" She was staring at him like he was a bug she'd never seen before.

Ridge gnashed his teeth. It would work better just to show her. "Tell me a number."

"Four."

"A bigger one."

"Four hundred and thirty-two."

Ridge could clearly see the numbers in his mind's eye and he used his forefinger to write them on the table. Four. Two. Three.

"That's four hundred and twenty-three, Ridge," Emma corrected.

He shook his head stubbornly. "It's four hundred and thirty-two."

Emma nibbled her lower lip. "You changed the numbers around."

"It doesn't look that way to me."

Her expression was more puzzled than disbelieving. "What about if I would write a number?"

Another shrug. "Go ahead."

He watched her finger move across the table. Five. Eight. Seven. "Five hundred and eighty-seven."

"Exactly," Emma said, smiling with victory. "You *can* read numbers."

"Only if I watch you make them." Ridge had been through this before, too.

"Stay here." Emma scurried over to the wood and pried a piece of bark from one of the logs, then knelt on the floor and wrote something in the dirt. "All right. Come here."

Wary, Ridge crossed to her side and leaned over, his hands braced on his thighs. He gazed at the number she'd written. "Nine hundred and twenty-four."

She grabbed his hand and tugged him down beside her, then covered the last two numbers in the dirt. "What number is that?" she asked.

"Nine," he replied, barely restraining his exasperation.

"Now put a picture of the nine in your head," Emma instructed.

Ridge did so.

She put her hands over the first and last number. "This number?"

"Four."

She grinned, but only said, "Now place that one beside the nine in your mind."

Ridge narrowed his eyes as comprehension sank in.

Then she covered the first two numbers with her hands.

"Two," he said without prompting. He looked at the three numbers in his mind. "Nine hundred and forty-two."

Emma clapped her dusty hands. "That's right!"

Ridge sat back on his heels and gazed at the number on the floor. He pointed at it. "But that doesn't match the one in my head."

"Can I tell you another story?" she asked.

"As long as there's not a horse involved."

She grinned. "No horses, I promise." She shifted around so her slender legs were folded sideways beneath her and close enough to Ridge that he could feel her dress against his leg.

"I learned much of the Lakota language from the children because the adults were too busy," Emma began. "Thay'd draw pictures in the dirt and give the Lakota name to the thing or animal. Although they didn't have letters or numbers like we do, they used pictures to tell stories."

Ridge nodded, knowing this already from his own association with the Indians.

"There was a little girl named Sweet Blossom who would draw her story pictures out of sequence. But if you asked her to tell her story, she would do so correctly. But if I drew a story for her, she would 'read' it wrong. She actually saw the pictures in a different order than everyone else."

Ridge felt a kinship with the unknown girl, but kept his voice indifferent. "What happened to her?"

Emma smiled. "The Lakota saw her as gifted. She learned to read picture stories by watching others recite theirs; and everyone else learned hers the same way."

"But I can read and draw maps without doing it backward."

"If someone draws picture stories backward, why isn't it possible that another person could see words and numbers turned around?"

Hope, long dead, stirred to life. "So you believe me?"

Emma motioned toward the number drawn on the dirt floor. "The proof is right in front of us."

He studied the individual numbers, trying to separate them mentally as Emma had done physically. It made his head ache. "Knowing that doesn't mean I can learn to read or write," he stated.

"You're right," Emma said honestly. "But I think you *can* learn. It's going to take time and patience to find the right way to do it."

"And someone who understands to teach me," he stated bluntly.

Emma drew lines in the dirt with the piece of bark. "I understand that you see things differently, but I'm not sure how to make sense of what you see."

Ridge locked his hands together. "The number. The way you did that helped me to read it right. Maybe we can try it with words, too."

Emma gazed at him, her expression unrevealing of her thoughts. "For short sentences, maybe, but things like newspapers or books, it would take too much time and you'd lose both interest and patience. You said you can recognize some words?"

He nodded. "Ma used to read things to me over and over again, and after so long I just knew what some of the words looked like."

"So you memorized them." She thought about that a moment, then seemed to come to a decision. "I'd like to try some things this afternoon. That way maybe we can both come up with ideas on what might work."

Although doubts continued to plague Ridge, he suspected that if anybody could come up with a way to help him, it would be Emma. She was determined and intelligent, and too pretty for his peace of mind. Being stranded in the small cabin with her was sweet torture. He was no saint and temptation seemed awfully close in these four walls. He hoped her lessons would steer his thoughts in other directions, even if his body's compass kept swinging back to Emma.

Ridge stood and clasped her hand, tugging her to her feet. He miscalculated his strength and she flew upward, with a little cry of surprise, and into his arms. Her breasts flattened against his chest and his body reacted with all the subtlety of a tomcat in the springtime.

Startled, Ridge looked down into Emma's uptilted face expecting to find shock and disapproval. Instead, he was stunned to see the reflection of his own desire and he instinctively drew her flush against him. His open hands splayed across her lower back, over the rise of her soft buttocks. His masculine pride preened when she moaned ever-so-softly and a flush spread across her cheeks.

Emma was so close he could feel her heart thumping wildly and smell the first tendrils of her passion. Pleasure swirled through his brain, obliterating everything but his need, which had only risen in the hours spent alone with her.

"I want you, Emma," Ridge whispered.

Emma's legs wobbled but Ridge's corded arms kept her upright. She knew intimately what he wanted, as her own body begged for the same, but once they gave in to lust, it would be impossible to undo. The second time would be easier, then a third and fourth even easier. Two lonely people in the middle of nowhere. So easy . . .

But they would both regret it once they returned to civilization. Ridge because of his sense of honor, and Emma, heaven help her, because she would only want him more.

She felt his hardness against her belly and her breath caught in her throat. Long-denied desire surged through her blood, swamping her senses. Ridge's hands caressed her buttocks, cupping and squeezing gently.

Would it be so bad, just this one time, to feel like a woman again? To touch a man's body, to skim her fingers along silky heat and flexing muscles? To smell the heady scent of Ridge's arousal and feel his breath upon her face and breasts?

The choice was hers and her mind knew what she should do, but her heart and body railed against rationality and caution. Ridge wasn't like the others; he never treated her with anything less than respect, despite him knowing she was a "white squaw." And he wanted her.

Just as she wanted him.

It was as simple as that.

Tomorrow she would have to live with her decision, but today she would surrender to the dictates of her heart and body.

She lifted her gaze and shivered at the naked passion that darkened Ridge's eyes. She cupped his cheek and his whiskers rasped against her palm, making her shiver with longing. Drawing closer, she gazed at his lips—lips that had spoken kind, soothing words to her; lips that had defended her; lips she'd fantasized about as she lay in her bed late at night.

He lowered his head, tilting it so their mouths matched perfectly. She'd always imagined his lips would be firm like the rest of him, but they softened beneath hers. Their breaths mingled as the kiss grew deeper. Ridge's tongue swept across her lips and she opened to allow him entry, tasting him for the first time. He caressed her palette and played across her teeth and the inside of her cheeks. He was devouring her as she pressed closer, allowing him everything he wanted.

Ridge drew away and rested his forehead against hers, his breathing swift and shallow. "If you don't want this, Emma, say so now. I can't promise I can stop later."

Emma considered his words for only a second and wrapped her arms around his neck. "I don't want you to stop. Not now, not later," she whispered.

With one fluid motion, Ridge scooped her into his arms and carried her the short distance to the bed. He laid her down and straightened, gazing at her with hot, lust-filled eyes. He slipped his hands under his suspenders and drew them off his well-shaped shoulders. "I wanted you the first time I saw you walking down the road, your shoulders so straight and proud." Passion roughened his voice.

Emma's heart tripped and words abandoned her. Kneeling on the bed, she helped him remove his shirt, leaving him in a wool undershirt. She tugged it out of his waistband and glided her hands beneath the material, losing herself in the sensation of his smooth warm skin. Her mouth grew dry as he lifted the shirt over his head, baring a sleek, well-muscled chest.

Running her hands up his planed torso, Emma felt his nipples pucker beneath her palms. With a little smile, she leaned forward and latched onto one, sucking it to pebble hardness.

Ridge moaned and his hands cupped the back of her head, his fingers wrapping themselves in her silky hair. "Emma."

She kissed a line across his chest and teased the other crest with her tongue and lips. Growing bolder, Emma stroked his back and sides, and felt the goose bumps that arose on his fevered flesh.

Suddenly her shoulders were grasped and she raised her head. Ridge crushed his lips down upon hers, and she met him without flinching, matching his passion with her liberated desire. Clumsy fingers opened her blouse and a work-roughened hand slid under her camisole. He cupped her breast with a tenderness that belied the primal urgency of their bodies. He rolled her nipple between his fingertips and she broke away from his savage kiss, panting heavily as arousal pulsed through her body in unending waves.

With unspoken agreement, they quickly shed the remainder of their clothing. Emma tossed hers onto the floor, uncaring as to where it landed, only wanting to have Ridge's nakedness against her own.

She lay back on the bed and drank in Ridge's virile beauty. He stood at the foot of the bed, solid and self-assured, with his hands on his hips as he stared down at her, his hot gaze caressing every inch of her body. Curious, she brazenly inspected his impressive masculinity, hard and curved against his belly. There was a glimmer of moisture at the tip, and it tantalized her.

She shifted over on the bed and patted the mattress in clear invitation. Ridge immediately settled beside her, his arms coming around her waist as he drew her flush against him. They kissed for lingering moments, then Ridge began to nuzzle her jaw and neck, and lower. He worshiped her body with his hands and mouth, and Emma's breasts tingled beneath his devotion. Her womb felt swollen and damp, and the pressure within rose with each caress.

Ridge cupped the source of her heat and eased a finger into her wetness. He teased the nub, sending a bolt of lightning through Emma's loins. Gasping, she reached down between their bodies to encircle his erection. He throbbed within her fist and she brushed her fingertip across the drop of moisture.

Ridge's muscles bunched and he inhaled sharply. "Emma."

Her heart kicked against her ribs and she tried to calm her stumbling breath. She released him and clutched his rock-solid arms. "Yes. Now Ridge." She hardly recognized the needy voice as her own.

Ridge paused to gaze down at her, as if gauging her readiness. A moment later, he guided himself to her opening and teased her sensitive folds.

Emma pumped her hips upward, straining toward him as her fingers dug into his arms. "Now. Please."

Ridge planted his hands on the mattress on either side of her and raised himself up so they touched only where they were joined. He continued pressing inward at a snail's pace, moving forward with agonizing deliberation.

Emma tensed only for a moment, having forgotten how it felt to be filled by a man. But her body had no trouble welcoming him and opened fully to his breadth. Tears gathered in her eyes and she tried to blink them away.

Ridge froze and a tender finger brushed away one tear that escaped her. "Emma?" he asked with so much concern, she wanted to sob.

She wound her arms and legs around Ridge, drawing him so close not even air could get between them. "I'm fine. It's just so good. Been so long," she whispered.

After a moment's startled hesitation, he began to move. He inched out, then eased back into her moist heat. He had to fight his body's insistence to take her fast and hard, to release the tension gathering in his groin like thunderheads before a storm. But she felt so tight, so hot, and he wanted to bury himself in her, never to come out.

Emma grasped his buttocks, urging him deeper. He could feel her pulsing around him and he groaned.

Capturing her lips with his, he thrust with more force and speed. His urgency boiled hotter and hotter.

He focused on Emma's face—her closed eyes, her arched brow, and her swollen lips. She was so beautiful, so courageous, so giving.

Suddenly, she opened passion-filled eyes and they widened when they met his. She tipped her head back and her body arched upward as a low keen spilled from her parted lips.

Her flesh tightened around him and he thrust into her one final time, spilling his seed deep within her. His heart thundered and he gasped for air as he held his weight on trembling limbs.

Emma peered up at him, her face flushed and damp from her climax. There were no regrets, nor condemnation in her eyes, only warmth and gratitude. She reached up to brush a strand of hair behind his ear. The gesture was so artless, Ridge's throat threatened to close.

He eased out of her and shifted to her side to lie down. Emma immediately curled against him, her arm draped across his waist. Unwilling to surrender their intimacy too quickly, Ridge embraced her. Her breasts flattened against him, tempting him with their plump softness. His groin twitched, but that was all he could manage after his shattering release.

He caressed her thick braid, the motion cozy and soothing. The fire crackled in the stove and the wind rattled icy snow against the windows. Ridge couldn't think of a single place he'd rather be.

"Enapay was my husband," Emma broke the silence some minutes later.

Ridge's fingers stilled. Of course he'd known she wasn't a virgin when he'd entered her, but he hadn't expected her confession. " 'Was'?"

"He died during a raid over two years ago," she replied quietly.

The whispers about her back in Sunset weren't far from

the truth, and Ridge wondered why he wasn't outraged that she'd slept with an Indian. "Was he good to you?"

He felt her nod. "We were married when I was seventeen. He was twenty-one."

Ridge continued to stroke her hair as he digested her words. "Do your parents know?"

"No. You're the first person I've told." She turned onto her side and rested her cheek in her propped-up hand as she gazed down at him. "I thought you would understand."

Her trust in him humbled and touched him. "If he's dead, why do you need to find his people?"

She looked down and stroked his chest with featherlight fingertips. Despite himself, his nipples hardened and renewed desire arrowed to his groin.

"I want to see his family one last time to make sure they're safe and well." She lifted her gaze and sadness shadowed her brown eyes, and Ridge sensed something more in her hesitation. "He was a good man, Ridge."

Jealousy sucker punched him and he forced himself to breathe slowly and evenly. He didn't own Emma and he sure as hell shouldn't care that she'd been married to an Indian. "I reckon that's a good enough reason."

"Thank you." She leaned down and brushed a kiss across his lips.

Lightning arced through Ridge's veins and he rolled Emma on top of him, so he could feel her bare skin from chest to toe. Emma smiled impishly and wriggled against his growing hardness. All thoughts of her past lover disappeared as Ridge growled and, with one smooth motion, had her lying beneath him.

Emma laughed brightly and Ridge suddenly wanted her with a need that bordered on obsession.

TEN

EMMA awoke with a shiver, alone in the bed, and with a driving need that she had to *do* something. But no matter how hard she focused, she couldn't determine what that something was.

She blinked in the dwindling light of the afternoon and spotted Ridge wearing his trousers and untucked undershirt by the stove. He was adding another chunk of wood.

She lay unmoving, not knowing what he expected. After their second joining, both she and Ridge had collapsed from exhaustion and fallen asleep. Her body twinged pleasantly in places she hadn't felt since her husband died. But there was still an unappeased hunger biding within her, a hunger to lie again and again with Ridge. Although Enapay had been a considerate lover, she had always kept a part of herself separate from their lovemaking. But with Ridge, she didn't want to hide any part of her from him, and that frightened her.

Her prediction had been too true. Now that she and Ridge had made love twice, it would be so easy to succumb again. Watching him, his face reflecting the fire and his motions as graceful as a cat's, Emma wasn't certain how she would close her Pandora's box now that it had been unlocked.

Knowing she was only prolonging the inevitable, Emma sat up, hiding her nudity beneath the blanket. "Is the blizzard letting up?" Although she kept the question casual, the urgency she'd awakened with kept prodding at her.

Ridge turned, startled. His gaze slid over her covered breasts then back up to her face. Banked passion flickered in his eyes. "Some. It should quit tonight."

"Which means we can continue on our way tomorrow."

"If the snow ain't too deep for the horses." Ridge gave his attention to the embers. "You'd best get dressed, Emma."

With Ridge's gaze averted, Emma jumped up and tugged on her scattered clothing. The scent of their joining rose around her and embarrassment heated her cheeks. However, she had no regrets for what they'd done.

"I'll make supper," she said.

Ridge straightened and closed the stove. "Good idea." He turned his back to her as he tucked in his undershirt and drew on his wool shirt, then slipped his suspenders back in place. "I'll be back in a few minutes."

Emma nodded and sliced salt pork as Ridge donned his boots and warm outer clothing. He slipped outside without another word and the cabin felt empty without his presence. Emma wondered if he regretted his loss of control. Or perhaps now that he had time to think about it, maybe he was repulsed by her marriage to an Indian.

That thought troubled her as she went about finding something to eat. As she was preparing a batch of biscuits, the door swung open and Ridge entered, his head bowed. Snowflakes peppered his hair and shoulders.

"How're the horses?" she asked, anxious to fill the silence.

"Fine." He removed his coat. "The snow's definitely letting up. We should be able to leave tomorrow."

"That's good."

Now that Ridge knew about Enapay, Emma's conscience nudged her to tell him about Chayton. If he could accept that she'd been married to an Indian, wasn't it a small step for him to accept that she had a child? She opened her mouth to confess, but courage deserted her. She wasn't even certain Ridge *was* comfortable with her marriage to one of the People, and Chayton was tangible proof of that union.

Emma continued to prepare their supper and when Ridge acted as polite as he had before they'd made love, she began to relax. Half an hour later, they sat down to eat fresh biscuits with beans and pork.

Ridge swiped his plate clean with the last biscuit. "Thanks. That hit the spot." He gave her a shy smile reminiscent of the first time she'd met the man.

She smiled back. "You're welcome."

After washing and drying the dishes, Emma donned her coat.

"Where're you going?" Ridge sat by the table where he was working on a bridle by the light of two candles.

"I want to take a sponge bath."

Ridge rose. "I'll fill the pan."

Before she could argue, he was out the door. He returned less than a minute later.

"Thank you, but you don't have to wait on me." Emma took the kettle from him and placed it on the stove.

"We do for each other. You made supper and did the dishes," he simply said, and then returned to his task at the table.

Emma hadn't considered it that way, and suspected few men were as thoughtful as Ridge. Her admiration for him, already considerable, rose another notch.

Knowing it would take some time before the water heated, she joined Ridge by the table and opened her book. But instead of reading, she watched his fingers work the leather with sure, deft motions. Maybe he couldn't read or write, but he had other talents, such as mapmaking, tracking, and mending leather with infinite patience. Where had he learned those skills?

Frowning, she realized how little she knew about him despite the time they'd spent together. "So you fought in the war, Ridge?"

He nodded.

"Union?"

"That's right."

"You don't like to talk about it."

Ridge's gaze turned to something only he could see; something she suspected he wouldn't want her to see. "War isn't pretty, Emma."

She remembered the night the soldiers came to the People's camp—the screams, the blood, the dead and dying. "You're right, it's not," she said, her voice husky. "War. It's such an ugly word—rhetoric used to defend hatred."

"It's man's nature. To fight for what he believes is righteous."

"Who decides what's righteous and what's not?"

"Each person has to make his own decision."

Emma listened to the sizzle of wood in the fire, an oddly comforting sound. "You made the choice to leave the army. Why?"

His gaze dropped and it was a long moment before he answered. "The war changed and I realized I wasn't fighting for a righteous cause anymore."

She touched his sleeve lightly, ignoring the spark between them. "For what it's worth, I think you made the right choice."

"I made the only choice I could," he said quietly in his husky timbre. "Just like you did."

Emma nodded, unable to speak around the lump in her throat. Nobody else could understand that—not her parents, and certainly not the townsfolk.

"Shall we start your lessons?" she asked a few minutes later.

Apprehension flitted across Ridge's face, but he set aside the bridle.

Emma moved her chair next to his and tried to ignore his masculine scent and the curve of long eyelashes framing smoky blue eyes. "Did you say you memorized some words when your mother used to read to you?" she asked.

"That's right. Just smaller words, like 'the' and 'now.'"

"It sounds like memorization might be the best way for you to learn."

Emma wrote twenty-five words on the back of a poster she'd found in the shack. She read them and spelled them aloud twice, then had Ridge do it. He stumbled more than once, but was persistent.

"Now try writing them as you say them," Emma suggested, handing him the pencil.

He stared down at the list of words. "I ain't going to get them right."

Emma cupped her hand over his. "What matters is that you keep trying, Ridge." She smiled tenderly. "You're not a quitter."

Ridge took a deep breath and nodded gamely.

Emma wanted to hug him, like she'd done to Chayton when he needed reassurance, but settled for giving his hand a gentle squeeze. She rose and removed the large kettle from the stove. The water was just right for a sponge bath. She glanced back at Ridge who was concentrating on his task. She took a moment to simply look at him, to admire the strong slope of his forehead and nose, to remember the softness of his hair, which brushed his shoulders when he turned his head, and to recall the lines of muscle beneath his clothing. But right now, it was his intense concentration that she found most compelling. For a little while, that look had been aimed at her as they'd pleasured one another.

Her heart fluttered in her chest even as liquid heat poured into that place beneath her belly. How could she have thought that lying with him twice would slake her desire for him? That she could forget his protective embrace and his body's coiled strength?

She halted the dangerous line of thought and physically turned away. Clearing her mind, she unbuttoned her blouse, then dipped the cloth in the water and squeezed out the excess. She ran the damp cloth around her neck and across her chest, refusing to dwell on why her puckered nipples were so sensitive.

She rebuttoned her blouse and glanced over her shoulder to see Ridge's attention on the words and not her. She chastised herself for feeling a twinge of disappointment. After removing her stockings, she leaned over and trailed the damp cloth up her left leg, then her right. She bunched the front of her skirt in her free hand and held it up as she carefully washed the juncture of her thighs. She closed her eyes at the unintentional pleasure the gentle friction created.

A tingle at the top of her spine caused her to look over her shoulder . . . and her gaze collided with Ridge's. His eyes smoldered and Emma welcomed the heat. Without breaking eye contact, Emma dropped the hem of her skirt.

"How's the studying coming?" she asked huskily.

The corners of his lips quirked upward. "Depends on what kinda studying you're talking about, ma'am."

Ridge stood and ambled over to her. The heat from his body was far more intense than the stove, and Emma swayed toward him. He settled his hands on her hips and she braced herself on his arms.

"Seems to me the student needs some more private tutoring," Ridge said, need underlying his rasping voice.

Emma knew she shouldn't, but knowing and doing weren't always the same. "I happen to know a tutor who'd be more than willing to give you private lessons."

Ridge undid the first button of her blouse.

THE wolf cuffed her cub playfully, and the youngster yipped and raced around his mother. Lying on her side to soak up the sun, the wolf watched her son as his attention was snatched by a hovering butterfly. The cub dashed toward it, but the butterfly fluttered away. The young wolf chased after it, disappearing into the brush.

The female wolf sat up and listened intently for her cub, her nose twitching nervously. She could hear him pad

*across the fallen leaves and dry twigs. She scented the air
and the hair at her nape lifted.*

Danger!

She plunged into the brush after her cub.

A lion roared . . .

Emma jerked upright, her heart thumping in her throat.

An arm came around her waist. "Easy, Emma."

She blinked and focused on Ridge, who lay beside her
in the narrow bed. Caught between her dream and waking,
she simply stared at him.

Ridge pushed himself to a sitting position and the
moonlight gilded his face and long, thick hair. "Nightmare?" he guessed softly.

She gulped air. "Yes."

"Want to talk about it?"

Emma merely shook her head. Hanging onto one of the
blankets, she swung her feet to the floor to stand by the
window. She gazed out into the pale night. A three quarter
moon hung amidst a sky filled with diamond-like stars, and
their light reflected off the fresh white snow. She shuddered at the otherworldly scene, half expecting a mountain
lion to charge out from the wavering shadows.

Ridge rose and joined her. He stood quietly, offering
silent support. The lump in Emma's throat wasn't all due to
her nightmare.

"I dreamt of a mountain lion," she finally confessed.

"We did hear one a couple days back," Ridge said.

Emma shook her head. "That wasn't the first time I've
dreamed of a mountain lion."

Ridge turned his head and one side of his face held an
ethereal glow from the night's luminescence. "People
dream about things that scare them."

Her knuckles whitened as she clenched the blanket between her breasts. "The People say dreams are the spirits
talking to you." She studied his steady eyes. "What do you
dream about?"

His jaw muscle jumped into his cheek. "I don't dream."

"I envy you."

"Don't." Ridge crossed his arms. "I don't have dreams; I have nightmares."

She leaned against his side, offering him comfort. "I'm sorry."

He wrapped his arm around her shoulders and she rested her head against his chest. Did she dare ignore her visions? To do so might cause death or harm to befall her son, and that she could never live with.

Cold air eddied across her bare feet and she shivered.

"I'd add more wood, but we're running low," Ridge said quietly. "We'll have to make due with our body heat."

Emma stared up at his profile, at the shadows that painted his cheekbones and jaw. She'd never met a man so beautiful both inside and out. She traced his lips with a light fingertip, surprising herself by her audacity.

Ridge's nostrils flared and he caught her hand, then kissed the center of her palm. "Let's go back to bed."

When Ridge slid into her body for the fourth time in less than twenty-four hours, Emma promised herself it would be the last.

A chinook wind had blown down from the mountains overnight, and the snow was already melting when Ridge went out to saddle the horses. He paused on the porch, squinted at the rising sun, and listened to the plink-plink of melting snow dripping off the roof.

He stretched, relishing his body's satisfaction. He went weeks, oftentimes months, without female companionship. Stuck one day in a cabin with Emma Hartwell and he lost the iron control he'd always possessed—and not just once. Even thinking about the things they'd done brought a surge of blood to his groin.

But what of the future? What about when he returned Emma to her father's ranch? Would she tell Hartwell that Ridge Madoc had his way with his daughter?

No, Emma wasn't like that. She wouldn't demand marriage and she would keep their secret, just as she'd kept an even more dangerous secret all this time. A white woman married to a Lakota. Just like a chinook wind, it was unexpected.

He wasn't certain about his own feelings toward her confession. He'd known many Indians, had even lain with a few of the pretty sloe-eyed women, and he'd never disrespected them afterward either. They'd come to him and he'd been encouraged by his newfound friends to accept what was offered. He'd been young and full of wild oats to sow. Hell, hadn't he considered marrying a Sioux maiden years ago? So who was he to judge Emma?

No, he didn't begrudge Emma her marriage. So why did his gut twist up like a mad rattler every time he thought about Emma and her Enapay?

Paint whinnied, snapping Ridge out of his thoughts. Ridge settled his slouch hat on his head more firmly and went to ready the horses. He had a job to do and two hundred dollars waiting at the end of it. One hundred from Hartwell, and one hundred from Emma, whom he'd taken to bed without thinking out the consequences of his actions. But he wasn't a man to waste time worrying about what he'd done. He could, however, ensure he didn't take advantage of her passionate, generous nature again.

Ridge saddled the horses and led them across the damp snow to the front of the line shack, where he loosely tied their reins to a porch post. He took a deep breath and entered the cabin.

Emma was checking the straps on her saddlebags and she glanced up, startled by his entrance. Then she smiled that part shy, part seductive smile and he damned near forgot all his noble intentions.

"I'm ready," she announced. Her gaze traveled around the small cabin, paused a moment on the bed, then continued on, and finally settled on Ridge. The intensity of her soft brown eyes stirred his blood. "I'll remember this place fondly."

Ridge knew he'd never forget this shack and its

cramped bed either. "We'd best move out. The going'll be slow and I want to put in at least thirty-five miles today."

Emma carried her saddlebags in the crook of her arm as she marched to the door, Ridge's oversize moccasins slapping lightly on the dirt floor. "I'm ready."

Ridge tossed his own bag over his shoulder and picked up the cloth sack that held the remains of their foodstuffs. He ushered Emma onto the porch and took one last look at their refuge, then followed her to the horses.

Ridge made a cradle with his hands and gave Emma a boost into the saddle. She smiled her thanks and he tried to squelch the foolish grin that kept creeping across his face.

After mounting Paint, Ridge led the way north, allowing his horse to pick his path across the snow. They wouldn't cover a lot of ground today but they were back on the trail and away from the cabin.

And that damned tempting narrow bed.

BY dusk, Emma was more than ready to call it a day and set up camp. She'd gotten through the initial stiffness of traveling soon after she'd left her father's ranch, but riding after the interlude in the cabin had given her a different kind of ache. Making love with Ridge had been thrilling, but sitting on a horse for ten hours the next day was downright unpleasant.

A few times during the day she'd tried starting a conversation with Ridge to divert her discomfort, but it was obvious he didn't want to talk. Not about reading lessons, not about where they were headed, and definitely not about what had transpired between them in that deserted line shack.

Ridge had been wary all day, his gaze constantly moving from side to side, and dropping to the ground occasionally. But they'd seen nothing but a herd of pronghorns, two mule deer, four squirrels, one waddling skunk they'd steered clear of, and an assortment of birds. However, Emma was well aware of how Indians could seemingly rise out of nowhere. If she and Ridge came across a raiding party or a group of angry braves, she wasn't sure how they would be treated.

It was nearly dark when Ridge finally called a halt for the day. "We'll stay here tonight."

Later, after they'd eaten more beans and biscuits for supper, Emma glanced at Ridge, but he seemed more relaxed than he had been during the day. A twig snapped and her head swung around sharply, her gaze trying to pierce the darkness beyond their circle of light.

"Rabbit, maybe a squirrel," Ridge said quietly.

Emma drew her attention back to the flames, but the hairs at her nape prickled. To take her mind off her unaccountable jumpiness, she asked, "Would you like another lesson?" The dark blue eyes that caught hers flared and her cheeks flamed. "A *reading* lesson?"

The heat in his eyes disappeared and after a moment's hesitation, he answered, "All right."

Emma dug her book out of her saddlebags and motioned for Ridge to join her on the log. Then, with her leg touching his, she began to read as he followed along.

RIDGE swayed to Paint's rocking gait and fought the sun's lure to close his eyes. He'd slept little last night after enduring Emma's proximity as she'd read from her cherished book. He shouldn't have agreed to another lesson, but the temptation had been too powerful. He truly did want to learn, but to be so close to Emma and not touch her was pure torture.

He'd known once they were back on the trail, they couldn't repeat their cabin tryst. But he'd spent too much time thinking about how he wanted to stroke Emma's softness and taste her sweetness. His physical ache had only increased as he'd sat next to her in the evening, listening to her honey-smooth voice and remembering that same voice hoarse with desire as she'd welcomed him into her body.

He shifted uncomfortably in his saddle. It had been hell

lying there last night with Emma little more than an arm's length away. He'd listened to her soft steady breathing, imagining her tucked in his arms like she'd been the night before.

A hawk's cry startled him out of his lusty musings and he sharpened his gaze, searching the panorama. Most of the snow had melted, leaving puddles scattered here and there among the brown scrub and sparse grass. Up ahead lay rocky slopes with canyons tucked into them—perfect camps for a people who didn't want to be found.

"This looks familiar," Emma said quietly, staring at the pockmarked land stretched out before them.

"I got a feeling we're getting close, but whether they're your band or not—" Ridge shrugged. "That's hard to say."

An indistinct movement far ahead caught Ridge's attention, and he narrowed his eyes, but he couldn't see anything amiss. He knew they were being watched, but when he searched the horizon for a plume of smoke or anything that might give away a village or a group's approach, he could spot nothing.

"What is it?" Emma asked.

He tugged his slouch hat lower on his brow, to hide his eyes. "Stay close, Emma. I got a feeling—"

Horses' hooves and bloodcurdling screams suddenly erupted around them. A dozen or so Indians raced toward them from the cover of huge boulders along a hill's slope. Ridge's first reaction was to turn tail and run, but he doubted they'd be able to outrun the expert horsemen.

"Stay where you are and keep your hands in plain view," Ridge ordered Emma.

Although her face paled, she nodded resolutely. She kept Clementine under a tight rein as the mare tugged at the bit. Ridge found Paint just as anxious as the bronzed riders thundered toward them and he focused on keeping calm. Why the hell had he agreed to this fool plan of Emma's? A man couldn't use an extra hundred dollars if he was dead.

Ridge glanced at Emma and was surprised to see her relaxed features. He'd thought she'd be terrified, but then Emma never reacted the way he expected.

Atop their sturdy ponies, the warriors surrounded Emma and Ridge. Their long black hair was divided into two braids with a scalp lock festooned with feathers and quills. Many of them wore necklaces made of animal claws and teeth. Deerhide breechclouts and leggings with moccasins covered their legs and feet, and a few men wore an incongruous gingham shirt. Every warrior carried a bow and arrow; half of them displayed recently obtained scalps.

Ridge's heart hammered in his chest, but he raised his chin. The Indians respected bravery among all peoples. One of the warriors reached out to pluck Ridge's rifle from its scabbard and his revolver from his holster. Ridge didn't argue.

The silence was more harrowing than the earlier war cries. They were definitely Lakota, probably a band of Brules, and they were definitely not pleased to see them.

Ridge easily picked out the leader, a man a few years older than himself with two glossy black braids and a broad face painted with lines and designs of red, black, and yellow. The other warriors, as well as the ponies, were also painted. The leader's piercing brown eyes roamed across Emma, and then Ridge, who met his gaze squarely. The two men parried looks and the horses stamped impatiently as a minute, then two, passed.

"Tuwe?" the leader finally asked.

"I am Winona," Emma replied in Lakota. "Adopted daughter of Fast Elk."

Ridge frowned, irritated by her forthrightness. Within the Sioux society, it was frowned upon for a woman to speak unless directly spoken to.

The leader's eyes narrowed, but he appeared more startled than insulted. He nodded toward Ridge.

"Madoc," Ridge answered the unspoken question. "I lived with your people many winters ago."

The brave scrutinized them, trying to determine if they spoke the truth. Another warrior brought his horse closer to the leader and spoke in a low tone Ridge couldn't distinguish. But when the leader's gaze flickered to Emma, Ridge wondered if maybe she'd been recognized.

"*Ihakob.*" The leader whirled around and a path was made through the other Indians to allow him through.

Ridge and Emma exchanged somber looks, then followed the Lakota. The riders closed in around them as they rode.

"Do you think they're taking us to their camp?" Emma asked Ridge, keeping her voice low.

"I think so. Do you recognize any of them?"

Her brow furrowed as she looked at those warriors she could see without turning in the saddle. "I don't know. Maybe one or two, but it's hard to tell with the war paint. How about you?"

Ridge shook his head.

Emma lapsed into silence as they journeyed. They rode through noon and on into the afternoon, with the Indians keeping a steady pace. There was no break for lunch or to drink from a canteen. Ridge's mouth grew parched and his tongue felt swollen.

The sun wasn't far from the western horizon when Ridge and Emma followed the stoic warriors through a twisting narrow trail between rocks. Ridge scanned the ledges high above them and noticed four boys, not more than eleven or twelve years old watching them closely. They stood with their feet planted apart, a bow in their hands and a quiver of arrows slung across their backs. It was a sure bet the entire village knew they were arriving.

The vista suddenly opened into a valley with a river running through it. Maybe twenty-five buffalo hide lodges were scattered across the greening grass. Dogs raced out from behind the tipis, dancing and barking around the horses' legs. Young and old women wearing deerskin dresses decorated with quills and beads paused in their tasks to gaze at them with impassive features. Groups of children stopped their games and stared at the new arrivals, their dark eyes round with curiosity. Pit fires lent little smoke into the air, but Ridge could smell food cooking and his stomach growled, reminding him it had been a while since they'd eaten a breakfast of cold biscuits and jerky.

Old men with scraggly gray hair and creased faces sat cross-legged in front of lodges and around fires. There were no other men the age of the raiding party warriors around the camp, but Ridge figured another group might be out hunting. Fresh meat would be needed for the celebration of a successful raiding party.

Suddenly the warriors began whooping and racing around the village on their ponies, their horsemanship skills never failing to amaze Ridge. Those few with scalps held them up as evidence of their prowess and success. As if a switch had been thrown, the children joined in the merriment, then the women. The older men remained dispassionate, but Ridge could see the past in their eyes as they relived their own youth through their sons and grandsons.

Situated at the peripheral of the excitement, Emma and Ridge seemed to be forgotten. However, Ridge knew better. If he or Emma tried anything untoward, they'd be surrounded in a matter of seconds.

He glanced at Emma, standing in her stirrups as she scanned the Indian faces. Since her husband was dead, she couldn't be looking for him. She had also talked about adoptive parents—was she searching for them?

"Is this your band?" Ridge asked her.

He could see her frustration in the shake of her head. "I'm not certain. I don't see Talutah or Fast Elk or—" she broke off. "Or anybody else."

Ridge frowned, certain she was going to say another name. But whose? Had she lied about her husband? Was he still alive? That possibility sent jealousy and possessiveness thundering through him. The intensity of his emotions shocked him, and he shoved them aside. There'd been no words exchanged between him and Emma, only mutual pleasure.

Emma suddenly stiffened and he followed her wide-eyed gaze to where an older squaw stood with a young boy who wore miniature deerskin leggings and a tunic. His long dark hair was braided into two plaits and his brown eyes were alive with mischief. But there was something about him, something Ridge couldn't put his finger on. . . .

Emma scrambled off Clementine and scooped up the boy in her arms. Confused, Ridge dismounted and positioned himself in front of the horses with the reins clutched in his hand.

Emma hugged the older woman, who was less demonstrative, although it was obvious she was pleased to see Emma. As they spoke in rapid Sioux, Ridge tried to puzzle out the riddle. It took him only another minute to detect what was odd about the boy—his skin was the color of watered down whiskey instead of the rich bronze of the Lakota.

The boy was half white.

He was Emma's secret.

ELEVEN

EMMA'S vision blurred as tears filled her eyes. She held her son close as she breathed in her little boy's familiar scent. She couldn't tell if Chayton remembered her, but at the moment all that mattered was she'd found him, safe and healthy.

"He's going to be a brave warrior like his father," Talutah said proudly. "Fast Elk says he will make Chayton's first bow and arrows soon."

Although she knew each Lakota boy started training to be a warrior at a very young age, her heart twisted at the thought of her son doing the same. She couldn't even imagine a grown-up Chayton as part of a raiding party like the one that had found her and Ridge.

Ridge.

She'd forgotten all about him when she'd spotted Chayton. Still holding her son, Emma looked over her shoulder. Ridge was standing in front of their horses with one knee slightly bent and his leather-covered shoulders at a relaxed slant. Anybody would've thought he was perfectly at ease, but she knew better. He was observing, noting every tiny nuance, from the way she held Chayton, to the affection between herself and her adopted mother.

Ridge Madoc was a good man. She prayed he wouldn't detest her too much for keeping this truth from him.

Chayton yanked her braid, bringing Emma's attention back. She grasped his fisted hand. "Let go," she said firmly in the Lakota language.

The young boy laughed and the sweet sound traveled clear to the depths of Emma's heart. His fingers, no longer pudgy, remained twined in her hair but she couldn't be angry and smiled at his mischief.

"Hiya," Talutah scolded the boy.

He released Emma's hair. *"Kuta?"*

She lowered him to the ground as he'd asked, and he immediately dashed off to join a group of children his age.

Emma's gaze followed him, and she fought the urge to scoop him back up and never let him go.

"He's grown so much," she said to Talutah.

"Ha. Soon he will begin his training with a *leksi."* Pride was evident in the older woman's tone.

Chayton didn't have an uncle in the white man sense, but according to Lakota definition, every warrior in the village was Uncle. Just as any male elder was Grandfather to everyone in the tribe.

"Who will train him?" Emma asked, trying to keep her voice steady.

"Hotah has offered."

Emma frowned. She remembered him as a bold warrior with a wide streak of cruelty. His bloodthirsty exploits were often told around the fire. He was also one of the few who had disapproved of her living among them.

"Why can't Fast Elk teach him?" Emma asked.

"He is old. He says it is a young man's duty." Talutah shrugged. "I know you do not like Hotah, but he is a skilled warrior. Chayton will learn well under him."

Not if I can help it.

Emma sought Chayton and spotted him dashing around, his legs a blur. She couldn't help but smile at his antics.

"He is always running, and keeps the young girls from becoming lazy in their task," Talutah commented, obviously noting the direction of Emma's gaze.

It appeared Chayton had flourished among his Lakota family. Emma should've been relieved and pleased, but the realization that he'd been fine without her saddened her.

"I saw you fall under a white soldier's blade," Talutah said, her eyes troubled. "Everyone believed you did not live."

Emma dragged her attention away from her son. "I was wounded. They carried me back to my white parents where it took me many moons to heal. Finally, I was able to come look for Chayton. I am grateful you cared for my son."

Talutah shrugged matter-of-factly. It was the way of the People. "Who is this *wasicu* who rides with you?"

"A friend." Emma decided there was no reason to expose the details of their meeting and subsequent journey together.

"He is not like the others?"

"No. He is honorable and brave."

Talutah called over a boy maybe eight years old. "Take care of their horses."

Puffing out his chest, the boy nodded solemnly. He trotted over to Ridge and without a word, took the reins from his hand. Ridge relinquished the horses with a nod at the boy, and strolled toward Emma, his expression unfathomable.

"I take it you found your people," Ridge said.

His drawl caressed Emma's insides. "Some of them. Ridge, I'd like you to meet my adoptive mother, Talutah."

He touched the brim of his hat while the woman bowed her head.

"My husband will be back from the hunt soon," Talutah said.

"I look forward to meeting him," Ridge stated in the native language.

"I will prepare a lodge for you, and find clothing for my daughter." Talutah left them standing there.

"Something you forgot to tell me, Emma?" There was a razor's edge to his casual question.

"Would you have brought me here if you'd have known?" She crossed her arms stubbornly.

"Probably not."

"That's what I thought."

"You have any more surprises?"

"No. At least, none I can think of right now."

"That ain't very comforting," Ridge growled. "We can't stay here long. Even though those scalps were from another tribe, next time they might be white scalps."

"I lived with them. They won't hurt us."

"Those who knew you then might not, but them young bucks that brought us in are itching to count coup. I figure it's only a matter of time until they throw in with Crazy Horse."

A stooped man with straggly gray hair hobbled over to them. A colorful blanket was draped over his thin shoulders and he limped noticeably, but his eyes were penetrating and intelligent.

"Come," the elder merely said.

He led them to an ornately painted lodge and entered, motioning for them to follow. Emma's eyes adjusted quickly to the dim light and she seated herself close to the tipi wall, leaving Ridge and the chief to sit nearer the fire pit in the middle of the floor. Moments later a squaw carried in two bowls of stew. She set them in front of Ridge and the chief.

As the men began to eat with their fingers, Emma surveyed the lodge and noticed Ridge's weapons on a pile of hides behind the leader. She suspected they'd stay there until Ridge left.

Another bowl was brought in and placed in front of Emma. Although her stomach was in knots from wanting to be near Chayton, she couldn't insult their host, especially the leader.

They ate in silence and after they were finished, a pipe was lit and the two men shared puffs for a few minutes before the elder began.

"I am Akecheta, leader of the Wolf band of the Brule

Lakota," the man said. He gazed at Emma shrewdly. "You are Winona of the Elk band, and Chayton is your son."

"Yes," Emma replied, trying to hide her apprehension.

"Your band was attacked by soldiers. Some died; many were taken to the white man's reservation. They escaped and we welcome them." He puffed in silence, the smoke wreathing his lined face and then rising lazily toward the opening at the top of the conical-shaped lodge.

Emma and Ridge exchanged looks, but knew better than to hurry the meeting along. It would be a grave discourtesy to press Akecheta.

"Why do you return?" Akecheta finally asked, his dark eyes pinning Emma.

"To see my son," she stated firmly.

"You have seen him."

Her gaze flickered to Ridge, but he only shrugged. His expression clearly said, *You wanted to find him and you did. Now what?*

"You cannot stay. We want no reason to bring the soldiers to our village. We are a peaceful band and we do not want war," Akecheta said.

Although Emma hadn't planned on staying, she hated to have the option taken away. Still, she was relieved the chief preferred peace to war. "I understand. I would like to visit my family and friends before I return. Is that allowed?"

Akecheta smiled, exposing brown stumps of teeth. "A visit is allowed."

"Thank you." She barely restrained a shout of victory.

The wise elder aimed a piercing look at Ridge. "You wear the face of a white eyes scout."

Suddenly frightened for Ridge's safety, Emma opened her mouth to speak, but Ridge shook his head curtly and she swallowed her words.

"I am no longer a scout for the white eyes," he said to the leader.

Akecheta scrutinized him silently and Ridge held his gaze. Then the chief set the pipe down and nodded. Their meeting was over.

Emma and Ridge rose quietly and slipped out of the lodge. Dusky shadows had fallen while they'd been in the tipi.

"How long, Emma?" Ridge asked.

She pretended not to hear him and continued walking, intent on finding Chayton.

Ridge grasped her wrist. "You made a promise, and I aim to hold you to it."

She jerked out of his grip. "Don't worry, Ridge, you'll get your two hundred dollars."

"I'm not worried about getting it; it's the when I'm thinking of."

"You gave me one week."

Ridge's jaw muscle jumped and his eyes narrowed. "One week. Unless Akecheta tells us to leave sooner."

"If you'll excuse me, I'm going to see my son."

She wove her way between cooking fires and tipis, following the sound of children's laughter. She'd prayed for this day for so long, it was difficult to believe it had arrived.

Now came the second part of her plan—keeping Chayton with her.

RIDGE sat outside, close to the lodge he and Emma had been offered, blending into the deep shadows of the night. He listened to the rhythmic cadence of the drums and the rise and fall of singing voices; he observed the swirling bodies as the Indians—both men and women—danced around the camp. Their skin reflected the firelight, making them appear like night creatures, dipping in and out of the shadows.

He raised a crude cup to his lips and swallowed some of the bittersweet drink. He knew it would make him muddle-headed if he drank too much, so he only sipped small amounts. Being in the Lakota camp he had to remain alert even though the chief had given them his consent to visit.

Ridge patted his belly, which had been more than satisfied. Besides the food he'd eaten in the chief's lodge, he'd also partaken of the fresh venison, which the successful hunters had brought back. Emma had pointed out Fast Elk, her adopted father, a husky man with strands of gray in his long black hair and a stoic face that revealed little. His gaze was direct and although he was wary of Ridge, he didn't appear hostile . . . which was more than he could say for the majority of the young bucks.

Fourteen years ago Ridge had come and gone among the Sioux, counting many of them friends and he'd not worried about his safety. But times had changed.

He leaned back against the stretched buffalo hide wall, but his wariness didn't fade. He and Emma were far too vulnerable in this village, although Emma had some protection from her adopted parents. He hoped she would remain safe.

She sat with her son between Talutah and another woman beside a nearby lodge. The three women were talking and smiling, no doubt trading gossip just like all females, no matter the color of their skin. Emma was wearing a buckskin dress with a hide tossed over her shoulders for extra warmth, and moccasins that fit better than the pair he'd loaned her. Her golden-brown hair was braided into two plaits and if not for the color, and her lighter skin, she could've passed for a Lakota squaw.

Emma turned her head and caught his eye. Heat shot through Ridge's blood at her raw beauty and the memory of what lay beneath the soft deerhide dress. She said something to Talutah then rose gracefully and guided her sleepy son toward Ridge. She sank down beside him, her legs folded to the side beneath her. Chayton immediately curled up with his head on her thighs.

Ridge took the time to study the boy whose droopy eyes had closed the moment he laid down. After leaving Akecheta's lodge, Ridge had checked on their horses, and then strolled around the camp. He hadn't had a chance to really look at Emma's son until now.

"He's a handsome boy, Emma," Ridge said quietly.

"His father was tall and handsome," she said proudly.

Her smile faded. "There were many who thought Enapay should have married one of the Lakota maidens, but he chose me. He was a stubborn man." She paused, her gaze softening. "You remind me of him. He never spoke much either, but he was brave and honorable."

Ridge glanced away, uncomfortable with both the praise and being compared to her husband. "Were you forced to marry him?"

Her eyes widened. "Of course not." Her sight turned inward. "He would play his flute for me in the evenings, then drape a buffalo skin over us." She smiled self-consciously. "It was so different from what I'd grown up with. Mother would've had a fit if I sat outside in the dark with a young man without a chaperone." She laughed, the sound like bells tinkling in the breeze. "Enapay seemed so shy at first and I wasn't certain what I was supposed to do, but together we figured it out."

Ridge remembered how open she'd been during their lovemaking. She'd obviously learned a lot with her husband. "Did you love him?" The question slipped out before he could bridle it.

Emma gazed down at her son and brushed a dark lock from his smooth brow. "He provided well for Chayton and me." She took a deep breath and her troubled eyes met Ridge's. "I remember the first time he came back from a raid carrying a bloody scalp. I thought I was going to be sick. Talutah scolded me, told me that I would embarrass my husband if I didn't celebrate his victory with him. I joined in, but I hated every time he came back with one of his prizes. And then there were the times when he would return with a book or two for me. I tried not to think about how he'd gotten them or who they'd belonged to, but it was getting harder and harder to ignore the killing.

"Enapay was respected and admired in the tribe, and I was proud he was my husband. But love?" She shook her head sadly. "No, I don't think I loved him like a wife should love her husband. He deserved better."

Ridge wrapped his arm around her shoulders, pleased

by her confession yet knowing how much it hurt to admit her shortcoming. Relishing the warmth of her against his side, he said quietly, "But you cared for him and gave him a son. He had more than a lot of men ever get out of life."

"Is that what you're looking for? A woman who'll care for you and give you children?" She seemed to peer straight into his soul.

"I'm looking for a woman who'll work with me to raise our children and build something that'll last," Ridge corrected.

"But what about love?"

He gazed down into her shadowed face, noting the fire reflected in her eyes and her full, glistening lips. "I don't remember much about my real pa, but I do recall how he used to tease Ma and how she used to giggle like a young girl. Then he'd hug and kiss her, and they'd talk in low voices. I didn't understand back then, but I figured out later, a few years after Pa died, that was love. My friend Colt loved his wife, too, but she was killed. Damn near drove him over the edge." He took a deep breath. "I don't ever want to go through the pain they did when they lost their loved ones."

Emma's brow furrowed and Ridge resisted the urge to brush his thumb across the wrinkles.

"But doesn't the joy of loving outweigh the sadness of losing that love?" she asked.

Ridge rested his palm on the boy's head, surprised by his hair's softness, and then gazed at the woman deliberately. "You tell me, Emma."

She looked down at Chayton and her heart did a little roll at the sight of Ridge's large but gentle hand resting atop her son's crown. She forced herself to consider his question. "I wouldn't trade anything for having borne him," she replied firmly. "And loving him."

Emma couldn't see Ridge's eyes, but she suspected he was startled by her vehemence. Chayton was her heart and soul, and during those times she despaired of finding him alive, she wasn't certain she'd survive the torment. But now, with her precious son in her arms, she recognized the depth of her love for him. She took a shaky breath. "I think the higher the reward, the higher the risk. It's like a poker game. The more money that's in the pot, the higher the stakes of winning or losing."

After a moment, he lifted his head. "So how did you learn to play poker?"

She smiled. "How else? From a book."

Ridge laughed, and the rare sound filled Emma with both longing and pleasure.

"You have a beautiful laugh," she said.

His laughter faded, replaced by a man's hunger for a woman. He stroked Emma's cheek with a featherlight touch and shivers coursed through her body to land in a hot pool in her belly. It would be so easy to surrender to passion again, but their talk of love reminded Emma of more important matters, like caring for her son. If she got with child, it would make planning for the future even more difficult. She only hoped she didn't already bear the result of her reckless behavior in the cabin.

Ridge drew back, frowning. "What is it?"

He must've sensed her sudden anxiety.

"I should be getting Chayton settled for the night," she said, hoping he didn't notice the huskiness in her voice.

"I'll carry him," Ridge offered.

Unable to resist, Emma nodded and allowed Ridge to lift him into his arms. He rose carefully with Chayton sleeping openmouthed against his shoulder. Holding Chayton with one arm under his backside, Ridge offered his other hand to Emma to help her to her feet. She released him and opened the flap of their tipi, allowing him with his precious burden to enter first. Emma let the flap fall behind her, muting the drums and chants of the celebration.

She remembered nights like this vividly, except it was Enapay, not Ridge who accompanied her into the lodge. And after Chayton was asleep, Enapay would take Emma, usually gently, but sometimes fiercely, although he was always careful not to hurt her.

But tonight, Emma would sleep with her son, and Ridge would have a separate skin. She couldn't afford to let her body's demands dictate her choices anymore.

"Lay him down over there," Emma said, pointing to a pile of buffalo hides on the far side of the fire pit.

Ridge gently laid the boy down, and remained squatting beside him. With one callused finger, he traced Chayton's cheek. "He looks like you," he whispered.

Despite herself, Emma knelt beside Ridge and gazed down into the beloved boy's round face. "I always thought he looked like Enapay."

"He's got your stubborn chin and cute button nose," Ridge said.

Emma's throat felt thick and she rested her hand on Ridge's forearm, feeling the muscle cord beneath her fingers. He made her feel like a young girl again, giddy and awkward, yet with a woman's knowledge of what could be if she allowed it.

"Emma," Ridge said, his warm breath fanning across her cheek. "We should get some rest, too."

She nodded jerkily and withdrew her hand from his sleeve. "It's been a long day," she managed to say. "I'll sleep with Chayton."

"Good idea."

He crawled over to the other pile of buffalo hides, pulled off his moccasins, and removed his coat. He slid between the thick skins and turned his head toward the tipi wall.

Emma's palms moistened, urging her to glide down beside Ridge's hard body and join with him. They would both enjoy pleasuring the other, and even just after one night together, Emma found she missed sleeping with him spooned behind her with an arm draped around her waist.

She sighed and tugged off her moccasins, then lay beside her son. For the first time in five months, she could sleep knowing Chayton was alive and well.

* * *

RIDGE awoke, instantly alert, but heard nothing but the wind whispering through the budding trees and low snores emanating from nearby lodges. It took him a moment to figure out it was the absence of sound—the drums and chanting—that had awakened him.

The fire in their tipi had burned down and a chill seeped in. Ridge took a deep breath, preparing himself for the cold air, and threw back the heavy hides. He added some wood from the small pile beside the pit and watched a tiny flame flicker to life, only to die and struggle to return. He leaned down and blew gently across the embers, which flared and the added wood burst into flame. This time it remained alive, and Ridge held his cool hands above the growing fire.

A movement from the other bed caught his attention and he spotted Chayton crawling out from between the buffalo hides.

Ridge intercepted the boy before he could slip out of the tipi, and lifted him into his arms. "Where're you going, little fella?"

Chayton pointed down at himself.

Ridge grinned wryly. "I'll go with you, pard," he said quietly, not wanting to wake Emma.

The boy bounced in his arms. *"Wana."*

"Okay, now." Ridge swiftly carried Chayton outside and set him on his feet. The boy lifted his tunic out of the way and aimed toward a bush. While he relieved himself, Ridge shrugged and did the same.

Ridge closed his trousers and adjusted Chayton's tunic, in the pre-dawn's gloom. Another hour or two and the Lakota would be rising.

"Chayton," came Emma's fearful call.

"C'mon, cub, we'd best get back inside before your mama has a fit," Ridge said.

Chayton only yawned and knuckled his sleep-filled eyes.

Ridge took the boy's hand and led him back into the lodge, where Emma was readying to leave, her expression frantic. She gasped and dropped to her knees in front of

Chayton, hugging him close and kissing him.

"You frightened me, Chayton. I didn't know where you were," Emma said hoarsely.

"He had to go outside so I went with him," Ridge explained. "I thought you were asleep."

With her arms still around the boy, she gazed up at him. Fear filled her eyes. "I woke up and he was gone. I thought—" Her voice cracked.

"It's all right, Emma," Ridge reassured her awkwardly, not liking the haunted expression in her eyes. "Chayton's just fine."

She bowed her head, revealing the pale skin at the back of her slender neck. Ridge remembered how sweet her soft skin had tasted there, and her breathy moans of pleasure as she'd begged for more. He dug his fingernails into his palms to keep from reaching for her, to offer her comfort, and anything else she might need. Or want.

"After I was brought back to my parents' ranch, I had nightmares. I couldn't save him no matter how hard I tried." Emma's voice was muffled by Chayton's shoulder. The boy protested her snug grip and she immediately loosened her hold. She drew a hand across her eyes and Ridge could see the effort it took to smile at her son. "Sleep," she said in Lakota to her son.

As Emma resettled Chayton and herself in their bed, Ridge slid back between his own furs and laid on his side, facing them. She sang quietly to her son, and Ridge closed his eyes to listen to her achingly sweet voice. Just as with reading, Emma's singing was easy on his ears and made him recall the only time in his life when he'd felt loved and protected.

Once Chayton's breathing evened out, Emma's song faded away. A hollow yearning filled Ridge, along with bittersweet memories and wishes that were best left locked away.

"I had one of his moccasins in my pocket when the army took me from the village."

Emma's confiding voice startled Ridge out of his musings. He opened his eyes and focused on the dim oval of her face.

"I managed to keep it hidden from my parents," she continued. "But every night when I'd go to bed I'd take it out of its hiding place and hold it against my chest, imagining I was holding my son. It kept me from going crazy."

Merely thinking of Emma's anguish made Ridge's gut ache. He could picture her in her room late at night, the tiny piece of hide clutched to her breast.

"Why didn't you tell your family about him?"

She laughed softly but bitterly. "What do *you* think my father would've said if I had told him?"

Ridge could only imagine, and what he did imagine wasn't fit for a lady's ears.

"I'm fearful about taking Chayton back there," she confessed.

Ridge levered himself up on an elbow. "You're planning on taking him back to your father's ranch?"

"Of course. He's my son."

"He's Lakota."

"He's as much white as he is Lakota."

As much as Ridge understood her dilemma, he also knew how she and her child would be shunned. He had personally seen how white women with half-Indian children were treated. "Have you thought this through, Emma? I mean, folks ain't going to take to him."

"I'll protect him," Emma said and Ridge could almost see her chin jut out stubbornly.

And who'll protect you?

"What about school? No one's going to let a half-breed attend school." Ridge deliberately used the slur others would use as a dirty word.

"I'll teach him myself." He could feel the burn of Emma's glare across the lodge floor. "Why are you saying these things? Once I found my son, did you think I would just abandon him again?"

"He's happy here."

"He's my son! Where I go, he goes." Emma rolled over, turning away from Ridge, and effectively ending their conversation.

Ridge lowered himself back to his bed. Emma was serious about raising Chayton in a world that had little compassion for someone like him. Couldn't she see how much better off he was here with people who loved and cared for him?

Ridge was intimately familiar with how hurtful other children could be to someone who was "different." He wouldn't wish that kind of childhood on anyone, especially an innocent boy like Chayton.

Closing his eyes, Ridge tried to sleep, but found slumber elusive. His eyes flew open as another thought struck—would the People even allow one of their own to be taken away? Even by the boy's own mother? The Lakota treated their children as children of the tribe, and they belonged to everyone, not just the parents who brought them into the world. Children were raised together and women looked after all of them, regardless of blood relationship. Mothers allowed other babies in addition to their own to suckle from their breasts.

Ridge gnashed his teeth. If he'd known Emma's real motive for finding her band, he would never have allowed her to bribe him with one hundred dollars. Chayton was better off here than he would be in a world that would treat him no better—probably even worse—than a stray dog.

TWELVE

EMMA straightened from her task of scraping an antelope hide and stretched her back, hearing a collection of pops along her spine. She'd forgotten how toilsome the day-to-day drudgery could be, but she was determined not to be a burden.

When Fast Elk had handed Emma over to Talutah all those years ago, she had vowed to carry her own weight in spite of being frightened and homesick. The tall, grave Indian had saved Emma's life and she owed him for that. However, as she gained more and more knowledge of the language and their ways, she realized she wasn't a slave, but an adopted daughter. And dutiful daughters were expected to help their mothers with everyday tasks.

However, after spending months away from this life, she ached from her exertions, but being able to look up and see Chayton playing with the other children was more than worth the labor. He and a handful of boys and girls had sticks they used to hit rocks back and forth. Soon, the boys would begin the first stage of their training. Chayton and the others would learn how to trail game, starting with squirrels and rabbits, then they'd begin to practice with

their bows to bring down those same small animals they
tracked, as well as birds and rodents. By wrestling with his
playmates, Chayton would learn how to defend himself
and how to defeat an enemy in hand-to-hand combat. All
of his fighting skills would be learned under the guise of
games, and in a dozen years or less, Chayton would join
the ranks of the warriors for his first raid.

Emma used the back of her hand to push aside strands
of sweat-dampened hair that stuck to her brow. She would
take Chayton away before he even began his training; her
son would not die as young as his father had.

"You have become soft like a *wasicu,*" Talutah teased.

Emma smiled at her adopted mother who was chopping
tubers into the venison stew that would simmer above the
fire pit all day. "Yes. It has been a long time since I've prepared a hide."

Talutah knelt beside her to help. "Your world is different than ours."

When Emma understood enough of the Lakota language to follow a conversation, she'd been intrigued and a
little shocked by their beliefs. At the time, she'd been too
shy and wary to speak of her own world. Now, however, it
saddened her to realize how far apart their cultures were.
There seemed to be no middle ground and she was fearful
the Indians would lose their way of life, which relied heavily upon open range and wild game, especially buffalo.

Emma sighed and continued her backbreaking work.
Shimmering Water, whom Emma had known before,
joined her after Talutah left. Emma described her return to
her parents and subsequent escape to find Chayton.

Then their talk turned to gossip, both serious and amusing, and the work didn't seem quite as difficult.

One time Emma glanced up and saw Ridge playing a
game of dice with three men, including Fast Elk. She
couldn't help but notice with a note of pride, that Ridge
had the most sticks piled in front of him. He caught her eye
and winked, and her cheeks bloomed with heat. Her reaction didn't go unnoticed by the other woman.

"He is handsome for a *wasicu*," Shimmering Water commented, elbowing Emma. "I would take him to my skins if my husband asked it of me." She batted her eyes in Ridge's direction.

It wasn't uncommon for a husband to share his wife with a visitor if he wanted to impress him or make him feel welcome. Emma had never been comfortable with that practice and fortunately, Enapay had never asked it of her. She wondered, however, what her reaction would've been if he had. She suspected Enapay wouldn't have liked her response.

She glanced at her friend, who had smooth skin with almond-shaped brown eyes and glossy black hair. Would Ridge accept her company if given a chance? What man wouldn't?

The thought of him lying with Shimmering Water stabbed her heart. She didn't want to imagine him with any other woman, bestowing those same gentle touches as he had given to her with his lips and hands. She didn't want another woman to feel him enter her body as she had rejoiced in feeling him deep within her. She had no right to be possessive, but couldn't deny the jealousy that made her fists clench and her head pound.

Shimmering Water sighed. "His mouth is very nice and I have never seen eyes such as his—the color of a night sky." She ducked her head closer to Emma. "He would look very good in only a breechclout, would he not?"

Emma's gaze traveled to Ridge's backside and pictured him in what Shimmering Water described. She mentally shook herself and returned her attention to her task, refusing to be drawn in. The fact was she didn't want to share Ridge with anyone.

The sun was high when the children and men drifted toward the kettles over the fire pits. Women returned to their tipis to eat stew or soup. Chayton dashed over to Emma's fire and the stew Talutah had made that morning. Emma could almost hear her son's stomach growling. Smiling, she filled a bowl for him and then one for herself. She broke off chunks of flat bread Talutah had made earlier and left on a stone close to the fire. Sitting beside her son, she asked him about his morning as they ate.

When Ridge joined them, Emma was refilling Chayton's bowl. She readied one for Ridge and handed it to him.

"Thank you." He slipped his hat off his head to hang down his back by the drawstring, and sat across the fire from them.

"You're welcome," Emma said, glad he'd come to their fire instead of going to someone else's, like Shimmering Water's. "You seem to have made yourself at home."

He shrugged and swallowed before answering, "In some ways, the Lakota haven't changed at all. They play the same games and brag about victories. But in other ways, they've changed a lot. There's more distrust, and there's more talk of war against the whites."

Emma nodded, having noticed the same changes herself just between the time she lived with them and now. It was sad and frightening, as well as inescapable.

The sun appeared from behind a cloud and caught Ridge's long thick hair, exposing strands of reddish-gold among the maple-brown. Emma tried to imagine him in short hair, like her father's, but couldn't. Before living with the Lakota, she'd daydreamed about beaux with trimmed mustaches and wearing suits and opera hats. Now when she allowed herself to woolgather, she thought of Ridge Madoc with his unfashionably long hair, moccasins, wool trousers, suspenders, buckskin jacket, and slouch hat. Ridge, with his midnight blue eyes, that when turned in her direction, could make her knees feel like honey.

Chayton's empty bowl slipped from his hands, and Emma smiled fondly at his drooped head and closed eyes.

"All that running around tuckered him out," Ridge said quietly. "I'll carry him inside if you'd like."

"Yes, please," Emma replied.

Ridge scooped the child into his arms and ducked into the opening of the tipi. Emma followed but stayed by the entrance with crossed arms as she watched Ridge settle the boy on a pile of skins. He tucked a flung-out thin arm under a hide, then adjusted the blanket under Chayton's chin and smoothed his hand across the boy's hair. Emma wasn't surprised by the man's tenderness—he'd never been anything but gentle with her. Except for the time he'd tied her up, but she didn't blame him for that.

He rose gracefully and Emma backed out of the lodge.

"Most of the children will sleep for an hour or two, then they'll be back at it," Emma commented.

Ridge didn't reply but picked up the bowls they'd used and hunkered down beside a pail of water sitting in front of the tipi. He ducked the dirty dishes into the water to wash them.

"I should do that," Emma said.

He grinned mischievously, making him appear not much older than Chayton. "Worried your friends'll scold you for making your man do a woman's chore?"

Her face warmed. "You're not my man," she responded tartly.

"No, but everyone sees us that way."

His gaze roamed across her, and her body responded as if he'd touched her intimately.

"Does that bother you?" he asked huskily.

"Does it bother *you?*"

"Why should it? You're a beautiful woman, Winona."

His drawl made her Indian name sounded oddly lyrical and Emma's heart tripped in her breast. Here, in the middle of a Lakota village, the white world with all its stuffy rules and harsh prejudices seemed a million miles away. It would be so easy for Emma to ask Ridge to share her furs, but they had to someday return to their own world. They'd already gone beyond civilized boundaries in the cabin; she didn't dare risk it again.

"Thank you," she said stiffly. "But you and I both know it's not that way." She turned away to needlessly stir the remains of the stew. "If you're offered a woman, don't turn her down on account of me."

Strong fingers gripped her shoulders, startling her. She hadn't even heard him approach.

He turned her around to face him. "I don't want any woman but you."

Emma gasped at the heat in his words and the need in his flashing eyes. She stared at his lips, his mouth, and fought the hunger in her own body. One touch, one look— that was all it took for Ridge to set her on fire. She hadn't bargained on her attraction growing after they'd yielded to their passion.

She trembled as she fought the overriding desire, but knew it would be a losing battle if Ridge didn't release her. It would be so easy to remain in his arms and be led into their lodge and join their bodies upon the soft skins. But Emma was under no illusions—if they were back in Sunset, Ridge wouldn't be treating her this way.

"Are you willing to marry me?" she asked, amazed that her voice remained steady.

Ridge released her as if she were scorching hot and growled a curse. "I ain't ready to get hitched."

At least not to me, she added silently with a stab of remorse.

"Then we'll not be lying together again either," she stated.

"Fine," he said curtly. He tugged his hat onto his head. "Fast Elk invited me to race this afternoon. I'd best go ready Paint."

Ridge's stride was fluid, but Emma noticed his clenched jaw and knew she'd made him angry.

She sagged. She'd never force him to marry her for what they'd done or what they might've done again if he had pressed her. But she wasn't strong enough to deny him, and she hated herself for that weakness. If he'd kissed her, she would've been lost, so she'd gambled on his honor. She'd expected his rejection, but it still hurt.

Terribly.

IN the Lakota culture, men were the hunters and warriors, and every activity they engaged in was geared toward being better hunters and better warriors. Emma had seen the men race their ponies countless times in the past and she'd long since lost her fascination with their riding skills. However, knowing Ridge was to participate, Emma made certain she faced the direction of the meadow where the race would take place.

"Is your man good?" Talutah asked.

Emma glanced at the woman sitting beside her who was sewing quills on a shirt for Fast Elk. "Yes," she replied. Although not as certain as she sounded, she knew Ridge possessed a natural grace atop a horse, and suspected he could easily match the other warriors' prowess.

Emma tried to keep her attention on her own sewing task, but her gaze kept shifting to the warriors and horses at the far end of the field. Ponies stamped and snorted as the men lined up in a single row. A boy whooped the signal to start. Horses and men exploded in a blur of motion.

Hoofbeats pounded the hard-packed earth and Emma picked out Ridge near the far end of the group. Her hands fisted and she leaned forward, silently urging him on.

Paint lengthened his stride and began to gain ground, moving forward to overtake the middle of the pack, then passing them. Only four riders were ahead of Ridge, and Paint ate up the ground between them. Finally, there was only one warrior who outdistanced them. Emma shaded her eyes to pick out the brave's features.

Hotah!

Talutah had told her he'd been on a scouting trip, but it appeared he had returned.

"Go Ridge," she murmured, her gaze riveted to the unfolding drama of racing horseflesh and skilled horsemen.

Clods of new grass were thrown back by sharp hooves as Ridge and Hotah leaned low over their horses' manes.

Paint drew neck and neck with Hotah's chestnut horse. Emma could make out flecks of spittle on both animals' muzzles and the faint tremble of the earth from the thundering gait. Just as they crossed the finish line, Ridge and Paint surged ahead to win by less than a head.

Emma clapped and smiled so widely her mouth hurt, but it couldn't lessen her exhilaration at Ridge's victory over Hotah.

A motion caught her eye and she turned to see Chayton standing on a tall boulder some two hundred feet away, jumping up and down as he, too, cheered Ridge's win. Her elation disappeared, replaced by dread at her son's precarious position. If he slipped, the fall could injure him badly, or even kill him. She rose, intent on getting him off the rock before he lost his balance.

Suddenly, Chayton's arms flailed wildly and he stumbled back to disappear behind the boulder. His shrill cry chilled Emma to the bone.

Talutah caught Emma's wrist. "You must allow him to learn on his own," the older woman said sternly. "Do not shame him in front of the others."

Emma's mouth gaped. "He's not even four summers old." She tugged free of the older woman's strong grasp. "How can such a young one be shamed?"

Talutah shook her head in disapproval. "You have changed, Winona. You think more like a *wasicu* than one of the People."

"If being one of the People means I cannot go to my son when he is hurt, then maybe it is better to be a *wasicu*," she said angrily, fear sharpening her words.

"Go then," Talutah said flatly. Her gaze dropped back down to her sewing.

Torn between apologizing to her adopted mother and her need to check on her son, Emma wavered, but her maternal instincts overrode her momentary indecision.

Running, she followed the trail the children had taken

earlier which led to the river's edge. She spotted the group of youngsters with Ridge already in their midst.

"How is—" Emma began, but broke off when she caught a clear view of her son sitting on a rock. He had blood running down the side of his face. She sank to her knees in front of Chayton, her heart jumping into her throat.

"It looks worse than it is," Ridge reassured. "He's a mite dazed, but he wasn't knocked out, and the bleeding's slowed. His head's gonna hurt some, though. And I think his ankle's twisted, but nothing looks broken."

Ridge untied the dark blue bandanna from around his neck and rose to dip it into the edge of the river. When he returned, he handed it to Emma, and spoke to the children. "Chayton will be fine. Go."

The dark-eyed girls ushered their charges away and in a few moments, the children were once again playing and laughing.

"This is one of the reasons I can't leave him here," Emma said hoarsely to Ridge, although her attention was riveted on her task as she wiped the blood from her son's face.

"Don't mollycoddle him. It's not their way."

Emma snapped her gaze to Ridge, her disagreement with Talutah adding fuel to her frustration. "This is *my* way!"

"Look at him, Emma," Ridge ordered. "Go on. Look! He's Lakota."

Reluctantly, Emma scrutinized her son, from his pale complexion to his struggle to remain unmoved by his injuries. There were two tear tracks down his dusky cheeks, but no more were being shed. He reminded Emma too much of Enapay after he'd been injured during a raid—the same withdrawn expression and impassive eyes.

She pressed her lips together and handed Ridge back the bloodied bandanna. "Could you rinse this for me?"

Emma had less than a minute alone with her troubling thoughts before Ridge returned. She continued to wipe away the blood, more than a little shocked that the boy hadn't spoken since she began.

"Does it hurt?" she asked him.

He finally focused on her. "No. I am not a baby."

"I know, Chayton, but I am your mother and I worry about you."

He stared at her, his eyes the same color Emma saw when she looked in a mirror. *"Ina?"*

She nodded solemnly. "Yes. I am your *ina*." She hadn't tried to explain to him yesterday, hoping that he might remember on his own. "I had to go away for a little while, but I'm back now."

Chayton studied her, almost frightening Emma by his intensity, which was far too profound for a boy his age. "You will stay?"

"I don't know." Emma brushed the gash on his head with the cloth and involuntary tears slid down Chayton's face, his stoic expression giving way to a little boy's pain. He whimpered and Emma drew him into her arms. She was surprised and pleased when his arms wound around her neck.

"If I go, I want to take you with me," she whispered in his ear.

Chayton raised his head. "Where?"

"To see your white grandfather and grandmother."

The boy grasped Emma's hand and stared down at their intertwined fingers. *"Wasicu?"*

She nodded, her throat full.

"Lakota," Chayton exclaimed fiercely, jabbing a thumb into his chest.

"Yes, you are. But you have as much *wasicu* blood as Lakota blood."

The boy raised his gaze to Ridge, as if asking him to deny her words.

Ridge nodded slowly. "Your ma's right, Chayton."

The boy's brow furrowed and for the first time, Emma considered Chayton's feelings about his mixed heritage and leaving his home. There was no doubt he'd heard stories about the whites and their treatment of the Indians, but how much did he understand? The warriors would've embellished atrocities the *wasicu* committed, while cele-brating their own victories. Emma's sympathies lay with her adopted family, but she wasn't blind to their fierce tendencies.

"He'll be all right, Emma," Ridge reassured. "It looks like the bleeding's stopped."

Emma eased Chayton back to the rock and raised her-self on her knees to tie the cloth around his head. "There. Let's go back to our lodge and you can lie down."

Chayton brushed the back of his hand over his moist cheeks and nodded. Before Emma could help him up, Ridge hoisted him into his arms.

"His ankle's already swelling. When we get back, you need to put a cold cloth around it," he said quietly. "Could you lead Paint back?"

Emma nodded and hurried to gather the horse where he stood with his head lowered. Dark patches on the horse's coat showed where he'd sweat, and his skin rippled occa-sionally from quivering muscles.

When Emma returned with Paint, she was gratified to see Chayton slumped in Ridge's arms, with his head on the man's shoulder. Leading Paint, she walked behind them on the narrow trail back to the camp, trying not to notice how her son's head rested against Ridge's cheek, or how care-fully he walked so he wouldn't jar Chayton.

Ridge abruptly halted and Emma nearly ran into his back. She raised up on her tiptoes to see over his shoul-der. A broad, flat-nosed warrior stood in the middle of the path. Her breath caught in her throat and she had the overpowering urge to grab Chayton and run in the oppo-site direction.

The cruel eyes rested on Ridge a moment and Emma could see he was furious to have lost the horse race to a white man. Hotah's lips thinned and his gaze moved across Chayton to Emma. He reached for Chayton, but Ridge shifted away so the warrior couldn't touch him. Hotah snarled and his shoulders stiffened as his hands fisted at his sides.

Emma stepped forward. "He will carry Chayton. Let us pass," she said firmly, hoping Hotah would listen to a mere squaw.

The warrior remained long enough to prove he could, then stepped to the side. Ridge passed first and Emma retrieved Paint and followed after him.

When they arrived at their lodge, Emma left Paint ground-tied outside the tipi. She removed Chayton's moccasin, nearly crying when the boy whimpered again. She was aware of Ridge building up the fire.

"I need to heat some water," she said quietly.

Ridge nodded and ducked out to retrieve some.

Emma wrapped her son's swollen ankle with a rabbit skin. She brushed her fingers across his cheek. "How are you feeling?"

"Head hurts," he whispered.

Emma swallowed back her tears. "I'll make something that will help."

Chayton bit his lower lip and nodded slightly.

Ridge returned with the water and set the kettle above the fire. He knelt in front of Chayton. "You're a brave warrior," Ridge said to the boy in Lakota.

Emma smiled gratefully at the man and retrieved her saddlebags to pull out her collection of herbs. As she waited for the water to warm, she listened to Ridge speak softly to Chayton.

"I'll bet you've never heard the story of the boy and the wolf, have you?" Ridge asked Chayton.

He shook his head, his amber eyes wide.

Ridge settled into a cross-legged position in front of the boy. "Many winters ago there was a boy who was called Dakota. Even though Dakota was only six summers, he took his bow and arrow and went hunting because his people were starving. He came upon a beautiful gray wolf who growled and snarled and showed his big sharp teeth. Dakota was very frightened, but he was also very brave like you. He did not run but spoke to the wolf. 'Why are you so mean?'

"That wolf stared at him for a long time, trying to decide if he should eat the foolish little boy. But he respected Dakota's courage, so he replied, 'I have a spine in my paw and I cannot get it out.'"

Emma leaned forward as Ridge's low, somewhat husky voice, drew her into the story.

"Dakota, who also had a kind heart, thought for a minute. 'I will help you if you promise not to hurt me.' The wolf nodded and laid down on the ground. Dakota carefully examined the wolf's paw. He found the sharp spine and gently removed it. The wolf was so happy he promised Dakota he would stay with him and protect him always.

"Then the wolf helped Dakota bring down deer and rabbits so Dakota's people wouldn't starve, but the people didn't understand how a little boy and a wolf could be friends. So they threw rocks at the wolf and chased him away. Angry and heartbroken, Dakota went after his new friend and never returned to his village. It is said that Dakota and his gray wolf still run through the woods together and if a person is lucky enough to see them, they will be blessed with a good hunt."

"I want a wolf," Chayton said.

Ridge smiled. "Maybe someday."

Emma stirred some herbs into a cup of warm water and carried it to her son. "Drink."

Chayton took the cup between his small hands and drank over half of it. The boy's eyelids drifted shut and Ridge settled him in the bed. Chayton hadn't napped earlier so Emma was fairly certain his drowsiness was caused by lack of sleep, rather than the bump to his head.

"That was a beautiful story," Emma said softly to Ridge.

He ducked his head. "Ma used to tell me one about a lion and a little boy. I figured Chayton would like a wolf better."

Emma stared at the cup in her hands, knowing it was time to tell Ridge of her dreams. She struggled to find the right words. "Remember when I told you I dreamed of a mountain lion?"

Ridge nodded slowly. "It was our last night in the cabin." His gaze caressed her face, and then flickered down to her breasts and back to her eyes.

The familiar curl of desire unfurled in her belly and she gripped the cup tighter to keep from reaching for Ridge. "The night before I left my parents' ranch, I had a dream about a wolf cub and a mountain lion. The frightened cub was being toyed with by the lion. A full-grown wolf tried to save the cub, and the wolf and the lion fought."

"What happened?"

She shook her head, feeling the urgency rise again. "I don't know. I woke up." She took a deep breath. "I've had the dream more than once since then."

"You think it's some kind of vision?"

Emma met his skeptical gaze without flinching and nodded. "Yes. That's why I had to find Chayton."

"You think he's the cub?"

"Yes."

"But you found him and he's safe."

"For now. In my dream, the moon is always full."

Ridge frowned. "There's a full moon tomorrow night."

Emma's heart leapt into her throat. "I know."

The fire crackled and Chayton snuffled restlessly. Outside the lodge, men and women talked, and children laughed. An occasional bark or whinny added to the peaceful sounds.

"Why didn't you tell me this earlier?" Ridge asked.

She smiled without humor. "Would you have believed me?" His silence gave Emma her answer. "The medicine man said I had a dreaming gift. He used to help me figure out what my dreams meant." She tucked a wayward strand of hair behind her ear as she gathered her courage. "I'm afraid for him, Ridge. I can't let him out of my sight for the next few nights."

"I'll help you watch him."

"I thought you didn't believe me."

"I admit it's kinda hard to swallow, but I've seen a lot of strange things in my time, Emma. I guess this ain't all that different."

Ridge's warm understanding threatened to bring tears to Emma's eyes. It would be so easy to fall in love with Ridge Madoc. No other man—not even Enapay—had been so tender and thoughtful. Among the Lakota, Winona had been Enapay's wife and Chayton's mother. Winona was expected to do her duties with no complaints and be there when her husband or son needed her.

But what about Emma?

She wanted to be Chayton's mother, but Emma wanted more than Winona. She wanted her husband's respect, and she wanted to be involved in decisions affecting her. She wanted—no, needed—to be loved by the man she would share her life with. Winona had accepted less; Emma would not.

She laid her hand on Ridge's and squeezed it. "Thank you."

Ridge merely nodded and then rose. "I'd best take care of Paint. After that race, he needs a good rubdown."

Emma smiled. "By the way, congratulations."

Ridge studied her, his eyes hooded. "Are you glad I won, or glad I beat Hotah?"

"Both."

$\mathcal{T}$HIRTEEN

RIDGE felt the hostile gaze drill his back as he led Paint back to the rope corral. He wasn't surprised someone was watching him. Ever since he and Emma had arrived yesterday, their freedom around the camp had been an illusion. Emma might not see it, but Ridge did. At least one warrior was always guarding him. He didn't think it was the chief's doing, but the men in the village who didn't trust a *wasicu*.

He kept his pace unhurried as he used Paint's saddle blanket to rub the gelding's withers, back, and flanks. He knew he was a fast horse, but hadn't realized how swift until the race. A smile tugged at his lips. The braves had been impressed by the weak white man.

Ridge rested his arms across Paint's back and stared out across the village. Two weeks ago when he'd left Sunset to find Emma Hartwell, he hadn't suspected half of what he'd learned about her since then. Discovering Emma was a widow had been surprising, but even more shocking was her son.

Taking Chayton back to Sunset was only inviting more trouble. Her life would be hell and old man Hartwell would try to cover up Emma's sin as quickly as possible by ridding himself of her and her half breed son. He might even force Emma to give up Chayton and then send her off to live with some far-off relative, like he'd planned before Emma had run away.

Bitter bile rose in Ridge's throat as he imagined the proud woman being forced to bend to her father's will. Emma would break before doing so, but what kind of life would she have? Would she end up in one of the cribs in the part of Sunset that everybody deliberately overlooked, where desperate men went looking for even more desperate women?

Merely imagining Emma lying on a dirty mattress, allowing every kind of man to rut with her made him want to puke. But hadn't he used her? She'd asked him about marriage, but he couldn't offer that to any woman until he had a good start on his ranch.

Would he have asked Emma if he was ready to take a wife?

The near-silent approach of someone made Ridge stiffen and strain to hear who it was. He turned slowly, expecting Hotah, but was pleasantly surprised to see Fast Elk.

"*Hau,*" Ridge greeted.

"*Hau,*" Fast Elk replied, his expression somber. "You raced well."

Ridge inclined his head in acceptance. "My horse is strong and fast."

Fast Elk crossed his arms and stared off into the distance. Ridge waited patiently.

"When I found Winona, she was frightened but she did not give in to tears," Fast Elk began. "Our daughter died when she was fourteen summers. Because she was strong and brave, I chose Winona to become our daughter. She never shamed us, but I knew she missed her white home. After the soldiers came, we thought we would never see her again."

"She wished to return to find her son and see her family," Ridge said.

"We lost many of our people that night and there was

much wailing. Some blamed Winona for their coming."
Fast Elk took a deep breath and exhaled slowly. His dark
eyes overflowed with regrets. "She can no longer live with
us. The young warriors are angry. War will come and we
will have to fight, but we will not win."

Ridge wanted to offer him hope, but Fast Elk would recognize his words as a lie. "What of Winona's son?" he
asked instead.

"He is Lakota."

"Winona wishes to take him to her white home."

Fast Elk's eyes flashed. "No. He will learn the ways of a
warrior as his father did."

"But you said you will not win the war."

"It does not matter. To die honorably in battle is our way."

"She loves him."

"Then she must do what is best for him." Fast Elk
turned and strode away noiselessly.

But who was to say what was best for Chayton? Emma
wouldn't leave her son without a fight.

Ridge patted Paint's neck and headed back to his lodge.
Again, he could sense suspicious eyes on him and knew
someone, maybe even Fast Elk, was observing him.

He passed two young squaws who kept peeking at him
and giggling. He smiled and tipped his hat toward them,
which resulted in more laughter and more heated looks. If
Ridge was ten years younger, he might've fished for an invitation, but there was only one woman who tempted him now.

And she was the one woman he couldn't have.

RIDGE dropped the last armload of wood beside the
lodge and grinned as he listened to Emma give her son,
who'd awakened feeling better, strict orders to stay out of
trouble. From what Ridge could recall, that meant a challenge to see how much trouble the boy could get into without his ma finding out.

"Kids are tougher'n they look," Ridge commented as
Chayton ran off, his limp barely noticeable.

Emma made a face. "Especially that one."

Ridge chuckled and sat down by the fire. Emma bent her head over her task and one honey-brown braid fell across her shoulder and draped down the front of her deerskin tunic. He could see a hint of her bare knee between the top of her moccasins and the bottom of her dress.

"Are you wearing your knife?" Ridge asked.

Emma glanced up. "Yes." She turned her attention back to sewing beads upon a shirt.

Ridge picked up a stick and drew random letters and numbers in the dirt. "I got the impression you and Hotah have a history."

She wrestled with her bone needle, forcing it through a double layer of deerskin. "You're an observant man, Mr. Madoc."

"You're trying to change the subject, Winona." He tossed his stick on the small fire. "Don't you think you've kept enough secrets from me already?"

Her cheeks flushed. "Hotah never liked me. He would taunt me, call me names, when no one was around. I didn't tell anyone." She shrugged. "After I married Enapay, Hotah stopped bothering me, but I could tell he still didn't like me."

"Did he ever hurt you?" Ridge asked, rage simmering in his veins.

"No, but I never felt comfortable around him." She smoothed her hand across the soft deerhide she'd laid in her lap. "Talutah said Hotah wants to be Chayton's teacher."

"But Chayton's part white."

"I know." She shook her head, bewildered. "It doesn't make sense, unless it's his way of hurting me."

"Can't Fast Elk choose someone else?"

"He could, but there may not be anyone else." Emma squared her shoulders. "It doesn't matter. I'm taking Chayton with me when we leave."

Ridge didn't tell her that Fast Elk wouldn't allow it. Besides, the stubborn set of her jaw told him it would do no good to argue.

CAPTAIN Colt Rivers lowered himself to a log beside the campfire, carefully balancing the tin cup of hot coffee. He resisted the urge to stare into the flames and lose himself in their hypnotic flickering. Instead, he pressed his flat-brimmed cavalry hat back and gazed at the stars, picking out Orion, the Big Dipper, and the North Star.

Strange how some things never changed, like the stars, and the rising and setting of the sun. The day-to-day struggles, like birth and death, survival, and the gut-deep pain of losing a loved one didn't so much as make time blink from one moment to the next.

He took a deep breath of the night-fresh air, hoping to blunt the crushing ache in his chest. He'd been married for less than a year, but even after three years, he missed her. He'd gotten drunk for a week after it happened and nobody had dared approach him during that time but Ridge Madoc. He owed the man his life and his sanity.

So why was he following an order he knew his friend would hate? Because, Colt thought bitterly, he was in the army and had to obey his orders no matter how much they rankled him.

Sergeant Gabe Sanders strolled over to join him, easing his considerable frame down beside Colt. "Four guards are set up with changeover every two hours, sir."

Colt nodded at the man who was at least ten years older than himself, and who had experienced most everything a soldier could. "We're in Lakota Territory now."

"Yes, sir," Sanders said neutrally, not meeting Colt's gaze.

Colt sighed. "Spit it out, Gabe."

The sergeant held his big hands up to the fire. "Why the hell are we doing this? So what if a few Indians got away and came up here. Ain't nobody cared before."

Colt stared off into the darkness as he answered in a voice that bordered on sarcasm. "General Mason is coming to visit the fort and Colonel Nyes wants him to think he's got everything under control."

Gabe snorted. "Brown-nosin' son of a bitch."

Colt wasn't surprised by Gabe's contempt. There was no love lost between the seasoned sergeant and the ass-kissing colonel. Bound by military protocol, Colt had to keep his agreement with the sergeant's opinion to himself. "It doesn't change our orders. Bring 'em back, dead or alive."

"Dead, if Cullen's got any say."

Icy apprehension settled between Colt's shoulder blades, and he looked around, searching for the scout. "Cullen's acting too damned sure of himself, like he's got a secret. I have a feeling he and the colonel had a chat before we left."

"Nyes wants another Sand Creek," Gabe stated flatly.

"And I'm his scapegoat if things go south."

"Cullen can't do much by himself and if he starts shootin', I'll kill him myself."

Colt suppressed a smile, but couldn't hide it from his voice. "I'll pretend I didn't hear that, soldier."

"Pretend all you want, Cap'n. I ain't going to have the blood of womenfolk and young 'uns on my hands."

"Nobody will if I can help it."

Another soldier joined them, sitting across the fire on another log.

"Our illustrious scout is missing, sir," Lieutenant Preston Wylie announced softly, his Carolina drawl more apparent than usual.

"Dammit! Any idea *when* he disappeared?" Colt demanded in a low voice.

"His horse was corralled with the others at supper-time. An hour later and it was gone, sir."

"Maybe we're closer than we thought," Gabe commented, his gray eyes glinting silver.

"What can one man do by himself?" Preston asked.

"Not much," Colt replied. "But with a rattlesnake, you never can tell."

"I can try to pick up his trail," Gabe offered.

Colt thought for a moment, then shook his head. "You'll end up stumbling around in the dark and one of the guards might have an itchy trigger finger. No, we'll just let Cullen hang himself."

"If he does," Preston added quietly. "As much as I abhor the degenerate, he always seems to land on his feet. And if you confront him about his departure, he will probably tell you he was merely doing his job and reconnoitering the area."

Although he hated to admit it, Colt recognized the truth in Pres's fancy speech. For a moment, Colt idly wondered anew about the lieutenant's background. Pres never spoke about his past, but it was obvious he had come from a family who could afford an expensive education. It was also clear he was from the South, but had chosen to fight on the Union side.

"Pres is right," Colt said. "There's nothing we can do about him. Yet."

"What if he stumbles upon Ridge?" Pres asked.

"Ridge can take care of himself, son," Gabe reassured.

They were friends of Ridge, and knew of the animosity between him and Cullen. By now, Ridge should've found Emma Hartwell and returned the woman to her father. At least, Colt hoped so. He had no wish to run into Ridge. Although he was a good friend, Colt didn't agree with his friend's views on the Indians. Not that Colt would ever condone a massacre, but sometimes force was required to contain the savages.

Maybe if they'd killed a few more down in Texas, Colt's wife would still be alive.

EMMA awakened early the following morning to cramps in her lower belly. She restrained a groan and carefully extricated herself from the buffalo blankets so she wouldn't wake Chayton. Quietly, she crawled over to a pile of small animal skins and picked out two, as well as some rawhide laces. She stood and walked bent over at the waist to the closed flap.

"Everything all right, Emma?" Ridge asked in a low voice.

"Fine," she reassured quickly, her face warming with embarrassment.

Emma slipped out of the tipi, surprised to see Talutah already up and coaxing the cookfire back to life. She nodded toward her adopted mother and the older woman returned a smile. But Talutah's smile faded when she noticed the skins in Emma's hands.

Emma would've preferred that nobody learned of her condition. In a Lakota village, when a woman had her monthly, she had to stay in a lodge set apart from the rest of the tipis.

However, she wanted to stay near Chayton. How could she do as Lakota beliefs demanded when her son was in danger?

Her hands trembling, Emma merely ducked her head and hurried into the brush. At least her joining with Ridge hadn't resulted in a baby, and for that, she was grateful.

Talutah stood in Emma's path on the way back to her lodge.

"Gather what you will need and go," Talutah said softly.

Emma stiffened her spine. "I cannot. I must stay with Chayton."

"I will watch Chayton."

Emma's heart pounded with fear and she clenched her fists at her sides. "I dreamt of danger for him."

"He will be safe among the People."

She thought of Hotah and wasn't so certain. "Will he? I'm afraid."

Talutah patted her cheek. "Do not worry about that which you cannot control, Winona."

How many times had Talutah given her the same advice

over the years? But just as with all the other times, Emma doubted if she'd be able to heed it.

"Chayton will stay with Ridge, if he agrees," Emma said.

She ducked back into her tipi and found Ridge sitting by the small fire. Keeping her face averted, she gathered her sewing items and placed them in a hide pouch.

"I have to go away for a few days," she finally spoke to Ridge, although she didn't meet his gaze.

"Why?"

If a Lakota had asked her the question, she wouldn't have been so mortified. But Ridge was white, and they'd been raised in the same culture, in a society that didn't speak of such personal matters.

"I have to go to the women's lodge," she said rapidly.

"Oh."

Now she did turn to him and almost smiled at the deep flush on his face that she was certain matched her own. "I should be back in two or three days. Could you—"

"I'll take care of him, Emma," Ridge answered the anticipated question without hesitation.

"Thank you," she whispered past the lump in her throat. It would be impossible not to worry about Chayton, but with her son in Ridge's capable hands, she wouldn't fret nearly as much.

Ridge rose and approached her. When he cupped her jaw and his thumb brushed her cheek, Emma closed her eyes and leaned into his touch. Over the past two weeks, she'd come to trust this man more than any other. He was proud, steadfast, and stubborn, but wasn't afraid to be tender and vulnerable with her. She knew confessing his reading and writing problems had been more than difficult—it had required trust in her and she felt humbled by that trust.

"I'll miss you," Ridge said, his voice husky. Then he kissed her forehead. "You'd best go before you're accused of stealing the medicine man's power."

Emma's eyes widened slightly. He obviously understood as much about Lakota beliefs as she did. Although curious about his past, it was the tender press of his lips on her brow that stayed with her long after she entered the seclusion of the women's lodge.

THROUGHOUT the day Ridge kept his distance from Chayton and the other children, but always ensured he had a clear view of Emma's son. He didn't mind the task, and actually enjoyed the boy's antics. Even though he was half-white, and wasn't the biggest or the oldest, Chayton tended to be a leader among the young children. He excelled at the games they played and often won, but even if he didn't, he never grew short-tempered or angry.

Chayton resembled his mother, from his stubborn chin to his flashing amber eyes. Occasionally, Ridge would catch an expression or a mannerism that reminded him of Emma's, and some unexplainable emotion would tighten his chest.

He found himself debating whether he had the right to convince Emma to leave Chayton behind. How would he feel if Chayton were *his* son? Would anybody be able to convince him that his child was better off with somebody else?

After Chayton ate some of Talutah's stew at noon, Ridge guided him into Emma's lodge to take a short nap. Ridge sat cross-legged on his pile of buffalo skins, a knife and piece of wood in his hand as he carved and kept watch over the boy. He'd promised Emma he would protect him, and he had no intention of breaking that promise.

Chayton slept for an hour, and then was ready to rejoin his young friends in the warm spring day again. Before he could escape, Ridge removed the bandanna from the boy's forehead and examined the injury. The bump was red and angry-looking beneath the gash, but fortunately it looked like it had decreased in size. By the time Emma returned, the swelling should be nearly gone and only a faded bruise and scab remaining. Since the wound would heal better in the open air, Ridge didn't replace the cloth.

"I want you to be careful not to fall on your head again, cub," Ridge warned the boy in Lakota.

Chayton giggled. "I am not a bear or wolf."

Ridge tousled the boy's hair, which was the color and texture of Emma's. "But you are a cub, cub," he teased. Suddenly not looking forward to sitting around the rest of the afternoon, Ridge asked, "Would you like to see if we can track down a wolf or a bear?"

Chayton's eyes widened. "Maybe I will find a wolf like Dakota."

Ridge chuckled and led the boy toward the river. It would be the best place to find tracks and begin Chayton's education in identifying animal's paw prints. Ridge slowed his pace considerably so the small boy could keep up with him.

As they walked, Ridge would stop and show Chayton different plants, giving their names both in Lakota and English, and explain to him how they were used by the People. The boy took the lessons seriously, repeating Ridge's words in both languages and taking the time to study the plants' leaves and flowers.

They passed by Chayton's group of playmates and, although they called out to him to join them, Chayton refused. He told them his *leksi* was teaching him many new things. Although Chayton's voice was smug, there was also pride, which made Ridge wish he truly could be the boy's uncle.

By the river's edge, Ridge squatted down and was immediately joined by the boy, who copied his pose, down to the elbow on the knee and chin in his hand. Ridge focused on the animal track in the mud. "What does this look like, Chayton?"

The boy's lips puckered as he thought. "A dog?"

"Look closer."

He leaned down so his nose was only a scant few inches from the mud. "Not enough toes."

Ridge grinned. "That's right, cub. A dog has only four, this one has five. And there is some webbing, too. And look at the line in the mud behind it—that's where its tail dragged. If you trail it backward, you'll probably find something else, too." Ridge rose and slowly backed up until he found what he sought. He pointed to the small pile of droppings. "See the shiny things in it?"

Chayton gazed at the scat and nodded.

"Those are fish scales. This animal swims in the water and eats fish, but also comes out onto land."

The boy's eyes lit up. *"Pta."*

Ridge's smile broadened. "That's right, Chayton. *Pta*, which means 'otter' in the white man's language."

"Aa-ter," Chayton repeated.

"That's right. Otter. Shall we find more?"

They found numerous signs of spring—prints of mice, porcupines, beavers, and even a blue heron. Nearly a mile upriver from the village, Ridge spotted small hoof indentations in the dirt.

"Tahca," Chayton spoke up.

"Yes. *Tahca.* 'Deer.' "

"Deer," the boy repeated, then scrunched up his face. "Why must I learn the whites' language?"

"Because you carry *wasicu* blood."

Chayton thought about that for a moment, then Ridge could almost see him shrug. The youngster skipped after the trail the deer had left behind. Ridge followed, allowing the boy to find more signs on his own.

A horse's approach caused both Ridge and Chayton to pause as the horse and rider neared them. Ridge squared his stance and hooked his thumbs over his belt.

"Hotah," Ridge greeted with a nod.

The stocky warrior, wearing only a breechclout and moccasins, peered down at him. "You have wandered far from camp."

Ridge shrugged nonchalantly. "I didn't realize I couldn't leave. Me and Chayton here were just doing some tracking."

"I want to find a wolf like the one *Leksi* told me about,"

Chayton announced to Hotah, although his adoring gaze remained on Ridge.

Hotah's jaw clenched and the knuckles of his hand that held his reins whitened. He narrowed his eyes, but the anger shown clearly through the slits. "What does a *wasicu* know about tracking?"

"As much as he knows about horse racing." Ridge smiled darkly.

Hotah's face reddened with rage.

"What are you really doing here, Hotah?" Ridge asked, dispatching of his polite facade.

"It is time I begin to train Chayton." His lips curled into a sneer. "The way a true Lakota trains a warrior."

"Winona asked me to watch over Chayton. I gave her my word."

"Your word." He spat on the ground. "Your word is worth nothing."

Chayton shuffled backward and bumped into Ridge's legs.

Ridge grasped the boy's shoulders. "My word is my bond." He met and held Hotah's hostile glare without blinking. Finally, the warrior glanced at the boy.

"Come with me, Chayton," Hotah ordered.

The boy pressed more firmly against Ridge and shook his head.

"He doesn't want to, Hotah. We will return before the sun sets," Ridge said.

Hotah glared at him over his haughty nose. "One day you and I will fight, *wasicu,* and then we shall learn who has more power."

"Name the time and place and I'll be there."

"It will come," Hotah said, then reined his horse around and galloped away.

Ridge stared at his receding back, knowing he'd made an enemy. But Hotah wasn't the first, and Ridge was still breathing.

FOURTEEN

EMMA paced the tipi, ignoring the glares from the other two women also temporarily residing in it. They hadn't known Emma before, and she explained how she'd been adopted by the Elk Band, but it did little good. Because of her skin color, she was treated with suspicion and resentment, just as she'd been treated in Sunset after her return. It appeared bigotry itself was color-blind.

Unable to endure their cold looks any longer, Emma slipped out into the evening's dusk. The lodge was far enough away from the main village that she couldn't make out individuals, but she could hear the sounds of singing and laughter. Men would be playing the hand game, while women huddled together tossing dice in the air. Songs often accompanied the contests, and Emma could tell the pace of the game simply by the excitement in the singing voices.

She had seen neither Chayton nor Ridge all day, and her frightening dream visions were never far from her thoughts. However, she reassured herself, if something had happened to her son or Ridge, Talutah would've told her.

Emma spotted a shadowy figure walking toward her and

tensed even as she unobtrusively laid a hand on her thigh, beside the hidden knife.

"It's me, Emma," Ridge called out softly in English.

Emma's hand fell away from her weapon as her heart tripped in its chest. She wanted to run to him and throw herself in his arms. Instead, she strolled over to stand in front of him and allowed her gaze to caress him instead of her hands. They'd been apart only twelve hours, yet to Emma it felt like twelve days.

"I'm glad to see you, Ridge." She couldn't keep the pleasure from her voice. "How's Chayton?"

"He's eating with his grandfather and grandmother." His gaze swept over her. "How're you doing?"

Emma crossed her arms beneath her breasts, oddly comforted by speaking English again. "I'm bored and I miss Chayton." She paused, then added softly, "And I miss you."

Ridge looked down and his hair obscured his expression. "We miss you, too."

Emma hugged her sides and wished it was Ridge's arms around her and not her own. "How's Chayton feeling? Is he in any pain?"

Ridge chuckled. "He's so busy, he hardly notices."

"He'll probably be fretting and overtired tonight. If his head hurts, mix some of the herbs I left out with warm water. It'll help him sleep."

"I'll do that."

They stood in awkward silence.

"What did you and Chayton do all day?" Emma asked, wanting to prolong his visit.

"Chayton played in the morning, and after he slept some this afternoon, him and me went looking for wolf tracks." He smiled boyishly, and Emma fought her body's insistence to move closer. "We didn't find any."

"And what would you have done if you had found a wolf?" Emma asked in amusement.

"I suppose we would've brought it back to the village as Chayton's pet."

Emma's mouth dropped open, but Ridge's soft huff of

laughter revealed his teasing. She chuckled. "Heaven help us if he ever finds one." Sobering, she asked, "Did you see Hotah?"

"I saw him."

His short reply told Emma there was more to it than a simple exchange. "What happened?"

He shrugged. "He wanted to begin Chayton's training. I wouldn't let him."

Emma gripped his arm as fear spilled through her veins. "What did he do?"

"Nothing."

Ridge was hiding something from her and she considered his choice of words. "What did he *say*?"

He glanced away and rubbed his clean-cut jaw. "He's got a grudge against me. I figure it'll come down to a fight one of these days."

Emma gasped. "You can't!"

"Fast Elk and some of the others'll make sure it's a fair fight."

"Hotah's bigger than you."

Ridge stiffened. "I can handle him."

She'd insulted his masculinity when all she'd done was express her concern. She forced her muscles to untense and kept her voice calm. "Please, stay away from Hotah. If you don't cross paths, he won't have reason to challenge you."

"I'm not afraid of him."

Emma rolled her eyes at his stubborn male pride. "That's not the issue. This is Hotah's home. If you beat him here, he'll be forced to leave."

"So now you're worried about *him*?" Ridge shook his head, exasperation in his shadowed features. "Make up your mind, Emma. You can't have it both ways."

"You don't understand."

"Damned right I don't." He settled his hat more firmly on his head. "Goodnight." Ridge spun on his heel and strode away.

Emma took a step to follow him, but halted. Ridge was too angry to listen. And what would she say? It was his

safety she was concerned about. If he and Hotah fought and
Ridge won, Hotah would seek revenge against the white
man. Hotah wouldn't care anymore about honor, because if
he lost to Ridge, he'd lose whatever honor he possessed.

Then there was the possibility Hotah would defeat
Ridge, which would be just as disastrous, because Hotah
wouldn't stop at beating him. The cruel warrior would deliver a killing blow.

Upset and anxious, Emma was angry with herself for involving Ridge in her personal quest. If only he hadn't found
her, or had let her go on by herself to find Chayton. Now, if
something happened to Ridge, the fault would be hers. And
Emma wasn't certain she could live with the guilt.

*THE black velvety darkness surrounded her, cocooned her,
and she was tempted to sink into it and never emerge. It
would be so easy; she'd been tired for so long now.*

*An owl's hoot startled her and she raised her head. Two
yellow eyes peered down at her, but she could make out nothing else in the pitch blackness. Dread riffled through her, but
the owl's steady gaze held no danger. At least not to her.*

*The sensation of movement made her rise up on four
legs and feral cat scent stung her nose. Moments later, low
growls and higher-pitched mewling sounds filled the air.
Using her nose and ears, the female wolf tried to determine
from where they came.*

*"Lisssten well for the angry one issss near," the owl
spoke in a sibilant whisper from its high perch.*

"Tell me where!"

"Closssse."

*A cloud slid away, revealing a full moon and illuminat-
ing sharp brambles surrounding the female wolf. Blinking,
she focused on movement beyond the thorny bushes and
spotted a mountain lion sitting in regal comfort, a weakly
struggling wolf cub in its mouth.*

*White-hot pain ripped through the female wolf and she
charged through the brambles, but the thorns tangled in*

*her coat. She fought to escape, but the needles dug deeper,
into her skin, and blood flowed from numerous gashes.*

*Still, she surged forward, unmindful of the profusely
bleeding wounds and the accompanying torment. She had
to rescue the cub, her child, her . . .*

Emma's eyes flashed open and she lay motionless, her
heart pounding and sweat coating her skin.

Where am I?

A long minute later, the answer tumbled back and
Emma sat up, throwing off her cover. The other two
women were asleep, and Emma tiptoed out of the lodge
into the moonlit night.

Raw urgency impelled her to see Chayton, to reassure
her he was safe and unharmed, unlike the wolf cub in her
dream. Keeping to the shadows, Emma ran in a half-
crouch to the lodge she shared with Ridge and her son. She
hesitated only a moment, then slipped inside and remained
by the opening, allowing her eyes to adjust to the dimness.

Chayton was a lump beneath the buffalo hides and
Emma silently passed Ridge's sleeping form. She knelt beside her son and eased the blanket down so she could see
his face, which was smooth and peaceful as he slept
soundly. Biting back a sob of relief, she stretched out beside him on top of the skins.

"Another dream?"

The low voice startled her and she raised her head to see
Ridge sitting with his arms wrapped around his drawn-up
knees.

"I didn't mean to wake you," she whispered.

"I wasn't sleeping much anyhow," Ridge admitted. He
kept his eyes on the low fire as he stirred it with a twig.
"Wanna talk about it?"

She settled back down on the soft buffalo skin and
wrapped an arm around her son. "Same dream, but different." She sensed Ridge's confusion. "This time I *was* the
female wolf. I couldn't see anything but I could hear the
lion and the wolf cub. Then the full moon came out and I

was trapped in sharp thorns." Emma paused, then whispered hoarsely, "I couldn't save him."

Ridge didn't speak and Emma closed her eyes. She inhaled the pleasant scent of soapweed on Chayton's skin, and she was soothed by his sleep snuffles.

"If you want to stay here the rest of the night, I'll wake you early enough to get back to the lodge before anyone catches you," Ridge offered.

His understanding filled her eyes with moisture. "Thank you," she said huskily.

She listened to him lie back down and remembered how she'd slept spooned against him with his arms holding her close.

Would she ever feel that safe again?

RIDGE was as good as his word, and Emma was back in the women's lodge before the sun rose the next morning, as well as the following two mornings. The night of the full moon came and went, and the dire dreams didn't return. Immensely relieved, Emma prayed it was because the vision had been averted.

By the afternoon of her fourth day of seclusion, she returned to the lodge she shared with Ridge and Chayton. After seeing her son was safe with the other children, Emma made a pot of stew to hang over the cookfire.

Light footfalls alerted Emma and she turned to see Ridge joining her. Pleasure coursed through her and she smiled warmly.

"Smells good," he said with a boyish grin.

"Are you hungry from playing all day?" she teased.

"I'm always hungry." Ridge winked.

He suddenly tensed and Emma followed his line of sight. Hotah prowled toward them, his lips curled in a sneer.

Uneasiness settled in Emma's belly.

"You will leave now," Hotah announced.

"Akecheta will tell us when it is time to leave," Ridge said coolly.

"He thinks like an old woman."

Emma gasped. To insult a chief was tantamount to treason. She glanced around but found no one near enough to overhear the warrior.

"Does Akecheta know you speak of him that way?" Ridge asked calmly, although Emma could see his lips tighten in anger.

"He knows I do not agree with running like rabbits."

"We do not run!" Akecheta and Fast Elk came out of Fast Elk's tipi, which was close enough for them to overhear Hotah's words.

The chief's words were loud enough to draw the attention of many of the villagers. Hotah flushed, but didn't retreat from Akecheta's glare.

"We do not fight," Hotah shot back. "We run like children if there is word of whites drawing nearer."

"We live! If we die there will be no one to carry our past and our people will disappear," Akecheta argued, his voice strong despite his frail appearance.

"We live like animals, hunting for a burrow when we should fight for what is ours."

Emma sidled closer to Ridge as she listened to the two men. It was obvious this wasn't the first time Hotah and the chief had argued, but it did appear this disagreement was more intense. And this time they had an audience.

"*I* speak for our people," Akecheta stated, his nostrils flaring.

"What of these two?" He pointed to Ridge and Emma. "They are not of the People." Hotah's hand fell to his knife handle. "They are *wasicu*, the enemy."

Emma stiffened with indignation, but Ridge squeezed her arm and she snapped her mouth shut. The People surrounding them shuffled and murmured, but no one interrupted.

"They are guests. You will not harm them." Akecheta lifted his chin. "Perhaps *you* have become the enemy."

Hotah jerked as if slapped. He narrowed his eyes and rage rolled off him in waves. "I will not hide like a coward."

The insult was clear to Akecheta, who stared at Hotah, his black eyes giving away nothing. "Leave this village. You no longer belong."

Gasps and mutterings broke out among the Indians, but Emma could tell it wasn't in protest of the chief's decree. Most of them also wanted to remain at peace.

Hotah straightened his spine and pulled his shoulders back. He glared at the chief, then shifted his fierce look to Ridge and Emma. "I will not forget," he vowed in a tone that sent dread through Emma's veins.

He pivoted and a line opened between the People to allow him through. He swaggered away, leaving shocked silence in his wake.

Akecheta gazed at Ridge and Emma, his lined face impassive. "One more day."

The chief retreated to his lodge, and after a few moments, the crowd dissipated quietly. Fast Elk and Talutah were the last to return to their tipi after a long, lingering look filled with sadness and resignation.

For the first time since she'd been accepted by the tribe years earlier, Emma felt the sting of being an outsider.

She remained standing beside Ridge, fighting tears. "At one time, these were my people, my family." Her voice broke. "Now, it's as if they're strangers."

Ridge cupped her face in his palms. "You can't change your skin color, or the way you were raised. And with the whites pushing the Indians again, lines will be drawn according to those differences."

She knew he spoke the truth, but the realization didn't lessen the pain.

"It's been nearly a week anyhow, Emma. We need to be getting back," Ridge said. "Day after tomorrow, we'll leave early in the morning and get a good start."

Emma nodded. She had one day to prepare her son to leave the only family he'd ever known.

* * *

RIDGE lay awake, his crossed arms pillowing his head as he stared up at the black sky through the smoke hole in the center of the lodge. Restlessness vibrated in his bones. After the confrontation with Hotah, Ridge had wanted to gather Emma and leave immediately. At least Hotah would no longer be a threat to Chayton—some other brave in the village would train the boy.

Chayton snuffled and shifted in his sleep, causing Emma to move also. Ridge closed his eyes against the memories her presence made impossible to forget—the feathery light caress of her hands; her warm, firm lips upon his; and her needy whispers begging him to touch her and fill her.

He shoved the randy thoughts away, but a soft, passionate cry sifted through the stillness from another tipi, bringing unwelcome images. Ridge smothered a groan, not wanting to listen to the amorous coupling, but he couldn't shut the sounds out. Heated blood shot to his groin and it took everything he had to ignore the temptation to bring relief to himself.

"Ridge."

Emma's quiet whisper startled him and he was glad for the darkness that covered his flushed face. "Yeah?"

She remained silent for so long, Ridge thought maybe he'd imagined her voice, confusing it with the breathy murmurs coming from the nearby lodge.

"When we get back home, we can't see each other again or folks will talk even more," she said softly.

Ridge stiffened, angry that she'd think he would further sully her reputation. "I'm not going to give them any more call to gossip, Emma."

He heard her roll over and turned his head to find her peering at him. "That wasn't what I meant."

Even in the dimness, Ridge could see frustration in her pale features.

Across the night air, a loud moan spilled from a man's

lips, echoed by a woman's cry. Emma's head turned in the direction from which the loving sounds had come. When she gave her attention to him once more, tension radiated from her body.

"I won't ever marry again."

Confused, Ridge offered, "You don't know that."

"Yes, I do," she stated firmly. "No man will want me."

"If you move away from Sunset, no one will know. You can say you're a widow."

"With Chayton, everyone will know." Ridge opened his mouth, but she held up a hand. "I don't want to argue with you tonight." She paused and he had the impression something else was on her mind. Something that both frightened and excited him. "I'm a widow, Ridge. I know what I'm giving up when I say I'll never be a wife again, and I most certainly won't be anyone's whore either."

Her use of the vulgar word and the vehemence in her quiet voice surprised him, but before he could speak, she continued.

"Despite what many folks in Sunset believe, I've lain with only two men—my husband and you. Enapay is dead, and you have your own life to return to when we get back to town. But now—" She stuttered to a halt, as if her courage deserted her.

Ridge took a deep breath and hoped he was reading her intentions correctly. His conscience nudged him, but his need for Emma was far too powerful to ignore. He raised one side of the buffalo hide blanket in mute invitation.

After ensuring Chayton was sound asleep, Emma crawled over to join him. She knelt in front of him and lifted the doeskin dress over her head, then tossed it aside. She wore nothing beneath it and her pale skin reflected the orange glow of the embers. Her nipples, surrounded by dusky circles, hardened as he watched. Unable to resist, he reached forward to roll the hard flesh between his thumb and forefinger.

Emma's head fell back, baring her throat and thrusting her breasts toward him. Ridge rose up to embrace her. He nipped and kissed the slender column of her neck as his hands roamed up and down her silky back and sides. Her tiny moans were accompanied by puffs of warm, moist air across his cheek.

How had he thought he could get enough of Emma in just one day? Her rising musky scent teased him and his body responded instinctively to the invitation to mate. But he recognized it as more than mere animalistic urges. He cared for Emma and admired her more than any woman he'd known.

As he gently lowered her to his bed and covered her body with his, something else pierced the lusty fog in his brain.

He was falling in love with her.

EMMA fisted her hands and laid them on her thighs, willing herself to remain calm in the face of Talutah's stubbornness.

"He is my son. He belongs with me," she said, keeping her tone steady.

"He is Lakota. He belongs with his people." Talutah's dark eyes narrowed. "You take him to the *wasicu*'s town and he will be killed."

"No one will hurt him! I will protect him."

"Pah! You will not be able to protect him from words or hate. He will wither and die."

Emma blinked back tears of frustration. "You cannot stop me. He is mine!"

Talutah studied her with a flat gaze that gradually gave way to sympathy. "Think of Chayton. Here he is free to run and play among the other children. Here he will become a respected warrior. But in your world, he will always be a *half-breed*." The term was spat out. "He will wallow in your whiskey and his thoughts will scatter. No longer will he be strong and swift."

"I won't let that happen to him. I will shelter him from the taunts and hatred."

Talutah shook her head sadly. "You are only a woman, Winona, and Chayton needs a *leksi* to teach him what it is to be a man."

Visions of Ridge instructing her son brought a bittersweet swell in her chest. She squared her shoulders and straightened her backbone. "Chayton will leave with me in the morning."

Talutah scowled, but she didn't continue the argument. Emma knew that the older woman could speak to the chief about keeping Chayton here in the village, but doubted her stepmother would. For all her stubbornness, Talutah loved her, just as Emma loved her.

Emma rose gracefully although her body twinged from the night's pleasures in Ridge's arms. Twice they'd joined and she'd flown to the stars each time. Ridge was a skillful lover, who could be gentle or fierce, whichever she wished him to be. She already longed for his touch again.

She slipped out of her adopted parents' lodge and looked around in the afternoon sunshine. Spotting Ridge and Chayton by the river, she smiled and walked toward them.

As she drew nearer, Ridge turned as if sensing her presence. His welcoming smile warmed her and sent a pang of desire through her. He was so handsome, so confident, and so gentle. If she hadn't left Sunset, or if her father hadn't hired Ridge to find her, or if he had given up after she'd escaped him, she would have never known his loving.

"What are you two doing?" she asked in Lakota.

"Searching for frogs," Ridge replied in English.

"Frogs," Chayton repeated exuberantly as he held up a squirming green and black one in his small fist.

Emma gaped at her son. "You know English?"

The slippery frog escaped Chayton and splashed into the water. The boy knelt at the edge of the stream to watch it swim away.

"He knows a few words." Ridge answered her question. "I gave him the English name for plants and animals we came across."

Touched by Ridge's considerateness and generosity, she

couldn't speak. However, knowing he'd be embarrassed if she made too much out of it, she merely said, "Thank you."

"It wasn't any hardship, Emma. He's a good boy."

And she could see the sincerity in his eyes, as well as the fondness he held for her son. Maybe it wouldn't be so difficult to convince him it was best for all involved if Chayton returned to Sunset with them.

With that glimmer of hope, Emma smiled. "Would anyone like to go for a walk?" she asked in Lakota.

Chayton scrambled to his feet and the excitement in his eyes gave Emma her answer.

"Ridge?" she asked quietly as Chayton skipped ahead.

Ridge smiled and guided her down the path after the boy.

Emma focused on Chayton, who squatted down and intently studied something on the ground. She spotted the pile of animal droppings and wrinkled her nose.

Ridge chuckled over her shoulder. "What animal is it, Chayton? Answer in English."

"Rabbit," he replied with an impish grin.

Pride rolled through Emma. Her son was a fast learner.

She followed a few paces behind Ridge and Chayton, listening as Ridge alternated between speaking Lakota and English as he taught the boy more than just a new language. He told Chayton about ice cream and buildings taller than ten men. Maybe Ridge would spend time with Chayton when they returned and continue the informal lessons.

Her good mood vanished as she imagined Ridge being taunted for befriending a half-breed boy. Ridge had endured too much ridicule in his life, and to be seen with Chayton or herself would surely heap more on him. No, it was better if they made a clean break once they arrived back home.

Some time later, she and Ridge sat atop large rocks across from one another while Chayton stretched out on a sun-warmed bed of soft pine needles. He was asleep within moments.

"How did your talk with Talutah go?" Ridge asked neutrally.

Emma drew her knees up and wrapped her arms around them. "Badly. She thinks Chayton is better off staying with the tribe."

"She's right."

Ridge had never been a mother. He couldn't understand the bond a woman developed for the child she carried within her womb for nine months. To abandon her son again would kill her as surely as a bullet to her heart. "What about his mother?" she asked.

"She'll be better off without him, too," Ridge said, his voice gravelly.

Enraged and terrified by his matter-of-fact words, she glared at him. "Have you ever cried yourself to sleep night after night because you missed someone so badly you couldn't *not* cry?" Tears filled her eyes, which she dashed away in embarrassment.

Ridge glanced away, but not before Emma caught a glimpse of soul-deep pain. "Yes. After my ma died. One night my stepfather caught me crying. He whipped me until I passed out, said it wasn't manly to cry. I never cried again."

Emma's fury vanished, replaced by compassion and empathy. She slid off the rock and went to him, placing a hand on his shoulder. "I'm sorry."

He wouldn't—or couldn't—look at her. "It was a long time ago."

"You're still hurting."

"A lot of things hurt, Emma." Ridge finally turned to her and clasped her hand resting on his shoulder. "A person just learns to live with it."

She tried to pull away, but Ridge held firmly to her hand, and she surrendered. "There are some hurts a person can't learn to live with," she said tremulously.

"Can you live with all the hurts Chayton will get from the other children, as well from grown men and women who'll hate him just because his father was a savage redskin?"

Although his words were intentionally cruel, she could hear his concern clearly. "I'll protect him."

"You can't be his shadow every minute of every day, Emma. And as he gets older, he won't want you beside him. He'll have to burden all the narrow-minded insults by himself. Can you do that to him? To your own son?"

She jerked out of his grip, hating what he said and hating him more for being right. "No! I'll take him far away from those kind of people. We'll live off by ourselves if we have to."

Ridge walked up behind her—she could feel the heat radiating from his body.

"And how will you survive? What if one or both of you get sick? What kind of house will you live in?" Ridge pressed.

"I know how to gather food and store it, and I have my herbs if we get sick. We can live in a tipi," Emma replied, her voice rising despite her intention to remain calm.

"And what'll you do when someone stumbles across your place? If it's an Indian, you'll be killed because you're white and he'll take Chayton as a slave. If it's a white man, he'll use you, then probably drag you around for a while until he's tired of you. Then he'll kill you, like he killed Chayton because a half-breed's life is worth less than a dog's."

Rage like she'd never known filled Emma and she whirled around, her arms flailing and her fists striking Ridge's hard chest. "Damn you! Why are you saying such horrible things? Why? Why? Why?"

Each "why" was punctuated by blows against Ridge, blows he didn't fend off or try to stop. He accepted them in stoic silence, which made Emma even angrier. How could he be so calm when she was losing her son?

Emma had no idea how long the blind fury burned, and then suddenly it was gone. And like the aftermath of a fire, only barrenness remained.

Her arms fell to her sides and her head dropped. She turned away from Ridge, but had no strength left for anything more. Numbness spread through her and the sunny afternoon became gray and dark as she stared at nothing.

Ridge's solid hands settled on her shoulders and massaged gently. Part of her wanted to lean back into his touch, but she didn't even have the will to do that.

"You're Chayton's mother and you have to do what's best for him." His mouth was close to her ear, and his voice was raspy, as if he'd been hollering for a long time. "Think long and hard about your decision, Emma, because life doesn't give you second chances."

She closed her eyes, emptying her mind and merely feeling Ridge's fingers kneading the tight muscles in her neck and shoulders. She didn't want to think right now, and didn't want to make a choice that tore Chayton from her forever.

Her son awakened, postponing her decision. He relieved himself before joining Emma and Ridge.

"Walk?" he asked in English.

Despite the sharp ache in her heart, Emma smiled and nodded. "Walk," she confirmed.

Before Chayton could run ahead, she took his hand and followed the narrow game trail. As he walked beside her, he proudly pointed out plants, insects, and objects that he called by their English names.

Even if Chayton remained living with the Lakota he would need to know English in the years ahead. Years that Emma was certain would be filled with more bloodshed and an eventual conquering of many Indian tribes. If Chayton knew English, he could help his people with treaties and ensure they wouldn't be cheated.

She sniffed. Foolish thoughts. She and Ridge would leave tomorrow and nobody would continue Chayton's lessons.

Emma refused to dwell anymore on the future, but focused on the present. Chayton tugged away from her and she followed his every movement with a greedy gaze, storing pictures in her mind to bring out as cherished memories in the days, months, and years down the road.

Chayton making a face over an especially smelly pile of skunk scat. Chayton with wide eyes studying a piece of pink quartz. Chayton giggling as a furry caterpillar marched up and down his knuckles.

In some small part of her mind, she was aware of Ridge walking behind them, allowing her time alone with her son, but close enough he could protect them.

Hours later, after Chayton and Ridge had eaten, and darkness had fallen, Emma guided her sleepy son into their lodge. She settled him on the bed of skins and hugged him until he wriggled in protest. Keeping her expression bright, she tucked him in and sat beside him as he fell asleep, adding more portraits to her memory.

She glanced up when Ridge ducked under the flap and watched as he removed his hat and moccasins. He settled cross-legged on the ground and fed more pieces of wood to the fire. The flames leapt up, illuminating Ridge's handsome, square-jawed face.

"Talutah and Fast Elk will raise him as their own," she finally whispered.

She expected Ridge to smile and nod his agreement. Instead his expression overflowed with compassion and sorrow. He opened his mouth as if to speak, but nothing came out, then he extended a hand toward her.

She crawled over to him and he enveloped her within his arms. Her grief came in ratcheting sobs as Ridge held her close and whispered soft words that could do nothing to soothe her anguish.

FIFTEEN

RIDGE woke before the sun and reluctantly extricated himself from Emma's limbs. She'd cried herself to sleep, and although his grief was only a shadow of hers, he'd felt the sting of tears for the first time in years. Emma was making a sacrifice no mother should ever have to make.

He tugged on his moccasins, then paused beside Emma to study her puffy eyes and pale complexion. Aching for her, he brushed her velvet-soft cheek with his thumb and fought the impulse to kiss her slightly parted lips. "It'll get better, Emma," he whispered.

Ridge grabbed his hat and left the confines of the tipi. Pausing outside, he stretched and his backbone popped. He and Emma wouldn't get far today, not after the restive night. But it was better to make a clean break rather than stay another day and allow the wound to fester.

Talutah dumped an armload of sticks on the ground and knelt to build up her cookfire. Ridge squatted beside her. She kept her gaze averted, but he knew she was aware of him, and probably had been since he'd stepped outside.

"Take care of him for her, Talutah," he said softly in Lakota.

She stilled, then settled a leathery palm on his forearm and met his gaze. "Take care of our daughter."

Ridge grasped the hand that rested on his arm. "I will if she allows it."

Talutah flashed him a gap-toothed smile and returned to her task.

Ridge disappeared into the brush, and after taking care of his personal business, he saddled Paint and Clementine. After nearly a week of lazing around, the two horses were spirited and didn't want to take the bits. But with a little friendly persuasion from Ridge, they finally gave in, then he left them in the rope corral with their reins wrapped around a bush.

He dragged his feet, unsure how Emma would react this morning. After her grief was spent last night, she'd fallen into an exhausted sleep. He'd lain awake long after, savoring her warmth but only wanting to comfort her.

As Ridge rounded a corner, he spotted Emma standing beside Talutah. It was strange to see her wearing a gingham skirt and blouse again with a wool coat over them. Her hair was no longer braided but was pulled back and bound with a leather tie. The only remaining sign of Winona was the moccasins on her feet.

She glanced up at him but quickly averted her gaze. Ridge sighed. Peace would be long in coming for her, and he doubted she'd ever feel whole again. But she'd made the right decision, difficult as it had been.

Ridge nodded at Talutah and Emma, and slipped into their lodge. Chayton lay on his back, his mouth open as he continued to sleep. The familiar soft flutter of his breathing brought an unexpected lump to Ridge's throat. He, too, would miss the boy. Although Chayton was more Lakota than white, he possessed many of his mother's traits.

Blanking his thoughts before he became too maudlin, he quickly shoved his belongings into his saddlebags. After a last look at Chayton, Ridge left the lodge. An old woman with scraggly gray hair hobbled toward him. As she drew closer, he recognized her as the chief's first wife.

"Akecheta wishes to see you before you leave," she said to Ridge, her lively dark eyes belying her age.

Ridge nodded once, and she turned away, satisfied with his answer.

"What did she want?" Emma asked as she joined him.

"The chief wants to see me."

She crossed her arms and watched the elderly woman duck into the tipi in the center of the village. "I'll go with you."

Ridge didn't bother to argue. Emma had more right than he did to visit with the elder one last time.

Talutah handed him some pemmican, which he washed down with water. Emma refused to eat, which earned her a concerned glare from her adopted mother. Instead, Emma returned to their lodge to say her final goodbye to her son.

"Her heart will take time to heal," Ridge said to Talutah.

"*Ha*. But you will help her," Talutah replied firmly.

Ridge doubted Emma would allow him to. What would she do? Bury herself in her father's house and never come out? Or maybe leave Sunset altogether?

The last choice would be the best for Emma, yet Ridge couldn't find it in himself to favor it.

There was a third option, one he'd wrestled with long into the night. He could marry her.

However, his place wasn't big enough for a wife, and all the money he made was to be put into cattle to start his herd, and to buy back the land Hartwell had basically stolen from his stepfather. He couldn't afford a family yet. Would Emma wait for him? Did he want her to?

In all the plans he'd made lying on the hard ground near battlefields and in the wilderness over the last dozen years, he'd never imagined marrying someone like Emma. It had always been someone like Grace Freeman, a gentlewoman whose father was a respected member of the community. Of course, in the eyes of the townsfolk, that applied to Emma's father, too, but Emma herself had lost her respectability the moment she'd been rescued from the Lakota.

Ridge rubbed his aching brow. He had to separate pleasure from practicality. Leaving Sunset would be best for
Emma and, despite her claim about never marrying, she'd
have no trouble finding a husband.

So why did his gut feel like he'd swallowed glass when
he thought of her lying with another man?

Emma ducked out of the tipi and Ridge was relieved to
see her eyes were dry. She'd probably cried all her tears
last night. She picked up her saddlebags that she'd left lying outside the lodge.

"I'm ready," she announced in a surprisingly strong
voice.

But when Ridge looked into her amber eyes, he read the
depth of her sorrow. He quickly turned away and nodded to
Talutah in farewell. He'd spent an hour talking with Fast
Elk last night, and in their own way, had traded unspoken
farewells. The Lakota believed all were connected through
the earth, and even if they were apart, they were never truly
separated. It was a comforting thought, but Ridge wasn't
certain he believed it. A belief did little to soothe a
mother's loss of her son.

Or a son's loss of his mother.

He led the way to the chief's tipi and paused outside the
door. *"Hau."*

"Timá hiyúwo."

Ridge entered the lodge and Emma followed. His eyes
took a moment to adjust to the dimness. The tribe's elderly
chief sat cross-legged by the fire while the wife who'd
summoned Ridge stood a few feet behind him. In her
hands was Ridge's gunbelt and knife that had been taken
from him when they'd arrived in the village.

Akecheta motioned for them to sit. Emma lowered herself to the ground behind Ridge.

"You will not be welcome here again," the gray-haired
man began without preamble.

Ridge heard Emma's sharp intake of breath and his own
chest squeezed painfully. He kept his expression emotion-

less. "We understand." He licked his dry lips. "Winona's son remains."

"He will be cared for and taught our ways."

Ridge nodded. "Thank you."

Akecheta grunted. "Go. It is time."

The stooped woman offered Ridge his weapons. *"Pila-mayaye."*

He nodded his thanks and she merely lowered her head and returned to her previous subservient position. Ridge buckled the gunbelt around his waist, then ushered Emma out of the tipi. The sun was just beginning to inch above the coral-, orange-, and rose-hued horizon. No clouds blotted the lightening sky. It would be a warm spring day, but he and Emma would be hard-pressed to appreciate its beauty.

As they rode, Ridge darted concerned glances at Emma, but she kept her gaze aimed forward and didn't even turn for one last glimpse of her adopted family. However, the strain was plain to see in her pale, drawn face. Knowing he could offer nothing but meaningless words, he merely rode beside her in silence.

THROUGHOUT the long day, every bone and muscle in Emma's body urged her to turn around and return to her son. However, she'd made her decision, though there was little comfort to be found with that choice. The only comfort was Ridge's solid, reassuring presence beside her. Without him, she wouldn't have had the courage to do the right thing. Still, it didn't prevent her from hurting or worrying. Nothing short of having her son with her would fill the hollow anguish.

Emma followed Ridge blindly, her sight focused inward. She was aware that the sun was shining and that birds flitted past, but she took no pleasure in it, as she'd done on their journey to find Chayton.

She'd had hope then, hope that she'd find her son and they wouldn't be parted again. Emma was glad that Chayton was loved, healthy, and safe, but her loss and guilt at leaving him wouldn't let her take satisfaction in that knowledge.

At noon, Ridge stopped so the horses could rest and graze. He offered Emma some jerky, but her stomach lurched at the sight of it and she shook her head. She was relieved he didn't argue but remained by the horses as his hawk-like gaze scoured the craggy bluffs around them.

They traveled throughout the afternoon, stopping only once to water Clementine and Paint. As the sun slid toward the western horizon, Emma finally began to notice their surroundings and the stillness became intrusive.

"How—" Her voice broke after not being used for so long and she cleared her throat. "How far have we traveled?"

Ridge slowed Paint so Emma could ride beside him. " 'Bout twenty miles." He shrugged. "I didn't push it."

Emma took a ragged breath. "I appreciate it."

Ridge lifted a shoulder in acknowledgment.

"I didn't think anything could hurt so much," she admitted softly. "Even when I almost drowned and thought I'd never see my family again."

"He's your son, your flesh and blood."

Emma's throat swelled and she glanced away until the lump in her throat wasn't choking her anymore. "You were right. He'll have a better life with the Lakota. He'll be free to grow into a fine man."

"He'd be a fine man no matter where he grew up," Ridge said quietly.

His confident assurance touched her and she reached over to clasp his hand, which rested on the saddle horn. "Thank you."

Ridge's expression seemed to ease and a crooked smile quirked his lips. "You're welcome."

He found a campsite a couple hours before sunset where they could settle for the night. Emma was grateful to stop early and did her share by getting the fire going, and cooking a meal of biscuits and beans. A pot of coffee was boiling over the fire when Ridge returned with a final armload of wood.

They ate in tranquil companionship, listening to the birds in the trees and the scuttle of squirrels in the thatch of shrubs behind them. After the dishes were cleaned and repacked in the saddlebags, Ridge made a last check of the horses and the perimeter of their camp.

Emma watched him circle around, his figure shadowed by the dusk. His steps were stealthy, his limbs loose, and she recognized the tilt of his head as he used all his senses to search for danger. Despite her physical and mental exhaustion, her body tingled and warmed.

When Ridge returned, Emma retrieved her book, which she hadn't touched since they'd arrived at the Lakota camp. She needed something to take her mind off Chayton, at least temporarily.

"Would you like me to read aloud?" she asked Ridge.

He frowned. "I figured you'd be tired."

"I am, but I won't be able to sleep." She glanced away. "Not right away, anyhow."

"Sure." He smiled crookedly. "I could listen to your voice all day and not tire of it."

Despite her embarrassment, she managed an impudent grin. "I never knew you were such a sweet talker."

His face reddened, endearing him even more to her.

"I never had much practice at sweet-talking a gal," he admitted.

She squeezed his work-roughened hand. "You're doing just fine."

He grinned, then glanced deliberately at her book.

She picked up the volume and shifted around to get the best angle of firelight across the pages. As she read, her own tension eased and before long, she reclined against Ridge's side. He curled an arm around her waist and his forearm brushed the underswell of her breasts, causing her words to falter for a moment. She couldn't draw in a full breath and her voice grew husky.

Ridge made tiny circles across her belly with light fingertips, further undoing her faltering concentration. When his thumb grazed her nipple, she gave up the pretense of reading. Allowing the book to fall to her lap, she leaned her head against Ridge's shoulder.

He dropped a gentle kiss to a sensitive spot beneath her ear and she shivered with passion. She tilted her head, allowing him more access to her neck and he trailed a tender line of kisses to her collarbone. He undid the top three buttons of her blouse and slid his hand inside, beneath the camisole and cupped her breast.

Emma wished she was strong enough to stop his seduction, but she couldn't deny the ever-growing attraction. She laid a hand on his thigh and roamed upward, to feel his hard length beneath his trouser buttons. She squeezed him intimately, and he throbbed beneath her palm. He moaned and his warm moist breath wafted across her neck.

He grasped her hand, putting a halt to her teasing touch. "You're going to be the death of me yet, Emma," he said breathlessly.

She kissed his whiskered jaw. "Then we go together," she said, her own voice hoarse with passion.

Ridge groaned and flipped Emma around so she lay on the ground beneath him. With deft fingers, he undid the remaining buttons on her blouse and tried to remove it as Emma struggled to get rid of her confining skirt and heavy stockings.

Emma laughed at their clumsy haste, but they finally had her clothes tossed pell-mell around them. She raised herself up on her elbows and pressed her lips to Ridge's Adam's apple, then licked and nipped it playfully.

Ridge rolled off her and she immediately missed his warm, reassuring weight. But when his fingers moved to his own shirt, Emma rolled onto her side with her head in her hand to watch him.

Firelight created planes and angles across his hewn features and his nostrils flared with desire. Keeping his sultry gaze locked with hers, he stripped. His pants came off last, and Emma allowed herself the luxury of perusing his masculine form at leisure. Little strands of hair graced his chest, but it began to thicken to a line at his waist which trailed down to form a triangle of coarse brown hair. From that nest jutted his erection, which curved toward his belly. Emma licked her suddenly dry lips.

In one graceful motion, he brought his flesh against hers and she ensnared him within her arms. For one brief moment, she thought of Chayton and her heart tripped, but she focused on Ridge's heated skin and his caresses. She kissed the hollow where his neck met his shoulder and dragged her tongue downward until her lips found his nipple. After sucking and licking until Ridge was squirming above her, she switched to the other side.

Suddenly Ridge rolled to his back, tugging Emma with him so she ended up lying on top of him. His hard length dug into her hip and she shifted until she had him poised at the juncture of her thighs. She gripped his biceps and raised her hips until she felt his tip brush her moist flesh.

"Oh God, Emma," Ridge breathed.

He found the tie at the back of her head and released her hair from its confines. She shivered when he buried his fingers in the long tresses and clutched handfuls of it to steer her mouth to his. Their lips met and opened, and his tongue explored her palate in maddeningly slow, delicious flicks.

Emma rocked her hips against him, and he responded by thrusting upward to meet her. Her breasts grazed his chest, and the sweet friction of his chest against her nipples scattered her thoughts. The driving need to join with him brought Emma up on her knees and she reached down to guide him into her.

She lowered her body over the blunt head and closed her eyes as he slowly filled her. She locked her gaze on his lust-filled eyes, which reflected the pleasure she herself experienced as their bodies joined. Once he was buried within her, Emma remained seated upon him, simply feeling his solid body in and around her.

Ridge gripped her hips and she raised herself up inch by inch, then lowered herself equally as deliberately. Emma wanted to prolong the ecstasy, but their needs were too demanding.

She threw back her head and rode him, excited by both the control she wielded and Ridge's obvious enjoyment of it. His fingers tightened on her thighs and Emma's breath gusted in and out as her heart sped out of control.

Ridge thrust upward and stiffened, firing Emma's release that immediately followed his.

"Ridge," she hollered as her body bucked and spasmed around him.

Her strength abandoned her and she fell forward onto him. His arms encircled her and hugged her close.

Sweat-coated and spent, Emma curled against Ridge's side. She laid her arm across his waist and used his shoulder as a pillow. His musky, masculine scent filled her nostrils, stirring her anew, but sleep tugged at her.

She was vaguely aware of Ridge covering them with their blankets. Lips pressed to her forehead just as she drifted into slumber. A small, bittersweet smile claimed her lips.

EMMA bolted upright, coming all the way to her feet. She stared at the darkness around her, but flashes of crimson-red and the echoes of screams surrounded her.

"What's wrong, Emma?"

She blinked, her mind disentangling from her dream, but the feelings caused by the dream remained as powerful, if not more so. "Something's happened."

Ridge stood and she became aware that they were both naked. However, that bothered her little compared to the afterimages that continued to make her stomach roil and her head spin. She clutched his forearms and knew she was digging her fingernails into his skin but couldn't stop.

"What is it?" he demanded.

"Chayton, the village. Something horrible has happened."

Ridge's eyes widened in disbelief. "How do you know?"

"I-I saw it. A vision." She snatched up her clothes and hastily tugged them on. Her limbs trembled, making it difficult to dress quickly.

"We can't go back there. You heard the chief. We're not welcome there anymore."

"I'll go by myself."

Ridge grabbed her wrist, halting her frantic motions. "The hell you will," he swore. "We're going back to Sunset."

She jerked out of his hold. "I can't. Chayton could be dead or hurt."

"Dammit, Emma, you had dreams before and Chayton turned out to be fine. This one's no different."

"Yes, it is." Emma's fingers shook so much she could barely find the holes for her buttons. "I can't explain it. I only know what I know."

Ridge stared at her, his hands on his trim hips. If Emma wasn't so shaken, she might have enjoyed the sight. But she couldn't think of anything but Chayton and the horrific vision that had visited her.

Once dressed, Emma quickly moved to saddle Clementine. She could hear Ridge tugging on his clothes and muttering under his breath, and she was glad she couldn't understand what he was saying.

By the time she had her horse ready to go, Ridge was tightening the girth on Paint's saddle. She mounted her mare and gazed down at Ridge impatiently. "Are you coming or not?"

"Yes, dammit," he growled back. Ridge leapt into the saddle without the use of his stirrups and gathered the reins in one hand.

Ridge didn't look at her, but reined Paint around to go back in the direction from which they'd traveled yesterday. Emma followed, gritting her teeth against the reminder of the previous night's loving as her mare shifted into a trot.

If she hadn't been so busy with her selfish needs, maybe she would have experienced the vision earlier. What if they were too late because she'd allowed her body to lead her mind?

Her temples pounded with the rhythm of the horses' hooves, and she chanted as they rode.

Let him live. Let him live. Let him live.

IT was nearly noon when Emma spied the first signs of the village's fate. Ridge had forced her to stop, insisting the horses needed a rest. He was right, but Emma chafed at the delay. She held the mare's reins as Clementine drank from a narrow, but swiftly running stream. Searching the horizon ahead, Emma spotted a curl of smoke rising into the blue sky. Fear clogged her throat until she thought she'd suffocate.

Ridge joined her, his gaze locked on the same sight. "It could be anything."

Emma shook her head, her heart thumping a harsh cadence. "It's happened again. Another massacre."

"You don't know that."

"Yes, I do," she whispered.

Feeling as if her sore, travel-abused body was separate from her mind, Emma mounted her mare and kicked Clementine into a gallop. She was aware of Ridge calling her name, but she simply ignored him.

Ridge caught up with her just as she came to the entrance to the camp. No Indian boys stood guard in the rocks and that chilled Emma to the bone.

Ridge tugged on Emma's reins and moved ahead to take the lead. Although irritated, she didn't have time to argue. She followed closely even though she dreaded what they would find.

They rounded the last corner and froze at the scene in front of them. Half the tipis had been destroyed and soldiers dressed in the blue uniform of the cavalry milled around, keeping guard on a circle of braves, some of whom appeared to be dazed and wounded. Another group watched over a collection of women and children.

The only sounds were voices speaking English and horses snorting occasionally. The Lakota were mute, and even the children were silent.

Rusty splotches on the earth were evidence of spilled blood. Emma's vision tunneled and she swayed in the saddle. A strong hand caught her arm and held her upright.

Had Chayton survived one massacre only to die in this one?

SIXTEEN

RIDGE'S nostrils filled with the nauseating stench of blood and burnt flesh. His stomach heaved, but he managed to choke back the nausea. He glanced at Emma, whose face was the color of ash. She pressed a hand to her mouth as she gagged uncontrollably.

Ridge looked away, afraid he'd lose the bit of control he'd managed to gain. Then he thought of Chayton, and guilt and fear sliced his chest. If he was dead, it was Ridge's fault. He was the one who'd talked Emma into leaving him behind.

He frantically searched for Emma's son among the women and children, but they were clumped together so closely he couldn't make out individuals. He swore under his breath and urged Paint forward.

"Ridge!"

The sound of his name caused him to pull back on the reins. Preston Wylie's uniform was usually spotless and flawlessly creased, but now it was splotched with brown and his left sleeve was cut off, exposing a makeshift bandage around his upper arm.

Ridge glared down at him. "What the hell's going on?"

Pres's jaw muscle clenched, exposing his own anger. But before he could speak, Emma launched herself out of her saddle and ran toward the circle of captives. Chayton tottered at the edge of the group. He appeared unhurt, but groggy and shaken.

Light-headed with relief, Ridge watched her fall to her knees and hug her son. The boy only stood there, his arms limp at his sides, and Ridge recognized shock in his features.

Renewed anger flooded through him and he turned back to the lieutenant. "What the hell happened?"

"Captain Rivers led the patrol," Pres began, his voice weary. "He—"

Before Pres could finish, Ridge caught sight of Colt, the commanding officer whom he'd counted as a friend. He dismounted and strode toward Colt.

The captain's eyes widened. "Ridge, what're you doing—"

Ridge's fist connected with Colt's jaw and he felt the impact all the way from his knuckles to his shoulder. Colt stumbled back and his hat fell to the ground, but the officer remained on his feet. Two soldiers grabbed Ridge's arms and bent them behind his back. Pain shot through his shoulder blades but he only glared at Colt.

The captain raised his head and glared back at Ridge as he used the back of his wrist to wipe away the trickle of blood at the corner of his mouth. "Why the hell did you do that?" Colt demanded, fury reddening his face.

Ridge motioned with his chin toward the captive Indians. "Did Nyes promise you a nice promotion? Or did it depend on how many savages you killed?"

Colt's mouth closed, his lips forming a thin slash across his face. His pulse throbbed in his neck and it was a long moment before he asked in a flat tone, "What're you doing here?"

"We figured something had happened," Ridge replied, unwilling to share Emma's vision with a man who'd become a stranger.

"We?"

"Emma—Miss Hartwell and me."

"You found her?"

"Yeah, I found her. Mind calling off your guard dogs?" Ridge deliberately looked at the men imprisoning him.

After a moment's hesitation, Colt waved the two soldiers away. Ridge flexed his arms and shoulders gingerly.

Gabe Sanders joined them, his face made grimmer by a streak of dried blood across his brow. "I got him trussed up tight, sir," he said to Colt, then turned to Ridge. "You're a long way from home."

"Who do you got trussed up?" Ridge asked.

"Pony Cullen. Son of a bitch tried turning this into a massacre. If Cap'n Rivers hadn't winged him, it might've happened."

Ridge stared at Colt, who met his gaze without flinching. "Why didn't you say so?"

Colt's eyes glittered ice blue. "You didn't give me a chance."

"When I saw—" Ridge broke off. "Me and Emma lived in this village for a week. They're not part of a war party."

Gabe and Colt's gazes flickered to the side and Ridge turned to see Emma walking toward them. She carried Chayton, who had his head tucked against her shoulder and his legs wrapped around her waist. The boy didn't even look up when Emma stopped in front of the men.

"Miss Emma Hartwell," Ridge said, reverting back to formality. "This is Captain Colt Rivers and Sergeant Gabe Sanders."

Colt and Gabe tipped their hats politely.

Despite the paleness of her complexion, her eyes blazed with rage. "These people were no threat to you. All they wanted was to be left in peace."

"Yes, ma'am," Colt replied. "But we were ordered to find those who left the reservation. We followed them here."

"So you decided just to kill them instead of going

through the trouble of taking them back?" Her voice trembled with derision.

"We were attacked," Colt explained. "We defended ourselves."

"You'd attack people who invaded your home, wouldn't you, Captain?"

Ridge squelched a smile of admiration. "She's right. These folks were only defending their home."

"Cullen reported that some of the warriors here had ridden with Crazy Horse," Gabe added.

"And you believed him?" Emma asked.

Gabe shook his leonine head. "If we believed everything he said, ma'am, everyone in this here village would've been killed."

Colt held up a hand. "Cullen tried to incite the men to a massacre. We stopped him, but there were casualties."

"Fast Elk was one of them," Emma said, her anger replaced by grief.

Ridge snapped his gaze back to Emma, whose eyes filled with tears. Without thought, he hugged her and Chayton. Emma leaned heavily against him and the boy roused enough to wrap a thin arm around his neck.

"I'm sorry, Emma," Ridge whispered, massaging her back soothingly.

Chayton began to whimper and Ridge cupped the back of his head. "You're safe, cub," he said in Lakota.

Chayton quieted and laid his head back down on Emma's shoulder.

"Who's Fast Elk?" Colt demanded.

"My adopted father." Emma raised her chin defiantly.

"We're taking them back," Colt replied stiffly.

"Why? They're not hurting anybody."

"We have our orders, ma'am."

"Orders ain't always right," Ridge interjected. "They're mostly women and kids."

"I can't leave them here," Colt stated.

Clenching his jaw, Ridge steered Emma toward what remained of the lodge they'd used and lowered her to the ground. He knelt beside her, unsure of what to say.

He lifted his head and took in the carnage. A dog's carcass, barely recognizable, had been trampled into the ground, and two dead horses lay at the edge of the village. The chief's tipi, along with another half-dozen were completely destroyed with only ashes and tufts of buffalo hide marking where they had been. The pit fires were cold and the embers scattered. Kettles were upended and their contents spilt across the ground. Skinny dogs were lapping up the food, growling at anyone who came near them.

Naked children around Chayton's age were held tight in women's arms. Tears stained both young and old ruddy cheeks, and shoulders hitched with sobs that were eerily silent. There were two dozen men and boys being guarded, and many of them were bloodstained. It appeared their wounds had gone untended.

"How's Talutah?" Ridge asked Emma.

"Grieving." Her red-rimmed eyes stared past him.

Ridge restrained a sigh. "I'm sorry."

"Tell them." She made a wide arcing motion toward the People.

"I'm going to see what else I can find out," Ridge said. "You stay here."

"No, I'm going to help."

"You'll be safe here."

Emma's laugh was brittle. "From who?"

Ridge gritted his teeth. He'd noticed the soldiers' disrespectful gazes at Emma and he knew it was only the beginning. Once the cavalry unit returned to their post, word would spread fast about Emma and her son. She would be accosted like a whore and her son taunted with cruel barbs.

"Could you get my saddlebags? I need my herbs," she said.

He muttered an oath and helped her to her feet. "What about Chayton?"

She hesitated only a moment. "I'll leave him with the women."

Emma was arguing with one of the men guarding the warriors when he returned with her saddlebags.

"I'm only going to take care of their wounds," she snapped at the soldier.

"Nobody's allowed near them," the guard repeated.

"Who said that?"

"Captain Rivers."

Emma turned her glare on Ridge. "He's your friend."

The way she said "friend" made Ridge cringe inwardly.

"What does she want?" Colt Rivers's voice startled Ridge.

" 'She' wants to treat their injuries since you don't seem to care whether they live or die," Emma replied curtly.

Colt fixed his frigid gaze on Emma. "If you're willing to risk your life, go ahead."

"They won't hurt me," she argued.

"You don't know that, ma'am. But like I said, it's your neck."

Emma wavered only a moment. "I'll take that chance."

"I'll help," Ridge offered.

"Leave your weapons out here," Colt ordered.

Ridge reluctantly did as he said. Irritated, he followed Emma, aware of Colt's stare burning a hole between his shoulder blades.

Despite Colt's dire warnings, the warriors allowed Emma to examine their wounds. Four had been shot, while another had been slashed with a knife across his chest, and most all of them had minor cuts and bruises.

Akecheta, the old chief, had the most serious wound—a bullet in the chest. He'd been propped up with a rolled-up buffalo skin and his weathered face was washed-out and slack.

Emma examined the wound carefully, but even Ridge could see there was no hope. She sat back on her heels and her eyes welled with tears.

"My time has come. I will join those who have gone before me," the chief said, his voice so weak Ridge had to strain to hear it.

Ridge didn't bother with pointless platitudes. "You ruled your people well."

Akecheta coughed and blood flecked his bluish lips. "Help them," he wheezed. "Honor the dead."

Ridge had seen an Indian burial or two and knew of the ceremony, but he wasn't certain he could convince Colt to allow them time to take care of their dead.

"We will," Emma promised.

Ridge flashed her a dark look, but her gaze was locked with Akecheta's. Then the chief closed his eyes and his breathing grew labored, until it stopped altogether.

Ridge removed his hat and bowed his head as Emma touched his forehead, as if in a benediction.

"Good journey," she said in a husky whisper.

The guard closest to them called for two other soldiers to take Akecheta's body to lie with the others.

Although the sun was warm, a chill swept through Ridge. He raised his head and settled his hat back on his head. He followed Emma and assisted her as she diligently took care of the others' injuries.

Just as they finished, a woman's wail broke the silence, followed by another and another until the air seemed to vibrate with the unnatural laments. The mourning had begun.

He felt Emma shudder beside him.

"I hate that sound," she confessed. "When Enapay died, I mourned until I was so hoarse no more sound would come. I had nightmares every night for a week." She swallowed hard. "I expect the nightmares will last longer this time."

Ridge guided Emma past the guards, some of whom appeared irritated by the anguished cries. Most of the soldiers, however, kept their gazes averted from the Lakota. Ridge escorted Emma to the women and children, where Chayton was more than ready to return to her arms.

"I have to go talk to Co—the captain," Ridge said. "Will you be all right?"

She nodded but didn't meet his gaze.

Ridge went in search of Colt and found him by Pony

Cullen, along with Gabe and Pres. At one time, Ridge had called the three men friends. Now, he wasn't certain.

Cullen glared at Ridge. "If it ain't the Injun lover himself."

Gabe kicked the scout's outstretched legs. "Shut up, Cullen."

"What do you want?" Colt asked Ridge, his expression stony.

"Akecheta, the chief, just died. He asked me if his people could have proper burials."

Cullen snorted, but one look from Gabe ensured that the scout kept the rest of his comments to himself.

"How long is it going to take?" Colt asked.

"Probably a day, maybe two."

Colt scowled and swore under his breath.

"It's the right thing to do, Captain," Pres Wylie said in his soft Southern drawl. "I'll help them, sir."

Colt nodded sharply. "All right. Get them started."

"Yes, sir," Gabe replied without hesitation.

Pres and Gabe headed toward the survivors.

After a curt command to Cullen's two guards, Colt walked away in the opposite direction and Ridge followed. Once they were out of Cullen's hearing, Colt stopped.

"I didn't want this to happen, Ridge. In fact, I was hoping Cullen wouldn't find them," Colt admitted in a low voice.

"But he did, and you weren't able to maintain control of your men," Ridge said.

Two red splotches colored Colt's cheeks. "Dammit, Ridge, I did what I could."

"You could've done more."

"Do you actually think I wanted this to turn into a massacre?"

"Maybe it was payback for what the Indians did to your wife down in Texas."

Colt's face whitened and his eyes glittered with rage. "No!"

Ridge took a step toward him. "These Indians saved

Emma Hartwell's life and gave her a home. In fact, the Lakota who found her and adopted her was killed by *your* men." He punctuated his words with a forefinger to Colt's chest.

The captain grabbed his wrist in a bruising grip. "If you actually believe I could order the murder of innocent lives—Indian or otherwise—you don't know me at all."

Ridge stared into Colt's piercing blue eyes. "Maybe I don't," he finally said.

Colt released him with a flicker of disappointment, which he masked immediately. "Did you know about the Hartwell woman's son?"

"Not until we got here."

"Bastard?"

Ridge stifled his impatience. "She was married to the boy's father."

Colt's lips turned downward. "Once word gets out, her past few months in Sunset will have been a cakewalk compared to what's ahead."

"We left the boy here and were headed back to Sunset when—" he broke off, unable to explain Emma's gift. "When we had a feeling something was wrong."

"And now?"

"Now there's no way in hell she'll leave her boy behind to be raised on a reservation."

"Old man Hartwell's going to have a fit."

Ridge snorted, not giving a tinker's damn about Hartwell. "Good for the son of a bitch."

"What about Miss Hartwell and her son?"

Ridge only shook his head, unwilling to think about Emma's upcoming trials. "Me and Emma'll stay through the burials; then we'll be heading back. Emma will want to see Fast Elk laid to rest." Ridge turned to leave, but Colt's hand fastened on his sleeve.

"She's a squaw woman, Ridge," Colt stated. "With a half-breed son. She'll only bring you trouble."

Ridge's muscles bunched, but he managed not to take

another swing at Colt. Besides, Colt was only repeating the same thoughts Ridge had already had.

"I know." And with that, Ridge trudged back to Emma.

EMMA moved in a daze, helping prepare the bodies for burial by dressing them in their finest clothing and painting their faces. A little girl whom Chayton had often played with, was the only child casualty. However, four of the nine warriors killed were younger than Emma.

Smudges of pungent smoke that purified the living and dead surrounded the women as they silently performed the final preparations for the burials. Two of the soldiers, those whom Emma had seen Ridge speaking to, helped the Indians build the wooden platforms for the bodies. She was grateful for their help but it still took the rest of the day and into the evening to complete them.

Once she'd walked within ten yards of Pony Cullen, outwardly ignoring his taunts but barely controlling the impulse to take a knife to his heart. She'd never felt such overwhelming hatred for another person, and it frightened her to know she could.

As she worked, Chayton slept with the other children on a buffalo skin pallet in the middle of the camp. Four young girls watched them closely. Every few minutes Emma would glance at him to reassure herself he was alive.

Emma was concerned with Talutah's stoic silence as the older woman prepared Fast Elk for his final journey. She didn't even seem to know Emma was there, nor did she search out Chayton. Talutah focused entirely on her husband of many years.

A long shadow fell across Emma and she looked up.

"How's Talutah doing?" Ridge asked softly.

Emma followed the woman's deliberate motions with growing trepidation. "Not very well."

"Once the shock wears off, she'll be able to grieve and move on."

Emma shook her head. "She was only able to give Fast Elk a daughter, and she died. I remember her telling me how she urged him to take another wife to bear him a son, but he wouldn't." Emma absently wiped away a tear rolling down her cheek.

Ridge shifted uncomfortably. "Indians don't show their feelings much, but I know Fast Elk loved you like you were his flesh and blood."

More tears coursed down her cheeks, but she wasn't crying. "I know."

Ridge took Emma's arm and helped her to her feet. He remained standing close and cupped her face to wipe away the tear tracks with his thumbs. She grasped his wrists and lowered his hands.

"Would you mind staying close to Chayton tonight?" Emma asked. "I'll be sitting with Talutah."

"I'll watch him," Ridge reassured. He lowered his hands to his sides and opened his mouth as if to say something more. Instead he spun around and strode away.

Too tired to look away, Emma followed his progress across the camp. He didn't pause until he joined Captain Rivers.

She didn't know who to trust. Although she'd treated their wounds and helped them with the burial preparations, the Lakota avoided her like the plague, and Talutah was lost in misery. Most of the soldiers were eyeing her like she was a bottle of whiskey in a dry town.

Emma rubbed her throbbing brow and pulled her hand away, only to notice dried blood across her knuckles. She wondered whose it was.

She lifted her gaze to Chayton and a tiny shimmer of light broke through the black sorrow. Her resolve strengthened. No matter what anyone said, she wouldn't leave him behind again.

THE long night passed, underscored by the survivors' grieving for their dead. Moans rose and fell, interspersed with an occasional wail which ululated through the camp. Fires flickered brightly, but smoke hazed the air and the cloying scent of cedar infiltrated everything.

Ridge lay on his side facing Chayton who slept restlessly beside him. Every time Ridge closed his eyes, he saw blood being lapped up by the earth beneath still bodies. He couldn't distinguish between memory, reality, and nightmare. The massacre he'd unwittingly been involved in last fall blurred with the one that had occurred twenty-four hours ago. Unknown victims took on the faces of those killed here.

As an army scout, Ridge had believed in what he was doing—making the wilderness safer for the incoming tide of settlers. However, on his last scouting mission, he'd been ordered to find a band of renegade Indians who'd attacked a wagon train. Ridge tracked them to a village. Instead of culling out the guilty, the army unit had ridden into the camp with guns blazing and swords flashing. Ridge had tried to stop the bloodlust, but he'd only been able to watch in horror as women and children were cut down, screams dying in their throats as their bodies fell under bullets and blades. He would never forgive himself for his part in the bloody massacre.

Ridge sat up, careful not to wake Chayton. As exhausted as he was, Ridge knew he wouldn't be able to go back to sleep any time soon. He added some wood to the fire and settled beside its warmth.

A figure emerged out of the shadows and Ridge tensed until he recognized Emma's slumped figure. She sank to the ground beside Chayton, her legs folded to the side. Gazing down at her son, she brushed her hand across his long, straight hair.

Ridge didn't break the companionable silence, leaving that to Emma if she was inclined to talk.

"Sergeant Sanders ordered me to get some sleep," she said, minutes later.

Ridge smiled. "He's hard to ignore."

Her lips curved upward, but the smile was fleeting. "I like him."

Ridge felt a stirring of jealousy. "He doesn't judge folks by the color of their skin."

Emma continued to stroke her son's hair. "What'll happen to them?"

"They'll be taken to the reservation."

"Will your friend let them take their belongings?"

"He's a fair man. He'll give them time to get their things together."

"If he's so fair, he'd let them stay here."

"He's only doing his job, Emma." Ridge felt compelled to defend him.

"He should find another job," she shot back.

After the somber task of preparing bodies for burial, Ridge was glad to see some of her spirit returned. "Colt's got his reasons for what he does."

"Maybe so, but it doesn't make it right."

Ridge sighed and lifted his gaze to the star-filled sky. "I didn't say it did."

Low voices crawled through the night and a muffled snore or two came from the soldiers who slept some forty yards away. The Lakota's wrenching moans continued unabated.

"Get some sleep, Emma. After the dead are put to rest, we're leaving for Sunset," Ridge said.

"With Chayton."

"With Chayton," Ridge repeated.

Emma was too tired for little more than a nod. She curled up beside Chayton and was asleep in moments.

Ridge rose and covered mother and child with his blanket, then watched over them until morning.

Seventeen

FROM atop his horse, Ridge watched the Lakota prepare to leave the camp at noon the next day. Despite the resentment of some of the soldiers, Colt had given the Indians time to dismantle the remaining tipis and pack their things. The dogs were put into harness to pull the travois loaded with the Lakota's sparse belongings.

Emma had helped Talutah with her preparations. Any other time the older woman wouldn't have accepted her assistance, but since they'd left Fast Elk on his burial platform early that morning, Talutah had become distant and unresponsive. Ridge saw the fear in Emma's face, as well as Chayton's confusion, at Talutah's uncharacteristic behavior.

A horse trotted up and he turned to see Colt draw up alongside him.

"When are you and Miss Hartwell leaving?" he asked without preamble.

Ridge fingered the reins of Emma's horse, which stood docilely beside Paint. "As soon as Talutah has her belongings ready to go."

Colt shifted in his saddle. "I'm sorry things turned out this way, Ridge."

"It only takes one man to rouse up the bloodlust. We've seen it before," Ridge allowed. Violent memories stirred and he mentally shook his head to rid his mind of the images.

Colt cursed under his breath. "I should've shot him as soon as we left the fort."

Ridge's gaze traveled to Cullen, who watched the activity with contempt from his bound position atop a horse. "You ain't a cold-blooded murderer like him."

"You thought I was."

Ridge's gaze flickered across his friend's swollen and discolored jaw. "Hell, Colt, I wasn't thinking straight."

"Yeah, I noticed," Colt said dryly. "When it comes to Miss Hartwell you got the same problem. She's got you where you don't know up from down, and you don't even know it."

Ridge stiffened. "What's between me and her is none of your concern."

"The hell it isn't. I don't want to see you lose all you've been working for because of her and her kid."

At least he hadn't said *half-breed*.

"Leave it alone, Colt," Ridge warned.

The captain narrowed his eyes and pursed his lips. He looked away. "We'll be behind you, but I won't be pushing them. There's too many wounded and old folks."

"That'll ease Emma's mind," Ridge said stiffly.

"It'll ease *my* mind when you two head out. But watch yourselves."

"Are you going to be all right without a scout?"

"Sarge is pretty good about picking up sign." Colt scanned their surroundings. "I know you and Nyes don't see eye-to-eye, but if we don't make it back tell him what happened."

Guilt nudged Ridge's conscience. "We could ride with you and I could scout."

"No. You need to get Miss Hartwell back to her father's ranch and give her some time before the rest of the town hears about her situation. And you can bet when we get back the gossip's going to start flying."

Colt was right. The townspeople would ravenously devour the newest tidbit about the fallen Miss Hartwell. If they made it back before the cavalry, that gave Emma's family time to overcome their shock and decide what to do. No matter what Ridge thought of old man Hartwell, he did seem to care for his daughters.

"All right," Ridge agreed reluctantly. "Keep your powder dry, pard."

"You, too."

Each placing a hand on the other's forearm, the two men said goodbye, but it lacked the warmth of past farewells.

Colt wheeled away to see if the caravan was ready to move out. Ridge watched him until his attention was drawn by Emma's approach. If possible, she looked more tense than yesterday. Her wan face and lank hair gave the impression she was ill, but it was a sickness of the heart, not body.

Ridge dismounted and went to her side. He helped her onto Clementine while Chayton leaned against his leg. Then Ridge lifted the boy onto the saddle in front of Emma. His little hands wrapped around the pommel and his hollow eyes lit with delight. Ridge's heart missed a beat at the boy's obvious pleasure. He patted Chayton's knee before climbing into his own saddle.

"Is Talutah any better?" Ridge asked.

Emma shrugged listlessly. "She does what she's told, but doesn't seem to know what's going on."

It was hard for Ridge to imagine the tough woman so beaten, but losing Fast Elk had been a terrible blow. "Is someone with her?"

"Shimmering Water said she would stay close to her."

"Good. Colt said he wouldn't push them."

Emma snorted in disbelief. "Just like he didn't lead the charge on the village."

Caught between loyalties, Ridge didn't comment. "We'll go on ahead of them."

"No. I want to make sure Talutah is all right."

"You said Shimmering Water will take care of her. We

need to get you back before the soldiers arrive." Ridge took a deep breath. "The truth of the matter is as soon as Colt's unit gets back, word's going to spread like wildfire about you and Chayton. If we can get to your folks beforehand, that'll give them some time to get used to the idea before tongues start wagging."

If possible, Emma's face paled further. "I hadn't thought of that."

"It's no wonder. You're exhausted and grieving." He glanced around to see the last of the caravan winding out of the camp. "We'd best head out."

Ridge felt the hostile looks from both sides—Lakota and white—as he and Emma trotted past them. He glanced at Emma and noticed the stern set of her chin. If he hadn't been looking so closely, he wouldn't have noticed the accompanying quiver.

Chayton fell asleep not long after they began their journey. Ridge and Emma didn't speak, but not because of the sleeping boy. Talking about what had happened would be pointless.

At dusk, they made camp. Chayton roused long enough to eat some food, then dropped off again. Drained emotionally and physically, Ridge and Emma fell asleep soon after the boy.

The following morning was brisk and they ate quickly. While readying their horses, Ridge noticed Emma pause and stare back in the direction from which they'd come. Guilt creased her brow and Ridge could do nothing more than give her shoulders a sympathetic squeeze.

They traveled steadily through the day despite the dreary gray clouds and occasional light showers that felt more like a cool mist. During the midday break, the sun burst through for a few minutes of relief from the dampness. Chayton regained much of his energy and spent the respite chasing bugs and searching for odd-shaped rocks. Ridge challenged him to a foot race and let the boy win, which delighted Chayton and brought a smile to Emma's haggard face.

They crossed rolling brown hills broken by massive gray jagged rocks thrusting up from the earth, and plodded through temporary ponds formed from the spring melt. Knowing their destination, they made better time traveling back. It had taken nearly two weeks to find the Lakota, but by Ridge's reckoning, it would take only five days to return to Sunset.

Chayton grew more animated and excited, probably thinking of it all as a big adventure. He buoyed Emma and Ridge's spirits with his childish questions and enthusiasm, but he also exhausted them. By the third night, Emma and Ridge were both relieved when Chayton went to sleep.

Sipping coffee, Ridge glanced across the fire at the boy's dark head, which peeped above his blanket. "You're going to have your hands full with him."

Emma, leaning against her saddle with her legs outstretched in front of her, nodded. "He's going to miss playing with other children."

Ridge looked at the woman and saw sadness lingering in her eyes. "I s'pect he will. Have you thought about what you're going to do when we get back?"

"It depends on my father." She rubbed her suspiciously bright eyes. "If he can accept Chayton, things won't be easy, but they won't be impossible either."

"And if he doesn't?"

She granted him a small smile. "I'm hoping my aunt in St. Paul will be willing to take us in. Maybe I could find a job in the city."

Ridge considered the jobs Emma might be able to get. He didn't think much of any of them. "Do you think your father will throw you out?"

"I don't know."

He barely heard her soft words. Ridge's stepfather had beaten him, but he hadn't cast him out. Could John Hartwell actually disown his daughter?

"I don't want your money for finding the village," Ridge finally spoke.

Emma snapped her head up to meet his gaze. "We made a deal."

Ridge shifted on the unforgiving ground. "You can use that hundred dollars to make a new start."

"I always keep my word," she said stubbornly.

"And I'm releasing you from it."

"You can't do that."

"It's my hundred dollars. I can do anything I want with it."

"Buy some cattle, or better yet, buy back some of your land from my father. It would serve him right."

Ever since he returned to Sunset and claimed his inheritance, Ridge had wanted nothing else. But now, he couldn't bring himself to take money from a woman and her son whom he'd come to care about far too much.

He held his tongue, but the argument wasn't over. Besides, even if her pride demanded he accept it, he'd find a way to give the money back.

"We'd best turn in," he said. "We'll be covering a lot of miles tomorrow."

Emma lay down beside her son, just as she'd done since they'd started back. Ridge stretched out on the other side of the fire and tried to ignore the cold emptiness beside him. And inside him.

He had a feeling it'd be a long time before he stopped missing Emma's warmth.

IT was the afternoon of the fifth day when Emma caught sight of her father's imposing home. They'd passed cattle with the Hartwell brand in the morning, but they had to ride some distance before arriving at the ranch house itself.

They paused on a rise a quarter of a mile from the buildings. Emma saw three men around the corral, working with unbroken horses. She heard the whoops and hollers, but couldn't understand the words. She could imagine them, though.

Chayton shifted in front of her. "What is that?" he asked in Lakota as he pointed toward the ranch house.

"That's where your white grandfather and grandmother live," Emma replied in the same language. "Remember how to say their names in English?"

"Gran-fa-ter and gran-ma-ter," Chayton said after a moment.

Emma patted his small shoulder. "Good. Do you remember your aunt's name?"

Another pause as the boy's face scrunched in thought. "Sarah."

Emma had been teaching him English throughout the trek, giving the boy's lively mind something to focus on during the long hours in the saddle. She wanted him to greet her family in their own language, hoping to make a good impression. Not that it would help if her parents were bound and determined to despise their own grandson.

Emma sighed heavily.

"Are you ready for this?" Ridge asked quietly.

"No," she said huskily. Ridge's long, cool fingers brushed hers and she clutched his hand. "Thank you. For finding Chayton and for—" She glanced away. "Everything."

Ridge's eyes burned with passion, as if remembering those nights filled with "everything." Attraction blazed and flared to settle as an ache in her chest.

Emma released his hand and asked with forced brightness, "Shall we?"

"Follow me," Ridge said.

Puzzled, she waited for him to go ahead. He led her down a circuitous route to the kitchen door at the back of the house. Realizing he did it so the ranch hands wouldn't see Chayton or herself, she wasn't certain if she should be grateful or upset. She wasn't ashamed of Chayton. He was her son. But she understood his reasoning—it was the same one used for going ahead of Captain Rivers and his unit.

Ridge dismounted and walked around the horses to lift

Chayton from Emma's saddle. Once Chayton was safely on the ground, Ridge wrapped his hands around Emma's waist and eased her down, drawing her body along his as he lowered her. His thumbs brushed the sensitive skin beneath her breasts and she gasped at the bolt of desire.

Quickly stepping away from Ridge, she took Chayton's hand in her sweat-dampened one and pushed open the door. She was relieved when Ridge followed them inside. Since it was too early to begin supper, no one was in the kitchen. Chayton tried to see everything at once as he pressed closer to Emma.

She took a deep breath and looked back at the man who'd unintentionally claimed her heart. She took strength and comfort in his solid presence, and walked through the swinging doorway into the dining room. Footsteps on the stairs made her turn to the wide staircase to see Sarah descending.

"Sarah?" she called softly when her sister reached the bottom of the stairs.

Sarah turned and froze, her eyes huge and her mouth agape. "Emma?" she whispered hoarsely.

"I'm home." Emma's voice trembled with anxiety.

Sarah raced across the floor and flung her arms around Emma, who hugged her sister with equal enthusiasm. Sarah stepped back, but clung to Emma's hands. "Are you all right? Where have you been? Everyone's been sick with worry."

"I'm sorry. Ridge—Mr. Madoc found me and brought me home," Emma said. Her heart pounding like a smithy's hammer, she released her sister and put a hand on Chayton's small shoulder. "He's why I had to leave."

Sarah's shocked expression would've been comical if Emma hadn't been on pins and needles. "An Indian boy?"

"This is Chayton, my son." Emma paused. "Your nephew."

Sarah's face paled and she swayed. Ridge caught her arm to steady her.

"Sarah, are you all right?" Emma asked with concern.

"Sarah?" Chayton piped up.

Emma looked down at her son's curious and excited expression. "Yes, Chayton. This is your aunt," she said in Lakota. "Sarah."

"Oh my," Sarah whispered. "Oh my."

"Do you need to sit down, ma'am?" Ridge asked.

"I think that might be a good idea," Sarah replied weakly.

Ridge led her to a heavy oak dining room chair and eased her into it. Emma and Chayton followed and stood in front of Sarah.

The younger girl stared at Chayton, lifted her gaze to Emma, then returned to study Chayton. "He has your chin and nose," she finally said.

"That's what Talutah, my adopted mother, always said, too." Emma fought the lump in her throat. "My husband Enapay said our son had my eyes, too."

"Your husband?" Sarah squeaked out the question.

"Yes. He's dead. I'm a widow," Emma said, trying to hold a tremulous smile.

"Sarah," Chayton said again with a wide grin. He tugged on her hands and raised his arms.

"I think he wants you to pick him up," Emma translated.

For a long, heart-pounding moment, Sarah stared at the boy. Then, with a radiant smile, she lifted Chayton onto her lap. Sarah's eyes sparkled with unshed tears. "I'm an aunt."

Emma stepped closer to Ridge, wanting to share her relief and happiness at Sarah's acceptance. Ridge smiled back, understanding without words like he so often did.

"How old is he? What does his name mean? Are you both going to live here now?" Sarah started throwing out questions as Chayton stared in fascination at her blond hair.

Sharp footsteps sounded on the polished wood floor and Emma turned to see her father and mother enter the dining room.

"Emma!" Martha Hartwell cried and hugged her daughter.

Dazed, Emma wrapped her arms around her mother. The familiar scent of rose water wafted around her, reminding her of long-ago days. "I've missed you, Mother."

Emma glanced over her mother's shoulder at her father to find his gaze locked on Chayton. She drew away from the older woman and moved to Sarah and Chayton's side. Trembling, Emma announced, "Mother, Father, I want to introduce Chayton. My son."

Her mother's eyes rolled upward and she collapsed. Ridge lunged toward her and managed to partially catch her, saving her from a bump on the head.

"Get some water," her father ordered. He shoved Ridge away from her, as if he thought Ridge intended to murder her.

Emma lifted Chayton into her arms and Sarah bustled into the kitchen for the water. She returned carrying a glass and a damp cloth. Glowering, Ridge kept his distance, turning the brim of his hat around and around in his hands.

Her mother roused and glanced around in confusion, but when her gaze settled on Emma and Chayton she let out a moan. Sarah and their father helped her into the chair Sarah had vacated.

Her father's lips thinned and his eyes were stormy. "Explain yourself, Emma."

Although she bristled at the command, Emma knew they deserved an explanation. "I'd been living with the Lakota for two years when Enapay began courting me. I had given up on ever being found and brought back home. I cared for him and we married three months later. Chayton was born a year after our marriage. My husband was killed during a raid when Chayton was less than two years old."

"You married a—a savage?" her mother asked, shock evident in her lined features.

"Yes, Mother, I married a 'savage' who loved me and treated me well. He even spoiled me." She smiled tenderly, remembering the times Enapay would return, bearing some gift for her.

Her father's face deepened to scarlet and a vein pulsed in his brow. "He was an Indian, for God's sake."

"He was a decent, honorable man." Emma lifted her chin and met her father's gaze head-on. No longer was she a girl, and no longer would she cower under John Hartwell's dictates.

He cursed loudly and fluently, drawing shocked looks from Sarah and their mother. Chayton buried his face in the curve of Emma's neck. "And now you want to raise your half-breed bast—"

"Hold on, Hartwell," Ridge broke in, stepping forward. Every taut line in his muscular body radiated furious indignation. "Chayton's parents were married so he's no—" He crushed the brim of his hat in his fists. "He's an innocent little boy who don't deserve your narrow-minded insults."

Emma's throat tightened and her eyes smarted. If she didn't love Ridge already, she would've fallen for him at that moment.

Timidly Sarah stepped forward, her hands twisting together in front of her. "Mr. Madoc is right," she stated, shocking Emma with her mettle. "Emma and Chayton have had a long journey and would probably like to clean up and rest before dinner. Isn't that right, Emma?"

"Yes, thank you, Sarah," Emma managed to say past her shock at her sister's newfound assertiveness.

Sarah smiled, but when she laid an ice-cold hand on Emma's arm, Emma knew how terrified she was defying their father.

"Could you take Chayton upstairs?" Emma asked her sister. "I'll be up shortly."

Sarah's smile wavered for only a moment. Emma spoke some soothing words to Chayton and passed him to his aunt. Once Sarah and Chayton were out-of-sight, Emma faced her parents. Never before had she felt so many mixed emotions—anger, disappointment, resentment, and fear. But it was anguish which prevailed and enveloped her heart.

"When do you want us gone?" Emma asked her parents bluntly.

Her father's jaw muscle clenched. "Why didn't you tell us?"

Emma laughed bitterly. "After your reaction to Chayton you have to ask?" Out of the corner of her eye, she saw Ridge shift uncomfortably. "Maybe you should pay Mr. Madoc so he can leave and not be witness to any more of our family squabbles. Oh, and you owe him another hundred dollars."

"Why?"

"I promised him a bonus for bringing Chayton back," Emma said. She figured Ridge would accept the hundred from her father more readily than from herself, and she would pay her father back. Someday.

"Did you come through town?" her father asked with a scowl.

Emma shook her head, immediately guessing the reason for his question. "No. And Mr. Madoc brought us around to the back door so none of the hired men saw us either."

"Emma, go upstairs. Madoc, come with me into my study," her father commanded. He gave his wife's shoulder a reassuring squeeze. "Keep the cool cloth on your brow, Martha, and don't try to rise until I return."

"What are you—" Emma began.

"I'll pay him. Go upstairs."

Emma didn't like being ordered about like a child, but the long journey had exhausted her. A bath and clean clothes were also enticing. It seemed like she'd been living in the same skirt and blouse for months rather than days.

Realizing she might not see Ridge again, her heart skipped a beat. For three weeks they'd not been far from one another. Thinking of the nights they'd lain together, Emma shivered with longing. But she reminded herself she'd known it couldn't last. Ridge had his own life to attend to, and she had a son whose needs came before her own.

"Thank you for everything, Mr. Madoc," Emma said

formally, refusing to give her father another reason to hate Ridge Madoc.

His warm blue eyes caressed her but he kept his expression bland. "You're welcome, Miss Hartwell. You take care of yourself and that fine boy of yours."

"I will," Emma whispered, her emotions overcoming her.

Before she did something she'd regret, she hurried up the wide staircase. Suddenly weary beyond words, Emma wanted to ensure Chayton was all right, then sleep for a week.

She only wished it would be in Ridge's bed.

$\mathcal{E}$IGHTEEN

RIDGE'S gaze followed Emma until she disappeared from view and a sharp ache arrowed through him. Already he could feel unfamiliar loneliness, the kind he hadn't felt since his ma had died. But Emma didn't need him anymore. Her sister would stand beside her, and hopefully her parents would come around to accept her son.

Suddenly weary, Ridge followed John Hartwell into his fancy office. Books lined the bookshelves that covered two of the walls, and Ridge had this vision of a young Emma sneaking in here to search for one to read. A fireplace encompassed much of the third wall, and the fourth was dominated by large windows.

Hartwell sat behind his desk, looking like some king presiding over his kingdom. He didn't invite Ridge to sit, but Ridge did so anyhow, and earned a scowl from Hartwell. After dropping into a brown leather chair, he eyed Hartwell's cool mask.

"The boy wasn't part of the deal," Hartwell said.

Ridge shrugged. "I didn't even know about him until we found the village."

"'We?' You were only supposed to find Emma and bring her home immediately."

Cursing his unintentional slip, Ridge propped his elbows on the chair arms and steepled his fingers, effecting a nonchalance at odds with the tight coil in his gut. "You didn't say *when* you wanted her home. I signed on to find her and bring her back. I fulfilled my end of the bargain." He inwardly flinched at the inference that Emma was merely a business matter—the subject of a black-and-white contract. She'd long ago ceased being a means to an end.

Hartwell slumped back in his chair and his face sagged, as if he'd aged twenty years. "Do you realize what kind of life she'll have raising a half-breed child?"

Ridge felt a fleeting sympathy for the man. "Yes, sir. For what it's worth, I tried to talk her out of bringing him back."

The rancher blinked in surprise, but quickly covered it with a scowl. "When people find out, she's going to be turned away from businesses and respectable folks won't want anything to do with her. Her son won't be allowed to attend school and the children will tease him, and worse."

"She knows." Ridge narrowed his eyes. "What about you? You gonna turn her away, too?"

Irritation sharpened Hartwell's features. "She's my daughter."

"And Chayton's your grandson."

Hartwell flinched. "I can send them away someplace where no one will know about her unfortunate past."

"You might be able to hide her past, but Chayton can't be hidden away and Emma won't be parted from him. He's her flesh and blood." Ridge paused. "Unless you're only getting rid of them because you're embarrassed by her."

"Emma's my daughter!" Hartwell spun his chair around to stare outside, hiding his face from Ridge. "I'll do what's best for her."

"She's not your little girl anymore, Hartwell, and she won't take kindly to you making her decisions."

Silence filled the room.

Finally, Hartwell opened a desk drawer and counted some bills. He held them out to Ridge. "Two hundred dollars. The one hundred we agreed on, and another hundred to keep your mouth shut. It'll get out soon enough but as long as her bast—her boy stays inside, nobody will find out."

"You can't hide him away forever."

"No, but the longer I can keep him out-of-sight, the longer I can protect Emma."

Ridge debated whether to tell him about the soldiers who had seen Emma and Chayton together in the village, but decided that was Emma's business. If Hartwell wanted to pay him an extra hundred, he wasn't going to argue. In fact, he even felt a measure of satisfaction. Hell, the man owed him that and more for cheating Ridge out of his rightful legacy.

"I won't tell anyone," Ridge promised. He stood and pocketed his money, then walked to the door. Halting, he looked at Hartwell over his shoulder. "Instead of being ashamed of her, you ought to be proud of her."

With that quiet remark, Ridge strode out by way of the kitchen to gather Paint and lead Clementine over to the hostler. As he rode away from Hartwell's ranch, loneliness settled like an iron mantle across his shoulders.

THE following days dragged for Ridge. With the needed money in his pocket, he sent a telegram to the seller of the bull in Cheyenne and told him he'd be down to purchase the animal soon. The only reason Ridge didn't leave Sunset right away was because he'd promised Colt he'd pay a visit to Colonel Nyes if the captain didn't show up.

Five days after returning to Sunset, Ridge dropped by the hardware store to talk with Howard Freeman and ended up taking his daughter Grace to lunch at the café. By the time their meals were served, Ridge was certain he'd go crazy with Grace's prattling on about this person's dress and that person's hair. When Grace clumsily turned the subject to Emma Hartwell, Ridge recognized the baited hook.   •

"I just can't imagine living among the savages like she did," Grace said, round-eyed and a little too innocent. "Why on earth did she want to go back to them?"

Ridge wiped his mouth with his napkin as his appetite fled. "You'll have to ask Miss Hartwell."

"Oh, I could never. Some things just aren't discussed in polite conversation."

Ridge bit the inside of his cheek to refrain from biting off the girl's feather-brained head. To his way of thinking, bustles and coiffures weren't polite conversation either.

"Nobody's seen Emma since she's been home," Grace said.

"She probably needed to rest up," Ridge replied. He'd kept his word and told nobody about Emma's son, but it wasn't Hartwell's money that bought his silence. It was his sense of protectiveness toward Emma and Chayton. "I'd best be getting back to my place."

Grace deliberately looked down at her nearly full plate. "I haven't finished yet."

You would've if you hadn't been running off at the mouth, Ridge thought peevishly. He forced a smile that barely made it past a grimace. "Don't hurry. I'll pay the bill on my way out." He stood and grabbed his hat before she could argue. "Good day, Grace."

He paid for the two meals and escaped outside. Why had Grace's chattering bothered him so much today? He'd spent some time with her before, and had managed to nod and utter the right comments at the right moment. But this time, her high-pitched voice and endless claptrap had nearly driven him crazy.

His gaze strayed up the road, to where Emma Hartwell and Chayton were hidden from prying eyes at her father's ranch. At least a dozen times a day he had to talk himself out of riding over to see how they were faring.

Be honest. You want to see Emma.

He thought the pang of missing her would fade, but it

only gnawed at him, like the hollow left by a pulled tooth. If Colt would just return, Ridge could take off to Cheyenne and pick up the bull. Time and distance would help him get past his pining for Emma.

Disgusted with his weakness, he stepped off the board-walk onto the main street. Puffs of dust arose around his moccasins. While he'd been chasing after Emma in the wilderness, the snow had melted and the ground had dried, leaving the town coated with a fine layer of grime.

He climbed into his saddle and, without making a con-scious decision, headed toward the fort, which lay seven miles east. Maybe Colt had made it back last night, thus freeing Ridge from his obligation. Forty-five minutes later he could tell by the signs that no unit with a passel of Indi-ans had come near the fort. He veered Paint away from the military post and rode in the direction from where they'd be coming. If they weren't far off, Ridge could leave for Cheyenne with a clear conscience.

After an hour of steady travel, he spotted a plume of ris-ing dust. Another hour and he called out to Colt who rode at the front of the column. Dust coated the captain's face and uniform, but his smile was welcoming when Ridge ap-proached him.

"You never were much on waiting," Colt said.

Ridge ignored the familiar jibe. "Any trouble?"

Colt shook his head. "Quiet as a horse thief after a hanging. How about you and Miss Hartwell?"

"No problems unless you count her ma fainting when she saw her grandson."

"How was old man Hartwell?"

"Just what you'd expect. He's only worried about how it'll reflect on him." Ridge stood in his stirrups to study the column. "I see you still got Cullen tied up."

"Gagged him, too. Son of a bitch wouldn't stop cussing. Every time we took the gag off, he'd start in on how the colonel's going to have my bars."

Ridge studied his friend who had dark crescents be-neath his eyes. "Any truth to it?"

Colt looked away. "It isn't a secret that me and the old man don't see eye to eye. That was one of the reasons I was surprised he assigned me this mission. Nyes also knows I have no respect for Cullen."

"And Nyes and Cullen are thick as thieves," Ridge interjected.

"Yep. The problem is I don't have any proof Cullen was intending to kill every man, woman, and child in that village. All I got is my gut, and Nyes isn't going to accept that."

"But Sarge and Pres—they'll stand behind you."

Colt dragged his bleak gaze to Ridge. "Nyes also knows they're loyal to me."

Ridge shook his head slowly, pondering something that had been stuck in his craw since he and Emma arrived at the destroyed camp. "How'd you get past the sentries? They had a natural defense with that narrow trail into the valley and guards always watching it."

Colt shrugged. "We didn't run into anybody until we almost stumbled into the camp. The lookouts must've been sleeping, or maybe they thought they were safe enough without them."

"Maybe." Ridge didn't think it likely but he couldn't come up with a better excuse. "You're close enough to the post now that you shouldn't have any problems."

"You in a hurry to get somewhere?"

"Cheyenne. I'm going to pick up my bull."

Colt grinned. "Congratulations. It won't be long until you're an honest to God rancher."

Ridge chuckled. "I need more than a bull for that, but it's a good start."

"Good luck to you."

"Thanks." Ridge paused and fixed a serious gaze on his friend. "I know you and me don't agree about Miss Hartwell, but could you keep an eye on her? With the soldiers back, things might get ugly."

Colt narrowed his eyes. "She really got under your skin."

Ridge scowled and shifted his backside on the saddle. "Would you do it?"

"Yeah, but I doubt old man Hartwell will be letting her out of her cage."

That's probably what the ranch felt like to Emma—a gilded cage with everything but the one thing she truly wanted—her and her son's freedom.

"Thanks. I'll stop at my place, then head out. I should be back in a week, maybe ten days," Ridge said. "Good luck with Nyes."

Colt grimaced. "I'll need it."

Ridge glimpsed Talutah in the line of Indians, and he gnashed his teeth at her weary shuffle and slumped figure. "You mind if I talk to her a minute?"

Colt shook his head, his face somber. "You're welcome to try. She doesn't speak to anyone. I'm not even sure she knows where she's going."

"She knows," Ridge said softly.

He nodded to Colt and trotted closer to the Lakota woman. Dismounting, he fell in step with her. Her hair, which she'd hacked off during her mourning for Fast Elk, lay uneven and straggly across her shoulders.

"Winona and Chayton are safe and well," Ridge said to Talutah in her language.

A slight stumble in her plodding shuffle was Ridge's only sign that she heard him. He continued walking beside her, leading Paint. Finally, Talutah raised her head. Ridge was shocked by the grayness of her pallor and the lifelessness in her eyes.

"It is good," she said, her voice hoarse from disuse. "Chayton will grow strong, like his grandfather Fast Elk."

"*Ha*. You taught Winona well the ways of the People. She will honor you and Fast Elk, as will her son."

Talutah grasped his hand with cold, bony fingers. "Be well and live with honor."

Ridge gently squeezed her painfully thin hand. "I'll do my best," he whispered.

She released him and her gaze dropped to the ground

once more. Ridge stepped out of line and watched the rag-
tag Indians pass by in silence. A group of soldiers brought
up the rear. They glanced at Ridge curiously, but they, too,
seemed to understand the sad injustice done to their Lakota
captives.

Once everyone had passed, Ridge reined Paint around
to ride back to his home.

THE slant of the sun told Emma she could wait only five
more minutes. She'd been pacing outside Ridge's small
cabin for the last twenty minutes, hoping to speak to him
one more time. When she'd arrived, she'd called out his
name but he wasn't around. Neither was Paint. He might
have already left for Cheyenne to pick up the bull he'd
proudly told her about some nights ago. It was the reason
he'd come to find her—he needed the money to buy the animal. After everything that happened on their journey, she
wondered if he regretted taking the job, and shuddered at
the thought of someone like Pony Cullen coming after her
instead.

Emma spied a rider coming down the road, and the
black-and-white horse was easily recognizable as Ridge's.
Relief made her shoulders slump, and awakened awareness
made her heart race. Although she thought of him often, it
couldn't compare to seeing him in the flesh, his lean, muscular body flowing smoothly with his horse's gait. Awareness of the man brought flutters to her belly, and her
breasts became heavy and more sensitive. Glancing down,
she could see her hard nipples clearly outlined by her
dress.

Scolding her body's wanton response, she smoothed
back her hair and attempted to gather her composure as she
watched him approach.

He kicked Paint into a ground-eating canter and jumped
out of the saddle before the horse came to a complete stop.
"Is something wrong? Is it Chayton? Are you all right?
What happened?" he asked in alarm.

Emma shook her head and almost put her palm to his mouth to halt his questions, but doubted she could withstand the temptation of his lips against her skin. "Chayton's fine. I'm fine. Nothing's wrong." That wasn't exactly true, but she couldn't afford to weaken.

"Where's Chayton?" Ridge looked around.

"Sarah's watching him."

He removed his hat, wiping his brow with his forearm. A hat mark flattened his hair in a circle around his head, giving him a boyish look, which made Emma smile with affection.

"Do you want to come inside? I can warm up a pot of coffee," Ridge said.

"I can't stay long," she said with genuine remorse. "I just wanted to be certain Father paid you."

"He did. All two hundred dollars."

"I'm glad. He may be a stubborn man, but he does pay his debts."

Ridge rested a gentle hand on her shoulder and she nearly wept with the tender feeling that swept through her. "Has he been able to accept Chayton?"

"Yes and no," she replied.

"Let's go inside and sit down."

Emma should have argued with him, but after being apart for so long, she craved his company—the sight and sound of him. He guided her into his tiny cabin and she perched on a straight-back chair. After slipping his hat off his head, Ridge placed the other chair in front of her and sat down, their knees brushing.

"Tell me," he commanded gently.

His compassionate eyes invited her to lay out all her troubles, but she steeled herself against the seduction of his kindness. "He doesn't talk to Chayton directly, but doesn't ignore him either. He had Sarah buy some clothes for Chayton, and I cut his hair." She smiled wryly. "It's a good thing all the hands were out working when I did, or they would've come running in to see who was getting killed.

I'm still trying to convince him that since we live with the *wasicu* now, we have to act and dress like them."

"I'll bet he doesn't like that one bit." Ridge sent her a crooked grin.

"You'd win that bet. Getting him used to wearing so many pieces of clothing has been even harder. The first time he took them off faster than I could put them on him. The second time they stayed on for all of ten minutes. I followed the trail of clothes to find him naked in the dining room. Mother had a fit." Emma laughed, remembering her prudish mother's expression when she'd caught sight of Chayton running atop the oak table without a lick of clothing.

Ridge chuckled. "That must've been quite a sight."

"Oh, it was." She sobered. "Until Father showed up to see what all the commotion was about. He had Chayton in tears by the time he was done, and Chayton didn't even know what he was saying."

Ridge's strong hand covered Emma's clutched ones. "I'm sorry."

Emma embraced his concern and acceptance, fighting the yearning to unload all her fears and worries upon his broad shoulders. "Don't be. It's not your doing."

"Have things gotten better?" Ridge asked.

"They haven't gotten worse," she answered evasively, and then forced a smile. "What I came over for was to give you something." She rose and went back outside.

Ridge followed her to her horse, where she opened one side of her saddlebags and tugged out a cloth bag. She handed it to him. "I want you to use this to practice reading and making your letters."

He took the bag from her and, with a puzzled expression, withdrew the book. She'd put the papers he'd practiced writing the alphabet, between the pages. "It's the same one you read from."

She nodded, ignoring the lump threatening to clog her throat. "It's my favorite."

He thrust the book back in the bag and held it out to her. "I can't take it."

"I want you to have it," she argued, pressing it back to him. "If nothing else, keep it as a remembrance of our time together."

"I don't need anything to remember you, Emma," Ridge said huskily. He cupped her face with his free hand, and slid his fingers into her hair as his thumb stroked her cheek. "I don't think I could forget you if I tried."

Emma's heart threatened to gallop out of her chest and she didn't know where she gained the strength to step away from him. She even managed light laughter. "You'll forget me easily enough once you find the right woman. Then you'll have a whole wagonload of beautiful children with dark blue eyes, who'll do you proud and carry on your name."

She quickly mounted Clementine, overtly aware of Ridge's hand above her elbow as he helped her. Intending to leave before he suspected her feelings, she reined her mare around. But Ridge caught the horse's bridle.

"I saw Talutah. They should be at the reservation tomorrow," he said quietly.

Emma's stomach dropped. "How was she?"

Ridge glanced down and shook his head. "Not good. Sounds like she's willing herself to die."

Emma squeezed her eyes shut and her breath stammered in her chest. It didn't come as a complete surprise, but she'd been hoping and praying that Talutah would overcome her sorrow and grief. "I'll go see her after they're settled."

"That wouldn't be a good idea."

She glared down at him. "I don't care what people think."

"What about Chayton? Do you care about him?"

Bitterness welled in her throat. "Nothing I say or do will change anyone's mind about a half-Indian, half-white child."

Ridge dropped his forehead to her thigh for just a moment, but it was long enough to inflame the smoldering spark between them. She ignored the bittersweet ache.

"Think about it before you go, Emma," he said quietly. "Just promise me that."

The reins cut into her palms. She nodded. "I'll think about it."

The furrows in Ridge's brow eased. "I'm headed to Cheyenne to pick up the bull. I should be back in a week."

Emma's heart clenched. A full week with no chance of seeing him, even from a distance. "Have a good trip," she said. "Goodbye."

She kicked Clementine's flanks, urging the mare into a trot. Although she felt Ridge watching her, she didn't dare turn around for one last look, afraid he'd see in her face what she had to keep hidden.

"TAKE him to the stockade, Sarge," Captain Rivers ordered.

"With pleasure, sir," Gabe Sanders replied with a jaunty salute.

"Not too much pleasure, Sergeant."

Gabe merely smiled crookedly.

Colt watched Sarge escort Cullen to the stockade, then turned to his men in formation behind him. "Dismissed," he commanded in a strong voice.

The exhausted soldiers headed to the corrals to take care of their equally tired horses.

Colt smiled at Pres, who remained beside him. "That order was for you, too."

"Would you like a corroborating witness when you beard the lion in his own den?" Pres asked.

"If Nyes won't listen to me, he won't listen to you either." Colt held up his hand before Pres could argue. "Go on, clean up, get something to eat at the mess, and then get some sleep. Something tells me we're going to be busy with the general showing up later this week."

Pres snorted. "Busy polishing our boots."

"Whatever needs to be done," Colt said. "Go on."

Reluctantly, he left. Colt remained sitting atop his horse in the middle of the parade ground for a moment longer.

Five minutes later he took a steadying breath before knocking on Colonel Nyes's door.

"Enter," the colonel barked.

Colt marched in, stood at attention, and saluted his commanding officer. He held the position until Nyes saluted back.

"Our mission was successful, sir. The Indians have been returned to the reservation."

Nyes smiled widely. "Good, good. I knew I could count on you, Captain. How many of the savages were eliminated?"

Colt stiffened. "I believe our mission was to return the Indians to the reservation, not kill them, sir."

The colonel's smile vanished. "The more we're rid of, the less to make trouble. How many, Captain?"

His muscles taut with anger, Colt replied tersely, "Ten killed, including the chief of the village."

"Well done, Captain Rivers. Obviously, Cullen was able to track them to their lair."

"He's in the stockade, sir."

Nyes rose and leaned forward, flattening his palms on his desktop. "Why in blue blazes is he there?"

"He incited the men to murder everyone, including the women and children, in the camp, Colonel."

"Can you prove this?"

"I know what I saw and heard, sir," Colt stated curtly.

"Perhaps you misinterpreted."

"I don't believe so, Colonel."

"You don't *believe* so?" Nyes roared. "Cullen has done an exemplary job as a scout. You can't have him arrested for something you can neither corroborate nor quantify, Captain."

Colt remained silent, his hands clasped at the base of his spine. Too angry to look directly at the colonel, Colt gazed out the window, over Nyes' shoulder.

"Corporal," Nyes boomed out.

The clerk in the outer office scurried in and saluted. "Sir?"

"Have Pony Cullen released from the stockade immediately."

The enlisted soldier bobbed his head. "Yes, sir."

Colt clenched his jaw, fighting the urge to countermand his commanding officer.

Nyes sank back into his chair. "Perhaps you should take some time off, Captain," he suggested coolly. "Maybe think about what you want to accomplish in the military."

"Yes, sir." Taut with suppressed anger, Colt barely managed a civil tone.

"You're dismissed, Captain."

Colt saluted sharply and marched out of the office. Back on the parade grounds, he paused to watch Cullen swagger out of the stockade. The scout spotted him and made a bee-line toward him.

"You better sleep with one eye open, Rivers, 'cause I ain't gonna forget what you done," Cullen threatened.

"That's *Captain* Rivers," Colt said, his tone low and warning. "And you're not the only one who won't forget."

Colt pivoted on his heel and strode to his quarters. He'd take the time off and keep his word to Ridge by checking on Miss Hartwell.

And maybe make some long overdue decisions in the process.

NINETEEN

RIDGE made thirty miles before nightfall and set up his sparse camp like he'd done uncountable times in the past. Only the memory of those times he shared with Emma remained the sharpest in his thoughts.

Sitting cross-legged by the fire, he sipped a cup of coffee. A faint sense of unease made Ridge's gaze survey the surrounding shadows. He had the impression someone was watching him from the darkness, but Paint would've made a fuss if something or someone was out there, and he was placidly foraging at the edge of the camp.

Unable to find any reason for his disquiet, Ridge set aside his empty tin cup and reverently opened the bag containing the book Emma had given him. He drew it out and something dropped onto his leg. He picked it up, recognizing it as Chayton's moccasin that Emma had held close for months. It must have gotten into the sack by accident.

He fingered the soft, supple deerskin, noting the intricate bead design across the top. Emma had obviously spent a fair amount of time sewing it.

As he reluctantly placed the small boot back in the sack, he felt something within the moccasin. Pulling the small shoe back out, he peered inside to find a folded piece of paper. Staring at the confusing mix of words, Ridge struggled to read the note. He recognized his name at the top, but then had to focus, using the tricks Emma had taught him to figure out the remainder.

Finally, after long frustrating minutes, he was able to piece the words together.

Ridge. Remember Chayton and me with fondness, and may his moccasin bring you the good fortune it brought me. Yours, Emma.

He clutched the moccasin in one hand, rereading the message over and over until he had it memorized. That Emma had given him something that meant so much to her humbled him. Nobody had given him a gift since he was Chayton's age, but it was nothing like this one—a gift that couldn't be bought.

The book and his lessons forgotten, Ridge stared into the fire's flames, the moccasin cupped within his palm.

IT didn't take long for the news about Emma's son to circulate once the soldiers returned. Her father was furious she hadn't told him about meeting them at the Indian village. She refused to explain the circumstances, but John Hartwell wasn't stupid. He'd figured it out through her non-answers.

Sitting on the porch one warm spring afternoon a week after she'd arrived home, Emma watched Chayton play with a litter of kittens. His trousers were already dirt-stained, but at least he had stopped removing them. His dark hair, once covering his back, was trimmed above the collar of his blue plaid shirt. It had taken Emma more time than Chayton to get accustomed to his short hair.

Only old Rory the hostler was left in the ranch yard, which was why she and Chayton were allowed outside. When the ranch hands started returning, she and Chayton would be relegated to the house again, which was growing increasingly frustrating.

What did it matter if they saw Chayton? Everybody knew. Cullen made sure of that, spreading the rumor with, according to Sarah, sadistic enthusiasm.

What Emma wanted to know was why the murderer had been set free. The last time she'd seen Pony Cullen he was a prisoner, arrested for inciting a massacre. She'd taken solace in the fact the captain was Ridge's friend and hoped he would see justice done. But it seemed Captain Rivers wasn't any better than many others who believed the only good Indian was a dead Indian. So why had he gone through the trouble of pretending to restrain the scout? The most painful question, however: Was Ridge part of the deception?

Movement on the road caught her eye and her pulse quickened. Had Ridge returned early? She shaded her eyes against the glaring sun and her excitement died. It was only one of the ranch hands coming in.

Disappointment weighed heavily upon her although she knew she had no right to feel that way. She had no claim on Ridge Madoc despite her heart's insistence.

Already accustomed to staying out of sight, Chayton joined her on the porch. "Go in?" he asked.

Emma stopped herself before nodding. "No, not this time." She was tired of acting like a wanted outlaw around her own home. "You can stay outside if you'd like."

Chayton grinned impishly and ran over to the corral to watch the man ride in. Emma recognized the ranch hand but didn't know his name. She stood and leaned against the porch post to watch closely and to ensure that the man didn't get ugly toward her son.

Although she couldn't hear the words, Emma saw Chayton's mouth moving and the startled man replying. When the hired hand smiled, Emma relaxed. And when he lifted Chayton onto his horse to give him a ride around the yard, tears filled her eyes with gratitude. She'd thank him later for his kindness.

"Are you all right, Emma?"

She turned to see her sister standing behind her, and

dashed the moisture from her eyes. "I'm fine, Sarah. Better than fine, actually."

Sarah's gaze found Chayton and his new friend. She smiled. "Father won't be very happy."

"Not happy at all," Emma agreed with mock severity.

Emma and Sarah looked at each other and broke into laughter.

"It's nice to hear you laugh, Emma. I've missed that," Sarah said after their mirth faded.

"I haven't had much to laugh about. I've been so worried about Chayton, but I was afraid to tell anyone about him," Emma admitted. "Ridge didn't even know about him until we rode into the village where Chayton was."

"Mr. Madoc?"

Emma warmed under Sarah's scrutiny. "Yes."

"Was he angry?"

"Not that I had a child. He was upset that I hadn't told him."

"Father doesn't like Mr. Madoc, but I always thought he was nice and kind of shy."

Emma chuckled. "He's not really shy—just quiet. He and Chayton got on like two peas in a pod when we were at the village. It was Ridge who started teaching him English. He has a way with children."

"Why, Emma Louise Hartwell, I do believe you're sweet on him," Sarah teased.

Much to her chagrin, Emma's cheeks burned with embarrassment. "Like you said, he's a nice man. He treated me like a lady, even after I knifed him."

Sarah gasped. "What?"

Emma reluctantly told her about the night Ridge found her, and how she used herbs to put him to sleep. Then she kept on talking, telling Sarah about him finding her again, tying her up, how she fell in the river, and finally locating the Lakota. She left out their nocturnal activities in the cabin, and the other nights she'd willingly crawled into his arms.

"You love him," Sarah said softly.

"I've only known him a month," Emma argued, keeping her gaze on Chayton who was now petting the hired man's horse through the corral poles.

"Did you tell him?"

Emma sighed, wishing Sarah wasn't quite so perceptive. "He doesn't love me."

"How do you know? Did you ask him?"

"He brought me back and hasn't tried to see me since we returned. That isn't what a man in love does."

"Did Mr. Madoc kiss you?"

"Sarah! You're impossible." Emma descended the porch steps. "I'd best get Chayton inside. The rest of the men will be coming in soon."

Emma ignored her sister's speculative gaze as she gathered her son and returned to the house. The coolness of the interior made her shiver, or maybe it was the occupants who chilled her.

Her mother walked into the front room. "Sarah, is that—Oh, it's you, Emma."

"Yes, Mother, it's only Emma," she said churlishly. "And don't forget her son Chayton. Oh, that's right. You *are* trying to forget him."

"Emma Louise Hartwell," her mother rebuked.

Twice in less than half an hour she'd been called by her full name. She was either being especially peevish today or her family was growing increasingly impatient with her. Perhaps both.

She sighed. "Did you want something, Mother?"

"Would you like a cookie, Chayton?" the older woman asked her grandson.

Chayton nodded eagerly. Cookie was one of those words he'd quickly learned. After a moment, Martha Hartwell extended her hand to Chayton. He took it eagerly with a shy smile.

Emma followed them into the kitchen, unable to believe her eyes. Although Emma had caught her mother watching Chayton numerous times, she hadn't gone out of her way to get to know him.

The older woman had Chayton wash up first, then sat
him down beside the small table in the corner. Emma's
mother placed two molasses cookies on a plate and poured
him a glass of milk. She placed the snack in front of Chayton and tentatively laid a hand on his head.

"I'm sure you're hungry after playing with the kittens,"
she said with a smile. "When your mother was your age,
she enjoyed playing with the animals, too." She smiled
wryly. "Of course, I tried breaking her of the nasty habit,
but her father only laughed and said I should leave her be."

"I didn't know that," Emma said quietly.

"You don't know a lot of things, Emma." Her mother
busied herself with punching down the rising bread dough.
The scent of yeast wafted through the kitchen. "You don't
know how I prayed day and night for your safe return after
you disappeared. You don't know that I never gave up, even
when your father insisted you were dead. You don't know
the nights I had to wake your father from a nightmare as he
called out your name." She wiped her floury hands on a
sackcloth. "When you were returned to us, we called it a
miracle. But your father couldn't bear people talking about
you after what you'd been through. He's the one who decided to keep you away from town after you recovered
from your wounds. He didn't want you hurt by those who'd
once been your friends."

She walked over to Emma and laid her hands on her
shoulders. "When you left to find the Indians, your father
was devastated. He swallowed his pride and asked Ridge
Madoc to find you—that's how worried he was. Then you
came back with a child and told us you were married to one
of those people who kept our daughter from us for seven
years." Her voice faltered and she cleared her throat. "How
do you expect your father and me to feel?"

Had she been that selfish to not even notice her parents'
grief? She'd learned of Sarah's the night before she'd run
away to find Chayton, but she hadn't even considered her
father and mother's feelings. She'd only seen their unbend-
ing strictness and assumed they were ashamed of her.

"I'm sorry," Emma whispered. "I didn't know."

She embraced her mother, who hugged her back, and something inside Emma fractured and broke. All the lost years; years she'd matured while her parents prayed they'd find their little girl. Only the Emma who came back to them had evolved into a widow with a child of her own. The adolescent her mother and father prayed for no longer existed. It was no wonder they seemed like strangers to her, too.

"More cookie?"

Emma glanced down to see Chayton standing beside them. She smiled. "What do you think, Mother? Would another cookie spoil his appetite?"

Martha Hartwell, her eyes shimmering with moisture, but with a smile much like her daughter's, thought for a moment. She stepped over to the tin and handed him a cookie. "This is the last one for now, Chayton."

The boy's face lit up. "Thank you, Grandmother."

"You're welcome—" She glanced at Emma then back at her grandson. "Chayton."

"Thank you," Emma mouthed.

Her mother turned away to surreptitiously wipe her eyes. "I don't feel like a grandmother. I used to call my grandmother Nana." She faced her daughter once more. "Do you think Chayton would mind calling me Nana?"

"I think he'd like that." Emma looped her arm around her mother's. "I know I would."

ALTHOUGH Emma was tired, her mind raced. She rolled onto her back and placed her hands behind her head to stare at the whitewashed ceiling. From the trundle bed beside her, Chayton murmured in his sleep. She thought she heard the word "Nana" and smiled.

Only her father remained to be won over by his grandson. Emma suspected that would be a near-impossible task, despite what her mother had confessed earlier.

While eating dinner, she'd tried to see behind her father's stoicism. However, when he'd scolded Chayton for using his fingers to eat a piece of chicken, she decided her mother was simply making excuses for his callous nature. Emma had argued with her father, pointing out that Chayton was doing extremely well with a spoon and fork considering he'd never used either until the previous week. She'd ended up getting the cold shoulder the rest of the meal.

The clock downstairs struck twelve.

Emma sighed. Although she hadn't had one of her dream visions since the night Chayton's village was attacked, her sleep had been restless. Waking often, she found herself reaching for a hard, warm body, but found only cool sheets. She missed Ridge, especially during the long nights. She missed the tickle of his hair against her nose while she lay on his shoulder, and the deep vibrations in his chest when he laughed quietly. But mostly she missed how he made her feel when they joined.

Desire encircled her, heated her blood, and made her body ache. She pressed her thighs together, determined to overcome the need.

She wondered if Ridge missed her even a little bit.

ALTHOUGH it was late, Ridge remained awake. The bull he'd bought that morning stood tethered to a twenty-foot rope far enough away that he wouldn't bother Ridge, but close enough that he could hear the animal if something bothered it. Ridge also trusted Paint to let him know if a dangerous predator—two- or four-legged—came close. The bull was foraging, and alternated between contented snorts and chewing the tender sprouts of spring grass.

Ridge had traveled longer that day than he planned, but he'd felt a sense of urgency that had only increased as the hours passed. It wasn't anything he could pin down, but a general feeling of unease. He didn't think it involved his home, but suspected it was more Emma who drew him.

During his long hours in the saddle, she was never far

from his thoughts. What was she doing now? Was she being shunned in town?

He had no doubt everyone now knew about Chayton, which meant they probably knew his part in finding her son and bringing them back to Sunset. Surprisingly, it didn't bother him. What troubled him the most was the fact Emma was facing the gossipmongers alone.

He ate a piece of jerky and washed it down with water. His stomach protested even that small amount of food.

After scouting around his camp and checking on Paint and the bull one last time, he settled into his bedroll. As if of its own accord, his hand found the leather moccasin beneath his saddle that he used as a pillow. He fingered the child's soft boot, as well as the scrap of paper within it.

Yours, Emma.

He savored the entire note, but especially those two words. He rolled them around, over and over in his head, and had even spoken them aloud where only Paint and the bull could hear him.

He was acting like a lovesick fool. Emma had no intention of marrying again, and even if she did, her father would never allow her to wed him.

Ridge crushed the moccasin and the note in his fist, and shoved them back under his saddle.

"I don't think this is a good idea."

The trepidation in Sarah's voice made Emma wish she hadn't asked her sister if she wanted to accompany them to the reservation.

"Nobody will know," Emma reassured. "With Father and Mother gone all day, and Rory thinking we went on another picnic, we won't even be missed."

"But what if someone sees us? Or Father and Mother return early? Or—"

"You can stay here if you want, but Chayton and I are going," Emma said firmly.

Sarah stood beside the buggy for a long moment, her expression undecided.

Chayton grinned down at her and clapped his hands. "Go for ride, Aunt Sarah."

Emma smiled as Sarah surrendered to her nephew. When it came to Chayton, Sarah had no defense against his innocent charms. Their mother, too, was fast becoming a willing subject of her grandson. It seemed all Chayton had to do was smile and gaze at them with his big brown eyes and they'd do his bidding.

For Emma, her mother and sister's acceptance was a miracle. The only stumbling stone was her father, who spoke to Chayton only when necessary and not a word more. His hardheadedness aggravated Emma and confused Chayton.

Emma slapped the reins against the horse's rump and the sturdy sorrel headed down the road. As Sarah answered Chayton's endless questions and added to his rapidly expanding English vocabulary, Emma allowed her thoughts to wander.

She'd been home ten days and this was only the second time she was leaving the ranch. The first had been to give Ridge the book and that had only been a short foray. Her father had forbade her to set foot off Hartwell land and her mother agreed with him, although her reasons were bound with affection rather than censure. The smidgen of guilt Emma felt for disobeying now was inspired by her mother's loving concern rather than her father's strictness.

Emma was worried about Talutah. She'd had a dream last night for the first time in over two weeks. A spotted owl had come to her with a tiny mouse in its talons. The mouse moved feebly within the owl's grasp. When Emma had awakened and the dream vision faded, Talutah was heavy in her thoughts.

The drive to the reservation took two hours and by that time, even Chayton was tired of riding. The boy brightened at the sight of the tipis, but Sarah's pinched features revealed anxiety and fear. "I've never seen so many Indians," she whispered.

"It's all right, Sarah. They won't hurt us," Emma reassured.

"How can you be so sure?"

"Because many of them are friends," Emma replied with more confidence than she felt.

Emma spied Shimmering Water and stopped the buggy. She hopped down and turned to help Chayton, only to find him on the ground, already beside Sarah and holding his aunt's hand. Emma smiled at her son's protectiveness.

"*Ha*, Shimmering Water. We have come to visit." Emma greeted her friend, the Lakota words sounding awkward across her tongue. In addition, Emma's clothing—a brown calico skirt and white muslin blouse with a twilled silk shawl and a matching bonnet—made her feel out of place among those she'd lived and worked with. She introduced Sarah to her friend.

The sparkle in Shimmering Water's eyes was gone, and her dark hair lay dull and lifeless across her shoulders. "Winona. I did not expect to see you again."

Emma heard the flat censure in her voice and, although she wasn't surprised, it still hurt. She glanced at Sarah who was staring at her like she was a stranger.

Chayton suddenly pointed at two children his own age and Emma recognized them as former playmates of her son's. "Play? Please?"

Emma smiled. "Yes, but don't stray far."

He released Sarah's hand and scampered away to join the children. When they began to play together, Emma gave her attention back to Shimmering Water. "How is Talutah?"

Shimmering Water's eyes were blank. "Gone."

Emma's heart skipped a beat. "Gone?"

"Her spirit has joined her husband's."

Moisture filled Emma's eyes and a tear rolled down her cheek in a maddeningly slow trickle. Images of her adopted mother teaching her, scolding her, laughing with her flooded Emma's mind. Fast Elk and Talutah had saved her life and she'd come to love them. Now they were gone. Just as Enapay and Ohanzee, the shaman who'd helped her understand her gift of dream visions, were gone. Only Chayton remained.

"What is it?" Sarah asked, unable to follow the conversation.

"Talutah, my adopted mother, died," Emma replied, her throat thick with tears.

"Oh, Emma, I'm so sorry." Sarah hugged her and Emma was glad her sister had accompanied them.

After a few moments, Emma turned back to the Indian woman. "Was her death mourned?"

"Yes." Shimmering Water's eyes softened. "She spoke of you and Chayton at the end."

Emma closed her eyes, willing her tears away. Talutah was with her husband. Neither of them would have to live caged on a reservation, but would now roam the plains with their ancestors.

She drew a hand across her face and surveyed the Lakota's new home. Lodges of various sizes and quality were scattered like scabs across the flat, greening earth. In some ways it didn't look that much different from the village in the wilderness where she'd lived with them. Women continued to stir stews and soups over small fire pits, and sew beside their tipis. Children still ran around, chasing the dogs and one another. The men played dice in the shade of the lodges.

However, where there would've been chanting and singing, there was only silence and subdued tones. The Lakota's heart no longer beat in this place.

She glanced up to see Shimmering Water gone and the truth struck Emma. No longer would Winona be welcome here.

"She didn't even say goodbye," Sarah commented with a frown.

"It's the Lakota way," Emma said absently. "Our visit is over."

"Don't you want to see her grave?"

"They don't bury their dead. They place them on platforms." Emma swallowed back her grief. "I don't think I could handle seeing her that way."

Her chest tight, Emma gathered Chayton and climbed into the buggy. Sarah kept a hand around her nephew's shoulders as she gazed out across the quiet camp.

"I never imagined Indian villages were this—this sad," Sarah said.

"This is a reservation, Sarah. It's different. The village I lived in, the People were content—they were always laughing and singing." Emma motioned to the disarray. "Here they're prisoners, so they have nothing to laugh or sing about."

"It's not fair."

Emma squeezed her hand. "I know, but there's nothing we can do."

"There should be."

"Maybe you'll think of something."

Sarah met her gaze squarely, her chin raised. "Maybe I will."

Pride flared in Emma at her younger sister's new maturity. Sarah had even begun questioning their father's dictates.

After one last look at the somber camp, Emma flicked the reins over the horse's rump. She thought of Talutah and Fast Elk, but the images were from seven years ago. They had no children left to repeat their stories nor remember them, except Emma and Chayton.

"Do you remember the story Grandmother used to tell you of White Buffalo Woman, Chayton?" she asked her son.

His dark eyes lit with excitement and nodded. "Tell again?"

"Many, many summers ago, two young warriors went hunting because the People were starving. A beautiful

woman dressed in white buckskin approached them. Now
one of those men thought bad thoughts about her, but the
other one thought she was holy," Emma began.

Both Chayton and Sarah listened intently to the story of
how the holy woman brought the Lakota the sacred Buffalo Calf Pipe and instructed the People in the ways to
pray to Wakan Tanka. Emma described how the holy
woman rolled four times as she walked away from the village, and how she turned into a black buffalo, then a brown
one and a red one, and finally a white female buffalo calf.
And after she was gone, great buffalo herds appeared to
give the People food and clothing and everything they
needed to live.

"That's beautiful," Sarah said when Emma was done.

"It is, isn't it?" Emma swept her hand across her eyes.
"It's part of Chayton's legacy and I want to make sure he
knows the Lakota teachings, and learns how to read and
write in my world."

Sarah brushed a strand of hair from Chayton's forehead.
"I'd like to learn more about the Indians, too."

Emma smiled and opened her mouth to speak, but a
rider in the distance caught her attention. She watched as
the horse drew nearer, until she could make out an Indian
mounted on the pony. Frowning, she eased back on the
reins and halted the buggy.

"Do you know him?" Sarah asked.

The brave's face grew clearer and Emma worried her
lower lip. "It's Hotah. He's from the village Ridge and I
stayed at."

"Why isn't he on the reservation?"

"He was banished the day before it happened."

Hotah stopped his horse close to the buggy, his dark
face impassive but his gaze raking up and down both
Emma and Sarah.

"What are you doing here?" Emma asked in Lakota,
hoping he couldn't hear the frantic beating of her heart.

Hotah narrowed his eyes. "I have come for Chayton."

Emma instinctively shifted to shield Chayton from Hotah's possessive gaze. "He is my son."

"I will teach him to be a warrior so he may ride with his people."

"No. He stays with me. With *my* people."

Although Sarah didn't understand the words, she comprehended the tone and wrapped an arm around Chayton's waist, holding him snugly against her side.

"He is one of the People," Hotah said, his nostrils flaring.

"He is also white." Although trembling on the inside, Emma met his gaze. "Leave us, Hotah."

His lips curled in a sneer and he pressed his horse closer to Emma. He grabbed her wrist. "Chayton is Lakota. I will take him and join Crazy Horse."

"No!" Emma twisted to escape his grip, but his fingers dug into her skin cruelly.

"Let her go!" Sarah shouted.

Hotah glared at Sarah.

The sound of galloping hooves startled Emma and Hotah released her. He leaned close. "He is not yours. I will have him." Then he kicked his horse's flanks, escaping as the other rider neared.

Emma's heart pounded against her ribs and her breath came in stuttered gasps. She didn't know if she was more angry or frightened. Blinking, she focused on the arrival who was dressed in black trousers and a gray shirt, with a wool vest.

"Miss Hartwell, are you and your son all right?" the blond man asked.

Emma nodded, recognizing him as Ridge's cavalry captain friend out of uniform. "Yes, thank you, Captain Rivers," she said stiffly. She couldn't forget nor forgive what he'd done to her Lakota friends.

Captain Rivers looked at Sarah. "How about you, ma'am?"

"I'm fine, thank you," she murmured.

"Who was that?" Rivers asked Emma.

"He lived in the village you attacked," Emma answered tartly.

The man's jaw muscle clenched. "What did he want?"

"Chayton."

"Your son?"

Emma nodded, the fear expanding once more. Her fingernails dug into her palms. "What're you doing here?"

Rivers placed his crossed wrists on his saddle horn and grinned. "I was just out for a ride."

Emma narrowed her eyes. "Why don't I believe you?"

He shrugged indolently. "Believe what you want, Miss Hartwell." His gaze flickered over Sarah and back to Emma. "What're you doing out here?"

"We were visiting friends."

"Talutah?"

The name brought a rush of fresh grief. "She's—" Emma glanced at Chayton "—passed away."

Rivers shifted uncomfortably. "I'm sorry, ma'am. Ridge told me how much she meant to you."

"Maybe it's better this way," Emma said quietly, then had to ask, "Why did you release Pony Cullen?"

"I didn't. Colonel Nyes wouldn't hold him on my word and released him."

"He's a murderer!"

"You don't have to convince me, but it wasn't up to me." Captain Rivers's face became as hard as granite.

Emma searched his features for a sign of deception, but there was only cool anger. It was obvious Rivers didn't agree with the colonel, which meant he and Ridge hadn't deceived her. The captain had planned on prosecuting Cullen.

"Thank you for your assistance, Captain Rivers," Emma said with more warmth.

"My pleasure. If you don't mind, I'd like to ride alongside for a little while."

Although Emma wasn't certain about his motives, she did see the wisdom in his suggestion. "We don't mind."

Rivers touched the brim of his hat and moved to Sarah's side of the buggy. As they traveled down the rutted road, Rivers made small talk with Sarah and Chayton, allowing Emma to ponder her own thoughts.

TWENTY

IT was early afternoon when Emma caught sight of Sunset. She halted the buggy and Chayton, who'd fallen asleep against Sarah's side, awakened. He rubbed his eyes and yawned. At that moment, he looked no different than any other sleepy child, white or Indian.

"Would you like to see a town?" Emma suddenly asked.

"Emma," Sarah spoke up. "We can't."

"Why not?" Although Emma's suggestion had been impulsive, she found herself wanting to defy all those people who felt it was their right to judge. What did they know of her experience with the Lakota? For that matter, what did any of them know about Indians, besides what they'd read in dime novels and newspaper articles that were meant to shock and titillate?

"Your sister's right," Captain Rivers said seriously. "Folks here won't like having a half-breed boy shoved in their faces."

"We're hardly shoving anybody in anyone's face," Emma retorted coldly. "Women bring their children into town all the time."

Sarah folded her hands in her lap and remained silent.

"What's a town?" Chayton asked, oblivious to the adults' undercurrents.

She pointed to the gathering of buildings half a mile away. "That's a town, where the whites—we—gather to buy food and supplies, and attend dances and socials."

Chayton's blank expression made Emma smile. She gave him a one-armed hug as she looked at Sarah and Captain Rivers. "Gertrude has known us ever since we were children. We could eat lunch there."

"I still don't think it's a good idea," Rivers said skeptically.

Sarah's gaze jumped from Emma to the captain and back to her sister. Her backbone straightened. "I'll do whatever you decide."

Emma's stomach fluttered. Now that she actually thought about it, she was uncertain. She peered at Chayton, noticing the excitement in his expression as he stared at the town.

Taking a deep breath, she hiyahed the sorrel and steered it around the edge of the town to enter on the side closest to Gertrude's restaurant. She wished Ridge were with her instead of Captain Rivers. Ridge's presence calmed her, made her feel as if nothing could harm her, including words.

People paused on the boardwalk and stared at her and Chayton. Fortunately, the boy was too busy oohing and aahing the unfamiliar sights, but Emma noticed. So did Sarah and Captain Rivers.

She drew the buggy to a stop in front of the restaurant. She'd been coming here with her family since she was Chayton's age. Surely Gertrude would treat her decently.

The cavalry captain dismounted and assisted Sarah down from the buggy, then Chayton. Rivers walked around to her side since no one offered to help her. It wasn't because there was a shortage of men. Most of them were gaping at her—some with disgust, others with curiosity, and a small number of them with something akin to lust.

Bees buzzed in her belly, but Emma pasted a smile on

her face. She thanked Captain Rivers and joined Chayton and Sarah on the boardwalk.

One woman standing in front of the restaurant swept her skirts aside so they wouldn't touch Emma or Chayton. Lifting her chin, Emma eyed her coolly until the woman looked away and whispered something to her companion.

The moment they stepped inside Emma realized she'd made a mistake. The interior grew silent and everyone stared at them as if they were part of a circus.

Gertrude met them at the door.

"I can't serve you in here, Emma," she said furtively.

"You've known me since I was a child," Emma argued.

Gertrude wrung her hands. "If it were up to me, I would do it, but if I serve you and your son, I'll lose business. Folks don't want his kind in here," she whispered as she deliberately looked down at Chayton.

"Thank you for your honesty, Gertrude," Emma said, her throat thick.

Emma, Sarah, and Chayton returned to their buggy, where Captain Rivers helped them into it. He placed Emma and Chayton in the backseat, then tied his horse's reins to the end of the buggy and joined Sarah in the front.

"Hungry," Chayton complained.

Relieved he hadn't noticed the disgust aimed at him, Emma wrapped her arm around his shoulders. "We'll eat when we get home."

Chayton pouted, but didn't fuss.

As Captain Rivers drove the buggy out of Sunset Emma stared down at her hands, which were the same hands she'd always had, and then looked at her laced-up shoes, skirt, blouse, and shawl. From the outside, she was the same as everyone else in town, yet a chasm of experience separated her from the others—experiences that made her different and alien. A stranger. She'd experienced the same sense of dispossession the second time she'd been among the Lakota, and even more so at the reservation.

With startling clarity, she realized it was only with Ridge that she felt like she belonged.

* * *

RIDGE made it back to his place in six days. The bull had shed some weight with the rushed journey, but the animal could spend the rest of the spring and summer grazing and growing fat.

Once home, Ridge got the bull settled in its pen and the lean-to he'd built while waiting for Colt to return. He planned to comb the government-owned broken hills to the west for unbranded cattle to start his herd. Ridge hoped to use the open range since he didn't own enough land to graze them. If Hartwell hadn't bilked Ridge's stepfather out of his land, Ridge wouldn't need the open range.

By evening, Ridge was restless. Although it'd been a long day, he saddled Paint and rode into Sunset. He claimed a table in the saloon, ordered a thick steak, and a shot of whiskey with a glass of beer. As he waited for his supper, he sipped his beer, and it eased the burn of the stronger liquor. He listened to the muted conversations around him, ignoring most until he heard Emma Hartwell's name.

"I heard she came into town today with her half-breed boy. Gertrude threw her and her nit out of the restaurant."

Ridge recognized the man who spoke as the foreman from the Circle C, where he'd worked before taking off to find Emma. Sam Pesant was a fair man, treating all the hired hands, including Ridge, equally. It surprised Ridge that he was bandying around Emma Hartwell's name in a saloon like she was less than a lady.

Unable to stop himself, Ridge leaned his chair back and said to Pesant, "Miss Hartwell know you're spreading rumors about her?"

The foreman turned toward Ridge and his ruddy face was flushed. "I'm not saying anything that ain't already been said. That scout, Cullen, has been pretty free with his words."

"Cullen? I thought he was in the stockade."

Another man playing poker with Pesant barked a humorless laugh. "Cullen? Word is he's got Colonel Nyes wrapped around his finger."

Nyes. Ridge should have known. Nyes was going to protect his ass, which meant he had to protect Cullen.

"Damn shame about Miss Hartwell, though," the foreman added. "Too bad the Indians weren't taken care of years ago before one of the sons of bitches got her with child. Nobody wants a squaw woman with a half-breed bastard. She would've been better off if she'd died instead."

"Hell, maybe she enjoyed it," a man with a missing front tooth said with a crude gesture.

"That's enough, Harley," Pesant warned.

"I don't know what Cullen's been saying, but Miss Hartwell wasn't used like that. The Lakota adopted her, treated her like their own," Ridge refuted sharply.

"If that's so, what about the kid?" the foreman asked with more curiosity than meanness.

"That ain't for me to say," Ridge replied, afraid he already let too much slip. "I was with her in the village for almost a week before the soldiers came. They treated Emma respectfully, which is more than I can say for anyone in this town."

Ridge thumped his chair back around to his table. Josey, the waitress, set a plate covered by a thick steak in front of him.

"Anything else I can get you?" she asked with a deep-throated purr.

Ridge shook his head at her obvious invitation. "No thanks, ma'am."

Josey's practiced smile was replaced by the girl beneath the face powder. She patted his arm. "You enjoy your steak, Ridge. I made Floyd give you the biggest one he had."

"Thank him for me, Miss Josey."

"I will. You need anything else, just holler."

Ridge cut into his steak.

"You know, you oughta take her up on her offer sometime. Might make you less ornery."

Ridge smiled as Colt joined him.

"Maybe you oughta take your own advice," Ridge bantered.

The two men shook hands over the table.

"You just get back?" Colt asked, slumping in his chair.

"This afternoon."

"Pushed pretty hard."

"The bull's in good shape." Ridge forced himself to chew a piece of steak. "What's this I hear about Emma Hartwell?"

Colt propped his elbows on the chair arms and clasped his hands. "What'd you hear?"

"That she and her son were in town today."

"You heard right. Her sister was with her." Colt described the short, but disastrous visit.

"I s'pected that'd happen, but it doesn't make it go down any easier." Ridge stared at his steak, his appetite gone. "I heard about Cullen, too."

"Hell, I'm lucky Nyes didn't throw me in the stockade when he let Cullen walk out."

Josey brought two beers to their table and took away the empty one in front of Ridge.

"You know an Indian named Hotah?" Colt asked.

"Yeah. How'd you hear about him?"

"He was bothering the Hartwell sisters and the boy on their way back from the reservation."

Ridge swore. "I told her not to go there."

"That old squaw you talked to died."

Ridge scrubbed his face with his palms. "Dammit. How did Emma take it?"

"'Bout how you'd expect. Good thing her sister was with her. She seems to be a levelheaded gal. Pretty, too." Colt finished his beer and called for another. "It'd be better all around if Emma and her son left town."

"Where the hell would they go?"

"Any place has to be better than here. No one wants anything to do with her."

"That's not true," Ridge said quietly.

Colt took a sip from his second beer that Josey brought. "I hope you're not thinking what I think you're thinking."

Ridge angled a scowl at his friend. "What if I am?"

"First off, old man Hartwell won't allow it. Second, if you manage to get past Hartwell, folks around here won't be forgiving. Third, that boy's going to be running into even bigger problems as he grows up."

"She started helping me figure out words and numbers."

"I thought—"

Ridge angled a look at him. "I just see things different than other people."

Colt shook his head, obviously catching the double meaning. "You always have." He sighed. "If you're hell-bent on doing this, I'd be wasting my breath trying to talk you out of it."

Ridge grinned. "That's what I like about you, Colt. You never did like wasting time."

"Except when I'm in a saloon with a beer."

Ridge chuckled and found his appetite had made a rebound.

"I'm gonna take a walk out back," Colt said. He wended his way to the door that led to the outhouse.

Ridge continued eating the steak, washing it down with warm beer. He finished the entire slab and pushed his plate away with a quiet burp.

Just as he began to wonder what was taking Colt so long, Josey scurried over to him, her face pale and eyes wide.

"Captain Rivers is hurt," she whispered hoarsely.

Ridge grabbed his hat and followed the woman out the back door into the alley. A dark figure lay on the ground and Ridge could smell the coppery scent of blood. He dropped to his knees beside Colt as Josey hovered anxiously.

"Go get the doc, Josey. Hurry!" Ridge hissed.

The girl dashed away.

Dark liquid pooled on the ground beside Colt and Ridge frantically searched for the wound. He found a stab wound above the heart, which continued to beat slowly.

Someone had tried to kill him, and might very well have succeeded.

WINGS fluttered almost soundlessly in the darkness. Only the sigh of air across feathers gave away the owl's presence. It swooped onto a tree branch, its talons curling around wood with innate grace.

The female wolf peered upward, into the crown of the tree where the owl perched. "I've come."

"The lion is gone."

"The pup?"

"Gone."

"Where?"

"Must find."

The wolf growled. "How?"

"The search must be yours alone."

The wolf lifted its muzzle to the full moon and howled.

Emma lurched up, struggling to breathe past the crushing weight on her chest. She crossed her arms as she bent at the waist, her forehead touching her drawn-up knees.

It was happening again.

The same messenger animals, the same full moon, the same breath-robbing fear.

Her heart gradually slowed its frantic pace and the sweat began to cool, causing her to shiver. She leaned back against her pillows and tugged the blankets up to her chin.

The last time she'd dreamt of the wolf and the owl, the full moon came and went without a ripple of trouble. The trouble had come three nights later when the soldiers found the village.

She mentally calculated the number of days before the next full moon. Would her dreams become increasingly vivid over the next week? Or was this only a remaining fragment of the former vision, meaning nothing?

A horse galloped into the yard, startling Emma. She jumped out of bed and pressed aside her curtain. Blinking against the morning sunlight, she focused on the horse and rider. She recognized the black-and-white horse immediately.

Ridge.

Why was he here? And why at such an early hour?

She donned her dressing gown and tied the sash snugly around her waist. She heard the pounding on the door as she flew down the stairs. Her father, who'd been eating breakfast, made it to the door seconds before Emma and swung it open. His scowl deepened.

"What do you want?" her father demanded.

"Captain Rivers has been hurt," Ridge replied coolly. "I need to talk to your two daughters."

"Why? They don't even know him."

"Yes, we do," Emma said as Sarah, also dressed in her robe, joined them. "What happened, Ridge?"

"Girls, return to your rooms and put on decent clothing," their father ordered.

Martha Hartwell glided in from the dining room wearing her morning wrapper. "Don't be silly, John. Mr. Madoc wouldn't have come calling so early if it weren't important. Come in, Mr. Madoc."

Despite the situation, Emma had to restrain a smile at her mother's graceful maneuvering.

Ridge stepped across the threshold and removed his hat. Sooty smudges lay beneath his eyes and whiskers shadowed his lower cheeks and jaw. Rust-colored stains on his buckskin jacket and tan trousers appeared to be bloodstains.

Concerned, Emma grasped his hand, which was shockingly cool. "What happened?"

"Colt was stabbed in the alley behind the saloon. I think someone was waiting for him," Ridge explained grimly. His shoulders slumped. "I was talking to him right before it happened. He told me he'd spent time with you and your sister and Chayton yesterday."

Her father's lips thinned as he brought his glare of disapproval to bear on Emma. "What was he doing here while we were away?"

Emma didn't hesitate to correct him. "He didn't come

to the ranch. I took Chayton and Sarah to the reservation, then we stopped in town. Captain Rivers escorted us from the reservation to Sunset and then home." She was more worried about Ridge and his friend than her father's pique.

"He said Hotah was bothering you," Ridge pressed.

Emma tightened her grip on his hand as anxiety washed through her. "Hotah showed up out of nowhere. He wanted Chayton. He wants to train Chayton to be a warrior in Crazy Horse's camp."

Her father was staring at her as if she'd sprouted a third eye.

"When we were at the village, I heard talk among some of the young bucks that they were going to join up with Crazy Horse," Ridge said. "Hotah might've had a hand in stirring them up. It would explain why there was already bad blood between him and the chief."

"Yet it was Akecheta's village that was attacked by Cullen and the soldiers." Emma felt sick to her stomach.

"One Indian's the same as another to most white folks," Ridge said quietly. "Did Colt have words with Hotah?"

Emma focused on the dilemma at hand. "No. Hotah rode away when he saw Captain Rivers riding toward us."

"How is he, Mr. Madoc?" Sarah asked, her doll-like face marred with worry.

"Doc says he was lucky. He was stabbed in the back. An inch lower and it would've gotten his heart," Ridge answered, his jaw taut.

"Have you been with him all night?" Emma asked.

Ridge gazed down at her and Emma floundered in the eyes she'd seen filled with impatience, exasperation, shame, humor, affection, and desire. And she realized she knew this man better than she'd known her own husband.

"Yeah. It was close," he finally replied with a raspy voice.

"You're going to keel over if you don't rest and have something to eat," Emma scolded gently.

"Emma," her father growled in warning.

"Emma's right. Join us in the dining room," her mother

insisted, overruling her husband without a flicker of hesitancy.

John Hartwell balked, his fists clenched at his sides.

"Father, are you coming?" Sarah asked innocently as she wrapped her arm around his.

Their father glared at Ridge, and Emma stepped between them defiantly. Her father deflated before her, and allowed Sarah to lead him into the dining room. Emma and Ridge followed.

"When did you get home?" she asked Ridge.

"Yesterday afternoon. You and Chayton should come by and see the bull," Ridge said, attempting a smile, but too tired to complete it.

"We'll do that. Will Captain Rivers be all right?"

"Doc thinks he will. He lost a lot of blood." Ridge took a shaky breath.

Emma considered Ridge's suspicions about the Lakota warrior. "As much as I'd like to blame Hotah, it doesn't sound like something he'd do—stabbing a man in an alley. Hotah might use a knife on him, but not in the back. He has his own sense of honor and I don't think he'd kill a man without facing him. Besides, he wouldn't come into Sunset. He would've ambushed Captain Rivers between the post and town."

"Yeah, I thought about that, too," Ridge admitted reluctantly. "Did you see Cullen yesterday?"

Emma shook her head, recalling too well her hatred of the scout, which far surpassed her dislike of Hotah. "That doesn't mean *he* didn't do it. Stabbing someone in the back sounds more like his style," she said bitterly.

"I think I'll have a talk with him."

"Be careful, Ridge. Cullen reminds me of a mad dog."

She guided him to a chair by the table then went to retrieve a plate of food from the sideboard for him and herself. As she returned, Chayton with his hair tousled and wearing a nightshirt, joined them.

"*Leksi*," the boy shouted. He threw himself at Ridge, who caught him and plopped him on his lap.

"What did he call you?" Emma's father demanded.

"Uncle," Emma replied. "It's a term Indian children use for a man who teaches them. Ridge taught Chayton his first English words." She didn't think her father needed to know those were learned over animal tracks and piles of scat.

Father studied Ridge, his expression blank but his gaze oddly speculative.

"You going to live here, too?" Chayton asked Ridge.

Emma choked on her coffee. Ridge leaned toward her and patted her back. After a minute, she nodded that she was fine.

"This isn't my home," Ridge answered Chayton after he settled back in his chair. "Maybe someday you'll see my place."

Chayton bounced on Ridge's lap. "Today?"

"I don't think so, cub. Maybe next week."

Emma leaned over Ridge's arm. "You should eat breakfast, Chayton. I'm sure Mrs. Wright would make up a special plate for you if you ask nicely."

The boy scrambled off Ridge's lap and scampered toward the kitchen.

"I'll go with him and make sure she doesn't spoil him." Sarah rolled her eyes. "He could charm the spots off a cat."

Ridge, Emma, and her mother laughed, and Emma was surprised to see a flicker of amusement in her father's face.

Ridge leaned close to Emma and whispered in her ear, "I think your father might be warming toward Chayton."

Emma nodded, oddly pleased that Ridge had noticed, too. It was like sharing a secret—another secret—with him.

Sarah and Chayton returned from the kitchen, bearing a plate piled high with hotcakes and syrup—Chayton's favorite, which the cook had obviously made special for him.

"It's a good thing you went with him, Sarah," Emma teased her sister.

Sarah's cheeks flushed and she shrugged helplessly.

Emma glanced at Ridge, who grinned and winked, sharing the good-natured jest.

The family ate in companionable silence and Emma's

father even stopped glaring at Ridge. Far too soon, empty dishes were pushed aside. Emma was glad, however, that Ridge ate everything on his plate. His haggard expression had lessened and his face had more color to it.

"Thank you, ma'am," Ridge said to her mother. "I guess I was hungrier than I thought."

"You're welcome, Mr. Madoc. Besides, it's the least we could do considering what you've given us—our daughter and grandson," the older woman said.

Over the past few days, Emma's mother had become more spirited and didn't blindly agree with John Hartwell anymore. Emma found it oddly disconcerting, although she approved wholeheartedly. Maybe her mother had just needed a reason to stand up to him.

"I'd best get going," Ridge said, pushing back his chair and standing. "I want to check on Captain Rivers before heading home."

"Emma, why don't you escort him to the door?" her mother suggested.

Emma smiled. "I'll do that, Mother."

She walked Ridge to the door and picked up his hat from the table where he'd left it. She handed it to him and their fingers brushed.

"Tell Captain Rivers we're thinking of him and praying for his swift recovery," Emma said.

Ridge's shy smile made Emma's heart quicken. "Thanks. I will." He fiddled with the brim of his hat. "Colt told me what happened yesterday in town. I'm sorry, Emma."

The sour tang of humiliation rose in her throat. "You warned me. So did my parents and Captain Rivers, but I'd hoped . . ." She shrugged, although she hardly felt indifferent. "I'm not sure what to do. I don't want to leave Sunset, but I don't have a choice. Father's contacted Aunt Alice, but we haven't heard back from her. Maybe she doesn't want anything to do with me anymore." Unwelcome tears stung her eyes and she savagely ignored them.

Ridge lightly stroked her cheek with his knuckles. "It's

not you, Emma. It's them and you can't make folks change their minds. It's something they got to do themselves." He took a deep breath. "You have another choice, Emma."

"I'm not Catholic so I don't think a convent would take me," she joked weakly.

A slow, sweet smile curved Ridge's lips. "You could marry me."

Emma's heart tripped and stumbled, then pounded with joy and hope. She hadn't even allowed herself to think about being Ridge's wife—it hurt too much. But now he was offering . . . and she couldn't accept. "No. If you marry me, you'll be treated the same or worse than Chayton and me. You don't deserve that, Ridge."

"That doesn't matter—"

"Yes, it does," Emma argued. "You won't be able to buy your supplies in town anymore."

"I'll get them in Redfield."

"Until they find out about your squaw wife and her half-breed boy." Emma kept her tone caustic.

"Not everybody is like that." He grabbed her shoulders. "Dammit, Emma, I want to protect you."

"I can protect myself," she snapped. "Besides, it's too big a sacrifice for you to make."

"I'm a grown man and I can make my own decisions. I'd be honored to have you as my wife."

Ridge didn't say he loved her, but he seemed sincere in wanting to marry her.

"If I say yes, Chayton and I get a home and your name. But what do you get, Ridge?" she asked softly.

"I get a son to raise like he was my own, and I get Emma Hartwell in my bed every night."

Lightning arced through her veins and settled beneath her belly. Suddenly too aware of her thin nightclothes and Ridge's masculinity, she took a step back. She smiled through her misery. "Sounds like you're getting the short end of the deal."

His heated gaze traveled down her body, pausing at her

breasts, and then moved back up to her face. "I don't see it that way."

She peered at him, at the crow's feet at the corner of his eyes, his generous lips, and thick tawny hair. What lay beneath his handsome exterior, however, was infinitely more attractive—his honesty, integrity, honor, and shy tenderness. There was no doubt he'd honor their marriage vows and treat her and Chayton well. But what of love? Where did that figure? Or was she asking too much?

"Madoc has a point, Emma."

She swung around to see her father coming around the corner. It was obvious he'd been listening to their conversation.

Ridge straightened and met her father's gaze. "I'd like your permission to marry your daughter, Mr. Hartwell."

Emma's mouth gaped as John Hartwell seriously considered Ridge's request. "No, I won't let him do it, Father," she said.

"I'd say you don't have a lot of choice in the matter, Emma," her father said.

"He's right," Ridge added, although she could tell he didn't like her father's cutting bluntness.

Emma glared at one man, then the other. "I can't believe you two are actually agreeing on something."

Her father scowled. "I'm only stating the obvious. Madoc isn't the man I would've chosen for you, but considering the circumstances, he's probably the best you can do."

Furious indignation clouded Emma's thoughts. "How dare you! Ridge Madoc is a decent and honorable man. He doesn't cheat men out of their land or treat people like dirt just because they weren't as fortunate."

Father's eyes glittered with anger, but his voice was steady, almost calm, when he spoke. "It sounds to me like you wouldn't mind becoming Mrs. Ridge Madoc."

Emma's mouth fluttered open, then snapped shut, and her face burned with embarrassment. Her father struck too close to the truth.

"I only asked your permission, Hartwell," Ridge said. "It's up to Emma whether she agrees or not. I won't marry her because you order her to."

Emma found her voice. "Don't worry, Ridge, he can't force me. I'll make my own decision." She crossed her arms, suddenly chilled. "I have to think about it."

"How long?" Ridge asked.

"Two days."

"That's fair enough. I'll come calling Wednesday afternoon."

"Come at five. You can have dinner with us," Emma said. She sent her father a pointed look. "Isn't that right, Father?"

His lips pressed together, he nodded once.

Emma turned back to Ridge. "Is Captain Rivers at the doctor's office?"

"Yeah," he replied somberly. "I'm hoping he woke up so I can talk to him. I want to find out if he saw who did it."

"Be careful," Emma said.

He lent her a wan smile. "I will. Goodbye."

"Bye." It was difficult to ignore the passion that sparked between them, but Emma did so, ensuring they didn't touch as he walked out.

She closed the door behind him and peered up at her father. "He didn't have to offer marriage," she stated.

He glanced away. "I know."

"It's not fair to him."

Her father's gaze shot back to her. "What about you? You didn't ask to be in this position."

Emma stiffened her backbone. "I made the decision to marry an Indian and I willingly had his child. If that's a sin, it's mine to bear, not Ridge's."

She marched up the stairs, needing to be alone to think and make a decision that would directly impact two lives other than her own. It was a responsibility she feared almost as much as she loved Ridge.

$\mathcal{T}$WENTY-ONE

THE doctor had closed the curtains so the corner room was dim and gloomy. Colt lay still and pale in the single bed, but the rise and fall of his chest assured Ridge he was alive.

"Any change?" Ridge asked Dr. Harold Winters.

"He's breathin' easier," the gray-haired doctor replied. "And the wound's stopped bleedin' completely. I've been tryin' to get him to drink some water, but more comes out than goes in. Once he wakes up, we gotta get some in him to replace that blood he lost."

"So he'll make it?"

"I reckon. He's young and strong."

Ridge breathed a sigh of relief and leaned one shoulder against the wall. Crossing his arms and ankles, he asked, "Has anybody else checked on him?"

"The sheriff stopped by 'bout an hour ago. Said he didn't have much hope in findin' whoever did it."

Ridge sighed. "Doesn't surprise me. Nobody saw anything and the bastard didn't leave anything behind."

"You got any idea who might've done this?" Dr. Winters asked.

"One or two," Ridge answered coolly.

"Don't you be doin' somethin' stupid, Ridge Madoc. I only got one bed."

"Don't worry, Doc."

"Goes along with the job, Ridge." Winters removed his glasses and wiped the lenses with his handkerchief. "Pony Cullen is a poor excuse for a human being," he suddenly commented. "And it's no secret that he and Rivers don't see eye to eye."

Ridge smiled darkly. "Nope."

Colt shifted and moaned. Ridge straightened as he watched his friend fight his way to consciousness. A low groan accompanied his opening eyes.

"Lie still, Captain," the doctor ordered.

Colt focused on Winters. "Wha—"

"You were stabbed, Colt," Ridge said, stepping up to the side of the bed.

Colt peered blearily up at Ridge. "Stabbed?"

"We were in the saloon having a drink. You went out to use the privy and someone put a knife in your back," Ridge explained.

"Remember goin' out . . . then heard something." He frowned. "Turned, but—" Confusion clouded Colt's eyes.

"Did you see who it was?"

His eyelids drooped. "Smelled—"

Ridge leaned nearer. "Smelled what?"

"Dirty. Sweat, stink."

"That would describe Pony Cullen," Dr. Winters said dryly.

"Do you remember anything else, Colt?" Ridge asked. "Anything at all?"

"Hurt. Blood."

Ridge touched his arm. "It's okay. I'll find him."

"You need to drink somethin', Captain," Dr. Winters said, holding a glass of water to Colt's lips. The officer drank it all, then closed his eyes and his breathing evened out.

"Best thing for him now is rest," the doctor said quietly.

"I'll be back tomorrow," Ridge said.

"See that you are, and in one piece."

Grinning, Ridge waved and strode out. Once he stood on the boardwalk, his smile turned feral.

CLOUDS slid across the night sky, obliterating the nearly three-quarter moon and casting a pall over the shantytown. Nearly every post had a nearby shantytown where laundresses and others whose main trade was with the soldiers lived. Some of the women who took in laundry also took in men at night, making more money on their backs than sweating over the washtubs during the day. But the washing kept them reputable and out of trouble with the post commander.

Ridge had paid a laundress once for more than cleaning his uniform, but even as his body had gained its release, his conscience hadn't let him enjoy it. It was a sad life for the women, many of whom were widows of soldiers who'd been killed doing their duty, and they had children to feed and clothe. Doing what they did was the only way to keep their babies from starving.

Emma might very well have ended up as one of those women if her parents had disowned her. Ridge's gut churned at the thought of Emma lying on her back to make enough money to keep her and Chayton alive.

Shaking the morbid thoughts away, Ridge focused on one specific shanty, a small lean-to with just enough room inside for a bed and little else. From what he'd gleaned from talking to people, Cullen's current squaw lived there. She was like Chayton, part Indian and part white. Cullen had bought her from her father with a jug of whiskey and put her in the dilapidated building so he could visit her whenever the urge took him. Word was the urge took him pretty much every night, so Ridge figured he'd be showing up soon.

A nearing horse caught Ridge's attention and he squinted to make out the rider in the dim light. It wasn't a soldier this time. Cullen. Finally. The scout reined his horse in front of the shack and dismounted. He rubbed his crotch as he wound the reins around a crooked post. Ridge would give Cullen time to get down to business, then make his appearance.

After a few minutes, he heard a loud steady thumping and a woman's muffled cries. Swallowing the bile in his throat, Ridge darted across the open ground and to the shanty's door. He kicked it open with a thunderous crash.

Before Cullen could recover, Ridge grabbed his greasy ponytail and jerked him off the woman. Her eyes widened and she quickly covered her bruised and emaciated body with a thin, dirty blanket.

The fully clothed Cullen struggled to escape, but Ridge tightened his grasp and forced Cullen's head back as he caught the scout's left arm, bending it behind him.

"What the fu—" Cullen growled, awkwardly tucking himself into his grimy trousers with his free hand.

"Sorry to bother you at such a delicate time," Ridge said with sarcastic apology. "But I wanted to have a little talk with you and this just seemed the most private place to do it."

"What the hell are you doin' here, Madoc?"

"Didn't you listen? I said I wanted to chat," Ridge scolded.

"About what?"

"Where were you two nights ago, about nine o'clock?"

"Here. Just ask her." He motioned to the terrified girl who didn't appear more than fifteen or sixteen years old.

Ridge pressed Cullen's pinned arm upward, and the scout cursed. "She's so scared of you, she'll say anything you want her to, you son of a bitch." He slowly eased his grip on Cullen's arm. "Let's try this again, where were you two nights ago around nine o'clock?"

"I don't know," Cullen replied sulkily.

"Let me help you remember. You were behind the saloon where you waited until Captain Rivers came out, then you stabbed him in the back like the craven coward you are." Ridge's anger climbed and he fought the impulse to break Cullen's arm. It would be so easy, a bit more pressure and . . .

"You're gonna break my arm," Cullen said through thinned lips.

"That's the idea," Ridge stated coldly.

Cullen hissed and Ridge reluctantly loosened his grip.

"Tell me where you were," Ridge reiterated.

"I was in town, yeah, but I didn't stab Rivers. But I wouldn't mind shakin' the hand of the man who did."

Ridge shoved Cullen away, afraid he'd kill the man. "You're lying."

Cullen flexed his twisted arm as he glared at Ridge. "You can't prove it."

"I *know* you are, and I'm going to keep digging until I find the proof." Ridge paused, fighting for control. "Or I get a confession out of you."

"Don't hold your breath, Madoc."

"Be damned glad Captain Rivers didn't die or I'd just be shooting you down instead of trying to put you in jail."

"Yeah, I hear you're good at shootin' down men," Cullen baited. "Got enough practice when you were bounty huntin'."

Ridge clenched and unclenched his hands at his sides. He hadn't broken the law bringing in outlaws dead when they were wanted dead or alive, but he wasn't proud of what he'd done either. He'd been a kid back then, not much older than Cullen's squaw.

"I'm gonna be keeping an eye on you, Cullen." Ridge pivoted on his heel and stalked out of the filthy hovel.

He wended his way back to Paint and stood for a moment, leaning against the gelding's side. Ridge had no doubt that it was Cullen who'd stabbed Colt, but to prove it would be damned near impossible. If only Colt could identify Cullen as his attacker, but the captain hadn't seen anything.

Cullen may not be bright, but he was smart enough to

hide his tracks. If Ridge was the same person he'd been fifteen years ago, he would take justice in his own hands, but he couldn't do that anymore. It was simple—he'd have to get Cullen to confess.

Simple. Right.

EMMA rocked gently on the porch, the chair making soothing creaks with every forward motion. Her gaze followed Chayton who was "helping" Rory take care of the horses. Although she hadn't seen Hotah since the confrontation on the way back from the reservation, he was never far from her thoughts. She made certain Chayton was either in her sight, or in her sister or mother's. Hotah might be desperate enough to come into the yard to steal him away, and Emma couldn't bear the thought of losing her son ever again.

Rory had taken a shine to Chayton, and didn't hold his Lakota blood against him. More surprising since it was Indians who had been the cause of the hostler's crippled leg. A half-dozen of the other hired hands, including the foreman Bob Tucker, had warmed toward her son, too, but the majority of the men ignored him. Only one or two were openly antagonistic, but Tucker had given them fair warning and the cruel jibes had stopped.

Although pleased with Chayton's well-being, Emma had worried herself sick the past two days as she wrestled with Ridge's marriage proposal. With the growing acceptance of Chayton, her fears had lessened about their future. Her father wouldn't force her to leave the ranch, especially since Emma's mother was firmly in her and Chayton's camp. But living with her parents for the next twenty or more years didn't set right with Emma, either. She wanted her own life and, if truth be told, she wanted to share it with a man she loved.

And that man would be arriving in less than five minutes expecting her answer. But how could she allow Ridge to sacrifice so much for her and Chayton? She couldn't deny his sincerity in wanting to marry her, but was it only because he'd enjoyed their lovemaking as much as she had? Or did he have deeper feelings?

She shook her head at her own foolishness. There was no doubt Ridge cared for her and Chayton. There would be fondness and passion in their marriage, of that Emma was certain. And on her side, there would be love. But would that be enough to withstand the criticism and hostility of the townsfolk? Or would tolerance come with time just as it had at the ranch?

A movement down the road caught her attention. It was Ridge and he would arrive at the house in a matter of minutes. Her stomach lurched, knowing her time for making a decision was rapidly approaching.

Gathering her composure, she stood and called for Chayton. He scampered across the ranch yard to join her on the porch. When he caught sight of Ridge, Emma had to restrain him from running out to greet him. Only after Ridge dismounted did she allow her son to race over to his *leksi*.

Emma's pace was much more controlled as she joined them, and her gaze drank in the sight of the man. Dressed in a dark suit with a white shirt and black tie, Ridge didn't resemble the buckskin-clad man with whom she'd spent so much time. But she couldn't find fault in his appearance— no matter what he wore; the sight of him always left her feeling like her corset was too tight.

Holding Chayton, Ridge swept off his black broad-brimmed hat and smiled at Emma. "Good afternoon, Miss Hartwell. I do believe we have a dinner engagement."

Emma laughed, enjoying this playful side she'd never seen before. "I do believe you're correct, Mr. Madoc. Won't you come inside?"

"After you." He motioned for her to precede him, and scooped Chayton into his arms.

Emma smiled as she listened to Chayton tell Ridge all about the kitties and the horses, as well as his new friends. His words came jumbling out as he mixed English and

Lakota, but Ridge didn't have any trouble interpreting the constant stream.

Once in the house, she took Ridge's hat and placed it on the foyer's receiving table. Ridge lowered Chayton to the floor and the boy finally paused to take a breath.

"Hello, Mr. Madoc," Sarah said as she came down the wide staircase.

"Miss Hartwell," he greeted.

"How's Captain Rivers?"

Ridge grinned. "The doc is threatening to tie him down."

Sarah laughed. "I have to go into town tomorrow. Maybe I'll stop by to see him."

"He'd like that."

"So would Sarah," Emma whispered loud enough for Ridge to hear.

"Dinner will be ready in half an hour," Sarah announced. She held out her hand to her nephew. "Come on, Chay. I'll help you change for dinner."

With a wave to Ridge and Emma, Chayton took Sarah's hand and they ascended the stairs.

"He's settling in well," Ridge commented.

"Better than I expected. Sarah and Mother have made a big difference." Suddenly alone with him, Emma's mouth grew dry. "Uh, would you like to go into the parlor?"

"Sure."

Ridge offered her his arm, and she threaded her trembling hand through the crook and rested her palm on his forearm. Even through the wool suit, she could feel his planed muscles.

"Have you found out anything more about the attack on Captain Rivers?" she asked in an attempt to postpone the marriage proposal conversation. She felt his muscles bunch beneath her touch.

"I paid a visit to Cullen. He admitted to being in town the night Colt was stabbed, but said he didn't do it," Ridge said disgustedly.

"You don't believe him?"

"No. That sorry excuse for a human being did it, but I can't prove it."

"Captain Rivers didn't remember anything?"

Ridge shook his head. "He remembers going out to the alley, and the stink of dirt and sweat, but that's it." He sighed and raked his fingers through his thick, wavy hair.

Emma caught a whiff of soapweed scented with sage, reminding her of happier, more carefree times spent with the Lakota. "So what can you do?"

"If it was anyone but Colonel Nyes, I'd go to the post commander."

They entered the parlor, where flames flickered invitingly in the fireplace. Emma motioned to the loveseat. He waited until she sat down, then perched on the stiff cushion at the other end.

"Father was telling me that a general is coming to visit the fort," Emma said.

"General Mason. He showed up this morning."

"Would he listen to you?"

"I doubt it. I don't know him."

"I do," John Hartwell said as he entered the room.

Emma curbed her irritation at his intrusion. By all rights, she and Ridge should have a chaperone, although after all they'd gone through together, it seemed a ridiculous issue.

Her father sank into the high-backed, floral chair across from them. "He's a fair man, intelligent, not like that idiot Nyes."

Emma couldn't help but smile. "That makes two things you're both in agreement on."

Ridge scowled, but it was halfhearted. "What's his stand on the Indians?" he asked her father.

"He'll do what he's ordered to do, but doesn't condone killing for the sake of killing, unlike Nyes."

"And Cullen."

"The one you think backstabbed the captain?"

Ridge nodded grimly.

"Talk to General Mason," the older man suggested. "Maybe he can help."

Emma leaned back, amazed that her father was having a civil conversation with Ridge, as well as offering assistance. But, then, Ridge had offered to take responsibility for her and Chayton, a burden John Hartwell would be glad to be rid of.

Ridge scowled, but it was directed at himself rather than her father. "I don't see how. It's my gut feeling against Cullen, and he's backed by Nyes."

"How about setting a trap?" Emma suggested.

"What're you talking about, Emma?" her father asked.

She leaned forward and her hands flowed with her words. "Ridge said Captain Rivers didn't remember anything, but what if his memory miraculously returned? What if the rumor was started that the captain knew who did it, but would only speak to General Mason? What do you think Cullen would do?"

"He'd try to finish the job he started," Ridge murmured.

"But what if he doesn't?" her father asked.

Emma shrugged. "We're in the same place we are now—nothing gained, nothing lost."

Ridge's eyes glittered. "It just might work. Do you think General Mason would agree to help?" he asked her father.

"If I'm with you when you talk to him, he might." He stroked his chin. "I might even mention to him how Colonel Nyes refused to send out a search party for Emma."

Ridge smiled with reluctant admiration.

"I'll set up an appointment with him and let you know when it is," her father said. "I'm looking forward to bringing Nyes down a notch or two."

Emma's mother stepped into the parlor. "Dinner is served."

The meal passed in lively conversation, with her father and Ridge even managing to discuss ranching without raising their voices. Emma's father seemed sincerely interested in Ridge's plans, and although Ridge was cautious, he answered his questions honestly. Emma wondered how much of it was because he might very well become Ridge's father-in-law.

After everyone was done eating, Ridge asked Emma to accompany him on a stroll outside. Emma's pulse skittered out of control. The moment of truth had arrived.

Emma wrapped a heavy shawl around her shoulders since the evening had cooled considerably. Ridge guided her out the door with his fingertips resting lightly at her waist. They walked in silence to the corral and stopped to watch the yearlings prance around. The sun still peeped through the mountain range in the distance, but it wouldn't be long before it disappeared completely.

"Your father surprised me," Ridge said.

"Me, too," Emma admitted. "I wonder what his ulterior motive is."

Ridge shrugged. "Maybe he just wants to help."

"Maybe." Emma shivered.

Ridge stepped behind her, his chest to her back, and wrapped his arms around her waist. Almost against her will, she leaned into his strong embrace and covered his clasped hands with hers.

"What's your decision, Emma?" he whispered, his lips caressing her ear.

She couldn't think, couldn't do anything but feel his hard body flush against hers and his breath wafting warmly across her neck. All sensation shifted to her breasts and between her thighs as longing flowed through her like thick molasses. Ridge's groin pressed against her backside, and even through all the layers of clothing, she felt his desire.

"I-I don't know," she said huskily.

He kissed the underside of her jaw. "What's your answer, Emma?"

Her knees wobbled like a newborn foal and the temptation to press her lips to his freshly shaven cheek was almost overwhelming. "Why-why do you want to marry me?"

"I told you. I want you in my bed and I want to raise Chayton as my own. In exchange, you'll have my name and protection. Not to mention—" He licked a path from beneath her ear down to where her shoulder met her neck. "*Me* in *your* bed every night."

Emma trembled, wishing she could deny his body's claim over hers, but that was the only thing she was absolutely certain of. Ridge Madoc knew her body better than she knew her own, and she knew his—every delicious nook, cranny, and hard muscle.

Physical love was better than no love at all.

She nodded. "Yes. Yes, Ridge, I'll marry you."

Without releasing her, Ridge shifted around until she faced him. His eyes glowed and his smile brought creases to the corner of his eyes. "Thank you, Emma. I promise I'll make you happy."

They weren't the words she wanted to hear, but they were close enough.

"You already have," she whispered, then wrapped her arms around his neck and brought his head down so she could taste his lips.

After long minutes of kissing and fondling, Emma drew away. Panting, she laid her forehead against Ridge's chest. "When do you want the wedding?"

Ridge pressed his lips to her hair and rubbed his groin against her belly. "The sooner the better."

Emma laughed. "I have this feeling we'll be spending an awful lot of time in bed."

He cupped her buttocks. "Or in the grass or beside the river or in the barn."

Emma smacked his chest playfully. "Let's start with a bed—a bed wide enough for both of us," she said, recalling the narrow bed in the cabin where they'd first made love.

Ridge kissed the tip of her nose. "I can do that."

They remained standing with arms around one another, drinking in the quiet of the evening before returning to the house to share their news.

THE meeting with General Mason and John Hartwell went amazingly well. Between Hartwell's criticism of Nyes and Ridge's own experiences with the colonel, the general's eyes had burned with angry indignation. He'd even promised to sow some seeds of gossip with Nyes and around the post. If Cullen was responsible for the attack on Colt, the scout was bound to get nervous. Hopefully, nervous enough to make another attempt on Colt's life.

As Ridge and Hartwell rode away from the post, silence surrounded the two men, but it wasn't uncomfortable. Emma had provided a bridge between them, and although Ridge doubted Hartwell would ever be a good friend, they could now be in the same room together without wanting to kill one another.

"Why did you offer marriage to my daughter, Madoc?" Hartwell asked after they'd traveled a mile or two.

"Why wouldn't I?"

Hartwell's face flushed and he tugged his hat brim lower on his brow. "You know why."

"I lived with the Indians off and on before I joined the cavalry. I got nothing against them."

"But—" Hartwell cleared his throat. "Emma laid with one."

"She was his wife." Ridge grinned with wry amusement. "Seems to me when a man and a woman are married, they're going to lie together. It doesn't matter what color they are."

Hartwell studied him. "You really don't care that she was married to an Indian and has a half-br—half Indian child?"

"Do you love her less than before she disappeared for seven years?"

"No, of course not. She's still my daughter."

"That's right, she is." Ridge took a deep breath and let it out slowly. "Emma braved the weather, the rivers and mountains, the Indians, and her own family to find her child. No man could ask for a stronger, more loyal and courageous daughter. And I want that woman to be my wife."

Hartwell swallowed and quickly turned his gaze away.

Ridge allowed the man his semblance of privacy and rode in contemplative silence.

* * *

"YOU think he'll come tonight?" Colt whispered from his bed in the doctor's office.

Ridge restrained a yawn. "It's been two days—the word's been spread. It'll happen soon."

"*If* it was Cullen."

Ridge, hidden in a corner filled with dark shadows, leaned forward in his chair. "Now you don't think it was?"

Colt muttered under his breath. "I don't know anymore. Maybe it was Hotah or one of a few dozen other men who have a grudge against me."

"You said Cullen threatened you when he was let out of the stockade. Do you think he meant it?"

"Yeah," Colt admitted. "I just hate laying around and waiting."

Ridge grinned, knowing full well how his friend hated inactivity. "You can thank Emma later. She's the one who came up with the plan."

"Emma Hartwell?"

"Yep."

"Oh." Colt grew silent, but Ridge could tell he remained awake. "I heard a rumor about you and Miss Hartwell."

Ridge flinched. "It's true. The wedding's next Sunday out at Hartwell's ranch."

"So when were you going to tell me?"

Ridge shifted on the hard chair, trying to relieve the soreness of his backside. "I didn't figure you wanted to know."

"You figured wrong. Do you love her?"

"I care for her."

"Do you love her?" Colt demanded in a low tone.

"Hell, I don't know. I've never been in love before."

Colt's deep chuckle startled Ridge. "Damn, you've got it bad, pard."

"Shut up," Ridge said without force.

Colt was quiet for so long Ridge thought the healing man had finally fallen asleep.

"Don't I get to be your best man?" Colt suddenly asked.

"You want to be?"

"Hell, yes."

"All right, as long as you don't pass out during the vows." Ridge smiled. "Get some sleep. Sarge and Pres are outside. If Cullen can get through them, he's still gonna have to go through me."

Midnight came and went. Colt snored softly from the bed across the room. Ridge's eyes closed and his chin dropped to his chest, startling him awake. He raised his arms above his head, stretching to relieve the kinks in his back and shoulders.

Surely if Cullen was going to make his move, he would've done so by now. Maybe he'd been wrong about the scout being behind the attack.

He sensed movement and scanned the room, but there was nothing to see. His nape tingled. There. By the window. A shadowy figure reaching out to raise the pane. Only a small screek betrayed the intruder's presence.

Keeping close to the wall, Ridge padded around to the window. The man lifted one leg over the ledge, then swung his upper body through and stood up in the room, a knife held in his right hand. The intruder stunk—like old sweat and dirty buckskins.

Ridge eased back the trigger of his revolver and held the barrel to the man's head. "Drop it."

The man froze, but held onto the knife.

Ridge nudged him with the barrel. "I said drop it."

The knife clattered to the floor, awakening Colt.

"What's going on?" the captain asked sleepily.

"Light the lamp, Colt. We got him," Ridge replied with smug satisfaction.

A match flared and Colt lit the lamp's wick.

Pony Cullen glared at Colt. "You shoulda died the first time, you son of a bitch."

"I would say that's a confession, wouldn't you, Captain?" General Mason entered the room, followed by Sarge and Pres.

"Yes, sir," Colt said with a grin.

"Lieutenant, place the manacles on Cullen and escort him to the stockade," the general ordered.

"Yes, sir," Pres said with a sharp salute.

"And don't let Colonel Nyes release him this time," the general added with a satisfied smirk. "You can also tell the colonel I'll be speaking with him in the morning about a new assignment."

"Yes, sir."

Ridge allowed Pres and Sarge to bind Cullen and take him away. As they left, Dr. Winters slipped inside to check on his patient.

General Mason shook hands with Ridge. "It's been a pleasure working with you, Madoc. If you ever want your old job back, just let me know. The army can always use some honest scouts."

"Thank you, sir, but after Sunday, I'll be a married man," Ridge said.

"That's right. It's been a long time since I've attended a wedding. I'm looking forward to it." Mason turned to Colt. "And you, Captain, hurry up and heal. I'd like to present you with your gold leaves personally."

General Mason pivoted sharply and left the two men alone with the doctor.

"I'll be damned. Congratulations, Colt," Ridge said with a wide grin. "Or should I say *Major* Rivers?"

Colt appeared dazed by the rapidity of the events. "What the hell just happened?"

"Cullen's gettin' his due and you just got promoted," Dr. Winters replied curtly. His old face creased with a smile. "And I didn't even have to sew anyone back together again."

Ridge grinned and met Colt's gaze. Things were finally looking up.

$\mathcal{T}$WENTY-TWO

"GOODNESS gracious, the dress will never be ready on time. Why on earth couldn't the wedding have waited one more week?" Martha Hartwell chirped in agitation.

"Because Ridge couldn't wait that long," Sarah replied, her eyes twinkling with mischief.

Emma managed to smile despite the headache that had plagued her since the early morning when her dreams awakened her. She patted her mother's shoulder. "Don't worry. Everything will work out."

"Easy for you to say. You just have to state your vows and look beautiful," her mother chided with an affectionate smile. She sighed from her place at the dining room table where they'd been finalizing the wedding details. "I have to talk to Mrs. Wright about the food and make sure she has everything she needs." Still muttering to herself, her mother and her list disappeared into the kitchen.

Emma propped her elbows on the table and buried her face in her hands. But closing her eyes only made her remember the dream visions with more clarity.

A hand settled between her shoulder blades. "What's

wrong, Emma?" Sarah asked with quiet concern. "Are you having nightmares again?"

Emma raised her head and peered blearily at her sister. "How did you know?"

"I've heard you cry out, but every time I go to your room, you get quiet again." Sarah's eyes clouded with worry. "What are your nightmares about?"

Emma waved a hand. "Just nightmares."

Sarah leaned closer. "I don't believe you. There's something you're not telling me."

"There might be a good reason I'm not telling you."

"You're scaring me, Emma. What's wrong?"

Emma slumped back in her chair and stretched out her arms on the table. She stared at a framed picture of the mountains on the wall, although her vision was directed inward.

The dreams always began the same way, with the owl flying out of the night to land in an oak tree. The wolf cub played innocently below on the ground until the mountain lion pounced, batting around the cub with malicious amusement. Sometimes Emma thought the lion's face changed shape to something more human, but she could never see the details clearly. And always, when the female wolf arrived, the lion attacked her. The fight would be brutal, but the cat would gain the advantage. That's when the eagle would swoop down and Emma woke.

Over the last two nights the dreams had changed subtly. Emma now had a sense of another creature in the shadows, but its intentions were unclear, which worried her even more.

She blinked back to the present and found Sarah's troubled countenance in front of her. Emma smiled and patted her sister's hand. "It's probably just wedding collywobbles. I'm sure all brides have them."

The furrows in Sarah's normally smooth brow remained. "Do you love him?" she asked.

Emma considered lying, but found she couldn't do that to her sister who'd been nothing but supportive since Emma had returned with Chayton. "Yes, but it's not returned."

Sarah's mouth gaped. "Any fool can see he's head over heels in love with you."

"I'm not a fool, Sarah," Emma said with a pained smile. "He has feelings for me, but not those kind."

Sarah clucked her tongue. "Think what you will, but the only fool here is you, Emma Hartwell." She stood and shook the wrinkles from her skirt. "I'm going to see if Rory is tired of Chay following him around."

Folding her arms on the tabletop, Emma laid her cheek on them and closed her eyes. She didn't want to think about weddings or love or the future. She just wanted to sleep without dreams.

The sound of her father's office door opening and closing brought Emma's head up from her uncomfortable position. She hoped he was only going outside, or to talk to her mother. Although he'd been more civil toward her and Chayton lately, she wasn't ready to lower her guard.

He entered the dining room and appeared surprised to see her. "Emma, I'd like to have a word with you."

"What about?" she asked suspiciously.

He joined her at the table. "I think it's time your son started learning how to ride."

Her wariness didn't fade. "He's been riding since he was old enough to stay on a horse by himself."

Her father's eyes widened. "Why didn't you tell me?"

"You never asked." She failed to keep the bitterness from her voice.

He dropped his gaze and twined his fingers together. Emma stared at his hands. She'd always assumed they were smooth, but there were numerous small scars and his fingers had obviously done more than hold a pen.

"I'd like to give him one of the new foals after it's weaned," he said. "I know you'll be living with Madoc, but I wouldn't mind coming by to help the boy work with it."

"The boy's name is Chayton, or Chay, whichever you prefer to call him," Emma said sharply.

He stood and glared at his daughter. "If you don't want *Chayton* to have a horse, that's fine. He's your son."

Emma's anger died as quickly as it flared, and she said quietly, "He's also your grandson." She thought about what he'd said. "Are you serious about helping him train the foal?"

"I wouldn't have offered if I wasn't."

Emma noticed the flush in his cheeks and the uncertainty in his face. *This* was the man who'd embraced her and shed tears when he'd seen his daughter for the first time in seven years after she was believed dead.

Emma rose and walked up to him. "I think Chayton would like his own pony, and he'd like his grandfather to teach him."

Her father's eyes glimmered suspiciously, and Emma reached out and hugged him. "Thank you," she said, her throat tight.

He returned the hug, enfolding her within his arms. "You're welcome, Emma."

His voice was as husky as hers.

THE day before the wedding Emma awakened with a scream trapped in her throat. She gasped and panted as her heart beat a harsh tattoo against her breast. The dream had been so real—she could almost smell the lingering feral scent of the mountain lion and the wolf.

The dim light in the room told her it wasn't even dawn, and she could sleep another hour or two, but the dream's memory was too vivid. She leaned over to glance down at Chayton, assuring he was safe. His mouth was open as he snored softly in his trundle bed. Smiling, Emma rose quietly and peeked out her curtain. The fat moon hung high in the sky—tonight it would be full.

Just as in her dreams.

Her smile disappeared and her stomach clenched. She had to talk to Ridge. He was the only one who would believe her.

After donning a split riding skirt and plain tan blouse, Emma tiptoed out of her bedroom, carrying her boots. She wrote a short note telling her family where she'd gone, then pulled on the boots and a jacket in the foyer. Tightening the chinstrap of her wide-brimmed hat, Emma stepped out into the morning's tranquillity, a sharp contrast to the dream visions which continued to haunt her.

Even Rory was still asleep when Emma saddled Clementine. By the time she led the mare out of the barn and mounted her, a rose tinge was dusting the eastern sky. As she rode to Ridge's, she watched the mountains transform from dark blue to coral and pink, and by the time she arrived at his place, the sun peeped above the horizon.

The cabin's door opened and Ridge stepped out wearing brown trousers, moccasins, and an unbuttoned undershirt, with a pair of suspenders hanging down the side of his lean legs. For a moment, she could only stare as her mouth grew dry at the tempting sight.

"Emma, what're you doing here?" Ridge demanded, hurrying over to grab Clementine's bridle.

She smiled, already feeling the crushing weight of her nightmare easing. "I know it's early, but I need to talk to you."

Ridge's hands spanned her waist as he helped her to the ground. "I just put some coffee on. It should be ready in a minute or two."

He took her hand and she curved her fingers around his. Despite her exhaustion and fear, the intimacy warmed her and reassured her that she'd made the right decision in agreeing to marry him, even if he didn't love her. Once inside the cabin, Ridge urged her into a chair and she thankfully sank down onto it.

As Ridge retrieved two cups and poured the coffee, Emma took the time to examine the one-room cabin that would be her home after tomorrow. A ladder led up to the loft, and she envisioned Chayton climbing up to his bed every evening. It was a cozy, homey picture.

An Atlantic Box stove, used for heating and cooking, sat in the center of the cabin. A table and four chairs had obviously been made by Ridge's meticulous hands, and smoothed by his sensitive fingers. They were solid and steady, much like the man who'd created them.

Her attention wandered to the bed. The cot that had been there was replaced by a store-bought four poster bed, large enough for two to sleep—and make love—comfortably.

"Coffee?" Ridge's voice broke into her musings.

Startled, she jerked her attention back to him and accepted the cup with a murmured "thank you."

"I know this place ain't much, but I already have plans to make it bigger," Ridge said awkwardly.

"No, it's fine, truly," Emma assured, then grinned mischievously. "It's bigger than a tipi, and the bed's not on the ground."

An endearing blush stained his cheeks and he sipped coffee to cover his embarrassment.

"You bought a new bed," she commented.

A roguish grin stole across his lips. "I thought you'd like it."

"I do," she said softly. "But you didn't have to do it."

"I wanted to." He shrugged. "I had some money left after buying the bull."

"But you were going to start buying your land back from my father."

"I will someday."

Emma blinked back tears and wished she dared confess how much she loved him. "Thank you," she whispered, clasping his hand across the table.

Ridge brushed his thumb across her knuckles. "Tell me why you rode over here so early."

Emma gathered her thoughts, reluctantly setting aside

the infinitely more pleasant ones involving Ridge and the new bed in the corner. "Remember when I had the dreams?"

"You were worried about Chayton. You thought something would happen the night of the full moon."

"I-I'm having those same dreams again, but this time they're even more frightening." She went on to describe them and was relieved when Ridge listened without comment, his expression somber.

"What do you think it means?" he asked as he continued to caress Emma's hand.

"That something will happen to Chayton tonight," she replied unhesitantly.

Ridge frowned. "And maybe you, too. But who's the mountain lion?"

"I don't know." Frustration laced her voice. "I don't know who the eagle is either."

"Easy, Emma. Last time, nothing happened. Maybe it'll be the same this time."

She shook her head vehemently. "No. This feels different, more real and more menacing."

Before Ridge could say anything, the sound of an approaching horseman broke the morning's quiet. Emma exchanged a puzzled glance with Ridge, and they rose together and went out to face the visitor.

Preston Wylie galloped into the yard and reined sharply in front of the shack. The usually fastidious officer's uniform shirt was misbuttoned and untucked. He spotted Emma and his eyes widened slightly in his dirt-streaked face.

"Where's the fire, Pres?" Ridge asked.

The lieutenant dragged his gaze away from Emma and replied, "Cullen's escaped. Whoever helped him killed the guard."

Emma inhaled sharply.

"Is someone watching Colt?" Ridge demanded.

"Sarge."

"Where's Nyes?"

"Back at the post. General Mason's questioning him now. The general wants you to track down Cullen."

"Cullen and whoever got him out of the stockade," Ridge said grimly. "I'll grab some supplies and ride over."

Pres touched the brim of his hat and said to Emma, "Ma'am."

Emma managed a nod and the officer rode away.

Ridge grasped her shoulders. "I have to go, Emma."

Again she nodded, unable to speak past the irrational fear lodged in her throat.

"Are you all right?" Ridge asked, ducking to peer into her face.

"Yes."

Ridge didn't appear convinced, but he drew back, his reluctance obvious. "I have to see if I can track down Cullen before his trail gets cold, but I'll come back to the ranch before nightfall so we can figure out your dreams."

"All right."

Although Ridge was anxious, he remained with Emma. "I'll escort you back to your place before I ride over to the post."

Emma mentally shook herself. "No. That'll add eight miles. You need to find Cullen and lock him up again before he hurts someone else."

She could see the fiery determination in his expression, but his eyes were uncertain. She gave him a little shove. "Go! I'll be fine."

After another moment of indecision, Ridge kissed her. It was brief but fierce—a promise he'd return to her as soon as he could.

He walked her to Clementine and gave her a boost into the saddle. He laid his hand on her leg and gazed up at her anxiously. "Are you sure?"

She leaned down and feathered a touch across his whisker-roughened jaw. "Yes. Now go."

He grinned, a crooked, wry grin that never failed to

arouse Emma's passion. Stifling a moan, she tapped her heels to the mare's flanks and the animal sprinted away.

RIDGE hunkered down, tipping his head from one side to the other as he tried to make out the footprints in the dirt. He had no trouble distinguishing Cullen's from the soldiers' since the scout wore moccasins. Except there was a second set of moccasin prints, slightly smaller than Cullen's. Ridge's first thought was Cullen's squaw had broken him out, but the prints were too big for a slip of a gal like her.

"Anything?" Pres Wylie asked, standing a couple yards away from the tracker so he wouldn't mess up the ground with his own boot prints.

"I'm not sure," Ridge replied. "It looks like whoever killed the guard and busted him out was wearing moccasins."

"There aren't many so-called civilized folks who wear them," Pres remarked.

Ridge glanced at his own comfortable, knee-high moccasins. "Yeah. Me, Cullen—" he broke off as a stray thought struck him. "Did you have any trouble getting into that village a couple weeks ago?"

Pres blinked owlishly at the change of subjects. "No, not that I can recall. Cullen led us through a serpentine trail that cut through rock. I remember thinking it was an opportune place for an ambush."

Ridge pushed himself upright. "While Emma and I were in the village they always had sentries stationed up there."

"So where were the sentries?"

"That's a damned good question." He strode back to Paint, his mind racing with possibilities. "Who's coming with me?"

"General Mason's authorized ten men for the search. I'm the ranking officer."

"Is someone guarding Colt?"

"Sarge is in charge of the guard detail."

Despite the gravity of the situation, Ridge smiled. "Betcha Colt's having a fit. Being out of the action is going to do what Cullen didn't—kill him."

Pres laughed. "I don't know about that, but Sarge is threatening to bind and gag him."

Ridge shook his head in amusement, but the moment passed and he sobered. "I'll meet you and your contingent outside the gate."

By late afternoon, Ridge was using every trick he knew to find the trail. At first the stolen horses' tracks were easy to follow. But as Cullen and his accomplice moved into rockier terrain, the prints disappeared. Ridge had to search for darker soil spots, which were exposed when a stone was disturbed; or a metal-gray slash on a rock from the graze of a horseshoe; or the fresh break of a twig. It was time-consuming and laborious.

Ridge gripped his saddle horn and shifted his stiff backside on the unforgiving leather saddle. He rubbed his eyes, which were sore from intently studying the ground for hours on end.

"Any ideas?" Pres Wylie asked, setting his horse beside Ridge.

"Yeah, but I don't like any of 'em."

Pres pushed his hat off his forehead. "If it wasn't another white man wearing moccasins, it was an Indian."

Although it wasn't a question, Ridge replied, "Yep. And I've got a bad feeling I know who it was."

"Who?"

"Hotah. He was from the village you attacked." He couldn't hide his simmering resentment.

Pres's gaze hardened. "We were under orders to recapture the natives and return them to the reservation. It wasn't our intention to do battle."

Ridge took a deep breath to dispel his anger. "It was Cullen, who somehow got Hotah to help him get the detachment into the camp without being seen."

"Why would this Hotah assist Cullen in murdering his people?"

"Revenge, maybe. The chief banished him from the village the day before the attack. Hotah didn't like that the chief wanted peace, not war." A lead ball settled in Ridge's stomach. "I could be wrong. I ain't never heard of an Indian turning on his own before, but if Hotah is hell-bent on stirring things up, this is a good way to help it along."

"Maybe Cullen offered him some incentive."

"What kind?"

"Half a dozen repeating rifles and boxes of shells were stolen from the armory the night before Colt was stabbed."

"Shit," Ridge swore. "Those would kill a lot of soldiers and settlers." He stiffened his backbone. "Let's get back to it. If Hotah and Cullen have those rifles, we need to stop them."

Determination driving him, Ridge led the small group of soldiers and hoped he was on the right trail.

EMMA trudged downstairs after trying on her wedding dress for the umpteenth time. This time, however, it fit perfectly, much to her mother's relief. Mrs. Wright was frying chicken and Emma's stomach growled, reminding her she'd eaten little during the day. Between her nightmares and her fear for Ridge with Cullen on the loose, she'd simply been unable to force food into her rebelling stomach.

She entered the front room and found her mother and Sarah with their heads bent over something as they sat on the comfortable sofa.

"What're you doing?" Emma asked.

The two women jumped in guilty surprise and Sarah moved to block her mother from Emma.

"Doing?" Sarah repeated too brightly.

Emma crossed her arms. "What's going on?"

"We have no idea what you mean, dear," her mother said innocently.

Emma suspected it was some surprise for the wedding

tomorrow, and didn't have the heart to spoil it for them. "Where's Chayton?"

"He went out to help Rory," Sarah replied.

"How long ago?"

"A half an hour or so."

"I think I'll go find him and let you two get back to doing nothing." Emma smiled sweetly.

She refrained from laughing at Sarah's loud sigh of relief as she left them to their scheming. Outside, the sun was dropping toward the mountains. It wouldn't be long before twilight came and went, which meant the rising of the full moon. She shivered uncontrollably and wrapped her arms around herself.

Where are you, Ridge? You said you'd be here.

Emma spotted Rory leading a bay gelding that had cut his front right fetlock two days earlier. She was pleased to see the horse's limp was barely noticeable now.

"Rory, have you seen Chayton?" she called out.

The old hostler shook his head. "Ain't seen him since early this afternoon."

"Sarah said he came out here half an hour ago."

"Ain't seen him," he repeated with a frown, a deep crease between his eyebrows. "Check the barn. Maybe he's just playin' with them kittens."

Emma was panting by the time she arrived at the barn and threw open the door. The kittens were nowhere to be seen. Neither was Chayton. Emma's anxiety turned to dread and her heart pounded so hard it made her dizzy.

"He ain't there?" Rory asked, limping up behind her.

"No. Where would he go?" she asked, her voice climbing.

"I'll start lookin' around and as soon as the boys start comin' in, I'll have them help." Rory patted her shoulder awkwardly. "Don't you worry, Miss Emma. He probably just found a new place to play."

Emma managed a nod and raced back to the house. Her cry brought her father out of his office, as well as Sarah and her mother from the parlor.

"Chayton's missing," Emma announced, her voice thready. "Rory hasn't seen him and he's not in the barn. When he's not with Rory and the horses, he likes to play in the barn with the kittens, so I thought he'd be there, but he wasn't." She knew she was rambling, but it was either that or fall apart completely.

"I'll get the men out looking immediately," her father assured, his mouth set in a grim line. "We'll find him, Emma."

He grabbed his hat on the way out the door, his stride purposeful.

"I'm sorry, Emma," Sarah cried. "I should've gone with him and made sure he made it over to Rory."

"I'm sure he'll be fine, Emma," her mother reassured, although her face was wan. "Why, I'll bet they'll find him curled up someplace taking a nap."

"I'm going to change clothes and help look for him," Emma said, her voice stronger.

Without waiting for a reply, Emma flew upstairs and changed into the same split riding skirt and blouse she'd worn that morning to Ridge's. Within ten minutes, she was searching the ground for a sign of a scuffle. Although she wasn't a tracker like Ridge, she'd learned a few things from him and Fast Elk.

Behind the barn Emma found what she was seeking. She called to her father, who joined her. She showed him the marks in the dirt—small boots and a larger set of footprints that weren't boots. Rather, they were moccasins.

Hotah.

Emma swayed and her father caught her arm.

"Emma, are you all right?" he asked, wrapping a steadying arm around her shoulders.

"It was Hotah, the Indian I told you about that Captain Rivers chased away."

"You said he wanted Chayton. Why?"

"He thinks Chayton should grow up to be a Lakota warrior. Hotah never liked me and when I took Chayton away, he must've followed me back here."

Her father scowled. "I'll have one of the men ride to the fort and tell General Mason what happened. He should be able to assign some soldiers to help us search."

Emma nodded absently, wishing with all her heart that Ridge were here. He would be able to make sense of the tracks. Besides, his confident presence would be a balm to her hysteria threatening to escape.

Her father led her back to the barn and joined some of the hired hands who had just returned from the range. Emma waited until his attention was on them and then slipped into the barn to saddle Clementine. A rifle leaned up against a stall and she slid it into the scabbard on the saddle.

She led the mare out the back door of the barn, hidden from the men, and began to follow the faint moccasin prints left behind. It would be night soon and she'd lose the trail in the darkness . . . except there was a full moon. More light. More danger.

Tonight her vision would come to life.

TWENTY-THREE

RIDGE cursed the bad luck that had him arriving at the Hartwell ranch after sunset. As he rode closer, he noticed the activity around the outbuildings and corrals. Lanterns bobbed about, carried by men who appeared to be looking for something.

Looking for what?

He dismounted in front of the house and his blood grew cold when he saw the door standing open. He took the steps with one leap and strode into the foyer.

"Emma! Emma, where are you?" he shouted in the house.

Sarah scurried around the corner, her eyes red-rimmed. "Ridge, I'm so glad you're here."

He grasped her cold hands. "What is it, Sarah? Where's Emma?"

Sarah shook her head, strands of blond hair falling around her face. "We don't know. First it was Chayton, and now Emma's missing, too."

The air in Ridge's lungs whooshed out as if he'd been gut-punched. He led Sarah to the front room and set her down in a chair. "Tell me everything."

Sarah described how Chayton disappeared, then Emma an hour later.

"Who saw Emma last?" Ridge asked, trying to keep his impatience reined in.

"Father, I think."

Ridge turned to leave, but Sarah latched onto his wrist. "Find her and Chayton. Just like you did before," the girl pleaded.

Ridge gave her hand a squeeze and managed a shaky smile. "I will. I promise."

Outside, Ridge found Hartwell saddling up with a dozen hired hands.

"Madoc, I'm glad you're here," Hartwell said with sincere relief. "Emma and Chayton are missing."

"Sarah told me. Were there any tracks?"

"Emma found some. I was getting the men organized to follow them and the next thing I know, she's gone." Hartwell's eyes couldn't hide his grief.

"Show me the tracks."

Two minutes later, Ridge knew. "It was Hotah or Cullen—both of them wear moccasins."

"Emma said it was Hotah," Hartwell said.

Ridge gazed down at the track, noticing it was the smaller of the two moccasin prints he'd been following all day. He nodded. "I think she's right." He pointed to the shod horse's tracks beside it. "And that's Emma's horse. I recognize the chipped shoe on the left rear foot."

"She must be following them herself."

Ridge curled his trembling fingers into his palms. Hotah wouldn't hesitate to take Emma if he knew she was behind them, alone.

Struggling to curb his rage and foreboding, Ridge led the search party through the increasing darkness. He glanced up to catch an eyeful of the full moon, which would give him enough light to follow the trail. It also reminded him of Emma's dream, which was starting to make sense. Hotah was the mountain lion, intent on stealing the cub Chayton.

But who was the eagle? Cullen?

* * *

THE only thing Emma could hear was the pounding of her heart. The nocturnal creatures had gone silent, even the nighthawks that usually began to skirl as soon as it darkened. Emma had managed to keep on the trail, although it was nonexistent in some places. But she'd been able to pick it up again each time, and knew deep down inside that she was on the right track.

An owl hooted and Emma froze, her gaze flitting across the branches of the scrub oak around her. There. Twin orbs reflected golden light.

"Whooo-whoooo."

The owl from her vision. Which meant Chayton was near. She peered through the brush and spotted a dim light—a small campfire. Her pulse doubled and Clementine shied, sensing her nervousness.

"Easy girl," Emma soothed, running a calming hand along the horse's withers.

Emma dismounted and let the reins drop to the ground. Cold fire licked through her veins. She should go back and get her father and the others, but what if Chayton and his kidnapper left? Or she couldn't find her way back?

She would get closer, but not try anything herself. Hotah could easily overpower her, just as the mountain lion overpowered the wolf.

Grabbing the rifle from the boot, Emma crept nearer to the fire, keeping low on the ground and ignoring the scratches from twigs and branches. As she approached, she could see a small bundle lying on the ground. She paused to look more closely and recognized Chayton curled up, his upper body moving up and down with his even breaths. He was probably exhausted.

Biting her lower lip against tears of relief, Emma shimmied closer until she was lying behind a growth of brush and could see Chayton's kidnapper.

Only it wasn't Hotah. It was Cullen's greasy buckskins and long stringy hair.

"Come on out, Emma," Cullen suddenly hollered out. "I know you're there."

Emma's breath caught and her heart skipped a beat, then another. She remained motionless.

"Don't play games. You don't come out, I hurt your bastard." He grabbed Chayton's arm, jerking the boy up and against his chest.

Emma's hands closed on the rifle and she lifted it to her shoulder. Sighting down the barrel, she found Chayton too close to Cullen to risk taking a shot. Her hands shaking, she closed her eyes briefly, her chest squeezing and her mouth desert-dry. She set the rifle on the ground and pushed herself to her feet slowly. "I'm coming. Don't hurt him."

On legs that felt like they belonged to someone else, Emma staggered into the fire's circle of light. She stopped shy of Cullen's reach.

His lecherous gaze roamed over her, making her feel soiled. "Get over here, Emma. I been locked up for four days and I'm hornier'n a toady frog."

Emma felt like throwing up. One glance at his crotch confirmed his words. She stepped back reflexively.

"Ina?"

Chayton's frightened voice grabbed her attention and her heart thudded at the lost look on his face. "Yes, Chay, I'm here."

"Home?" he murmured.

"Soon," she promised.

"Don't bet on it." Cullen wrapped his arm around Chayton's small neck.

Emma started toward them. "No! Leave him alone!"

"You don't do as I say, and I'm gonna have to hurt him again."

In the fire's flickering light, she spotted a bruise forming on her son's right cheekbone and a swollen lower lip.

Rage buried her fear. "What did you do to him?"

"Bastard tried to run off after I got rid of Hotah." Cullen laughed, the sound like glass on a blackboard. "Stupid Injun said he had to have the kid before we left the territory.

Threatened to slice my neck iffen I interfered. He's the one who ended up with a knife in the back."

"You murdered Hotah? Just like you tried to kill Captain Rivers."

Cullen shrugged. "The Injun wasn't useful no more. And now I got me six repeatin' rifles to sell. Figure it's a good deal all around."

"Except for Hotah."

"Why're you cryin' over him? He's the one who stole your kid from the ranch. I told him not to bother, but the stubborn redskin didn't listen. And now I got me a kid to sell, too. Too young to bring much, but I'll get somethin' for my time."

Emma's eyes widened and her insides twisted into a knot. What Cullen planned to do was so appalling, so horrible that she was robbed of speech.

"Get over here, Emma. Now!" Cullen tightened his hold around Chayton's neck and the young boy's mouth gaped as he clawed at Cullen's arm. The brute didn't even notice his struggles.

Emma obeyed immediately, falling to her knees beside the foul-smelling Cullen. "I'll do anything you want! Just stop hurting him."

Cullen released Chayton, who dropped to the ground and Emma swooped him into her arms. He was trembling and she could feel his heart pounding in his chest. "Shhhh, it's all right, Chayton. You're safe now."

"Not for long if you don't do like I tell you," Cullen growled.

More terrified for Chayton than herself, she leaned as far away from Cullen as she could and eased her arms away from her son. "Run away," she whispered in his ear. "Find *Leksi*."

As she turned back to Cullen, she heard Chayton scramble to his feet and into the brush.

Cullen roared and jumped up to chase the boy. Emma grabbed one of his legs, unable to trip him, but stopping him from his pursuit. Cruel fingers twisted in her hair and tugged her to her feet. Tears filled Emma's eyes, but as long as Cullen was busy with her, the more time Chayton had to escape.

"You'll pay for that, squaw woman." He backhanded her and the world spun crazily, nearly driving her to unconsciousness. She struggled to clear her muddled thoughts as her cheek throbbed from the blow.

She had no illusions about what he planned for her, and she knew without a doubt the mountain lion would beat the wolf. But what of the eagle?

RIDGE cursed as he rolled the body over. Hotah. He'd been killed by a knife to the back—same method Cullen had tried with Colt. But this time he'd succeeded.

"Who is it?" Hartwell asked from atop his horse.

"Hotah."

"The one Emma thought kidnapped Chayton?"

"The same."

"Who—?"

"Probably Cullen. Double-crossed Hotah." Ridge rubbed his brow, wishing he could press the ache away. It robbed him of his usual alertness and made him impatient, tense, and he needed his wits if he was to find Emma and Chayton. "Have one of your men take the body back."

Hartwell's frown was evident in the moon's glow. "I'm not going to send a man back who can help search."

"Look, Hartwell, the trail pretty much ends here. Between what little light we got and the rocks, we ain't going to be picking up a trail until morning." Although Ridge fully intended to remain searching for Emma and Chayton, he figured a dozen men bumping into each other in the dark would only hinder him.

"I'm not leaving my daughter and grandson out there with a murderer."

Ridge's irritation was diminished by Hartwell's concern for both Emma and Chayton. "I don't want to do it anymore than you do, but we don't have a choice unless we just want to stumble around blind."

"We can split up, each man taking a section. If someone finds Emma, it'll be two shots; Chayton, three."

Although Hartwell's suggestion was like shooting fish in an ocean, Ridge reckoned it was better than doing nothing and he wouldn't be saddled with a crowd trailing after him. He nodded. "We'll do it your way. Just make sure your men go slow and easy."

Hartwell seemed surprised by Ridge's acquiescence. "All right."

After giving the orders to his men and having one of them take Hotah's body back, Hartwell turned back to Ridge. "Good luck, Madoc."

Ridge nodded once. He listened to the men move away, keeping their horses to a walk. He climbed back into Paint's saddle and patted the horse's neck. "Let's go find 'em, fella."

Paint snorted and they continued the search. Half an hour later, Ridge removed his hat and raked his hand through his hair in frustration. He might as well be riding in circles for all the good he was doing. He hadn't caught a glimpse of anything remotely resembling a trail.

With Hotah dead, why had Cullen kept Chayton? The scout had wanted Emma at one time, but not her boy. Unless he had some use for him.

What if Cullen had both Emma and Chayton? After seeing how Cullen treated his squaw, Ridge knew what awaited Emma. Loathing surged up from his belly. He couldn't stop. He had to find them.

The rustle of an owl's wings caused Ridge to swivel in his saddle. He spied the large bird flying between a patch of scrub oak to land on a high branch. A chill settled down Ridge's spine and he urged Paint forward, toward the tree where the owl perched. As soon as Ridge neared it, the owl leapt from the branch, opened its wings and dipped past Ridge to fly ahead.

Without hesitation, Ridge urged Paint after the owl. He wasn't certain he believed Emma's dream visions, but he did believe in his gut, and it told him to follow the owl. Twice Ridge thought he lost the bird of prey, but the owl reappeared in front of him both times. Afraid to think about it too much, Ridge just concentrated on keeping it in sight.

Finally, the owl landed on another scrub oak and began to preen itself. Ridge stood in his stirrups and looked around the silver-gilded wilderness. A light flickered in the distance. Ridge urged Paint on once more, until he came to another horse, saddled and ground-reined. He dismounted and examined the mare closer. Clementine.

A woman's cry broke the silence. Cold fire froze Ridge's blood and he shoved through the underbrush toward the camp. One look told him everything: Emma, trying to kick and claw Cullen as the son of a bitch ripped at her clothes.

Ridge charged toward them.

AN eagle's scream froze Emma. For a split second, Emma stared into the black eyes of a sharp-taloned eagle as it dove toward them. Then the eagle was gone and in its stead was Ridge, colliding with Cullen. The villain released her as he tried to defend himself and Emma rolled away. Terror pumped blood through her veins as she scuttled backward on her hands and knees.

Her breath came in fast, jerky gasps as she watched Ridge and Cullen roll around on the ground. Ridge landed a fist in Cullen's face. The taller man barely flinched and brought up his knee between Ridge's legs. Ridge rolled away, grimacing and panting. Cullen jumped up and attacked Ridge with a roar of fury. Ridge bounced to his feet and spun away, causing the other man to pause.

Ridge delivered a right punch, then a left. The first snapped Cullen's head back and the second sent him staggering backward. Ridge followed him, pressing his advantage with a blow to Cullen's belly. The murderer doubled over and Ridge moved in again, but pulled up sharply when Cullen straightened, holding a knife in his right hand. Emma was certain it was the same one used to wound Colt and kill Hotah.

Cullen swung the blade at him and Ridge sucked in his gut as he jumped back. The knife's tip barely missed him. Cullen tried again, but Ridge grabbed the wrist of Cullen's hand holding the knife. His face reddened as he struggled to force Cullen to drop the weapon. Cullen brought up his other hand and slugged Ridge in the face, but Ridge managed to hold onto Cullen's wrist.

Ridge hooked a leg behind Cullen's and shoved, tumbling the two men to the ground. The knife disappeared between their bodies and Emma struggled to her feet, her lungs fighting for air. She had to do something. Cullen could kill Ridge.

Suddenly the two men froze in a tableau of shock, then they both collapsed, Ridge on top of Cullen. They lay still and silent.

A scream crawled up Emma's throat and she swallowed once, twice to stifle it. She staggered over to them and fell to her knees, her hand hovering an inch above Ridge's back.

"Ridge?" she whispered.

A movement, then a groan and Ridge rolled off Cullen. There was a circle of scarlet blood on Ridge's shirtfront and Emma trembled with horror.

"It's not mine, Emma," he reassured her.

She stared at him, trying to comprehend his words.

Ridge sat up, but didn't touch her. "It's not my blood. It's Cullen's."

Emma's gaze shifted to Cullen's motionless body. "H-he's dead?"

"Yeah."

Emma tugged her ripped blouse tight across her breasts and satisfaction brought her chin up. "Good. I'm glad."

Ridge helped her to her feet and led her away from the

body, ensuring her back was to the grisly sight. "Are you all right? Did he—"

Emma shook her head, her own shock dissipating as the shakes settled in. "No. He wanted to. Tried to. But you got here before—"

Her shoulders shuddered as the sobs she'd been restraining broke free. Ridge enfolded her in his arms, smoothing a hand up and down her back. "It's all over now, Emma. He can't hurt you or Chayton anymore."

She jerked up. "Chayton. Did you find him?"

"No. Where is he?"

"I t-told him to run . . . I d-distracted Cullen. I told him to find you," she stammered out. "He's out there all alone."

As if in reply, three gunshots sounded, breaking the night's stillness. Ridge's smile was brilliant in the moonlight. "Someone just found Chayton. Three shots was the signal for him."

Hope flooded through Emma, replacing her despair. "Who?"

"Your father has most of his men out looking for you and Chayton. I lost Cullen's trail about an hour ago and we split up. The signals were three shots when Chayton was found, and two for you." Ridge brushed her cheek with his fingertips. "I suppose I'd better signal them."

With the danger gone and Chayton safe, Emma slumped against Ridge in exhaustion. "Could we maybe wait a few minutes? I'd like to be able to stand on my own when they get here."

"Anything you want, Emma. Anything you want," Ridge whispered, holding her close.

Emma wrapped her arms around Ridge's waist, reveling in the scent and feel of him. After Cullen's obscene pawings, Ridge's gentleness was seductive yet calming.

"An owl brought me to you," Ridge said after some moments of companionable silence.

Emma drew away from him, but stayed close enough to remain in his embrace. "My dream." She smiled gently. "You were the fearless eagle."

"I don't know about fearless," Ridge said with a wry chuckle. "I was plenty scared for you." He framed her face in his palms. "You could've been killed."

"But I wasn't." Emma took a deep breath and smiled, giddy with relief. "And I still have a chance to make you fall in love with me."

Ridge swallowed hard. "Colt asked me the other night if I loved you. I told him I didn't know, that I'd never been in love before so didn't know what it felt like." Naked devotion shown in his deep, dark blue eyes. "I think I figured it out."

Emma's heart soared and her voice trembled as she spoke the words she'd hidden away for so long. "I love you."

"And I love you, Emma Louise Hartwell." Ridge lowered his mouth to hers, teasing her lips open with the tip of his tongue.

Joy bubbled through her until she could no longer contain it and she broke away from Ridge's too-tempting lips, smiling. "If we don't signal them, we may not get to it until morning and my mother will have a fit. All her wedding plans would be totally ruined."

Ridge laughed. "Your family's going to take some getting used to."

"But it's going to be all right."

Ridge's amusement faded. "Things will be far from perfect, Emma, but we'll have each other and your family, plus some good friends. We'll carve out a home for us."

"I'm not worried. As long as I have you and Chayton, I'll be home."

ALTHOUGH the ranch yard was far from overflowing with guests, those who attended were genuinely happy for Emma and Ridge. Among them were most of the ranch hands; General Mason; the hardware store owner Howard Freeman, his wife and daughter; Gertrude Manning, who couldn't stop apologizing and promised a free meal the next time they were in town; Lieutenant Pres Wylie,

Sergeant Gabe Sanders, and the newly promoted Major Rivers, who managed not to pass out during the ceremony; and a handful of other townsfolk who went out of their way to tell Ridge and Emma they were more than welcome in their homes and businesses. The banker and his son were even there, although Emma suspected it was more her father's threat to take all his money elsewhere than well wishes toward the bride and groom that had them in attendance.

Smiling, Emma adjusted the wildflower garland perched on her head—a surprise from Sarah and her mother—and watched Chayton play with George and Sally Orton's children. Emma knew there would be hard times ahead, but she was also confident the good would outweigh them.

Arms came around her waist from behind and lips pressed against her ear. "A penny for your thoughts," Ridge whispered.

Emma leaned back and clasped his hands. "They're not worth nearly that much." He huffed a laugh and warm air wafted across her neck. She shivered and told her body to behave. She watched Sarah, her cheeks pink and her eyes glowing, lean close to Colt Rivers. "Did you notice how Sarah is hovering around Colt?"

"And that Colt doesn't mind her hovering?"

Emma laughed. "It's too bad he's not resigning his commission."

"He would've if General Mason hadn't talked him into accepting a staff position."

"The promotion was an added incentive, too."

Ridge nodded. "The army needs more officers like him."

Someone cleared his throat behind them and they turned as one to face John Hartwell, who had an amused glint in his eyes. Ridge kept his arm around Emma's waist as he nodded at his new father-in-law. "Hartwell."

The older man flinched slightly. "Since we're related now, you could call me John."

Ridge smiled wryly. "That'll take some getting used to."

Her father chuckled. "I imagine it will . . . Ridge." He withdrew an envelope from his suitcoat pocket and handed it to his son-in-law.

"What's this?"

"A wedding present."

Frowning, Emma watched Ridge open the envelope flap and withdraw an official looking piece of paper that read *Certificate of Deed* at the top. Ridge glanced at her, a question in his eyes. Although he was learning to read, the progress was slow and vexing. She skimmed the form and her eyes widened.

"He's deeded back all the acres he bought from your stepfather," Emma announced. "And a hundred more, for a total of five hundred acres."

Ridge caught his breath and his gaze shot to the older man. "Why?"

Her father straightened his shoulders and met Ridge's gaze. "I was wrong to cheat him out of that land and I apologize." He held out his hand.

Emma held her breath as Ridge stared at it for a long moment. Then he reached out and clasped her father's hand in a firm grip.

"Thank you, Hart—John," Ridge said with a genuine smile.

The older man turned an affectionate gaze to Emma. "Thank your wife. She's an extraordinary woman."

Emma's eyes filled with tears, and she kissed her father's cheek and hugged him. "Thank you," she whispered.

She released him and stepped back into Ridge's waiting arms.

"I'd best go ask your mother to dance or I'll never hear the end of it," her father said with a wink.

Emma followed his progress through the small throng and smiled as he whisked her mother into his arms.

"Did I tell you about my dream last night?" Emma asked, watching her parents dance.

Ridge's eyes widened slightly as he shook his head.

"There was a female wolf and four young cubs curled

up beside her, with an eagle perched above them, guarding them while they slept."

Ridge appeared dazed. "Four?"

"Too many?"

He gazed down at her affectionately. "Not nearly enough, Emma Madoc."

She grinned. "Then we'll have to work on that."

He wrapped her in his strong arms and kissed her tenderly.

DANNI Hawkins juggled a Chinese takeout bag, her backpack, a jumbo iced tea, and two cans of soda as she tried to open the door to the office. Just when she succeeded in turning the knob, the tea tipped, splashing across her tan trousers and onto the cracked sidewalk in front of the door.

"Son of a—" Biting back the rest of her frustration, she righted the cup, stepped over the tea puddle, and entered the office of B. MARSHAL, ATTORNEY AT LAW and D. HAWKINS, PRIVATE INVESTIGATOR.

She scurried past Cathy Miller, who sat behind the reception desk, and down the hall to a small break room that doubled as a storage area. She slid her backpack onto a chair and deposited the white bag and two colas on the Formica-topped chrome table, then stepped into the bathroom. As she tried to remove the brown stain from her pants, Cathy appeared in the doorway.

"Having some trouble?" the petite paralegal asked, her arms crossed.

"No," Danni shot back with as much sarcasm as she could inject into one word. She glanced at the spot and found it had only spread further across the material. "Damn!" With more force than necessary, she flung the damp cloth into the chipped porcelain sink. "Is the one o'clock still on?"

"As far as I know. He hasn't called to cancel." Cathy's expression softened. "Are you sure you're up to this? You should've taken the whole week off."

"I'm fine." Danni regretted her sharp tone the moment she spoke. "I'm sorry. I have a lot on my mind." Afraid to meet Cathy's eyes, Danni slipped by her to return to the break room. "Hungry?" she asked with forced brightness. "I brought Sesame Chicken and General Tso's from Lucky Ling's."

"Does a pig like mud?"

Danni laughed, a rusty but welcome sound after the somberness of the past few days. "I brought enough for Beth, too."

"She had an appointment at twelve-thirty—the kid your father referred to her." Since Cathy worked for both Beth and Danni, she knew both their schedules.

"The juvie who tried to fence a laptop?"

Cathy nodded. "He has two priors. Nothing serious, but the kid's almost eighteen and the D.A. wants to try him as an adult."

Having been a cop for two years, Danni could easily imagine the type. Danni's father had spent much of his off-duty time combating the gangs' influences by working with streetwise teenage boys. His colleagues had respected him for his dedication and sacrifice.

It was too bad his daughter had fallen into the "sacrifice" category.

Danni and Cathy emptied the white takeout boxes onto two mismatched plates and nuked the first one in the microwave, which was perched on a stack of Xerox boxes.

Cathy stashed one of the colas in the fridge, then popped open the other over the sink. She held it away from her as it exploded and overflowed into the drain. "Did you shake this or what?"

."Not on purpose. Sorry," Danni answered absently as she watched the plate go round and round in the microwave.

A touch on her shoulder startled her back to the present. "Why don't you take more time off?" Cathy asked gently. "After all, he was your *father*."

Danni's throat tightened and she shook her head. As long as she stayed busy, she could pretend her father was still alive and that she might someday make him proud of her. "I have work to do. I'm already too far behind as it is."

Heavy silence compressed the room. Danni wished she could simply ignore the fact that her father had been buried yesterday with full police honors. Ignore the fact that he'd committed suicide. Ignore the fact that they'd been taking the first tentative steps toward rebuilding their father-daughter relationship.

Danni's stomach twisted and suddenly the food didn't look nearly as appetizing as it had when she'd picked it up on her way to the office. "Maybe you're right," she murmured. "There's a lot to do."

"Have you gone to the house yet?" Cathy asked.

"The funeral director needed a suit to bury him in. Being a cop was his life so I figured I'd just have him buried in his service uniform." Her eyes felt hot and scratchy, but there were no tears. There hadn't been, not when the bugler had played taps, and not when she'd walked away from the cemetery with a folded flag in her arms and her father's bronze casket sitting above the ground like some lonely sentry.

Cathy put her arm around Danni's shoulders and gave her a half hug. "Go home. I'll call your one o'clock and reschedule."

Danni was tempted, but she'd already been out of the office for four days. "I can't. I have to start tagging Warner this afternoon."

"Do it tomorrow."

"The sooner I can prove he's screwing around, the sooner we get paid."

Danni had opened her private investigator's business almost two years ago. Even though she split overhead costs with Beth, it was only in the past few months that Danni could afford to eat somewhere that didn't have plastic sporks or offer ketchup in pump dispensers.

The second plate of food finished reheating and the two women sat down to eat. But the quiet gave Danni too much time to think. "How's Ashley doing?"

Cathy shrugged. "Fine, for an alien."

Danni tipped her head to the side in a mute question.

"Once she hit puberty, it's like she was taken over by a hostile alien," Cathy explained.

"You've been watching too many *X-Files* reruns." Danni waved her fork and sent a lone grain of fried rice skittering across the tabletop. "You need to get out more."

"Look who's talking." Cathy grinned conspiratorially. "Hey, why don't we go clubbing this weekend? Ashley will be at her father's." Her smile faded. "That is, if you're up to it."

"Sure, why not?" But Danni couldn't meet Cathy's eyes. "I mean it's not like it's that much different now. I actually didn't see Dad that much before he—" Much to her embarrassment, her voice broke and she cleared her throat. "Before he died."

"He was still your father."

An ember of anger sparked Danni's tongue. "Sometimes I wondered if *he* knew that. He was never around when—" Her rage vanished as swiftly as it had appeared. "It's not fair."

Cathy gave her forearm a gentle squeeze, but wisely didn't offer any empty platitudes.

The phone rang and Cathy hurried out to answer it. Danni tried to listen to the one-sided conversation, but only heard snatches. She forced another forkful of General Tso's into her mouth, but even the spicy chicken—her favorite—didn't bring much enthusiasm to her taste buds.

Cathy's heels on the tiled floor alerted Danni to her return.

"Damn reporters," she muttered as she plopped down without her usual panache. "Bob Carlyle from KMCX wanted to interview you for the evening news." Her eyes flashed. "I told him where to go."

Cathy's protective zeal brought Danni a small measure of comfort. Cathy might be petite, but she was as fierce as a mama bear when it came to protecting her family and friends.

"Let me guess. He wanted to unravel the mystery of why a man with a distinguished record who came from a long line of cops would commit suicide," Danni guessed bitterly. "I've been getting calls from reporters at home. I'm actually surprised it took them this long to call here."

Shoving aside her melancholy thoughts, she glanced at her watch. She had five minutes before her appointment arrived. Cathy helped her clean the break room in record time and placed the leftovers in the antiquated refrigerator.

"Don't you have a change of clothes here?" Cathy asked, eyeing the prominent stain on Danni's trousers.

"I forgot to bring in another set after the SUV repo."

"Ahh," Cathy said knowingly. "He was the one who thought you were a carjacker."

Danni scowled. "Yeah, like he didn't hear me explain the three missed payments or how the bank sent me to repossess it." The bastard had played dirty, but Danni had some tricks up her sleeve, too. He had ended up in the hospital with a broken collarbone.

"Did the one o'clock say what he wanted?" Danni asked, pausing in her office doorway.

Cathy shook her head. "He said he'll tell you in person."

Danni shrugged, closed the door, and crossed to her desk. Pulling open the lower drawer, she placed her backpack inside. She felt the hard line of her Smith & Wesson in the pack and debated placing the revolver in a more accessible location in case her next appointment was some psycho. Hell, it'd happened before. A delinquent father she'd tracked down had stalked in, waving a knife and threatening to kill her for forcing him to meet his financial responsibilities to his children. She'd disarmed him using defensive moves her father had taught her when she was fourteen years old in case some boyfriend got a little too friendly.

Danni slumped back in her chair and closed her eyes. Not all her memories of her father were unpleasant. She remembered the first time she'd ridden her bicycle without the training wheels. Her dad had hauled her into his big arms and swung her around until she was laughing so hard she almost lost her earlier snack of chocolate cookies and grape Kool-Aid. Years later, when she'd graduated from the police academy, her father's proud smile and tentative hug had made her feel the same way.

But it was the memory of his disappointment when she'd turned in her badge that had made her sick to her stomach.

The intercom buzzed, startling Danni out of the eclipsing memories. She leaned forward and stabbed a button. "Yes?"

"Nick Sirocco is here to see you."

"Send him in."

Cathy opened the door and Danni stood, catching the wink and smirk the paralegal sent her. Then Nick Sirocco strode forward and Danni understood Cathy's signals.

Danni had been expecting a middle-aged man trying to get the goods on a cheating wife, not someone who looked like he'd just stepped out of a Chippendales gig. Nick Sirocco was a good two or three inches over six feet with broad shoulders that tapered to a narrow waist and hips. Faded blue jeans that hugged muscular thighs and a taut gray T-shirt beneath a weathered brown bomber jacket brought Danni's hormones scampering out of hibernation.

"Danielle Hawkins?"

His deep timbre sent her gaze to his face, only to have her attention captured by startlingly clear blue eyes beneath a high forehead and closely trimmed honey brown hair. A sense of familiarity washed through her, but she dismissed it. She wouldn't have forgotten meeting someone like Nick Sirocco.

"Yes, I'm Danni Hawkins." She mentally chided herself for reacting like a sex-obsessed teenager. "Nice to meet you, Mr. Sirocco." She extended her hand over her desk and he crossed the short distance to shake it. His strong, warm grip sent pleasurable currents rushing through her and jump-started parts of her body that had been out of commission for too long.

"Call me Nick." His smile brought creases to the corners of his eyes and mouth.

He glanced down and she followed his gaze to the tea stain on her trousers. Her face burned and she quickly lowered herself back to her chair, grateful for the desk's cover.

So much for first impressions.

"Would you like something to drink?" Danni asked. "Coffee? Soda?"

"A glass of water would be good."

"I'll get it," Cathy offered and closed the door behind her.

Sirocco had obviously made an impact on the paralegal. Cathy was usually adamant about not playing gofer.

He lowered himself to his chair with an animal-like grace.

Danni wasn't used to dealing with drop-dead gorgeous men in her office. The majority of her clients were women, and the few men who sought her help looked like over-the-hill jocks with more gut than hair.

She lifted her gaze to his summer sky–colored eyes. "What can I help you with, Mr. Sirocco?"

"Nick," he insisted.

Danni usually remained professional with her clients, but if Sirocco preferred less formality, who was she to argue?

"What can I do for you, Nick?" she reiterated.

A crease appeared between his eyebrows and the discomfort that crossed his features made Danni tense.

"I knew your father," he said.

Danni narrowed her eyes as adrenaline leaped into her veins. "A lot of people knew my father."

"I saw you at the funeral."

She studied him more closely, trying to remember if she'd seen him at the service or the gravesite. But she'd kept her gaze downcast throughout most of the funeral and could recall few of those who'd attended.

"You were the only family Paddy had," Sirocco added.

Paddy. Was Sirocco just another bloodsucking reporter who'd dug a little deeper than his colleagues?

A soft knock on the door gave Danni a momentary reprieve. "Come in."

Cathy entered with two glasses of ice water, handing one to Sirocco and placing the other on the desk in front of Danni.

"Thank you," Sirocco said.

Danni murmured the same and Cathy left them alone. Although Danni hadn't asked for the water, she was grateful. Sirocco's little announcement had given her a case of dry mouth.

"So, how did you know him?" Danni asked after taking a sip.

"He helped me when I needed it." Sirocco shrugged, but his eyes were crystalline. "I owe him."

"It'll be hard to pay him back now." She kept her tone intentionally blunt.

Startled, Sirocco stared at her like he was trying to discover something within her. His lips turned downward as if he didn't find it. "You don't sound like you're real broken up about his death."

Rage tightened its icy claws around Danni's chest, making it hard to breathe. "You don't know anything about me, Mr. Sirocco, so don't you dare presume to know how I feel about my father."

Sirocco's eyes widened minutely, but enough to tell Danni he got her message, loud and clear. "You're right. I don't know you." His voice was cool and flat.

"Why are you here?"

He took a long moment to answer her question. "I need your help."

"Why?"

"Because you have access to people and places I don't."
Sirocco set his glass on a stone coaster on the corner of the
desk. "I want to find the man who murdered your father."

Three years ago, Danni had been kicked in the belly by
a suspect accused of stealing from his employer. He'd been
wearing steel-toed boots at the time and she recalled her
desperation when she couldn't catch her breath and how
her heart raced as she'd lain on the grimy gray and tan
linoleum floor, her arms clutched around her middle. She
felt much the same way now.

"I don't know what kind of sick game you're playing.
My father was upset about being forced to retire in a few
months. His gun was found in his hand and there were
burns around the entry wound on his forehead. Powder
residue was found on his hand," Danni said, keeping her
hands clasped lest he see her trembling. "If he couldn't be
a cop, he had nothing left to live for."

"Bullshit." Sirocco's quiet expletive held more intensity
than a loud bellow. "If you knew your father at all, you'd
know he would never take the easy way out."

If you knew your father at all . . . That was what this all
came down to, wasn't it? *Had* Danni known her father?

Her heart clamored in her chest and she forced herself
to breathe deeply to allay her sudden dizziness. At the time
she'd been informed of his death, she'd questioned the suicide ruling. But all the evidence pointed to that determination.

"Why would someone kill him?" Danni managed to ask
in a calm voice.

Sirocco glanced away, then brought his sharp gaze back
to her. "I don't know. That's why I need your help."

Danni's throbbing head joined in her heart's pounding
tempo. "My father is dead. Why can't you let him rest in
peace?"

"Because his murderer is walking around out there scot-
free." Sirocco dragged a hand over his short hair. For the
first time, she noticed dark smudges beneath his eyes.

"Paddy left a message on my answering machine the night he was killed. He said he had to talk to me about something important, and that he'd try me in the morning if I didn't get back to him. By the time I got his message, he was already dead."

Danni looked away to regain control of her jagged emotions. Her father had called Sirocco instead of his own daughter the night he committed suicide. But if it was murder . . .

"If he was planning on killing himself, why did he say he'd call me back in the morning?" Sirocco pressed, leaning forward in his chair.

She shoved the old hurts back down into their tattered box. The man had a point. "What's your connection to my father?"

"I've known him for a long time, ever since I was seventeen. He—" The man took a shaky breath. "I was headed down the road to prison when he turned me around."

Danni's eyes widened as a lightbulb flared and realization dawned. "You were one of them. One of the boys he tried to help."

"*Did* help. Like I said, he straightened me out, helped me get into the army. He changed my life."

Danni's life had been changed, too, by her father's involvement with troubled street teens. But it hadn't been for the better. She'd gone with him to the gym until her body began to fill out and "his boys" had started noticing her. At that age, she'd been foolish enough to encourage the attention. After two of the boys had started a fight over her, Danni's father had ordered her to stay home, but he never stayed home with her. He'd always chosen *them* over her.

That decision had been the start of the disintegration of their relationship.

"How nice for you." Danni's rapier sarcasm sliced the air between them.

Sirocco frowned. "I didn't see him for about twelve years. When I got out of the army, I moved back here and started writing books."

Danni noticed a slight hesitation in his speech, as if he were glossing over something, or leaving something out of his explanation. She listened more closely.

"We went out to eat a few times. He talked me into helping out with the youth group, giving a hand where I could. You know, coaching some baseball, refereeing some b-ball games, just being there if someone wanted to talk," Sirocco explained with a shrug. "I found I liked it, and it made me feel pretty good to be able to give something back."

Danni swallowed a block of bitterness. Her father had never asked her to help. Not even after she'd donned the brothers-in-blue uniform.

"Two months ago, I asked Paddy if he'd help me with a novel I was working on," Sirocco continued. "I needed technical assistance with proper police procedure, and I wanted to use some cop slang to give the book a more realistic feel. He was excited about it and agreed to be my official consultant." A smile played on his lips. "We met once a week to discuss details."

Danni willed herself to remain calm on the outside, despite the emotional hurricane raging within her. "What evidence do you have, Mr. Sirocco?"

His eyes blazed with impatience, and he braced his forearms on his thighs. "He wouldn't kill himself. And if you would take a few minutes to think about it, you'd know that, too."

He truly believed in her father. For a second, she hated Nick Sirocco. She hated that he had more faith in her father than she did.

She hated him because he'd had what she'd been denied.

"Who had a motive?" Danni asked, trying to remain objective even as her adolescent memories rose, ugly and spiteful inside her.

"I don't know." Sirocco's words came out clipped and harsh. "You're the private investigator—you know the ins and outs of this stuff."

Unable to sit any longer, Danni rose and paced the small

space between Sirocco's chair and the door. Her insides felt like fire ants had taken up permanent residence.

Sirocco shifted in his chair so he could watch her. "He was your father," he said softly.

Danni paused, took a deep, shaky breath, and shoved her fingers through her hair, snagging the curls and tugging them back, away from her face. "I didn't know him very well, Mr. Sirocco. He had his life and I had mine. His ex-partner, Sam Richmond, was more like a father to me than he was."

Sirocco looked like he wanted to ask a question, but instead, he pressed his lips together. "Your dad told me all about you."

Danni's vision blurred with unwelcome moisture. Why couldn't he have talked *to* her instead of *about* her?

"Help me find the person who murdered him." Sirocco's piercing blue eyes demanded her agreement.

Murder. It was such an ugly word, and even uglier when applied to someone she'd known. Her own father.

If there was even a possibility of foul play, Danni had the responsibility to find his killer. Maybe she didn't owe him like Sirocco did, but despite everything, she'd loved him.

And maybe somehow her father could see her and finally be proud of her.

More entertaining romance Texas-style
from **USA Today** bestselling author

Jodi Thomas

"Jodi draws the reader into her stories from the first page...
She's one of my favorites."
—Debbie Macomber

*Available wherever books are sold or
to order call 1-800-788-6262*

B936

BERKLEY SENSATION
COMING IN AUGUST 2004

Sweetheart, Indiana
by Suzanne Simmons
Socialite Gillian Charles has inherited a town. The only catch is she has to live there. What can a small town offer a Big City girl? For starters, a handsome, single man named Sam Law.

0-425-19779-4

Undead and Unemployed
by MaryJanice Davidson
Betsy Taylor may be the Queen of the Vampires, but she still has bills to pay. But landing her dream job selling designer shoes won't help this undead royalty stay out of trouble.

0-425-19748-4

The Heiress of Hyde Park
by Jacqueline Navin
A governess's daughter and a young lord have fallen in love, but he must marry an heiress. If only they had a fairy godmother to secure their fate...

0-425-19778-6

Goddess of Spring
by P.C. Cast
To save her failing bakery, Lina trades souls with Persephone, the Goddess of Spring—and starts to fall for hunky Hades.

0-425-19749-2

Available wherever books are sold,
or to order call: 1-800-788-6262